GREEN, WHITE, AND RED

GREEN, WHITE, AND RED
The Italian–American Success Story

by
DOMINIC J. PULERA

L'ITALO-AMERICANO
San Marino, California
2009

ISBN 978-0-615-26851-4
Library of Congress Control Number: 2008943413

L'ITALO-AMERICANO
745 Sierra Madre Boulevard
San Marino, CA 91108

Design and production by Capital A Publications, LLC
Spokane, Washington

CONTENTS

Prologue

AMERICAN AND ITALIAN

Frank D. Stella enjoys drinking Rocchetta bottled water—it comes from his ancestral hometown of Gualdo Tadino. This Umbrian community is well known to the people of Jessup, Pennsylvania, where Stella was born in 1919 and lived until 1937.[1] Jessup, a small town in the Lackawanna Valley near Scranton, Pennsylvania, attracted many Italian immigrants a century ago due to the recruitment practices of the area's coal mines. During Stella's youth, Jessup's large Italian population from the Province of Perugia (particularly such communities as Gubbio, Scheggia, Gualdo Tadino, and Sassoferrato) was just beginning to assimilate into American culture.[2] It is because of his Umbrian-immigrant parents that Stella developed a lifelong passion for Italy in general and Umbria in particular. Over the years, he remained in contact with Gualdo Tadino, a town that honored him when it celebrated Frank D. Stella Day on October 27, 1984.[3]

The fourth youngest of thirteen children, Stella was born in Jessup, Pennsylvania, on January 21, 1919. He, his parents, and his siblings lived in an Italian-speaking household. However, Stella remembers that the young people "spoke only English outside the home." The members of his large family observed many Italian customs and traditions. They washed their faces in water laden with roses on St. John's Day. And they often ate polenta with lamb, pork, grouse, rabbit, sausage, and chicken.[4] During the 1920s and 1930s, Stella remembers that Jessup was Irish, Polish, and Italian.[5] The residents of this predominantly Catholic town in northeastern Pennsylvania lived in ethnically homogeneous neighborhoods, but Stella himself never experienced any ethnic discrimination.[6]

Frank D. Stella is the son of Italian immigrants whose descendants have achieved the American Dream. His father left Gualdo Tadino as a young adult. The elder Stella went to Jessup, where he found employment with a cousin "who was a mining contractor." Later, Stella's father returned to Umbria. He married Stella's mother and then they went to the United States. Frank Stella left Jessup in 1937 when he enrolled at the University of Detroit. He received his bachelor's degree in 1941, whereupon he was drafted into the U.S. Army. After World War II, Stella launched a successful career as a businessperson and entrepreneur.[7] His signature business is The F. D. Stella Products Company, a Detroit institution that describes itself as "Michigan's foodservice & dining equipment headquarters."[8] An elegant man with silver hair and a graceful bearing, Stella and his late wife, Martha, had seven children. Today he has seventeen grandchildren.[9]

Approximately one century ago, Frank D. Stella's parents arrived in the United States with few material possessions; now their son is an influential and well-connected figure in Michigan and beyond. He enjoys relationships with decision makers at the highest levels of academia, Corporate America, the Catholic Church, U.S. politics and government, and countless civic groups and advocacy organizations.[10] In addition, this consummate insider is a veteran of high-level Republican politics, one who has held various appointments in local, state, and national government. Stella received appointments from Presidents Richard Nixon, Gerald Ford, Ronald Reagan, and George H. W. Bush. And he has been an invited guest at numerous state dinners over the years. A recipient of the Ellis Island Medal of Honor, Stella is well known for his long-standing interest in different ethnic, racial, and religious groups. He regularly receives honors from civic, political, business, religious, and advocacy organizations.[11]

This proud son of Umbria maintains close ties to Italy and numerous Italian figures. Frank D. Stella frequently makes trips to Italy, where he comes into regular contact with high-ranking Italian governmental officials. A deeply religious man, Stella continues to be very involved in the Catholic Church. He is Founding Director for Life of Legatus, an organization for the Catholic elite, and he remains close to the Franciscans of Assisi. Stella, too, has advised a number of academic institutions with ties to Italy. Moreover, he holds the title of Grand'Ufficiale in the Ordine al Merito della Repubblica Italiana, an honor that recognizes his contributions to positive U.S.-Italian relations and tireless work to help the Italian-American people.[12]

Stella is a central figure in the history of the National Italian American Foundation (NIAF), one of Italian America's most significant advocacy organizations. A charter member of NIAF in 1977, Stella served as president of NIAF (1979 to 1989), vice chairman of the board (1989 to 1991), and NIAF chairman (1991 to 1999). Stella and his fellow ethnic advocates focused attention on such matters as Italian-American representation in government and Corporate America. In the early years of NIAF, John Volpe and Frank Stella perused corporate annual reports for Italian surnames at various companies. Then they contacted corporate officers to advocate on behalf of more Italian-American executives.[13] Years later, NIAF continues to be a rich cultural and political resource for Italian Americans and others.

Frank D. Stella earns plaudits from Italian Americans for his significant and pioneering contributions to Italian-American culture. This opera enthusiast and patron of the arts remains involved in Italian-American affairs through his continuing role in NIAF and membership in such organizations as Americans of Italian Origin and the American Society of the Italian Legions of Merit. "In the last 25 years," observed Stella in a 2004 interview, "Italian Americans came into being in every nook and cranny of this country."[14] He himself personifies the Italian-American success story. Indeed, the trajectory of his life reflects the tremendous progress that Italian Americans have made during the last century.[15]

I. The United States of America is a country named for an Italian (Amerigo Vespucci) and whose European antecedents can be traced to the ocean voyages of an Italian (Cristoforo Colombo). Furthermore, such explorers as Giovanni Caboto (John Cabot) and Giovanni da Verrazano played important roles in the European exploration of North America. And students of the American Revolution credit Filippo Mazzei with providing ideas to Thomas Jefferson while Francesco Vigo helped to bankroll the Americans' drive for independence. Two individuals of Italian descent—Caesar Rodney and William Paca—signed the Declaration of Independence. Italian immigrants began coming to the United States in small numbers in the seventeenth century. Until the last years of the nineteenth century, however, the Italian-American population remained relatively small and primarily northern Italian in origin.[16]

Italian immigrants, mainly from the south of Italy, started arriving in the United States in large numbers during the 1890s. The figures for Italian immigration to the United States, by time period, illustrate these developments strikingly: 1789 to 1870 (25,000); the 1870s (55,000); the 1880s (267,000); the 1890s (603,000); 1900 to 1914 (3,035,000); 1915 to 1924 (585,000). Immigration to America from Italy halted almost completely for decades after 1924, due to U.S. immigration restrictions. All told, 4.5 million Italians entered the United States between 1880 and 1924.[17] Most Americans of Italian descent trace their ancestry to these individuals, although many thousands of Italians have immigrated to the United States since the end of World War II.

Over the years, Italian Americans integrated into the general population, due to such factors as their wholesale support for and their large-scale participation in World War II, the emphasis on assimilation and Americanization during the Cold War, and the popularity of Frank Sinatra, Joe DiMaggio, and other Italian-American heroes of U.S. popular culture.[18] "By the 1970s Italians were thoroughly interwoven into the fabric of American life," observes Michael Barone. "It took eighty years."[19] Today the discrimination of the past is largely a matter of history. "Once a marginalized, despised minority," writes George Pozzetta, "Italian Americans are now among the most highly accepted groups according to national surveys measuring 'social distance' indicators (Italians ranked fourteenth in 1926, but fifth in 1977). All of the statistical data point to a high level of structural assimilation in American society, although Italian American ethnicity has not disappeared."[20]

It is currently fashionable to identify as an Italian American, as evidenced by the number of people selecting "Italian" as a response to the ancestry question on the U.S. census form. "Indeed," notes Richard D. Alba, "Italian-American identity is more salient than that of most other white ethnic groups."[21] The number of Italian Americans went from 12.1 million in 1980 to 14.7 million in 1990 to 15.7 million in 2000. These increases seem to be attributable, in part, to more self-reporting of Italian ancestry, not greater amounts of Italian immigration or higher birth rates among Italian Americans.[22] Continuing this trend, the American Community Survey in 2005 found that 6.0 percent of the U.S. population (17,235,000 individuals) was of Italian descent in that year.[23] There is now greater cachet associated with Italian ancestry in the United States, just as the current climate makes it more acceptable to identify with one's ancestral origins.

These developments parallel the virtually complete assimilation of Italian Americans into mainstream American culture and society. This social, economic, and cultural integration has occurred to the point that full-blooded Italians are now outnumbered by individuals of mixed ethnic origins in the youngest generations of Italian Americans.[24] Yet, at the same time, many Americans enjoy celebrating their dual Italian/American identity. Indeed, two flags (those of Italy and the United States) are often used to symbolize this dual identity in our nation—and other countries of the Italian diaspora—in all manner of media, from T-shirts to address labels. Moreover, the green-white-and-red imagery of the Italian flag often colors ads for Italian-American clubs, festivals, restaurants, and Web sites. This imagery may or may not be juxtaposed with the red-white-and-blue American flag. These instances of ethnic iconography remind us that the United States is home to a large and vibrant Italian population.

Italian Americans celebrate their heritage with gusto and pride, even though they differ as to how overtly "Italian" they choose to be in their daily lives. Some individuals are Italian in name only. Many Americans of Italian descent take pride in their heritage, but they spend relatively little time celebrating it or focusing on ethnic issues. Others live in worlds that are thoroughly shaped and defined by their ethnic heritage. In any event, there are different ways of referring to people with Italian backgrounds, as in *Italian*, *Italic*, *I.A.* (in the shorthand), *Tally* (a colloquial term), *American Italian*, *Italian American*, *Italo American*, and *American of Italian origin, descent, or extraction*, and others. While each term has its proponents with their rationales, *Italian American* is certainly the most frequently used umbrella phrase for people with Italian ancestry.

In the United States, Italian Americans often use the stand-alone identifier "Italian" to describe themselves—and they use the term *nationality* to refer to their Old World antecedents. A proud American, then, might say that his nationality is "Dutch" or "Italian" or "Polish." Americans began to use the term *ethnicity* in lieu of, or perhaps alongside, *nationality* during the 1960s.[25] Paul Andriulli reports that in the New Jersey of his youth, people often asked each other, "What are you?" Andriulli knew he was an American, of course, and he always identified as "Italian" in response to this question about his ethnic identity.[26] Andriulli's self-description is typical among Americans of Italian extraction. To be sure, after decades of integration and assimilation, there are some individuals with Italian backgrounds who want to be seen solely as Americans.

Today the Italian-American identity is highly individualistic and specific to particular people, places, and generations. Italian-American culture is a fascinating potpourri of customs, experiences, and traditions that differ by gender, generation, geography, political ideology, socioeconomic status, and other factors. There are multiple variants of the Italian-American experience.[27] All are legitimate and all should be recognized as such. Of course, certain continuities exist for different aspects of the Italian-American experience, as in the usage of the term "backhouse" and the practice of chaperoned dating among young people, memories of which are still fresh for people in their sixties and older. These continuities also show up internationally as well, particularly in such English-speaking countries as Canada, Australia, New Zealand, and the United Kingdom.

Middle-aged and elderly Italian Americans often have had remarkably similar experiences, regardless of where they grew up or live today. Peter Balistreri aptly characterizes such individuals, including himself, as members of the "bridge generation" of Italian Americans. The sixtysomething attorney and grandson of Sicilian immigrants is part of the first generation of Italian Americans to be fully American in their outlook. Yet they continue to be closely attuned to the Old World customs and traditions as a result of their childhood experiences with their Italian-born family members.[28]

II. Father John J. Richetta reports that he once went into a bank in Kenosha, Wisconsin, and told the teller that he wanted to send money to a foreign country. When the young man learned that Richetta was sending money to Italy, he responded with mock indignation that Italy was not a foreign country. This bank teller, in all likelihood, traced his ancestry to Italy and viewed the boot-shaped nation with warmth. It is very likely that the bank teller was the son, grandson, or great-grandson of Italian immigrants and that he had grown up in Kenosha, home to one of the largest and most vibrant Italian-American communities north of Chicago. Father Richetta's experience at the bank symbolized the extent of the ties between Kenosha and Italy (specifically, Calabria).[29] These connections matter to many of the parishioners at Our Lady of Mount Carmel Church, the heavily Italian parish in Kenosha that the Italian-speaking Richetta served as pastor from 1966 to 2005.[30]

Kenosha is a thriving community of approximately 93,000 residents in southeastern Wisconsin about fifty-five miles north of downtown Chicago.[31] According to the Census of 2000, people of Italian descent account for 12 percent of Kenosha's population, and many of them have Calabrian forebears. At one time, some Italian Americans felt left out of the mainstream of this once-industrial city. An older Italian man told me that he remembered when the Italians of Kenosha were considered, in his opinion, to be only good for "drinking wine and making babies." After generations of socioeconomic mobility, though, one finds Italian Americans in virtually every one of Kenosha's institutions. One woman told me that membership in Kenosha's venerable Italian-American Society is now valued by local businesspeople for its networking opportunities.

Now the city is very Italian-friendly. Tenuta's Delicatessen and Liquors, a Kenosha institution, ranks among the most comprehensive Italian markets in the United States. Moreover, Alfred De Simone of Kenosha is one of southeastern Wisconsin's most enduring businesspeople, civic leaders, and philanthropists, with an encyclopedic list of accomplishments to his name (including service on the University of Wisconsin Board of Regents). And in 2003, Kenosha's Bradford High School and Tremper High School began offering Italian-language courses.[32] Kenosha has long had a sister-city relationship with Cosenza, Calabria, the city that is "home" to so many Kenoshans of Italian origin. A delegation of Calabrian dignitaries journeyed to Kenosha for a landmark visit in 2004 to promote cultural, economic, and intellectual exchanges between the two nations.[33] At the same time, one sees numerous examples of young Italian-American Kenoshans who want to learn more about their ancestral heritage and culture.

The University of Wisconsin–Parkside is an institution that serves the community and promotes ties between Kenosha and Calabria. UW–Parkside was founded in 1968; Italian Americans were instrumental in creating this campus in Kenosha. There are buildings at UW–Parkside named for local Italian Americans, and the student body includes many people of Italian extraction. The University of Wisconsin–Parkside is linked through an exchange agreement to the Università della Calabria in Italy. This agreement promotes cultural and academic links between the two institutions. UW–Parkside is the only university in America to have this exchange with Calabria. Each year there is a fund-raising event (the Celebrazione Italiana) at Parkside to support the UW–Parkside/Università della Calabria Student Exchange Program.[34]

I have a special interest in Kenosha because my Italian relatives have lived there for more than a century. My great-grandfather Leonardo

Pulerà left Roccabernarda, a small town in the mountains of central Calabria, for the United States in 1902, when he was in his late twenties. He arrived in America on May 3, 1902, exactly seventy-two years before I was born. The ship manifest lists his occupation as "peasant" and indicates that he could not read or write. The records show that he came back through Ellis Island again in 1907, but this time he listed his residence as the United States. I do not know when, exactly, my great-grandmother—she was a Seminara—arrived in the United States. In any event, one of their American-born children was my paternal grandfather, Frank Joseph Pulera, whose birth occurred in 1915, in Kenosha, Wisconsin.

My other Italian great-grandfather, Pasquale (Charles) Puntillo, left Arcavacata, a small town near Cosenza in northern Calabria, for the United States in 1911, when he, too, was in his twenties. He lived and worked in the United States for ten years before sending for my great-grandmother, Divina Puntillo (née DeFranco) and their two children, Michelina and Salvatore. After Divina arrived in the United States in 1921, she and Pasquale had three more children. Mary, my grandmother, was their first American-born child. She was born in Kenosha, Wisconsin, in 1924. The Great Depression marked a difficult time for the Puntillos, when Pasquale Puntillo died and Michelina and her husband, Anthony Parise, provided for her young siblings.

Mary Puntillo and Frank Pulera were married in 1941. Apart from my grandfather's military service in the South Pacific during World War II, they spent all their lives in Kenosha. My father, Eugene Leonard Pulera, came into the world in 1946. English is his mother tongue, even though both his parents spoke dialectal Italian as their first language, and he knows dozens of Italian words and expressions. Like so many Italian Americans in his generation, my father's parents only spoke Italian around him when they did not want him to understand their conversation.

My father left his hometown of Kenosha in the 1960s to complete his bachelor's degree at the University of Wisconsin–Madison, where he met my mother, Margaret Lux Pulera, who traces her ancestry to Germany, in 1971. My sister, Maria, and I grew up in a household in rural southeastern Wisconsin. Our parents stressed our German and Italian heritage—and I take pride and interest in both sides of my family history. As youngsters, Maria and I visited our Aunt Michelina in Kenosha. A demonstrative and redoubtable woman, Michelina Parise was the matriarch of our Italian-American family and our living link to the Italian-immigration experience until her passing in 1995.

The research for this book has been a wonderful learning experience for my family and me. We discovered that our surname is actually spelled Pulerà and pronounced "poo-lair-UH," with the accent on the last syllable, during a visit to Roccabernarda, the Calabrian town that is ground zero for the Puleras. Similarly, we gained knowledge about family history, trivia (I have the same birthday as Frankie Valli and Niccolò Machiavelli), the meanings of various dialectal terms that my father picked up as a youth, and, most importantly, the stories of hundreds of people throughout the world.

As part of the research for this book, I traveled extensively throughout the United States, visited Italy on six occasions, and went to the other parts of the globe where there are significant concentrations of people of Italian descent. During my research and the writing process, I delivered more than two hundred talks on Italian-American issues to audiences in various venues in the United States (forty-five of the fifty states) and the world (Asia, Europe, Oceania, and North America).[35] And in 2003 I addressed several audiences of students at the Università della Calabria in Italy (where I focused on race relations in the U.S.A.) and delivered a public lecture about race, culture, and language at the Language Learning Centre on campus. Over the course of several years, my Italian-American research has received coverage from journalists and media professionals in a variety of print publications and on a number of media programs, here and abroad.

❁ ❁ ❁

The Italian-American success story matters to all of us, regardless of where we live or where we or our ancestors came from in the Old World. This is true for two reasons. Firstly, anything that affects one group of us as Americans in one part of America affects all of us in some way or another. Secondly, Americans of Italian descent are important figures in our national institutions—the military, entertainment, politics and government, the corporate world, the Supreme Court, and elsewhere—and they make decisions that affect all of our lives. I believe strongly in this message. Therefore, I went to a wide variety of places to speak, share ideas, and learn about people's perspectives on the Italian-American presence in our nation.

While researching and writing *Green, White, and Red*, I came into contact with a large number of warm, welcoming individuals, Italian and non-Italian, here and abroad. I met people who remember when Italian Americans experienced discrimination, when a local company would not hire them, a particular club would not admit them, or a person from another ethnic group would not or could not date them. I also interviewed many folks who have no Italian ancestry. They are an important part of this story, because the people of the Italian diaspora live in multiethnic (and, in many cases, multiracial) countries and communities.

Italian Americans are blessed with an extraordinarily rich array of culturally valuable stories, experiences, and institutions. This book does not aspire to be an encyclopedic treatment of the Italian-American experience; it is, of course, impossible to cover every subject and community in great depth. I tried to choose representative anecdotes and vignettes that highlight various aspects of life in Italian America. During my research on this book, I spoke to hundreds of individuals in the United States and other nations about their experiences and perspectives. While I could only mention the names and stories of a small percentage of these respondents in the text, their stories, insights, and anecdotes informed my coverage of Italian-American success. The tone of this book is not entirely dispassionate, as I believe strongly in America and what is possible here.

Over several generations, Italian Americans reached parity with other European-American ethnic groups. They faced stereotyping and discrimination over the years, but these factors had declined significantly by the 1980s and 1990s. "It wasn't fashionable to be Italian," remembers Susan Rienzi Paolercio of her youth during the 1950s and 1960s.[36] Today older Americans of Italian origin sometimes marvel at the extraordinary changes that they have observed during their lives. There are Italian Americans, to be sure, who have not prospered economically or who feel they still encounter subtle bias and stereotyping, but the vast majority of them are achieving success as they define it. Indeed, Italian Americans are admired, valued, and respected members of communities throughout the United States. More and more Americans than ever before have firsthand familiarity with people of Italian origin: They are our friends, our neighbors, our colleagues, our classmates, and, increasingly due to intermarriage, members of our own families.

This is a unique point in Italian-American history. Americans of Italian descent are still an identifiable ethnic group, but the assimilation process has proceeded to the point that it is almost entirely finished for most people of Italian origin in this country. Except for the physical characteristics of many Americans of Italian descent, there is little else that would make them interchangeable with an Italian in Italy. At the same time, it is still possible to speak to first- and second-generation Italian

Americans, those who experienced poverty and discrimination firsthand. Meanwhile, there continues to be a vibrant Italian-American ethnic culture; the Italian-American identity is still noted, celebrated, and caricatured in American society.

Now it is accurate to speak of the Italian-American success story (as a whole), due to the significant socioeconomic mobility that Americans of Italian origin have enjoyed over the last three to four generations. Italian Americans are more successful than ever before. They can be found in almost every occupation, in virtually every major institution, and doing almost every type of worthwhile endeavor. While this book focuses on a particular American ethnic group, it is really a story about America: A narrative that affirms and celebrates our nation and, as importantly, what is possible here. This work could be the history of 30, 40, or 50 different American ethnic groups. These stories of overcoming poverty and discrimination are by no means unique to the Italian-American experience.

Green, White, and Red describes and interprets the Italian-American success story. Part One offers the social and economic context for this treatment of Italian-American progress. Part Two highlights the assimilation and integration process for Italian Americans. Part Three, then, describes the cultural geography of Italian America. And Part Four depicts various aspects of contemporary Italian-American culture, particularly those that involve the ancestral heritage of people from Italian family backgrounds. Finally, the Epilogue focuses on the future of Italian America and Italian Americans in our multiethnic nation.

Part I

SOCIAL AND ECONOMIC INDICATORS

Chapter 1

COMING TO AMERICA

At one point in the popular film, *Meet the Parents* (2000), Greg Focker (Ben Stiller), engages in a driving contest with his girl-friend's father, Jack Byrnes (Robert De Niro). At the conclusion of Focker's car race with Byrnes through the streets of Long Island, one of the men from his party says to him, sarcastically, "Nice driving, Mario." This offhand remark in *Meet the Parents* illustrates the racing legend Mario Andretti's ubiquity in American popular culture.[1] It includes no reference to Andretti's surname or anything else that would identify "Mario." Yet viewers of *Meet the Parents* could simply assume from the context that an instantly recognizable reference to Mario Andretti, the iconic Italian/American racecar driver, was in order.[2]

Mario Gabriele Andretti was born in Montona, a town on the Istrian Peninsula of Croatia, on February 28, 1940.[3] He lived the first eight years of his life there. Then, in 1948, his parents, Alvise Andretti and Rina Ben-vegnu, were faced with a wrenching decision because Istria had become part of Communist Yugoslavia. Their choice was to "stay or you do not own anything," or they could leave and retain their Italian citizenship.[4] Ninety percent of the Italians in Montona departed from Yugoslavia at this time, an exodus that included the Andretti family. From 1948 to 1955 the Andrettis lived in Tuscany, where young Mario grew up in a refugee camp in Lucca.[5] Eventually, the Andrettis decided to go to the United States, where one of Rina Benvegnu's uncles—they knew him as Uncle Tony—had lived since the early 1900s.[6]

The Andretti family corresponded with Uncle Tony, who resided in Nazareth, Pennsylvania; he sponsored them to immigrate to America.

Alvise Andretti went to the United States for five years and then the rest of his family followed him here. Mrs. Andretti and the three Andretti children came to America on June 16, 1955. Mario Andretti, an Italian Catholic, did not speak any English upon his arrival in Nazareth, a town that had been founded by Moravians. He and his twin brother, Aldo, had studied English in school, though, so he could understand some of the language. During the summer of 1955, Andretti and his brother practiced their English at their Uncle Louie's filling station in Nazareth. The go-getter vowed to speak proper English by Christmas 1955. He achieved this difficult goal.[7] Later, in 1964, he became an American citizen.[8]

The Andretti family has had roots in Nazareth for approximately one century. When the European Andrettis came to Nazareth in the 1950s, the Italians congregated in the West End of town. Alvise Andretti built a home for his family on the prominent side of town in 1957, at a time when few Italians lived there. In doing so, he "broke that tradition." Nazareth is proud of its most famous resident (Andretti continues to make his home there), and the town has supported him since he established himself as one of the world's top racecar drivers during the 1960s. Nazareth's Market Street became Victory Lane, a sign of how the community was proud that Andretti brought international attention to this small town in eastern Pennsylvania. Nazareth also held a major parade after he won the Indianapolis 500 in 1969.[9]

Over the years, Andretti earned a well-deserved place in the pantheon of international sporting greats. "Mario Andretti's stature in the history of motorsports remains unparalleled," wrote his biographer Gordon Kirby in 2001. "Despite his roots in Italy and its racing tradition, Mario is regarded by many as the greatest American driver ever. He won races and championships in a more diverse range of cars than anyone else and survived competitively at the top level of the sport for thirty years, much longer than any of motor racing's other great superstars."[10] "But Mario's seemingly endless catalog of victories, titles, and records [is] more than just the result of his immense natural gifts as a driver," continues Kirby. "For Mario, doing it all always included making whatever extra effort was needed to compete on or off the track, whether it meant testing new equipment, reengineering a problematic car, or studying a new track or his fellow drivers."[11]

Andretti, meanwhile, remains quite committed to his Italian heritage, one of the constants of his life. He reads, writes, and speaks standard Italian—and he converses in the Veneto dialect as well.[12] His Nazareth,

Pennsylvania, home is called Villa Montona.[13] The Formula One World champion periodically returns to Montona, the "capital of truffles," where he is very well received by the locals. Today the Andretti Winery has a reserve, "The Montona," that is served in Montona, among other places.[14] Mario Andretti frequently receives honors that recognize his stature; for instance, he was the grand marshal of the Columbus Day Parade in New York City in 2004. In 2006, similarly, he was part of the U.S. delegation to the Winter Olympics in Turin. He embodies the Italian/American connection: His wife, Dee Ann, is a native Pennsylvanian, and they have three children (Michael, Jeffrey, and Barbara Dee).[15]

Nowadays Mario Andretti continues to be one of the most enduring icons of modern American popular culture. Recording artists from a wide array of musical genres make reference to the legendary racer in their lyrics, including the Beastie Boys, Charlie Daniels, D. J. Jazzy Jeff & the Fresh Prince, Amy Grant, Ice Cube, Alan Jackson, and Gwen Stefani.[16] The Andretti family, too, continues to be prominent in the top tier of motorsports. Mario Andretti's sons, Michael Andretti and Jeff Andretti, his nephew, John Andretti, and his grandson, Marco Andretti, have all been successful racecar drivers.[17] Now retired from racing, Mario Andretti is an entrepreneur, one whose businesses include the Andretti Winery, Andretti Green Racing, and the Andretti Gordon Racing School. Indeed, he speaks with great passion and conviction about the opportunities that America "presented" to him. "I can truly say that I have lived the American Dream," notes Andretti.[18]

I. At the time of her passing on February 8, 2007, Josephine Bardelli was one of America's oldest citizens of Italian origin. A native of northern Illinois, Bardelli (née Scandroli) was born in Freeport, Illinois, on April 27, 1899. Three months later, her Lombardian-immigrant parents moved to Rockford, Illinois, her home for the next 107 years. Mr. Scandroli worked for the gas company in Rockford; he and his wife spoke the Lombardian dialect at home. Josephine, their eldest child, was fluent in both English and dialectal Italian. Consequently, she served as an interpreter for her parents as well as the neighborhood families. People came to the elder Scandrolis and asked for their daughter's assistance as an interpreter. In return, they gave a loaf of bread or some other groceries to the family.[19]

Bardelli demonstrated an amazing ability to recall the details of life in the early 1900s. Her father was a winemaker, and she remembered the intricate process that the Italians used to make homemade *vino*. She explained that her remarkable life span stemmed from a healthy diet. The Scandrolis, like many Italian families, had a garden. When Mrs. Scandroli made soup, her children went to the garden and selected the necessary vegetables for dinner that evening. Rockford's most senior resident recalled making hard bread every day: The family consumed the bread with soup. During an interview at the age of 107 in June 2006, Josephine Bardelli remembered life before indoor plumbing, automobiles on virtually every street, and the advent of supermarkets with pre-packaged foods. She shared such experiences as using a washboard for laundry, going to the cinema for five cents, working at a knitting mill for five dollars in salary every two weeks, and sledding down a hill onto the Rock River during Rockford's cold winters.[20]

Throughout her life, Bardelli lived in an organic community, surrounded by her family members and fellow Italians. Her neighborhood in Northeast Rockford was predominantly northern Italian, while the southern Italians lived in South Rockford. Bardelli's classmates at St. James School in Rockford were mainly Italian, too. Josephine Scandroli married her late husband, Stephen Bardelli, in 1917. He was an immigrant from northern Italy who lived in the same neighborhood. They had one son and four daughters. Bardelli's culinary repertoire included such foods as ravioli, risotto, cornbread, pasta fagioli, handmade tortellini, and polenta with rabbit. For years, she and several other ladies prepared spaghetti for the Sunday dinners at the Verdi Club in Rockford. Bardelli lived for ninety-eight years in the same Northeast Rockford neighborhood before she moved to an assisted-living facility elsewhere in the city. Her residence had three paintings from northern Italy that she brought back with her to the United States after a 1950 trip there.[21]

Due to her extraordinary longevity, Bardelli had firsthand memories of events, customs, and lifestyles that most Americans know about only from history books, family folklore, or television documentaries. This engaging centenarian noted with pride that her family included five living generations.[22] As a great-great-grandmother, Bardelli observed the births, baptisms, confirmations, and marriages of her descendants. They came to see her frequently and cherished their time with the family matriarch, whose life had taken place in three centuries.[23] During her 107 years of life, the

United States became a global power and the Italian-American people became an integral part of our nation.

Americans, of course, are an important component of the Italian diaspora.[24] Donna R. Gabaccia writes:

> Between 1870 and 1970, over twenty-six million persons—roughly the popula-
> tion of Italy in 1861—left home to work or live abroad, many of them temporar-
> ily. Between 1876 and 1914 a third of Italy's fourteen million migrants went to
> North America (mainly the United States) and a quarter to South America,
> mainly to Argentina and Brazil. (The rest migrated within Europe and, in far
> smaller numbers, to Africa and Australia.) Today, about sixty million persons
> of Italian descent live outside Italy, about equaling the number of Italy's mod-
> ern inhabitants. Two-thirds of this Italian diaspora live in the Americas.
> Roughly half of modern Argentines and 10 percent of Americans in the United
> States have Italian forebears.[25]

Most Italian Americans trace their ancestry to the immigrants from Italy who entered the United States between 1876 and 1930, 80 percent of whom were from southern Italy. The tens of thousands of pre-1876 Italian immigrants to the United States were mainly from northern Italy.[26] According to Joseph Lopreato, "Official Italian figures show that 5,058,776 Italians migrated to the United States in the 1876–1930 period. Of these, 4,034,204, or 80 percent of the total, were southerners, and only 1,024,572, or 20 percent, were from the central and northern regions."[27] Nearly 69 percent of the Italian immigrants who came to America during the years from 1876 to 1930 hailed from five regions of Italy: Sicily: 1,205,788 (23.8 percent); Campania: 1,105,802 (21.8 percent); Abruzzi and Molise: 652,972 (12.9 percent); and Calabria: 522,442 (10.3 percent).[28] The amount of immigration from Italy to the United States declined significantly between the mid-1920s and mid-1960s, in response to the immigration restrictions that limited significantly the number of Southern and Eastern European immigrants who could come to America.[29]

Many, if not most, Italians immigrated to the United States during the period from 1876 and 1930 because they sought greater economic opportunities. The conditions in southern Italy (the *Mezzogiorno*) in the late nineteenth and early twentieth centuries were akin to those in the poorer nations of the developing world today. The southern Italians confronted poverty, disease, illiteracy, corruption, crowded living conditions, and many other disadvantages.[30] Maldwyn Allen Jones, for one, describes the conditions in southern Italy a century ago. According to Jones, "the region as a whole presented a picture of chronic poverty unparalleled in Europe."[31] As innumerable books and articles have documented in great detail, the United States offered employment opportunities for the Italian immigrants that did not exist for them at that time in Europe. The typical American of Italian origin, then, is descended from people who came to the United States with little more than their hopes, dreams, and aspirations.

The Italian-American family stories about the process and, at times, ordeal of immigration continue to be compelling narratives that are passed down from generation to generation. Genealogical research has allowed many Americans to flesh out the details—and enhance the accuracy—of these stories. Most elderly Americans of Italian origin and many middle-aged Italian Americans have some familiarity with the experiences of their immigrant forebears. The immigration experience was undoubtedly diffi- cult for many Italians (even if they never said so later). An Italian father often came over here first and then earned enough money to pay for his wife and children to join him. Many Italian men commuted back and forth to work across the Atlantic Ocean. They often returned to live in Italy, as they had never intended to relocate to America permanently. The various accounts remind us that the Italian immigrants experienced feel- ings of deprivation, dislocation, and homesickness, while entire families were divided forever by immigration.[32]

Michael Petta shares one particularly poignant story from his family's history. It involves New Orleans. Louisiana's best-known city was once a port of entry for early Italian immigrants, many of them from Sicily. Thus Americans of Sicilian descent sometimes note that their ancestors entered the United States through New Orleans, not Ellis Island. Michael Petta remembers hearing about how his grandfather and great-uncle immi- grated from Sicily to New Orleans many years ago. The two brothers were both in their early twenties at the time. In all the commotion, the Sicilian newcomers were accidentally separated from each other at the port of entry in New Orleans. Neither man had any facility with the English lan- guage. So they were unable to enlist any American authority figures to help them find each other. For the rest of their lives, there was no further contact between the two men.[33]

Regardless of when and where the Italians arrived in America, the tenacity and perseverance of these immigrants continue to resonate with many of their descendants. George Silvestri Jr., an attorney in Marin

County, California, takes care never to forget his Italian-immigrant roots. As Silvestri relates, "I have a collection of framed certificates on my wall above my desk, which include my college and law school diplomas, my bar admission, and my state and federal court admissions (including, by the way, the United States Supreme Court). In the center column and higher than any other certificate is my Tuscan grandparents' U.S. citizenship certificate, which also names my father and uncle." This certificate of naturalization dates back to 1914 or 1915.[34]

George Silvestri Jr. arranged the documents on his office wall in this way to remind himself that none of the achievements symbolized by the other documents would have been possible unless his grandparents had made the decision to immigrate to the United States and become naturalized American citizens. Silvestri was the first member of his family to go to college (St. Mary's College in Moraga, California). He also graduated from the Hastings College of Law in San Francisco. Over the years, Silvestri has been involved in numerous Italian-American activities, including his service on the National Italian American Foundation's Board of Directors. He maintains ties to Italy as well. In 1993, the Camera di Commercio in Lucca, Italy, awarded its Medaglia d'Oro to George Silvestri Jr.[35] The Silvestri family, after all, found opportunities in America that did not exist in Europe more than a century ago.

Not all of the Italian immigrants to the United States, of course, came from modest socioeconomic backgrounds. A person of my acquaintance remembers how a professional mentor once described her as "the child of Italian immigrants," and did so in a well-meaning but paternalistic fashion. While many, if not most, Italian Americans are descended from immigrants who arrived in America with few resources and take great pride in their families' subsequent successes, such narratives certainly do not describe the experiences of every Italian immigrant family. "The child of Italian immigrants" mentioned above is of Tuscan extraction. She comes from a well-to-do family with aristocratic origins, and her story exemplifies the great diversity of the Italian-American experience. To be sure, this individual respects and celebrates the accomplishments and contributions of all Americans of Italian descent, regardless of their regional origins in Italy or the socioeconomic backgrounds of their ancestors.

During the twentieth century, Italians and others often made demarcations between "Americans" and "Italians," or Italians and other ethnic groups (e.g., the Irish or the Germans). This type of verbal dichotomy described the delicate cultural balancing act for the American-born children of immigrants in their day-to-day lives. As Jerre Mangione writes in *Mount Allegro*, "We gradually acquired the notion that we were Italian at home and American (whatever that was) elsewhere. Instinctively, we all sensed the necessity of adapting ourselves to two different worlds. We began to notice that there were several marked differences between those worlds, differences that made Americans and my relatives each think of the other as foreigners."[36] Older Americans of Italian origin made—and, to some extent, continue to make—distinctions between "Italians" and "Americans." Even today, they periodically use the terms "American," "Americans," and "Americano/i" to refer to non–Italian Americans.[37]

Depending on the context, these types of distinctions may assume semi-racial dimensions. As Matthew Frye Jacobson points out in *Whiteness of a Different Color*, "Immigrants were often as quick to recognize their racial distance from the Anglo-Saxon as vice versa."[38] Contemporary Italian Americans may refer to ethnically homogeneous European Americans (in contradistinction to Italian Americans) as "whites" or "white people," or some variant of these terms. I have encountered Italian Americans, who are unmistakably Caucasian, who use the phrases "white person" and "white people" to describe assimilated individuals of Northern European descent. Some individuals even write in "Italian" on the school forms that ask respondents to identify themselves by race; I have heard of this practice in such places as Ohio, Illinois, and West Virginia. One middle-aged Ohioan told me that he puts down "Italian," rather than "white," on any forms that ask for demographic information because of his discomfort with the idea of racial and ethnic counting.

Recent scholarship has focused on the racially ambiguous status of Italians, particularly southern Italians, in American history. While the Italians were always considered to be white in a legal sense, there is anecdotal evidence to suggest that not every Italian was seen as white—in every situation, at least—during the late nineteenth and early twentieth centuries.[39] Matthew Frye Jacobson writes, "In certain regions of the Jim Crow South Italians occupied a racial middle ground within the otherwise unforgiving, binary caste system of white-over-black. Politically Italians were indeed white enough for naturalization and for the ballot, but socially they represented a problem population at best."[40] Furthermore, Jacobson notes: "It was not just that Italians did not look white to certain social arbiters, but that they did not *act* white."[41] The Italian immigrants sometimes violated the social norms and mores of white supremacy in the decades of segregation—and they consequently encountered suspicion and discrimination from some white Southerners.[42]

During the Jim Crow era, dark-skinned Italian Americans were, on occasion, seen as "black." This phenomenon probably occurred with the greatest frequency during the summer months, when people spent more time outdoors and had bronzed skin as a result. Indeed, the legendary football coach Vince Lombardi said he was asked to leave one segregated southern restaurant because the restaurateur mistook him for a black man.[43] An Italian-American Virginian told me about how her grandfather missed the birth of one of his children because he was an active-duty service member. Upon seeing his baby for the first time, he initially denied being the infant's father on the grounds that she was black (due to her dark complexion). Several years ago in suburban New Orleans, a thirtysomething Sicilian American referred to his skin tone in a conversation with my father and me. He pointed to his arms, which were light brown in color, and said, "I have Italian arms." This fellow also mentioned his brother's dark complexion: He described him as one of "the black Italians."

The limitations and complexities of racial classification become evident in those instances where Italian Americans have been mistaken for persons of color. People of Italian origin will note that some members of their group may take on a racially ambiguous appearance in the summer when they go out into the sun on a regular basis. One Italian-American man of my acquaintance is known as "Blackie" to his friends. In the summer, he tans to the point that, in a visual sense, he resembles an African American. Such visual perceptions indicate that Americans cannot always pigeonhole Italian Americans into neat categories: They might be seen as Arabic, Latino, Armenian, Middle Eastern, or as members of other ethnic groups.

The Italian people and, to a large extent, Italian Americans are characterized by remarkable visual diversity: It is attributable to Italy's complex history of migration, conquest, and intermingling. We Americans frequently view the Italians as looking a certain way, primarily because most Italian Americans trace their ancestry to the regions south of Rome, where people often have dark hair, dark eyes, and different shades of olive skin. To be sure, Italian Americans take note of their varying skin tones, hair colors, and eye colors, but they often do so in a jocular fashion. I regularly hear stories about and from fair-skinned Italian Americans whose light-colored eyes and hair lead them not to be seen as "Italian" in the United States.[44]

❋ II.   John DeMary remembers that World War II brought people together in Rivesville, West Virginia, for two reasons.
Firstly, there was widespread bartering in this coal mining town because
of the wartime rationing. The "American" and "Italian" residents of
Rivesville traded with each other and intermingled while they did so. Secondly, people from different ethnic backgrounds worked together during
the war. Due to the wartime shortage of humanpower, women from many
different ethnic groups entered the paid workforce and labored side by
side in the factories. Likewise, Rivesville's men worked together on the
home front and served together in the military.[45] As a result of the G.I.
Bill, some young men from Rivesville went on to higher education and
became professionals.[46]

World War II and the ensuing emphasis on national unity contributed
to positive ethnic relations in Rivesville. Many of Rivesville's old-stock residents of Northern European descent considered the Italians and the other
Southern and Eastern Europeans to be "foreigners" during the 1910s, 1920s,
and 1930s. John DeMary remembers how people once described
Rivesville's Italians as "spaghetti eaters" and "garlic snappers." Old-stock
residents of Rivesville said that "hunkies and dagos" lived in the community's Greentown section, according to DeMary. (The "hunkies" traced
their ancestry to Russia, Poland, Hungary, and Lithuania.) At the same
time, the Italians were largely self-sufficient during the Depression.[47]

Minnie Rote, who is in her nineties, describes how attitudes toward the
Italians have changed over the years in Rivesville. Her father, Giuseppe
Cavallaro, settled in Rivesville in 1911. She says that her father became "the
first foreigner" to come to this lightly populated community in northern
West Virginia. Filomena—everyone knows her as "Minnie"—Rote was
born in Rivesville in 1912, the daughter of a Calabrian-immigrant father
and a Sicilian-immigrant mother. Rote, who remembers being called a
"dago" and a "garlic snapper" in second grade, has lived in the same
Greentown home since 1919, except for the one year that she spent in New
York City. Minnie Rote and her family operated Cavalier's State Novelty
News for more than four decades. Rote herself has attended virtually all
of the Rivesville Town Council meetings since the 1930s.[48] This fact led
her to receive a plaque from the Rivesville Town Council in 2005 that recognized her as "The Heart of Rivesville."

Residential segregation once existed in Rivesville's different neighborhoods. The Highlawns section of town was mainly Protestant and popu-

lated by people from old-stock, Northern European backgrounds. Rivesville's Greentown neighborhood was the province of the Italians and other Southern and Eastern European ethnics, many of whom were Catholic.[49] Alfred Bossi remembers that his Piedmontese-immigrant father, John Bossi, had a general store in Greentown from 1911 to 1929. Later, John Bossi operated a Rivesville bakery. Alfred Bossi's mother, Margaret Bossi, was well liked by both Catholics and Protestants. This Piedmontese immigrant cooked for all of Rivesville's churches when they had benefits. Alfred Bossi left Rivesville for Las Vegas during the postwar years, but he still returns to his hometown for visits.[50]

John DeMary himself has lived in Rivesville since 1938. His Italian-immigrant father, G. Pete DeMary, founded DeMary's Market, a Rivesville business, that year. John DeMary, who was born in 1919, took over his father's Rivesville general store in 1946. (This family business continues to be a staple of Rivesville's retail landscape.) Four years later, John DeMary built a home in the Highlawns section of Rivesville. Some old-timers were not happy about having an Italian move into their neighborhood. By the time John DeMary's children went to school, however, the Highlawns-Greentown distinction had no ethnic or religious significance whatsoever.[51] Today 169, or 18.6 percent, of Rivesville's 911 residents are Italian Americans, and everyone gets along well.

Over the generations the Italian immigrants and their descendants have integrated into American culture. As is common for immigrants from many ethnic, racial, and national backgrounds, the Italian-born adults who came to the United States often remained very Italian in their customs, outlook, language, and lifestyle. In many respects, they were *Italians who lived in America* more so than *Italian Americans*. However, the American-born children of these immigrants—as well as the Italian-born youngsters who went to American schools, where they were socialized as Americans—often became as American as someone whose ancestors came here centuries ago.[52] The Italian immigrants often insisted that their offspring follow Italian customs and traditions at home. At the same time, the newcomers differed as to whether they resisted, accepted, or applauded the fact that, outside the realm of family, their children and grandchildren became fully American.

World War II in particular played an indispensable role in facilitating the acceptance of Italian Americans *as Americans*. The general population saw how Italian Americans served their country honorably in the military and on the home front—and they saw how Italians of all ages flew the American flag, purchased war bonds, and in other ways signaled their unequivocal support for the United States. At least 500,000 and perhaps 1 million–plus Americans of Italian extraction served in the U.S. military during the war, 13 of whom received the Congressional Medal of Honor for their heroism. World War II answered conclusively the questions that some Americans may have had about the loyalties and allegiances of Italian Americans during the 1920s and 1930s.[53]

The book *Italians in America: A Celebration* describes how people of Italian origin became accepted members of mainstream American society after the war ended. Cataldo Leone and his co-authors write: "The postwar years also were a time when Italian Americans in general assumed a higher profile in American society. The patriotism and devotion they had shown during the war earned them the respect of the larger American public that their immigrant parents might have merited but did not enjoy. This new generation of Italian Americans, fluent in English and armed with high-school and university educations, was ready to become an integral part of American society."[54]

The Thanksgiving holiday that typifies Americana was another way in which the Italian immigrants and their descendants embraced American culture. By doing so, they signaled their acceptance of an important American holiday and, more broadly, the mores and customs of the United States. The lessons about the Pilgrims in our schools helped the young first- and second-generation Italian Americans to see themselves as part of the American culture and mainstream, even as they preserved certain Italian customs and traditions at home. Michele Tuberosa Misci remembers that her Italian-American family in East Boston always had turkey on Thanksgiving during the 1940s and 1950s, although it was never a stand-alone meal. Misci and her kinfolk enjoyed their turkey with lasagna or baked ziti, while they concluded their Thanksgiving meal with desserts of apple pie and ricotta pie each year. She summarizes the reasoning behind these American/Italian Thanksgiving meals as follows: "We cherish our American nationality and we value our Italian heritage as well."[55]

Such ideals have been evident among many of our country's most visible Italian Americans, those individuals who have achieved prominence in sports, the arts, and entertainment. In fact, figures from these fields played an important role in helping Italian Americans to gain acceptance from the broader population, as they earned the respect and admiration of Americans from many different backgrounds. By the 1940s and 1950s, one could point to a fair number of American celebrities who hailed from Italian family backgrounds. Their prominence occurred at a time when Italian Americans still experienced exclusion and discrimination in different parts of the United States.[56]

Thomas J. Ferraro delineates how Italian Americans emerged as major figures in American institutions during the twentieth century. Ferraro writes:

> It was at mid-century that Italians, in significant numbers, made their first great breach into legitimate America—into ward and city politics (Fiorello LaGuardia and Vito Marcantonio), into sports (baseball especially, but also Vince Lombardi and others in football), and, most importantly, into arts and entertainment—as character actors, classical musicians, big band instrumentalists, graphic artists, theater and film production folk of all sorts (including directors Frank Capra and Vincente Minnelli), but, especially, as makers of popular music.[57]

Now Italian Americans are so thoroughly part of the mainstream popular culture that most people probably do not even notice they are Italian. Jay Leno is the longtime host of the *Tonight Show with Jay Leno* and a popular figure on late night television. Except for his surname, though, there is really nothing overtly "Italian" about the Scottish-Italian Leno or his public persona. The same holds true for so many other prominent Americans of Italian origin. Over the years, a large number of Italian-American celebrities have adopted a wholly "American" approach to their work and lives and, by doing so, appealed to mainstream audiences.[58]

The episodes of *Everybody Loves Raymond*, a popular and critically acclaimed sitcom that aired on CBS for nine seasons from 1996 to 2005, included regular Italian-American cultural references and dynamics with a particular emphasis on food and family.[59] Italian-American names, words, foods, people, places, subtleties, cultural nuances, and identifying characteristics are an integral part of the program. *Everybody Loves Raymond* casts an Italian-American clan from Long Island, New York, as a universally American family: Frank and Marie Barone, the patriarch and matriarch, respectively; Robert and Raymond (Ray) Barone, their two sons; and Ray's Irish-American wife, Debra, and their three children. Robert Barone is an NYPD officer, while his younger brother, Ray, works as a sportswriter for Long Island's *Newsday*. The program's star and namesake, Ray Barone (Ray Romano), is an American Everyman who happens to be Italian.

Most episodes of *Everybody Loves Raymond* never explicitly reference the Italian connection. The Italian-American dynamic is thoroughly part of *Raymond*—it appears in many ways, including the mention of a neighbor's Italian surname, the types of food that Marie prepares for her family, and the Italian words and phrases that surface in the characters' dialogue. Indeed, Italian-American culture is shared with *Raymond*'s viewers in such a way that virtually every American would enjoy, appreciate, and understand it. If anything, the Italian-American dimension of this long-running television program heightened its popularity. *Everybody Loves Raymond*, in short, underscores how fundamentally American that Italian Americans and Italian-American culture have become in recent decades.

To be sure, some episodes of *Raymond* were overtly and explicitly Italian in their storylines. During an episode in the second season, a supposed relative from Italy came to visit the Barones in their Long Island, New York, home. At one point in this episode, all the adult members of the Barone family (except for Debra Barone) speak Italian without subtitles. Similarly, the two-part opening episodes during the fifth season of *Raymond* focused on the Barone family's trip to Italy, complete with Italian humor, subtitles, cultural nuances, and gorgeous settings. This storyline contributed to the show's cultural authenticity and did not detract in any way from the program's unmistakably American vibe.

While Ray Barone represents the typical middle-class American suburbanite, Rocky Balboa continues to be one of America's most enduring icons of Italian origin. The actor Sylvester Stallone has brought this fictional character to life in six films: *Rocky* (1976), *Rocky II* (1979), *Rocky III* (1982), *Rocky IV* (1985), *Rocky V* (1990), and *Rocky Balboa* (2006). Rocky Balboa is an Italian American from Philadelphia, one who rises from a dead-end life to become a world-class heavyweight boxer. His boxing nickname ("The Italian Stallion") leaves no question as to his ethnic heritage. In recent decades, Rocky Balboa has come to be identified with anyone who succeeds after s/he confronts serious odds—by virtue of much determination, great perseverance, and an exceptional work ethic.[60] Public figures, including the tennis star Serena Williams and Secretary of State Hillary Clinton, have invoked Rocky to underscore their unswerving resolve.[61]

III. Gaspare Pipitone spends much of his time working with and on behalf of Italian immigrants.[62] A native of Sicily who immigrated as a young man to the United States in 1969, Pipitone is employed by Patronato Epasa in the Glendale section of Queens, New York. According to its mission statement, "Patronato Epasa is an organization dedicated to providing people with assistance in obtaining pensions, whether it be of old age, disability, or survivor benefits." One finds this organization in different sections of Italy in addition to such nations as Canada, Belgium, Germany, Australia, Switzerland, and the United States.[63] Many Italians live in Glendale, New York, where Pipitone's office on Myrtle Avenue gives them an important connection to Italy and its complex government bureaucracy.

Pipitone was born in Sicily on November 29, 1945; he left his hometown of Camporeale after the devastating earthquake of 1968. Today he and his wife live in Queens, where she teaches at a local public school. Pipitone is involved in Com.It.Es, an Italian acronym that stands for the "Council of Italians Living Abroad." He serves as vice president, director of public relations, and president of the Language and Culture Commission of Com.It.Es of New York and Connecticut.[64] The New Yorker also hosts a Thursday morning radio program, "Patronato Epasa Informa," on the Italian Communications Network in Queens. And he writes articles as a correspondent for *America Oggi*, the Italian-language daily newspaper. On a regular basis, Pipitone travels from Queens to other parts of the New York City metropolitan area to meet with the Italians there.

In his personal life and professional activities, Gaspare Pipitone focuses mainly on Italy, Italians, and Italian culture. This friendly and outgoing man speaks fluent English, of course, but he usually communicates only in Italian with his clients. Pipitone's two daughters were born in the United States, and they remain deeply rooted in the Italian community. Their father takes pride in his heritage: He displays a photograph of the road sign to Camporeale in his Glendale, New York, office. Indeed, Pipitone lives and works in a world that blends the Italian and American cultures effortlessly and virtually seamlessly.

Italian immigration to the United States has slowed to a trickle during the last twenty-five years, now that Italy is one of the richest countries in the world. Discriminatory regulations limited the amount of immigration from Italy to America from the mid-1920s through the mid-1960s. Soon after the significant limitations on this immigration were lifted, Italy's economy began to soar and relatively few Italians wanted to immigrate to the United States anymore. Italians used to go abroad in search of opportunities; these days they typically stay in Italy. As Loretta Baldassar writes, "Northern Italy is now considered by its inhabitants as the 'America' migrants originally set out to discover."[65] Consequently, the current population of Italian Americans now largely consists of people who were born, reared, schooled, and socialized in the United States.

By analyzing data from the last eight decades, we can see how Italian-born individuals once accounted for a sizable number of Americans. In 1930, people from Italy constituted the largest group of foreign-born Americans, as 1,790,000 Americans had been born in Italy. The same was true in 1960, when 1,257,000 Americans were Italian natives, and as recently as 1970, a year in which the U.S. census counted 1,009,000 individuals who had come from Italy. In 1980, there were 832,000 Italian-born Americans; they constituted the fourth-largest source of foreign-born people here. By 1990, the number of Americans born in Italy had dropped to 581,000 and their rank among foreign-born Americans was eighth.[66] Italian-born individuals now constitute only a small percentage of the entire Italian-American population.

During the last quarter-century, there has been little immigration from Italy to the United States. Between 1981 and 2000, 55,500 Italians immigrated to America. Moreover, the United States received 9,700 Italian immigrants between 2001 and 2004. Far larger numbers of immigrants come to the United States from Asia, Latin America, and other parts of the world.[67] To be sure, there are multiple sources of immigrants with Italian backgrounds (besides those individuals who hail from Italy). The latest group of Italians to immigrate to this country comes from Latin America, particularly individuals from Brazil, Argentina, and Uruguay, countries with sizable numbers of people with Italian ancestry. Of course, the immigrants from Spanish-speaking Latin America may be seen as Hispanic more so than Italian, at least according to our nation's current classification schemas.

Italians from Italy still immigrate to the United States, just in far smaller numbers than in yesteryear. The current Italian immigrants go to America to work as actors, scientists, physicians, researchers, restaurateurs, entrepreneurs, fashion designers, computer programmers, and in other positions. Now they are often well-educated professionals who usually come to the United States with certain marketable skills. Contemporary Italian immigrants often see little in common with native-born Italian Americans (and vice versa). Italian-born individuals who were socialized in Italy, and who went to school there, have a different outlook and perspective than native-born Italian Americans or those Italian immigrants who came here at very young ages. The new Italian immigrants blend in easily in Multicultural America, where they benefit from and contribute to the glamorous reputation that Italy enjoys in the United States.

I have met some Italian Americans who were born in the United States, went to live in Italy at a young age during the 1920s or 1930s, and eventually returned to America after World War II. One such individual, Donato Federico, was born in Elizabeth, New Jersey, in 1921. He and his family went to Italy (specifically, the Province of Benevento) in 1923 because his grandfather had a large farm and he needed people to help him cultivate the land. Federico wanted to return to the United States in 1935; however, he could not do so because of the ongoing Italo-Ethiopian War. This American-born Italian was conscripted to serve in the Italian Army from 1940 to 1944. Once the geopolitical conditions allowed him to reenter the United States, Federico permanently returned to the land of his birth in 1946.[68] In addition to narratives like Donato Federico's transnational story, one hears about older Americans of Italian extraction who lived in Italy as children for a period of time before their families decided to come back to the United States.

Some Italian Americans were born as U.S. citizens in Italy and lived the first part of their lives there. Rose and Domenick Guarnieri hail from the same hometown—Roccella Ionica in Calabria—even though they met each other in the United States.[69] Both individuals were born as American citizens in Italy, because their fathers, Peter Meli and Felice Guarnieri, had served in the U.S. Army during World War I and consequently became naturalized Americans. Meli and Guarnieri then returned to Italy, where they started their families. Rose Guarnieri (née Meli) came into the world on November 27, 1928. She and her family immigrated to the United States in 1932; they settled in Brooklyn. Meanwhile, Domenick Guarnieri was living in Italy. He was born in Calabria on December 6, 1921. Throughout the 1930s his father, Felice Guarnieri, planned on taking his entire family—which included six children by 1940—to live in the United States.

In 1940 Felice Guarnieri and his oldest son, Domenick, set out for the United States; they expected that the other members of their family would join them once they found a permanent home in America. Domenick

Guarnieri, an American citizen, was eighteen years old when he visited the United States for the first time. Rose Guarnieri describes what happened next: "Shortly after Domenick and his father arrived in the United States, World War II broke out, and all travel and communication between America and Italy ceased. His mother and five siblings remained in Italy for the duration of the war. In the meantime, Domenick was drafted and served in the U.S. military during World War II. The family was reunited after the end of the war."

Domenick Guarnieri and Rose Meli were married on September 26, 1948, at Brooklyn's beautiful Regina Pacis Church. Guarnieri met Meli, a graduate of Brooklyn's Bay Ridge High School, in Brooklyn. Their fathers knew each other. The Guarnieris lived in Brooklyn until 1959, when they relocated to southern California. The temperate weather in Orange County, California, where they make their home, resembles the pleasant climate of Roccella Ionica, Italy. Today the Guarnieris grow lemons, oranges, tomatoes, and other fruits and vegetables in their backyard. They stay in close contact with their sons, Donald Guarnieri and Richard Guarnieri, and their grandchildren, all of whom live in southern California. In 2008 the Guarnieris celebrated six decades of marriage; they have a network of family and friends that extends from California to the East Coast and beyond to Italy and Australia.

As a rule, Italian immigrants report that they deeply appreciate the opportunities available to them in the United States. Anthony Polsinelli immigrated to the United States from a village in Lazio at the age of seventeen in 1968. From the beginning, he has enjoyed his time in America, where people have received him well. Now Polsinelli co-owns his own business, Saturn Bronze Inc., in McMechen, West Virginia, and he gives back to the community through his involvement in such activities as the Upper Ohio Valley Italian Festival. The fiftysomething entrepreneur uses the metaphor of gold as a proxy for the opportunities that exist in his adopted homeland. Polsinelli says, "If you're willing to try, you will find gold here. The gold is still here." He says of himself: "I have found the gold mines."[70]

Similarly, Renato Turano is an American entrepreneur, philanthropist, and political leader who gives back to the community through his civic leadership and public service. Turano was born in 1942 and lived until 1958 in Castrolibero, a town in northern Calabria.[71] His father, Mariano Turano, immigrated to the United States in 1955 upon the advice of his brother, Carmen, who had come here many years earlier. In America,

Mariano Turano first worked as a laborer in the sewers. Due to his feelings of cultural and economic dislocation, he returned to Calabria. Soon, however, Mariano Turano went back to America.[72] Renato Turano, his mother, Assunta, and his brothers, Umberto and Giancarlo, followed their father to the United States in 1958.[73] "My father dreamed of returning to Italy, but he knew that America was the place where his children would have a better future," remembers Turano.[74] "So, like so many others before him, he left his dream of Italy behind to build a new dream in America."[75]

Mariano Turano worked with his three sons to build a successful business, beginning with his purchase of a Chicago bakery in 1962. This shop was the forerunner of what is now known as the Turano Baking Company. Renato, Umberto, and Giancarlo Turano all worked in the family-owned bakery business and built it into a multimillion-dollar behemoth. Currently, the Turano Baking Company operates five plants, three in the Chicago suburbs of Berwyn, Bolingbrook, and Bloomingdale—and two new plants in the South (Florida and Georgia, respectively). Renato Turano serves as chairman of the board of the Turano Baking Company, while Umberto Turano is president—production and operations and Giancarlo Turano is executive vice president—sales and marketing.[76] In addition, he is the immediate past chairman of the board of directors of the American Bakers Association.[77]

Besides his thriving business ventures, Renato Turano has been deeply involved in Italian-American activities for decades. In the late 1960s, he and several other individuals started the Italian American Civic Organization of Berwyn. Over the years, Turano has led such organizations as the Columbian Club of Chicago, the Calabresi in America Organization, the Italian American Civic Organization of Berwyn, and the Italian American Chamber of Commerce—Midwest. Turano, moreover, is a co-founder and the first chairman of Casa Italia in Stone Park, Illinois, and a member of the board of directors of *Fra Noi*, the Italian-American newspaper in Chicago. A generous supporter of Italian-American causes, events, and activities, Renato (many Americans know him as "Ron") Turano is a dual citizen of Italy and the United States.[78]

Turano maintains close ties to Italy in general and Calabria in particular. As a member of the Italian Parliament earlier this decade, he spent much of each year in Rome on legislative business.[79] Furthermore, this son of southern Italy returns to Calabria, on average, three to four times each year.[80] In 1995 Turano became, in the words of *Fra Noi*, a "*consultore* to the Region of Calabria, representing the interests of Calabresi in America at annual conferences in Italy."[81] Indeed, the Chicago resident is strongly committed to keeping the connections alive between Italy and North America. He astutely notes that the family ties that connect Italians and Italian Americans were once closer and more immediate than they are today. In response to a question about America forty years ago, the average Calabrian might have replied that he had an uncle in America. Now the typical Calabrian is more likely to say that he may have some distant cousins in the United States.[82]

To promote transatlantic ties between Italy and the United States, Turano engages in numerous activities. Most notably, he served as an Italian senator from 2006 to 2008. During this period he represented a constituency that encompassed the Italian citizens of Canada, the United States, Mexico, and Central America.[83] Turano's multifaceted platform emphasized the importance of reinforcing the cultural and economic ties between Italians in Italy and the Italians abroad.[84] "We look to Italy to provide us with language lessons, better consular services and cultural programs," says Senator Turano. "We look to Italy to help us stay in touch with our heritage and pass that along to our children."[85] At the same time, Italy gains, too, from allowing the Italian citizens abroad to elect representatives to the Italian Parliament.[86] "As programs increase and services improve," notes Turano, "Italy will build even stronger bonds with its descendants living abroad, and those bonds will have economic benefits that are equally strong."[87]

❀   ❀   ❀

There are countless family immigration narratives that contemporary Italian Americans remember with feelings of pride, gratitude, and appreciation. Pasquale Pesce remarks that he admires his immigrant parents, who passed through Ellis Island, for their pluck, courage, and determination to pack up and leave Italy for a new country.[88] Ellis Island, of course, is a significant reference point for many Americans, as 40 percent of us have family narratives that include a forebear or forebears whose immigration experiences involved being processed there.[89] Not every Italian American, of course, has a family story about Ellis Island. John Scara, for one, notes that his Italian-immigrant grandparents entered the United States before Ellis Island became a port of entry.[90]

Ellis Island and the Statue of Liberty hold particular meaning for Ernest Marinelli because his father, William (Willy) Marinelli, had immigrated to the United States from Italy. During the Independence Day Weekend in 2006, Ernest Marinelli and his wife, Pat, visited New York City to take part in the International Tyrolean Trentino Organization of North America (ITTONA) Convention. At the time Marinelli was the president of the Tirolesi-Trentini Del Colorado. The Marinellis went on a tour of New York and environs. The tour enabled them to travel past the Statue of Liberty and visit Ellis Island.[91]

Ernest Marinelli writes of his reaction to seeing the Statue of Liberty: "The first stop was the Statue of Liberty. As we approached this magnificent Lady of the Bay, standing tall as a sentry guarding the bay, my chest puffed out with pride. As I looked up at her, as we were not allowed inside, I thought how great she is, representing the liberty and freedom our ancestors and so many other foreigners so desired. You have to wonder, allowing a tear or two to well up in your eyes, did my dad stand here and look at her, what did he think?"[92]

After the Statue of Liberty, Ernest and Pat Marinelli went to Ellis Island. It was a poignant period of time for Mr. Marinelli. "My father," noted Ernest Marinelli, "was processed here when he came to America." The younger Marinelli characterized the legendary port of entry in the following terms: "The island of hope, the island of dreams, and for me the island of forgiveness."[93] As he stood on the sidewalk at Ellis Island and took in the awe-inspiring New York City skyline, this Italian-American Coloradan thought about his father's experiences as an eighteen-year-old immigrant. "I wondered if I might be standing on or near the spot where my father might have stood, thinking of what the future might hold for him," says Ernest Marinelli. "I am sure he wondered . . . if he would meet a nice girl and have a family, and maybe he shed a tear or two, wondering about the future and thinking about the family he left behind."[94]

Marinelli had an emotional epiphany at Ellis Island, as he contemplated the meaning of his father's life, legacy, and fateful decision to leave Italy.[95] He writes: "I began to realize my dad did this and much more for me, and I know now I really did not appreciate what he did. Like most young kids we do not think. I may not have been the best son, but his dream did come true and I miss him. Now I must see that his Trentini heritage is carried on and not forgotten for the good life he has given to me. What would this country have been if not for the hard work of these immigrants? What courage they had."[96]

Now let us turn to Barbara Tenaglia Abela's perspective on this topic.

Abela's father, Raffaele "Ralph" Tenaglia, was born in Abruzzi in 1914. He came to the United States when he was five years old. Abela happened to be accompanying her father and mother on a cruise as they went by the Statue of Liberty and Ellis Island in the late 1980s. "My father stood there on the ship looking at the statue with tears coming down his face," remembers Barbara Tenaglia Abela. She asked her father what was wrong, and he explained his emotional reaction to the Statue of Liberty. "You don't know what that statue means to people who come from the other side," Ralph Tenaglia told his American-born daughter. Tenaglia's reflections on his immigrant background left an indelible imprint on Barbara Tenaglia Abela's mindset.[97]

In fact, Ralph Tenaglia's perspective guides Abela in her role as president of LIADO—Le Italo-Americane Di Oggi/The Italian-American Women of Today, a Florida-based organization that holds a San Gennaro Festa every year. Through their monthly meetings, their regular cultural activities, and their popular annual festival, Abela and her colleagues revere the Italian traditions of their immigrant ancestors while they seek to make these Italian customs relevant to contemporary Italian Americans. LIADO's San Gennaro festival is organized, designed, and led by women who are, in many cases, the children and grandchildren of Italian immigrants. In doing so, they seek to promote the Italian-American heritage and carry it forward. They also present a positive impression of Italians, one that counteracts what they see as the stereotypical images of *The Sopranos* and similar programming. The festival, furthermore, is an important fundraiser for local charities—one example, among many, of how Italian Americans sustain the communities in which they live.[98]

Chapter 2

STEREOTYPING, DISCRIMINATION, AND ACCEPTANCE

John Stossel of ABC News interviewed Dona De Sanctis and other Italian Americans for a *20/20* segment on Hollywood and ethnic stereotyping that aired on September 8, 2006.[1] In the broadcast, Stossel notes: "Most Italian Americans have nothing to do with organized crime. But you wouldn't know that watching TV. This angers some Italian activist groups."[2] After Stossel's initial commentary, De Sanctis appears on camera: "We are among the few ethnic minorities that it's still okay to make fun of and that's not right. Our young people don't want to be identified with the guys who talk like this, because that's not them."[3] In the same program, the actors Vincent Pastore and Pat Cooper offered perspectives that were uncritical of Mafia imagery in American popular culture.[4]

The Italian-American dialogue on ethnic stereotyping continued in the *20/20* segment. De Sanctis appeared again in the program to respond to Cooper and Pastore: "I have to say to people like Pat Cooper, I'm sorry, your portrayals are influencing public opinion. The popularity of a stereotype doesn't justify it. Cowboy and Indian movies were wildly popular for generations, but that doesn't make the stereotype right."[5] De Sanctis's interview with John Stossel was in keeping with her role as a prominent advocate for Italian Americans. She is regularly cited and contacted by journalists for her perspective on Italian-American issues, culture, and controversies. Indeed, this native New Yorker has spent much of her professional career in fields involving Italy and Italian/American culture.

During her childhood in Brooklyn, Dona De Sanctis recalls that she "fell in love with the Italian language and culture."[6] Her grandparents were born in Campania, and they came to the United States in 1880. A graduate of New Utrecht High School in Brooklyn in 1959, De Sanctis remembers when relatively few Italian Americans went to college. She herself graduated from Brooklyn College in 1963 and went on to earn a doctorate in Italian and Comparative Literature. As a graduate student, the third-generation Italian American received a Fulbright Scholarship to go to Italy for one year, where she studied at the University of Rome. "Then," De Sanctis notes, "I married an Italian and lived in Rome for eight years." After her first husband's passing, she returned to the United States with her son, Leonardo. For years she "taught Italian at various colleges here and in Italy." De Sanctis eventually moved to Washington, where she engaged in public relations work and journalism, had "much experience in magazine writing," and became deeply involved in a number of Italian groups.[7]

Since the early 1990s De Sanctis has worked for Italian-American advocacy organizations. In 1992 the National Italian American Foundation had an opening for the position of Director of Communications at the organization's Washington headquarters. The job was a "perfect fit" for De Sanctis, due to her proficiency in Italian and media and journalistic experience. At the National Italian American Foundation, she was responsible for media relations, research and reports, NIAF's *Ambassador* magazine, antidefamation activities, and the organization's bimonthly newsletter. In 2002 she became deputy executive director of the Order Sons of Italy in America (OSIA) in Washington. At OSIA, De Sanctis had similar duties to her position at NIAF. She wrote research reports, engaged in antidefamation work, discharged administrative responsibilities, and served as editor-in-chief of OSIA's quarterly magazine (*Italian America*), among other activities.[8] Then, in 2007, De Sanctis resigned as OSIA deputy executive director. Still, she continues to serve as editor-in-chief of *Italian America* and produce *OSIA Nation* (the organization's quarterly newsletter), along with periodic project work.[9]

Dona De Sanctis and her colleagues have conducted "much research to educate the public" and counter any existing stereotypes about Italian Americans. They regularly write research reports in order to answer individual questions and/or address current events.[10] In 2005, for example,

Dona De Sanctis and Research Assistant Krissy Ellison compiled *Italian American Crime Fighters: A Brief Survey*.[11] "As this report reveals," write De Sanctis and Ellison, "Italian Americans have enforced the law as police officers, detectives, criminal prosecutors, district attorneys, U.S. attorneys general and judges at federal, state and local levels."[12] *Italian American Crime Fighters* mentions such individuals as Catherine Abate, Charles Bonaparte, Geraldine Ferraro, Louis Freeh, Rudolph Giuliani, Nancy Jardini, Frank Panessa, Joseph Petrosino, Joseph Pistone, Frank Serpico, and Judge John J. Sirica.[13]

There are numerous viewpoints on defamation and stereotyping within the Italian-American community, a subject that De Sanctis discusses with sensitivity. This granddaughter of Italian immigrants notes that OSIA seeks "respect," not "the mantle of victimhood," in its efforts to combat bias and stereotyping against Italian Americans. She observes that older Italian-American men particularly "don't embrace victimhood." Some are "too proud" to think of themselves as the victims of bigotry—consequently, they do not always support specific antidefamation efforts.[14] While Italian Americans may differ on the impact and magnitude of stereotyping, it is undeniable that the advocacy and educational efforts of OSIA and other Italian-American organizations have made a real difference in improving the image of the ethnic group as a whole.

De Sanctis herself spent more than 15 years actively working professionally on antidefamation issues.[15] "On the plus side," writes this long-time ethnic advocate, "I believe the media, the American public and Italian Americans themselves are far more aware of the sting of stereotyping than they were 10 or 15 years ago."[16] She cautions, however, that stereotyping is still an issue for Italian Americans; "examples can be found in *Italian America* magazine's ironically titled column, 'It's Only A Movie,' that shows how stereotyping has invaded all levels of our society from children's books, to political campaigns, to high school sports."[17]

Looking toward the future, De Sanctis sees cultural grants at a community level as an effective means of promoting positive images of Italian Americans. Such grants could be used to sponsor exhibits and conferences about Italian-American culture and history; purchase multimedia materials (books, DVDs, and other items that showcase Italian Americans in a positive light) for public schools and libraries; and fund the travel expenses of an educator's summer studies in Italy, in order to enhance her or his linguistic skills and lead to improved teaching and higher enrollments in

Italian-language classes.[18] These creative suggestions reflect Dona De Sanctis's lifelong commitment to education and her dedicated advocacy on behalf of the Italian-American community.

I. Before he became an American cultural icon during the 1960s, the fabled football coach Vince Lombardi had his own experiences with anti-Italian bias. His biographer, David Maraniss, writes:

> Lombardi had been keenly aware of the sting of prejudice long before his supposed *Black Like Me* experience in Winston-Salem. He had gone through life being called a dago and wop and guinea because of his dark skin and southern Italian heritage. Throughout his school years he had struggled to overcome the lower academic expectations that society seemed to have for Italian boys. In high school and college he had tried to dress more sharply, scrub cleaner, keep his hair trimmer and maintain a more businesslike appearance just so that he would not be defined by stereotypes. At Fordham, he had risked suspension from the football team by tackling and punching a teammate who had taunted him in the shower with ethnic epithets. At various points during his long apprenticeship in coaching, he had suspected that his advancement had been slowed by bias against Italians. But the world teems with people who are sensitive to prejudice only when it is against them, not when they are inflicting it on others. Lombardi's concern seemed universal, not merely self-centered.[19]

Today Vince Lombardi is one of America's most revered coaches of all time. During the 1960s, he achieved national prominence by taking the Green Bay Packers to victories in Super Bowls I and II, among other triumphs. The native New Yorker, too, transcended sports to become a significant public figure, one who stood for traditional American values during a tumultuous time in U.S. history. With his close-cropped haircuts, uncritical celebration of America, and emphasis on winning through teamwork and discipline, Lombardi won plaudits from many on the Right. Yet this racially tolerant coach enjoyed friendships with the Kennedys and considered himself to be a Democrat. Republican presidential candidate Richard Nixon, who privately voiced derogatory views of Italians, even considered Lombardi as his running mate in 1968. At the time of his death in 1970, Lombardi's prominence symbolized—and contributed to—the increasing integration of Italian Americans into the mainstream of American life.[20]

Until the 1960s and 1970s, people from Italian backgrounds regularly encountered discrimination and stereotyping that affected their life chances. Initially, the masses of Italian immigrants did not win acceptance easily for a variety of reasons, including their relative poverty, Roman Catholicism, cultural values, lack of proficiency in English, and other identifying aspects of foreignness. Their skin tones, facial features, and visual characteristics were often different from those of the Americans from Northern and Western European backgrounds. The Italian immigrants encountered hostility, too, because native-born workers were concerned that they offered competition for jobs and depressed wage scales in a number of industries. And their sheer numbers led nativists to take note of them.[21] "It was the unfortunate fate of Italian immigrants to be the largest nationality of 'new immigrants' at a time of a thriving anti-immigrant sentiment that characterized the late nineteenth and early twentieth centuries," according to Salvatore J. LaGumina.[22]

The prejudice and discrimination against Italians were quite acute during the era of mass immigration from Italy to the United States. "It was at the turn of the twentieth century, a time of dramatic increase in Italian immigration and a period of economic crisis, that anti-Italian sentiments flourished," notes LaGumina.[23] The levels of discrimination varied, to some extent, in different parts of America. In the Midwest, the Northeast, and other parts of the country, one found employers who would not hire Italians, fraternal organizations that would not admit them, and residential developments that excluded them. These experiences did not always occur frequently or, for that matter, occur in every community.[24] Yet there were a number of instances of mob violence against Italians in the United States between 1874 and 1920, most prominently the lynching of eleven Italians in New Orleans in 1891.[25]

Since the 1920s there has been a consistent decline in discrimination against Italian Americans. The gradual assimilation and integration of people from Italian family backgrounds during the 1920s, the 1930s, and particularly the 1940s led to greater acceptance for them. After World War II, Italian Americans became more affluent, better educated, and part of suburban America in significant numbers. The bias, prejudice, and discrimination that they encountered were subtler and less overt than in the past. As a result of the ethnic mobilization of the 1960s and 1970s Italian Americans founded organizations to counteract any existing discrimination against members of their ethnic group. These developments, coupled with the rising numbers of Italian-American decision-makers, further reduced the like-lihood that individuals of Italian descent would face barriers based on eth-nicity. By the 1970s and 1980s the stereotyping of Italian Americans in pop-ular culture (particularly the frequent depiction of Italians as criminals or buffoons) had become the primary obstacle that remained for them.[26]

There are numerous stereotypes that have affected Italian Americans over the years. In his book, *The things they say behind your back*, William B. Helmreich lists several stereotypes of Italian Americans: "Belong to the Mafia"; "Cowards in battle"; "Family-oriented, clannish, distrustful of outsiders"; "Great shoemakers"; "Great singers"; "Stupid, ignorant, suspi-cious of education"; "Talk with their hands"; and "Violent and quick-tem-pered."[27] Of course, these stereotypes of Italian Americans have certainly diminished in significance over the years, as a result of their exceptional accomplishments in many fields and full-scale integration into the Amer-ican mainstream.[28]

The stereotype of Italian-American criminality, violence, and Mafia involvement is an enduring American archetype that dates back to the nineteenth century.[29] Italian-American gangsters are a staple of American popular culture; their frequent appearances in films, novels, and television programs make them universally recognized figures. These hoodlums and mobsters have been portrayed in such well-known media as *Little Caesar* (1931), *Scarface* (1932), *The Untouchables* (1959 to 1963), *The Godfather* novel (1969), *The Godfather* films (1972, 1974, 1990), *Goodfellas* (1990), *Donnie Brasco* (1997), *Analyze This* (1999) and *Analyze That* (2002), and *The Sopra-nos* (1999 to 2007).[30] "The mass media preoccupation with Italian Ameri-can mobsters sustains the illusions that the Mafia myth can be extrapo-lated to all Italian Americans," contends Donald Tricarico.[31]

The American Mafia, to be sure, has had a very real presence in our nation. Thomas Reppetto is the author of a two-volume history of this distinctively American entity of Italian-American criminals who have like-minded associates from a wide variety of ethnic groups.[32] There are many different types of criminals that receive public attention. "Yet the American Mafia is more than just another group of criminals," writes Reppetto.[33] "Since the 1920s it has been the heart and soul of American organized crime. As such it has exercised significant influence on the political and economic life of the country."[34]

In his books, Thomas Reppetto traces the gradual development, period of significant influence, and eventual decline of this criminal empire.[35] As he notes: "That an organization that never had more than five thousand full-fledged members could exercise such immense power is one of the most phenomenal accomplishments in the history of the United States. It was not, however, a lasting achievement."[36] Due to its very real power in past decades, continuing presence in the underworld (however attenuated), and enduring notoriety in popular culture, the American Mafia remains the best-known criminal entity in our nation and a constant source of stereotypes for Americans of Italian origin.[37]

In addition to the stereotyping stemming from the Mafia, such terms as *wop*, *dago*, *guinea*, and *greaseball* have been used over the years to denigrate, disparage, and downgrade Americans of Italian origin.[38] These insults have been heard less commonly in recent decades. "Processes of assimilation and upward mobility contradict insulting ethnic epithets, especially for the generations born after World War II," notes Donald Tricarico.[39] As with many epithets today, the offense given and taken by using such terms can be contextual. Sometimes friends may use an epithet like *wop* among themselves and there is no offense given or taken. In recent years, the word "guido" has emerged as a term for Italian-American males; it can be derogatory, depending on who says it and in what context.[40] Similarly, one who describes the Verrazano-Narrows Bridge in New York City as "the guinea gangplank" is unlikely to win many friends among Italian Americans. Many Americans, too, pronounce the word "Italian" with a long "I" on the first syllable, a pronunciation that does not always meet with favor from people of Italian descent.

The extent to which discrimination and stereotyping have affected the life chances of Italian Americans depends on the individual, the context, the time period, the geographical area, and other considerations. Sometimes siblings in the same family (who are from the same cohort) did not experience the same feelings of exclusion and discrimination. To be sure, the stories of anti-Italian bias in decades past still come up regularly in conversations with older people from Italian backgrounds. Even the perception of Italian heritage could be enough to hinder someone. Anti-Italian discrimination once existed in the workplace, where the relatively low social status of Italian Americans during the first half of the twentieth century could hinder their ability to get ahead. I have heard stories from the 1930s and 1940s of men who were not hired for jobs because of their Italian names; after failing to gain employment, they went back to the same places seeking employment with more "American"-sounding names and found work. And, of course, there are many stories of Mob-related stereotyping, past and present, in Italian America.

The stereotyping of Italians went beyond the Mafia, of course, and could involve a subtle disdain for people of Italian origin. One of my respondents from Maine recalls an experience during the late 1940s where a woman did not want her daughter dating any *guineas*. An Italian-American man remembers when his non-Italian wife-to-be received advice from her parents not to marry an Italian, on the grounds that "they beat their wives" and "they cheat on them." Her father later apologized to him, but her mother never saw any need to do so. Elsewhere, an American of Italian descent in his early nineties remembered some commentary involving a new home in his Ohio neighborhood approximately fifty years ago. The neighborhood observer reportedly said: "There is a beautiful house being built down the street, but, you know, they're Italians." The home-owners' Italian background apparently diminished the value of their home, at least in the eyes of this man.

Italian Americans also share anecdotes about not being accepted: these stories do not refer to overt discrimination per se, but rather the idea of being outsiders in a given context. An Italian American recalls moving to Somerset County, New Jersey, several decades ago with his wife. After the couple introduced themselves to their new neighbors, everyone was polite to them, yet they were never invited to any of the parties that people had at their homes. He also recalls when there was an unspoken understanding that an Italian American would never rise above a certain executive level in his company. Today New Jersey is a state in which Italian Americans are, of course, an essential part of the mainstream culture and institutions.

At the same time, the narratives of anti-Italian discrimination are by no means universal. One Italian immigrant told me that he never encountered any ethnic bias when he came to the United States during the 1950s. Not surprisingly, anti-Italian discrimination was often a nonissue in those places with substantial numbers of Italian Americans. An older woman of Italian origin recalled that there were no concerns about anti-Italian discrimination in her South Philadelphia neighborhood because virtually everyone was Italian there. Likewise, an older man in Providence, Rhode Island, said that the Italian Americans in his cohort encountered no problems due to their ethnic names or Italian lunches. Their numbers were such that they could acquit themselves quite well if anyone mocked or challenged them.

Some Americans of Italian descent report that their athletic abilities helped them gain acceptance from the general population. Middle-aged and elderly men mentioned this observation to me in different parts of America, from northern California to Indianapolis, Indiana, to Millinocket, Maine. As a young Tuscan immigrant to the San Francisco Bay Area in the 1950s, Emil Bagneschi was exposed to baseball during physical education in the sixth grade. A fellow student showed him how to hold and use a baseball bat and he took to the sport immediately. In high school, Emil Bagneschi was selected as an "ALL-PAL" (Pacific Athletic League) Player and to be on the "All Star" Team in Burlingame, California.[41] Bagneschi reports that his athletic successes, particularly in baseball, "gave me confidence to excel at other things."[42] By participating in their schools' teams, Bagneschi and the other Italian-American amateur athletes garnered favorable publicity that reflected well on the entire Italian-American community.

II. Since he immigrated to the United States from England in 1948, Jim Rahilly has had long-standing social, family, and business relationships with Italian Americans. This English immigrant of Irish origin came to the United States as a teenager with his family. Rahilly married his Italian-American wife, Lucille, during the 1950s; thus he is part of an extended Italian family. For a number of years, Jim and Lucille Rahilly lived in South Brooklyn, the setting of *Moonstruck*, where they owned their own house. Mrs. Rahilly's mother and sister and her brother, sister-in-law, and their children lived in different sections of this house. Other relatives resided in a renovated home nearby. "As you can see, I was very involved with Italians," remembers Jim Rahilly.[43]

Appropriately enough, this "Italian By Marriage" offers some interesting observations about ethnic stereotyping. Jim Rahilly writes:

> I had an insurance agency on Long Island and insured a lot of Italian contractors. If they were very successful I was asked if they were "connected." The people did not know that most of the owners worked very hard for years to build their businesses. One, in particular, had a fleet of cement trucks but he still lived in the same house and had the same lifestyle. I asked him what he was doing with all of the money from his business. His answer: "I am building it for my sons." When buying a large life insurance policy, he listed his occupation as a truck driver. I said, "You are the president of a substantial corporation." His answer, in an Italian accent: "I still drive the truck sometimes." A very humble, hardworking Italian.[44]

Jim Rahilly's extensive familiarity with Italian Americans and his appreciation of their cultural heritage enable him to comment insightfully on how people of Italian descent have become part of mainstream America. He remembers when, as a young man, he worked with several older Italian Americans at a New York City insurance company. These men shared with him the story of how they had adopted non-Italian surnames upon joining this firm years earlier.[45] Indeed, Rahilly enjoys the company of people from different ethnic backgrounds, and his sensitivity to the stereotyping of Italian Americans reflects his inclusive and open-minded perspective. Today people of Italian origin are well accepted in our country, in part because millions of non-Italians like Jim Rahilly have embraced their Italian friends, neighbors, colleagues, classmates, and family members.

Now, after more than one hundred years of progress, Italian Americans differ over the extent to which they face any remaining stereotyping and even discrimination.[46] Many Americans from Italian backgrounds consider overt or covert bigotry against Italians to be a thing of the past. Yet I still hear current stories, anecdotes, and examples from my respondents that relate to subtle prejudice against Italians. One man told me that he continues to encounter negative stereotyping related to the Mafia and positive stereotyping about his mother's cooking. "Your mother must be a great cook," people tell him. In his case, for certain, there is no truth to either stereotype. And Italian Americans with non-Italian surnames and appearances report they have heard negative comments about Italians in their presence. Apparently, their interlocutors felt free to make such remarks because they thought no one would take offense.

Over the years, opinion surveys have documented that a significant percentage of the American public may give credence to stereotypes that conflate the Mob with Italian Americans as a group.[47] Italian Americans have had their life chances affected by stereotypes about their supposed involvement in the American Mafia (perhaps in the form of diminished social standing relative to their professional achievements).[48] Likewise, some well-known Italian-American political figures—Geraldine Ferraro and Mario Cuomo chief among them—once confronted enervating rumors about their families and possible connections to organized crime.[49] Rudolph Giuliani, however, has encountered relatively few issues on this front. As U.S. attorney for the Southern District of New York during the 1980s, Giuliani prosecuted mobsters, dishonest politicians, and inside traders on Wall Street.[50] "His national prominence as a racket buster also shielded Giuliani from the stigma of the Mafia, which had affected the election campaigns of a number of other Italian Americans," notes Stefano Luconi.[51]

The fallacious notion that many Italian Americans are "connected" to the Mafia continues to be salient in a variety of contexts. Americans with the surnames of Capone and Gambino report having encountered Mob-related jokes, comments, and innuendoes, due to Al Capone's infamy and the Gambino crime family's prominence in underworld circles.[52] Folks sometimes jokingly say that an Italian-American migrant to a place with relatively few Italians (e.g., Nashville, Tennessee, Springfield, Missouri, or Green Bay, Wisconsin) is actually part of the Witness Protection Program. Moreover, northeasterners from Italian backgrounds report being asked about their "connections" in such places as Florida and Colorado. Older Italian Americans remember how, at one time, some people in Buffalo, New York, might hint that successful Italians had possible Mafia ties—and those "connections" helped them to get ahead. Even today, affluent Italian Americans describe their periodic encounters with individuals who insinuate that they have made their money illegitimately through machinations and nefarious methods.

The organized-crime stereotype for Italian Americans shows up internationally, as it has been disseminated around the world through American films and television programs. One of my respondents told me that his Italian relatives are fascinated by stories about the American Mafia. Moreover, I interviewed an Italian-born American who recalled how the Mafia stereotype surfaced in his tour group during a trip he took to Mexico. There was a point when everyone on the tour introduced himself to the entire group. After this man said his name was "Tony," the Mexican tour guide started humming the theme music from *The Godfather*. In my travels, I have heard jokes, comments, and observations about the stereotypes involving Italian Americans and organized crime in such nations as Italy, Brazil, Lebanon, and Pakistan.

There are divergent Italian-American reactions to the organized-crime stereotype. Many people ignore or dismiss it. After all, it is not uncommon for Italian Americans to enjoy films and television programs that involve Italian-American gangsters. Others are angered and irritated by this kind of stereotyping—and what they feel it does to minimize the accomplishments of Italian Americans as a group. While many Americans are sharply critical of organized crime, it is possible to encounter individuals who take a nuanced view of the Mafia and even speak positively about certain aspects of its activities. Some older Italian Americans will say that the Mafia kept their neighborhoods safe. At one of my talks, an elderly Italian-American man said, "We brought class to the rackets."

Northern Californians of Italian descent often report that they have experienced little, if any, discrimination and stereotyping in their lives. George Silvestri Jr. notes that northern California's Italian-American communities typically date back to the nineteenth century "when the State was only a few decades old." They developed in a context where, except for World War II, there were relatively few instances in which native-born Italians felt a sense of estrangement from the mainstream culture. In fact, Silvestri remembers that he once had a conversation with a fellow attorney, an Italian American from Connecticut with what he describes as "a far different experience." "Frank," Silvestri said to his colleague, "you should come to California. We are the Yankees." At the same time, Silvestri tells his coethnics in northern California that they should support antidefamation efforts at the national level because stereotyping still affects Italians elsewhere in the country.[53]

Likewise, many Italian Americans in northern California trace their ancestry to northern Italy, in contrast to most Americans of Italian origin. William Cerruti is the grandson of Ligurian immigrants; the Sacramento, California, attorney and ethnic advocate notes that the media portrayals of Italian-American criminals typically highlight people from southern Italian backgrounds. Cerruti posits that antidefamation efforts matter just as much for Americans of northern Italian descent as they do for people of southern Italian extraction. In his opinion, the media portrayals of southern Italians (e.g., *The Godfather* trilogy and *The Sopranos*) and resultant stereotypes affect all individuals with Italian surnames. Therefore, he believes that Americans with northern Italian backgrounds should join their southern Italian compatriots in fighting bias and discrimination.[54]

Some Americans of Italian descent draw upon their experiences—and those of their parents and grandparents—to explain their views about multiculturalism and diversity issues. I have heard numerous examples of people with Italian backgrounds who supported the civil rights movement of the 1960s (in contrast to other European Americans of their acquaintance) because of their own experiences with discrimination and stereotyping. A man from an Italian background told me he will never use the N-word because he knows what it is like to be called a *wop*. Indeed, some Italian Americans draw upon their ethnic group's history (and/or their family history) to explain their progressive positions on immigration, diversity programs, and other multicultural issues. "I would argue that our experience has taught us firsthand of the evils of racism and nativism," says Rudolph Vecoli.[55]

Other Italian Americans espouse conservative viewpoints on multicultural topics along the lines of former Colorado Congressman Tom Tancredo. Italian Americans will sometimes distance themselves from our nation's complicated racial history on the grounds that their ancestors arrived on these shores after slavery had ended in the United States.[56] Recently, a middle-aged Italian-American native of New York described to me his experiences with anti-Italian prejudice during his childhood. He says that the Italian Americans had persevered and overcome numerous obstacles by dint of their hard work and philosophy of self-reliance. "We're moving forward," said this self-made man about his coethnics as a group. Like many American conservatives, he contends that the members of historically disadvantaged groups should focus on the future, not the inequities and disparities of the past and present.

III. Tony Soprano is a well-known fictional character in American popular culture. The actor James Gandolfini brought Tony Soprano to life in *The Sopranos*, the eponymous HBO series that featured a New Jersey Mafia chieftain and his respective families (at home and at work). The noted series, which consisted of original episodes that aired from 1999 to 2007, is a staple of our nation's popular culture. Its characters, story lines, and even venues have become instantly recognized aspects of Americana. David Chase (né De Cesare) is the creator and an executive producer of *The Sopranos*; this New Jersey native wrote numerous episodes of the program, too.[57] The broadcast of the last original episode of *The Sopranos* aired in June 2007. Millions of *Sopranos* fans eagerly anticipated and speculated about what would happen to Tony Soprano in the final episode. However, David Chase delighted, infuriated, and perplexed fans of *The Sopranos* with a deliberately ambiguous conclusion that offered no definite answers about Tony Soprano's future.[58]

In June 2007, Alessandra Stanley of *The New York Times* offered the following reflections on *The Sopranos*:

> The ending was a reminder of what made David Chase's series about New Jersey mobsters so distinctive from the beginning. "The Sopranos" was the most

unusual and realistic family drama in television history. There have been many good Mafia movies and one legendary trilogy, but fans had to look to literature to find comparable depictions of the complexity and inconsistencies of American family life. It was sometimes hard to bear the encomiums—the saga of the New Jersey mob family has been likened to Cheever, Dickens and Shakespeare; scripts were pored over as if they were the Dead Sea Scrolls. But its saving grace was that the series was always many different things at once.[59]

The Sopranos, for all its popularity among the critics, has been deeply controversial within the Italian-American community.[60] Leading Italian-American activists and organizations roundly condemned the program for what they saw as its glorification of organized crime and reinforcement of existing stereotypes that many Italian Americans are involved in the Mafia. It is not uncommon for Italian Americans to say they have never watched Tony Soprano and his colleagues, antagonists, and family members. The critics of *The Sopranos* contend that the program offers negative images of New Jersey, serves as a guidebook on misbehavior for young people, and provides a primer on Italian-American lifestyles for the residents of states with few Italian Americans.[61]

Many Italian Americans, to be sure, are fans of *The Sopranos* or feel ambivalent about the program. In 2005 a young Italian-American Rhode Islander told me he enjoyed watching *The Sopranos*. I asked him what his response would be to those individuals who said the program stereotyped Italian Americans. His response: "Turn it off." Similarly, in 2006, a middle-aged Italian-American North Carolinian said that he had friends who subscribed to HBO solely because they wished to see *The Sopranos*. Another respondent contends that there is "enough" positive news about Italian Americans "to offset" the stereotypical images that may stem from *The Sopranos*. Indeed, these discussions demonstrate that Italian Americans differ dramatically over the extent to which mob films and television programs harm the image of their ethnic group—and what their reaction should be to those portrayals.

The Italian-American Mafia, meanwhile, is steadily decreasing in relevance. A number of factors have resulted in the gradual demise of the Mob, including the extensive investigations and successful prosecutions of gangsters; the sharp decline of many traditional rackets and revenue streams for Mafiosi; vigorous competition from other ethnic groups and organizations in the underworld; and the general prosperity of Italian Americans and the disappearance of the impoverished neighborhoods that once proved to be recruiting areas and havens for the Mafia.[62] "It seems ironic that the mafia is flourishing in popular culture at a time when Italian American organized crime is on the decline," observes George De Stefano.[63] "But while some Italian Americans fume about mafia stereotypes," contends De Stefano, "most pop-culture consumers find the Corleones, the Sopranos, and various other fictional wiseguys colorful and entertaining, familiar figures who pose no real threat to anyone but each other."[64]

George De Stefano describes the American public's continuing interest in the American Mafia in his book, *An Offer We Can't Refuse* (2006). To be sure, there are many films and television dramas that focus on the Mafia.[65] The mass media, after all, sometimes make celebrities out of gangsters due to their fearsome personas, colorful nicknames, and outlaw lifestyles. Today the late John Gotti's daughter, Victoria Gotti, enjoys some minor celebrity as a novelist, columnist, reality-television star (*Growing Up Gotti* on the Arts and Entertainment Network), and long-time celebrator of her father.[66] In addition, there are journalists, former mobsters, and retired law-enforcement authorities who write books about organized crime. There are even Web sites about the Mob for those netizens who find the topic interesting.[67]

American English now includes various references to the Mob, Mafia, and organized crime in non-criminal contexts. Italian words with Mafia connections have begun to appear in the mainstream culture. Journalists frequently use the Italian word *consigliere* to refer to a prominent person's advisor (Karl Rove's relationship with President George W. Bush) and, less commonly, the word *omertà* (to describe a code of secrecy) in mainstream contexts. And, in American English, *Merriam-Webster's Collegiate Dictionary* defines one meaning of the word "mafia" as "a group of people of similar interests or backgrounds prominent in a particular field or enterprise."[68] When it comes to crime, moreover, the term "mafia"/"Mafia" increasingly describes non-Italian criminal organizations: Albanian, Bulgarian, Chinese, Colombian, Indian, Israeli, Japanese, Nigerian, Russian, Turkish, Ukrainian, and other ethnic and national mafias.[69]

Despite the decline of Italian-American organized crime, *The Godfather* novel and *The Godfather* films have introduced a number of phrases, expressions, and fictional characters (what some observers describe as "Godfatherisms") into the American lexicon. These "Godfatherisms" include references to and analogies involving characters from *The Godfather* novel and *The Godfather* films, particularly Vito Corleone and his sons, Fredo, Santino/"Sonny," and Michael Corleone. Another popular expression in American English involves the idea or action of "making someone an offer he can't refuse." In 2005, for example, the prevalence and popularity of Mafia imagery in U.S. popular culture led to the following headline in *The Christian Science Monitor*: "An offer Hollywood can't refuse."[70] The enduring popularity and continuing cultural significance of *The Godfather* novel and *The Godfather* films are such that journalists, cultural observers, and others can use "Godfatherisms" and expect the references to be commonly understood by American adults.[71]

Some law-abiding Italian Americans enjoy, joke about, and embrace the depictions of Italian-American gangsters in *The Godfather* novel, *The Godfather* films, and similar fare. It is not uncommon to hear people of Italian origin say that *The Godfather* accurately portrays many aspects of Italian-American culture (except for the criminal activities, of course).[72] Likewise, one of my respondents told me, "*The Sopranos* do a lot to promote Italian awareness." To this end, one finds movie posters from gangster flicks in certain Italian delis and restaurants. There are even Italians who want to be seen as "connected" for the purposes of self-aggrandizement, in order to elicit respect and admiration from their peers.[73] Yet the *Godfather/Sopranos* connection certainly does not appeal to everyone. I have spoken to many Italian Americans who are tired of people making Mafia-related comments around them and/or applying the Mob stereotype to them.

One such anecdote comes from Florida in the early 1990s. A fellow on the west coast of Florida was speaking about the Italians and the Mafia (in a derogatory fashion) around an Italian American of his acquaintance. After the first or second time he made his biased statements, this American of Italian origin said to him: "I am very offended by those comments." He brushed aside her concerns. Initially, she backed down, while the man continued talking about how Italian mobsters would authorize hits on people. Finally, in exasperation, she told him, "That's right. If you don't cut it out, I know someone who would take you out in a New York minute." He took her admonition seriously. After that exchange, he never made any untoward comments about Italian Americans in her presence ever again. Later, she felt angry with herself for going to his level.

Likewise, James Tognoni, a law-abiding businessman who works in telecommunications, reports that his daughter, Amanda Tognoni, periodically encountered two questions as a student at Southwest Missouri State University in Springfield, Missouri. Initially, classmates would ask her:

"So you're Italian?" (They invariably pronounced the word Italian with a long "I" on the first syllable.) Then they would query her: "Is your father in the Mafia?" The Italian-surnamed undergraduate always answered affirmatively to the first question about her heritage, but she eventually tired of addressing the second question amid her peers' Mafia innuendoes. Finally, Amanda Tognoni began to answer their questions about her family's supposed involvement in organized crime with the following non-committal reply: "My father does not discuss his business with me." The other college students left her alone after that, as they interpreted her tongue-in-cheek response to mean that her father observed a code of silence regarding his putatively illicit activities.[74]

IV. Dr. Emanuele (Manny) Alfano will not tolerate bigotry or prejudice of any kind. Alfano himself relates several examples of subtle ethnic bias that have occurred to him. During the 1960s, for instance, he wanted to move into a particular New Jersey neighborhood (one with few Italian Americans). The locals were not keen on having him there. As one person said, "We don't know what kind of people he's going to be bringing into the neighborhood." Alfano recalls another incident from the late 1960s or early 1970s, when UNICO members had purchased a tricycle for a young person with special needs. When someone asked an adult about the origins of the tricycle, she said "that Mob group down the street" had been the benefactor. In the late 1970s, Dr. Alfano would encounter Mafia innuendoes when he dropped his children off at school, as this genial chiropractor was wearing a suit and driving a Cadillac. Some people erroneously thought he was a gangster, due to his attire and vehicle.[75]

Today Manny Alfano is a leading voice against the defamation and stereotyping of Italian Americans in politics, advertising, and popular culture.[76] Alfano, a son and grandson of Sicilian immigrants to the United States, grew up in a heavily Italian neighborhood: the Fourteenth Ward of Newark. This Bloomfield, New Jersey, resident remembers Italian-American schoolteachers "who had changed their names to get work" as well as the Italian boxers in his neighborhood who assumed Irish names when they entered the ring. On Career Day at his wife's high school, certain guidance counselors encouraged the students to attend vocational school instead of matriculating at a university. Manny Alfano himself was a first-generation college student. As a young teacher in Newark during the 1960s, Alfano wondered why there was not more coverage of Italian-American history in the textbooks. He cites *The Godfather* and, later, Alex Haley's *Roots* as important cultural catalysts in his development as an Italian-American activist.[77]

Since the 1990s Alfano has been involved in a number of antidefamation activities. He currently serves as chairman of the UNICO National Anti-Bias Committee. And he is the chairman of the Italian-American One Voice Coalition, "a national network of activists enabling the Italian American community to act as one united voice when dealing with defamation, discrimination and negative stereotyping."[78] This organization dates back to 1993. It releases *The Alfano Digest*, an online publication that covers breaking developments related to Italian-American issues and imagery. Alfano and his colleagues monitor advertisers, politicians, corporations, news media outlets, and pop-culture purveyors for any instances of stereotyping and defamation of Italian Americans. In addition, they affirm those who promote positive images of Italian Americans. Over the years, these dedicated activists have enjoyed numerous successes as a result of their e-mails, letters, faxes, and telephone calls.[79]

The Italian-American One Voice Coalition closely tracks the portrayals of Italian Americans in American culture. Manny Alfano cites Will Girardi, the character played by Joe Mantegna on the now-canceled *Joan of Arcadia*, as an example of a positive Italian-American character on television.[80] From 1999 through 2007, Dr. Alfano and his colleagues consistently lobbied against *The Sopranos*.[81] Alfano notes that television programs with Italian-surnamed gangsters might have Italian-American cops, in order to inoculate the shows against charges of ethnic bias. Likewise, Manny Alfano reports that when companies are challenged for advertisements that include stereotypical images of Italian Americans, an Italian-American employee (or an "Italian By Marriage" on staff) will be dispatched to say that s/he is "not offended" by this particular depiction of Italians.[82] Such reactions come as no surprise to the Italian-American antidefamation activists, who sometimes cite their coethnics' apathy as one of the reasons why Italians may still encounter some stereotyping in America.

Alfano's activism and perspective are national and international in scope. He believes that Italian Canadians have experiences with stereotyping and defamation that resemble those of Italian Americans. He points out how the East Coast gangsters on *The Sopranos* affect the image of Italian Americans throughout the United States and around the globe. To this end, Alfano's perspective elicits a series of reactions from people in the United States, Canada, Australia, and the United Kingdom. Some individuals tell him, "Come on, lighten up." Others say, "You're right."[83] Through their advocacy, Dr. Manny Alfano and the activists of the Italian-American One Voice Coalition play an important role in the grassroots efforts to present accurate and positive images of Italian Americans in our national culture.

The Italian-American antidefamation advocates are vigilant for any negative depictions or portrayals of Italian Americans in politics, advertising, business, the media, popular entertainment, and other fields. They commonly decry what they see as the pervasive stereotyping of Italians in U.S. popular culture and contend that no other ethnic group is treated this way. Over the years, the Italian-American activists have protested against *The Untouchables*, *The Godfather*, *The Sopranos*, *Shark Tale*, and other films and television programs that they felt stereotyped Italians.[84] Similarly, the Italian-American actors, writers, producers, and directors involved in Mob films and television programs—and those people of Italian origin who enjoy such fare—have come under fire from some Italian-American advocates.

A variety of national Italian groups are active in antidefamation efforts. These organizations include the Columbus Citizens Foundation, the Italian-American One Voice Coalition, the Italian American Task Force on Defamation, the Italic Institute of America, the National Italian American Foundation, the Order Sons of Italy in America, and UNICO National. OSIA has a Commission for Social Justice (CSJ); the CSJ operates a Positive Image Program and monitors the news media, advertising world, and entertainment industry to evaluate their coverage of Italian Americans.[85] Elsewhere, Bill Dal Cerro, the vice president of The Italic Institute of America, operates a Web site—"Stereotype This! Debunking Hollywood's Italian Stereotypes and Myths."[86]

Italian Americans often seek to overcome negative stereotypes by promoting knowledge—and positive images—of Italian and Italian-American culture. Dr. Carmine Paolino, for example, is responsible for some innovative Italian cultural programming in Waterbury, Connecticut. The longtime Italian-language educator at Waterbury's Kennedy High School tries to counteract the stereotypical portrayals of Italian-American gangsters with a focus on the Italians, including Dante and Michelangelo, who have contributed much to Western civilization. "We want to reflect the good things, the positive things, the contributions," Paolino notes.[87] Indeed, Italian Americans regularly form and develop institutions and organizations to promote positive images of Italians through their cultural and charitable activities, among other objectives. Sometimes they do so without explicitly engaging in antidefamation activities.

The Museo ItaloAmericano/Italian American Museum in San Francisco owes its origins to efforts to "improve the image" of Italian Americans, remembers Paola Bagnatori, the Museo's managing director. It was founded in 1978 by Giuliana Nardelli Haight, an immigrant from Trento. "Nardelli Haight wanted to present another image of Italians by showcasing Italian American artists," says Bagnatori. The Museo ItaloAmericano promotes knowledge of Italian art and culture and simultaneously presents a positive image of Italian Americans through its events, exhibits, and cultural activities.[88] The Museo's events include symposia, movie premieres, cultural tours to Italy, classical music concerts, and CIBO COME CULTURA— Food As Culture. This San Francisco institution, moreover, offers such cultural activities as Italian films, regular lectures, and Italian-language classes. In addition, the Museo provides free art programs for thousands of young people through the CIAO (Children's Italian Art Outreach) Program, where they learn about Renaissance art and history.[89]

Besides cultural-enrichment activities, Italian Americans also counteract the Mafia stereotypes through their extensive involvement in law enforcement. To be sure, Americans of Italian extraction have long been involved in fighting crime, a fact documented by the OSIA report, *Italian American Crime Fighters: A Brief Survey*. Many of these law-enforcement personnel focus on crimes that have little, if anything, to do with Italian gangsters. They serve and protect the public and defend us from lawbreakers in almost every conceivable realm. At the same time, a goodly number of the Mafia's nemeses in the law-enforcement community are themselves Italian Americans.[90] Three such individuals, Ralph Salerno, Jules Bonavolonta, and Rudolph Giuliani, have recounted their family histories of experiencing mistreatment at the hands of gangsters.[91] Giuliani, interestingly, is an avowed fan of *The Godfather*, *The Sopranos*, and similar films and television programs.[92]

During the 1980s Giuliani used the word "Mafia" publicly as U.S. Attorney for the Southern District of New York (despite receiving criticism for doing so from certain Italian-American organizations).[93] He writes about his viewpoint on this topic:

I do feel sensitive about the pressures on Italian Americans regarding organized crime—it's a burden for them (and for me, too). But the more I thought about it, the more I decided that the way forward was not to be afraid of the word "Mafia," but to use it and explain what any reasonable person already knows: that the Mafia is made up of an extremely small percentage of Italians and Italian Americans. It's roughly the same percentage in which every ethnic group commits crimes. Ultimately, "Mafia" says only that Italians and Italian Americans are human beings. Once we acknowledge that, we take much of the mystique out of it.[94]

Louis Freeh is another person of Italian origin who has publicly reflected on how organized crime can affect the image of Italian Americans as a group. Freeh, whose mother is of Italian descent, served as director of the Federal Bureau of Investigation from 1993 to 2001.[95] He writes about how his Italian-American mother, Bernice Freeh, encountered discrimination as a young woman; she was told by one prospective employer: "We'd like to employ you, but we don't hire Italians."[96] Louis Freeh, a first-generation college student, comes from New Jersey. He remembers how the college counselor at his Catholic high school made an unflattering judgment about his academic potential. The upwardly mobile Eagle Scout went on to earn a bachelor's degree and a law degree and spend twenty-six years in public service. Freeh began his career as an FBI agent. Later, he worked for the U.S. Attorney's Office for the Southern District of New York, where he spent years prosecuting cases involving organized crime. Freeh eventually served as a U.S. district court judge before becoming the FBI director in 1993.[97]

In his autobiography, *My FBI*, Louis Freeh addresses the Mafia issue. He writes:

> Being an Italian-American and having spent a career prosecuting La Cosa Nostra cases, I became deeply sensitive to the heroism and gifts that countless Americans of Italian heritage have bestowed on our nation. My involvement in the National Italian American Foundation and with its charitable and educational good works is how I try to balance the equation of the cases I prosecuted. Great jurists, warriors, doctors, captains of industry, benefactors, FBI agents, and entertainment pioneers . . . have more than made up for the misdeeds of a tiny minority of this great heritage.[98]

Freeh's eloquent comments underscore how the contributions of millions of Italian Americans to our country certainly negate the criminal activities of several thousand mobsters with Italian backgrounds.

❦ ❦ ❦

To some extent, there are generational differences in terms of how Americans of Italian ancestry might experience perceptions of anti-Italian bias. I have had older people tell me that while overt discrimination against Italian Americans is a thing of the past, they think that subtle prejudice against Italians may still exist. These respondents hail from various communities, including Pueblo, Colorado; Erie, Pennsylvania; Rochester, New York; and Madison, Wisconsin. They remember when being identifiably Italian could be a disadvantage in certain contexts. Younger people, of course, have never experienced the feelings of exclusion that lead their elders to hold these opinions. In sum, the various generations of Italian Americans may have differing, but equally legitimate, viewpoints on anti-Italian discrimination that take into account their different experiences as Italian Americans.

Now we have reached the point where many Americans do not even notice another person's Italian ancestry, positively or negatively. Time and time again, people in different parts of the United States have told me that they do not ever think of Italian-surnamed individuals as being "Italian" or in any way different from anyone else. Once, after I gave a presentation about the themes of Italian-American progress, a middle-aged man of Northern European descent shared the story of his college roommate, who had a clearly Italian surname. Then he asked me: "Do you think he was Italian?" I answered affirmatively—and noted how his roommate's identifiably Italian surname had been a matter of no consequence to him. Such sentiments are borne out by the successes that Italian Americans have achieved (and are achieving) in many places and institutions with relatively few people from Italian backgrounds.

Still, the stereotype of Italian-American involvement in organized crime lives on, to some extent, as measured by anecdotal evidence. In 2006, a transplanted New Jerseyite in Virginia related an anecdote to me about a local man who came to work on his home. The tradesman told the Italian-American homeowner that he would do good work. If he did not do so, after all, he figured that something might happen to him—an unsubtle reference to his erroneous perception that his client had Mob ties. These types of remarks lead Italian-American leaders and advocates to emphasize the continuing need to counteract such stereotyping. "We, the heirs of a great cultural patrimony, cannot be content to let the media, the entertainment industry and politicians define us as a lesser people— ignorant, violent and criminal," said Lawrence Auriana in a 2005 speech.[99]

To be sure, people still make jokes about Italian Americans and the Mafia. In 2005, for instance, I mentioned to a middle-aged white man that West Virginia had recently elected an Italian American, Joe Manchin III, to the governorship in November 2004. Upon hearing the news, this fellow pantomimed the movement of a man reaching inside his coat for a gun, as if a mythical mobster had coerced West Virginians into voting for an Italian American. Moreover, he jokingly said that there were legions of these gun-toting men who had gone all over West Virginia and influenced the voting choices of people in the Mountain State. He implied that Mafia-like activity accounted for the fact that Manchin won the election with 63.5 percent of the vote as a non-incumbent, running twenty points ahead of his party's presidential candidate. Some, but certainly not all, Italian Americans might interpret the aforementioned story as an example of how members of their ethnic group continue to be marginalized in certain contexts, even today.

Milwaukee, Wisconsin, attorney Peter Balistreri knows what it feels like to be an outsider. Balistreri was born in Milwaukee in 1941, and he spent the first seven years of his life in a heavily Italian neighborhood there. In 1948 his family moved to nearby Shorewood, an upscale suburb of Milwaukee. Young Peter entered St. Robert School, a Catholic institution where most students traced their ancestry to Ireland and Germany. He felt a profound sense of difference in this environment and initially was "fearful," "frightened," and "standoffish."[100] The other students, after all, had little familiarity with his cultural heritage.

When his teacher conducted a mock presidential election in 1948, the results confirmed Balistreri's feelings of difference. Twenty-nine students in the class voted for Republican presidential candidate Thomas Dewey— and one student (Balistreri) backed the Democrat, President Harry Truman. It was a secret ballot. Therefore, his classmates puzzled over the identity of the lone Democrat among them. After Harry Truman's remarkable upset victory in November 1948, Balistreri proudly informed his classmates that he had been the sole Truman voter. Eventually he became acclimated to Shorewood and won acceptance from his Irish-American and German-American peers.[101]

A perceptive man with a keen interest in history, Balistreri says that Italian Americans do not confront much bias anymore. While he has experienced periodic prejudice on the basis of ethnic origin, he contends that Americans currently make distinctions between real-life Italian

Americans and the stereotypical portrayals of gangsters that they see on television and in popular films. Balistreri's inclusive perspective extends to other ethnic groups and draws upon his experiences in Milwaukee, a multiethnic city where blacks and whites coexist uneasily at times. He readily notes that he had it easier in parochial school as an American of Italian descent than he would have had if he were an African American. Balistreri believes that intermarriage is the principal factor driving the decline in bias against Italian Americans over the years. It is harder for one to feel negatively about a group, posits Balistreri, when s/he is related by marriage to some of its members.[102]

Balistreri cites examples from his own family background to support this theory. His wife is an Austrian American. Her family had no interaction with Italians before their marriage. In addition, Balistreri notes that his fortysomething son is married to a woman of Irish and Polish descent. The younger Balistreris have three sons, all of whom are one-quarter Italian with Italian surnames. Before Peter Balistreri's son married his Irish-Polish spouse in the mid-1990s, her parents had no contact with Italians, while their children knew Italian Americans and members of other ethnic groups in school. Balistreri points to the upsurge in ethnic and racial intermarriage as a hopeful sign that we Americans will eventually bridge some of the divisions that presently exist in our nation.[103]

Chapter 3

SUCCEEDING IN AMERICA

Shortly after he became the First Marine Expeditionary Force's new commander in 1994, General Anthony Zinni went to Camp Pendleton in southern California for a ceremony to mark "the change of command for the artillery regiment."[1] As he and his wife, Debbie, were "walking down the center aisle" to the ceremony, "an elderly man stepped out of the center aisle" and blocked his path. Zinni first stepped around him. But then the "man stepped out again with tears in his eyes." "General, I just want to look at you," he said to Zinni. The older man told the general that he had looked at the military brass on the field—and all the top authority figures happened to be Italian Americans. It was a very different situation when this particular veteran served in World War II; at that time, he and his compatriots were far more likely to be found as privates than as members of the military hierarchy. "I never thought I'd ever see the day" when there would be Italian-American colonels and generals, he said to the I MEF commander on that day in 1994.[2]

Zinni himself had never thought of the Italian-American advancement in the military in this way before. But he then surveyed the field, where one found Colonel Tony Palermo, the Division Commander; Major General Frank Libutti, the Air Wing Commander; and Major General Paul Fratarangelo. "The top three generals on the field" were of Italian descent, remembers Zinni. In subsequent weeks, he reflected on the prevalence of Italian Americans in high-ranking military posts. Later, the native Pennsylvanian saw General Carl Mundy (the Commandant of the United States Marine Corps from 1991 to 1995), the one who "makes the assignments" for the Marines. Zinni described to Mundy what had happened at Camp Pendleton, along with his reflections on Italian-American successes in the military. General Mundy replied that he "never thought about it." Zinni was impressed that "we had reached the point where people did not even think about it." Non-Italians, in fact, took pride in the Italian-American presence in the Marine Corps' hierarchy.[3]

Zinni's reflections on this topic gave him a "sense of how far we had come." During his Italian-immigrant father's military service in World War I, Italians were "mainly enlisted men." By World War II, there were Italian-American junior officers in addition to enlisted men, but few people of Italian origin were then found in the military's higher ranks. By Zinni's generation, though, Italian Americans were becoming colonels and generals. "Three generations of Italians gradually worked their way up the ladder," according to Zinni. He traces the trajectory of the Italian-American people, from the "low pay," "few opportunities for education," and "some discrimination" of the past to the remarkably positive developments of the present. The "immigrants proved themselves" and "others followed in their footsteps," observes Zinni. Indeed, he remembers that his parents and people beforehand "laid the groundwork" for his myriad successes.[4]

Zinni's parents, Antonio and Lilla, were natives of Italy. His father, Antonio Zinni, was born in Abruzzi in 1896 and came to the United States with his mother, Christina Zinni, in 1910. (Antonio Zinni's father, Francesco Zinni, was already working in America.) A World War I veteran who served in France, Antonio Zinni labored in the mills, as a landscaper, and, finally, as a chauffeur. His formal education ended with the third grade. Antonio Zinni's future wife, Lilla DiSabatino, was born in Abruzzi in 1903. She came to America at the age of three with her mother, Cecilia DiSabatino. (Her father, Zupito DiSabatino, preceded them in coming to the United States.) Lilla Zinni had an eighth-grade education, and she found employment as a garment factory worker. The Zinnis lived in Conshohocken, Pennsylvania, while the DiSabatinos were residents of South Philadelphia. Antonio Zinni and Lilla DiSabatino married in 1927. Anthony Zinni was the youngest of their four children. He was born in September 1943 and raised in Conshohocken, a mill town just west of Philadelphia with large Irish, Italian, Polish, and German populations. Zinni grew up in a loving, close-knit Italian Catholic family.[5]

The tradition of military service runs deep in Anthony Zinni's family, as his father, brother, cousins, and brothers-in-law were all veterans.

Antonio Zinni served in the U.S. military during World War I and received his American citizenship as a result.[6] Anthony Zinni enrolled at Villanova University in 1961. As he had no vehicle and Villanova was seven miles from his home in Conshohocken, he walked or hitchhiked to school during his undergraduate years. When the future four-star general entered the United States Marine Corps in 1961 (he joined the Marines on his first day at Villanova), he was vigilant for signs of bias from the predominantly Southern Anglo officers there. Zinni found no such treatment, only a relentless focus on performance. "Performance is key in the Marines," notes the Villanova graduate.[7] Throughout his thirty-nine years of military service, Zinni led American troops during significant periods of recent world history, ranging from the Vietnam War in the 1960s to the military efforts to contain Saddam Hussein in the late 1990s.[8]

During the 1990s Zinni became one of America's top military leaders, a man with global stature and an enviable reputation in dozens of countries. The capstone of Zinni's military career came in 1997, when he was named Commander in Chief of United States Central Command (CENTCOM).[9] The countries covered by CENTCOM comprised "a diverse region that spanned an area from East Africa through the Middle East to Southwest and Central Asia and into the Indian Ocean."[10] Zinni served as the Commander in Chief of CENTCOM until his retirement from the Marine Corps in 2000. Since then, he has been busy with such activities as teaching, public speaking, consulting work, international business, writing best-selling books, service on corporate boards, and most prominently, peace mediation and a role as the U.S. envoy to the Middle East peace process.[11] A forceful and articulate voice on military and foreign-policy matters, Zinni regularly appears in the media to discuss his views about the appropriate use of American power in the world. His two books, *Battle Ready* (2004) and *The Battle for Peace* (2006), outline the decorated Vietnam veteran's remarkable story and insightful perspective on geopolitical matters.[12]

Meanwhile, Anthony Zinni preserves his Italian heritage in a wide variety of ways. He cooks Italian food, travels to Italy, conducts genealogical research, and works to make his children conscious of their Italian roots. Zinni himself has been honored by the Italian government: He holds the prestigious Italian title of Commendatore, one of the many forms of recognition that he has received from institutions and governments throughout the world. Today this son of immigrants from Abruzzi continues to lend his cachet to numerous Italian-American events, activities, and organizations.[13] "Be proud of your heritage and use it to strengthen your ties to America," advises Zinni.[14] Now in his mid-sixties, Anthony Zinni exemplifies the enormous contributions that Italian Americans have made and continue to make to the U.S. military, American culture, and our national institutions.

I. During the early 1940s, Arthur Castraberti became one of the first class presidents at Medford High School in Medford, Massachusetts, who hailed from South Medford rather than West Medford.[15] South Medford was the less-affluent side of town, where the residents lived in double- and triple-decker homes. West Medford was more affluent than South Medford, as the residents had single-family homes there. Castraberti and his future brother-in-law, John Bucci, campaigned among the Irish-, Italian- and Portuguese-American students of South Medford and, consequently, he won the class office. His symbolically significant victory resonated with the South Medford youths, most of whom came from modest socioeconomic circumstances.

Their class president went on to have a successful career in business and as an entrepreneur. His father, Oreste Castraberti, was a Neapolitan immigrant who came to the United States alone at the age of sixteen. Arthur—he was christened as Arturo—Castraberti was born in 1924; he went to college on the G.I. Bill of Rights and earned bachelor's and master's degrees in the sciences. A devoted family man, he and his late wife, Rose, have three children: Steven, Paul, and Linda. After working in the corporate world, Castraberti purchased Prince Pizzeria and Bar in Saugus, Massachusetts, in 1961, and he turned it into a multimillion-dollar enterprise.[16] Castraberti worked seven days a week, fifteen hours a day, to transform the business (Prince Pizzeria was failing when he purchased it) into a great success.

Prince Pizzeria is what the *Boston Globe* recently described as "a Route 1 landmark."[17] The restaurant, which is located at 517 Broadway Street in Saugus, encompasses 12,000 square feet. It seats 650, has 140 parking spaces, includes a comedy club on the premises, and boasts a Leaning Tower of Pizza. Prince Pizzeria sells an average of 7,000 pizzas each week, for a total of 15 million pizzas since 1961. Families from many ethnic backgrounds enjoy an affordable Sunday dinner at Prince Pizzeria. Currently, the establishment is owned by Steven Castraberti; he purchased it from his father in 2005.

The story of Arthur Castraberti's life affirms the significance of education, highlights the value of hard work and entrepreneurial activity, and upholds the importance of generosity to one's family and community. For decades Castraberti has been active in community affairs. Among his many civic responsibilities, he served as a member of the advisory boards of the University of Massachusetts and Salem State College, respectively. In addition, he founded and served as the president of the Route One Businessmen's Association (now the Saugus Chamber of Commerce).[18]

Over the years, Castraberti has been generous to people and organizations that require assistance. Today the charming entrepreneur and his wife, Claire, divide their time between Gloucester, Massachusetts, and Sarasota, Florida. During his time in Florida, Arthur Castraberti volunteers five days each week in the cardiac-rehabilitation ward of a local hospital. And he has served as a longtime leader of the Gulf Coast Italian Culture Society in Sarasota (including two years as the organization's president), a role that allows him to promote positive images of Italian Americans. In his golden years, this grandfather of six enjoys spending time with his family, celebrating his Italian heritage, and doing good works in the community. His three children, too, have impressive educational accomplishments, all of which testify to the successes of the Italian-American people.[19]

As with Arthur Castraberti, the vast majority of Italian Americans are descended from immigrants who came to this country during the period between 1880 and 1924. They sought economic opportunities that did not exist for them in Italy at that time. Many, if not most, of these immigrants would be seen today as poor or close to being poor. The pre-1880 Italian immigrants in America were from a diverse set of regional origins and often hailed from upper middle class and professional backgrounds. The post-1880 Italian immigrants to the United States, however, included large numbers of laborers and peasants, along with a few professionals and some artisans. These Italian immigrants typically found employment in menial and manual positions, which paid them relatively little compensation.[20]

Several factors affected the progress of Italian Americans over the years. For one, the Italian immigrants were not familiar with much upward mobility in Italy. At the same time, they often sent remittances back to relatives in Italy. Consequently, it could be difficult for them to break out of poverty quickly, due to the fact they had few additional funds to spend on their own entrepreneurial activities. Initially, many of the Italian immigrants were skeptical about education as a means of climbing the

American socioeconomic ladder. The first-generation Italian immigrants were most likely to be found employed as laborers or manual workers.[21] Many older Italian Americans still recall the social discomfiture that they experienced as a result of growing up in poor or not-so-affluent families with parents who had little formal education.

To be sure, the first- and second-generation Italians in America who experienced success and upward mobility did not do so, for the most part, because of formal education. The Italian immigrants often resisted education for a variety of reasons, some of which related to their Italian antecedents and some of which had to do with their lives in America. There was not a sophisticated educational system in the southern Italian towns and communities many of them left in the period between 1880 and 1924. Public education was chronically underfunded and not especially significant in the rural parts of southern Italy during those years. Nor did members of the political class, as a general rule, assert themselves in favor of educating the poor. Education funding came from the local taxes, so the government schools were funded by taxes paid by members of the community (who already faced high taxes). For these reasons, southern Italy had high illiteracy rates: 90 percent (1871) and 70 percent (1900). The rate of illiteracy in northern Italy was lower than that in southern Italy.[22]

Formal education often did not resonate with the southern Italian immigrants to the United States. In southern Italy at the time the educated nobles and their surrogates mistreated the masses; consequently, the typical southern Italian did not take to education, in part because s/he considered it to be the province of the elites. Another reason the southern Italians initially did not stress formal education was that children of a certain age (say, those in their early teens) could earn money to help support the family, as they did in those days. This idea carried over to the United States, where the Italian immigrants usually needed every able-bodied member of the household employed in the workforce. The typical Italian immigrant was employed in unskilled or semiskilled labor. These jobs did not pay much, so a youth's earnings (however small) made a difference to the entire family. Moreover, the Italian-immigrant parents thought that their children would gain training and knowledge to advance occupationally in the workplace, not the classroom. In this context, formal education might be seen as optional and dispensable.[23]

The permanence of their residence in America affected the Italian immigrants' attitudes toward education. In many cases, they fully expected to return to Italy. Such individuals typically wanted to amass financial resources, not go to school, in America. Of course, when Italians concluded they were going to stay in the United States, they had more of a positive attitude toward formal education here. At the same time, their American-born and -raised children began to see the value of education as part of a broader shift away from the Old World attitudes and traditions. As the chronological distance grew between Italy and the Italian immigrants and their descendants, they were more likely to change their attitudes about the value of education. Italian Americans, then, started to take a pragmatic approach to education, due to the role it played—and plays—in allowing for socioeconomic mobility.[24]

Professor Philip J. DiNovo relates his family's experiences with eminent domain to illustrate how Italian immigrants sometimes lost out on opportunities because they did not understand fully the intricacies of the American political and economic system.[25] His paternal grandfather, Filippo DiNuovo (the family surname became DiNovo in the United States), immigrated to the United States from Sicily in 1901 at the age of twenty-two. After working and earning money, he returned to Sicily to marry Antonina Arrigo DiNovo. The DiNovos initially made their home in Pennsylvania before they moved to Albany, New York. They worked tirelessly, conserved their resources, purchased land, and supported their nine children. By the 1940s, Filippo DiNovo had a forty-acre truck farm on which he grew vegetables, particularly parsley, within the city boundaries of Albany. DiNovo was known as "The Parsley King," and his parsley supplied many of the hotels in New York's North Country.

During the 1950s the State of New York claimed the DiNovo family farm under eminent domain to construct the Harriman State Office Campus. The DiNovos only received a modest amount of money for their land, as Filippo DiNovo lacked the political connections necessary to challenge the state's assessment of the value of his beloved farm. The Albany Country Club abutted the DiNovo property. It, too, faced an eminent-domain claim from the State of New York. The leaders of the Albany Country Club, whose members included attorneys and physicians, subsequently challenged the state's assessment of the value of their land and received a larger amount of money than was originally offered to them. Over the decades, Filippo DiNovo bought rental properties as a result of his careful saving and investing. When the DiNovo family patriarch passed away in 1970, he left behind a respectable estate for his heirs.

This story about eminent domain continues to be part of the DiNovo family lexicon. Indeed, it shows what a difference money and education can make in terms of affecting a person's life chances. Philip J. DiNovo's American-born parents, August (Gus) DiNovo and Rose Sgarlatta DiNovo, never had the opportunity to go to high school. "If they had had an education, imagine what they would have done," says their son many years later. He himself was the first person in his family to earn a four-year college degree. The Albany native spent his professional career as an academic. Professor DiNovo was the founder and chairman of the Department of Business Administration at what is now Morrisville State College in New York. Moreover, he "taught a number of Departmental courses over a 32-year period." In retirement, DiNovo works to preserve the history and culture of Italian Americans in Albany and beyond, an objective that led the Italian government to confer the honor of Cavaliere upon him.

During the last century Italians have enjoyed remarkable socioeconomic mobility in the United States.[26] "By the 1960s Italian-Americans had risen above the national average in income," writes Michael Barone, "even though they still had fewer years of schooling than average. That latter statistic had changed by the 1970s, as the educational level of young Italian-Americans reached the national average."[27] By 1990 Italians had reached or exceeded the national average on many important socioeconomic indicators.[28] The median family income for Italian Americans in 1999 was $61,297, compared to $50,046 for America as a whole.[29] It is now clear from many socioeconomic indicators that Italian Americans have achieved a significant amount of upward mobility.[30]

There are two principal factors that explain the tremendous progress of the Italian immigrants and their descendants during the last century: Italian Americans themselves and the American system itself. The Italian immigrants and their descendants have done everything you are supposed to do to make it in America: They have worked hard; played by the rules; had strong families; contributed to their communities; embraced America, the English language, and our national culture; saved their money; started businesses; and, particularly in recent decades, encouraged their children and grandchildren to go on to higher education. At the same time, we must give equal credit to America for their successes, for having a culture, an economy, and the institutions that afford immigrants significant opportunities for prosperity.[31] The United States is a critically important part of the Italian-American success story, as this country has provided opportunities for the Italian immigrants and their offspring that did not exist for them in Italy many decades ago.

Today Italian Americans are well-regarded residents of towns, cities, villages, and states across the country, and not just in places where there are large numbers of Italian Americans. We have reached a point in American (and Italian-American) history where people of Italian origin occupy significant positions in communities and institutions throughout the United States. With the diffusion of Italian Americans to different parts of America, many ethnic milestones pass with little or no fanfare. An educator might become the first Italian principal of her school. A construction worker may become the first Italian-American foreman of his job crew. A businessperson might be selected as the first Italian to head the local chamber of commerce. A civic leader may become the first Italian American elected to a city council or a county commission. These modest milestones may not receive much attention, but they represent the complete integration of Italians into mainstream America.

II. Every year there is a "Bite Night" in Rock Springs, Wyoming, when the locals pay fifteen dollars for a ticket and then they have the opportunity to sample food from thirty to forty different restaurants in town. The Italian-American contribution to "Bite Night" includes twelve batches of *bagna calda*, a dip that contains such ingredients as a cube of butter, seven cloves of garlic, a cup of olive oil, four ounces of anchovies, and a teaspoon of vinegar. Bagna calda can be enjoyed with French or Italian bread or such vegetables as celery, cabbage, broccoli, or cauliflower. It is popular with people from all ethnic groups in Rock Springs. Indeed, the Italian-American purveyors of the delicious spread cannot keep enough of it in stock.[32] There is "more and more each year," according to Mary Joe Kaumo, a Rock Springs resident who helps prepare the bagna calda for the annual event.[33]

The popularity of Italian-American fare on "Bite Night" typifies the acceptance of Italians in Rock Springs, a town where people of Italian origin are admired, valued, and respected members of the community.[34] Rock Springs has a sizable Italian-American population in large part because of the recruitment practices of the local coal mines many decades ago. This southwestern Wyoming community bills itself as the "Home of 56 Nationalities." The ethnic diversity and multicultural harmony in Rock

Springs stem, in part, from the fact that many different groups of people came to Rock Springs and Superior in Sweetwater County, Wyoming, to work in the mines.

A large number of the Italian Americans in Rock Springs trace their ancestry to the Italian region of Trento-Alto Adige. In fact, the Italians of Sweetwater County often cook Austrian and Slovenian foods, an unsurprising fact considering the geographical location of their ancestral homeland.[35] The community includes immigrants from Italy, as in Lilia Albertini, who hails from the Province of Trento. Her daughter, Shirley Albertini, is the head bookkeeper at Rock Springs National Bank. Shirley Albertini grew up speaking Nones, a dialect of Trento, as her native tongue. Her younger sister, Diane Albertini, learned English from her older sibling. (Diane Albertini is currently an associate professor of English at Dixie State College of Utah in St. George, Utah.)[36] The Albertinis participate in the Tyrolean Trentini of Wyoming. This local organization preserves southwestern Wyoming's Italian customs and traditions.

Over the years Italian Americans have thrived in Rock Springs. The late Teno Roncalio came from Rock Springs; Roncalio represented Wyoming in the U.S. House of Representatives for five terms during the twentieth century.[37] In 2000 Italian Americans accounted for 8.1 percent of Rock Springs' 18,968 residents. The town's mayor, Tim Kaumo, is of Italian descent. Josephine Profaizer, another Italian American, is a well-regarded local educator. Karen Bonomo, moreover, served as the 2006–2007 president of the Rotary Club of Rock Springs. Today Rock Springs is a model of Italian-American progress and prosperity, a place where the Italian immigrants and their descendants make up an integral part of the community.

Throughout the United States, most Italian Americans now have good opportunities to achieve success as they define it. These days one finds Americans of Italian origin well represented among the ranks of middle class, upper middle class, and affluent Americans.[38] In 2000 Rocco Caporale described and analyzed the socioeconomic progress of Italian Americans for an entry in *The Italian American Experience*.[39] Caporale noted the significant advances of his coethnics: "The most recent studies, conducted by scholars using the census data and data from the General Social Survey, indicate that Italian Americans as a group enjoy one of the highest per capita and per family income[s] in the country, although they may not occupy positions of prestige and power in all professional and occupational areas in proportion to their numbers."[40] In any event, the idea that Italians are usually successful (as they define it) took some time to penetrate the mass consciousness.

Father Vincent Bommarito knows firsthand what it is like to encounter the fallacious notion that Americans of Italian origin continue to be concentrated in low-wage, low-status occupations. Bommarito's parents never attended high school. In those days, many Italians left school prematurely because their families needed them in the workforce. To be sure, the elder Bommaritos strongly advocated education. Father Bommarito's older brother was the first family member to earn a college degree. This milestone received much attention in the Bommarito family at the time. Father Vincent Bommarito himself has a master's degree. As with many Italian Americans in the Baby Boom generation, the fiftysomething Missourian celebrates and appreciates the value of education. Indeed, this grandson of Sicilian immigrants testifies to the role that formal education has played in creating opportunities for members of his family.[41] At present, "Father Vince" (as many of his parishioners refer to him) is the beloved pastor of Saint Ambrose Church, a traditionally Italian parish, in Saint Louis, Missouri.

During Bommarito's tenure as associate pastor at Saint Ambrose from 1981 to 1987, non-Italians sometimes called the church asking for references for people who could cook and clean. They assumed that, at an Italian church, there would be a ready supply of people willing to do such work. These periodic phone calls to St. Ambrose "infuriated" Father Bommarito, as they completely ignored the great progress that Italian Americans had made over the preceding decades—and reflected stereotypical thinking on the part of the non-Italian callers. At one time, many Italians worked as cooks and housekeepers (and they had done so with honor and dignity). By the 1980s, though, it was unusual to find people of Italian origin in those occupational categories—in Saint Louis and throughout the United States.[42] Education and entrepreneurship were key factors that facilitated their upward mobility.

By the 1960s, after all, many Italian Americans had left the ethnic enclaves and were going on to higher education and success in mainstream American society. Frank Joseph Schiro is one such individual.[43] He grew up on the South Side of Rockford, Illinois, during the 1950s and 1960s.[44] This American of Sicilian descent only realized that he was "American" in the second grade, a reflection of the demographic composition of his

heavily Italian neighborhood. At the time Italian Americans were beginning to move up the socioeconomic ladder in Rockford, as elsewhere in
America. A scholarly youth and a hard worker (he had jobs of some kind
from the age of eight), Schiro became the first member of his immediate
family to go to college and graduate school. His parents, John George
Schiro and Mamie Delores Schiro, were factory workers who spoke
"imperfect English" and had "no more than a sixth-grade education." He
appreciates the sacrifices that the members of the Schiro family—John
and Mamie Schiro chief among them—made to help him during his
youth.

In the 1960s Frank Joseph Schiro matriculated at Northwestern University in Evanston, Illinois. For the first two years of his education, he
remembers feeling out of place; his attire, socioeconomic background, and
outlook on the world were different from those of many of his privileged
classmates. Over time, however, the Illinois native came to be accepted by
and popular with his peers. His involvement with a campus dance group
contributed to his popularity and social acceptance at Northwestern University. Schiro remembers feeling a bit sheepish about the prospect of having his fraternity brothers meet his parents. But John and Mamie Schiro
were quite popular with their son's fraternity brothers. Their warmth,
authenticity, and down-to-earth attitude went over well with the young
men.

After graduating from Northwestern University in the mid-1960s, Frank
Joseph Schiro moved to Milwaukee, Wisconsin. He continued his education at Marquette University Law School in Milwaukee, where he was part
of the Class of 1969. From 1970 to 1976 Schiro served as an Assistant District Attorney in Milwaukee County, Wisconsin, at a time when relatively
few Italian Americans held such positions there. Now Schiro is a successful attorney in Milwaukee and an Italian-American leader in southeastern
Wisconsin. He currently serves as president of the OSIA Filippo Mazzei
Greater Milwaukee Lodge #2763 in Milwaukee. In addition, Schiro is a former officer and current board member of the National Italian American
Bar Association. He promotes an inclusive model of Italian-American
identity, one that transcends social class and Italian regional origins.

We can reflect on the progress of Italians in America by examining the
topic of literacy, an important issue for the Italian immigrants. Patty Koch
remembers that, in 1956, her Italian-born grandmother learned to write
her name (Angelina Bellezze) in her granddaughter's junior high school

yearbook. It was an important event in the family.[45] One man told me that his two grandfathers were illiterate when they came to the United States; he is a physician. Another man, a retired dentist and professor, describes how his grandfather signed his name with an "X" when he became a naturalized citizen. Indeed, it was not uncommon for Italian Americans of the older generations to have grown up in homes with few, if any, books. Today Italian Americans' personal narratives often refer to the limited amount of formal education that their parents and grandparents had in Italy or America, as benchmarks of how far they and the Italian-American community have come over the years.

Stories of economic deprivation are intertwined with the history of Italian America. Shoes can be an important point of reference in this regard. An elderly woman told me the story of how her hardworking father went to the local thrift store to purchase shoes for his children. Decades later, she remembered how he came home with the shoes for the youngsters. Her anticipation turned to dismay when she learned that there were only boys' shoes in his bag for her to wear, because there had been no girls' shoes for sale at the store. An older man told me how he never had his own pair of shoes to wear until he was thirteen. Another fellow, who is middle-aged, remembers having only two pairs of shoes as a youth. Now that this gentleman has a well-paying, professional job, he purchases many pairs of shoes. In 2009 the typical Italian-American youth enjoys the material abundance of the world's foremost consumer society. Such narratives of economic deprivation seem difficult to believe to youngsters; they are part of a history that is comfortably distant.

Mary McGarry relates a heartwarming story from her childhood. The Ohioan was born in 1920 and grew up in Kantner, Pennsylvania. Her parents, Francesco Vaccarino and Giovanna Di Pasquale Vaccarino, were immigrants from the Province of Messina in Sicily. McGarry's father operated a store in Kantner; it served everyone in the ethnically diverse community. As with many Italian families at the time, the Vaccarino household was rich in love and not-so-rich in money. There were five girls and three boys in the family. They had a big garden, so no one ever went hungry. Despite the economic hard times, the Vaccarinos generously shared their food with less-fortunate individuals. When hobos journeyed through the area during the Depression, Mrs. Vaccarino made sandwiches for them.[46]

In the 1920s and 1930s, traveling salesmen regularly came to Mr. Vaccarino's store in Kantner. Sometimes, remembers Mary McGarry, her mother invited them to visit the Vaccarino home for dinner.[47] In those days, after all, there were relatively few diners and restaurants. The salesmen enjoyed and appreciated her food and the convivial atmosphere in which she served it to them. One Christmas, Mrs. Vaccarino received a large box of toys from the grateful diners. The traveling salesmen sent the gifts to her children as tokens of their appreciation for her graciousness. The Vaccarino children cherished the toys, as they had never received any playthings before.[48]

To this day Mary McGarry remembers the wonderful surprise that the salesmen sent to her home. "We were amazed," recalls Mrs. McGarry as she thinks about the joy that the children felt when they opened the box of toys.[49] Indeed, the box contained the only toys that Mary McGarry and her siblings ever received during their childhood. Over the years Mrs. McGarry has told and retold this poignant story to her children and grandchildren.[50] Today her granddaughter, Lisa Dimberio Nelson, is a wife, mother, and entrepreneur in northeastern Ohio. She notes that her grandmother "has been telling me the story since I was a very small child. I would say, though, that it did not truly sink in until I was an adult with children of my own."[51]

The personal stories of Italian-American advancement continue to be passed from generation to generation. Telling such stories can be quite moving and emotional experiences for the people who share them with others. During one discussion, an Italian-American man became emotional as he described how the G.I. Bill had given him the opportunity to attend college in the 1950s, as it did for many Italian Americans.[52] In another discussion, an Italian immigrant choked up as he described with pride how he had built a prosperous small business. Older Italian Americans often recollect how they overcame poverty and prejudice to become successful. As a rule, Italian-American elders take pride in their achievements and the fact that they surmounted great odds, in many cases, to prosper in this country.

III. Public service, community leadership, and philanthropic activity are arenas in which Italian Americans give back to America. In towns, cities, and states throughout the United States, Italian Americans can be found in various activities to develop and maintain a viable civic life. People of Italian origin are involved in service clubs;

their children's schools; their parishes, congregations, and synagogues; and other activities in the community. The amount of philanthropy by America's Italians is becoming increasingly visible, too, in response to the growing amounts of wealth in this demographic group. Now let us focus on the examples of Alessandra Di Cicco Higgs and Robert Barbera, two Italians in North America who have achieved significant successes and currently spend their time helping others through charitable works.

Florida entrepreneur Alessandra Di Cicco Higgs has an inspiring and heartwarming story that reflects, in a microcosm, the remarkable achievements of the Italian immigrants in the New World.[53] Di Cicco Higgs was born in March 1939 in Valleluce, a little village near the city of Montecassino in the Region of Lazio.[54] During World War II, her father and uncle served in the Italian Army. In late 1943 the German soldiers came to Valleluce, whereupon they destroyed many homes, sacked the village's food supply, and raped many of the young women. Alessandra was eating her favorite breakfast (corn bread with goat's milk) when the soldiers evicted the Di Cicco family from their residence. Since Valleluce was temporarily uninhabitable, Alessandra, her mother, her maternal grandmother, her baby brother, and a group of approximately fifty refugees headed for nearby Abruzzi. As they trekked through the mountains, the intrepid villagers remained vigilant for hostile aircraft that might bomb them.

Her experiences as a homeless refugee made an indelible impression on Higgs. The travelers from Valleluce were only able to carry whatever they could bring with them. The adults positioned Alessandra, who clutched her pillow from home, in front of their ragtag procession. They thought the four-year-old should be first because she was too young to have committed any sins. Therefore, they viewed her as an angel who would protect them. When the refugees reached Abruzzi, some Good Samaritans allowed them to sleep in a large barn there. On occasion, little Alessandra and her two older male cousins begged for food from the *abruzzesi*. They spent the cold winter months in the unheated barn. Finally, the Di Ciccos returned to Valleluce after having been on the road for almost six months. Due to these traumatic experiences, Higgs could not talk or think about the war for many years. Today she empathizes with the little girls in war-torn areas whom she sees on television.

Alessandra and her family lived in Valleluce until 1953. (Alessandra herself is the oldest of three children.) She babysat her brother while her mother and grandmother cultivated the crops. They had no radio, no electricity, and no indoor plumbing. Alessandra left school at age eleven because Valleluce was too small to offer classes for students in the higher grades—and there was no transportation for her to attend the educational institution in another village. To give his children more opportunities, Angelo Di Cicco immigrated to Ontario, Canada, in 1951. His family joined him two years later. The Di Ciccos departed from Naples, Italy, on February 19, 1953. Valleluce's newest expatriates arrived in Halifax, Nova Scotia, on March 4, 1953 (Alessandra's fourteenth birthday). From Halifax, the *vallelucesi* took the train to London, Ontario, where they arrived two days later.

Life was not easy for the Di Ciccos in their early years in Canada. Angelo Di Cicco had a job with the railroad, and on the weekends, he worked in a vegetable market. His wife, Domenica Di Cicco, labored in a laundry that lacked air conditioning. For two years the Di Ciccos lived in a boardinghouse with limited amenities. Alessandra, meanwhile, took care of her younger siblings and another boy. She attended a Catholic school in London, Ontario, for six months. On her first day of school in Canada, the young immigrant became discombobulated and began to cry in the classroom. Within days, however, Alessandra learned basic English vocabulary from friendly classmates, who tutored her one-on-one. Her formal education ended in the fall of 1953, as Alessandra left school permanently to enter the paid labor force. After a series of factory jobs, she went to work full-time at Sophie's, a dress shop. The Di Cicco family purchased a three-bedroom home around 1955; they could do so because Angelo, Domenica, and Alessandra Di Cicco held jobs.

As a teenager, Alessandra discovered that she had a knack for sales. John Stronski, a Polish immigrant who was the father of the talk-show personality Jenny Jones, owned Sophie's, where Alessandra honed her sales skills. When she was only twenty, in 1959, Alessandra and her then-husband started a construction business with a post-hole digger and a twenty-dollar typewriter in their living room. By the early 1970s they owned a successful roadbuilding enterprise as well as an asphalt plant and two Ready-Mix companies in Ontario. Alessandra worked for the business full-time: She was the "people person" and the "front person." The Higgses relocated to Naples, Florida, in 1973, where their enterprises continued to flourish. The Canadian transplants built seven high-rises and many subdivisions in southwest Florida. Alessandra handled sales and development for their business. In addition, she operated her own thriving real-estate company that sold condominiums and other properties developed by the Higgs family corporation.

To achieve great success, Higgs surmounted serious obstacles related to social class, national origin, and gender. "All my life I had to fight to survive," she recalled in a recent interview. Indeed, Alessandra hailed from a modest socioeconomic background. Her hardworking parents crossed the Atlantic Ocean in order to provide their children with a higher standard of living. As a youth in Italy, Alessandra had little schooling because of the patriarchal notion that young women did not need much formal education, since they were expected to raise children and do housework. Upon coming to Canada, Higgs learned to speak English largely on her own. (She proudly remembers her first sentence in English: "Give to me a bottle of milk.") Due to her gender, people frequently underestimated this redoubtable businesswoman, even though she began dealing with bankers at the age of twenty or twenty-one. Moreover, she sold the family's three Ready-Mix companies herself. Higgs achieved success in a man's world; as a builder, developer, and co-owner of a concrete business, she was the only woman in the room during many negotiations.

Alessandra Di Cicco Higgs presently spends much of her time on charitable activities and community work. During the last two decades, she has been involved with such nonprofits as Hope for Haiti, St. Matthew's House, St. Anne Catholic Church, the David Lawrence Foundation, Catholic Charities-Collier County, the National Italian American Foundation, and the Italian Cultural Society and the Italian Cultural Foundation in Naples. This warm, dynamic, and stylish woman characterizes herself as a "consultant," a description that takes into account the advisory role she plays for many charities. In the best Italian tradition, she stays "very close" to her parents, children, and grandchildren. Higgs is modest about her exceptional accomplishments and compelling personal story; she prefers instead to focus attention on worthy causes.[55]

California real-estate mogul Robert Barbera, too, is deeply committed to his Italian heritage, and he is very involved in promoting American values and culture. Barbera's parents immigrated to the United States from Sicily. His father, John Salvatore Barbera, left the Sicilian town of Masala for the United States in 1908. John Barbera enlisted in the U.S. Army during World War I; consequently, he received his U.S. citizenship. Robert Barbera's mother, Rosalina Barbera, came from Carini, a town near Palermo, in 1920. John and Rosalina Barbera met and married in the

United States. They had two children: Henry (who became a sociologist) and Robert. A native of New York City, Robert Barbera grew up in Brooklyn and Queens. From 1932 to 1953 he lived in three communities: Bensonhurst, Brooklyn; St. Albans, Queens; and the Jamaica Estates section of Jamaica, Queens.[56]

After two years in Charlotte, North Carolina, Barbera went to California in 1955. He has been there ever since. Robert Barbera pursued a college education and received a degree in accounting from California State University–Los Angeles. This was a big accomplishment for him. Initially, says Barbera, "I saw no value in education." His early mentor was Dr. Murphy, the dean at Cal State. She "loved Italians" and encouraged him to develop his potential and explore his interest in Italy.[57] Over the years, Barbera worked for a number of government agencies and in private enterprise, as he expanded his property business (which he started in 1956). He presently serves as chairman of Barbera Property Management, a company that owns and operates twenty-six apartment houses in California's San Gabriel Valley.[58]

From 1956 until her passing in 2001 Barbera's closest ally and confidant was his wife Bernice, a Mexican-Portuguese native of Hanford, a town in California's Central Valley. They have three children: Ann, John, and Patricia.[59] A quiet and very bright woman, Bernice Barbera was a staunch patriot. Robert Barbera notes that "the Italian Americans received Bernice very well."[60] She cooked Italian food and had a number of Italian-American friends. Likewise, Bernice Barbera learned Italian quickly, due in part to the similarities between Italian and Spanish. At the same time, she quietly endured discrimination throughout her life. Robert Barbera notes that it "pains" him "that she was not considered to be American by some people" due to her Mexican appearance.[61]

Barbera himself has experienced subtle discrimination on the basis of ethnic origin. A fellow Italophile once described him to his face as "the Godfather." Bernice Barbera immediately challenged the man for his ethnic slur. Another time, at a Pepperdine University board meeting, he and two other Italian-American Trustees were discussing various issues, when a non-Italian Trustee walked by and remarked, "There's the Mafia." Due to Barbera's considerable success in real estate, some people pointedly attribute his wealth to organized crime—they cannot accept the fact that he has done so well legitimately. Barbera cites other examples where his ethnicity may have worked against him, as in the Irish priest who never

acknowledged his presence at church, even though he had been a parish-
ioner there for ten years and was a teacher of Confraternity of Christian
Doctrine (CCD). Regardless, the rebuffs in his life have made him "work
harder."[62]

As an American, Barbera takes great pride in the land of his birth. He
remembers that his mother was ecstatic on the day in 1940 that she became
an American citizen. During World War II, Rosalina Barbera sent him to
school to buy Liberty Bonds. In doing so, she "demonstrated her commitment to America," remembers her son. He had the highest amount of purchases of Liberty Bonds in his entire school. A Republican and a savvy
entrepreneur who "bought and sold houses," Rosalina Barbera had only a
fourth-grade education. She taught her son how to save, invest, deal, and
negotiate from a very early age. Moreover, she showed him how to purchase and manage real estate.[63] Currently, Barbera is chairman of the board
of the Americanism Educational League, an organization that promotes
American values and traditions through its videos, essay contests, and edi-
torial materials.[64] He celebrates America for many reasons, among them
the tremendous socioeconomic mobility that is possible here.[65]

Barbera himself enjoys a well-deserved reputation as a generous man in
Los Angeles County and elsewhere. By his own estimates, he "has raised
millions of dollars for different institutions" in Los Angeles and numerous colleges and universities in southern California. Barbera's top goals
include promoting access to higher education.[66] Accordingly, he offers
numerous awards and scholarships at local educational institutions,
including Pepperdine University and California State University–Northridge. Barbera does so for three reasons: he wants to "help other kids go
to school"; he knows firsthand "the difference that schooling can make for
you"; and he cites "the feelings of how people" treated him as an Italian.
Indeed, this philanthropic activity is a "response to the negativism that has
been hurled at him" over the years.[67]

Barbera and his wife, Josephine Volpe Barbera, continue to be deeply
involved in Italian and Italian-American events and activities.[68] He and
Mrs. Barbera married in 2003; both of them had been widowed.[69] A longtime participant in and leader of such organizations as UNICO and Federated
Italo-Americans of Southern California, Robert Barbera generously supports the Italian Cultural Institute in Los Angeles and the Italian program
at California State University–Northridge. Furthermore, Barbera owns and
serves as head publisher of *L'Italo-Americano*, the venerable Italian-Ameri-

can publication that dates back to 1908. Today the Barberas host numerous events at their elegant San Marino, California, home. In addition, they are significant donors to the Pepperdine Campus School in Florence, Italy.[70] Robert Barbera, meanwhile, is president and founder of Lingua Viva, an organization that promotes the Italian culture and language in Southern California.[71] In sum, the Barberas celebrate their Italian heritage while simultaneously embracing and reinforcing the commonalities that bind us as Americans.

❄ ❄ ❄

The trajectory of Italian-American success in Easton, Pennsylvania, reflects the achievements of Italian Americans throughout our nation. In 2000 people of Italian origin accounted for 14.1 percent of Easton's multiethnic population of 26,000-plus residents. Anthony Noto is an Easton native whose life story parallels the progress of the Lehigh Valley's Italian population. Noto was born in the United States in 1920. As a young child, he spent three and one-half years in Sicily. When Noto returned to the United States, he was six years old and had no facility whatsoever with the English language. He "picked it up quickly," however. By 1941, Noto had graduated from Lafayette College and been elected to Phi Beta Kappa; the twenty-one-year-old educator was teaching English at Easton High School.[72]

On a weekday in 1941 the school district census taker visited the Noto family's home. He asked about the occupations of the family members. When Noto's Sicilian-born mother told him that Anthony Noto worked at Easton High School, the census taker asked, "Is he a janitor?" He automatically assumed that no resident of the Noto family's modest neighborhood would hold a white-collar position.[73] "At the time our home was in a somewhat ethnically mixed but predominantly Italian neighborhood that consisted of rowhouses, some still with outhouses," writes Anthony Noto. "Townhouses now stand in the two-block area that once included our family residence."[74] Many years later, Anthony Noto shares this anecdote to underscore the advances that Easton's Italians have made over the last seven decades.

The story of the Mamana family also illustrates how Italian Americans have flourished in Easton. Joseph Mamana Sr. was a Notre Dame graduate and one of the first Italian-American teachers in the Easton public schools.[75] Mamana spent much of his career as a school principal; his distinguished record of educational leadership in Easton resulted in dozens of awards over the years.[76] He and his wife, Julia Cericola Mamana (who taught elementary school at St. Phillip and St. James Catholic School in Phillipsburg, New Jersey), always emphasized education at home to their five studious, hard-working children, who were born and reared in Easton. Indeed, the accomplishments of the younger Mamanas—Joseph Mamana Jr., James Mamana, Dr. John Mamana, Dr. Julianne Mamana Boyd, and Dr. June Mamana—testify to the power of education. The five Mamana siblings count an attorney, an educator, a physician, and two theater directors among their ranks.[77]

At the same time, Italian Americans are well represented among Easton's civic, political, and economic leaders. Salvatore Panto is once again the mayor of Easton; he previously served in this position from 1984 to 1992. As of 2006, four of the five Easton City Councilmembers were of Italian descent: Council President Sandra Alercia Vulcano, Council Vice President Pamela (Piparato) Panto, Councilmember Carole (Scarito) Heffley, and Councilmember Dan Corpora. Heffley, who is one-half Sicilian, remembers hearing stories about the bias that her Italian relatives encountered decades ago. Her Italian family background, among other factors, motivated her to sponsor successfully an anti-discrimination ordinance in Easton in 2006.[78] More than a century after the Italians began coming to Easton, they enjoy acceptance throughout the community (as is the case for Italians all over America).

Easton residents John and Pamela Richetta celebrate the Italian-American traditions in Pennsylvania's Lehigh Valley through their community activities and the events and radio programs produced by their company, Richetta Promotions. The Richettas are relentlessly positive boosters of Easton and its ethnic and cultural diversity; in 2006 John Richetta was elected president of Easton's Pomfret Club.[79] A veteran musician and disc jockey, John Richetta is currently a radio personality and the drummer in King Henry & The Showmen, a popular band on the East Coast. Richetta Promotions' signature program, "Tempo Italiano with John Richetta," began airing on Sundays on AM 1400 WEST in Easton in January 1998. John Richetta quickly established himself as a popular radio personality in the Lehigh Valley. In 2007 "Tempo Italiano" shifted to WSAN 1470 AM, where it airs from 9:00 A.M. to 3:00 P.M. every Sunday.[80]

"Tempo Italiano" is a bilingual, interactive program with significant audience participation and community involvement. Every Sunday the listeners request and dedicate songs as well as make comments and share anecdotes on the air. John Richetta's playlist includes traditional Italian music, contemporary Italian singers, and Italian-American artists. "Tempo Italiano" has approximately forty advertisers; it is a top-rated radio program in its time slot in eastern Pennsylvania.[81] "Tempo Italiano," too, helps to raise money for various organizations in the Easton area. Pamela and John Richetta enlisted their listeners and advertisers to collect the requisite funds to open Villa Tempo Italiano in downtown Easton.[82] "The grand opening in July 2001 introduced two bocce courts, fountains, trees, benches and gardens for the entire community to enjoy," according to the Tempo Italiano Web site.[83]

To be sure, the Richettas have developed a series of events, activities, and publications around "Tempo Italiano." They sponsor the Tempo Italiano Bocce Rollers Association league and bocce tournaments (including the yearly Tempo Italiano Heritage Day Bocce Tournament). There are periodic Tempo Italiano trips to Italy, regular Tempo Italiano day trips by bus, the annual Lehigh Valley Italian American Celebration, and Tempo Italiano Supper Clubs at local restaurants three times each year. All of these events and activities have an Italian or Italian-American connection.[84] For five years, John and Pamela Richetta authored the *Italian Tribune*'s "Tempo Italiano" page.[85] And in 2005 they published the *Tempo Italiano Memories Cookbook*: It includes photos, recipes, and family stories.[86] Through all of their activities, the Richettas seek to preserve and promote the Italian-American culture and heritage for future generations.[87]

Part II

ASSIMILATION
AND
INTEGRATION

Chapter 4

THE ETHNICS

In the late 1960s Joseph Maselli played golf regularly at a certain country club in southeastern Louisiana. Eventually he decided to apply for membership there, but the club rejected his application.[1] This affront surprised Maselli, who had already achieved considerable success in business by this time. Thereafter, the proud Italian American became active on many fronts to fight discrimination and advocate on behalf of his coethnics. During the last forty years, he has expended a considerable amount of his time, energy, and resources in these pursuits. His family, meanwhile, prospered and became part of the local elite. Maselli's daughter now belongs to the country club whose leadership once slighted her father. His children, in fact, are members of top-flight country clubs in the New Orleans area.[2] The club's unfortunate decision to exclude Maselli benefited Americans of Italian descent, as it inspired him to commit his formidable talents to Italian-American causes.

The oldest son of a Pugliese immigrant (Frank Maselli) and a Sicilian immigrant (Mary Iannetta), Joseph Maselli was born in Newark, New Jersey, on May 30, 1924. He grew up in the heavily Italian communities of Newark, New Jersey, and Belleville, New Jersey. Both Newark and Belleville had sizable numbers of Italian immigrants. Maselli spoke only Italian until he entered the public schools, and he lived in predominantly Italian neighborhoods as a youth.[3] "By the time I was twenty, I felt American," reports the native New Jerseyite.[4] He experienced this evolution from Italian to American when he served in the U.S. military during World War II.[5]

Joseph Maselli came to Louisiana in the 1940s, and he has made his home in the Pelican State for more than six decades. The former pugilist graduated from Tulane University after the war; the G.I. Bill of Rights enabled him to go to college. (His father had only a third-grade education in Italy.) Maselli married Antoinette Cammarata in 1946. As with the vast majority of Louisiana's Italians, she traces her ancestry to Sicily. The Masellis have three sons and one daughter. Over the years, Joseph Maselli's business interests have included liquor distribution, apartment complexes, and strip malls.[6] Maselli's business acumen and subsequent financial independence enabled him to focus on ethnic issues and become one of the nation's preeminent Italian-American leaders.

Since 1970 he has been actively involved in the Southeast's Italian-American events and organizations.[7] In 1973 Maselli founded the organization that eventually became known as the American Italian Federation of the Southeast. The same year, Maselli and his associates started publishing the *Italian American Digest*, a quarterly newspaper that describes itself as the "Italian American Voice of the South."[8] During the 1970s and 1980s, he created and developed the American Italian Renaissance Foundation Museum and Library, an institution that is located at 537 South Peters Street in New Orleans.[9] Likewise, the dynamic businessman cofounded the magnificent Piazza d'Italia, the "living monument" (Maselli's words) to Italian Americans next to the Museum and Library.[10] And in 2004 he published a book about the Italian-American population of Greater New Orleans.[11]

Maselli has a lengthy record of involvement in numerous state, regional, national, and international Italian and Italian-American organizations. For many years he served as vice chair of the National Italian American Foundation. Maselli, moreover, advised Presidents Ford, Carter, and Reagan on ethnic issues. The longtime New Orleanian enjoys excellent political connections, a fact that benefits Italian Americans in the Crescent City and environs. Top state officials attend the American Italian Renaissance Foundation's annual dinner for the Louisiana American Italian Sports Hall of Fame. The recipient of many honors from different ethnic groups, Maselli is a knight of Malta and a Grand'Ufficiale.[12] As a humanitarian, he played an integral role in Italian earthquake relief efforts in 1973 and 1980.[13]

This proud Italian American protects, preserves, and perpetuates the Italian-American heritage and culture in many different ways. As one who personally felt the sting of ethnic bias, he defends Americans of Italian descent from negative characterizations. Maselli notes that the pop-culture stereotyping of his coethnics particularly affects their image in those contexts where people have little familiarity with Italian Americans as a group. Thus there are few competing images and impressions to counteract the negative ones. On the home front, Maselli and his colleagues in New Orleans have helped Italian Americans to learn about their roots, specifically the Sicilian towns where their ancestors originated. The New Orleans business leader also records oral histories and clips local death notices for the Italians of southeastern Louisiana.[14]

Today Maselli reflects on the progress that Italian Americans have made over the years.[15] "Over a period of sixty to seventy years it [discrimination] has diminished to the point of being almost nonexistent," notes the pioneering ethnic advocate.[16] (As recently as 2005, though, someone referred to him as "the Godfather," a comment that angered Maselli for obvious reasons.)[17] He rightfully takes pride in the successes of his children. "They're all workaholics," reports Maselli. "They're all stand-up people."[18] Every one of his children married non-Italians, a development that mirrors trends throughout Italian America.[19] Meanwhile, Louisianans and others benefit from Joseph Maselli's enduring commitment to Italian-American culture and his admirable record of service and leadership in the Italian-American community.

I. Thomas Ragona remembers that Irish Americans dominated the local establishment in Bridgeport, Connecticut, when he was growing up there in the 1920s and 1930s. They accounted for the majority of Bridgeport's teachers, politicians, police officers, and businesspeople. Ragona and his fellow Italian Americans then represented approximately 40 percent of the city's population, but they remained underrepresented in the ranks of Bridgeport's authority figures. Not surprisingly, the ethnic tensions of the time spilled out into the playgrounds of Bridgeport. As a youngster in the late 1920s and early 1930s, Ragona engaged in weekly fistfights with an Irish-American friend. Their ethnic backgrounds figured prominently in these fights—the two young men traded ethnic insults while they pummeled each other.[20]

In 1933 Ragona had an incident in physical education class that reflected the Irish-Italian conflicts of the era. As he went to jump the horse in a gymnastics exercise, an Irish-American bully stuck out his foot and tripped him. The son of Eire compounded the indignity by intoning, "You wop," as he tripped Ragona. An indignant Ragona promptly went to the gym teacher and said, "I want to fight him." The teacher said, "He's bigger than you." (The young Irishman was 6' 2", while this son of Italian immigrants measured 5' 10".) The height differential did not deter Ragona. So the youngsters laced up their gloves. Little did anyone know that Ragona's uncle, Henry DiJulio Sr., was a successful professional boxer. (His grandfather, Alphonse DiJulio, had a boxing ring in his basement. Male family members settled their disputes there.) The other students gathered around them—and then Ragona administered a beating to his classmate, who ended up with a black eye and a bloody nose. The two young men became good friends after their bout of fisticuffs.

Two years later, Ragona once again encountered anti-Italian discrimination, this time when he applied for a job with the telephone company in Bridgeport. Every weekday for about three months he went to the company's office to inquire about his employment application. Each day he received a noncommittal answer. At first, Ragona thought nothing of his inability to land a job with the telephone company. Few employment opportunities existed in 1935, the height of the Depression. After a while, though, Ragona noticed that his Irish-American classmates, who had similar qualifications, were being hired, but not he. One day the Irish-American employment manager advised Ragona to stop wasting his time—the telephone company only wanted to hire Irish Americans. Ragona remembers his experiences with no apparent rancor; the Irish-Italian conflicts of his youth have faded into history.

Over the years the ethnic relations between Italian Americans and other European-origin groups have improved dramatically to the point that there are few differences between and among native-born European Americans anymore. In general, the ethnic conflicts of the past have subsided as the differences that separated Italian Americans from other white Americans diminished significantly because of such factors as ethnic intermarriage and the assimilation process. One finds that older people still remember the ethnic tensions of their youth, but they also acknowledge how much has changed in the last forty to eighty years. As recently as the 1960s and 1970s an interethnic marriage involving an Italian would raise eyebrows, both inside and outside the Italian-American community, in certain parts of the country. At the same time that Italian Americans became largely accepted by other European Americans, racial issues came to the fore in American society due to the civil rights movement and other catalytic events.

During this period, in the late 1960s and early 1970s, the Italian Americans and others of Southern and Eastern European descent became known as "white ethnics." John D. Skrentny writes:

> Who are the white ethnics? As with the affirmative-action minority groupings, there never has been a clear definition of exactly who is in this category. The core groups are the mostly Catholic immigrants or persons with ancestry from eastern or southern Europe, such as Italians, Poles, Hungarians, and Slovaks. Orthodox Christians such as Greeks and Serbians are usually included, while Jews and Catholic Irish Americans are on the boundaries. American political commentators usually group Latinos separately, though they are often white. White ethnics are generally Americans of those nationalities that were disfavored but not excluded by American immigration policy between the early 1920s and 1965. WASPs and Scandinavians are therefore not in this category.[21]

Italian-American ethnic pride and advocacy organizations flourished during the 1960s and 1970s, as an outgrowth of the civil rights movement, the women's rights movement, and other social movements that heralded the emergence of previously ignored, marginalized, or quiescent groups of people in American society.[22] As John D. Skrentny notes, "in the late 1960s and early 1970s an extraordinary ethnic revival took place, especially in older northeastern and midwestern cities. Like Latinos and other groups, white ethnics formed organizations, lobbied, even engaged in some protest."[23] In recent decades, some Italians have adopted the language of equity, inclusion, and multiculturalism to promote Italian-American issues, causes, and activities. To be sure, while the Italians and other Southern and Eastern European immigrants once experienced poverty and faced social discrimination in many contexts, they rarely, if ever, encountered the demeaning forms of discrimination endured by African Americans and other people of color.

Discussions regularly occur among Italian Americans about their role in American society and culture. Some older Italian Americans still consider themselves to be minorities and, to some extent, outsiders in American society. There was a time in which Italian Americans were less likely to celebrate their ethnicity publicly: It was controversial to do so six, seven, and eight decades ago. Likewise, some Italian Americans felt a sense of difference that made them sheepish about, embarrassed by, and even at times ashamed of their ethnic background, as they wanted to minimize any sense of difference from the mainstream culture. In any event, many Italian Americans of a certain age remember what it was like to be out-siders in WASP-dominated settings and contexts.[24] Now individual Italian Americans will sometimes complain about what they see as disunity in their community and then compare Italian Americans to members of other ethnic groups (those that mobilize their resources and political power more successfully, in their opinion).

Italian-American ideas and individuals play important roles in shaping what we define as mainstream American ideas and culture—and the images of ourselves that we transmit to the world. The Italian-American cinematic icons Rocky Balboa and Michael Corleone are in many respects as *American* as they are *Italian American*. At the same time, many Americans of Ital-ian descent do not feel "ethnic" much or any of the time. "I'm not too eth-nic," one Italian-surnamed man in suburban Buffalo, New York, told my father and me in 2005. Americans of Italian descent, to be sure, express their pride in the form of lighthearted ethnic chauvinism. They may do so by using Italian and Italian-American decals, T-shirts, credit cards, address labels, affinity pins, and license plate holders that celebrate their Italian-American identity.[25]

In *Ethnic Identity*, Richard Alba describes how Italian Americans and other long-established white ethnic groups relate to their ethnic heritage. Alba writes:

> The general outlines of symbolic ethnicity offer a far better fit to the emerging nature of ethnic identity—essentially in the desire to retain a sense of being eth-nic, but without any deep commitment to ethnic social ties or behaviors. Sym-bolic ethnicity is concerned with the symbols of ethnic cultures rather than with the cultures themselves, and this seems true also of the cultural commitments of ethnic identity: the cultural stuff of ethnicity continues to wither, and thus ethnic identity tends to latch onto a few symbolic commitments (such as St. Patrick's Day among the Irish). Symbolic ethnicity makes few and intermittent demands on everyday life and tends to be expressed in the private domain of leisure-time activities. These characteristics have been amply demonstrated for the ethnic identities of most whites.[26]

Since Italian Americans increasingly are of mixed ethnic origins, they have multiple choices as to when, where, and how they identify as "Italian."[27] There are a wide variety of indicators as to how Italian Americans relate to their ethnic heritage. Such indicators include whether they consume Italian foods, speak the Italian language, live in a heavily Italian neighborhood, belong to Italian-American organizations, have regular Italian cultural experiences, interact socially and enjoy friendships with their coethnics, and identify as Italian in their day-to-day lives and encourage their children to do so.[28] Many Americans of Italian origin from ethnically mixed families are genuinely biethnic or multiethnic in their identity and outlook.

Remo Minato reports that his six children, who are one-half Italian, toggle between their Italian and Oregon-pioneer backgrounds in terms of how they self-identify in an ethnic sense. Minato himself is the American-born son of Anselmo and Maria Minato, who immigrated from the Veneto to the United States. His late wife, Joanne Carolyn Minato, was a fifth-generation Oregonian of Irish-Scottish descent. Sometimes their children identify as Italian Americans, especially when they observe and celebrate various Italian customs and traditions. On other occasions the younger Minatos identify with their mother's heritage, particularly when they attend her large family's annual reunion.[29] These Italian-surnamed residents of the Beaver State offer a flexible, ecumenical, and, above all, very American perspective on ethnic identification.

Jessica Lyons articulates a viewpoint—along with that of her husband, Tom Colosi—on Italian-American life that reflects the experiences of many Americans of Italian descent.[30] "My husband and I think of ourselves as Italian-American," writes Lyons. "But neither Tom nor I speak the language. And we've never been to Italy. We eat plenty of pasta, but Tom's red sauce and my eggplant are original recipes."[31] Lyons also notes that she and her husband find "mob-genre stories" fascinating. Moreover, she invokes the holiday traditions in their Italian-American family: wine, Sinatra, ravioli, many cousins. At the same time, the Monterey County, Californian notes the difficulty of articulating what being Italian American is or what it means today.[32] Lyons writes: "Tom and I both struggle with what our Italian culture means beyond good food, close families and a strong work ethic. We also don't want to lose it, whatever it is."[33]

As we explore the issue of ethnicity, one comes to the topic of whether Italian regional differences matter anymore in Italian America. The Old World dynamics once structured Italians' identification patterns and how they were perceived by other Italians and, to some extent, native-born

Americans in the United States. The Italian immigrants usually identified first with their region of origin and then, secondly, as Italians or Italian Americans.[34] The northern Italian/southern Italian distinction continues to have some significance in the United States, but it is less important than it was, say, fifty years ago. It is still salient in Italy, where there are regional terms that the Italians use to describe—and derogate—each other.[35] The subject of Italian regional origins regularly surfaces in Italian-American contexts, too. This subject seems to matter the most to recent immigrants, elderly and middle-aged people, and those individuals who maintain close ties to Italy.

Even today, there are internal stereotypes within the Italian-American community. One still hears lighthearted jokes and the occasional mean-spirited comment about the fabled traits and characteristics of each region's people. At least one person told me that he believes the Italians north of Rome are not the "real Italians." Other people may stereotype the southern Italians in different ways. In Italian-American contexts, individuals regularly ask each other about their ancestral origins in Italy, more so out of interest and curiosity than any other reasons. Intra-Italian intermarriage, the simple passage of time, and the development of a pan-Italian identity in America are some of the factors that have diminished the importance of Italian regionalism among Italian Americans. Italian regional identities still matter, of course, to many Americans of Italian descent, but they do not necessarily take precedence over the pan-Italian identity anymore.

II. Italian Americans now have the best of both worlds: They can enthusiastically celebrate their Italian heritage and not be seen in any way, shape, or form as un-American for doing so. Sometimes there will be a continuum of different ways of identifying with one's Italian heritage in a given family. One sibling might be a devoted Italophile, while another barely notes her Italian ancestry. All approaches reflect the diversity of opinion in Italian America. Fifty years ago, an Italian American might have downplayed his ethnicity because of the prevailing melting-pot ethos. Today if he does so, it is more a matter of personal preference than a reflection of external pressures to assimilate into the broader society. To be sure, the stigma attached to being an Italian American has disappeared (or is rapidly disappearing) in most contexts.

The connection between "Italian" and "American" is developing to the point that it is now difficult to disentangle the two identifiers in many cases. World War II marked the last period in U.S. history when any noticeable percentage of the American population may have questioned the patriotism of Italian Americans. Indeed, Italian Americans can wave Italian flags, observe Italian Republic Day, sing the Italian National Anthem, and celebrate Italy's victory in the 2006 World Cup with few, if any, instances of hostility from other Americans. Nowadays virtually no one suggests that Americans of Italian descent are anything but Americans. The examples of two individuals who represented New Jersey in the U.S. House of Representatives—Frank Guarini Jr. and Marge Roukema—offer valuable Italian-American perspectives on American identity.

Former Congressman Frank Guarini Jr. remembers hearing the stories about how his Italian-born grandmother, Clementina Lemi Guarini, successfully "studied to be a midwife by the light of a fireplace" in Jersey City, New Jersey. During her subsequent career as a midwife in the early twentieth century, Clementina Guarini attended to the mothers of thousands of babies in the Jersey City area. There were few physicians at the time and, in any event, many people could not afford the expense of a doctor. Consequently, Mrs. Guarini's services were in great demand among the Italian immigrants and their families.[36]

Frank Guarini recalls that his grandmother also advised many Italian immigrants on different matters. Clementina Guarini wrote letters for the Italian newcomers and read aloud the letters that came to them from Italy (many Italian immigrants were illiterate). In short, she was a central figure in Jersey City's Italian community, one who was "very much respected" by the other Italian immigrants. Decades later, the main Post Office in Jersey City, an expansive building in the Italian Renaissance style, was named in honor of her grandson, Congressman Frank J. Guarini—the very post office where she mailed her letters on behalf of the immigrant families. The Post Office also now bears her name.[37]

Clementina Guarini would undoubtedly take pride in the significant accomplishments of her grandson, Frank Joseph Guarini Jr., a successful attorney, seven-term Member of Congress, and former chairman of the National Italian American Foundation. She came to America at the age of three in 1876. Clementina Guarini married a fellow who had arrived in the United States during the 1880s. Their son, Frank Joseph Guarini Sr., was born in New York City in 1892; he traced his ancestry to Campobasso in what is now Molise. Frank Joseph Guarini Jr.'s maternal relatives came from a village near Catanzaro in Calabria. His mother, Caroline Loretta Critelli, was born in Niagara Falls, New York. He himself was born on August 20, 1924, in Jersey City.[38] During his youth, he remembers that the "Italians were very much downtrodden."[39]

A native of Jersey City, Guarini embraced education, made a fortune as an attorney, and later entered public service. As a young man, he earned a bachelor's degree from Dartmouth College and two degrees (the J.D. and LL.M., respectively) from the New York University School of Law. During World War II, Guarini was commissioned as a Lieutenant in the U.S. Naval Reserve and saw action in the South Pacific, earning the Navy Commendation Medal and three battle stars. The New Jerseyite entered electoral politics because of his desire to improve the quality of the political system in Hudson County. Guarini, who was a state senator from 1965 to 1972, won election to the U.S. House in 1978. This moderate Democrat served as a congressman from 1979 through 1993 from a district in Hudson County, New Jersey.[40]

A popular representative who posted large reelection margins, Guarini focused on taxes and trade during his fourteen years in Congress. He served as a member of the House Ways and Means Committee. Indeed, Guarini played an important role in enacting the Tax Reform Act of 1986. This advocate of universal health care also served as a member of the House Budget Committee, where he headed the Task Force on Urgent Fiscal Matters. In addition, Guarini has visited many of the countries around the globe on trade missions and other official business. To this end, he regularly meets with heads of state and top governmental officials. Guarini, too, highlights the multiethnic character of America: He enjoys a close friendship—and often travels with—former New York Congressman Benjamin Gilman, who is Jewish, and House Ways and Means Committee Chairman Charles Rangel, who is African American.[41]

Since the early 1990s Guarini has been one of America's top Italian-American figures. He served as president of the National Italian American Foundation for six years (1993 to 1999) and chairman of NIAF for six years (1999 to 2005). During Guarini's leadership of NIAF, he sought to strengthen the ties between the Italians in Italy and Italian Americans. Moreover, he tried to develop "links and networks between people of Italian origin." And Guarini focused on developing close relationships among the Italian-American organizations. This American of Italian descent loves Italian food, design, music, poetry, history, architecture, and the performing arts. The "splendors of Italy pervade every field," says Guarini. He characterizes himself as "very American in my manners and very Italian in my culture."[42]

Frank Guarini Jr. toggles seamlessly between his globetrotting schedule and lifelong commitment to his hometown of Jersey City.[43] His fifteenth-floor office in Jersey City overlooks Ellis Island, a symbolically resonant detail considering his ethnic background and efforts to create opportunities for all Americans. Guarini himself is the recipient of numerous honors, including four honorary doctorates and the prestigious Italian title of Grand'Ufficiale. In addition, one finds the Guarini Center for Governmental Affairs at Saint Peter's College in Jersey City, the Congressman Frank J. Guarini Library at New Jersey City University in Jersey City, the Guarini Institute for Public Affairs at John Cabot University in Rome, Italy, and Dartmouth College's Congressman Frank Guarini Language School in Rome. With his philanthropy and commitment to public service, Guarini follows the admirable example set many years ago by his grandmother, Clementina, and underscores the integral role that Italian Americans play in our nation's culture and politics.

Similarly, former U.S. Representative Marge Roukema has often emphasized the unifying concept of American identity throughout her long and distinguished career in public life. Roukema (née Scafati) was born on September 19, 1929. She is the granddaughter of Italian immigrants. During the early 1900s her father's family, the Scafati clan, came to the United States from Abruzzi, while her mother's forebears (the D'Alessios) left Campania for America. Roukema herself grew up in West Orange, New Jersey, which was mainly Irish/English at the time, with "very few Italian Americans." She describes West Orange as a "very integrated community," one in which she had friends of Irish, English, and German descent. In a 2005 interview she remembered her relatives as being patriotic and proud of their American nationality.[44]

"America," says Marge Roukema, "is the land of promise, opportunity, and liberty for all the people of the world."[45] Her father, Claude Scafati, lived the American Dream. Originally he was a garage mechanic, then later a service manager, and finally a partner in Gasner Motor Company—it became Dodge Montclair—in Montclair, New Jersey. By his example, he taught his daughter, Marge, how one works her or his way up the ladder in American society. Claude Scafati and his wife, Margaret, also emphasized to their daughter that she should pursue higher education. "They believed in public education," remembers Marge Roukema. She graduated from Montclair State University in 1951. Later, her uncle, Dr. Edward D'Alessio, served as president of Seton Hall University.[46]

During the 1950s, 1960s, and 1970s, Roukema focused mainly on civic affairs and her responsibilities as a full-time parent. After college, the lifelong New Jersey resident taught U.S. history and government for four years. She instructed her students in the fine points of American citizenship and the responsibilities that accompanied America's leadership role in the world. Then she became a full-time mother, one who raised three children. Her husband, Dr. Richard Roukema, is the son of Dutch immigrants. In fact, he is the only child in his family who was born in the United States. He grew up in Prospect Park, New Jersey, which was heavily Dutch at the time. Dr. Roukema's family came to the United States in the 1920s. The son of a widowed mother, Richard Roukema graduated from medical school and became a respected authority in the field of psychiatry. While he was in medical school, he and his wife, Marge, lived with her parents. She supported the young couple by teaching school.[47]

Marge Roukema entered electoral politics in the 1970s—doing so was an extension of her previous work as a teacher of American history and government. She was a civic leader in Bergen County, New Jersey, and served on the Ridgewood Board of Education from 1970 to 1973. Marge Roukema first ran for Congress in 1978 at the urging of her friends and associates in Bergen County. In 1980 she was elected to the U.S. House as a Republican from a district in northern New Jersey and served there until her retirement in 2003. A social moderate and fiscal conservative, Roukema believed in compromise and consensus-building; this approach enabled her to be an effective and productive lawmaker, even as she sometimes clashed with more conservative members of her party. Throughout her twenty-two years in Congress, the savvy legislator focused especially on banking, education, and family issues.[48]

Roukema's outlook and perspective emphasize our commonalities as Americans and underscore the importance of international issues. She was a key player in the efforts to pass the Family and Medical Leave Act, in part because of her experiences when her late son, Todd, had leukemia in the mid-1970s. Thus she worked tirelessly for eight years to pass the Family and Medical Leave Act. Roukema was the lead Republican sponsor of the initiative, and it became law in 1993.[49] Throughout her lengthy legislative

career, Roukema says that she consistently recognized the importance of
"integrating all ethnicities together" in American democracy.[50] The New
Jerseyite, furthermore, is global in her mindset when it comes to promoting
American values. Appropriately enough, Ramapo College in Mahwah,
New Jersey, has opened the Roukema Center for International Education
in her honor.[51]

III. Dave TanCreti is probably one of the few Italian-American tourists ever to visit Rock Valley, Iowa. TanCreti
remembers that he and his two brothers went to Rock Valley in 1982 or
1983. They stopped to eat in a local tavern, and a discussion ensued with
one of the diners. In the course of their conversation, TanCreti introduced
himself. Upon hearing his surname, the Rock Valleyite asked him, "What
type of name is that?" When TanCreti replied, "Italian," the other person
said, "We have never had them up here before."[52] In the best small-town-
Iowa tradition, the two men then engaged in friendly conversation.[53]
Indeed, the outgoing and well-traveled TanCreti regularly encounters
people whose perceptions of Italian Americans he helps to shape.

TanCreti is descended on his father's side from Campanian immigrants. When his grandfather, Vincenzo Tancredi, came to the United
States many years ago, an immigration officer changed his surname to
TanCreti. Family lore suggests that the officer might have been Dutch. A
native of Naples, Italy, Vincenzo Tancredi had ten children with his
Campanian-born wife, Maria Cascio Tancredi. Vincenzo TanCreti went
to work in Vermont on the Vermont Central Railroad. One of his sons
was Alfred TanCreti (Dave TanCreti's father), who grew up in Hanover,
Vermont. There are currently 780 TanCreti family members in the United
States. Many TanCretis live in Vermont, Massachusetts, Rhode Island,
New York, and New Jersey. Dave TanCreti's mother, Irene Hensing
TanCreti, is of Prussian-German/Danish descent. His wife, Cheryl
Pierce TanCreti, comes from Austrian/German/Irish stock. They named
their son Angelo after a family friend.

Since he travels frequently, TanCreti regularly has interesting experiences
that relate to his Italian surname and background. Italian Americans often
take pride in his ancestry. He has had his coethnics make a connection with
him in such places as a Caribbean cruise, Gloucester, Massachusetts, the
Orlando International Airport, and in the Black Hills of South Dakota.

"He's one of us," commented one Italian American when she learned of his Italian heritage. On a recent trip to the Northeast, TanCreti observed the effects of ethnic affinity in action. Italian Americans responded with enthusiasm when they learned about his ethnic background. Northeasterners often told the Des Moines, Iowa, resident that they "did not know there were any Italians west of Chicago," or some variation of this theme.

The TanCretis, to be sure, periodically experience subtle discrimination. A graduate of Drake University who served in the Army Air Corps during World War II, Alfred TanCreti was a salesman whose route included Texas at one point. The elder TanCreti had a dark complexion, so some Anglo Texans perceived him to be of Mexican origin. To gain entry into certain body shops and wholesale paint stores, Alfred TanCreti asked a local man to vouch for him. These days Dave TanCreti regularly goes pheasant hunting in rural parts of central Iowa. In the past, he introduced himself to the farmers as Dave TanCreti and asked for permission to hunt on their property. Sometimes they allowed him to do so. On at least one occasion, however, he was denied permission to hunt on a man's land. One farmer even told him, "I don't want your kind here." Now TanCreti usually asks his hunting partner to speak to the farmers, on the premise that someone with a Northern European name will fare better with them.

Another discriminatory event occurred to TanCreti in 1982 at his then-place of employment—a major Des Moines hospital. TanCreti asked the supervisor in charge of maintenance if he could use some 55-gallon chemical drums as garbage receptacles at an Italian festival. The supervisor denied TanCreti's request. "I don't like you guys," said the blunt-spoken Iowan. "You Italians are always schemin' and scammin' somebody out of money, and you're all in the Mafia." TanCreti, not surprisingly, took umbrage at these comments. He replied, "If I were in the Mafia, I wouldn't be working here, dressed like this, working on cooling towers. I'd be driving a Cadillac and wearing silk suits." The irate supervisor responded by ordering him out of his office. Such unpleasant incidents rarely occur to TanCreti, as he is a personable man and talented raconteur who makes friends easily. His delightful stories and diverse range of experiences illustrate how a person of Italian descent fits into different contexts in our multiethnic nation.

The existing conceptions of quintessentially American looks, names, and even behavior stem from the fact that people of Northern European descent have accounted for a majority or near-majority of the U.S. population throughout most of American history. Many Americans once thought

of the archetypal "American" as being someone of Northern European origin. Today this perception is changing quickly, largely due to the rapidly
shifting demographics of Multicultural America. People of color now
account for more than one-third of the U.S. population, a percentage that
increases each year. Omniracial looks are "in style" these days throughout
much of America. Consequently, people whose Italian skin tones and
physiognomies once marked them as outsiders now fit in better than ever.

Alan Balboni, an academic from Nevada, notes that his light olive complexion periodically leads foreign-born individuals to perceive him differently than if he was a fair-skinned Northern European. On a trip to Mexico, for instance, the bilingual flight attendants spoke to him in Spanish,
not English, on the airplane. "¿Algo más?" they asked the tall, burly Massachusetts native to determine whether he needed anything else. Similar
experiences occurred to Balboni in Mexico City. In addition, Balboni
reports that when the inside of his Las Vegas home was being painted, the
Mexican-born contractor said to him, "You're a little bit dark. Maybe you
come from a different place?" Balboni responded by discussing the variety
of different skin tones that one finds among the Italian people. Another
time, in Sweden, an Iranian-born storekeeper struck up a conversation
with Balboni; he seemed to have a certain comfort level with him because
their skin tones were similar.[54] Indeed, Balboni's gregarious nature and
open-minded attitude enable him to cross cultural and national boundaries
with ease.

Meanwhile, Joseph Ordornez, a native of Spain who enjoys the culture
of Italy, is regularly mistaken for Italian. When Ordornez was three, he
and his family left Spain for Latin America. They eventually settled in the
United States. Ordornez grew up in a heavily Italian neighborhood in
Manhattan and he developed a lifelong love of Italian culture there. He is
very familiar with dialectal Italian and numerous Italian customs and traditions. (The longtime New Yorker teaches standard Italian to members of
the Italian American Society of St. Petersburg in Florida.) Ordornez
speaks English with a slight European accent, so his fellow Americans
periodically ask him, "Where are you from?" or some variant of this question. When he answers "New York," they inquire further as to his country
of origin. "Ninety-nine percent of the time," says Ordornez, they think he
is Italian.[55]

The experiences of the Noto family of Tampa indicate how one can
blend the Sicilian and Hispanic customs and traditions in a culturally con-

genial fashion. Al Noto is an American-born Floridian of Sicilian descent. His late wife, Dalia (née Rodriguez), traced her ancestry to Cuba. On December 24, Al Noto, Dalia Noto, and their children observed the Cuban tradition of "Noche Buena" by consuming rice, pork, yucca, and black beans. And on Christmas Day, they ate Italian foods and celebrated Italian customs. On Easter, moreover, the Notos blended the Sicilian and Hispanic traditions in a syncretic celebration that drew upon their Catholic faith. In keeping with their inclusive approach to holidays, the Tampans celebrated Thanksgiving in the American fashion. Moreover, during the last three decades, Al Noto and his family have been instrumental in organizing the St. Joseph's Feast Day that occurs in Tampa each March. This annual event reflects their Sicilian heritage, of course.[56]

There are several parts of the United States where members of the Italian and Spanish communities interact on a regular basis, as in Albuquerque, New Mexico. In fact, the Italian and Spanish commonalities in culture, appearance, and language appear to promote good relations between Italian Americans and Spanish Americans. During the early years of the twentieth century, Italian immigrants contributed to the ethnic diversity of Albuquerque. "In 1920 and 1930," writes Nicholas P. Ciotola, "more Italians lived in the city than any other foreign-born group besides Mexican immigrants, a testament to their significance to Albuquerque's immigrant past."[57] Nearly a century ago the Champion Grocery and Meat Market in Albuquerque, a store that was owned and operated by Italians, had English and Spanish signage.[58]

Likewise, St. Bernard Parish, Louisiana, is a place where one finds regular interactions between Italian and Spanish Americans. The parish's venerable community of Isleños (Canary Islanders) dates back to approximately 1780. This group of Spanish Americans receives attention for its fidelity to the linguistic and cultural heritage of the original Canary Islanders who came to southeastern Louisiana during the eighteenth century.[59] Italian Americans, too, constitute an important part of St. Bernard Parish's population. Before Hurricane Katrina dispersed most of the parish's residents in 2005, St. Bernard Parish was 20 percent Italian. The parish's civic and political leadership includes Italian and Spanish Americans. And there is an Irish-Italian-Isleños Community Parade in St. Bernard Parish each year. Similar experiences of cultural blending occur in such places as Tampa, Florida, Pueblo, Colorado, and El Paso, Texas.

One observes numerous examples of amicable Italian-Hispanic relations in Texas over the last two centuries. Some nineteenth-century Italian immigrants to Texas adopted Spanish or Spanish-sounding names, as in José Cassiano (Giuseppe Cassini).[60] The legendary El Paso bootmaker Tony Lama was an Italian American, but his name could very easily pass for Spanish or Mexican.[61] Richard Apodaca reports that the Italians who went to the El Paso–Juárez area a century ago "essentially became Hispanic" as a result of their marriages to Mexican-origin women.[62] Beginning in 1881, the Jesuit Fathers came to West Texas, where they spent much of their time working with and ministering to the Spanish-speaking community. Not surprisingly, some of these Italian priests (e.g., Fathers Carlos Persone, Carlos Pinto, and Francisco Tomassini) were known by Spanish, not Italian, forenames.[63]

In El Paso today, the legacy of Father Carlos Pinto—"Padre Pinto" to many El Pasoans—remains alive. A native of the Province of Salerno in Italy, Pinto was born in 1841. The Jesuit priest came to the U.S. Southwest after he completed his studies and training in France, Spain, and Maryland. In 1872 Father Pinto went to Colorado, where he spent the next two decades principally serving Hispanic Catholics. Then, in the spring of 1892, Father Pinto departed from Colorado for El Paso. He remained in West Texas, for the most part, until his death in 1919.[64] While in El Paso, Pinto served as a parish priest, received a variety of diocesan assignments, and led the Jesuits in the region. Pinto founded numerous schools and churches during his years in West Texas, beginning with Sacred Heart School in El Paso, which opened in 1892 to educate Spanish-speaking children. Then Sacred Heart Catholic Church was completed in 1893; this parish has served mainly poor Mexicans and Mexican Americans in South El Paso for the last 116 years. In West Texas, Pinto worked with both English-speaking Anglos and Spanish-speaking Latinos.[65]

Father Pinto left an indelible imprint on the Catholic community of El Paso. Enrique Medrano, an attorney who is a respected historian of Catholic El Paso, documents and publicizes Father Pinto's important role in El Paso's history. Medrano provides quantitative evidence as to the indefatigable priest's legacy: six "churches planned and built by Father Pinto"; six "churches built by other priests under Father Pinto's supervision"; and seven "schools established under the supervision of Father Pinto."[66] Father Rafael Garcia, a Jesuit priest who serves as the pastor of El Paso's Sacred Heart Catholic Church, is a driving force behind the efforts to recognize Padre Pinto's contributions to El Paso. Beginning in

2000, a committee of Anglos, Hispanics, Italian Americans, and others worked with Father Garcia to raise the money for a plaza and statue to honor Padre Pinto. In 2004, Padre Pinto Plaza opened at Sacred Heart Church; the impressive plaza includes a bronze, life-size sculpture of the Italian-born Jesuit.[67]

❀   ❀   ❀

Italian Americans regularly take note of the history, culture, heritage, and accomplishments of Italians in Italy and Italians in the New World. It is common for them to cite the achievements of Leonardo da Vinci, Michelangelo, Giuseppe Verdi, A. P. Giannini, and many others. To this end, they highlight the myriad Italian and Italian-American contributions to Western civilization in such books as Federico and Stephen Moramarco's *Italian Pride: 101 Reasons to Be Proud You're Italian* (2000) and Peter D'Epiro and Mary Desmond Pinkowish's *Sprezzatura: 50 Ways Italian Genius Shaped the World* (2001).[68] Italian Americans will celebrate the remarkable successes of Italians in Italy and in the New World alike, as exemplified by Angelo Bianchi's eloquent tribute to his coethnics ("I Am An Italian-American").

Elderly Italian Americans take note of the popularity of Italy, Italian culture, Italian products, and Italian people in our country. They remember a time when many Americans did not have very favorable views of such people, places, and things. After all, ethnic-specific activities (bocce) and ethnic-specific foods (polenta) have become chic, trendy, and fashionable. Indeed, the Italian and Italian-American influence currently pervades American life in many ways. Now Italian coffee-related terms, brands, and types, including latte, espresso, and cappuccino, are part of American English and an integral part of the daily routines of many Americans. Italian designers, as in Gucci, Prada, Ferré, Zegna, Brioni, Canali, Armani, Versace, Missoni, Valentino, Ferragamo, Bottega Veneta, and Dolce & Gabbana, are popular with fashion-conscious Americans. And Italian manufacturers of sports cars—Ducati, Bugatti, Ferrari, Maserati, Lamborghini, Alfa Romeo, and others—enjoy enviable reputations among many Americans. These types of status symbols, coupled with the popularity of Italian art, food, music, and culture, have helped contribute to positive images of Italian Americans.

In recent years, it has become fashionable, glamorous, and prestigious to be of Italian descent in some American circles. This development can be attributed to the positive image of Italy in American eyes, the visibility of Italian Americans in so many aspects of American life, the ability to celebrate openly one's ancestral heritage, and other factors. Youths who are one-half or one-quarter Italian often stress that part of their identity. Toni Andriulli, an educator in Maine, reports that her fifteen-year-old driver's education students highlight their Italian ancestry, regardless of the percentage.[69] Nor is it uncommon to hear about "wannabes," individuals who seek to identify with the Italian heritage and culture, even if they do not have any Italian blood themselves.[70] Not all people of part-Italian origin focus on the Italian element of their heritage, of course.

In any event, more Americans than ever before have some Italian ancestry, even as fewer and fewer Americans overall are 100 percent Italian. It will be fascinating to observe how the individuals with fractional amounts of Italian ancestry identify with their heritage and how their identification patterns affect the viability of different aspects of Italian-American culture. The Triangle Italian-American Heritage Association in Raleigh, North Carolina, takes into account the variegated nature of Italian ethnicity in America: Its scholarship recipients need only to be one-eighth Italian.[71] Indeed, Americans of Italian origin sometimes identify with Italy even as they have a diverse set of ancestral markers.

Italian Americans are now so well integrated into the broader American society that their ethnic identifiers and periodic expressions of ethnic pride no longer elicit much, if any, negative attention from other Americans. Few people today would question the loyalty of Italian Americans to their nation; hence there are none of the concerns about divided allegiances that existed decades ago. One sign that Italian Americans are a vital part of American mainstream culture is that the term "ethnic," as in white ethnic, is used infrequently these days, at least in a contemporary sense. Now that members of white ethnic groups have become part of the American Establishment, the term "ethnic" is used more commonly as a polite euphemism for people of color than it is for Americans of Southern and Eastern European origin.

On occasion members of some American ethnic groups, particularly Arabs and Middle Easterners, will claim to be Italian in order to win acceptance from others. It is not uncommon for Arab Americans or Armenian Americans and even the occasional Mexican American or Puerto Rican to say that they are of Italian descent. Due to the tremendous visual diversity of the Italian people, individuals from a wide variety of Mediterranean, Middle Eastern, and even South Asian backgrounds can plausibly pass as "Italian." The Iranian-American comic Maz Jobrani jokes about how he and his compatriots characterize themselves as Italians in the post-9/11 era.[72] There is an elderly Algerian American from Hoboken, New Jersey, who even changed his name because he wanted to sound Italian.[73] The aforementioned developments make it clear that Italians, who once were not accepted by everyone, now enjoy mainstream status throughout our nation.

As the numbers of immigrants and foreign-born people increase in America, many Italian Americans want to see members of these groups assimilate in the same way that they and their ancestors did in the past. To this end, they express their opinions that the newcomers should learn English, embrace American customs, and otherwise integrate into American society. Certain aspects of multiculturalism (bilingual signage and bilingual education, among them) are controversial in Italian America. In my talks in various venues around the nation, Italian Americans and others have described to me their belief that the recent immigrants are not playing by the same rules as did their ancestors. At the same time, other Italian Americans espouse tolerance toward immigrants, support diversity initiatives, and celebrate America's increasing ethnic, racial, religious, and cultural heterogeneity.

Daniel Cotroneo, for one, articulates an inclusive perspective that underlies his efforts to promote diversity in the Saint Paul Fire Department in Minnesota. The Saint Paul fire captain advocates on behalf of the efforts to recruit Hmong firefighters there. Cotroneo does so because he knows firsthand the benefits that Hmong police officers bring to public-safety efforts, when it comes to community outreach, pragmatic problem-solving, and increasing trust between Saint Paul's large Hmong population and its city departments. Consequently, he wants to see that Hmong applicants have equal opportunities to become members of the Saint Paul Fire Department. Cotroneo discusses how standardized tests may ask some questions that disadvantage Hmong applicants without reflecting on their qualifications to be firefighters.[74] In sum, his outlook on racial issues is nuanced, insightful, and takes into account the complex dynamics of multiethnic Minnesota.

Chapter 5

MARRIAGE AND FAMILY LIFE

D uring the early twentieth century, Enrico (Henry) DeRenzo left his native Abruzzi for the United States.[1] He went to America to earn money and then sent for his wife, Esterina (Esther) Giampaolo DeRenzo, to join him with their young son, Tony, who was born after his father had left Abruzzi. When his young family joined him in Pennsylvania, Henry DeRenzo had never seen his son before. The DeRenzos went to live with Italian friends in Reading, Pennsylvania, for approximately one year; thereafter they resided in Birdsboro, a small town in eastern Pennsylvania.[2] Henry and Esther DeRenzo had three sons, Tony, Dominic, and Pompeo, and one daughter, Theresa (Terry), who was born in 1933. They lived in a predominantly Italian neighborhood in Birdsboro. The DeRenzo family had one acre of land with ducks, chickens, and ample amounts of vegetables. They always had plenty of fresh food, including plums and peaches from their trees and applesauce from their apples.

Terry DeRenzo Noll remembers her youth as "a continuous, hardworking young life." Until she was sixteen, the youngest DeRenzo child pulled a plow to till the family's acre of land. She grew up in a home with no books, telephone, newspapers, or magazines. (Henry and Esther DeRenzo could not read or write.) Their daughter entered Birdsboro's public schools knowing no English, speaking only the Italian dialect of her immigrant parents. At the time, Italians were "less than important" in Birdsboro, remembers Noll. Certain children snickered when she initially did not know English at school. Today she recalls some prejudiced teachers as well as some educators who "embraced" her. As a result of her good work ethic and a voracious desire to learn, Theresa DeRenzo graduated fifth in her class at Birdsboro High School. Her home-economics teacher wanted young Theresa to go to design school in New York City. Noll's parents vetoed this possibility, however, as they did not want their seventeen-year-old daughter to be so far away from home. So she became a seamstress like her mother, Esther, and later an interior decorator.

Theresa DeRenzo met her future husband, Bill Noll, in 1955. At the time, she worked in a blouse factory. The attractive young woman, who had once placed second in the Miss Birdsboro Contest, served as secretary of the factory's union. One evening in 1955 she represented the union at a dance and met a handsome trumpet player named Bill Noll from Reading. His father, Wilson Noll, was a trumpet player, too, and the owner of a Reading bicycle shop. Interestingly, Bill Noll was not even supposed to attend the dance that night. The musicians called him at the last minute to substitute for someone else. In any event, Bill Noll and Theresa DeRenzo connected with each other immediately. One week later Bill Noll came to the DeRenzo home to meet Henry and Esther DeRenzo. Although Theresa DeRenzo had already agreed to go on a date with him, she warned the young Pennsylvania Dutchman to ask her father if he could take her out (in accordance with Italian tradition). He did so, and Henry DeRenzo assented to the polite young man's request.

The DeRenzos were tolerant and inclusive individuals, who wanted their children to choose their spouses based on compatibility, not ethnicity or nationality. In fact, the elder DeRenzos warmly accepted each new member of their family. To this end, Terry Noll reviews her older brothers' marital choices. Her oldest brother, Tony DeRenzo, married Ida, an Italian national. Another brother, Dominic DeRenzo, wed a Swedish-American woman named Ruthann. And her other brother, Pompeo DeRenzo, married Hildie, the daughter of German immigrants. She herself wed Bill Noll, who was a Catholic of Pennsylvania Dutch descent. "We got married at the Immaculate Conception Church in Birdsboro," remembers Terry Noll. The newlyweds made their home in the Lehigh Valley—specifically, the town of Easton, Pennsylvania—after their nuptials on June 27, 1959. The Nolls had three children: William David, Marlene Theresa, and Tiffany Irene.

Bill Noll's mother, Irene Noll, taught her daughter-in-law, Theresa Noll, how to cook Pennsylvania Dutch dishes. Meal time in the Noll household in Easton included such dishes as lima beans with smoked sausage, pork and sauerkraut, string beans and ham, and, chief among them, chicken pot pie or Chicken Bott Boi in Pennsylvania Dutch. "One time the pork and sauerkraut [dish] was so good, Bill said it was the best he had ever had," reminisces Terry Noll. "What a compliment to an Italian!" "Of course, chicken pot pie was the favorite in Bill's eyes," continues Mrs. Noll. "I would make enough to reheat for several times. Each time it got better." After years of cooking Pennsylvania Dutch food, Terry Noll reached a point where she prepared certain dishes better (in her husband's eyes) than his own mother. Marlene Noll, in turn, learned how to prepare chicken pot pie from her mother; the Pennsylvania Dutch dish wins praise from her husband's Italian-American family in Michigan.[3]

Bill Noll, to be sure, embraced Italian-American culture. "He had a deep respect for the Italians and what they had accomplished," says his loving wife. Her husband enjoyed playing bocce, eating homemade spaghetti, and fraternizing with the family's many Italian-American friends and business associates. Bill Noll worked in radio advertising, and he eventually became general manager of WEST, a radio station in Easton, Pennsylvania. When Mr. Noll met with a prospective Italian-American client, he would tell the individual that he was "part Italian." The nonplused businessperson might then ask him how he could be Italian with the name of Noll. Bill Noll usually responded by mentioning that his wife was Italian.

Since Bill Noll's passing in 2006, his wife continues to preserve her husband's memory after the five wonderful decades that they spent together. Indeed, Terry Noll and her late husband, Bill Noll, had a modern American love story. "My parents really loved him," remembers Mrs. Noll. She describes her late husband as "a kind, soft-spoken gentleman" who would sit and talk to his mother-in-law and father-in-law for lengthy periods of time. They enjoyed his company and always spoke highly of him. Bill and Terry Noll, along with so many others in their generation, created a warm, inclusive family environment that melded two different ethnic cultures and backgrounds. Their heartwarming story reflects the importance of marriage and family life in Italian-American culture.

I. During their childhood years in the 1940s and 1950s, Theresa Paterno and her younger sisters, Rosaria Salerno and JoAnn Serpico, grew up at 719 DeKoven Street in Chicago. They were raised on DeKoven Street, near the intersection of Taylor Street and Halsted Street, in what Rosaria Salerno characterizes as an "all-Italian neighborhood." The Salerno youngsters spent much of their time at the Salerno family home at 724 DeKoven Street in Chicago; they referred to this dwelling, which was across the street from their residence, as "The Big House." (It had been the home of their late grandparents, Rosario D. Salerno and Theresa Viapiana, both of whom died before Rosaria Salerno and JoAnn Serpico were born.) Theresa Paterno, Rosaria Salerno, and JoAnn Serpico were always at "The Big House," where they enjoyed the Italian meals, familial camaraderie, and loving atmosphere. Both of their parents, Joseph R. Salerno and Ella Cataldo, were born in the United States in families whose roots were in the Province of Cosenza (Calabria) and the Province of Avellino (Campania), respectively.[4]

The Salerno family was—and is—known in Chicagoland for its funeral-home business and extensive community involvement.[5] Rosario D. Salerno and Theresa Viapiana had eight children, all of whom were raised on DeKoven Street in a residence above the family's funeral home. Their only daughter, Marie, was a physician, and their youngest son, Philip, became an attorney. Six of Rosario D. Salerno's seven sons—Anthony, Frank, George, Joseph, Ralph, and Rosario—worked with him in the funeral-home business.[6] "My grandfather started the business and then took my father (who was the second oldest child) into the business," remembers Rosaria Salerno. "They were the original co-owners. It was my father's license that established the funeral home and it was my dad who took his brothers into it as they became of age."[7] The Salerno family was a large one, with eight children and numerous grandchildren. Consequently, Theresa Paterno, Rosaria Salerno, and JoAnn Serpico have many cousins.

Joseph R. Salerno and Ella Cataldo gave their three children a thoroughly Italian upbringing. Every major aspect of life (e.g., food, religion, holidays, and cultural traditions) for the Salernos involved the Italian culture and heritage. On DeKoven Street, the Italian Americans sat on chairs in front of their homes and chatted with each other on summer evenings. All the Salerno descendants gathered for Sunday dinner at "The Big House" at 724 DeKoven Street. Rosaria Salerno remembers playing with her cousins; she saw them as if they were her brothers and sisters. As a rule, the major holidays were important for the Salernos. Everyone came together at Christmas and on New Year's Eve.[8] Many years later, Theresa Paterno, Rosaria Salerno, JoAnn Serpico, and their relatives continue to maintain the close family ties that are a hallmark of Italian-American culture.

The Italian immigrants and their descendants typically have had strong, cohesive families. Of course, there were cultural conflicts for Italian families when they first came to America, as their cultural values and familial mores differed from those in the United States.[9] Elizabeth G. Messina writes: "Antithetical to the values of the mainstream American family cultural values, where independence, individual achievement, and privacy of the nuclear family are valued, the dynamics of the Italian American family have been characterized by a pattern of family relations in which family loyalty, affiliation, and cooperation are valued over pursuit of individual rights and feelings, confrontation, and competition."[10] In those days, the father/husband was the sole or principal breadwinner and generally seen as the head of the Italian-American family, while the wife/mother occupied an important (but less visible) role in family affairs. The Italian immigrants and their descendants eventually adopted many, if not most, of the behaviors, aspirations, and value systems of the United States.[11]

Whenever I ask Americans of Italian origin about the Italian and/or Italian-American traditions that they have followed over the years, family comes up as a consistent response. Indeed, Italian food and close family ties are staples of contemporary Italian-American culture. The dinner table was (and is) an important place in Italian-American culture. Therefore, the Sunday dinners after church and gatherings of family members that were once quite common in Italian America blended the two traditions well. Throughout the United States, holidays and family milestones brought Italian-American relatives together on a regular basis. Rosalie Galasso Caputo remembers growing up in a large Italian family in suburban Los Angeles during the 1950s and 1960s. Caputo's childhood was filled with birthdays, marriages, and First Communions. "Everything revolved around family," notes Caputo in a refrain that echoes throughout Italian America.[12]

Many Italian Americans also have rich memories of the time they spent with their grandparents (who were often Italian-born). As a youth in Connecticut, Carlo Giraulo frequently came into contact with his Italian-immigrant grandparents. They helped to shape his world view and personal development. Giraulo's grandparents spoke English with strong Italian accents. The Maine resident remembers vividly one day when he was approximately twelve years old and a neighborhood boy had his grandmother visit him. It surprised Giraulo to learn that the older woman spoke English without a foreign accent. Giraulo's family and cultural

environment were predominantly Italian; consequently, he had little contact with native-born American seniors.[13] Many middle-aged Americans
of Italian origin have had similar experiences, particularly those individuals who grew up in homes where their grandparents lived with them.

Italian Americans, of course, value their memories of being with their
grandparents. Shirley Sinclaire, who is of Italian and Norwegian descent,
reports that she identifies with her Italian side because she spent many
hours as a child with her Italian-immigrant grandparents. They passed
numerous Italian values, customs, and traditions on to her. Today the
Minnesotan researches her Italian genealogy and is active in UNICO: The
Italian American Club of the Twin Cities. Now Sinclaire transmits the
Italian customs (including the treasured family recipe for sauce) to her
adult children.[14] Similarly, Lisa Del Torto, a twentysomething doctoral
student at the University of Michigan, spent much time with her Italian-
born grandparents as a child. Del Torto's grandparents were her daytime
caregivers during her first five years of life. Therefore, the Connecticut
native learned to speak and understand dialectal Italian from her *nonni* as
a youth in the 1980s.[15]

During the twentieth century, endogamy helped to keep the Italian-
American culture alive. The Italian immigrants frequently settled in
American towns, communities, and neighborhoods where many of the
Italians came from the same part of Italy. Their children and even grandchildren often chose Italian partners, especially in close-knit ethnic communities. Frank Agostini is a third-generation American of Italian
descent. The native of South Philadelphia is 100 percent Neapolitan.[16] At
the same time there was a "melting pot" within Italian America, as people
whose ancestors came from different regions of Italy met and married
each other in the United States. More than a few native-born Italian
Americans are 100 percent Italian but they trace their ancestry to two or
more parts of Italy, e.g., the middle-aged woman who told me that her
ancestors came from Naples, Calabria, and Sicily.

One regularly hears stories that focus on the phenomenon of intra-Italian intermarriage in the United States, whereby people with different Italian regional backgrounds (say, an Emilia-Roman and an Abruzzese)
formed unions. The Italian immigrants brought their Old World mores
with them to the New World, and they sometimes described the unions
of Northern and southern Italians as "mixed marriages." Yet today one
finds such ethnic combinations as Tuscan/Sicilian, Venetian/Sicilian, and

Sicilian/Lombardian in Italian America. Italian Americans from different Italian regional backgrounds still joke and reminiscence about "mixed marriages." One middle-aged man of Sicilian and Calabrian descent remembers that his parents noted their regional origins during their arguments, as they invoked the stereotypical characteristics of people from their spouse's region while they criticized each other. These differences have largely faded into history for the younger, American-born Italians.

Older Americans of Italian descent remember when people from other ethnic groups might have been discouraged from dating and marrying them. There are numerous examples of Italians who encountered subtle or overt ethnic prejudice in the marriage market. An older man of German and Sicilian origin told me about how his non-Italian wife's grandparents never spoke to him again once they learned about his ethnic background. Due to his light complexion, they initially did not know he was Italian. At the wedding, however, they discovered his Italian background because of all his Italian relatives who attended the celebration. The German-Sicilian bridegroom never offended his grandparents-in-law, to his knowledge; these folks just did not like Italians.

There are numerous types of such examples in Italian America. I heard of a long-ago instance where a non-Italian described a family member as marrying "a black," meaning an Italian. Another fellow referred to his half-Italian grandchildren as "white n———rs" and wanted little to do with them. And a middle-aged Ohioan of Northern European ancestry related to me how when he went to Ohio State University in Columbus, he encountered Italian-American women for the first time. But his mother did not want him marrying one of them. His younger brother, however, later married an Italian American and she was accepted into the family.

Similarly, the Italian immigrants and their family members strongly encouraged the Italian-American youngsters to marry someone from their ethnic background. Many Italian parents expected their children to find a spouse within their insular ethnic community. And many Americans of Italian origin did so, particularly in the older generations. The partners in such marriages often value the fact that they share a similar Italian background in terms of foods, holidays, cultural issues, and religious matters. They enjoy their commonalities and feelings of cultural affinity.

Other Italians have had no interest in marrying someone from their ethnic group. One man of Italian extraction told me that he did not date Italian-American women because doing so was akin to dating his sister.

Likewise, an Italian-American woman said she would not date Italian men because they were too "controlling," in her opinion. A man of Italian descent described how he was the first in his family to marry outside his ethnic group. When he brought his girlfriend home to meet everyone in the early 1970s, his grandmother broke the ice by slapping the young lady on the posterior and welcoming her into the family. Thereafter, many other family members followed suit and married non-Italians as well.

As a result of their increasing affluence and a century of assimilation, Italian-American families have become similar to other American families in many respects. Now there is a significant amount of ethnic intermarriage in Italian America. Contemporary Italian Americans do not have markedly larger families than their counterparts from other ethnic groups. Divorce, though, seems to be considerably less common among Italian Americans than in the general U.S. population. Even today, Americans of Italian origin typically come into contact with their family members on a regular basis.[17] Meanwhile, gender-role traditionalism is subsiding among younger generations of Italian Americans.[18] Overall, the diverse family types in Italian America correlate to such factors as one's lifestyle choices, geographical location, socioeconomic status, amount of personal mobility, and degree of assimilation into American mainstream culture.[19]

II. Agnes Nese spent much time with her grandson, Dan Basalone, during the 1940s, 1950s, and 1960s.[20] Nese arrived in Los Angeles at the age of twenty-one in 1906; she left her hometown of Villa Latoria, near Naples, for California. As a child and young man, Dan Basalone valued the numerous opportunities he had to learn about his grandmother's life in Italy. Basalone was born in California in 1939, the grandson of immigrants from Campania (his mother's side) and Lazio (his father's side). His Italian-immigrant grandmother grew up on a farm in rural Campania. "She herded goats for her father," remembers Basalone. Agnes Nese once told a story to him about how she fought off a wolf that wanted to attack the goats.

In the best Italian tradition, Nese also came to know and love her grandson's wife, Carmen Basalone. Dan Basalone and Carmen Tetreault were married in 1960. Carmen Basalone's family moved from Quebec to Vermont when she was six. The Tetreaults later lived in Massachusetts. Carmen Basalone, a French-speaking naturalized American, "was immersed in Italian culture" in California after she married Dan Basalone. In the 1960s she learned Italian cooking, including such dishes as ravioli and "Easter bread," from her husband's grandmother Agnes and his aunt Josephine. Nese passed away in 1965. Then, from 1965 to 1990, Dan Basalone's Aunt Josephine was the matriarch of his father's family and a friend to her nephew's wife.

Carmen Basalone, to be sure, is thoroughly familiar with and apprecia-tive of Italian cultural traditions. Mrs. Basalone cooks "Easter bread" each year on the occasion of Easter. Moreover, she notes that the Basalones make their own sausage "around Easter and Christmas" and at other times "if we get hungry for it." Dan Basalone enjoys his wife's Italian cooking very much. "You can be from another culture," says the Californian, and "you can learn the Italian culture if you want to do so." The Basalones are close to their five children and ten grandchildren, all of whom value their Italian heritage and seek to keep their Italian-American culture alive. They do so through religion (they are Catholics), what they describe as "basic holiday activities," and other means.

At the same time, Dan Basalone notes the role that Italian organiza-tions play in helping to sustain the heritage and traditions of Italians in America. He is a longtime member and officer of the American Educators of Italian Origin United (AEIOU), an organization of Italian-American edu-cators in Greater Los Angeles. "Organizations allow you to do what many years ago your family did for you," says Basalone. The union administrator and former elementary school principal speaks highly of the friendships that AEIOU members enjoy with each other. And he celebrates the organi-zation's efforts to promote Italian culture, as in the scholarships they award to opera singers and high-achieving secondary school students. In his reflections on the importance of the AEIOU and similar groups, Basalone posits that "these associations allow you to keep your culture alive."

The high rates of Italian-American intermarriage in recent years offer compelling evidence that people of Italian descent are well-accepted members of American mainstream culture. Michael Barone discusses the intergenerational patterns of intermarriage and assimilation among Italian Americans:

> In the process, Italians have become much more likely to marry non-Italians. As late as the early 1960s, about 60 percent of Italian-Americans chose spouses

of unmixed Italian ancestry. By 1979 a majority were marrying non-Italians, and less than 20 percent of Italian-American children under age five were of entirely Italian ancestry. Of Italian-Americans born since 1950, more than two-thirds of those of entirely Italian-American parentage and four-fifths of those with partial Italian parentage married non-Italian Americans.[21]

The ethnic mixtures in Italian-American intermarriages often depend on the demographics of the communities in which people of Italian origin live; therefore, one finds many individuals of Irish-Italian descent in and around Boston, for example.

Italian Americans are a demographically complex group, in that some people of Italian origin are fully Italian while others come from ethnically mixed backgrounds. There continue to be some native-born American youths who are 100 percent Italian. Ethnic endogamy seems to occur most often for Italian immigrants and their children, individuals who reside in ethnic enclaves, and those Italian Americans who are deeply involved in Italian cultural activities. An Italian surname, of course, offers no guarantee that someone is fully Italian. Madonna is only part Italian, as are Susan Lucci, Liza Minnelli, Sofia Coppola, and Sylvester Stallone. Leonardo DiCaprio is reportedly one-quarter Italian. Likewise, Louis Freeh, Jimmy Kimmel, Susan Sarandon, Brooke Shields, Bruce Springsteen, and Steven Tyler all have Italian ancestry, even though their surnames do not make this clear.[22]

Richard D. Alba examines the effects of intermarriage on Italian-American culture. Writing in 2000, Alba observed:

> As a result of rising intermarriage, a massive shift is occurring in the composition of the Italian group, as is true also for some other white ethnic groups. In the recent past, most of the adults in these groups were individuals who, by virtue of their undivided ethnic heritage and their families' recency of immigration, had grown up in quite ethnic family and community environments. In the near future, this will no longer be true. Today, the majority of young people entering adulthood come from ethnically mixed families, belong to the third if not the fourth generation, and were raised outside of ethnic communities. Among Italians, more than three-quarters of those born during the late 1960s and the early 1970s, who are entering their early adult years during the last decade of the twentieth century, come from mixed ethnic backgrounds. By contrast, only about a quarter of Italian Americans born before World War II have mixed ethnic ancestry. This contrast implies a profound shift of cardinal impor-

tance for ethnicity. On average, persons with mixed ancestry are much less exposed in their upbringing to ethnic traits, from language to values, than are persons of undivided ethnic heritage.[23]

The extent to which ethnically mixed Americans of Italian origin identify as Italian Americans depends on a number of factors. Firstly, the matter of surnames assumes significance, as a person with an Italian surname may be more identifiable as an Italian. Secondly, there is the whole matter of appearance: in other words, whether a person looks "Italian." Thirdly, one's family heritage—what family members stress at home—can determine his identification patterns. Fourth, there are an individual's personal activities and preferences. Siblings in the same family may differ as to how "Italian" they act and feel. Fifth, there is the makeup of the community in which a person lives; one's Italian ancestry might be emphasized in a place with few Italians—or just be a matter of fact in a heavily Italian community. There are other factors as well, such as whether an individual's Italian heritage constitutes the single largest part of her ethnic background and whether her other ancestral identifiers have much salience in Multicultural America.[24]

When it comes to intermarriage, the Irish/Italian combination is particularly common today. In the 1930s, 1940s, and 1950s, Irish and Italian family members alike were often skeptical about Irish/Italian unions. A man of Irish descent told me that his mother was quite surprised when she learned (in the 1950s) that he was going to marry an Italian American. "You're marrying one of *them*?" she asked her son with incredulity. There was stereotypical thinking on the Italian side, too. "My wife's family asked her if I was a drinker," reports this genial and open-minded individual. He has been happily married to his Italian-American wife for five decades. They participate together in Italian activities.

To be sure, Irish Americans and Italian Americans have formed unions without any acrimony, particularly in recent years. An elderly woman in Youngstown, Ohio, the daughter of Irish immigrants, told me that she and her husband, the son of Italian immigrants, married in 1941. There were no ethnic issues or problems that ever separated their respective families. Likewise, I heard a story from an Irish American in Erie, Pennsylvania, about her Italian-American husband and their Irish/Italian children. She is a former president of the Italian-American Women's Association in Erie. During the late 1990s her children had sweatshirts made that read: "Half Italian, Half Irish, and All Perfect."[25] These shirts reflect their ethnic heritage and the significant family ties that bring together Irish Americans and Italian Americans.

It is not uncommon for Italian-American men to say that their non-Italian wives "are more Italian than they are," an indication of how thoroughly these spouses have embraced Italian-American culture. During the twentieth century, many non-Italian women who married Italian men became very "Italian," in that they picked up the customs and traditions (particularly in terms of food) of their Italian in-laws. Thomas Ragona, who is completely Italian, was happily married to his Slovak-American wife, Ann, for sixty-three years until her passing in 2006.[26] The Ragonas raised their Italian-Slovak son, Ronald Thomas Ragona, as an Italian American. That was their "family orientation," says Thomas Ragona. Ann Ragona celebrated her husband's Italian heritage and became a proficient Italian cook. In a 2005 interview, Thomas Ragona reported that "my wife is more Italian than I am."[27]

Likewise, there are Italian Americans whose family lives incorporate the customs and traditions of their non-Italian spouses. Bill and Bob Battista are the fiftysomething sons of Joe and Anita Battista, immigrants from Abruzzi; both brothers married women of Polish descent.[28] They grew up in King of Prussia, Pennsylvania, and now live in Madison, Wisconsin. Bill Battista left Pennsylvania to attend graduate school at the University of Wisconsin–Madison in August 1971. He has lived in Madison ever since. His younger brother, Bob, followed him to Wisconsin's capital city to attend college.

Bill Battista's wife, Alice (her maiden name was Nasielski), comes from a Polish-Croatian family. A native of King of Prussia's King Manor section, Alice Battista and her family attended a Slovak parish, Our Mother of Sorrows Catholic Church, in Bridgeport, Pennsylvania, where she went to parochial grade school. She and her husband graduated from the same public high school, Upper Merion Area High School, in King of Prussia. Their wedding shower was held in 1971 in a church hall at Our Mother of Sorrows Church.[29] The 125 people in attendance gave such gifts to them as a cavatelli maker, a ravioli maker, a spaghetti maker, and a pizzelle maker.

Today Bill and Alice Battista and their three daughters, Amy, Lori, and Beth, meld the Italian and Polish traditions seamlessly in their lives. "Most of the traditions we have carried on as a family come from Alice's Polish side," reports Bill Battista. Alice Battista participated in the Polish Heritage Club in Madison, Wisconsin, when her daughters were youngsters, as she wanted to expose them to Polish traditions. The family celebrates the holiday tradition of St. Nicholas each year. Stuffed cabbage rolls are a culinary vestige of Alice Battista's heritage that she brings to her household (mainly for Alice and her sister to eat, according to Bill). To be sure, Italian dishes are more common than Polish dishes in the Battista family's culinary repertoire: They regularly enjoy pasta, pizza, and other Italian foods. Jordan almonds, too, were an Italian aspect of their daughters' weddings. And on occasion there is good-natured ethnic bantering in the Battista family about which ethnic food is better.

Their Polish heritage is an important part of life for the Battistas. To this end, the Battista family members observe the annual tradition of communion wafers (*oplatky*) every December, whereby they put a communion wafer on everyone's plate at the dinner table on Christmas Eve. Then they say grace and break off a piece of the wafer for the person next to them at the table. While doing so, the tradition holds that they wish their seatmate peace. This Polish/Slovak custom dictates that the Battistas should leave an empty plate with a wafer for the departed members of their family. Consequently, they put out wafers for Alice Battista's father, the late Detective Sergeant Walt Nasielski, as well as for her mother, Mary, and Bill's parents, Joe and Anita.

Alice Battista, moreover, participates in the blessing of the food on the Saturday before Easter at Our Lady Queen of Peace Catholic Church in Madison. (One puts the food in a basket and the priest blesses it for him or her.) "This is a strong Polish tradition," says Mrs. Battista, who teaches third grade at Our Lady Queen of Peace School in Madison. Alice Battista brought this "old family tradition" with her from Pennsylvania to Wisconsin. It was she who initially suggested that the Easter-time blessing of the food should take place at Our Lady Queen of Peace Church. Now she reports that the custom "keeps getting bigger and bigger each year."

The Battista and Nasielski clans maintain close ties to each other. Alice Battista's sister, Nora, lives in Madison with her husband Tom, who went to high school with Bill and Alice. Bob Battista's wife, Cindy (née Gutkowski), is a Polish American from Milwaukee, Wisconsin. Bob Battista met his future wife because Alice Battista introduced her to him. Bob and Cindy Battista had a Polish-style wedding and reception in Milwaukee, one with the requisite polka band that is found at such events in Wisconsin. There were 250 guests at their wedding reception. Now Bob and Cindy Battista have two sons. As is the case in so many American families,

Bob Battista says there is nothing really "ethnic" about his household. His sons are aware of their Italian/Polish heritage, to be sure. But they are quintessentially American and, therefore, illustrate how people of Italian and Polish descent are thoroughly part of the American mainstream.

III. On Christmas Eve during the 1960s and 1970s, everyone in Jill Rose's immediate family went to her Aunt Maryann and Uncle Paulie's house on Staten Island.[30] Aunt Maryann cooked for weeks in preparation for this veritable feast, which was Jill Rose's "favorite day of the entire year." There was a rich cornucopia of Italian foods on the dinner table, along with lobster, scungilli, calamari, and other fish. "At Thanksgiving," writes Rose, "after eating the same types of Italian foods, turkey was served to show American tradition." Rose fondly remembers the "hours and hours of eating and talking and laughing" on Christmas Eve with Aunt Maryann and Uncle Paulie.

Every year during the holiday season, Jill Rose always reflects on her family's wonderful Christmas experiences in the 1960s and 1970s. Indeed, her mother, Winnie Conti, observed numerous holiday traditions that her children and other relatives enjoyed very much. "We have always baked a lot of cookies from scratch during the holidays . . . for the weeks ahead and we would give them out to neighbors and friends," notes Rose. "We also make from scratch a gingerbread house each year." Christmas Day in New Jersey was always Winnie Conti's bailiwick, where there were delightful festivities that included "lots of decorations" and "lots of presents." Then, the day after Christmas, the Conti family went to New York for an enjoyable meal of ham or roast beef, mashed potatoes, and peas with their Irish relatives.

Jill Rose comes from an Irish/Scottish and Italian family in New York and New Jersey. Her mother, Winnie Conti, is of Irish and Scottish descent. Her father, Frank Anthony Conti, is an Italian American. Jill Mary Conti grew up with her three siblings in New York and New Jersey. Her mother's Irish/Scottish family is "typically American," according to Rose. The Contis follow Italian customs and traditions; they enjoy ethnic foods and festivities. During the 1960s and 1970s Rose spent much time with both sides of her family. She remembers her Italian grandmother's home in Brooklyn as a place where the family matriarch, Phyllis Conti (Nanny to her grandchildren), and her aunt prepared wonderful smorgasbords of food and drink for their family members. Nanny Conti would always have a big pot of sauce—"gravy" to the Contis—in the house. There were eggplant, meatballs, pork products, and so many other delicious foods on her table. Phyllis Conti presented each course to everyone with "love and concern." She wanted her guests to eat and enjoy the food and to have smiles on their faces while they did so.

A warm, nuturing person, Jill Rose grew up in the Northeast and has lived in different parts of the country since then. Mrs. Rose, who was born in 1961 in New York, met her German-Scandinavian husband, Doug Rose, when she worked in hotel management in Minnesota. The Michigan State University graduate remembers that her Italian grandmother approved of Doug Rose immediately: Phyllis Conti lavished affection (and cannoli) upon him. Doug and Jill Rose now have two teenage sons, who have grown up in New Jersey, Minnesota, and South Carolina. Jill Rose continues to honor the customs and traditions of her loving family. As her busy schedule permits, she relishes the opportunity to make a big pot of homemade red sauce. The annual holiday tradition of making a gingerbread house continues, too, with Jill Rose and her family.

Rose also shares the Italian-American culture with her fellow South Carolinians. (The Roses have lived in the Palmetto State since 1997.) For Christmas, Rose is known to bake Neapolitan cookies and give bags of these treats as gifts to her co-workers. And she prepares eggplant parmigian for everyone in her office. Rose is rightfully proud of her time-consuming culinary handiwork, which wins praise from her Southern friends and co-workers. In 2006 she purchased a box of cannoli and took the pastries to a client in Columbia, South Carolina. In doing so, Rose introduced him to cannoli. It is no wonder that people call her "Mama Rose."

Doug and Jill Rose and their boys maintain close ties to their Italian-American family members. Recently the Roses took a trip to New York, where they stayed with Aunt Maryann and Uncle Paulie on Staten Island. During their visit, Uncle Paulie frequently purchased items (bagels, Italian ices, and Sicilian pizzas) for his grandnephews to enjoy. Their "generosity is unbelievable," says Jill Rose of her aunt and uncle. As an adult, Mrs. Rose marvels at the cost, time, and commitment required to prepare and host a feast like Aunt Maryann's Christmas Eve party. The transplanted South Carolinian, meanwhile, seeks to transmit the Italian customs and traditions to her two teenage boys.[31] At family gatherings, the

Contis typically play cards for pennies ("penny poker," in the family's parlance). Through this activity, they emulate the example of Phyllis Conti, who was an inveterate "penny poker" player. The members of the Conti clan live in different parts of the country now; yet they maintain their love, their common values, and their commitment to each other.

Family ties continue to be quite important for many Italian Americans, even as individualism, middle-class lifestyles, assimilation and integration, the disappearance of certain Italian enclaves, and the dispersal of Italians throughout the United States have made it more difficult to sustain the close Italian families of yesteryear.[32] Richard N. Juliani writes: "With the great attenuation of communal institutions that once organized their lives, family life may be more significant now than at any previous period for their personal identity and group cohesion as Italian Americans."[33] In any event, the heartwarming family memories from the past come up repeatedly in contemporary Italian-American oral histories. "We were poor. We were happy. We were family," remembers Michael Pastore of his childhood and young adult years in Portland, Maine, during the 1930s and 1940s.[34] Some younger Americans of Italian descent want to recapture these experiences: I know of at least one example of a younger Italian American who has revived the custom of the Sunday pasta dinners.

Italian family members, to be sure, often enjoy and sustain strong, healthy, and enduring relationships with each other. An elderly man in Providence, Rhode Island, related to me how he had taken care of his sister for ten years when she had Alzheimer's disease. When a physician remarked to him that he had made "a sacrifice" by doing so, this gentleman responded indignantly that it had been "a privilege" for him to be her caregiver. He loved his sister very much—and he cherished the chance to help her when she could no longer help herself. Likewise, Marianne Dalfonso Reali notes that her daughter, Julie Reali-Kopenga, named her daughter, Charlee Marie Kopenga. Little Charlee Kopenga was born in July 2006; she is named for her great-grandfather, Charles Dalfonso, who passed away in April 2005. Julie Reali-Kopenga had a significant bond with her grandfather. "She was extremely close to my father and wanted to honor him by naming her baby girl after him," says Marianne Dalfonso Reali.[35]

Turning now to Wyoming, two Italian-American women from two different generations offer us an inspiring model of how relatives care for each other. Flora Bertagnolli is close to her nephew, Buddy Kaumo, and his wife, Mary Joe Kaumo. Indeed, Flora Bertagnolli views Mary Joe Kaumo as her niece. Mrs. Kaumo stayed with her Aunt Flora while her husband, Buddy Kaumo, served in Vietnam. The Rock Springs, Wyoming, residents see each other on a regular basis; they can count on each other under any circumstances. As a token of her affection for her niece, Flora Bertagnolli once purchased a shirt with the slogan "Italian Pasta" and "Irish Potatoes" on it, a reference to Mary Joe Kaumo's Irish ancestry (she is one-half Italian and one-quarter Welsh, too).[36] The Bertagnollis, the Kaumos, and the other Italian-American families of Rock Springs continue to maintain a sense of community, one that encompasses a growing number of people from different ethnic backgrounds due to widespread intermarriage.

Similarly, the Silvestri family of northern California highlights the enduring nature of Italian-American family ties. Giorgio and Ida Silvestri were Tuscan immigrants who came to the United States in the early twentieth century. They were devoted to each other. In fact, Ida Silvestri "always prayed that God would take her too if anything ever happened to her husband, Giorgio," remembers her grandson George Silvestri Jr. One day in 1953 Giorgio and Ida Silvestri returned to their home after they visited another Tuscan family in Marin County, California. Giorgio Silvestri had a heart attack in the bathroom and passed away. Twenty minutes after losing her husband, Ida Silvestri "expired." George Silvestri Jr. was an altar boy at his grandparents' funeral at Saints Peter and Paul Church in San Francisco. Today he remembers the solemn occasion with emotion, for he loved his grandparents very much.[37]

George Silvestri Jr. emphasizes the closeness of his family members, here and in Italy. He reports that his father, George Silvestri Sr., "exposed" him to Italy. During the 1950s he learned about the Italian culture and language by listening to George Silvestri Sr. read letters from his uncle in Italy. Later, in December 1963, the younger Silvestri surprised his future wife, Valerie Scatena, and her friend by meeting them in Geneva, Switzerland, when they were traveling in Europe. George Silvestri Jr. surprised Scatena (who is one-half Tuscan) once again when he asked her to marry him on Christmas morning in 1963. He gave her an engagement ring in the Silvestri family's chapel—it dates back to 1609—in his ancestral Tuscan hometown. Currently, the Novato, California, attorney is very close to his relatives in Italy, particularly a cousin from his generation. George and Valerie Silvestri, meanwhile, spend much time with their children, grandchildren, and other relatives.[38] "Family is everything," notes George Silvestri Jr. "The most meaningful joys and sorrows of life involve family."

Likewise, Kathleen Maggiora Rogers hails from a close-knit Italian-American family in northern California.[39] Her Piedmontese family's roots in the Bay Area date back a century. In 1906 her great-uncle, Vincenzo Maggiora, immigrated to Richmond, California. Rogers' grandfather, Luigi Maggiora, came to America fifteen years later. Initially, the two Piedmontese immigrants worked in the construction business. "They moved to Sausalito, California, in 1926," notes Rogers, "where they bought real estate on Spring Street (homes to rent and empty lots for future homes)." In the ensuing years numerous Maggioras moved to this pleasant location as well.

During her childhood years in the 1950s and 1960s, Kathleen Maggiora Rogers' family life was centered on Spring Street in Sausalito and the Maggiora farm in Cloverdale, California. Luigi Maggiora himself started to live on Spring Street during the late 1920s, while Vincenzo Maggiora began to reside there in the early 1960s. Throughout Rogers' youth, twenty Maggiora family members lived on Sausalito's Spring Street; they saw each other frequently. Luigi and Vincenzo Maggiora also bought property in Cloverdale, California. They planted an orchard, a vineyard, and vegetable garden (during the summers) and built a home there. Members of the Maggiora family—Kathleen Maggiora Rogers among them—gathered at the Sonoma County farm each summer.

Today the Maggioras' homes on Spring Street in Sausalito hold special significance to the family's younger generation. Due to the closeness of their family and the fact that their grandfathers bought those residences, Rogers and her cousins would never sell the homes. In fact, she says they charge "below-market rents to keep people in the houses who are good tenants." "My mother lives on Pearl Street, just around the corner from Spring Street," reports Rogers. "She still owns the house she grew up in on Spring Street and the house she moved into when she was married and raised my brother and me in on Spring Street." Decades later, the San Francisco paralegal cherishes her childhood memories of how the Maggioras of Spring Street met at different homes for different holidays (Easter, Thanksgiving, and Christmas), where they enjoyed multicourse meals that included Piedmontese dishes.

In different parts of America, people of Italian origin are preserving and reinventing aspects of Italian-American culture in response to the backgrounds and cultural attributes of their non-Italian spouses. Vincent Lanzolla and Stephanie Angle Lanzolla are North Carolinians whose family life encompasses Italian and Southern traditions. Vincent Lanzolla is an

Italian American from the Bronx in New York City; his father came from Bari in Apulia. As with a growing number of Italians from the Northeast, he now makes his home in the Tar Heel State. Mrs. Lanzolla, meanwhile, is a native Southerner who hails from Charleston, South Carolina.[40]

The Lanzollas harmonize their respective traditions beautifully. At their wedding, they had equal amounts of Italian food and Southern food. Each year they have a seven-fish dinner on Christmas Eve. Then they enjoy pork, collard greens, and black-eyed peas on New Year's Day. Stephanie Angle Lanzolla relates well to her husband's interest (and pride) in being Italian because many southerners emphasize the importance of focusing on their heritage. The Lanzollas are active members of the Triangle Italian-American Heritage Association in Raleigh, North Carolina.[41]

Vincent and Stephanie Lanzolla describe their perspective on culture and tradition: "We are both very proud of our heritages, and love sharing in each others'. We both respect tradition, and while things we each enjoy get blended each day, we also try to keep some of them hallow and whole, hence the feast of the seven fishes and the pork, collards, and black-eyed peas. When we entertain, we will often either have a Southern theme, or an Italian theme."[42] Vincent Lanzolla, moreover, is a dual citizen of the United States and Italy. His wife shares her husband's attachment to Italian culture and his appreciation for ethnic diversity.[43]

※ ※ ※

The Lioi family of Baltimore, Maryland, has a story that typifies the evolution of Italian-American family life, from its origins in Italy to its thoroughly American dynamics today. Five-year-old Andrew Lioi immigrated with his mother, Rosaria, and sister, Catherine, to the United States in 1930. The Calabrians came to America, where Andrew's father, Bruno Lioi, was working to create opportunities for his wife and children. The Liois settled in Baltimore's Little Italy; eventually, Catherine and Andrew had four American-born siblings: Theresa, Paul, John, and Gerard. Andrew Lioi is a self-made man; the decorated World War II veteran put himself through law school and achieved success in business. He chronicles his family's history in a delightful autobiography, *Rosaria's Family*, which was published in 1997. Lioi appropriately names the book for his redoubtable mother, as it was her love, wisdom, and determination that united the Lioi family.[44]

Andrew Lioi's book covers his family's births, baptisms, courtships, engagements, marriages, divorces, military service, academic achievements, professional accomplishments, family events and reunions, illnesses, and deaths. Bruno Lioi, who lived until 1967, and his wife, Rosaria, enjoyed seeing the younger generations of Liois growing and thriving in America. Rosaria Lioi lived well into her nineties; she took great pride in the growth of her family and the myriad achievements of her children and grandchildren. Until her passing in 1989, Rosaria was the matriarch and focal point of her family, as the Liois gathered around her on holidays, Sunday afternoons, and other important occasions. Andrew and his wife, Gerry, were close to Rosaria. They never had any children of their own, so the lifelong Baltimoreans have been particularly involved in the lives of their nieces, nephews, godchildren, grandnieces, and grandnephews.

On the last page of *Rosaria's Family*, Andrew Lioi eloquently describes the cycle of life in his Italian-American family: "Together with the grandchildren and now the great-grandchildren there is created a body—a living entity that thrives and will survive the present and progress into the future. There exists a strand of genes that can be twisted, tied into knots or stretched. But it cannot be broken for it has no weak links. The qualities of family love, respect, honor and integrity, compassion and devotion have passed on from Rosaria and can be seen even in the youngest of the young."[45] The most youthful Lioi descendants now have multiple ethnic identifiers and they are unhyphenated Americans, yet their Italian heritage continues to guide their values and lifestyles.

The vast majority of young Italian Americans are, in actuality, only part Italian. Now there are American youths who have Italian surnames but who are only one-quarter Italian or even one-eighth Italian. During the coming years it will be interesting to see how these youngsters identify, if at all, with their Italian heritage. In 2003, for instance, a young man at Collins Hill High School in Lawrenceville, Georgia, told me that he was "half hillbilly and half Italian." Of course, finite amounts of Italian ancestry can be significant in terms of a person's self-identification. In 1990 one of my peers told me that his then-girlfriend was one-quarter Italian—and that, on the basis of her Italian ancestry, he thought she would be a good cook. Some American parents give names to their children that take into account their ethnically mixed backgrounds. Therefore, we see youths with such names as Marco McGavick and Liam Capozza.

Even with all the intermarriages that involve Americans of Italian origin, there is still some ethnic endogamy in the Italian-American community. Carl and Nancy Carani are natives of Highwood, Illinois, whose parents came from the Province of Modena in Emilia-Romagna. Carl Carani, in fact, serves as President of the Società Modenese di Mutuo Soccorso (Modenese Society), a mutual aid society based in Highwood. Many members of Highwood's sizable Italian population have roots in the Province of Modena. The Caranis' daughter recently married an American-born man with an Emilia-Roman background similar to hers.[46] Moreover, Americans of Italian descent sometimes marry Italians from Italy. There are interactions between members of both groups at universities, in the workplace, through cultural organizations, and elsewhere.

Now we are seeing an increasing number of Italian Americans who are biracial or multiracial, due to more interracial marriages and relationships. The ranks of biracial Italian Americans include such individuals as the late baseball star Roy Campanella, football great Franco Harris, the actor Giancarlo Esposito, musical impresario Alicia Keys, onetime professional basketball player Jayson Williams, and former Amgen Chief Financial Officer Richard Nanula. Some of these individuals identify with their Italian heritage. Leon Wynter writes about a young woman of Italian and African descent who qualified for and won a scholarship designated for an Italian American.[47] Conversely, a young woman in Dearborn, Michigan, who is half black and half white (mainly Italian with some Greek ancestry), told me that she identifies as black. She said there is no point in identifying as Italian because other people see her as African American. These types of decisions will almost certainly become more common in the future.

Young people who are adopted by Italian-American families often identify with Italian culture and carry on Italian traditions. Hank and Mary Marcello have two daughters of Korean descent: Jennifer Marcello and Allison Marcello. Their Italian cultural background is important to these twentysomething Wellesley graduates. They have taken courses in the Italian language and studied at universities in Italy.[48] Likewise, Dominick and Joan Filipponi recently became the grandparents of two Guatemalan-born girls. Their daughter, Christina Krueger, and her husband, Daniel Krueger, have three children: Alex, Micaela, and Victoria. Alex is their birth child; the Kruegers adopted Micaela and Victoria, who are first cousins, in Guatemala. All three children are being raised with an appreciation of their family's Italian heritage. These examples indicate how Italian-American culture can be inclusive, welcoming, and embraced by people from a broad range of ethnic backgrounds.[49]

Chapter 6

NAMING PRACTICES

D id you ever wonder where some of your Italian family or friends got their names?" asked Marianne Peri Sack in a 2004 newspaper column that ran in *Il Pensiero*, the Italian-American newspaper in Saint Louis, Missouri.[1] In writing this article, Peri Sack took her readers on a tour of the history of Italian-American naming practices. She described the places (schools, workplaces, ports of entry) where Italian names were anglicized to sound more "American." Her article included vivid personal examples that highlighted how the Italians conformed to American naming practices. Peri Sack writes that her cousin had a business called Pat Perry's Plumbing. In a conversation with Pat Perry, she learned that his surname, in fact, was changed by a teacher. The American educator altered the youngster's records so that his name read "Perry," not Peri. From that point on, he was known as Pasquale, or Pat, Perry. This development angered Pat Perry's father, who lacked sufficient clout to reverse the naming decision.[2]

Peri Sack's piece reviews the naming conventions of the early and mid-twentieth century as well as the immigrants' desire to become part of the American mainstream. She notes that the Italians often gave "American" names to their children and, on other occasions, had few opportunities to resist the name changes that were forced upon them by others.[3] In her article, Peri Sack discusses the name changes that sometimes complicated (and often simplified) life for Italian Americans. She takes on the issue of nicknames and ponders why different people had the same forename but varying nicknames. The Ballwin, Missouri, resident mentions three relatives who were named Ignazio. Two of them were known as Eugene. But many

people described the other Ignazio as Tony. "Many individuals had difficulty when they went to apply for Social Security since their name on their
birth record did not agree with the name on their school and work records,"
notes Peri Sack. Her Uncle Henry was really named Gabriele, while her
Aunt Sarah learned that her birth certificate listed Rosaria as her given
name. These discoveries surprised both individuals.[4]

Marianne Peri Sack, the English-language editor of *Il Pensiero*, is
strongly committed to preserving the Italian-American culture. Since
around 1990, this granddaughter of Sicilian immigrants has been deeply
involved in many activities in the Italian-American community of Saint
Louis and environs. A lifelong resident of Greater Saint Louis, Peri Sack
is president of the Misericordia Society and the person responsible for the
Columbus Day Parade and Festival Saint Louis. She grew up in a home
where her parents preserved many of the Old World customs and traditions. Her husband, Don Sack, is a German American, as are so many
people in the Saint Louis metropolitan area.[5] Peri Sack refers to herself by
her maiden name and married name, a common practice among Italian-
American women who have non-Italian husbands.

A number of Peri Sack's friends and colleagues know her as Marianne
Peri Sack, the "American" version of her given name, Maria Antonia Peri
Sack. The sixtysomething Missourian takes pride in her heritage and given
name. Thus she concluded the aforementioned column on names by advis-
ing her readers to reclaim their original names.[6] "If you are one of those
that lost their true identity with changes of this sort, take back your real
name even for just a day," writes Peri Sack. "It will probably make you feel
good. Please note that my byline reads Maria Antonia Peri Sack on this
article."[7] This particular column hit home with the readers of *Il Pensiero*,
who are familiar with the bias, stereotyping, and assimilationist pressures
that led many Italians to alter, modify, and anglicize their names.

Saint Louis, specifically that city's "The Hill" neighborhood, is a repository of the vital Italian-American tradition of nicknames. In 2005
Eleanore Berra Marfisi published a book, *Soprannomi*, that traces the nicknames of Italian Americans in this vibrant ethnic enclave.[8] Marfisi
describes the origins and utility of nicknames, which were helpful in a
community where many names resurfaced across the generations in Italian-
American families.[9] "No doubt, this could lead to a bit of confusion, especially when families get together," writes Marfisi. "Therefore, nicknames
were needed and played a major role in the community."[10]

Eleanore Berra Marfisi cites many nicknames in her book, some of which are in dialectal Italian while others are in American English. She isolates at least eleven types of Italian-American nicknames on the Hill: "unsung heroes," "physical traits," "Italian dialects," the same surname, "types of employment," "endearing eccentrics," "hometowns and sports," "particular preferences," "complacent personalities," "self-dubbed and childhood nicknames," and "names derived from given names and surnames." Such nicknames typically met with approval from the recipient as well as the broader neighborhood. By having such a nickname, one was seen as a vital part of an organic community. Take Joe Ponceroli's nickname "Ice": It stemmed from his role as the neighborhood's ice delivery man. Some Italian-American nicknames in Saint Louis are clearly dated. Furthermore, many individuals may not even recall the origins of the names. Yet the traditional nicknames still have staying power today and remain familiar to the Italians there.[11]

James Tognoni, an Italian-American leader in Saint Louis, discusses the significance of his ethnic heritage as it relates to names. In high school during the 1960s, Tognoni's classmates pronounced his surname in an anglicized fashion and often referred to him by nicknames (e.g., "T-Bone"). Tognoni has always pronounced his surname the Italian way and ignored the inevitable mispronunciations of it. At a recent high school reunion, though, some of his classmates were confused. "Why did you change your name?" they asked him. He had not done so—they had just never listened to the proper pronunciation of his name before. Tognoni, like many Italian Americans, has an interest in genealogy. Decades ago his great-uncle researched the family's Calabrian genealogy and its surname of Corea. He found that "the origin of the name was Correa," remembers James Tognoni. "They were Spanish pirates who had apparently been exiled and ended up in Calabria."[12] Tognoni takes pride in his family name and history, as do the other Italian Americans in Greater Saint Louis and, indeed, throughout Missouri and the United States.

In 2005 John Marino and his wife preserved a venerable Italian family tradition when they gave the name Raffaele to their firstborn son. Little Raffaele is named after his paternal grandfather, Raffaele Marino. In the Marino family, one typically names his firstborn son after his paternal grandfather.[13] A native of New Jersey, John Marino is the third child of immigrants from Campania. His U.S.-born older brother is named Giacomo after his paternal grandfather. The American family calls him "Jack." John Marino himself was named for his maternal grandfather, Giovanni. His formal name is John, though, not Giovanni. As a youth at home and in Italy, most people referred to John Marino as "joo-juan," the dialectal form of Giovanni. When Marino came into the world, his Italian-born parents, Raffaele and Angelina Marino, selected an American name for him, as they were more assimilated into American culture by this time. But the Marinos still observed the Italian custom of naming their second son for his maternal grandfather. They did so in such a way that reflected the realities of life in their adopted country.[14]

Raffaele and Angelina Marino immigrated as adults to the United States in the early 1960s. They come from Vatolla, a village of approximately five hundred inhabitants in the Province of Salerno. The elder Marinos have a home in Vatolla and maintain close ties to Italy. At the same time they love the United States and the opportunities here. John Marino's father framed his "Certificate of Citizenship" and hung it on the wall of the home where the family lived on the Jersey Shore. Marino grew up speaking Neapolitan dialect at home with his parents and siblings. He went to Italy during many summers as a youth, where the Italians often described him as the "americano." In Vatolla today, John Marino is warmly accepted by the locals due to his family connections to the town, knowledge of the local dialect, and work at the National Italian American Foundation.[15]

An engaging man in his thirties, Marino is a rising star in the Italian-American world. He was a junior college instructor before going to work at the National Italian American Foundation in Washington, D.C., in 2002.[16] "NIAF is an organization with a mission centered upon promoting the best of the Italian-American and Italian culture and heritage," says Marino.[17] The Italian-American advocate currently serves as Director of Government Relations and Public Policy at NIAF.[18] A multiculturalist, Marino reports that he "always felt a bond" with people of immigrant parentage. He has a good friend who is the son of Guatemalan immigrants, for example.[19] Through his commitment to inclusion and our nation's multicultural heritage, Marino honors his family name and carries it forward with dignity.

The naming process is something with which most Italian Americans are familiar, due to their experiences and those of their ancestors over the years.[20] John Philip Colletta describes the Italian custom of repeating names throughout the generations:

Since at least the sixteenth century, both on the mainland of Italy and the islands of Sardinia and Sicily, tradition has dictated how Italian parents name their children. For this reason the same given names reappear over and over in Italian families, generation after generation. A couple's first son is given the name of the father's father; the first daughter is given the name of the father's mother. The second son is given the name of the mother's father; the second daughter is given the name of the mother's mother. Subsequent children are usually given their parents' names, or the names of favorite or unmarried or deceased aunts and uncles.[21]

This custom persisted, to some extent, in the United States, although the names were often Americanized.[22]

Name changes were a significant and sometimes unsettling part of the assimilation process for the Italian immigrants and their descendants. "Many Italian surnames have been transformed in the United States— shortened, Americanized, spelled differently, changed completely," notes John Philip Colletta.[23] Likewise, Italian immigrants often gave their children the English-language equivalents of traditional European names: Mary (Maria) or Anthony (Antonio). Nor is it uncommon for Americans with Italian forenames to go by American-sounding names.[24] Nunzia might be known as Nancy most of the time. Likewise, Salvatore will often go by Sam in his day-to-day life. Even the spellings of traditional Italian names were frequently Americanized, as in Ugo (Hugo) and Filomena (Philomena). These developments helped the Italians win acceptance from their American neighbors.

Many Italian Americans have family narratives about the changing or anglicizing of their forenames and surnames that occurred during the 1910s, 1920s, 1930s, 1940s, and 1950s. On many occasions, I have heard about people who changed or anglicized their names to obtain work during the Depression and at other times. These name changes were done coercively at times. Cesarina Piscitello recalls that educators changed her name to "Jessie" when she entered the Pennsylvania schools at the age of five during the 1930s. From that point onward, Mrs. Piscitello has been known as "Jessie."[25] Likewise, Carlo Giraulo remembers the story of an Italian-American family named Jones in East Haven, Connecticut, whose surname was changed by an Ellis Island immigration officer who thought the "original name" had an overly complicated pronunciation.[26]

The pressure for the Italians to change their Italian names existed as recently as the 1950s and early 1960s. Romana Antonelli immigrated to the

United States in 1950. During her early years in America, people advised Mrs. Antonelli to call herself "Ramona" or "Romona." She emphatically rejected their suggestions. "My name is my identity, and I will never change that," states Antonelli. She gave Italian forenames to her children and bestowed Italian nicknames upon her grandchildren (Emily is "Emilia") as well.[27] A dynamic and enthusiastic proponent of the Italian culture and heritage, Romana Antonelli recounts how she maintained her name despite the pressures to make it sound more "American." Similarly, an Italian-American woman in Queens, New York, told me that her husband was advised to adopt a different name to find a job in the early 1960s.

During the late 1950s John Terravecchia received advice to change his name to succeed in the banking industry. When Terravecchia graduated from Northeastern University in 1959, he found it somewhat difficult to gain employment with the old-line Boston banks. One person even recommended that the American of Sicilian descent change his name to "Terry." John Terravecchia resisted such a move, as did his wife, Tina Terravecchia. He retained his polysyllabic surname and went to work in New Hampshire.[28] In the ensuing decades, he achieved significant success in the banking world as John Terravecchia. Now the Bedford, New Hampshire, resident is part of a group of bankers and investors who have launched a new company, Hampshire First Bank, in New Hampshire.[29] Terravecchia's unmistakably Italian surname—it contains five vowels—is a nonissue today.

As part of the assimilation process, Americans of Italian descent were not always aware that they had been given authentically Italian forenames. Dr. James Guttuso discovered as a teenager that his real name was Gioacchino, not James. Gioacchino is the name that appears on his birth certificate.[30] "My parents realized the English translation of Gioacchino was Joachim and they did not like it so they named me James," recalls Guttuso.[31] As a teenager, he submitted an application for a driver's license in his hometown of Buffalo, New York. Guttuso initially could not get his permit because of the confusion over his proper name. The future dentist, professor, and Italian-American leader put down James as his name on the application, but his birth certificate read Gioacchino.[32] Such stories are not uncommon among first- and second-generation Italian Americans.

Some Italians in America made a linguistic accommodation: They pronounced their child's American name in the Italian fashion. Ernest Manzo grew up in Millinocket, Maine, during the 1930s and 1940s. He was named Ernest instead of Ernesto. Nonetheless, his Italian father, Giuseppe, always pronounced the name Ernest as if it were Ernesto sans the "o." (Ernest Manzo's mother referred to him as "Ernie.") Likewise, Giuseppe Manzo pronounced his daughter Mary's name in the Italian fashion as well. Ernest Manzo eventually became a school principal in Millinocket; the gregarious educator has always been known by the American pronunciations of "Ernie" and "Ernest."[33]

Emil Bagneschi pronounces his Americanized forename the Italian way. He came to America from Tuscany with members of his family in 1952. During the late 1950s (specifically, his senior year at Burlingame High School in Burlingame, California), Bagneschi shortened the spelling of his forename from Emiliano to "Emil" at the time he became an American citizen. He did so in order to seem more "American." The name "Emil" has stayed with him throughout the subsequent decades. Now the real estate investor and retired Defense Department official serves as president of the Peninsula Italian American Social Club in San Mateo, California. Even today some members of the club do not know that Emil is a shortened version of Emiliano, Bagneschi's full name.[34]

Indeed, the spellings and pronunciations of Italian names frequently change in the United States. These changes occur to make the names confirm to Anglo-Saxon conventions. D'Alessandro, for example, may become Dallesandro in the American context. Likewise, many Italian Americans omit the space between the Di and the second word in their surname: The Italian Di Giorgio becomes the Italian-American DiGiorgio. There are different pronunciations of Lucia in America, as in Loo-shuh or Loo-SEE-uh instead of the Italian Loo-CHEE-uh. Such names as Mario and Carmine sound very different on the American tongue as opposed to what one hears in Italy. Moreover, many Italian surnames are pronounced quite differently in the United States than in Italy. Americans typically pronounce the name Schiavo as "SHY-voh," while the proper Italian pronunciation of the name is "skee-AH-voh." Similarly, many Americans pronounce the "g" in such Italian surnames as Croglio, Tenaglia, Battaglia, and Tagliavia.

Italian Americans, to be sure, are often aware of the anglicized spellings and pronunciations of their names. Hugo Tagli points out that the American spelling and pronunciation of his name differ dramatically from the customs and conventions of Italy. This son of Tuscan immigrants notes that his forename is spelled Ugo in Italy and that the Italians pronounce his surname as "TAHL-yee," not "TAG-lee" as in the United States.[35] Meanwhile, one periodically encounters people of Italian origin with non-Italian names at Italian-American events and in Italian-American venues. Ronald Little is a native of Upstate New York whose family name was changed from the Italian "Piccerillo" to Little decades ago. His Neapolitan surname translates to *little boy* in English. Ronald Little enjoys Italian-American culture and emphasizes his Italian background. To this end, he is a member and served twice as the president of the Triangle Italian-American Heritage Association in Raleigh, North Carolina. Little recounts the history of his surname to explain how he came to have an Anglo-Saxon name.[36]

Sometimes Italian Americans take on "American" names to integrate into a given context or community. Take the nickname "Charlie," for instance; it has been adopted by Italians with such names as Calogero, Carlo, and Carmine. Calogero Cascio immigrated from Sicily to the United States in 1956.[37] Many of the New Yorker's friends and colleagues know him as "Charlie." Carlo Dalla, likewise, is almost unanimously described as "Charlie" by his friends and associates in Colorado. Only his family members refer to him by his birth name.[38] Similarly, Carmine Russo, a native of New York, is known as "Charlie" in his hometown of Winchester, Virginia, a community with relatively few Italian Americans. His friends in Winchester's Sons of Italy Lodge refer to him as Carmine, however.[39] In all three cases, these individuals observe and celebrate Italian customs and traditions. Such examples indicate how Italian Americans accommodate the naming practices of mainstream America.

II.   Alicia Keys is one of the celebrities profiled in Nick Mileti's book, *Closet Italians: A Dazzling Collection of Illustrious Italians with Non-Italian Names* (2004).[40] The recording star and native New Yorker comes from an ethnically mixed background. Her mother, Teresa (Terri) Augello, is of Irish and Italian descent while her father, Craig Cook, traces his ancestry to sub-Saharan Africa by way of Jamaica. Alicia Keys was born as Alicia Augello Cook. She became an international star in 2001, after the release of *Songs in A Minor*, her debut album. Keys is one of America's top recording artists; her many honors include eleven Grammy Awards. During the last five years, she has released *The Diary of Alicia Keys* (2003), *Unplugged* (2005), and *As I Am* (2007).[41] Due to Americans' tendency to see someone of partial African descent as black, along with Keys's Anglo-Saxon stage name, many people do not know about the superstar's Italian background.

To be sure, there are numerous Italian Americans with non-Italian names. Nick Mileti's book, *Closet Italians*, documents this phenomenon by offering a kaleidoscopic list of such individuals from Western Europe and the United States. Mileti highlights a number of reasons why Americans' names do not always reflect their Italian heritage. For one, many Italian Americans have mothers, but not fathers, of Italian descent. A large number of Italian-American women have non-Italian surnames by marriage. Then there were the errors that occurred at Ellis Island. Many people adopted new names for professional reasons, particularly in show business. Other Americans changed their Italian names because of discrimination. And it was not uncommon for people to shorten long names or those that were difficult to pronounce. Finally, some individuals altered their names in order to win greater social acceptance.[42] Mileti points out that such name changes were not always painless. Take the comedian Pat Cooper, who was born Pasquale Caputo in Brooklyn.[43] "My father hated that I changed my name," recalled Cooper.[44]

The topic of Nick Mileti's book is a fun parlor game for Italian Americans. Mileti profiles a wide variety of individuals from music, sports, the arts, entertainment, and other fields who are readily known to the American public but not necessarily identified as Italian, as in Georgia O'Keeffe, Regis Philbin, Steven Tyler, Louis Freeh, and Dana Reeve. Not everyone knows that Hulk Hogan (profiled in *Closet Italians*) and Randy "Macho Man" Savage (né Randall Mario Poffo) are Italian Americans, for example.[45] The singers Chris Isaak and Tim McGraw are part Italian, but the general public probably does not see them in this light, in contrast to such men as Robert DeNiro and Sylvester Stallone (who are only part Italian, too). With the prevalence of intermarriage among Italian Americans, there are many Americans of Italian origin whose names give no clue as to their ethnic background. In the coming years, then, the subject matter of Mileti's volume will undoubtedly become even more relevant.

Italian naming conventions still matter to many Americans of Italian origin, particularly those individuals aged fifty and older. Certain forenames are particularly common among Italian Americans, including Gina, Mary, Frank, and Anthony. Indeed, it is not uncommon for middle-aged and elderly Italian-American men to have the name Frank Joseph. Similarly, the nickname "Dom" is a clear indication that one is Italian American: It could stand for Dominic, Domenic, Dominick, or even Domenico. Josephine is a name that is popular among women from many different ethnic groups; it appears with regularity in Italian America.

Now, with widespread intermarriage and the assimilation of Italian Americans, one finds far more Jasons and Jennifers than Salvatores and Concettas in the younger generations of Italian Americans. Many Italian Americans, as with parents from other ethnic backgrounds, choose the fashionable names of the moment for their children. One person of my acquaintance relates what she sees as the incongruity of the names that result when parents pair the *au courant* names (e.g., Cody, Tyler) with their Italian surnames. Likewise, we sometimes see children with Italian surnames whose other ethnic antecedents are reflected in their forenames, as in an Irish-American mother who gives Celtic names (Patrick, Bridget) to her Irish-Italian children. To be sure, one also sees this phenomenon occur in reverse, when an Italian-American mother with a non-Italian husband gives her children names (Santo, Angelina) that reflect the Italian part of their heritage.

Many non-Italian women have Italian surnames, after all, while a number of Italian-American women have non-Italian married names. Former Hewlett-Packard Chairman and CEO Carly Fiorina is not an Italian American, notwithstanding her Italian surname. Her husband, Frank Fiorina, is an Italian American. Carly Fiorina enjoys the status of an IBM ("Italian By Marriage"). Likewise, one regularly sees women with Italian forenames and non-Italian surnames. Top Hewlett-Packard executive Ann Livermore goes by her married name, so people do not always know that she is an Italian American whose maiden name is Martinelli.[46]

For some Italian-American women, their married names obscure their Italian heritage. The fact that women may keep their original names maintains this ancestral connection to some extent. Remo Minato notes that all three of his married daughters have retained the surname of Minato; their spouses are not Italian.[47] Some Italian-American women use their Italian surname mainly when they are involved in Italian-American activities. Others will use it as a middle name in their professional life, as in the case of the economist Laura D'Andrea Tyson. In Italian-American contexts, ethnically mixed Americans with non-Italian surnames may list their Italian surnames in parentheses as a matter of self-description. Someone from such a background might write her name as

Jane (Castello) Duncan. An Italian-American academic with an Anglo-Saxon surname (by marriage) is known professionally by her Italian and English surnames. On certain occasions, though, she uses only her English name. This particular individual is not concerned about anti-Italian bias. Rather, she wishes, at times, to minimize any sense of difference from mainstream culture by "passing" as an unhyphenated American.

John Koch describes himself as "John Buffa Koch" in his Italian-American interactions in Jacksonville, Florida. Koch is one-half Polish and one-half Sicilian, and his surname is a truncated form of the Polish name of his paternal ancestors. His wife, Patty Koch, is Irish and Italian. Although John Koch has deep roots in Italian-American culture, he periodically encounters people who question his Italian bona fides because of his non-Italian surname. During the 1960s, for instance, an Italian-American club in his native New York City refused to allow him to become a full member because he was not 100 percent Italian. After the Koches joined the Italian American Club of Jacksonville in 2001, a couple of individuals asked John Koch why he became a member of the club. "You're not Italian," they told this descendant of Sicilian immigrants. To alleviate any confusion about his ethnic identity, he now puts "John Buffa Koch" on his business card. Buffa is his mother's maiden name.[48]

Due to intermarriage, there are Americans of Italian origin with the quintessentially American surname of Smith. One Italian-American woman of my acquaintance has a daughter whose surname is Smith (her father's surname). Another woman mentioned the Smiths—they are one-half Italian—in her family to me as an example of the assimilation process at work. Some Italian-American women carry the name of Smith as a result of marriage. Lucy Basso Smith, for instance, is 100 percent Sicilian. The Dunedin, Florida, resident is a member of LIADO—The Italian-American Women of Today. Moreover, she and her husband, Charles (Chuck) Smith, have taken classes to learn the Italian language. A native of the San Francisco Bay Area, Basso Smith also maintains connections to her ancestral homeland. She is a dual citizen of Italy and the United States. Moreover, Basso Smith has passports from both nations.[49] This Italian/American writes: "My Italian passport only uses Basso as my surname. That is how they do it in Italy. My married name, Smith, is not on my Italian passport at all."[50]

When it comes to the pronunciations of their names, Italian Americans encompass many approaches and perspectives. Some Italian Americans are very accepting of different pronunciations of their names, as they defer to the speaker's preferences in this regard. Other Americans of Italian origin insist that their names should be pronounced in either an anglicized or Italian fashion. To be sure, there is diversity of opinion on this issue in Italian America. It is even possible to hear about Italian-American siblings who pronounce (or spell) their surnames differently. To be sure, numerous Italian Americans, including Intel CEO Paul Otellini, pronounce their names in the Italian fashion.[51] Nowadays, it seems more common for Italian Americans to prefer or even insist that their names are pronounced the Italian way. This phenomenon is undoubtedly an outgrowth of the resurgence of ethnic pride among many Italian Americans.

Pronunciations of names have always been a significant issue for some Italian Americans. One woman from an Italian family told me that she never responded, even as a youth, to mangled pronunciations of her beautiful Italian surname. Italian Americans, to be sure, are often familiar with mispronunciations of their melodious names. A lady of Irish-Italian ancestry related to me that she invariably knew when her teacher would be reading her name on the roll in school. The instructor always hesitated when she came to this particular student's name, since she did not know how to pronounce it correctly. Another woman shared her experiences involving a neighbor who has never learned the correct pronunciation of her Italian surname. Consequently, she introduces the Italian American to newcomers by her first name. Stories exist in the Italian-American community of telemarketers who mangle Italian surnames when they call people. Indeed, it is not uncommon for Italian Americans to insist upon correct pronunciations of their names from telemarketers and others.

In any event, there can be a certain amount of ethnic affinity associated with Italian surnames. Frank Sagona reports that his Italian surname and his father's reputation ensured that Italian Americans hired him for jobs during his youth in Pueblo, Colorado. When he went to apply for a job, would-be employers looked at his name (Sagona) and asked him, "Is that Italian?" After Sagona's affirmative answer, the prospective employer then asked, "Who's your father?" Upon learning that it was Sam Sagona, a well-regarded resident of Pueblo, the response was: "OK, when can you start?" This type of situation occurred to Frank Sagona numerous times in Pueblo during the late 1950s and early 1960s.[52] Likewise, Michael Illia reports that in his irrigation business, the older Italian-American farmers whom he works with in coastal California usually associate his surname with being

Italian. The ethnic connection is "an icebreaker" in certain situations, says the Pismo Beach, California, resident.[53] In essence, Michael Illia's Italian name allows him to establish rapport with some of the farmers from the very beginning of their business dealings.

Although people with Italian surnames in this country increasingly have little Italian ancestry, their surnames often structure how they identify themselves and are identified by others. Due to intermarriage and American naming conventions, it is not unusual to see people with Italian surnames who do not look at all "Italian." Likewise, there are Italian-looking individuals whose ancestors either changed their surnames or who have Italian ancestry but a non-Italian father or grandfather. Increasingly, many of the people we see as Italian Americans, as in Mario Batali and John Travolta, are only partly Italian. An Italian surname matters for Italian-American role models, even if the illustrious figure is only one-quarter Italian, according to Joseph Maselli. This is the case because Americans will readily identify the Italian-surnamed individual as an Italian and associate him or her with other people of Italian ancestry. Consequently, this person's accomplishments can serve to enhance the image of Italian Americans as a group.[54]

When it comes to role models for Italian Americans, one cannot always ascertain whether a surname is Italian or representative of another ethnic group.[55] As Truby Chiaviello writes:

> Just because the surname ends in a vowel does not mean the name is Italian. Vowel-ending surnames exist at times in other languages that evolved from Latin like Spanish, Portuguese, French, and Romanian. All these Latin based or Romance languages share the same vowels. The vowel-ending name may actually belong to one of these other languages instead of Italian. In some other cases, certain surnames belonging to Asian languages, like Arabic, Turkish, Farsi, and Urdu, have been shortened to where they end in a vowel and may resemble Italian.[56]

Chiaviello offers hints as to how someone can determine if a name is genuinely Italian. It is a matter of sleuthing, to some extent. "Focus only on the root word of the last name," advises the Italian-American journalist.[57] "The first name," continues Chiaviello, "can be misleading since most first names are based on religious figures, shared among Catholic countries."[58] Chiaviello advises genealogical researchers to concentrate on surnames— and to do so with an Italian atlas and an Italian dictionary at hand. If a person's surname is also an Italian place name, there is a high probability that the individual in question is at least part Italian.[59] Another way Chiaviello recommends to deduce whether someone might have Italian ancestors is to consult *un dizionario italiano*: "If the name or root of the name is mentioned in an Italian dictionary then that is strong evidence the person is Italian."[60]

Similarly, an American with a Venetian surname like Michelon may have to explain her family history in order to be recognized as an "Italian." Jennie Michelon relates that many Italian Americans initially do not view her as Italian because of her Venetian surname. Unlike most Italian surnames, Michelon's name ends in a consonant, not a vowel.[61] Nor does her forename, Jennie (her real name is Giovanna), readily indicate that she comes from an Italian background.[62] Once Italian Americans learn that Jennie Michelon identifies as an Italian with pride, then they think the Illinoisan dropped the vowel from the end of her surname (or that the Michelon family did so decades ago). Such speculation is incorrect, of course, as Michelon is an authentic Venetian name.[63]

III. Vincent Damian Jr. (né Damiano) has led a blessed life. He graduated from North Miami High School in 1956 and went to Princeton University on a full scholarship. The native New Yorker was part of Princeton's Freshman Council, a member of the University's varsity swimming team, and "chosen to be part of one of the elite eating clubs." "Princeton was beautiful for me," remembers Damian of the institution from which he graduated in 1960. He characterizes his experiences at Harvard Law School, which he attended from 1960 to 1963, in similar terms.[64] This scholastic standout never personally encountered ethnic discrimination or prejudicial treatment.

To be sure, Damian appreciates the different dimensions of the Italian-American experience. His father, Vincent Damiano Sr., was a New York City firefighter of Italian origin. His mother, Ruth Sears Harris, traced her ancestry to Northern Europe and came from an old-stock family in the Coney Island section of Brooklyn. Vincent Damian Jr. and his brothers lived in a Brooklyn neighborhood where white ethnics accounted for a majority of the population. In 1954 the Damiano family moved to South Florida, where they did not lead an especially "ethnic" lifestyle.[65]

Over the years Vincent Damian Jr. has learned about various aspects of Italian-American history. In 1964 he married Carol Esposito, who became an academic and respected art historian. Her father, Dr. Joseph Esposito, went to Yale University during the Depression. He was "terribly mistreated," remembers Vincent Damian Jr. many years later. It was "very, very hard for an Italian to be there" at that time, according to Damian. Esposito then went on to Columbia University Medical School, a meritocracy, and became a prominent radiologist in Fairfield, Connecticut.[66] During graduate school, Damian's future father-in-law gave to him a copy of Pietro di Donato's powerful novel, *Christ in Concrete*. The book left an "indelible" imprint on Damian's mind: It heightened his awareness of the obstacles that Italians had faced in America during the early twentieth century.[67]

Vincent Damian Jr. was known by the surname of Damiano until he changed it to "Damian" in the spring of 1963. He graduated from Harvard Law School at that time and decided to adopt the name Damian because he wanted to run for president someday. In 1963 he did not think that Americans were ready for a presidential candidate whose surname ended in a vowel. After the assassination of Robert F. Kennedy in 1968 (Vincent Damian worked for RFK's presidential campaign in Washington), the young Italian American left behind his political ambitions. He, his wife, Professor Carol Damian, and their family have lived in South Florida since then.[68] Over the ensuing decades, this region has become increasingly Hispanic and Italian Americans have become more accepted throughout our nation.

A surname with several vowels is no longer a disadvantage. It may actually be an advantage in certain contexts now. Today Damian's son and daughter tell their father they wish their surname was Damiano. But Vincent Damian Jr., Professor Carol Damian, and their children are "very well known in Coral Gables as Italians," so there is no need to return to Damiano for that reason. Moreover, the Miami attorney and Coral Gables civic leader says that all four members of the Damian family are well established as Damians in their respective professions. No one is going to return to Damiano now, as people would be confused if they adopted their original surname at this time.[69] Yet the fact that they could consider returning to Damiano illustrates how much progress has occurred for Italian Americans during the last forty-six years.

As part of the ethnic revival that began in earnest in the 1970s and continues in the present, Italian forenames and surnames have become popular, acceptable, and even glamorous in many parts of the United States. In the last three decades some native-born Italian Americans have given traditional Italian forenames to their children. Italian Americans do so as a matter of ethnic pride, to honor their ancestors, or just because they like the names. Today there are American youngsters named Rosa, Maria, Angelo, Santino, Massimo, Antonio, Giovanni, and Francesca. These youths with Italian names often carry the names of their Italian forebears.

Italian Americans, it should be noted, sometimes have American forenames and adopt (or are called by) Italian names informally. Vincent Sposato III is active in the Italian-American Society of Tulsa. A member of a venerable family in Tulsa's Italian community, Sposato goes by "Vincenzo" at the Society's meetings.[70] Since the late 1990s, Richard Floreani has been known as "Riccardo" to many of his associates. The New Hampshirite adopted the name in Italian contexts after he studied and explored his Friulian heritage in detail.[71] In Nevada, meanwhile, John Illia Jr. reports that his family often refers to his thirtysomething sons Anthony and Vincent as "Antonio" and "Vincenzo," respectively.[72] Such examples highlight one way in which Italian Americans preserve some connection to their ancestral heritage.

In California, George Silvestri Jr. refers to his thoroughly American grandchildren by endearing Italian nicknames, a reflection of the deep and enduring pride that he takes in his Italian family background. Silvestri christened his oldest granddaughter, Carlisle, as "Signorina Gambe Lunghe" (Miss Long Legs). Likewise, Silvestri gave her younger sister, Laughlin, the nickname of "Signorina Occhi Azzurri" (Miss Blue Eyes). Finally, their little brother Bryson is "Brisone," at least to his grandfather; Brisone, of course, is an Italian version of Bryson.[73] These naming practices are intriguing expressions of Italian ethnicity in America.

The pendulum has swung in the positive direction for Italian Americans, as manifested by the tendency of people of Italian origin to consider returning to their original names when they or their relatives had anglicized those names. While relatively few people take this step, the fact that the ethnic revival of the 1970s and beyond made it possible to do so (along with the immense popularity of all things Italian) is a sign of Italian-American progress, in and of itself. I heard of an example of a man who was named for his grandfather, Gaetano. To Americanize the name, his parents christened him Gaetan. Eventually he changed his name to Gaetano. On a similar note, Leonard DiTomaso comes from a family whose surname was once "Thomas." A number of years ago he took the initiative and changed his surname back to DiTomaso. Several family members followed his example and returned to DiTomaso as well.[74]

Carlo Dallapiccola reclaimed his ancestral surname, too. His grandfather, Bartolomeo Dallapiccola, immigrated to the United States during the 1920s. Due to the difficulties people had in pronouncing his name, Bartolomeo Dallapiccola shortened it to "Dalla" upon becoming an American citizen in 1940. His grandson, Carlo Dalla, graduated from college in 1983. At that time he officially reclaimed his full surname and became Carlo Dallapiccola. The younger Dallapiccola takes pride in his Italian heritage and sees the family name as a "beautiful name," according to his father. Carlo Dallapiccola underwent the process of changing his name before he entered graduate school, as it would be more complicated to do so later in life. Now Dallapiccola is a professor of physics at the University of Massachusetts and known to all by his original family name.[75]

The Italian spellings of Italian-American names seem to be more popular these days, as some Americans of Italian descent reclaim those spellings. A woman in Queens, New York, told me that she wanted to be called Teresa, not Terry; moreover, she insists that her name be spelled the Italian way (without the American "h"). Likewise, Professor James Divita offers some compelling reflections on the spelling of his family name over the years. A former president of the Italian Heritage Society of Indiana, he notes that his Italian grandfather's surname is listed as "Divita" after he arrived in the United States in the early twentieth century.[76] "My dad and two of his brothers continued to spell the name with the small 'v,'" writes Divita.[77] Then the Chicago native and respected historian describes the increasing tendency of people to capitalize the "v" in his surname. "One uncle returned to the capital 'V' because his wife thought that the capital letter made our name distinguished," says Divita. "Most of my mail from Italian-American organizations and people who do not know me will spell my name with a capital V, especially in recent years."[78]

These days it is not uncommon to meet Italian Americans who once Americanized their Italian forenames but who have returned to using their Italian names. Armando De Marino Jr. went by the name of "Armand" for a number of years. The Glendale, New York, real estate broker now proudly refers to himself as "Armando."[79] Pasquale Pesce's Italian-immigrant parents gave him a very Italian name (it means Easter in Italian). He remembers there was a time when he preferred to be called

"Pat" rather than Pasquale. Now the Bronx native insists on being called Pasquale, but his friends can call him "Pat."[80] The aforementioned examples highlight the changing attitudes in America toward people of Italian origin.

Similarly, the saga of Joseph R. Cerrell's surname illustrates the progress of the Italian Americans. The grandson of Calabrian immigrants, Cerrell was born Joseph Cerrella in June 1935 in Jamaica, Queens. In 1941, when he was six years old, his father, Salvatore Frances Cerrella, enrolled him at PS 49 in Middle Village West, Queens. While doing so, the elder Cerrella truncated the family name: He made it "Cerrell" instead of "Cerrella." Salvatore Cerrella took this action because of discrimination in his occupation (firefighting) from Irish Americans and his fears that there would be anti-Italian attitudes because of the impending war. From that point on, his son was known as Joseph (or Joe) Cerrell.[81] The student at PS 49 went on to become one of America's top political consultants, an important civic leader in Los Angeles, and an internationally known Italian-American figure.

Now Joseph R. Cerrell's grandson may eventually have the same name as his great-grandfather, Salvatore Cerrella. Cerrell's son, Joseph Walter Vincent Cerrell, studied Italian in Perugia. He is director of Global Health Advocacy at the Bill and Melinda Gates Foundation. His son, Salvatore Cerrell, was born in 2003. Joseph R. Cerrell advises the little boy's Italian-born nanny to teach her native language to him. In a 2005 interview, Salvatore's proud grandfather reported that there are going to be discussions about reattaching the "a" to the Cerrell name. Salvatore Cerrell could then become Salvatore Cerrella. The Cerrells want to preserve the Cerrella name in America, as there are few males to carry it forward.[82] Joseph R. Cerrell and his wife, Lee Cerrell, are also the proud grandparents of identical twins named Chase and Josephine, who were born in 2006. Little Josephine is named for one of her Calabrian ancestors.[83]

As a result of our interest in genealogy, more and more Italian Americans are researching the origins of their Italian surnames. The genealogical research can be quite complex and difficult, in part because of the repetition of Italian forenames through the generations.[84] Some Italian Americans make interesting discoveries about their ethnic backgrounds. Monsignor Dominic Bottino recently learned that his great-grandmother's maiden name (Ardis) was Greek, a finding that underscores the tremendous diversity of his ancestral Sicily.[85] Several years ago Peter Balistreri discovered that his late uncle Joseph's name was actually Onofrio after his daughter went to Ellis Island and learned that this name, not Giuseppe, appeared on the ship manifest.[86] One has to be a sleuth to track down the accurate names and histories of his or her Italian forebears, due to naming conventions, the Ellis Island experience, and the desire to assimilate by many Italian immigrants and their descendants.

Dr. Pete DePond is deeply involved in such genealogical research. His father, Pietro Di Ponte, was an immigrant from Santa Croce del Sannio in Campania. DePond's American-born mother was a Fazioli, but the family name was changed to Fazio at some point in America. Her parents came from Frosolone in Molise. The family name of Di Ponte—it means "of the bridge" in Italian—became DePond in the United States. Pete DePond began focusing on genealogy around 1999 or 2000. The retired dentist painstakingly reconstructed his family history. In doing so, he came into contact with relatives in Italy, Rhode Island, and the United Kingdom. The parish priest in Santa Croce del Sannio, Padre Enrico Narciso, even consulted the parish archives to locate information for the native West Virginian.[87]

DePond conducts much of his research online, often with fruitful results. He focuses on the three surnames related to him: Di Ponte, Fazioli, and Pollutro. In his research, he consults such sources as the Italian White Pages (*Pagine Bianche*), the Ellis Island Passenger Arrivals: American Family Immigration History Center Web site, and the excellent genealogical resources maintained by the Church of Jesus Christ of Latter-day Saints. DePond discovered the specific errors that the harried registrars made at Ellis Island when they processed his family members. For example, he learned that his great-aunt Immaculata was listed as "Tunnacalata" in one document. In addition, the family name of Pollutro was listed, alternately, as "Pallutri" and "Polluto" on various documents. And DePond ascertained that his father's name is spelled different ways on different papers (the "Declaration of Intention," the "Petition for Naturalization," and the "Certificate of Naturalization") during the naturalization process.[88]

To this end, genealogical research can even be helpful in attempting to solve medical mysteries. Judge Richard Marano relates a fascinating story from the mid-1990s about a discovery that an American made as a result of her research on the POINTERs (POINT—Pursuing Our Italian Names Together) Web site. There was a fortysomething member of POINTERs whose ten-year-old daughter had a rare blood disease. Decades ago this person's grandfather had changed the family name from Giancola to Jones (not her real name). Ms. Jones did not know about her original surname until her daughter became ill. Then her great-aunts told her that they really were not Joneses but Giancolas. Thus she contacted Marano through POINTERs to obtain information about her lineage and family history for her physicians. In doing so, they hoped to reconstruct her family genetic ancestry to help find a cure for the little girl's illness. With Marano's assistance, they traced her surname to a village in Molise that is the home base for Giancolas throughout the world.[89]

❊   ❊   ❊

Italian forenames seem to have become increasingly popular in recent times. Ralph Tambasco, for one, has observed this dynamic during the last ten to fifteen years. His brother, Gennaro, was always known as "Gene." Therefore, people thought his real name was "Geno." And in recent years they began referring to him as "Geno," in an effort to respect his Italian heritage. Ralph Tambasco, meanwhile, is named for his great-grandfather, Raffaele. These days some individuals ask the Indianapolis attorney why he sticks with the monosyllabic name Ralph instead of going with the more-mellifluous Raffaele. Tambasco is comfortable with his current forename. Still, he finds it interesting that traditionally Italian names seem to be fashionable now.[90]

Ralph Tambasco's son, Michael Tambasco, offers some insights on naming practices among young Italian Americans. The twentysomething Indianan grew up in Greenfield, Indiana, a town of 14,600 approximately twenty-six miles east of Indianapolis. He was one of only two Italian Americans in his high school. Tambasco has always been aware (and proud) of his Italian heritage. His distinctively Italian surname and appearance reinforce the ancestral connection. Tambasco, who sports an "Italy" tattoo on his right biceps, recounts coming across people in his generation with Italian surnames. He asks them, "Is that an Italian name?" More often than not, they respond, "I don't know."[91] Such examples indicate that the Italian connection has completely disappeared for some Americans of Italian descent.

Since the vast majority of Italian-American youths are of mixed ethnic origins, their surnames and forenames do not always indicate that they are at least part Italian. In any event, there are many American youths with Italian surnames who do not look "Italian," because they are only one-half, one-quarter, or even one-eighth Italian. Marianne Reali says that her half-Italian grandson, Dominic Reali, has an Italian name but he "looks very Scandinavian" (his mother's ethnic background). Conversely, Reali's grandchildren with "American" names look "Italian," in her opinion.[92] These youngsters represent the diversity of Italian America in the twenty-first century.

From time to time Italian Americans are mistaken for Latinos, due to some similarities in the naming practices and physical appearances of members of the two communities. The blurring of these ethnic boundaries may be increasing in frequency, due to the fast-growing population of Hispanics in the United States. Maria Baroco, an Alabamian of Italian descent, went to graduate school in Austin, Texas. She reports that people in Austin automatically assumed that she had a Hispanic background because of her name, the cultural context, and the large Latino population there.[93] Similarly, one Italian-American man, who is an administrator at a school with a predominantly black and Latino enrollment, reports that African-American students sometimes ask him, "What are you, Ferraro?"[94] This individual has a surname that ends in a vowel; consequently, some students cannot place him in an ethnic sense. To be sure, the Italian surnames ending in an "a" or an "o" are less distinctively Italian in many cases than those ending in an "e" or an "i."

Yet not all Italian Americans are mistaken for Latinos. Such experiences may not occur often in those places with few Hispanics. Memphis, Tennessee, has a small but growing Latino population. Still, Mario Bertagna, a Memphian of Tuscan descent, says that no one ever has mistaken him for Latin American in his hometown. They do, however, mispronounce his name on a regular basis.[95] Nor are Italians necessarily mistaken for Hispanic in those places where they live in close proximity to many Latinos. An example of this type of community would be Waterbury, Connecticut. Judge Richard Marano, an Italian American, notes that no one in Waterbury and environs ever thinks he is Latino.[96] In a place like Waterbury, where there are large numbers of Puerto Ricans and Italian Americans (16.9 percent and 23 percent of Waterbury's population, respectively), people may have greater familiarity with the different names that typify each ethnic group. Therefore, they would be less likely to blur the boundaries between Italians and Hispanics when it comes to naming conventions.

Italian Americans report varying experiences in this regard in Pueblo County, Colorado, where Italians and Latinos constitute 8.2 percent and

38.0 percent of the population, respectively. Frank Sagona, a retired educator of Sicilian origin, notes that he and his brother, Gary Sagona, find that Puebloans often refer to their surname as "Segura" (a common Spanish name in Pueblo) and consider it to be Spanish.[97] Conversely, Michael Salardino, a financial services executive of Italian descent, reports that he has been mistaken for Hispanic perhaps once in the five decades he has lived in Pueblo. He speaks warmly about the similarities between the Hispanic and Italian cultures. Salardino's peer group during high school in Pueblo was Hispanic, Slovenian, and Italian.[98] Pueblo, to be sure, is a community in which Latinos and Italians largely coexist in harmony.

Richard Apodaca of El Paso, Texas, bridges the Italian and Hispanic cultures well. He is descended from a soldier in Julius Caesar's Roman legions in Spain. When Apodaca's uncle conducted genealogical research on the family's history during the 1980s, he found that their progenitor's surname was "Apodacco" at the time of Caesar. The Apodacco family became Spanish during the ensuing centuries. "Over time one 'c' was dropped and the 'o' became an 'a,'" reports Richard Apodaca. His Spanish/Italian ancestors came to the New World hundreds of years ago. Today Apodaca celebrates his Spanish heritage and Italian ancestry. Since the mid-1990s he has been a member of the Italian-American Cultural Society of El Paso. Apodaca currently serves as the organization's treasurer. In addition, he oversees the preparation of all the Italian food for the Society's monthly luncheons.[99]

Chapter 7

LANGUAGE AND CULTURE

L*a Befana vien di notte/con le scarpe tutte rotte/va vestita alla romana/viva, viva, La Befana!*"[1] Every one of Josephine A. Maietta's elementary school students of Italian chants this poem in early January.[2] In Italian folklore, after all, La Befana is an elderly woman who visits the homes of children on the evening of January 5, right before the Epiphany (January 6). Well-behaved children receive goodies from La Befana, whereas their ill-behaved counterparts can expect nothing more than a lump of coal. "My students learn the poem and recite it the night before January 6, or during the entire week, hoping that La Befana will bring them a treat," says Maietta. The parents of Maietta's students reinforce this lesson in cultural diversity by putting a delectable gift on their children's desk or pillow, or somewhere else in the house. "La Befana also greets them upon their arrival at school on the morning of January 6," reports their irrepressible teacher. Maietta enjoys the legend of La Befana very much—it is a delightful custom that she grew up with in Italy.

A native of Sicily, Giuseppina Anna Buscaglia came to America at age sixteen with her mother, Antonia, and four siblings (Carmela, Giovanna, Nicola, and Gaspare). This young Italian immigrant spoke virtually no English when she arrived in the United States. A lifelong teacher who earned two master's degrees by her mid-twenties, Maietta began teaching ESL Adult Basic Education for the New York City Board of Education in 1971—she did so until 1982. From 1977 to 1982, Maietta taught fifth- and sixth-grade students, many of whom were Italian speakers, at PS 123K in Ridgewood, Queens. Then, from 1982 to 1996, Josephine Maietta was a full-time parent, one who participated in numerous Italian activities ranging from cultural events to charitable programs to international media. (She and her husband, Mauro A. Maietta, have two twentysomething sons, Mauro Salvatore and Joseph Anthony.) Maietta reentered the paid labor force in 1996 to teach Italian to elementary school students in the Syosset (New York) School District. Since 2001 she has been the world language coordinator and mentor for the Syosset School District's elementary schools.

Josephine Maietta is a dynamic and knowledgeable teacher of Italian. The West Hempstead, New York, resident uses an interdisciplinary curriculum, one that educates children about art, opera, the Euro, popular music, the geography of Italy, prominent Italians and Italian Americans, and so much more. All the while, Maietta makes her lessons about the Italian language and culture fun and lively. Her students sing frequently and play many games, including Tombola, a bingo-like activity. Actors dressed in period attire introduce the youngsters in Maietta's classes to such historical figures as Amerigo Vespucci, Christopher Columbus, and Leonardo da Vinci. And at Maietta's school, there are dual clocks (one for New York time and the other for Italian time) in the lobby. Not surprisingly, this exceptional educator inspires her students to do very well in Italian pronunciation contests.

Maietta, moreover, is a longtime veteran of the Italian-language media. While in college, she worked on Renzo Sacerdoti's Italian Program on WEVD, where she "enjoyed being in charge of programming." Then, in the 1980s, the onetime actress hosted "La Dolce Vita," a weekly Italian-language radio program that aired on Saturday afternoons on ICN Radio in New York City. "La Dolce Vita" was a very eclectic program: It included songs, music, recipes, interviews, beauty tips, health advice, notable quotations, and public service announcements. Nowadays Josephine Maietta periodically assists Giovanna with her Italian radio program, "Souvenir d'Italia," on Saturday mornings on WRHU–Hofstra University.[3] She participates in interviews and special events. In addition, she sometimes receives coverage in *America Oggi*.

Maietta comes from a close-knit Italian-American family—she and her relatives proudly honor the memory of her nephew, Anthony Calia. A graduate of Hofstra University, Calia managed Carmela's Ristorante Italiano in Franklin Square, New York. The 32-year-old restaurateur passed away in April 2004, after an auto accident. Eight hundred people reportedly visited him when he was in the hospital. Calia's funeral Mass at St.

Thomas the Apostle Church in West Hempstead was completely full; Monsignor Jim Lisante described him as "the prince of Franklin Square."[4] "They had to turn people away at the funeral home, because there were so many who gathered there," remembers Josephine Maietta. (Anthony Calia's photograph is displayed in the front window of Carmela's.) His family memorializes Calia in many ways, including a statue of St. Anthony when Baby Jesus appears to him by the renowned artist Sandro da Verscio in the Basilica Inferiore of St. Francis in Assisi, Italy, that was dedicated to him in May 2005.

Josephine Maietta, meanwhile, has received numerous awards, honors, and commendations over the years. These well-deserved encomiums recognize her remarkable commitment to teaching and her lengthy record of involvement in civic and community affairs. In 2003 she was the first recipient of the National Italian American Foundation's Teacher of the Year Award. Within the past few years, Maietta became a member and, later, commander of the Order Knights and Ladies of the Holy Sepulchre of Jerusalem and she was honored as a Cavaliere by the Italian president. The Sicilian American, too, served as president of the American Association of Teachers of Italian, Long Island Chapter.[5] For more than three decades, she has been actively involved in Italian and Italian-American charities and activities throughout the New York City metropolitan area. Indeed, this inspiring and compassionate educator works tirelessly to promote the Italian language and culture in many venues.

I. Seventy-five percent of the 150 members of Piemontesi nel Mondo Southern California "speak or at least understand" the Piedmontese dialect.[6] Ray Boggio, a leader of this organization, notes that Piedmontese often sounds similar to French. For example, the word for automobile is *macchina* in Italian and *voiture* in French and Piedmontese. Likewise, the word for wine is *vino* in Italian and *vin* in French and Piedmontese. Boggio and the other members of Piemontesi nel Mondo, many of whom are elderly, regularly converse in Piedmontese during their monthly meetings and the four or five functions that are held for the general membership each year. Their discussions focus on such cultural topics as Piedmontese music, poetry, cuisine, and literature. These gatherings allow the group's members to keep the Piedmontese dialect alive in southern California.[7]

Boggio's interest in Italy and Italian Americana stems from his parents, Alex and Maria Boggio. They hail from the same Piedmontese village and are, in fact, third cousins. Ray Boggio reports that his mother "was born in the Piedmont in a house that has been in different branches of the family since 1462." Alex Boggio is Michigan-born; he spent ten years as a youth in the Piedmont. The elder Boggio served in the U.S. Army during World War II. After the war, he ran an import-export business. Ray Boggio, therefore, spent much of his childhood in Rome. The middle-aged Californian is three-quarters Piedmontese and one-quarter Venetian (his mother is part Venetian). A tall, stocky man with silver hair and a goatee, Boggio speaks fluent Italian and he reads and understands Piedmontese. His mother speaks Piedmontese with the prestigious Torinese accent. In addition, Maria Boggio converses in Italian, French, English, and Intrese (a Lake dialect of Piedmontese).[8]

To illustrate the intricacies of how the Piedmontese dialect evolves in America, Boggio remembers a childhood anecdote involving his paternal grandmother. His Grandmother Boggio, who had been in the United States for forty years, spoke English with a thick accent. She used English, Piedmontese, and Italglish (the Italian-English hybrid tongue) in her daily speech. Once, when Ray Boggio visited her home, he wanted to jump over a chain-link fence. Grandmother Boggio sought to dissuade young Ray from doing so, and she said to him, "*Non jumpar la fenca.*" Her command included two Italglish words: *jumpare* and *fenca*. Moreover, because the Piedmontese "cut the vowels off" in their speech, Ray Boggio's grandmother pronounced the Italglish word *jumpare* as *jumpar*—in the Piedmontese fashion. Boggio immediately understood her instructions.[9] Decades later, he honors his grandmother's memory by preserving her native tongue through the activities of Piemontesi nel Mondo Southern California.

The Associazione Piemontesi nel Mondo of Northern California actively tries to preserve and perpetuate the Piedmontese dialect, too. Kathleen Maggiora Rogers, the president of this 250-member organization, notes that Piedmontese-speaking Californians often speak an "American" Piedmontese: It incorporates English loanwords and dialectal terms that are no longer commonly used in the Piedmont.[10] Piemontesi nel Mondo of Northern California offers Piedmontese classes in the fall, winter, and spring.[11] In 2007, moreover, this organization supported, financed, and released a CD compilation of Piedmontese songs and poems

(*Rèis Monfrin-e: Poesie e canson an Piemontèis*). Bobby Tanzilo compiled the CD, along with Gian Piero Morano and Vincenzo Marchelli.[12] These cultural-preservation efforts maintain the linguistic heritage that the Piedmontese immigrants brought with them to America many years ago.

Relatively few of the Italian immigrants who came to the United States during the period from 1880 to 1920 spoke standard Italian. "Italian, as a national language, was spoken in government offices, at universities, in industry, and commerce," writes Joseph A. Tursi of this period in Italian linguistic history.[13] Traditionally, Italy was a bastion of regional dialects; until the twentieth century, most Italians spoke their local dialect, not standard Italian. Benito Mussolini and his Fascist government promoted linguistic unity among Italians by requiring standard Italian to be the language of instruction in Italian schools.[14]

This development occurred after most Italian immigrants had already departed for the United States; initially, at least, the Italian immigrants from different regions of Italy sometimes encountered difficulties comprehending each other during their interactions here. Consequently, they needed a mutually understood medium of communication, as their usage of the different forms of dialectal Italian at times impeded communication between and among Italian Americans.[15] "Official Italian might fulfill this function, or an amalgam of grammar and lexicon from Italian, various dialects, and English could emerge as a lingua franca," according to Frances M. Malpezzi and William M. Clements.[16] "Italglish," a language that was neither completely Italian nor English but something in between, served as a means of communication for many Italian immigrants to the United States.[17]

Italian-immigrant parents often advised their children to learn and speak English well and, by doing so, become fully American and integrate completely into the mainstream culture. Middle-aged and elderly Italian Americans still remember how they were discouraged from speaking, or even forbidden to speak, Italian. I regularly hear about these experiences from native-born Italian Americans in their 50s, 60s, 70s, and 80s. Italian parents spoke in Italian about topics that the young people were not to hear or understand. At the same time, young Italian Americans might speak in English so as to keep things from their Italian-speaking elders.[18] The Italian immigrants were proud of their heritage, of course, but they knew that their children had to speak English well to succeed in this country. They wanted them to have the social and economic opportunities that exist for individuals with a perfect command of American English.

Time and time again, Italian Americans in their 50s, 60s, 70s, and 80s have told me that they wished their parents had taught Italian to them. Their parents, of course, only wanted to help their children assimilate into American society. They were well aware of the subtle social and, possibly, economic sanctions against those individuals who did not seem to be totally American. Numerous factors led Italian Americans to embrace English as their language. The American schools, in particular, emphasized the English language and reinforced the overall focus on unhyphenated Americanism in those days. The new immigrants and their descendants quickly grasped that their best chance to be accepted in the United States—and to prosper here—was to learn and speak American English as quickly as possible.

Not surprisingly, the Italian dialects have largely disappeared in Italian-American culture.[19] Linda Santarelli Susman writes:

> The average age of those who speak primarily dialect is 65 or older, and only 5 percent are under 17; of all foreign speaking populations in the United States, Italian speakers are the oldest. There is no replacement pool of dialect speakers because recent Italian immigrants to the United States are likely to speak standard Italian, the resident dialect speakers are aging, and the third and fourth generations of Italian Americans have not learned dialect. Social and political environmental changes in Italy and the United States have activated an extinction process, but fossils remain in the forms of names, personal correspondence, songs, and rhymes.[20]

Fewer and fewer Italian Americans, too, speak American English with international accents. Many Italians who immigrated to the United States by the age of nine or ten speak accentless American English. Those who entered the American schools at a young age usually are indistinguishable from native-born English speakers. Not surprisingly, the extent of an Italian immigrant's accent and the quality of his or her language acquisition are correlated to the amount of exposure that the person has to English-speaking people outside the home and in the workplace. It is possible to find a family in which two sisters have different amounts of facility in English—one speaks with a heavy Italian accent, the other does not—because one worked every day with native English speakers, and the other did not.

Every census, to be sure, shows a decreasing number of people who speak Italian on a daily basis. By 2003, there were 782,000 Americans who spoke Italian at home.[21] It is easy to see why Italian is not spoken much in Italian-American homes anymore. There are few Italian immigrants these days. At the same time, most Italian Americans now marry non-Italians: American English is the primary or exclusive medium of communication in their households. Even today, however, there are still Italian-language services in heavily Italian Catholic parishes in such places as California, Connecticut, the District of Columbia, Illinois, Massachusetts, Michigan, New Jersey, New York, Ohio, Pennsylvania, and Rhode Island.[22]

Since many Italian-American speakers of Italian trace their ancestry to the pre–World War II immigrants, their spoken Italian often sounds quaint and outdated to contemporary Italians. The Italian spoken by native-born Americans may not even be intelligible to a contemporary Italian; it is often the antiquated dialect of a particular Italian region. Italians in Italy may be surprised, delighted, perplexed, or baffled when they hear the dialectal Italian spoken by Italian Americans and other members of the Italian diaspora, as these New World Italians typically speak outdated dialects that were passed down to them by the immigrants of yesteryear. Yet an Italian American might define his ancestral patois as "Italian," although many qualify that they speak Calabrian or Sicilian or Neapolitan or some other form of dialectal Italian.

Currently, the Italian language is very well-regarded in the United States. American entrepreneurs may use such Italian words as *caffè*, *ristorante*, and *salumeria* to reinforce the Italian connection and perhaps to add a touch of exoticism to their venue, product, or service. Older Italian Americans sometimes describe their relatives with Italian terms, as in *nonna* (grandmother), *nonno* (grandfather), *zio* (uncle), and *zia* (aunt). In addition, the word "paesan," a variant of *paesano* (villager or countryman), is frequently used in Italian-American English. Many people, particularly those who are involved in Italian-American activities and organizations, will include Italian words, phrases, and expressions (e.g., *Ciao*, *Grazie*, *Saluti*, and the Italian equivalents of American names) in their speech and correspondence. They do so when they come into contact with people who are perceived to share their interest in Italian-American culture.

II. *America Oggi* is the sole daily Italian-language newspaper in the United States. This publication, whose name means "America Today" in English, appears every day of the week. It originates in Westwood, New Jersey. *America Oggi* dates back to November 1988. Most of its staffers worked for the venerable—and now-defunct—*Il Progresso* until 1988, when the new owners fired the entire workforce in a dispute over unionization. Then twenty-three former *Il Progresso* staffers raised $100,000 and started *America Oggi*. Andrea Mantineo, the editor of *America Oggi*, is a native of Messina, Sicily. Mantineo came to the United States permanently at the age of twenty-eight in 1970. That year he was hired by *Il Progresso* and worked there for the next eighteen years. *America Oggi* is an employee-owned publication, and the owner-journalists print the newspaper at their Westwood plant.[23]

Andrea Mantineo and his writers try to cover the broadest possible series of stories, in part because their readers, who are mostly first-generation Italian immigrants, live throughout the country. *America Oggi* focuses on politics, popular culture, sports (particularly soccer), and other topics. It frequently covers Italian-American affairs and events. In addition, the newspaper includes a weekly Sunday insert ("Oggi 7"), where the journalists devote in-depth attention to social and cultural issues. *America Oggi*, too, covers all the U.S. visits by high-ranking Italian officials. Mantineo reports that his newspaper's European perspective differentiates its coverage of national and international issues from that traditionally found in U.S. newspapers.[24] Now *America Oggi* partners with ICN Radio, the Italian-language radio network, to create multimedia content for America's Italian-speaking population.

Over the years, their Italian-language media options have helped the Italian immigrants adjust to life in the United States. The ethnic media (particularly radio programs and newspapers) promoted a sense of cohesion among Italian Americans, kept them in touch with Italian events and developments, and, at the same time, helped them to adjust to American culture and become full-fledged members of their respective communities. Naturally, as people from Italian family backgrounds integrated into the mainstream culture, the audience for such Italian-language programming has become ever-smaller. Many Italian-language newspapers and radio programs went out of business as their target audiences passed away or English became their dominant language.[25] Even now, one still finds Italian-language newspapers and radio programs in the United States, along with stores that sell Italian books, films, music, knickknacks, newspapers, periodicals, and greeting cards.

The Italian-American print media include dozens of weekly, biweekly, monthly, bimonthly, and quarterly publications. *Primo, Ambassador, Italian America,* and *In Buona Salute* are periodicals that appeal to Italian-American readers. And there are such newspapers as *Andiamo!* (Colorado), *Fra Noi* (Chicago), *Il Pensiero* (St. Louis), the *Italian American Digest* (New Orleans), the *Italian Times* (Milwaukee), the *Italian Tribune* (Michigan), the *Italian Tribune* (New Jersey), the *Italian Voice* (New Jersey), *La Gaceta* (Tampa), *La Gazzetta Italiana* (Cleveland), *La Voce* (Las Vegas), *La Voce Italiana* (Cincinnati), *La Voce Italiana* (Houston), and *L'Italo-Americano* (Los Angeles). In addition, hundreds of Italian-American organizations have bulletins or newsletters for their members. There are professional journals, too, that cater to specialized audiences. The aforementioned publications often appear completely or mainly in English, but there are a number of Italian/English newspapers that continue to exist.[26]

Likewise, contemporary Italian-American radio shows draw upon the sizable, if not cohesive, Italian-American communities that still exist in many parts of America. The hosts of Italian-themed radio shows vary from Italian immigrants to well-assimilated Italian Americans. Some programs are largely Italian in content and language, while others are a genuine blend of Italian and English, and still others are English-dominant and very Italian American. The content of such programs, not surprisingly, often centers around music.[27] One can find continuous (twenty-four hours a day) Italian-language radio programming on ICN Radio, based in Middle Village, New York. ICN Radio offers programming to listeners who have radios with a particular frequency in the Tri-State Area of New York, New Jersey, and Connecticut.[28]

Italian-American radio has proven to be resilient in a fragmented universe of many media options. Christopher Newton writes: "Italian American radio's advantages continue to be its relatively cheap operational costs and its ability to reach members of a community who have moved to a fragmented Little Italy. And even though community leaders continue to fear the disappearance of Italian American broadcasting because younger generations seem disinterested in traditional culture and old-fashioned technology, as generations grow older a surprising number return to tune in to a continually reinvented form of Italian American radio."[29]

Quality Italian-language programming draws upon strong community support, as exemplified by the success of Luigi Aiello, a veteran broadcaster in southeastern Wisconsin and northeastern Illinois.[30] Aiello spent his childhood in rural Calabria, where his family had a small farm. His formal education in Italy ended with the fifth grade. At the age of 26, in 1966, he came to live in Kenosha, Wisconsin, to be with his Calabrian-born wife, Gina. A retired foundry supervisor at Racine, Wisconsin's Case Corporation, Aiello emphasizes that immigrants should learn the English language and become part of America's mainstream culture.[31] He describes the Italian/American connection from his perspective: "My country is Italy. It is where I was born and raised. But I like to live the style of this country. I thank this country [for giving] me the opportunity to do whatever I can to better myself."[32]

As a longtime radio host with nearly three decades of experience in broadcasting, Aiello focuses on the trends, flavors, culture, and traditions of Italy. His current radio show, "La Voce D'Italia," is a two-hour program on Sunday afternoons that airs on WRJN–AM 1400 in Racine, Wisconsin. The Kenoshan's listeners are mainly people in the 35-and-older demographic. Mario Ruffolo, who himself immigrated to the United States from Calabria, participates in each program as an on-air personality. Joe Bisciglia, meanwhile, is responsible for the radio show's English-language content. "La Voce D'Italia" includes much music (Italian and Italian-American artists performing traditional and contemporary tunes); Italian news and sports (soccer, in particular); interviews with guests, some of whom are politicians; and other content.[33] Aiello's radio program reaches listeners in both the Chicago and Milwaukee metropolitan areas.

Until recently, there were limited television options for individuals with an interest in Italian and Italian-American programming. Some Italian Americans subscribe to RAI, the Italian television network, through their cable provider and keep up-to-date on Italian events in this way. Also, one can view ITALICS, a monthly cable television program that is sponsored by the John D. Calandra Institute in New York City.[34] "Currently," notes one source, "there is no cable channel in English that focuses exclusively on Italian and Italian American culture, fashion, travel, art, history, and entertainment."[35] The newly created Italian American Network (I A Net) seeks to fill this void. Due to its appealing concept, experienced leadership, and large potential audience, the Italian American Network has promising prospects.[36]

✳III.   Richard Floreani's Italian heritage is very important to
        him. His late father, Adriano Floreani, was an immigrant
from Friuli who taught his sons to appreciate their rich cultural background. Since retiring as an international airline pilot several years ago,
Floreani has devoted much of his time to traveling in Italy, learning the
Italian language, and promoting the Italian culture. The New Boston,
New Hampshire, resident encourages his grandchildren, who are one-
eighth Italian, to learn about and take pride in their family's connection to
Italy. To this end, they strongly identify with their Italian heritage. These
youngsters are enthusiastic soccer players whose pride in being "Italian"
increased even more after Italy won the World Cup in 2006.[37]

In recent years, Richard Floreani has learned the Italian language. As
someone who grew up in a thoroughly American household—his mother,
Eleanor Floreani (née Moravek) was of Czech origin—he never had the
opportunity to speak much Italian as a youth. This Friulian American
describes his linguistic odyssey:

> Shortly before my father died, he told me that the one thing he regretted was
> that he did not teach his two boys to learn Italian. You see, he married "una
> Americana," so English was the language of the home. Besides, in those days
> one wanted to homogenize into English quickly so as to blend in and advance
> economically. But, in his last years he spoke in Italian to me as often as possible
> and helped me understand it. After his death I have continued this quest and am
> now fluent in Italian. I love speaking in Italian! *Perché è la lingua del mio sangue.*[38]

Floreani's experiences are by no means unusual. They herald a growing
interest in the Italian language among Americans, many of whom have
ancestral connections to the Italian culture. Today there are many venues
in which one can learn to speak Italian, including K–12 schools; colleges
and universities; language schools; and Lago del Bosco, the Concordia
Italian Language Village. Italian-American organizations and community
centers regularly offer Italian lessons to their members and other interested individuals. The Italian language has tremendous symbolic significance for some Italian Americans; therefore, the efforts to teach it receive
much support from Italian-American organizations. Not surprisingly,
some of the ethnic advocates who endorse Italian-language efforts themselves never had the opportunity to learn to speak Italian.

In the global era, learning world languages (including Italian, of course) is an imperative with myriad cultural and economic benefits for American students. The arguments in favor of teaching the Italian language in America's schools focus on the importance of Italian culture in the Western world, the significance of Italy as an economic superpower, the relevance of Italian for a wide range of disciplines and professions, and related matters.[39] To be sure, there has been an important increase in the number of secondary school students taking Italian in recent years. In 2000, for instance, 4,057,600 American public high school students studied Spanish, 1,075,400 took French, 283,300 enrolled in German classes, 64,100 studied Italian, and 50,900 took Japanese. By 2000, one out of every 200, or 0.5 percent, of all American public high school students were enrolled in Italian courses.[40]

Italian programs at the secondary school level are particularly common in the Northeast, where, as Professor Christopher Kleinhenz points out, there are "major Italian-American populations" and the study of Italian "took root early on."[41] Outside the Northeast, one finds vibrant Italian programs in public schools in such states as Florida, Maryland, Colorado, Illinois, Wisconsin, and California. In certain states, however, no high schools offer Italian or there is only a single high school teaching it.[42] As part of the ongoing Italian-American cultural renaissance, Italian-language programs are developing in places where the opportunities for such studies were rare or even nonexistent ten, fifteen, and twenty years ago.

The Italian government, to be sure, has played an active role in promoting the study of the Italian language and culture in the United States and beyond. Maria Grante Roos notes that the Italian Consulates support "the learning and the teaching of the Italian language."[43] Several years ago, the Italian government provided significant financial assistance for the development of the course and exam for the Advanced Placement (AP) Italian Language and Culture Course.[44] The Italian Consulates also support and sponsor seminars and workshops on the Italian language and culture for Italian teachers. Furthermore, there is Italian governmental funding to help establish new programs in Italian in the K–12 schools.[45] "The Italian government also provides lecturers in Italian language to colleges and universities in the United States through an application process coordinated by the various consulates," writes Christopher Kleinhenz.[46]

Italian classes around the country often focus as much on Italian culture as they do on the Italian language. The Italian teachers employ inventive pedagogical techniques, as in playing bingo and interpreting song lyrics, to teach their students. Lisa Guido, an Italian-language educator, points out that Italian teachers are "not just teaching a language to their students." Indeed, the youngsters typically learn about history, politics, geography, self-expression, and other topics along with their language lessons.[47] Ethnic identification may—or may not—be a reason why students enroll in Italian-language courses. Rosalie Galasso Caputo teaches Italian at Centennial High School in Pueblo, Colorado, where three-quarters of her students have some Italian ancestry, while one-quarter of them are music students and/or Italophiles.[48] Conversely, the Hispanic population is the core of the Italian program in South Florida's public schools, according to Maria Grante Roos.[49]

Italian enrollments, to be sure, are growing in Florida's schools. Roos herself cofounded and served as the president of the Florida Association of Teachers of Italian. A native of L'Aquila, the capital of Abruzzo, Roos taught Italian at Miami Coral Park Senior High School from 1984 to 2005; during the 2008–2009 school year, she returned to teach at this institution after a sabbatical in Italy.[50] By January 2005, there were 2,800 Italian-language students in Miami-Dade County, Florida's public schools. In fact, most public high schools in Miami-Dade County offer Italian. Roos says that the elements for continued growth in Italian exist in South Florida, due to its similarities with Spanish; the continuing prosperity of Italy; the Italian government's financial support of Italian programs; the glamour of "Made in Italy" products, including Italian cars and fashion; and "the presence of Italians who have become investors in Florida."[51]

Antonella Albano is a nationally recognized teacher of Italian in Naples, Florida, who originally hails from Naples, Italy. Today Albano teaches Spanish and Italian classes at Gulf Coast High School in Naples. Her multiethnic group of Italian-language students (they are approximately one-third Latino, one-third Italian American, and one-third from other ethnic backgrounds) list a wide variety of reasons for studying Italian. Some young people cite their ancestral heritage and family backgrounds. Others are Italophiles who revere the Italian culture and intend to travel to Italy. Still other students find Italian a welcome addition to the language curriculum, simply because it seems more exotic than Spanish or French. Moreover, some of Albano's young scholars have professional goals that require facility with Italian. And, as elsewhere, the students of Italian in Naples, Florida, regard the language as sophisticated and fashionable.[52]

Italian, in many cases, essentially competes with the other world languages that are offered in a given school district, with French and especially Spanish receiving priority. There is generally little or no attrition for other language programs when students have the option to study Italian in the public schools.[53] According to Christopher Kleinhenz, "Students already taking another foreign language will simply add Italian to their program and will not stop taking the other language, and often students who opt to take Italian are not taking another foreign language."[54] Still, young people are often encouraged by their parents and teachers to take Spanish instead of Italian or some other language. Approximately thirty-five million Americans speak *español*, after all, and Spanish-language skills are a definite advantage in the job market. Veteran teachers of Italian at the high school level have confided to me the pressures they sometimes face to recruit students to take Italian courses and, in some cases, continually justify the existence of the Italian-language programs at their respective schools.

Bruna Petrarca Boyle knows well the perpetual challenges of maintaining enrollments in Italian-language programs. Boyle is the Regional Representative for New England—Connecticut, Massachusetts, Maine, New Hampshire, Rhode Island, and Vermont—for the American Association of Teachers of Italian (AATI). She reports that Connecticut, Massachusetts, and Rhode Island have excellent enrollments in Italian, while there are no Italian-language programs in Maine, Vermont, and New Hampshire. Boyle also served as the president of the Rhode Island Teachers of Italian Association; such cities as Warwick, Cranston, and Providence have thriving programs in Italian. In addition, the Warwick, Rhode Island, resident has authored four books to help students prepare for the AP Italian exam. She currently teaches Italian at the University of Rhode Island, where approximately 15 percent of her students are Italian Americans.[55]

To be sure, Italian is an increasingly popular subject to study at the university level. The "growth of Italian has been constant," reports Christopher Kleinhenz of the University of Wisconsin–Madison, who joined the faculty of this world-renowned institution in 1968. UW–Madison has the largest Italian program in the country, in terms of students and faculty. Kleinhenz notes that, for some time now, it has been considered "cool" and "chic" for students to take Italian.[56] The study of Italian in higher education, as at the secondary school level, continues to outpace the total growth in world languages. The number of students enrolled in Italian-language courses in America's colleges, universities, and graduate schools tells the story: 49,287 (Fall 1998), 63,899 (Fall 2002), and 78,368 (Fall 2006). From 2002 to 2006, there was a 22.6 percent increase in the number of undergraduate and graduate students taking Italian in U.S. academic institutions, compared to a 12.9 percent increase in world language enrollments overall.[57]

The teaching and preservation of standard Italian and, to some extent, its dialectal variants continues apace in the United States. The American Association of Teachers of Italian is the premier professional organization of Italian-language educators.[58] Christopher Kleinhenz, a former president of the AATI, describes some key developments affecting his profession:

> Despite the centuries-long debate over the "Questione Della Lingua" in Italy, in North America the "standard language" (i.e., Tuscan) is taught. Given the great influx of new Italian immigrants in Canada (especially in Toronto) over the past 40 years, the University of Toronto has developed courses in standard Italian for native dialect speakers. Interest in Italian dialects has led to the recognition of the need to preserve them, and indeed studies of dialect poetry, folklore, and literature are most important in this regard.[59]

Professor Gaetano Cipolla, for one, promotes Sicily and the Sicilian culture and language under the aegis of Arba Sicula. This New York organization publishes a newsletter (*Sicilia Parra*) and a scholarly journal (*Arba Sicula*); organizes and sponsors regular excursions to Sicily; and holds events, including poetry recitals and public lectures.[60] An author, editor, speaker, publisher, translator, and academic expert, Dr. Cipolla teaches at St. John's University in Queens, New York, where his courses focus on the Italian language, literature, and civilization. He serves as president of Arba Sicula and editor of the organization's academic journal. Cipolla regularly translates Sicilian poetry into English. Also, this expert on Sicily recently edited *Introduction to Sicilian Grammar*, a book by J. Kirk Bonner, among his many professional activities.[61]

IV. Approximately 100,000 listeners in New York City and environs tune into "The Italian-American Serenade" each week.[62] This popular three-hour radio program airs every Sunday from 11:00 A.M. to 2:00 P.M. on WVIP-FM 93.5 in New Rochelle, New York. Listeners enjoy the wide array of Italian and Italian-American music and the bilingual commentary of the program's host, Floyd "Uncle Floyd" Vivino. He started his radio program in 1987. And he began writing a weekly column with the same name for New Jersey's *Italian Tribune* in 1999.[63] Readers of Vivino's columns enjoy his keen insights, poignant recollections, and humorous observations related to Italian Americana. In addition, he regularly appears in Italian-American venues, including stage shows, dinner dances, fraternal halls, and ethnic festivals.[64] As a result, this proud son of Italy enjoys good name recognition in the Northeast's Italian communities, particularly in the New York City metropolitan area.

Florio Giovanni Vivino hails from a family of Italian-American entertainers. He was born on October 9, 1951, in Paterson, New Jersey. His father, Jerry Vivino, was a Calabrian immigrant who arrived in Paterson in 1929. Vivino's mother, Emily, hailed from Paterson; her parents came to the United States from Campania. A veteran entertainer, Vivino grew up in the heavily Italian-American Second Ward of Paterson. In New Jersey, he is well known for "The Uncle Floyd Show," a cable television program that aired from 1974 through 2001. Vivino and his castmates often filmed Italian-American episodes. There was a *Godfather*-like segment starring Don Goombah, while some programs featured Senator Stunata, a fictional contemporary of Julius Caesar. Other segments, moreover, took place in Pasquale's Pizzeria. These slapstick vignettes contributed to the popularity of "The Uncle Floyd Show."[65]

A self-described nostalgist and "traditionalist," Vivino would like to "never let go" of the rich and warm Italian-American culture that he grew up with in the 1950s and 1960s. He characterizes himself as "almost Norman Rockwellesque" in his efforts to preserve the music and culture of that period. As Vivino puts it, he is "trying to hold on to an Italian-American world that does not exist in Italy today and is vanishing in America today." He speaks a fair amount of Italian: His Italian is a "mixture of southern dialects," according to Vivino. It is an antiquated Italian, says Vivino, because he learned it from members of the generation of Italians born between 1890 and 1910, many of whom came to the United States. When he performs, the dialectal words often slip into his dialogue. "The audience loves it," says Vivino.[66]

Floyd Vivino honors the past of Italian-American comedic traditions, preserves this venerable heritage in the present, and may point the way to its survival in the future. As Salvatore Primeggia observes: "The significance of Uncle Floyd Vivino's success is the integration of the best of Italian American and American components in his comedy. Yet, as long as contemporary Italian American comics follow Vivino's lead of combining the two perspectives in their work, there is a future for Italian American humor."[67] Indeed, this entertainment virtuoso works tirelessly and with great dedication to preserve the Italian-American culture that he enjoys so much.

As part of their contribution to U.S. popular culture, Italian-American comedians have used standard Italian, dialectal Italian, Italglish, and, most commonly in recent decades, American English in their routines. For many years, the Italian immigrants and their descendants have enjoyed and supported professional comedians in their community, in such venues as feasts, vaudeville, coffeehouses, amateur clubs, and ethnic theater. Many of the comedic routines, those aimed at Italian-immigrant audiences, initially appeared in Italian and showcased Old World mores and storylines. In a development that paralleled the overall assimilation process, Italian-American comedians had begun to perform mostly in English by the mid-twentieth century (although they often used Italian-American themes and Italian words thrown in for good measure).[68]

Since the 1920s the history of Italian-American comedians has included humorists who focused mostly on reaching their coethnics, while others targeted general audiences. Italian-language radio served as a popular medium during the 1930s and 1940s for comedians of Italian extraction in the New York City metropolitan area. In the immediate postwar years, this type of programming became less popular due to television's growing influence and the decline of Italian immigration.[69] "Italian radio survived well into the mid-1970s, fighting an everlasting battle to survive," writes Floyd Vivino. "By the mid-1980s, it was just about over for the old Italian radio shows that survived."[70]

During the last nine decades, furthermore, a large number of comedians from Italian backgrounds have made their careers by appealing to the larger American culture as a whole—and by including a certain amount of Italian-American content in their routines. Jimmy Durante, for instance, was a thoroughly American comedian, but one who appealed to the general public while being clearly Italian. The first American comedians of Italian descent generally attracted largely Italian audiences, but they were succeeded by American-born humorists whose acts appealed to mainstream America.[71]

Lou Monte and Louie Prima were two such individuals. Monte, who lived from 1917 to 1989, recorded many English-language ballads, while

Italian images, sayings, and dialect infused "[h]is popular novelty songs." Similarly, when Monte performed, he often engaged in stand-up comedy and his program typically included dialectal Calabrian and Neapolitan words and phrases. As Lou Monte prospered in show business, New Orleans native Louie Prima himself achieved popularity in American mainstream culture. Prima's comedic songs and on-stage skits included many words from Italglish and Italian dialect. The Louisianan's Italian/American style won him many fans among the general American audience as well as among Italian Americans.[72]

Italian-American humorists remain popular in the United States and some of them continue to be rooted in a distinctive ethnic culture. The veteran Italian-American performer Pat Cooper's popularity with mainstream audiences and his fellow Italians dates back to the 1950s. His comedy routines usually encompass characters, references, and dialectal Italian words that resonate with people from Italian family backgrounds. At the same time, Cooper presents his material in such a way that non-Italians enjoy it, too. Cooper, along with younger comics of Italian descent (e.g., Joy Behar, Dom DeLuise, and Floyd Vivino), draws upon the Italian-American experience for humorous stories and sketches. Of course, today's best-known comedians of Italian descent mostly perform in venues with no discernible ethnic connection.[73]

Elsewhere in the entertainment world, Italian-American recording artists sometimes drew upon their ethnic roots (particularly in past decades) in their popular music.[74] Italian-American artists, including Julius LaRosa and Dean Martin, recorded songs with Italian lyrics and/or themes that appealed to people from a variety of ethnic backgrounds. Julius LaRosa's legendary song, "Eh, Cumpari!" (1953) was a major hit in mainstream pop culture.[75] "It is sung in a southern Italian dialect, with words common to Sicilian language and Neapolitan language," notes *Wikipedia*. "This leads to shortened or variant spellings even within the verses."[76] Dean Martin was particularly famous for including some Italian lyrics in his mostly English songs. Several Italian-oriented songs—"That's Amore," "Volare (Nel Blu Dipinto Di Blu)," "Innamorata," "On An Evening in Roma," "Non Dimenticar," and "Come Back to Sorrento"—were part of an album released by Curb Records in 1990 (Dean Martin—*All-Time Greatest Hits*).[77]

Indeed, Dean Martin's rendition of "That's Amore" has been a legendary song for more than fifty-five years. "That's Amore" was part of the soundtrack of *The Caddy* (1953), a film starring Jerry Lewis and Dean Martin.

Naples, Italy, is the setting of this song. In his rendition of "That's Amore," the Steubenville, Ohio, native invokes numerous Italian and Italian-American words and references: "Napoli," "signore," "Scuzza me," "pasta fazool," "a big pizza pie," "too much wine," "a gay tarantella," and, above all, "amore" (the word love in Italian). The word "fazool," incidentally, stems from *fasule* (Neapolitan dialect for beans).[78] According to *Wikipedia*, "Martin did not attempt to deliver the lyrics in an authentic Italian accent, but used the accent of an American trying to mimic Italian pronunciation."[79] This song continues to be a sentimental favorite for Italian Americans and others, years after Martin's passing.

Today's Italian-American artists usually record in English—and there may be little, if anything, that is distinctively "Italian" or even "Italian American" about them. Take, for example, Bruce Springsteen and Steven Tyler, who are two important figures in American rock music whose non-Italian names obscure their Italian heritage and whose music has no overt connection to Italian-American culture. Gwen Stefani, to be sure, is an Italian-surnamed artist, but she is not an Italian American in the same way that Dean Martin was one. Bruce Springsteen's career epitomizes how Italian-American artists use American English to reach fans from many different ethnic groups. The typical American of Italian origin, after all, was "Born in the U.S.A." (the title of Springsteen's legendary ballad from his 1984 album of the same name).

❀   ❀   ❀

Soon after 9/11, Luisa Potenza took a tour of Italian Americans to Basilicata, where they visited the capital city of Potenza.[80] During this particular trip, an Italian friend told Potenza that there would be a concert to honor the Americans and others who had fallen on September 11, 2001. On the day of the concert, the young Italian said to Potenza, "I want you to get up and address the people." At first, the New Yorker did not want to do so. But when her friend insisted that she speak to the assembled Italians, Potenza went to the front of the audience and addressed them in Italian. Potenza said, "We are happy to be here in Italy. We are very touched by this concert—that you are honoring the Americans who died." Potenza began to cry at this point. It was a deeply emotional moment for her, because of her New York roots and ancestral connection to Basilicata.

To be sure, the people of Basilicata seem to feel a kinship with Americans in general and New Yorkers in particular. On the same trip, Potenza and the members of her tour group went to Pietrapertosa, the highest point in Basilicata. A journalist from RAI interviewed Potenza and members of her party. The interviewer asked such questions of them as, "Who are you? What are you doing here?" This report subsequently aired throughout Basilicata. Thereafter, people in the region recognized them—and treated them as if they were celebrities. Italians stopped the American tourists in the street and asked them, "Do you know my cousin in Brooklyn?" Then they invited them into their homes for some pasta. Another interesting example of the ties between Italy and the United States occurred to Potenza when she took the tour group to her mother's hometown of Cirigliano, Italy. The motor coach stopped before the Americans descended into the village. As the U.S. tourists entered Cirigliano, they heard someone blaring Sinatra's "New York, New York" from a window.

Potenza's ancestors come from Basilicata (she prefers to describe the region using its ancient name, Lucania). A dignified woman who often sports hats in such hues as black, beige, and maroon, Potenza shares her surname with the largest city in her ancestral region of Basilicata. She is a native of the Bronx in New York City, the child of immigrants from Basilicata who met in America. Potenza herself understands dialectal Italian from Basilicata. She speaks standard Italian with an excellent Italian accent, too, as a result of her repeated visits to Italy and her extensive study of Italian over the years.[81]

Luisa Potenza has always been interested in Italian music and culture. Her radio program ("Italia Mia") dates back to 1999. Since June 2001, it has been broadcast on WALK 1370 AM out of East Patchogue in Suffolk County, New York.[82] The program airs for two hours, from 11:00 A.M. to 1:00 P.M., on Sundays. Potenza broadcasts in English and Italian, as "95 percent of [her] audience speaks English" as their primary or only language. Overall, there is much Italian music, some of which goes back to the 1930s, on "Italia Mia." Neapolitan songs are particularly popular with her listeners. As a rule, Potenza plays twenty-six songs on each Sunday.[83] Interviews with Italian-American luminaries and newsmakers are common on her program: They occur for twenty to twenty-five minutes during the second hour. "Italia Mia" also includes current news bulletins from Italy along with a serious story and then something lighthearted. Finally, there is a cooking segment at the end of each month on "Italia Mia."

Potenza's program fosters a sense of community among her listeners. Indeed, everything about "Italia Mia" (the host, music, guests, advertisers, and news and cultural content) heightens Long Islanders' awareness of Italian and Italian-American culture. Potenza's monthly events ("Luncheons with Luisa") occur in conjunction with her radio program. There are approximately one hundred people at each luncheon. These luncheons sometimes feature celebrities of Italian origin. Moreover, tour buses take Potenza's listeners on trips, as in their visits to the annual Sergio Franchi Outdoor Concert in Stonington, Connecticut. The people who attend these events and functions are usually middle-aged and elderly Long Islanders of Italian descent.

As with many Italian-American cultural figures, Potenza frequently visits Italy. In fact, she conducts regular tours there. Potenza visits Basilicata two times each year. Her tour groups consist of twenty to twenty-five Italian Americans, mainly individuals who trace their ancestry to Basilicata. They go for ten to twelve days and "travel by private motor coach." Each trip includes stops in medieval cities and a visit to the legendary caves of Matera. In addition, Potenza gives the people on her tours an opportunity to visit their ancestral hometowns on their own. Over the years, this daughter of immigrants from the Province of Matera has witnessed a number of emotional family reunions. "I definitely feel that I am home," says Potenza of her visits to Italy. The people on her tours, of course, are well received by the locals.

This Suffolk County, New York, resident tries to observe Italian and Italian-American customs and traditions in her life. Potenza herself used to write food articles for a newspaper. On occasion, she may get together with a good friend to make sausage and pasta. In doing so, Potenza follows in the footsteps of her aunts and other relatives. While she does not study family history, several of her cousins research the family genealogy. Her program, meanwhile, is heard each week in Nassau and Suffolk counties in New York, as well as in parts of Connecticut, the Jersey Shore, and the Bronx (by car). In sum, Luisa Potenza's radio programming, cultural activities, and tours of Italy contribute to our nation's enduring Italian/American heritage.

Part III

CULTURAL GEOGRAPHY

Chapter 8

ITALIANS IN AMERICA

When Innocente Illia Sr. immigrated from Italy to Argentina in 1867, he probably did not think that one of his grandsons (Arturo Umberto Illia) would become the nation's president nearly a century later. Martino Illia, the seven-year-old son of Innocente, accompanied his father to Argentina that year. The Lombardians stayed in South America for only three years, as their attempts to farm did not succeed. While he and his father went back to Italy in 1870, Martino Illia clearly remembered Argentina with fondness. In 1882 he traveled there again; the twenty-two-year-old settled in Argentina permanently and eventually had thirteen children over the course of two marriages.[1] He appears to have been known as Martín Illia in Argentina.

Martín Illia married Emma Francesconi, who was also a native of Lombardy. Their son, Dr. Arturo Umberto Illia, was born in Pergamino, Argentina, in August 1900. He became a physician and an elected official. Most prominently, Dr. Illia served as President of Argentina from October 1963 to June 1966. The Argentine military overthrew President Illia in 1966 and he died in Córdoba, Argentina, in January 1983 at the age of 82. This son of Lombardian immigrants personified the Italian presence in Argentina.[2] In fact, he certainly had one of the most Italian names of any Argentine president: his forename (Arturo), middle name (Umberto), patronymic (Illia), and matronymic (Francesconi) were all Italian. These names fit in well in Argentina, as the Italian influence is integral to the country's history and culture.

Innocente Illia Jr., a younger brother of Martino Illia's, went to the United States in 1892. In March of that year, the eighteen-year-old Italian came to New York. Then he traveled to California, probably by train, where he settled in Sonoma County. Innocente Illia went to Occidental, a Sonoma County community known for its Swiss-Italian presence. Then he married an Irish-American woman, Helena Redmond and, after some time, he became a major property owner. Throughout his life, Illia stressed thrift, family, hard work, and education (all five of his children went to college). Innocente Illia's son, John Illia Sr., was a well-regarded athlete and coach in northern California. He and his wife, Helen Marie Illia, had three children: Susan Browder, John Illia Jr., and Kevin Illia.[3]

Today Susan Browder, a granddaughter of Innocente Illia, owns and maintains the 320-acre family ranch in Occidental. "The ranch" or "the old home place," as it is known to the Browder family, came into the Illia family during the 1890s. Susan Browder's children, Greg, Gerald Jr., Seanna, and Suzanne, grew up in northern California, a place with numerous "Illia family relations" who visit the ranch.[4] According to Greg Browder, an engineer at the World Bank, the sizable Italian-American presence in Occidental "reinforces the Italian-American connection" for Innocente Illia's great-grandchildren.[5] Gerald Browder Jr. echoes his brother's sentiments. "The land that Innocente acquired (and which is still in the family) serves as a constant reminder of our proud Italian heritage," notes this avid student of genealogy, who has gone to Italy and Argentina in search of knowledge about his forebears.[6]

The U.S. Illia family remained in contact with their Argentine cousins for many decades. John Illia Jr., a Las Vegan who grew up in San Francisco and later lived in Reno, Nevada, remembers that the U.S. side of the Illia family took pride in their Argentine cousin's political prominence during the 1960s. His aunt, Hilda Pozzi, corresponded with the Argentine Illias and, consequently, the American Illias followed events in Argentina.[7] Any time Greg Browder encounters Argentines who work at the World Bank, he mentions that his grandfather was Arturo Illia's first cousin. The Argentines always react positively to these references to Dr. Illia from his German-surnamed relative. Greg Browder reports that his famous cousin is known for being "humble" and "honest and democratic."[8]

Earlier this decade, Gerald Browder Jr. went to Argentina for two weeks to learn more about the Argentine wing of the Illia family.[9] The San Jose, California, resident describes his experiences: "During my visit to Buenos Aires, everyone I spoke to (starting with the cab driver at the airport) also spoke warmly of Arturo Illia. He was known as a humble country doctor.

One person told me that when he was overthrown, they brought a car to the presidential palace to take him away. He refused their offer, grabbed his two suitcases, and set off walking down the street to find a public bus that would take him back to Pergamino."[10] These examples indicate President Illia's enduring reputation for dignity, honesty, and humility.

The descendants of Battista Illia, another branch of the U.S. Illia clan, preserve and celebrate the saga of their illustrious Argentine relative too. Battista Illia, a brother of Martino Illia and Innocente Illia, immigrated to the United States as a young man. Michael Illia cites the Illia family's Argentine connections in his genealogical research; the Pismo Beach, California, resident is one of Battista Illia's great-grandsons. He himself first learned about Dr. Illia as a student at California Polytechnic State University, San Luis Obispo. The Internet has made it easier for him to research the Illia family's genealogy. To this end, he prints articles and pictures from the Web.[11]

Michael Illia himself preserves various Italian customs and traditions in his family life. The irrigation engineer reports that salami and cheese are culinary staples of gatherings at his home. Winemaking is also an important part of his life. Michael Illia's paternal grandfather, Oliver S. Illia, made grappa on the occasion of each grandchild's birth (they still have the 1967 vintage grappa from the year Michael Illia was born). Oliver S. Illia resembled his first cousin, President Arturo Illia, according to his grandson. Now Michael Illia seeks to learn more about his Italian heritage and relatives in South America.[12]

It is not uncommon for Italian Americans to have distant family ties to Argentina, due to the fact that the South American nation was once a significant destination for Italian immigrants. Had Innocente Illia and Battista Illia gone to Argentina instead of the United States, the Illias and Browders would now be Latin Americans who speak Spanish as their native tongue. Indeed, the Illias of Argentina and the United States have a truly American story, in the global sense of the word. Their family connection forms a trans-American bridge that spans continents and thousands of miles; it is based on a common Italian heritage and culture.

I. The example of Sycamore, Illinois, resident Joseph V. Bussone illustrates how Italian Americans enhance community life throughout the United States.[13] Bussone's parents, Joseph E. Bussone and

Margherita Bussone, were immigrants from Venasca, a Piedmontese village ywenty-five miles from the French border, who came to the United States in 1920. They settled in Roanoke, Illinois, a town of approximately two thousand inhabitants in the central part of the Land of Lincoln. Joseph E. Bussone became an American citizen in 1925, as soon as he could do so (five years after arriving in the United States). Voting was very important to him. Joseph and Margherita Bussone's three sons were born in the United States and all of them served in the U.S. military during World War II. Their youngest son, Joseph V. Bussone, was born in December 1926; he is a veteran of the U.S. Navy.

Joseph V. Bussone flies the American flag on a 22-foot-long pole outside his Sycamore, Illinois, home. There is a light to illuminate the flag at night. Bussone flies the Italian flag, too, whenever he has Italian-American visitors. There is a memorial at the bottom of the flagpole. It reads: "In memory of my beloved father Joe E. Bussone/He loved his adopted country and its flag so very much." Joseph E. Bussone's patriotic example inspired his youngest son, Joseph V. Bussone. This World War II veteran grew up in Roanoke, Illinois, and graduated from Bradley University in Peoria, Illinois. In 1950 he married Evelyn Search, a nurse from an old-stock American background. (All of Mrs. Bussone's great-great-grandparents were born in the United States.) A product design engineer at General Electric for sixteen years, Joseph V. Bussone has owned and operated his own business, Bussone Engineering Sales Company, since 1967. He and his family moved to Sycamore, a community of 12,000-plus residents in north-central Illinois, in 1954.

People in his hometown know of Joseph V. Bussone as "Mr. Sycamore," a title that reflects his civic-mindedness and significant involvement in community affairs. His list of current civic activities includes: the Kiwanis Club of Sycamore, the Knights of Columbus, the DeKalb County Hospice, the Veterans of Foreign Wars, the Sycamore Chamber of Commerce, St. Mary's Roman Catholic Church, the Midwest Museum of Natural History, and the Ben Gordon Community Mental Health Center. Since 1961 Bussone has been responsible for the Veterans of Foreign Wars' "Voice of Democracy" contest in Sycamore, by which young people compete in an oratorical contest on patriotic topics. The intersection of California Street and Elm Street in Sycamore is known as "Bussone's Corner," because that is where this community elder stands to collect for various charities during the year. His fundraising at

"Bussone's Corner," in corporate contexts, and elsewhere has resulted in substantial contributions to area charities over the last 40 years.[14]

Italian Americans like Bussone live virtually everywhere in the United States, even more so now that migration patterns are taking people of Italian origin throughout the country. Traditionally, Americans of Italian descent were concentrated in the Northeast, the industrial Midwest, Colorado, Louisiana, and California. "The 1960 census indicated that 84 percent of Italian Americans still lived in the established areas of the Northeast and North Central United States," writes Phylis Cancilla Martinelli. "By 1990, however, this number had dropped to about 56 percent, with dramatic population growth in the West (Arizona, southern California), the Northwest, and Florida in the Southeast."[15]

As of 2003, 47 percent of Italians lived in the Northeast, 21 percent in the South, 16 percent in the Midwest, and 16 percent in the West.[16] The last federal census found that the states with significantly higher-than-average percentages of Italian Americans included Rhode Island (19.0 percent Italian); Connecticut (18.6 percent Italian); New Jersey (17.9 percent Italian); New York (14.4 percent Italian); Massachusetts (13.5 percent Italian); Pennsylvania (11.6 percent Italian); Delaware (9.3 percent Italian); and New Hampshire (8.5 percent Italian). The ten metropolitan areas with the largest numbers of Italian Americans were: 1) New York–Northern New Jersey–Long Island; 2) Philadelphia–Wilmington, Delaware–Atlantic City; 3) Boston–Worcester–Lawrence, Massachusetts; 4) Chicago–Gary, Indiana–Kenosha, Wisconsin; 5) Los Angeles–Riverside–Orange County, California; 6) San Francisco–Oakland–San Jose, California; 7) Washington, D.C.–Baltimore, Maryland; 8) Pittsburgh, Pennsylvania; 9) Detroit–Ann Arbor–Flint, Michigan; and 10) Cleveland–Akron, Ohio.[17]

Within a state, to be sure, the Italian-American population may not be evenly distributed throughout every community. Take Delaware, for example. The Italian Americans of Delaware are concentrated in the northern part of the Constitution State. In 2000 the federal census found that Italian Americans accounted for 11.6 percent of the 500,265 residents in New Castle County, the largest and northernmost of Delaware's three counties. New Castle County includes such communities as Elsmere (17.0 percent Italian), Hockessin (17.6 percent Italian), and Newark (13.3 percent Italian). Wilmington, Delaware, itself is a black-majority city with a well-known Little Italy enclave. Elsewhere in Delaware, one finds Kent County (5.4 percent Italian) and Sussex County (5.0 percent Italian).

Employment opportunities and chain migration have resulted in Italian communities in many different parts of America. "By the time large-scale migration ceased in the early 1920s, Italians settled in colonies—large and small, temporary and permanent—located throughout most states of the Union," notes Michael LaSorte.[18] While large central cities certainly attracted huge numbers of Italian immigrants, they also went to small and medium-sized cities and most locations where work existed in canals, sewers, seaports, railroads, construction, heavy industry, and road building. Italians, too, could be found in rural America, mining villages, and small factory towns.[19] Due to chain migration, the Italian Americans of some locales trace their ancestry mainly to specific villages, towns, cities, provinces, and regions in Italy.[20] Some heavily Italian municipalities are predominantly white (Webster, New York, and Wethersfield, Connecticut); others have multiethnic demographics (Vineland, New Jersey, and Poughkeepsie, New York).

The experiences of Italian Americans, of course, are shaped by their environments. For one, people of Italian origin speak American English with a wide range of regional accents. Also, the salience of ethnicity seems to differ for Italian Americans by city, state, and region. According to Toni Andriulli, in New Jersey you "always ask what someone's nationality is." She and her husband, Paul, now live in Portland, Maine. The transplanted New Jerseyites find that Mainers do not focus on ethnicity in the same way as do people in the Garden State.[21] Similarly, Rose Ann Rabiola Miele says that there is a difference between her hometown of Chicago and her current residence of Boulder City, Nevada: "No one is ethnic out here." Chicagoans, she notes, regularly remark upon their ethnic backgrounds.[22] Joseph Lo Casto, too, describes how many residents of the Nashville area see themselves as "Southern." The idea of being "Irish," "Italian," or "German," which is so common in his native Brooklyn, has little relevance in Tennessee.[23]

In any event, the Italian immigrants and their descendants found many opportunities in the Western states—and their experiences often differed dramatically from those of their urban Midwestern and Northeastern counterparts. Andrew Rolle delineates this perspective in his classic work *The Immigrant Upraised*, a book about the Italian-American experience in twenty-two states west of the Mississippi River. While the Italian immigrants may have encountered prejudice, on occasion, in the Western states, they often enjoyed better life chances than their coethnics in the urban East.[24] "Whether in mountains or deserts," writes Andrew Rolle, "the West was generally tradition-free. It offered the immigrant opportunities not available in the mills and factories of the eastern city."[25]

Chicagoland is an area where the Italian immigrants and their descendants have contributed mightily to Industrial America and, more generally, the U.S. economy. In 2000 seven percent of the 9,157,540 residents of the Chicago–Gary–Kenosha metropolitan area reported Italian ancestry.[26] Greater Chicago includes Kenosha County, Wisconsin (10.8 percent Italian); DuPage County, Illinois (12.0 percent Italian); and Will County, Illinois (10.7 percent Italian). In the Illinois suburbs of Chicago, one finds sizable Italian percentages in communities like Lake in the Hills (17.8 percent Italian); Melrose Park (18.8 percent Italian); Wood Dale (18.8 percent Italian); Bloomingdale (20.7 percent Italian); Highwood (22.6 percent Italian); and Elmwood Park (28.7 percent Italian).

Similarly, the Detroit–Ann Arbor–Flint metropolitan area is home to a large number of Italian Americans; they account for 5.9 percent of Greater Detroit's 5,456,428 inhabitants.[27] In particular, Macomb County, Michigan, is 13.8 percent Italian with 788,149 residents. This county in north suburban Detroit includes such locales as St. Clair Shores, where Italian Americans constitute 16.6 percent of the population. Clinton Township is a Macomb County community with an important Italian presence. In Clinton Township one finds such community institutions as Vince & Joe's Gourmet Market; San Francesco Catholic Church; the Italian American Cultural Center; and Bonaldi's—For A Little Bit of Italy.[28]

The historian Armando Delicato notes the evolution of suburban Detroit's "now far-flung Italian community."[29] Delicato writes: "Unlike many cities in North America, Detroit has no 'Little Italy' neighborhood. There are a few remnants downtown, in the Eastern Market area, along Gratiot Avenue, and in Cacalupo to remind visitors that Italians once lived there. A new center for the Italians has developed along Garfield Road between Seventeen and Nineteen Mile Roads in Clinton Township with Italian businesses including some that have moved with the community over the years."[30]

Northeast Ohio, likewise, is a bastion of Italian Americans. People of Italian origin account for 9.4 percent of the 2,945,831 residents in the Cleveland-Akron metropolitan area.[31] Lake County, Ohio (east of Cleveland) is 15.0 percent Italian; it includes such communities as Willowick (19.3 percent Italian) and Wickliffe (20.3 percent Italian). Elsewhere in

Greater Cleveland, one finds the likes of Mayfield Heights (26.1 percent Italian) and Highland Heights (31.3 percent Italian). Moreover, the Youngstown–Warren metropolitan area continues to have a substantial Italian presence, as 14.6 percent of the nearly 600,000 people there are of Italian descent.[32] Italian Americans remain quite common in such Youngstown-area communities as Canfield (23.1 percent Italian); Niles (23.9 percent Italian); Poland (26.8 percent Italian); Struthers (28.3 percent Italian); and Girard (29.5 percent Italian).

II. Patricia Anderson's Italian ancestors have been in southern Alabama for more than one hundred years. They came from Trentino in northern Italy. Southern Alabama has long had an Italian population, particularly in and around Daphne, a pleasant community near Mobile. Anderson, an engaging woman in her forties with the maiden name of Bertagnolli, is President of the Circolo Trentino di Sud Alabama and Secretary of the International Tyrolean Trentino Organization of North America (ITTONA). In the best Italian and Southern traditions, the members of the Bertagnolli family continue to be close to each other. Approximately one thousand people attended the 1998 Bertagnolli family reunion in suburban Mobile. In addition, Patricia Anderson and three of her four siblings presently live within five miles of their parents, Donald Bertagnolli and Charlotte Wright Bertagnolli, in Daphne.[33]

Maria Baroco works with Patricia Anderson in the leadership of the Circolo Trentino di Sud Alabama. Baroco is a Daphne native and an alumnus of the local parochial schools. The thirtysomething children's librarian reports that her father, Joe Baroco, is descended from Sicilian immigrants who came to the United States during the 1870s. Her mother, Helen Baroco, has ancestors who immigrated to this country from Trentino in the early 1880s. Being Italian in southern Alabama sometimes meant encountering minor indignities in past decades. As a young man, Joe Baroco was asked for his ID card on the bus. During her youth, other children called Helen Baroco names because of her Italian ancestry. Today, of course, such experiences do not occur anymore. At the same time, the Baroco and Bertagnolli families value the Italian customs and traditions of their forebears. "Everything is done around the kitchen table," says Maria Baroco. She is unsure as to whether this is specifically an Italian or Southern tradition.[34]

There are several Italian-American activities in Daphne, Alabama, each year. The Circolo Trentino di Sud Alabama offers a summer picnic, a Christmas Party (complete with a polenta meal), and wine and cheese receptions in the spring and fall.[35] Moreover, Christ the King Catholic Church in Daphne is a parish with many Italian-American parishioners. La Festa Italiana is held at the church each March, usually around the time of St. Patrick's Day (March 17) and St. Joseph's Day (March 19). This spaghetti dinner with cannoli and Italian cookies usually draws 300 to five hundred attendees every year. Pizza fritta, a mini-pizza, is a popular fundraiser at La Festa Italiana. The process of making pizza fritta draws the interest and enthusiastic participation of youths, Italian and non-Italian alike.[36] These activities illustrate how people from Italian family backgrounds are integrally part of southern Alabama's culture.

More generally, Italian Americans represent a growing percentage of the American South.[37] While there was not a large influx of Italian immigrants to the southern states (Louisiana excepted) during the period between 1880 and 1920, they could be found in every southern state. The Italians in Dixie often worked in mining and agriculture. They went to Birmingham, Alabama, for instance, to labor in the steel mills and coal mines. During the 1950s the Italian-American migration to the South began to pick up speed and continues to this day (as part of a broader national shift of people from the Northeast and Midwest to the South and West).[38] "Buoyed by postwar prosperity, newfound leisure and recreation, and pension and retirement benefits, Italian Americans came southward in increasing numbers, as tourists, new residents and workers, and retirees," notes Gary R. Mormino.[39]

Even today one still finds a minuscule percentage of Italian Americans in many southern states and communities. To this end, let us examine the percentages of Italian Americans in the eleven states of the Confederacy: Alabama (1.3 percent Italian); Arkansas (1.3 percent Italian); Florida (6.3 percent Italian); Georgia (2.0 percent Italian); Louisiana (4.4 percent Italian); Mississippi (1.4 percent Italian); North Carolina (2.3 percent Italian); South Carolina (2.0 percent Italian); Tennessee (1.7 percent Italian); Texas (1.7 percent Italian); and Virginia (3.6 percent Italian). According to the Census Bureau's definition, the South also includes Delaware (9.3 percent Italian); the District of Columbia (2.2 percent Italian); Kentucky (1.5 percent Italian); Maryland (5.1 percent Italian); Oklahoma (1.4 percent Italian); and West Virginia (3.9 percent Italian).[40] Currently, Delaware,

Florida, Louisiana, Maryland, and West Virginia are the southern states with the largest Italian communities—that is, as a percentage of the state population.

Indeed, there is a significant Italian presence in Greater New Orleans.[41] "Although New Orleans was settled first by the French and then the Spanish, by the 19th century the city had become a mecca for Italian immigrants," writes Joseph Maselli.[42] As in many parts of America, the Italian immigrants often came to Louisiana with little money, few marketable skills, and not much formal education. Initially, they encountered discrimination in the Pelican State, which, in its most virulent expression, led to the lynching of eleven Italians in 1891. Also, the Mardi Gras organizations, or Carnival "Krewes," refused to admit Jews, Italians, and African Americans during the 1920s and 1930s.[43] "Despite their hardships," notes Maselli, "most Sicilian immigrants were able to build better lives for themselves and their families in New Orleans. Here they found land they could afford to buy, a familiar religious community, and a natural climate similar to the one they left behind in Sicily."[44]

Over the decades, Italians became leaders of the New Orleans region and the entire state of Louisiana. Robert Maestri won the mayoralty of New Orleans in 1936. He was the first person from an Italian background elected to this position (and he served as mayor for nine years). Later, Victor Schiro held the mayor's job from 1961 to 1970. His administration enforced school integration at a critical time in New Orleans' history. Louisiana's elected officials with Italian roots from the New Orleans metropolitan area include U.S. Senator Mary Landrieu, onetime Louisiana Attorney General Charles Foti, former Louisiana Lieutenant Governors Bobby Freeman and Mitch Landrieu, and Louisiana Supreme Court Chief Justice Pascal Calogero Jr.[45]

Today Louisiana's Italian-origin population is concentrated in metropolitan New Orleans, particularly in the Crescent City's suburbs. Italian Americans account for 8.2 percent (109,710) of the 1,337,726 residents in Greater New Orleans.[46] Jefferson Parish, a county of 455,466 residents that directly abuts New Orleans, is 11.4 percent Italian. The city of Metairie is 15.9 percent Italian, with many Italian Americans among its 146,136 residents. And in nearby Kenner, Italian Americans account for 12.8 percent of the 70,517 residents. There are vibrant expressions of Italian ethnicity in New Orleans and its suburbs, including the Louisiana Irish-Italian Parade each March on the occasion of St. Patrick's Day and

St. Joseph's Day.[47] These celebrations reflect the clout and visibility of Italian Americans in the New Orleans area.

Oklahoma, by contrast, is only 1.4 percent Italian American. Yet there continues to be a particularly notable Italian presence in Pittsburg County, Oklahoma, as an outgrowth of the mining jobs that brought European immigrants to the region more than one hundred years ago.[48] Thirteen and one-half percent of Krebs, Oklahoma's 2,051 residents identified as Italian American in 2000. Krebs is currently home to such establishments as Lovera's Italian Meat Market and Grocery and Pete's Place (named for its founder, Pete Prichard, a.k.a. Pietro Piegari).[49] In nearby McAlester, Oklahoma, there is the Italian Festival each Memorial Day Weekend; this ethnic celebration originated in 1971.[50]

Elsewhere in Oklahoma, the Italian-American Society of Tulsa draws members from the state's second-largest city and its neighboring communities.[51] Many members of the Italian-American Society of Tulsa come from the Northeast, according to Salvatore Gargiulo, the Oklahoma representative for Com.It.Es. Gargiulo, an Italian-born New Jerseyite who moved to Oklahoma because of his involvement in the oil business, served as president of the Italian-American Society of Tulsa.[52] Similarly, Scott Brogna, another of the Society's past presidents, grew up in Boston. As an adult, he moved to Oklahoma. Brogna compares his migration narrative to the experiences of his Italian-immigrant grandparents.[53] There are native Oklahomans, too, in the Italian-American Society of Tulsa.

Mary Jo Tannehill (née Parenti) is a native Oklahoman whose Italian-American father, a Pennsylvanian, met her mother, who was one-half Cherokee, during his military service in Oklahoma. A former president of the Italian-American Society of Tulsa, Tannehill remembers that she and one other youth were the only Italian-surnamed individuals in her classes in the Oklahoma public schools. During her career as an educator, this descendant of Cherokee Indians and Italian immigrants taught at schools in Tulsa, Osage, Wagner, and Muskogee counties. There were few Italian Americans among her students. On those rare occasions where Mary Jo Tannehill encountered an Italian-surnamed youngster, she would tell the individual that s/he was Italian. The stock reply seemed to be: "I am?" Now Tannehill does cultural presentations about Italian-American issues at schools in and around Tulsa.[54]

Frank and Sheri Agostini are two of Tannehill's colleagues in the Italian-American Society of Tulsa. The Agostinis moved to Oklahoma in

1994. Frank Agostini, who has deep roots in South Philadelphia, teaches at Fort Gibson Middle School in Fort Gibson, Oklahoma. During the 2005–2006 school year, Mr. Agostini had 144 seventh-grade students, none of them with Italian surnames, in his technology education classes. This longtime opera enthusiast teaches his students about Italian-American culture. The Agostinis, moreover, remember how they used to bring Italian foods with them to Oklahoma after they visited South Philadelphia. Now Frank Agostini reports that three Italian families (including his own) are among the eight hundred families in St. Joseph Roman Catholic Parish in Muskogee, Oklahoma.[55]

III.   During the evening of Saturday, December 6, 1941, 23-year-old Tony Bacino and five or six other Italian Americans were refused entry to the Pioneer Hall in Pueblo, Colorado. The young men went up the steps to the dance hall, at which time the doorman asked them: "Where are your cards?" "What cards?" the would-be dancers responded. "You need a card to get in here," they were told by someone who undoubtedly only wanted "Americans" in his establishment. Indeed, a newspaper advertisement at the time for the Pioneer Hall said, "Strictly American," in terms of its preferred clientele.[56]

In a 2005 interview, Tony Bacino remembered when Italian Americans were refused admission to movie theaters, dance halls, skating rinks, and at least one fraternal organization in Pueblo. His wife, Kathy, says that is how it was on December 6, 1941. Everything changed for Tony and the Italians of Pueblo the very next day, when the Japanese bombed Pearl Harbor and the United States entered the Second World War immediately thereafter. "On December 7, 1941, Tony became an American when he went into the Army," notes Mrs. Bacino.[57] In other words, he became American—fully American—for the first time at the age of twenty-three.

Such experiences reflect the history of Pueblo's Italian Americans, who are largely descended from the Sicilian, Campanian, and Calabrian immigrants who came to southern Colorado in the late nineteenth and early twentieth centuries. Pueblo's large Italian population can be mostly attributed to the employment opportunities that brought Italian immigrants to southern Colorado's mines, farms, ranches, railroads, and steel mills. The "Goat Hill" neighborhood on Pueblo's East Side was traditionally a bastion of Italian Americans.[58] Tony Bacino, a son of immigrants from Lucca

Sicula in Sicily's Province of Agrigento, was born in May 1918 and lived until January 2008; this "Goat Hill" resident took pride in his heritage and neighborhood.[59]

The Pueblo Italians encountered significant prejudice and discrimination on nativist grounds in the decades preceding World War II.[60] "It was pretty bad before the war," notes Kathy Bacino, a German American who has interviewed the children of the Goat Hill immigrants, people in their eighties and nineties.[61] Older Puebloans from Italian families remember dance halls during the 1930s with signs that read: "No dogs or Italians allowed." Tony Bacino cited the example of a man named Sam Martellaro who wanted to work at the steel mill in Pueblo during the 1930s. When he identified himself as "Sam Martellaro," the Anglos would not hire him. However, he was hired when he called himself "Sam Martel."[62]

Ralph Montera, an elder in Pueblo's Italian-American community, remembers vividly the perceptions of Italians during the 1920s and 1930s. Montera was born in August 1915. This native-born American of Sicilian origin recalls that an Italian-American bandleader (who had many Italian bandmates) was playing Pueblo's Arcadia Dance Hall around 1935. Italians would go to the door of the Arcadia Dance Hall only to be told, "No *wops* allowed." Montera recollects that, in the prewar years, some Anglo Puebloans came up to him and said, "You're nothing but a *wop*."[63] They did so to downgrade and disparage him—and to reinforce their prejudicial feelings that Italians were not as good as they were.

"The biggest change came after the war," remembers Ralph Montera. Before World War II, Italians could only work as laborers at the Colorado Fuel and Iron (CF&I) steel mill, known locally as "the Mill," in Pueblo. During the war, the Mill was unionized and Italians began to be hired in the higher positions. Until World War II, the International Brotherhood of Electrical Workers (IBEW), Local 12 had one Italian member. By 1950 or thereabouts, Ralph Montera was President of IBEW Local 12 and there were many Italian members of this union. Moreover, his younger brother, Carl Montera, went to college and worked at NASA for 30 years. And his first cousin, Philip Cabibi, started working as a newspaper boy and eventually became a District Judge.[64]

To be sure, after World War II, the Italian-American veterans returned to Pueblo and began to change things for the better. Italian Americans graduated from colleges and universities and entered the professions in Pueblo. Other folks started successful businesses and prospered as entrepreneurs. Their energy and industriousness caused the other Puebloans to take note of them, says Kathy Bacino. "You could not hold them back," notes Mrs. Bacino. She remembers that in the 1940s and 1950s, a person's Italian ethnic background still mattered in Pueblo. If an Italian was successful in those days, observes this German American, some people would say, "He's Italian."[65] In doing so, they sought to minimize the person's accomplishments. This ethnic discounting appears to have disappeared several decades ago.

By the 1960s and 1970s anti-Italian discrimination had largely vanished from Pueblo's landscape. As recently as 1970, though, a female college classmate told Pueblo civic leader Michael Salardino that she could not go out with him because "her father would not allow her to date Italians." Salardino himself served on the Pueblo City Council from 1978 to 1990. "At one time," notes the financial-services executive, "four of the seven Pueblo councilmembers were Italian Americans."[66] Indeed, Italian Americans are part of the Pueblo elite—and they can be found in virtually every occupation, profession, and institution there.

Puebloans currently promote and preserve certain Italian customs and traditions, as they maintain ties to Italy. Father Ben Bacino notes that the tradition of the St. Joseph's Table has had a resurgence in Pueblo.[67] There is a venerable heritage of celebrating Christopher Columbus in Pueblo, too; it includes a yearly Columbus commemoration and a statue of the Genoan navigator. Pueblo itself is home to four Italian societies: La Famiglia Italiana, the Dante Alighieri Society, the OSIA Southern Colorado Lodge #2738, and the OSIA Cabrini Lodge #2826.[68] Also, Pueblo has two Italian sister-city relationships, one with Lucca Sicula and one between Pueblo City/County and Bergamo City/Bergamo Province. Puebloans Michael Salardino and Frank and Vivian Sagona have been deeply involved in the Bergamo Sister City relationship; they travel regularly to Italy.

More than ten years ago, Michael Salardino encountered an Italian tour guide, Paolo, who gave him some profound insights into the nature of opportunity in America. Salardino recounts his experiences:

> On my first trip to Italy in late 1998, I had an opportunity to walk around Rome on the first day of our arrival. I was in shock at the beauty and majesty of Rome. When I returned to the hotel, I saw our tour guide, Paolo, sitting at his desk. I sat down and asked him, "Why did my grandparents leave all of this to die young in the coal mines of Colorado?" He said (and I am paraphrasing), "They did not have all of this. They were probably poor farmers in southern

Italy and Sicily. They had no hope of doing better. They couldn't even dream of doing better.

I was in Chicago once at a conference and was looking down at the street from the top of a skyscraper. The people looked like ants and I realized that most of them would never eat in the fancy restaurant where I was. But they could dream and they could find a way through hard work to make their dreams come true.

Your ancestors couldn't even dream. But they wouldn't accept that. They had heard about America and the opportunities and they left Italy, not knowing if they could survive the journey and not knowing what to expect. But they had the courage to try. They didn't achieve the American Dream. They had to work in coal mines and they died there. But they made it possible for *you* to achieve the American Dream.

I have always felt that Italian Americans are the best. We know Italians have been blessed with talents, as you can tell from what so many of us have produced. Americans, like Italians, have courage and a winning spirit. So Italian Americans, I have always felt, have it all.

You owe your ancestors. They didn't get to live the American Dream. But, because of them, it became possible for you to have it. You better wake up every morning and do your best all day in their honor. Because you owe them!"[69]

Michael Salardino thinks about this inspiring and thought-provoking conversation every day.[70] Paolo's perspective provided him with a new lens through which to view the advances of Italian Americans that he himself has witnessed in his own life as well as in southern Colorado more generally.

IV. In 1986 Dr. James Vitale moved from Youngstown, Ohio, to the Island of Maui in Hawaii. A native of Youngstown, Vitale was born in 1945. He traces his ancestry to Calabria and Basilicata. This longtime physician lived for decades in a heavily Southern and Eastern European environment, one that is quite different demographically from his current home in Maui. When he first arrived in Hawaii, Vitale saw many surnames that he thought might be Italian. After all, certain Filipino, Japanese, and Portuguese surnames end in vowels. Vitale, of course, proudly embraces the multiethnic, multicultural nature of Maui and, more broadly, Hawaii. To this end, he reports that the Italian-American "culture is much more visible over there" on Oahu, compared to Maui.[71]

Dr. Vitale is passionate about his Italian heritage, and he promotes Italian-American culture through his family life and involvement in the Italian American Club of Maui. The former Ohioan speaks basic Italian—and he regularly visits his ancestral homeland. James Vitale's children, who are one-half Italian and have been raised in Hawaii, identify strongly with their Italian ancestry due to their family's taste for Italian cooking and observance of Italian customs. Vitale, moreover, cofounded and has served as president of the Italian American Club of Maui, a group that celebrates Hawaii's cultural diversity and inclusiveness. According to Dr. Vitale, "the aloha spirit permeates our Italian with a little Hawaiian flair."[72] Indeed, Italian Americans, many of whom are transplants from elsewhere in the United States, add to Hawaii's unique ethnic, racial, and cultural milieu.

These days Italian Americans, along with Americans from so many ethnic groups, continue to migrate to the southern and western states of our nation. As Phylis Cancilla Martinelli writes: "By the 1980s the trend of older generation Italian Americans was to leave the areas in which they had resided for lengthy periods and flock to the Sun Belt regions as their retirement locale of choice. The Carolinas, Florida, Arizona, New Mexico, and California have drawn these Italian Americans in great numbers."[73] Besides the South and West, Italian Americans migrate to such places as New Hampshire and Ocean County, New Jersey, too. Arizona remains quite popular as a destination for Italian Americans, who constitute 4.4 percent of the state's population. Scottsdale, Arizona, in particular has drawn Italian-American migrants from midwestern and northeastern states.[74] Now 8.5 percent of Scottsdale's residents come from Italian family backgrounds.

Nevada, meanwhile, is another western state with a visible Italian-American population. In 2000 people of Italian descent accounted for 6.6 percent of Nevada's residents. The Italian-American presence in Nevada dates back to the nineteenth century but it also includes large numbers of in-migrants during the last sixty years. These longtime Nevadans of Italian descent, whose ancestors have been in the Silver State for generations, often live in central and northern Nevada. Their progenitors engaged in mining, farming, ranching, and entrepreneurial pursuits. In places like Ely, Elko, Reno, and Winnemucca, people from Italian family backgrounds integrated into the mainstream culture relatively quickly.[75] Blanton Owen notes that "the visible evidence of Italians in the state is sometimes little more than a name in a phone book or on a mail box."[76]

Most Italian-American residents of Las Vegas and environs, as with most Nevadans in general, moved to Nevada during the last six decades (or had relatives who did so).[77] Alan Balboni, a Las Vegan who originally came from Massachusetts, writes about his coethnics in southern Nevada: "Italian Americans in Las Vegas today are a well-assimilated ethnic group. The assimilation process occurred more rapidly in Las Vegas than in the Eastern cities from which the great majority of southern Nevada immigrants came during the post–World War II years. No doors were closed to the Italian-American immigrants in the West."[78]

Neighboring California, too, is a state where Italian Americans have not encountered many closed doors.[79] The 2000 census counted 1,450,884 Italian Americans in California, an ethnic group that constituted 4.3 percent of the state's population. Contemporary Italian Californians span the spectrum from Italian-born professionals who arrived in Los Angeles last year to sixth-generation Californians whose ancestors came to the Golden State during the 1850s. In fact, there is a substantial population of Italians from Italy, many of whom live transnational lifestyles, who work and reside on the Westside of Los Angeles.[80] At the same time, numerous Italian Americans in the San Joaquin Valley are fifth-, sixth-, and seventh-generation Californians.[81]

Gloria Ricci Lothrop describes the history of California's large and diverse Italian-American community:

> This population could be classified into four categories based upon the period of arrival. The earliest, largely representing the northern regions of Italy, came in the mid-19th century as goldseekers and early agriculturists. The second group, representing the period of mass migration from 1870 to the passage of the Immigration Act of 1924 which reduced the annual quota of Italian immigrants to a mere 5,500, drew heavily from southern Italy and Sicily. The third category, arriving after World War II, consisted largely of war brides and Italian Americans migrating to California from America's East and Midwest. Most recent arrivals, who constitute the fourth category, are middle-class urban professionals. Many are the products of Italy's economic boom of the 1960s.[82]

Elsewhere in the United States, Florida continues to be a premier Sun Belt destination. Florida's Italian-American population keeps growing larger, due to the tremendous in-migration to the Sunshine State from other parts of the country. Florida has become progressively less "southern" over the years, a direct consequence of its large numbers of domestic migrants and foreign immigrants.[83] Still, Italian-American transplants sometimes had adjustment difficulties when they first came to Florida in the 1950s, 1960s, 1970s, and 1980s. One such individual—she moved to Florida in 1969—told me that, at first, she experienced "culture shock." (Florida was much more "southern" then than it is today.) Italian-American transplants have played a role in making Florida a "national" state that encompasses people from all over America—and the Americas. Recent censuses have recorded significant increases in Florida's Italian-American population: by 1990, there were almost 800,000 people of Italian origin in the state.[84]

More than 1,000,000-plus Italian Americans lived in Florida in 2000; overall, they accounted for 6.3 percent of Florida's population then. Of the 50 U.S. metropolitan areas with the largest numbers of Italian Americans, six of them are in Florida: 11) Miami–Fort Lauderdale; 13) Tampa–St. Petersburg–Clearwater; 27) West Palm Beach–Boca Raton; 44) Jacksonville; 46) Daytona Beach; and 47) Sarasota–Bradenton.[85] Two particular bastions of Italian Americans exist in Palm Beach and Broward counties north of Miami. In 2000 Palm Beach County, Florida, was 9.4 percent Italian with a total population of 1,131,184. Palm Beach County includes such communities as Jupiter (16.8 percent Italian) and Wellington (14.6 percent Italian). Similarly, 9.5 percent of Broward County, Florida's 1,623,018 residents were Italian Americans in 2000. Coral Springs exemplifies Broward County's vibrant Italian presence. This growing city of 130,000 residents was 14.2 percent Italian in the last federal census.

By 2000 there were numerous Florida counties and communities with sizable Italian-American percentages. The Florida counties where Italian Americans constituted at least ten percent of the population in 2000 included: Martin County (10.5 percent Italian); St. Lucie County (10.9 percent Italian); Pasco County (11.0 percent Italian); Hernando County (12.8 percent Italian); and Flagler County (12.9 percent Italian). In Florida, such communities as Palm Coast (15.3 percent Italian), Spring Hill (18.0 percent Italian), and Port St. Lucie (15.7 percent Italian) are among those with particularly high Italian-American percentages. Indeed, people with Italian ancestors are well represented in many parts of the Sunshine State, except for certain traditionally "Southern" places.

Many native Midwesterners and Northeasterners who live in Florida still maintain ties to such states as Ohio, Michigan, New York, and New Jersey. These Floridians regularly return to the Midwest and Northeast for holidays and special events. In the past, numerous people even brought such items as baccalà and Italian bread back to Florida after visiting the Northeast. In particular, there is a significant amount of New York–Florida traffic and migration, primarily by airplane and automobile along Interstate 95.[86] To be sure, one regularly sees Florida license plates in New York City and environs. New Yorkers account for the largest number of part-time residents in Florida, and people describe the Miami area as "the Sixth Borough" of New York City.[87] The typical middle-aged or elderly Italian-American Floridian, it seems, comes from somewhere else; s/he often speaks American English with midwestern or northeastern inflections.

Italian-American transplants to Florida often have interesting stories about what it was like when they first moved there. Ben Mercadante, for one, arrived in Florida in 1956. "When I came to Florida, there were few Italians," says Mercadante, who grew up in Utica, New York. Italian delis, bakeries, and restaurants were in short supply. The longtime Floridian is a former president of the Italian American Club of Greater Clearwater. His colleagues include Nick and Madeline Ciani and Tony and Amelia (Amy) Odorisio. In 1972 the Cianis departed from Staten Island for Florida. Two years later, the Odorisios moved to Florida from Totowa, New Jersey. In 1975 Tony Odorisio was a carpenter working on a job site in Clearwater. He heard later from his colleagues, "We all came around to see where you were working. We wanted to see what an Italian (pronounced EYE-talian) looked like." In addition, the Odorisios heard all the time that they spoke with accents when they first moved to Clearwater.[88]

As recently as the 1980s, Italian-American migrants to Florida experienced some difficulties in finding their ideal foods. In the mid-1980s one could not purchase certain Italian culinary items in Jacksonville, according to John and Patty Koch. Between 1986 and 1995, the Koches returned periodically to New York (their original home). Each time they visited New York, they put a cooler full of ravioli, salami, Italian bread, Italian cheeses, and Italian sausage in the trunk of their vehicle to take with them to Florida. Then Costco, Publix, and Sam's Club began to stock Italian foods in Jacksonville, once Italian Americans and others asked for them.[89] Now one can live in Jacksonville and purchase all the items needed to be on a Mediterranean diet.

The Koches' experiences were shared by other Italian-American transplants to Florida. Julie Calabrese and her spouse, Albert Calabrese, moved from New Jersey to the Tampa–St. Petersburg–Clearwater metropolitan area in 1989/1990. Initially, Mrs. Calabrese experienced "culture shock," in part because of the difficulties she encountered in finding Italian foods, particularly good Italian bread. Today she has numerous options to purchase the staples of an Italian-American diet, due to the stores that Italian-American newcomers have opened in the region.[90] Similarly, when Dominick and Joan Filipponi first came from Long Island to the west coast of Florida in 1989, they could not obtain ricotta, mozzarella, or certain types of macaroni locally. These foods are now available in their area, a reflection of the popularity of Italian cuisine and the growing presence of Italian Americans from the Northeast and elsewhere.[91]

☙ ☙ ☙

Italian Americans can be found throughout the United States, a demographic fact that alternately amazes, delights, and entertains people from the heavily Italian sections of America. Initially, they may be taken aback to hear about the Italian-American presence in such states as Iowa, Colorado, and Kentucky. One Kentuckian finds that people outside the Bluegrass State ask her with incredulity: "You're Italian, you're Catholic, *and you're a southerner?*" As a native of Wisconsin, I find people in other parts of America who are often surprised—and sometimes amused—by the Italian-American presence in the Badger State. One New Yorker told me how it makes him happy to know that Italians live virtually everywhere in the United States. He enjoys hearing that Italian Americans contribute to many different communities across our nation.

Italians in areas with small Italian-American populations have an especially important impact on their ethnic group's image. Fewer people come into contact with Italians as a group in such places. Therefore, they may draw their impressions of Americans of Italian descent at least in part from their interactions from the Italians of their acquaintance. Some Italian Americans have described to me how they thought about what it would be like to relocate to a new place with relatively few Italians. Before he moved there, one man imagined that Flagstaff, Arizona, would be barren of Italian-American culture. Another Italian American told me that her mother felt she might encounter prejudice or hostility when she went to live in a small city in Virginia. These initial apprehensions proved to be unfounded, however.

Good food can serve as a useful outreach tool for Italian Americans who are interacting with members of other ethnic groups. In June 2007, for instance, Italians from the OSIA Frances Cabrini Lodge in Winchester, Virginia, had a booth at Sacred Heart Catholic Church's Parish Fair, where they sold cannoli, along with pasta and Italian ice.[92] In the past, when Winchester's Sons of Italy members began selling cannoli at community events to raise funds, people came up to them and asked: "What is a cannoli?" Soon they became familiar with these delectable pastries. Now they come up to the Italians of Winchester and say: "Where are the cannoli?"[93]

Jacksonville, Florida, is another place where Italian Americans have used food as an outreach tool. The Italian American Club of Jacksonville won the "People's Choice Award" in Jacksonville's World of Nations Celebration in 2005. Many native southerners went to the festival. The southerners enjoy ketchup, mustard, and mayonnaise on their Italian foods. Consequently, the Italian-American transplants in Jacksonville joked with them, particularly concerning their habit of putting mayonnaise on sausage-and-pepper sandwiches. They engaged in lighthearted repartee and mimicked each other's regional accents.[94] These intercultural experiences contribute to positive impressions of Italian Americans, as the members of the Italian American Club of Jacksonville interact with individuals who may not have much contact with people of Italian origin.

To this end, the members of the Italian Cultural Association of Greater Austin focus on community events and charitable activities. They come to these venues to present a favorable image of Italian Americans. The Austin Italians had a booth with sausage-and-pepper sandwiches at an art festival in 2005, for example. "It was a learning experience for the locals," notes Robert Calvisi, a Detroit native who moved with his wife, Linda, to Texas in 1984. "People were looking for tacos." The Austin residents were curious about sausage-and-pepper sandwiches, and they wanted to know if you put mustard on them. Calvisi and his compatriots also have a periodic movie night with a free Italian film to invite the general public, in part as a means of educating non-Italians about Italian culture. "It is really cool to be Italian now in Austin," says Calvisi. "Things Italian," he continues, "are really hot."[95]

Atlanta, Georgia, is another part of the United States where Italian-American migrants are becoming increasingly common. Marge DeBenedetto, a Calabrian American from Minnesota's Iron Range, and her husband, George DeBenedetto, a Sicilian American from Louisiana, helped to cofound La Società Italiana Inc. in Georgia in 1986. Mrs. DeBenedetto says that most of the group's 152 members are transplants from such states as New York, New Jersey, and Connecticut. Atlanta, of course, is not exactly a bastion of Italian Americans. Marge DeBenedetto reports that she and her colleagues receive many inquiries, particularly e-mails to La Società Italiana's Web site, from people who may relocate to Georgia. They wonder if there are good Italian delis, bakeries, and restaurants in and around Atlanta. In general, the prospective migrants want to know more about the Italian presence in Georgia's largest metropolitan area; they seek to determine whether they would be comfortable living there.[96]

As a rule, the most heavily Italian parts of America will become less Italian in the coming years, just as the Italian presence increases elsewhere. Some communities with sizable Italian percentages may decline in population, if economic conditions lead younger people to move in search of opportunities to such states as Arizona, Florida, Georgia, and North Carolina. To be sure, Italians will remain a numerically significant ethnic group in the Northeast, industrial Midwest, California, Colorado, Louisiana, and elsewhere. The Northeast, moreover, will continue to have many of the institutional centers of Italian America, as well as many of the cultural opportunities that define what it means to be Italian in our country.

Chapter 9

ETHNIC NEIGHBORHOODS

Spanish and Italian speakers once worked side by side in the cigar factories of Ybor City, a section of Tampa, Florida, a century ago.[1] John Spoto remembers that his Sicilian-immigrant grandfather learned to speak English and Spanish in addition to his native Italian after he came to Ybor City to work in the cigar industry. The Cuban, Spanish, and Italian cigar workers communicated with each other in Spanish and Italian, and they even formulated some words that combined the two languages. Spoto and his friend, Vince Pardo, grew up using the Spanish words *mantequilla* for butter and *ventana* for window instead of the Italian words *burro* and *finestra*, respectively.[2] Similarly, Pete and Josie Noto of Tampa remember how their Italian grandmother used the Spanish word *leche* in lieu of the Italian *latte* for milk. Her seatmates at the cigar factory were Cuban. Rolling cigars was a monotonous task—and the workers spoke to each other regularly.[3] These conversations resulted in many friendships as well as linguistic and cultural exchanges among the Latins (as Cubans, Italians, and Spaniards were known in Tampa then).[4]

Tampa has been home to an Italian community for more than one hundred years, perhaps most notably in the city's Ybor City section.[5] The majority of the Tampa Italians—at least those whose roots there predate the tremendous in-migration to Florida from the other parts of the country—trace their ancestry to the Province of Agrigento in Sicily, particularly the towns of Cianciana, Alessandria della Rocca, and Santo Stefano Quisquina. These communities are not far from each other and they share a similar dialect.[6] Initially, the Italian immigrants were not always accepted by Tampans from Anglo backgrounds: In 1910 a mob lynched two Italian suspected criminals in Tampa.[7] Over the years, however, the Tampa Italians became a fully integrated part of the city's mainstream culture.[8] The list of Tampa's mayors includes such Italian Americans as Nick Nuccio, Dick Greco, and the city's current chief executive, Pam Iorio. Today there is a tangible Italian-American presence in Tampa, a place where people of Italian origin account for 5.6 percent of the population.

L'Unione Italiana (The Italian Club of Tampa) is an Ybor City institution that preserves Tampa's Italian-American culture; it dates back to 1894.[9] At one time, L'Unione Italiana was a "cradle-to-grave mutual aid society," according to Vince Pardo, who was born in Ybor City. He has been a member of L'Unione Italiana since his birth. Pardo is the fourth consecutive Vincent Pardo in a line of five Vincenzo Pardos that extends to his thirtysomething son, Vince "Enzo" Pardo.[10] His father, Vincenzo "Jimmy" Pardo, was president of the Italian Club of Tampa in the 1960s. Vince Pardo himself served as president of L'Unione Italiana during the 1980s. His grandfather played dominos there after work in the 1940s, 1950s, and 1960s.[11] All of Pardo's grandparents and great-grandparents participated extensively in L'Unione Italiana.

The Italian Club of Tampa transitioned out of its mutual-aid phase during the mid-1980s. Around this time, L'Unione Italiana's leadership started working toward the historic-cultural-preservation phase of the Club's history. The Italian-American preservationists earned some grants in the 1980s for the restoration of L'Unione Italiana's magnificent building on East Seventh Street in Ybor City. The Club's current events and activities include Italian-language classes, an Italian children's group, the Krewe of Italia for younger members, and the Sorrento Cheese Festa Italiana.[12] Vince Pardo brings in a dance troupe from Agrigento, Sicily, every other year for Tampa's Festa Italiana. Italian-American families host the Sicilian dancers in their homes.[13]

There is a Sister City relationship between Tampa and Agrigento. Vince Pardo, the manager of the Ybor City Development Corporation, founded the Agrigento Sister City relationship during the early 1990s. He did so in conjunction with the centennial of Ybor City. Pardo and his compatriots selected Agrigento as Tampa's Sister City, as it was the capital of the province that includes the ancestral towns of most Tampa Sicilians. Pardo continues to serve as chairman of the Tampa-Agrigento Sister Cities Committee. This committee offers regular tours of Sicily. These flexible tours allow the heritage tourists to rekindle family connections. The Italian-American visitors light up when they see their family name on a Sicilian street sign, for example. Such homecomings have involved marching bands, genealogical research, official receptions with local dignitaries, the flags of Italy and the United States, and even banners that read "Welcome Americans."[14]

Members of the Pardo family themselves regularly travel to Sicily. In 1992 Jimmy Pardo and his son, Vince, went to Sicily together. Jimmy Pardo had never been to his ancestral homeland before. "It was like a religious experience for him," Vince Pardo said of his father, as he reflected on this trip. In advance of their visit to Italy, Vince Pardo contacted his grandfather's cousin in Sicily; both men had written to each other over the years. The Sicilian cousin, it turns out, had saved all the letters from his American relative. He brought out the letters when the Pardos visited his Sicilian home. Since 1992 Vince Pardo has gone to Sicily numerous times.[15]

His Italian-speaking son, Vince "Enzo" Pardo, makes regular visits to Sicily, too. In 2005 Enzo Pardo married Maria Capitano, an American-born native of Tampa who is 100 percent Sicilian, in Sicily. Their wedding took place in Agrigento's "Valley of the Temples." The city's mayor married the two Floridians and, later, the newlyweds had a reception at L'Unione Italiana in Ybor City. (They met each other at the Italian Club.)[16] Enzo and Maria Pardo represent the vanguard of younger Americans who seek to maintain connections to Sicily and their Sicilian heritage.

The traditions of Sicily continue to be important in Tampa, particularly among middle-aged and elderly people from Sicilian backgrounds. Vince Pardo wears a pendant with the Trinacria—the symbol of Sicily and also L'Unione Italiana—around his neck. His father, grandparents, and great-grandparents are buried in L'Unione Italiana Cemetery/The Italian Club Cemetery in Tampa. Vince Pardo has purchased a crypt there as well. The next generations of the Pardo family continue to respect their ancestral customs and heritage.[17] For example, Vince and Enzo Pardo make wine together each year.[18] Both men take pride in their family's deep roots in Sicily and Ybor City alike. After years of decline, the Ybor City Historic District has become a fashionable area.[19] This venerable section of Tampa is an "ethnic neighborhood," a community in which people from different and identifiable ethnic backgrounds live, work, and socialize side by side.[20]

❋I.   The Cercone family's roots in Pittsburgh's Bloomfield neigh-
      borhood date back to 1922, the year Dan Cercone immigrated
from Abruzzi with his family to Pittsburgh at the age of twelve. When
Mr. Cercone opened his business (Dan Cercone's Barbershop) on Liberty
Avenue in Bloomfield during the early 1930s, an invitation to join the
Bloomfield Merchants, as they were called in that era, was not forthcom-
ing. As an Italian immigrant, he did not fit into what was then a heavily
German business community. Initially, business was a struggle for Cer-
cone because of his youth, his ethnicity, and the economic hard times.
Early on, though, Dan Cercone sponsored athletic teams in Bloomfield.
The teams proved to be very successful, and the Cercone name has been
on sports jerseys in Pittsburgh for more than seven decades.[21]

Eventually, Dan Cercone's barbering business flourished and he
became a member of the Bloomfield Business Association after World
War II. Cercone, a go-getter, served as a longtime leader of the organization, including the position of Chairman of the Board of Directors in
1984. In addition to his civic activities, this top barber sponsored new Italian immigrants during the postwar years. His wife, Mary D'Amico Cercone (who was the daughter of Abruzzese immigrants), found apartments
for the Italian newcomers and filled their refrigerators with Italian food.
Indeed, the Cercones were deeply involved in their community, the reason why Dan and Mary Cercone received the Key to the City of Pittsburgh.[22] Today Dan Cercone's Barbershop continues to be in business:
His grandson, Dennis Scullion, cuts hair in his late grandfather's chair,
where he himself had his first haircut.[23]

Meanwhile, Dan Cercone's daughter, Janet Cercone Scullion, is a
devoted promoter of Bloomfield. This lifelong Bloomfield resident currently serves as President of the Bloomfield Citizens Council and Executive Director of the Bloomfield Preservation and Heritage Society.[24] Scullion is also a member of the board of the John Heinz Regional History
Center—Italian American Center. She built the Cercone Village on the
Park, a three-story Medical Office Building that has created 100 new jobs
in this small community. Cercone Village on the Park also houses the
neighborhood History Center and pays tribute to America's immigrants.[25]

Each year Bloomfield, which is known as Pittsburgh's Little Italy, hosts
the Little Italy Days Festival. This three-day festival in late September
brings, on average, ten to twelve thousand people to Bloomfield. The visitors enjoy Italian food, listen to Italian music, watch bocce players com-

pete in a tournament, cheer on the contestants in the pizza eating contest, and attend the Italian Mass and view the street procession offered in conjunction with the festival.[26] "Produced by the Bloomfield Business Association," notes one account, "this event helps to nurture Bloomfield's Little Italy identity, to promote family values and the community to the region, and to encourage people to live, work, shop and play here in the future."[27]

Neighborhoods like Bloomfield, which are identified with Italian Americans and their culture, can be found in many towns and cities throughout the United States. The best-known Italian enclaves tend to be in America's larger urban areas. These Little Italy districts usually date back to the period of mass immigration from Italy, during which people from particular regional backgrounds often clustered together in an attempt to recreate the ambience of home and provide themselves with a certain amount of security. While these neighborhoods may have appeared "Italian" to outsiders, they were not always ethnically homogeneous communities. During the 1950s, 1960s, and 1970s, a number of the big-city Italian neighborhoods underwent substantial demographic shifts. These changes occurred due to such factors as urban renewal efforts, the empowerment of minority groups, and the movement of upwardly mobile white ethnics to the suburbs.[28]

There continue to be a number of viable Italian enclaves in our nation. They are referred to as Little Italys/Little Italies, Little Italy sections, districts, or neighborhoods, and by their particular names (Bloomfield, "The Hill," the North End, South Philadelphia). Sometimes the best-known street of the Little Italy neighborhood is commonly used as a shorthand for the entire enclave, as in Wooster Street (New Haven), Arthur Avenue (the Bronx), Mulberry Street (Manhattan), and Taylor Street (Chicago). Many well-known Italian-American neighborhoods—e.g., North Beach, Bensonhurst, and the Federal Hill section of Providence—are found in cities and regions with large and visible Italian-American populations. However, some Little Italy neighborhoods exist in states with relatively few Italian Americans, including Millinocket, Maine, The Hill neighborhood of Saint Louis, and the Greenbush section of Madison, Wisconsin.

Jerome Krase describes the demographics and cultural characteristics of Little Italy neighborhoods. Krase writes:

> The taken-for-granted ethno-territorial label "Little Italy" is generally applied in ordinary, as well as academic, parlance only to those urban neighborhoods whose appearances (physical structure and observable social life) are easily recognized

by passersby and social researchers alike, as meeting particular sensory criteria. Adding to the sociological mystique of the territory, however, is the fact that, for example, although Little Italys are frequently described as having *Old World Italian* airs, in most cases what is defined as *Old World*, or even *Italian* is arbitrarily ill-defined, if defined at all. People just seem to know when they are in a *real* Italian neighborhood.[29]

In America's traditionally Italian enclaves, there are numerous indicators of the districts' Italian heritage, including Italian-themed stores, events, festivals, restaurants, and cultural amenities. These neighborhoods often have green-white-and-red iconography, in such forms as banners and markings on fire hydrants, lampposts, and street signs. There are parks, streets, statues, and other landmarks named for local Italian-American dignitaries and nationally and internationally known figures of Italian extraction (particularly Christopher Columbus) in Italian neighborhoods. In addition, bocce courts exist in such places as South Philadelphia, Baltimore's Little Italy, and the North Beach neighborhood of San Francisco. These ethnic touches can make the Italian sections attractive to outsiders. Indeed, some Little Italy districts have become "destination points" or "destination neighborhoods," whereby tourists specifically visit them in search of Italian/American culture.

Marco Li Mandri offers an important perspective on Little Italy neighborhoods and other ethnic enclaves. The San Diegan's company, New City America, helps form assessment districts that fund efforts to revitalize businesses and neighborhoods in different parts of the United States.[30] "All in all, New City America has formed nearly fifty similar community benefit districts over the past ten years," writes Li Mandri. "However, Little Italy in San Diego is the only one they manage."[31] Li Mandri and New City America work in conjunction with the Little Italy Association to maintain San Diego's Little Italy.

As a veteran of community redevelopment efforts, Li Mandri discusses how ethnic enclaves can maintain and even enhance their vitality. He posits that there are four factors you need to rejuvenate a community: 1) vision, 2) leadership, 3) resources, and 4) time and place. In addition, the three types of Little Italy neighborhoods ("ascending," "neutral," or "descending") form a schema that Marco Li Mandri says can be applied to any neighborhood. This grandson of Sicilian immigrants notes how it is absolutely essential— a "key, critical component" of the redevelopment of any Little Italy—that the Italian-American property owners do not sell their property.[32]

San Diego's thriving Little Italy is a nationally recognized success story as to how an Italian neighborhood can maintain its authenticity while appealing to people from many different ethnic backgrounds.[33] During the last fifteen years or so, the Little Italy section of San Diego has evolved from a traditional ethnic community to an enclave where committed homeowners, civic leaders, and business owners have worked together to encourage tourism, initiate cultural activities, and develop the area's status as a recognizable "brand." Marco Li Mandri characterizes San Diego's Little Italy as "a twenty-first-century urban neighborhood" and describes this public space as having "a great heritage."[34] There are numerous events and activities there, including ArtWalk, Carnevale, Opera Nights, the Christmas Tree Lighting, the Italian Motor Sport Show, and the State of the Neighborhood Dinner. The annual Little Italy Festa in October draws 100,000-plus people on one day.[35]

As he notes the vitality of San Diego's Little Italy, Li Mandri describes other goals that he and his colleagues hope to achieve. They want to link the different generations of Italian-American San Diegans more closely, for example. In a 2004 interview, Li Mandri observed, "We are heading rapidly into a post–Little Italy world." He is working on "rebuilding the critical mass" and attracting Italian-American retirees and professionals to San Diego's Little Italy.[36] The San Diego example demonstrates how a venerable ethnic enclave can develop new life, even as its traditional raison d'être may have changed over the years.

Cleveland's Little Italy on Mayfield Road offers another example of a reborn and popular Italian enclave. The Little Italy Redevelopment Corporation is an important part of the revitalization of Little Italy, a Historic District in Cleveland.[37] Little Italy is on the east side of Cleveland, near some major hospitals and the Case Western Reserve University campus. In 2000, 3,500 residents lived in this neighborhood, many of whom were Asian-American students from Case Western Reserve University. According to the Master Plan, 80 percent of the businesspeople in Cleveland's Little Italy are Italian Americans. The "perception from the outside" is that the neighborhood is heavily Italian, according to Laurie Penca of the Little Italy Redevelopment Corporation. "Actually," Penca notes, "it is quite mixed."[38]

Little Italy, of course, is thriving in Cleveland. Penca observes that the "allure" of Italian culture and "the ethnic flavor" bring tourists and shoppers to the area. A native of Cleveland, Laurie Penca describes how "Little Italy has gone through different stages." This neighborhood "flourished" in the late 1800s. Penca notes that the community's reputation "went down a bit" from the late 1960s to the mid-1980s. Devotees of Little Italy worked together to revitalize the neighborhood and it "started flourishing again" during the 1990s. Currently, Little Italy has new housing, regular rental inquiries, rising real estate values, and a shortage of parking. The gentrification process in the Little Italy of Cleveland continues today, as community advocates seek stronger code enforcement and want to encourage more homeownership.[39]

II. The North Beach neighborhood of San Francisco regularly receives national and even international recognition.[40] In 2004 the "Project for Public Spaces chose North Beach as the No. 3 neighborhood in all of North America," according to Marsha Garland, the founder and executive director of the North Beach Chamber of Commerce in San Francisco. The same year, Garland remembers that the "*London Times* selected North Beach as San Francisco's No. 1 neighborhood." And the American Planning Association recently listed North Beach as one of the ten "2007 Great Neighborhoods in America."[41] These honors recognize the unique atmosphere and high quality of life valued by North Beach's residents and businesspeople (and enjoyed by the area's many tourists).

A native of a country market town just north of London, Marsha Garland is a longtime booster of North Beach. She immigrated with her mother, stepfather, half sister, grandmother, and aunt to the United States in the 1950s. Her father, a Royal Air Force officer in the Bomber Command, was killed near the end of World War II. Garland is one-eighth Italian: Her great-grandmother, Emma Di Maria, immigrated from Italy to Britain. In a 2005 interview, this English-born American recalled that her mother and aunt's Mediterranean complexions led some Californians to mistake them for Mexicans when they came to the United States. Marsha Garland values and identifies with her Italian heritage, and she describes herself as having been "involved in North Beach since the 1960s."[42]

The longtime San Franciscan characterizes North Beach as "a neighborhood and a tourist destination." Tourism definitely contributes much revenue to San Francisco's economy. Marsha Garland founded the North Beach Chamber of Commerce in 1986 to promote the culture and businesses of this ethnically diverse community. There is a substantial Chinese presence in North Beach: Garland reports that "60 percent of the properties are owned by Asians." Conversely, she says that "the merchant community is 70 percent Italian owned or with an Italian flavor." During the late 1980s, her marketing materials for North Beach included Chinese references because of the community's large Chinese population.[43]

Soon, though, Marsha Garland focused on North Beach as San Francisco's Little Italy—the Chinese activists supported her decision to market this neighborhood as an Italian enclave. After the 1989 earthquake in San Francisco, Garland and her colleagues concluded that the Little Italy references would attract the largest number of tourists to the neighborhood. Around 1990 local businesses began to embrace what they were doing to promote North Beach.[44] Today this culturally rich district enjoys a close association with San Francisco's Italian heritage and presence. It is, in essence, a Little Italy of the twenty-first century.

Garland has pursued an Italian connection for North Beach both as a matter of symbols and substance. Perhaps most prominently, the colors of the Italian flag are painted on the lampposts of North Beach's streets. And there are street signs marking Columbus Avenue as Corso Cristoforo Colombo in San Francisco's Little Italy. "By marketing North Beach as Little Italy, it became more Italian," reports Garland. "There are more Italian businesses opening here now." The merchants see that it makes economic sense to stress the Italian nature of the neighborhood, as this connection resonates with tourists. To preserve North Beach's distinctive character, Garland successfully challenged the introduction of several chain stores.[45]

This community leader always tries to ensure that North Beach plays a role in San Francisco events. During the Olympic Torch Run, for instance, the runners came down Columbus Avenue. Marsha Garland bought "many flowers, pulled off the petals, and showered them in front of the athletes."[46] Each year Garland produces the North Beach Festival, which at fifty-four in 2008 is the "oldest outdoor arts and crafts festival in the country." This festival draws seventy to eighty thousand people annually. Garland reports that she tries "to infuse some Italian culture into it," including Italian chalk street art (Arte di Gesso) and an animal blessing at the National Shrine of St. Francis of Assisi.[47] In sum, the vibrancy of San Francisco's North Beach neighborhood reflects—and contributes to—the popularity of Italian-American culture in our nation.

Little Italy neighborhoods have become glamorous in certain parts of America, as their symbols of Italian ethnicity draw people to shops, delis, restaurants, ethnic festivals, and cultural events. In recent years, there have been a variety of efforts (with varying amounts of success) to preserve, promote, and, in some cases, recreate Little Italys as a means of attracting shoppers and tourists to various communities. Some Little Italy neighborhoods are heavily Italian and see relatively few tourists while others are gentrifying rapidly and attract many visitors. Italian restaurants and Catholic churches continue to be popular components of the quintessential Little Italy districts. In addition, organizations (e.g., the Little Italy Merchants Association in New York City and the Little Italy Neighborhood Association in Wilmington, Delaware) promote the respective Little Italy neighborhoods.

The North End of Boston is one of America's best-known Little Italy sections and most celebrated ethnic enclaves. The North End was 95 percent Italian during the 1930s and 1940s, when the neighborhood's population reached as high as 42,000. As of 2000, the North End's population was 12,500 inhabitants—and Italian Americans accounted for approximately 30 percent of them. This fabled neighborhood draws a substantial number of visitors and residents with few, if any, ancestral connections to Italy or Italian-American culture. It includes expensive real estate, fashionable restaurants, and a charming ambience that appeals to many people. At the same time, the changing image and demographics of the North End of Boston have led some longtime residents to feel that the neighborhood's traditional sense of community is disappearing.[48]

In any event, the North End of Boston has become chic. Writing in 2000, Erla Zwingle noted:

> The North End is "hot." It started in the early eighties, when an area once considered a slum suddenly appeared as a great place: College students wanted a safe neighborhood, young couples who had traveled liked the European atmosphere, and driven professionals wanted to be able to walk to their jobs in the nearby financial district. Rents have shot up, and the resulting exodus of families has meant that schools and stores, and even churches, are closing. Shops keep turning into restaurants, and some of them, despite names like Rabia's and Il Villaggio, are actually owned by non-Italians, their kitchens full of anxious, silent workers from North Africa and Central America doing the work that their predecessors once were lucky to find. Real estate speculation, powerful as a tectonic plate, is moving everything around.[49]

Rising property values typify Chicago's Taylor Street neighborhood as well. Italian immigrants and their descendants have lived in this Little Italy on the Near West Side of Chicago since the late nineteenth century. With increasing affluence, Italian families left Little Italy in the postwar years to live in suburban Chicago (Franklin Park and Elmwood Park were favored destinations). Today the Taylor Street neighborhood continues to see ethnic and generational shifts: Students from the University of Illinois at Chicago are replacing older Italian Americans who relocate to the suburbs. Italian Americans, to be sure, continue to own many of the buildings in Chicago's Little Italy.[50]

It can be difficult to promote and preserve the genuine ethnic roots of a community such as Taylor Street, even while the area enjoys large amounts of gentrification, soaring real estate values, and a booming scene for Italian restaurants. The Taylor Street neighborhood is close to Chicago's downtown area. Consequently, during the real estate boom several years ago, one regularly saw veteran neighborhood residents selling their properties and moving elsewhere. As a result, some Italians on Taylor Street bemoan the irrevocable loss of the ethnic connections and the closeness of Italian-American community that once existed there.[51] "The neighborhood is on an economic upswing, yet progress continues at the expense of Little Italy's authentic ethnic heritage," write Matthew A. Paolelli and Craig Tiede. "The lingering question is whether the neighborhood remains a truly Italian community or is simply cashing in on a commercialized tourist version of a bygone era."[52]

Demographic changes, the gentrification process, and related dynamics have resulted in the evolution of Taylor Street's ethnic ambience.[53] "It's a different type of ethnicity," notes Professor John Betancur. "It's a gathering place. It's a symbol, but it's not the community itself as in the old days that was intimately linked, where residents bought from their own stores. The Italians are more scattered and they go there to eat, but they don't stay there."[54] Betancur contends that ethnic neighborhoods in Chicago are eventually going to symbolize the ethnic traditions of yesteryear, yet they will do so as commercial districts that draw tourists and residents from many ethnic and national backgrounds.[55] "What people identify as Little Italy is the restaurant now, but it puts our community on the map," says Christopher Provenzano, who serves as executive director of the University Village Association. "Those Italian-themed businesses always strike a chord with people. It gives the community an identity, a marketing and promotional tool, and there's still a strong base in the community."[56]

Even today there are a number of Little Italy neighborhoods in New

York City. According to the 2000 census, people of Italian ancestry accounted for 8.7 percent of New York City's 8,000,000-plus residents. By borough, the Italian-American demographics are as follows: the Bronx (5.2 percent Italian), Manhattan (5.5 percent Italian), Brooklyn (7.5 percent Italian), Queens (8.4 percent Italian), and Staten Island (37.7 percent Italian). By 2000, West Indian Americans outnumbered Italian Americans substantially in Brooklyn, a borough typically associated with Italian Americans. Still, after decades of out-migration by Italian Americans, there are pockets of Italians in the Big Apple. The Howard Beach section of Queens is 47 percent Italian, for instance.[57]

New York City continues to draw tourists to its Little Italy neighborhoods, particularly Mulberry Street in Manhattan and Arthur Avenue in the Belmont section of the Bronx. The Little Italy on Mulberry Street is one of America's best-known ethnic neighborhoods, even as it has become a tourist attraction more than anything else. "New York's Little Italy," writes Michael Powell, "has become almost wholly a marketing venture, its restaurant row snaking between wealthy yuppies of no particular ethnic flavor and an ever-expanding Chinatown."[58] Similarly, the Belmont neighborhood of the Bronx is fabled for being a bastion of Italian Americans. People flock to Arthur Avenue (its main thoroughfare) to dine at restaurants, shop for Italian foodstuffs, and attend Mass at Our Lady of Mount Carmel Church, which offers two daily Italian Masses.

III. Father Matthew Mauriello likes to reminisce about the Italian-American community of his youth. Indeed, he has a "longing for the days of yesteryear." "It was spectacular," remembers Mauriello of the rich and vibrant Italian-American culture of his childhood and young adult years during the 1950s, 1960s, and early 1970s. Now Mauriello regularly visits Italy and various Italian-American communities as he seeks to recreate the happy experiences of those bygone years. He frequently goes to the Bronx, where he purchases meat, cheeses, olive oil, and fresh ravioli in the Italian shops on Arthur Avenue. In addition, this grandson of Italian immigrants regularly shops in the Federal Hill section of Providence, journeys to the pastry shops of Brooklyn's Italian neighborhoods, goes to South Philadelphia's myriad Italian stores, often visits Wooster Street in New Haven to enjoy "the neighborhood feel," and travels to other "Italian heritage spots."[59]

A native of New Jersey, Mauriello was born on September 30, 1956. Both of his parents are native-born Americans of Italian origin. His father, Tony Mauriello, is the son of immigrants from Campania—specifically, the village of Sant'Andrea di Conza in the Province of Avellino. His mother, Susan Mauriello (née Fiore), is the daughter of immigrants from Tricarico in Basilicata's Province of Matera. Father Mauriello and his siblings grew up in a three-family home in an Italian-American neighborhood in Newark's Vailsburg section. His grandmother's home was nearby. He remembers a childhood filled with many relatives and close family friends ("non-genetic aunts and uncles"). Relatives from Italy came to visit the Mauriello household, where large gatherings were held on a regular basis. This devoted preservationist of Italian-American traditions was ordained as a Catholic priest in 1988.[60]

As the pastor of Holy Rosary Catholic Church in Bridgeport, Connecticut, Father Matthew Mauriello lives and leads in a formerly Italian neighborhood that is now mainly Latino and African American. There are approximately two hundred families in his parish; they live in the suburbs around Bridgeport. At least 75 percent of them are Italian Americans, including former Bridgeport Mayor Leonard Paoletta and former Connecticut Senate Judiciary Committee Chairman Salvatore DePiano.[61] The East Side of Bridgeport was once heavily Italian, and Holy Rosary Church was the center of the Italian neighborhood. Holy Rosary parishioners remember how people packed the Church in the past.[62] This is not the case anymore because Italian Americans have migrated to Bridgeport's suburbs as they gained more education and became increasingly affluent.[63] In 2000, nearly nine percent of Bridgeport residents reported Italian ancestry, a substantial decline from the Italian presence during the 1930s, 1940s, and 1950s. Italian Americans can be found in sizable percentages in the suburbs near Bridgeport, including Stratford (22.5 percent Italian) and Trumbull (29.5 percent Italian). At this time Father Mauriello notes that there are no weddings or baptisms—and only a few children—in his parish. He spends much of his time visiting hospitals, in nursing homes, and at funerals, but says "this is where I am meant to serve the Lord."[64]

Bridgeport used to be a heavily industrial city, one with many large Catholic parishes and a significant Italian-American population. The parishioners of Holy Rosary Church relate heartwarming stories of family, community, immigration, faith-filled lives, and hard work and gradual progress that are echoed throughout the United States.[65] Angie Staltaro, for one, describes the rich array of Italian-American cultural activities that took place on the East Side of Bridgeport in years past. The youngest and only American-born child of Calabrian immigrants, Staltaro remembers the shops, churches, societies, and block parties and picnics that once characterized life for Italian Americans on the East Side of Bridgeport.[66]

Holy Rosary Catholic Church continues to maintain an important place in the Italian Catholic culture of Bridgeport and environs. Father Mauriello values the opportunity to preserve and perpetuate Italian-American Catholic traditions at Holy Rosary. To this end, he designed a coat of arms for the parish. And he has an extensive Mariological collection that includes books and figurines of the Virgin Mary. Mauriello, moreover, served as the U.S. national director for—and was one of the speakers at—the World Apostolic Conference on Mercy (WACOM) in Rome in 2008. Closer to home, he organizes the Father Matt Lunch Club, a group of parishioners at Holy Rosary Church who participate in social and cultural activities throughout the year (including an annual bus trip to Arthur Avenue).[67] The Bridgeport area is presently home to many people who grew up on the city's East Side and have fond memories of the now-dispersed Italian community that previously flourished there.

Many of the Italian neighborhoods of yesteryear, to be sure, have disappeared or are only small-scale versions of what they were during the 1940s, 1950s, and 1960s. Take, for example, the North End of Portsmouth, New Hampshire, which once had a noteworthy Italian population.[68] Similarly, Akron, Ohio's North Hill section, a neighborhood with an Italian flavor, was only 15 percent Italian in 2000.[69] Today some traditionally Italian neighborhoods continue to be populated by sizable numbers of Italian Americans, but there is little or nothing that distinguishes these places from other area communities. Many American cities no longer have heavily Italian neighborhoods, due to such factors as the geographic mobility, socioeconomic advances, and full-scale integration of Italian Americans.

In communities throughout the United States, Italian Americans have migrated from the central cities to the suburbs during the postwar decades. As these individuals became more affluent in the postwar years, they moved out of the central city neighborhoods in such places as Chicago, Cleveland, Rochester, Hartford, Paterson, Newark, Providence, and Boston. Relatively few Italian Americans live in such cities as Newark and New Orleans anymore, yet the suburbs of those cities have large Italian-American populations. "While most Italian Americans resided in ethnic neighborhoods during most of the twentieth century, this is no longer the case," writes Judith N. DeSena. "Indeed, the stereotypical Italian neighborhood is now home to a distinct minority of the ethnic group."[70]

The traditional urban enclaves continue to be places where many Italian Americans will return to shop, visit, and worship. Many older Italian Americans grew up in urban neighborhoods (i.e., Canarsie and East Harlem) whose demographic composition has changed over the years. Still, they often maintain some sort of identification with "the old neighborhood." In a number of cases, Italian Americans did not voluntarily leave the Little Italy districts; rather, they were forced out by urban renewal. Such efforts significantly affected some traditionally Italian enclaves and, in certain situations, decimated these neighborhoods. In addition, Italian Americans have sometimes clashed with African Americans in the industrial Midwest and Northeast.[71]

There were once notable Italian-American populations in various New Jersey cities that now have large communities of color, including Camden, Newark, Paterson, and Trenton. In fact, Trenton offers an interesting case study of demographic change and residential mobility in Italian America. People of Italian descent have had a noticeable presence in Trenton since the 1880s. In particular, the city's Chambersburg section has a long-standing connection with Italian-American culture. With increasing socioeconomic progress and the rise of newly empowered minority groups in the 1960s and beyond, many Italian Americans left traditionally industrial cities like Trenton for the suburbs. The Italian-American community, meanwhile, continues to shrink in Chambersburg.[72]

Similarly, Erie, Pennsylvania, is a city whose Little Italy neighborhood does not have a sizable Italian population anymore. Erie's Little Italy is on the city's West Side. During its heyday, 16th, 17th, and 18th Streets were the principal roadways of this ethnic community. Ronald DiVecchio, a lifelong resident of Erie's Little Italy, remembers when the community "was blocks and blocks of Italians." "In the 1960s," says the seventysomething DiVecchio, "you could see that people were moving out" of the old neighborhood. Today there are remnants of what once was Erie's booming Little Italy district, including Columbus Park, an Italian deli/bakery, some Italian restaurants, and St. Paul Roman Catholic Church, an Italian national parish that dates back to 1891.[73]

Italian Americans return to Erie's Little Italy and go to St. Paul Church for Masses, dinners, festivals, and funerals. Most of St. Paul's parishioners have moved out of Little Italy, but they were baptized, confirmed, and married in this church.[74] "The Church is the focal point" of the Italian-American community, according to Ronald DiVecchio, who is a lector and Eucharistic minister there. "If we ever lost the church," says this son of Tuscan immigrants, "it would be a void that we could never fill." The parishioners feel "a sense of pride" and a sense of community. St. Paul Church hosts the meetings of such organizations as the Wolves, the Sons of Italy, the Mazzini Civic Association, and the Italian-American Women's Association. Even now, the parish is predominantly Italian and the parishioners are, on average, in their seventies.[75]

Farther east, Maine once had several Little Italy neighborhoods, with the best-known community of this type being located in Portland.[76] The Italian population in Maine's most populous city had its traditional hub around St. Peter Catholic Church, an important institution on Federal Street. This parish has a much-smaller membership today than in past years and for understandable reasons.[77] "As the next generation entered into more professional careers and moved up economically and socially," wrote Vincent A. Lapomarda, "parishioners moved to the suburbs and the population of the city parish declined."[78] To be sure, the Feast of the Assumption and St. Rocco's Street Bazaar at St. Peter's Church draws a large crowd every August.[79]

While the Little Italy of Portland, Maine, does not exist anymore, it remains alive in the memories of those individuals who once lived there. Marianne Dalfonso Reali, for one, spent her childhood in this neighborhood.[80] Reali is a longtime leader of the Italian Heritage Center in Portland, an institution that helps to preserve Italian-American culture there. "We tried to keep Little Italy going through the IHC because of everyone moving out of the city," notes Reali. Now there are extensive renovations going on at the IHC, which will remain in Portland. According to Reali, "We looked at potential locations outside the Portland area and then decided that our property is prime property and that's where the Italians feel most comfortable."[81]

Of course, Portland, Maine, is not the only American city to see its Italian enclave disappear: The Little Italy that used to exist in Reno, Nevada, approximately one hundred years ago is now part of history. Lake Street formed the nucleus of Reno's Italian district. This Little Italy included French-, Basque-, and Chinese-run shops within its boundaries. The district, to be sure, served a useful purpose for Reno's Italians in the

years before they fully entered the social and economic mainstream in
Nevada.[82] Albin J. Cofone reflects on the trajectory of Reno's Little Italy:
"The economic achievements of the hoteliers, store owners, and investors
meant that they could afford a better life. Reno's Little Italy, as well as the
tightly knit ethnic bonds that existed in Italian communities throughout
the state, were of a time and place. The images and values that allowed
Italians to perceive their social space in Reno as a Little Italy were transi-
tory. Once having gained acceptance, there was little economic incentive
to hold on to the past."[83]

Seattle, Washington, too, once had a "Little Italy" that no longer exists
today. This Rainier Avenue neighborhood was known as "Garlic Gulch."
It existed in full force from the "late 1940s to the early 1960s," remembers
Dennis Caldirola, who grew up there. Caldirola, the American-born son
of a Piedmontese immigrant and his Irish-American wife, spoke English
and Italian as a child. In fact, he "spoke to his barber and corner pharma-
cist in Italian." Fifty years ago, one regularly heard people conversing in
Italian on the street corners of Seattle's Little Italy. This neighborhood
eventually passed into history as a result of the Italian Americans' social
and economic mobility. Caldirola notes that "Italians went from Garlic
Gulch to the east side of Lake Washington," an observation that takes
into account their accomplishments during the last five decades.[84]

IV. Kathleen Fantazzi grew up in an "all Italian" neighborhood
in South Philadelphia. Indeed, Fantazzi remembers that
the Italian influence was "all-encompassing" there—and that one had to be
Italian to be baptized in her parish. She attended Saint Maria Goretti High
School, an all-girls school that was then 85 percent Italian (in her estima-
tion). When Fantazzi went to nursing school, it was her "first experience
with what was not a mainly Italian community." Then this daughter of
South Philadelphia, whose maiden name was Morelli, married an Italian
American from the neighborhood. Around this time there was a mass
migration of Italians from Philadelphia to the South Jersey suburbs.[85] Fantazzi herself stayed in Philadelphia for many years. She spent twenty-one
years as a registered nurse—nineteen years in Philadelphia and two years in
West Virginia—before she began practicing law in the mid-1990s.[86]

Fantazzi took her Italian-American culture for granted until she
entered middle age. This medical-malpractice attorney recalls that "all my

life I was trying to get away" from the Italian-American culture that had enveloped her as a child and young adult. When Fantazzi moved to West Virginia during the 1990s, however, she "started to realize that she missed" the rich ethnic culture of her youth. The Duquesne University School of Law graduate concluded that the Italian-American culture had "the things that I wanted the most." Consequently, she retained her surname of Fantazzi after marrying a non-Italian man. "I could not give up the 'i.' That was my identity," says Fantazzi.[87]

Around this time Kathleen Fantazzi also became involved in Italian-American activities in West Virginia. Since 2003 she has served as a board member of the Upper Ohio Valley Italian Festival Foundation. And in recent years, she has held such posts as president, chairman, and co-chairman of the Upper Ohio Valley Italian Festival. Today Fantazzi continues to be a key figure in the ongoing efforts to promote and preserve the Italian-American culture of the Upper Ohio Valley. At the same time, the native Pennsylvanian maintains contact with her Italian-American relatives who live in South Philadelphia, one of our nation's best-known Italian communities.[88]

During the heyday of Industrial America, European immigrants (the Irish, the Poles, the Italians, and others) and domestic migrants (African Americans from the South) played a major role in populating South Philadelphia.[89] For decades South Philadelphia has been characterized—and defined—by its Italian-American presence, which is exemplified by the shops of the Italian Market.[90] In recent years, moreover, immigrants from a wide range of countries, including China, Mexico, Russia, Vietnam, Thailand, and Cambodia, have settled in South Philadelphia.[91] Still, according to *Wikipedia*, "The area in general remains largely Italian American, and most neighborhoods in South Philadelphia are known as 'Little Italys.'"[92] Now, after decades of mobility and out-migration, many natives of South Philadelphia live elsewhere.

The renowned boxing trainer and longtime Floridian Angelo Dundee grew up in South Philadelphia during the 1920s, 1930s, and early 1940s. His parents, Angelo Mirena and Philomena Iannelli, were immigrants who came to the United States from the same Italian village (Roggiano Gravina in northern Calabria). Angelo Mirena had been a sheepherder in Calabria, and he could not read or write. He and Philomena Mirena had nine children, seven of whom lived to become adults. Angelo Dundee was their second-youngest child. Years later, he described his parents in the following way: "The mother was the angel, and the old man was the strength." The Mirena family resided at 8th and Morris (829 Morris Street) in South Philly.[93]

As with so many Italian-immigrant families, the Mirenas lived in an ethnic neighborhood where they were surrounded by others from similar backgrounds. Angelo Dundee was born on August 30, 1921, in the City of Brotherly Love.[94] "Really," remembered Dundee in his autobiography, "it was South Philly, sort of a city within a city filled with Old World Italians, many of whom, hardworking first-generation Italians with a working unfamiliarity with English, spoke only their native tongue."[95] He reminisces about "a caring, warm, loving family," one in which his father had a job with the railroad while his mother, a homemaker, created a nurturing environment on the home front.[96]

During his twenties Dundee decided to seek his fortune outside of South Philadelphia. In 1948 he went to work for his older brother, Chris Dundee, who managed fighters in New York.[97] "Sure, I could have stayed in South Philly like so many of my *paisanos*," wrote Dundee many years later. "But I decided to roll the dice. If it didn't work out, I could always go back."[98] In New York City, Dundee, who characterized himself as "a streetwise kid from the streets of South Philly," began the path that led him to global prominence in the boxing world.[99] At the same time in New York, Dundee met his future wife, Helen, a North Carolinian of Irish descent.[100]

Angelo and Helen Dundee moved to Florida in the early 1950s. Both of their children were born, reared, and schooled in North Miami, Florida. For years Angelo Dundee operated the 5th Street Gym in Miami Beach. He and Helen Dundee now live in Oldsmar, Florida, where they are close to their two children and six grandchildren. A humble man, Dundee says, "There is good in everyone." For years, he made his home in Weston, Florida, where he engaged in good-natured repartee with the neighborhood youths, whom he described as "future leaders," during his daily walks around the community.[101] The famed boxing figure, in essence, replicated the same type of neighborhood camaraderie for these Florida kids that he himself experienced as a youth in South Philadelphia.

When he relocated from the Northeast to Florida, Angelo Dundee legally took the surname "Dundee." For the first decades of his life he was known as Angelo Mirena (his name at birth). His older brother Joe was a fighter who assumed the Scottish surname Dundee because there had been three champion boxers with the name. Another older brother of his, Chris, also had adopted the surname Dundee.[102] "Little Dundee" was Angelo Dundee's childhood nickname—and he eventually took the name Dundee as a young man. Consequently, some people are surprised to learn that he is Italian. Dundee, to be sure, points out that his Italian forename should leave little doubt about his ethnic heritage.[103]

Angelo Dundee started working in boxing more than sixty years ago. During the 1950s he became a boxing trainer and soon established a sterling reputation in the world of pugilism.[104] According to Thomas Hauser, "Angelo Dundee was, and is, one of the most respected trainers in boxing."[105] Dundee has trained fifteen world champions, as in Carmen Basilio, George Foreman, Sugar Ray Leonard, and, most notably, Muhammad Ali.[106] Indeed, he is best known for training Muhammad Ali during his illustrious and historically important career as a heavyweight boxer. Dundee describes Muhammad Ali as "the very first fighter" who spoke in pithy sound bites to the media, as well as a "remarkable human being" and "the greatest heavyweight of all time."[107] Decades after Ali's retirement, the Philadelphia native continues to be active as a boxing trainer.

Dundee is enthusiastic about his Italian heritage and South Philadelphia roots. He enjoys Italian food in general and pasta in particular. Over the years, he has visited Italy and socialized with Italians in such nations as Zaire, Australia, and the United Kingdom. The boxing legend also regularly participates in Italian-American activities and organizations. His list of honors includes induction into the UNICO National Hall of Fame and the National Italian American Sports Hall of Fame, along with the One America Award (with Muhammad Ali) from the National Italian American Foundation. In addition, Dundee served as the Grand Marshal of the West Virginia Italian Heritage Festival in Clarksburg, West Virginia, on three separate occasions.[108] As he reflects on his life story, Dundee notes with characteristic modesty: "Not bad for a little kid from South Philly who got into boxing almost by default."[109]

❀   ❀   ❀

Due to the paucity of Italian immigration to the United States—and the upward mobility of Italian Americans—it seems very likely that most Little Italys will not grow in size in the coming years. Some Little Italy neighborhoods, to be sure, are thriving and being revitalized. Others are not thriving at all, and they are fading into history. The dynamics affecting a particular Little Italy depend on many factors, including the community's demographics, the nature of tourism in a given area, the interest of local leaders in promoting a Little Italy, and the organizational strength of the Italian-American population. The current initiatives to revitalize the ethnic enclaves take on new significance as central cities seek creative ways in which to attract tourists and promote economic development.

Salt Lake City, Utah, is one place where there are ongoing efforts to develop a full-blown Little Italy enclave. On the west side of Salt Lake City, one finds a neighborhood that includes Carlucci's Deli, Cucina Toscana, Tony Caputo's Market & Deli, the Italian Center of the West, and three bocce courts. (The Italian Center of the West currently offers films, parties, reunions, exhibits, lectures, language classes, and events to promote Italian culture in Salt Lake City and beyond.) Some people in Salt Lake City characterize this area as a "Little Italy," due to the Italian shops and activities there and the neighborhood's Greek and Italian heritage. Indeed, members of Salt Lake City's Italian population seek to enhance and develop further this Little Italy district.[110]

In 2003 Edward and Jinger LaGuardia initiated a yearly Italian street festival to coincide with the Ferragosto (the Assumption) in Italy each August. The Ferragosto in Salt Lake City is a volunteer-driven event with numerous food and entertainment options, along with games, music, dancing, arts and crafts, and cultural exhibits. It takes place in Salt Lake City's nascent Little Italy. Over the years, there has been strong support for the Ferragosto from Salt Lake City proper and numerous other entities, including Precious Cheese. This festival is "more of a cultural celebration than it is a religious experience," says Edward LaGuardia. Since perhaps 25 percent of Utah's Italian Americans are Latter-day Saints, the LaGuardias and their compatriots are careful not to make the Ferragosto into a Catholic religious event. Of course, the Ferragosto has been an integral part of Salt Lake City's developing Little Italy community.[111]

Not every area with a noticeable Italian-American population has a specifically defined Little Italy district. Take Des Moines, Iowa, for instance. Italian Americans accounted for 3.9 percent of Des Moines' 198,688 residents in the 2000 census. In particular, the South Side of Des Moines has concentrations of Italian Americans in certain neighborhoods. "The South Side, where Italian families built tight-knit neighborhoods from the early 1900s, sits just across the river from downtown," writes one observer of Des Moines.[112] "As many Italian-Americans have prospered, assimilated, and dispersed, the area's cultural fabric has thinned."[113] Des Moines may have a relatively small Italian-American population, but its members play an important role in the politics and business affairs of central Iowa.[114]

The Italian-American community in and around Des Moines is active, vibrant, and preserving the Italian customs and traditions in numerous ways.[115] Regular pan-Italian activities occur in central Iowa, including Festa Italiana (August), Italian Heritage Month (October), and events related to the Sisterhood Relationship between the Greater Des Moines Sister Cities and the Province of Catanzaro in Italy. Italian-American Iowans participate in such organizations as the Society of Italian-Americans and their auxiliary, the Società Vittoria Italiana and their auxiliary, Gruppo Il Trattenimento Italiano (the Italian Folk Dancers), and the Italian-American Cultural Center of Iowa, which serves as the umbrella of the above organizations.

The aforementioned Center offers numerous cultural, charitable, and educational activities. This Italian heritage site in South Des Moines encompasses a Museum, Photo Exhibit Hall, and Research Library with materials that help genealogists, family historians, and others interested in their heritage. And it sponsors lectures, conferences, study groups, and classes in Italian art, dance, cooking, and language. The Center, moreover, hosts St. Joseph Tables, sponsors an Italian day camp for children, holds a Santa Lucia Celebration, and organizes a party for La Befana each year.[116] In sum, there are continuing Italian-American cultural influences in Des Moines and environs.

The Mauro family in Des Moines, which currently numbers 135 living relatives, illustrates the closeness of Italian Americans in Iowa's capital city.[117] Two members of this family—Iowa Secretary of State Michael Mauro and his older brother, John Mauro, a Polk County, Iowa, supervisor—are important political figures in the Hawkeye State. Supervisor John Mauro, for one, has served as president of the Society of Italian-Americans and chairman of the Polk County Board of Supervisors. This grandson of Italian immigrants grew up on the South Side of Des Moines in a community with a significant Italian population. John Mauro and his 30 childhood friends maintain close ties today. He is part of La Macchina (*The Machine* in Italian), a civic and political organization that meets monthly. As of 2005, every member of La Macchina was of Italian descent; these savvy and community-minded politicos ranged in age from fifty-five to eighty.[118]

Chapter 10

THE ITALIAN BASTIONS

The New Jersey Italian and Italian American Heritage Commission exemplifies the clout that Italians wield in New Jersey, a state where 17.9 percent of the population is of Italian descent. The Commission promotes a wide variety of events and activities that highlight and celebrate New Jersey's Italian-American culture. Its mission is defined in the following way: "To build and strengthen the cultural identity of Italians and Italian Americans through public educational programs that preserve and promote an accurate, bias free, and non stereotyped understanding and awareness of historical and current contributions and accomplishments of people of Italian heritage."[1] The New Jersey Italian and Italian American Heritage Commission's influence extends to every part of the Garden State, from North Jersey to South Jersey, and from Sussex County in the northwest to Cape May County in the southeast.

North Jersey is home to many people of Italian origin. In North Jersey, Morris County (22.8 percent Italian), Sussex County (22.2 percent Italian), and Bergen County (22.0 percent Italian) are particularly popular with Italian Americans. To be Italian in such places as Nutley or West Paterson (two North Jersey communities with sizable Italian populations) is typical, commonplace, and thoroughly unremarkable. After generations of socioeconomic progress, Italian Americans are well represented in the affluent suburbs that dot northern New Jersey. Michael Barone and Richard E. Cohen write: "This area may look like WASP suburbia on the surface, but in fact it is home to successful people of all ethnic groups, many descended from those who first saw the Statue of Liberty from the steerage deck and passed through the inspection queues at Ellis Island."[2]

South Jersey, meanwhile, continues to be a heavily Italian part of America. Monsignor Dominic Bottino is very knowledgeable about the culture of South Jersey. A Sicilian American who was born in 1950, Monsignor Bottino grew up in Camden, New Jersey, where an Italian enclave existed in South Camden until the mid-1960s.[3] According to Bottino, Italians currently account for at least one-half of the Catholics in the Diocese of Camden.[4] In recent decades, some Italians have moved from South Philadelphia to the Philadelphia suburbs of Camden County and Gloucester County in New Jersey. These counties are known as "South Philly Removed," says Bottino.[5] Gloucester County, New Jersey, has a particularly sizable Italian presence; it is 24.4 percent Italian. Meanwhile, the South Jersey town of Hammonton, New Jersey, is the most heavily Italian community of 5,000 or more people anywhere in the United States. Fifty-four percent of Hammonton's 12,604 residents are Italians.[6]

The Jersey Shore, too, has a significant Italian-American presence. Monmouth County, New Jersey, is 23.2 percent Italian; this county of 615,301 residents is part of metropolitan New York City, along with neighboring Ocean County, New Jersey. More than one-quarter of the 510,916 Ocean Countians are Italian Americans. Ocean County encompasses such communities as Brick Township, where Italian Americans account for 30.4 percent of the 76,119 residents, and the Toms River CDP, where 31.5 percent of the 86,452 people are of Italian descent. Of course, people with Italian backgrounds are well represented in the ranks of Ocean County's leaders. Freeholder Joseph H. Vicari is a public official in Ocean County, New Jersey: His memberships include the Seaside Italian-American Club, the Italian-American Cultural Society of Ocean County, the Columbia Civic League of Ocean County, and the Central Ocean County Regional Italian-American Social Club.[7] Today Ocean County continues to be one of America's premier bastions of Italian Americans.

Mario Delano Jr. is a native of Bensonhurst who moved to the Jersey Shore when he was eleven years old in 1973. (He has lived in Ocean Township, New Jersey, since 2002.) According to Delano, people still referred to this area as "the country" during the 1970s. There are significant differences between Bensonhurst and "the Shore," as the residents describe it. On the Shore, there are Italian delis, to be sure, but one does not find the same concentrations of Italian pastry shops, pork stores, and pizza parlors as in Brooklyn. There is more space on the Shore than in New York. Mario Delano Jr. is deeply involved in civic activities, which include his role as

Cubmaster of Cub Scout Pack 36. Out of the 49 Cub Scouts in his troop in 2005, there were "fifteen to twenty boys who are at least half Italian." He describes his father, Mario Delano Sr., as a "big heritage person." For years the elder Delano has been involved in the Italian American Association of the Township of Ocean (IAATO). Mario Delano Jr. himself serves as the First Vice President of the IAATO and the Festival Chairman.[8]

The IAATO has 350-plus members, the majority of whom are 60 and older. Each August there is the Ocean Township Festival sponsored by the Italian American Association of the Township of Ocean. Typically, 80,000 people (who represent many different ethnic groups) will attend the Festival. In Ocean Township's public schools, students begin studying world languages—Spanish, French, or Italian—in the fifth grade. In addition, there are weekly Italian classes at the IAATO. Mario Delano Jr.'s oldest son takes Italian in school and at the IAATO, which offers three scholarships to high-achieving students of Italian at Ocean Township High School. Ocean Township has a Fall Fest, at which members of the IAATO may show people how to play bocce.[9] These examples demonstrate how Italians in the Township of Ocean successfully work to preserve their Italian culture and heritage. By doing so, the various generations of Italian Americans contribute to New Jersey's Italian feel, cachet, and ambience.

I. "Wow, I miss my culture," thought Joseph Lo Casto when he first moved to the Nashville, Tennessee, area several years ago because of his work in the music business.[10] Lo Casto is a middle-aged native of New York City, one who grew up in Brooklyn in a Sicilian family. During his childhood, Brooklyn was home to some of the country's largest and most vibrant Italian communities. Italian-American culture, therefore, was thoroughly part of his daily life. In fact, it would have been difficult, if not impossible, to differentiate the Italian from the American in his cultural milieu, so closely intertwined were the two. While Nashville, Tennessee, is a cosmopolitan city and the world capital of country music, relatively few Italian Americans live there.

This Sicilian American enjoys living in metropolitan Nashville, but he nevertheless misses the ethnic culture of New York and the ability to celebrate his ethnic heritage there. Lo Casto finds that Tennesseans often emphasize being American and "southern," without any sense of an ethnic identity. In the Northeast, however, one's ethnic background is a regular part of daily life. Consequently, in 2004, the Brooklyn native decided to contribute to the local culture by organizing a chapter of the Order Sons of Italy in America: The OSIA Giuseppe Verdi Lodge #2818 in Franklin, Tennessee. Its members include native Tennesseans and transplants from the Northeast and West Coast, among other places.

Joseph Lo Casto refers to the members of the OSIA Giuseppe Verdi Lodge as an "extended family." When his wife became ill recently, Lodge members cooked traditional foods for her. The Lodge's Mission Statement, to be sure, is very inclusive: "We're a diverse community of friends who believe in taking care of each other and helping others. And though many of us share a common ethnic heritage, we embrace anyone who shares our passion for all things Italian."[11] Lodge members enjoy playing bocce, volunteering for charities, and eating Italian-American cuisine.[12] Indeed, Lo Casto and his colleagues spearheaded the successful drive to install bocce courts in Granny White Park in Brentwood, Tennessee, in 2005. Over the last few years, their efforts to promote the Italian-American culture have received media coverage in Nashville and environs, a development that heightens the visibility of their ethnic community.[13]

Many of America's most solidly Italian counties and communities are in the Northeast and the industrial Midwest. With some exceptions, the U.S. counties with the largest Italian-American percentages continue to be found in the Northeast, as in Hunterdon County, New Jersey; Dutchess County, New York; and Putnam County, New York.[14] When one surveys the list of the nation's most heavily Italian-American communities, the largest number of such locales (those with percentages of 25 percent Italian or greater) can be found in New York and then New Jersey. Massachusetts, Rhode Island, and Pennsylvania have several such communities. Apart from the Northeast, one finds a number of places in the industrial Midwest—Niles, Ohio; Boardman, Ohio; Bloomingdale, Illinois; and Elmwood Park, Illinois, are examples—with sizable Italian populations. Not all of these heavily Italian communities are in the Northeast or the industrial Midwest, as evidenced by Follansbee, West Virginia (35.8 percent Italian) and Independence, Louisiana (29.5 percent Italian).[15]

In the aforementioned places, Italian Americans are typically found in schools, churches, workplaces, shopping malls, and other places and institutions. Virtually everyone has some degree of familiarity with Italian Americans and their culture, including their foodways and naming practices. There are many amenities, as in Italian delis, stores, parishes, and cultural opportunities, that individuals with Italian backgrounds take for granted in most of these areas. Such environments can be alternately affirming and limiting for Italian Americans. One man from an insular Boston neighborhood told me that he was a young adult before he learned there were others besides the Irish and Italians in the world. In the areas with large and politically powerful Italian-American groups, one often sees Italian events, festivals, activities, and Italian-language programs.

Generally, a community needs to have an Italian-American population that significantly exceeds the statewide average of Italians to be noteworthy in this regard. Pittsburg, Kansas, is known for its Italian-American connection. Five and one-half percent of Pittsburg's 19,316 residents have ancestral ties to Italy, while people of Italian origin account for 1.9 percent of Kansas's population. Let us now look at Massachusetts, where 13.5 percent of the entire state is Italian. For an Italian-American community to stand out demographically in Massachusetts, it must significantly surpass this statewide average, as do certain communities in the Boston area (Billerica, Revere, Saugus, and others) and in the Berkshires (e.g., Pittsfield and North Adams). It takes a much smaller percentage of Italians for a community to be demographically significant for Italian Americans in the Deep South or Great Plains.

Due to the migration of Italians to different parts of America, people with Italian backgrounds are settling in communities with small Italian-American populations. Many of these places are predominantly Protestant, particularly in the Southern states. One respondent of mine, a native of the Northeast, now lives in a part of South Carolina where she says there is a "Baptist Church on every corner." As a Catholic, she sometimes feels like an outsider in the Palmetto State. The paucity of Italian delis, stores, Italian-looking people, and other signs of home can make some Italian-American transplants to the South and Midwest feel out of sorts at first. A northeasterner of Italian origin remembers walking through a Minnesota mall; at the time, she lived in a community where many people traced their ancestry to Germany and Scandinavia. "I never saw anyone who looked like me," the Italian American noted as she reflected on her Minnesota experiences.

Italian Americans from ethnic neighborhoods in the Northeast have reported experiencing "culture shock" after they relocated to such places as Florida, Indiana, Tennessee, West Virginia, and North Carolina. Vincent Lanzolla, a Bronx-born Italian American in his early forties, recalls thinking, "I miss my culture," when he first moved to North Carolina.[16] Marie Spinner, an older Italian American from New York who now lives in North Carolina, remembers: "The minute I got to Raleigh, I said, 'Where are the Italians?'"[17] Sometimes Americans of Italian origin become actively involved in celebrating their ancestral heritage for the first time after they move to a place where the Italian culture and traditions are somewhat rare or unusual.[18]

Laura Frappollo and her husband, Albert Frappollo, are natives of Westchester County, New York. In the late 1980s, they moved to Winchester, Virginia, a community where Italian Americans account for 3.1 percent of the 23,585 residents. Laura Frappollo was always proud of her Italian heritage in Westchester County, but she did not think about it much there. Everyone in New York, it seems, is Italian, related by marriage to an Italian, friends with someone of Italian descent, or at least knows a person with an Italian background. When she moved to Winchester, however, Frappollo became "passionate" about her Italian heritage.[19]

The Italian-American community of Winchester, Virginia, is largely comprised of transplants from the Midwest and Northeast. Winchester's Italian Americans relate stories of bringing back Italian foods from the Midwest or the Northeast to their new homes in northwestern Virginia. Others had CARE packages containing Italian foods sent to them by their Italian-American relatives, particularly in the days when Italian foods were difficult, if not impossible, to find in the local supermarkets. The Frappollos are active in the OSIA Frances Cabrini Lodge #2723 in Winchester: Laura Frappollo is the lodge's past president and Albert Frappollo currently serves as the lodge's vice president. The members of this organization originally came from such states as Ohio, New York, New Jersey, and Connecticut.[20]

II. The DaVinci Center for Community Progress offers the people of Providence's North End multiple opportunities for learning and recreation and gives them the tools to gain employment and access basic public services.[21] According to its mission statement, "The DaVinci Center is a neighborhood, multi-purpose social service agency whose mission is to deliver needed services to residents of all ages in the North End of Providence and vicinity."[22] This community institution at 470 Charles Street in Providence helps people from a wide range of ethnic, racial, and national backgrounds.[23]

There are five areas in which the DaVinci Center provides services: health, education, senior citizens, community development, and ticket to work and counseling. John Deluca, a former high school guidance counselor, serves as executive director of the DaVinci Center. Five individuals, Deluca among them, incorporated the DaVinci Center in 1972. They did so to provide opportunities for the area's young people, some of whom were idle and getting into trouble, and its elderly residents, who needed innovative programming tailored to the needs of senior citizens.[24]

The DaVinci Center currently occupies an 8,000-square-foot facility in Providence, one that serves hundreds of clients each month.[25] "A variety of social service programs continue to thrive at the Center and many of the programs have been cited as models on a national and international level," notes the DaVinci Center's Web site.[26] This institution receives particular recognition for its Housing Programs and the Drop-Out Prevention Program.[27] As the DaVinci Center's Executive Director, John Deluca is a linchpin in the ongoing efforts to revitalize Providence's North End. This genial, committed, and compassionate man has devoted his professional life to helping people develop their human capital and improve the quality of their lives. In so doing, he contributes to civil society in multiethnic Providence, a city with a venerable Italian community.

Italians have had a sizable presence in Rhode Island for more than a century. In the 2000 census, 19 percent of Rhode Islanders said they were at least part Italian, the highest percentage of any state. For decades the Ocean State has been known as a bastion of Italian Americans, with such communities as Warwick and West Warwick having large Italian populations.[28] People of Italian origin account for 21.8 percent of the population of Kent County, Rhode Island, a place that includes Warwick and West Warwick. At Warwick's T. F. Green Airport, Italian Americans are ubiquitous. Moreover, the town of Westerly, a community of 22,966 in southwestern Rhode Island, is 34.2 percent Italian. Some of Rhode Island's—and our nation's—most heavily Italian-American communities are in suburban Providence: Cranston (34.5 percent Italian), North Providence (43.0 percent Italian), and the Town of Johnston (53.6 percent Italian).

The Manni family of Cranston contributes to the vibrant Italian-American presence in Rhode Island as well as the sense of family and community that one finds there.[29] Tilde Cornelia Ronci and Luigi Francesco "Frank" Manni were the matriarch and patriarch, respectively, of this large clan. Ronci and Manni hailed from Cave, a town near Rome. They became acquainted in Providence, though, and married in Rhode Island's capital city in January 1913. Tilde and Luigi Manni had ten children: Elsie Manni, Albert Manni, Armand Manni, Mary Marcello, Louise Tamagni, Mafalda Doglione, Angelina Renzi, Natalie Brandt, Frank Manni, and Fred Manni. They raised their family in the Knightsville section of Cranston. The Mannis had animals (a cow, a pig, rabbits, chickens) along with grape vines, fruit trees, and a vegetable garden on their property. Angelina Renzi recalls that she and her siblings grew up in a nurturing ethnic neighborhood. In an observation that Italians echo throughout America, she remembers that if a child broke the rules in her neighborhood, the errant youth's parents would learn about this instance of misbehavior almost immediately.

Today many members of the growing Manni Family still live in Rhode Island, while others reside in different parts of the United States. The living descendants of Tilde and Luigi Manni currently number 130: 10 children (7 of whom are alive), 36 grandchildren, 59 great-grandchildren, 17 great-great-grandchildren, and 10 great-great-great-grandchildren. In the postwar years, Louise Tamagni and Mafalda Doglione moved to California. Their spouses, John Tamagni and Domenic Doglione, are natives of the Golden State. Natalie Brandt, meanwhile, lives in Oklahoma with her husband, retired Colonel Henry Brandt. Angelina Renzi resides in Florida; her two living children dwell in Florida while her five grandsons make their homes in Florida, California, and New York.[30] "Even though we're scattered across the country," writes Renzi, "there's a sisterly and brotherly love and respect that brings us together whenever possible. Our children are welcome in all our homes too."

Sunday afternoons are an important time of the week for the Mannis who live in and around Cranston. On a typical Sunday afternoon, twenty to thirty-five members of the extended Manni family gather at Mary Marcello's spacious apartment in Cranston for dinner and conversation. "Aunt Mary" or "Auntie Mary," as she is called by her multitudinous relatives, is "the matriarch of the family," according to her younger sister, Angelina Renzi. Each Sunday afternoon is marked by a continuous series of people going into and out of Mary Marcello's home. Family members bring wine, fruit, breads, and pastries for these Sunday get-togethers. Mrs. Marcello cooks the dinner. After preparing the delicious meal, she relaxes, drinks wine, and engages in conversation with everyone. Angelina Renzi reports that Mary Marcello's Sunday dinners carry on a longtime Manni family tradition that dates back to the 1920s and 1930s.

Moreover, there is a Manni family reunion each July during La Festa di

Santa Maria della Civita. Santa Maria della Civita is the patron saint of Itri, a fishing village in Campania. Many residents of Knightsville trace their ancestry to Itri. Fred Manni and his wife, Solange, have an open house at their Cranston residence during the Feast. This festive occasion draws Mannis from throughout the country. Angelina Renzi says that "the Feast Day is like homecoming week . . . a time when out-of-staters come home to visit and thus a chance to meet those who have left too." Rhode Islanders from many ethnic backgrounds attend this venerable festival, where they savor "Doughboys" (the local term for fried bread pastry), enjoy the street festivities during the evening, and dance to music in the Bandstand.

Angelina Renzi, a transplanted Floridian who regularly returns to Rhode Island, enjoys the fact that the Ocean State is our nation's most Italian state. The retired real estate broker characterizes Rhode Island as an "Italian Heaven," and she celebrates Cranston's "wonderful schools." Beginning in the seventh grade, Renzi took Italian classes and learned to read, write, and speak standard Italian. She notes that Rhode Islanders respect the Catholic Church and Italian cultural traditions. Renzi herself moved to Florida in 1973 and she lived in Key Largo for three decades. Today the Boynton Beach, Florida, resident describes her visits to Rhode Island: "Everywhere you go, someone is Italian." Whenever Renzi reads a Rhode Island newspaper, the ubiquitous Italian surnames and the visibility of Italian Americans stand out to her. These successes—and, indeed, the achievements of her entire family—reflect the prosperity and accomplishments of Italian Americans in Rhode Island and beyond.[31]

There is considerable interest in preserving the Italian language and culture in Rhode Island, as evidenced by the successful Italian-language program at Narragansett High School in Narragansett, Rhode Island. Bruna Petrarca Boyle taught Italian at Narragansett High School from 1975 to 2006; more than one-fifth (20.6 percent, to be exact) of Narragansett's 16,361 residents are Italian Americans. Boyle arrived in America at the age of 11 in 1965, after she and her family emigrated from Molise. The Petrarcas settled in West Warwick, Rhode Island, where Bruna Petrarca Boyle entered the seventh grade speaking only dialectal Italian. Mrs. Rose, an English teacher, helped her to learn English after school. Within a year, Boyle was an honor student. She graduated from the University of Rhode Island in 1975 with a major in Italian and minors in Spanish and French.[32]

Narrangansett High School's Italian-language program originated as a result of a petition drive spearheaded by Narragansett native David

Cicilline, now the mayor of Providence, during the mid-1970s. There are approximately one hundred Narragansett High School students taking Italian at any one time. The high school has two Italian-language teachers (they also teach Spanish), with a program that includes four levels of Italian instruction. Narragansett High School's faculty includes Daniela Johnson, a native of Tuscany, and Gabriela McNamara, an Argentine who is part Italian. Over the years, Bruna Petrarca Boyle has earned a well-deserved reputation as one of America's top Italian-language educators. Boyle reports that many of her upper-level Italian students at Narragansett High School have gone on to visit Italy, study Italian at the university level, and even work in Italy and sometimes marry Italians.[33]

✻III. The South End of Hartford, Connecticut, continues to be well known for the Little Italy on Franklin Avenue. For decades there was a substantial Italian population in Hartford, one that supported the Italian markets, bakeries, restaurants, and social clubs of the city's Little Italy.[34] After decades of out-migration by people of Italian origin, however, there were only 4,345 Italian Americans in Hartford by the 2000 census. The city was 3.6 percent Italian in 2000. At the same time, tourists, suburbanites, and Hartford residents alike go to the South End to dine and shop in Hartford's Little Italy.[35] The Hartford metropolitan area, to be sure, is 16.2 percent Italian.[36] Presently, Newington (23.6 percent Italian), Rocky Hill (29.8 percent Italian), and Wethersfield (31.8 percent Italian) are three Hartford suburbs with large Italian populations. Connecticut itself continues to be a place in which Italian Americans help to shape, define, and affect the state's politics, economy, and cultural milieu.[37]

Italian Americans constitute 18.6 percent of Connecticut's population. Of all the U.S. cities of more than 100,000 residents, Waterbury, Connecticut, had the highest percentage (23 percent) of Italian Americans in the 2000 census.[38] The nearby communities of Watertown (34.1 percent Italian) and Wolcott (38.1 percent Italian) also have sizable Italian-American populations. Waterbury, Watertown, and Wolcott are all part of New Haven County, Connecticut, one of the nation's Italian-American bastions. Indeed, three counties in Connecticut—New Haven (24.4 percent Italian), Litchfield (21.7 percent Italian), and Middlesex (21.2 percent Italian)—rank among our nation's top twenty counties with the highest percentages of people with Italian backgrounds.[39]

Italians are well represented in such places as New Milford, a pleasant community of 28,000-plus residents in Litchfield County in western Connecticut. According to Catherine Killoran, there is a "large group of Italian-American gals" at the New Milford Senior Center in New Milford. Killoran, who serves as the Senior Center's Assistant Director/Program Coordinator, is one-quarter Italian by way of Genoa. The New Milford Senior Center has what certain elders have dubbed "the Italian Table" in the dining area; the people who gather there have Italian backgrounds. During some recent summers there have been Italian-language classes at the Senior Center in New Milford. The Italians came to New Milford a century ago to be employed as stone masons and railroad workers, among other occupations, whereby they and their descendants helped to build and develop modern Connecticut.[40]

Elsewhere in Connecticut, the late Sando Bologna, whose parents were immigrants from Sicily, chronicled the history, culture, and architecture of Waterbury in his books and articles. Mr. Bologna was the author of *The Italians of Waterbury: Experiences of Immigrants and Their Families* (1993) and *Growing Up Italian and American in Waterbury: An Oral History* (1997), the latter of which he co-authored with Richard Marano.[41] An author, journalist, local historian, world traveler, and freelance writer, Sando Bologna lived from 1915 to 2005. He and his late wife, Claire, were married in 1940. Claire Bologna was the daughter of immigrants from the Province of Avellino in Campania. The Bolognas had three daughters: Flavia DePolo, Sandra Maineri, and Anita Bologna. For years they were the only Bologna family listed in the Waterbury telephone directory.[42]

Now Anita Bologna in particular carries on her father's passion for Italy and Waterbury alike. She remembers how he encouraged her, as a child, to learn the Italian language by giving her a coin if she counted to ten in Italian. An inveterate Italophile who once lived in Rome for a year, Anita Bologna gained her Italian citizenship in 1996. Later, her sister, Sandra Maineri, and two of her nieces became Italian citizens too. Ms. Bologna, a reference librarian at Waterbury's Silas Bronson Library, had visited Italy thirty-two times by early 2009. She collects books on different aspects of Italian culture and regularly attends Italian events in Connecticut, as in the Festa of Madonna della Libera of Cercemaggiore.[43]

Judge Richard Marano, meanwhile, is a native Waterburian (and current resident of New Haven County) who has been involved for years in various Italian-American activities. Marano was born in 1960 and grew up in Waterbury. He graduated from the Seton Hall University School of Law in Newark, New Jersey, in 1985. Then the baby boomer returned to his hometown to develop a law practice and raise his family. After his mother's passing in 1990, he wrote a family history that led him to become involved in such organizations as UNICO and the Sons of Italy. Marano subsequently founded and served as the first president of the Connecticut Italian American Bar Association in 1993. And he was president of UNICO–Waterbury (the nation's first chapter of the Italian-American service organization) as well as president of the now-defunct OSIA Leonardo da Vinci Lodge #66. Currently, this published author is a Superior Court Judge in Connecticut. Judge Marano reports that it is "comfortable to be Italian" in Connecticut, due to the Constitution State's large Italian-American population.[44]

Many people in Waterbury look to the Campanian community of Pontelandolfo as their ancestral hometown. In fact, there may be as many as 15,000 *pontelandolfesi* in the Waterbury area. Even today, it is not unusual for two American-born residents of the Waterbury area to marry each other, and both of them trace their ancestry to Pontelandolfo. In west-central Connecticut, such surnames as Albini, Ciarlo, Daddona, D'Occhio, Fusco, Guerrera, Gugliotti, Mancini, Paternostro, Perugini, Polletta, Rinaldi, and Sforza indicate that one is, in all likelihood, descended from the *pontelandolfesi*. Many of the Pontes, as they are known, regularly visit the Pontelandolfo Community Club, a remarkable establishment at 380 Farmwood Road in Waterbury. The Ponte Club draws an estimated 200,000 visitors each year, due to its wide range of popular events and activities (particularly the Festa di San Donato, which honors Pontelandolfo's patron saint). In addition, Waterbury and Pontelandolfo enjoy a Sister City relationship.[45]

Waterbury is part of New Haven County, Connecticut, a place where nearly one-quarter of the 824,008 residents identify as Italian Americans. New Haven County includes such heavily Italian communities as West Haven (27.5 percent Italian), Hamden (28.0 percent Italian), Derby (33.4 percent Italian), Orange (34.5 percent Italian), North Haven (40.2 percent Italian), North Branford (41.1 percent Italian), and East Haven (50.5 percent Italian). The Wooster Square neighborhood of New Haven is a fabled Little Italy, with legendary pizzerias that receive national attention.[46] Today Rosa DeLauro, a Wooster Square native, represents much of New Haven County in Congress. Her parents, Ted and Luisa DeLauro, both served on the City Council in New Haven.[47]

Italian regional origins continue to matter in New Haven County, and many Italians trace their ancestry to Campania in general and Amalfi in particular.[48] As Nancy N. Cassella and William V. D'Antonio write, "the New Haven area counts more descendants from Amalfi (10,000 in the city and 27,000 in the metropolitan area) than actually live in Amalfi itself."[49] Appropriately, there is a Sister City relationship between Amalfi and New Haven.[50] The Italians of Greater New Haven have contributed to projects in Amalfi, including the refurbishing of the town's cathedral. Atrani is another Campanian town that sent immigrants to New Haven. Now Americans of Atranian origin account for "several thousand" of Greater New Haven's residents.[51]

In the Wooster Square neighborhood of New Haven, five religious societies represent the specific communities of origin for New Haven's Campanian immigrants and their descendants. The five religious societies and their corresponding Italian hometowns are: Santa Maria Maddalena Society (Atrani), St. Andrew's Society (Amalfi), St. Catello (Castellammare di Stabia), Santa Maria della Vergine (Scafati), and Saint Trofomina (Minori). These societies work together. Saint Andrew is the patron saint of Amalfi, and the Society of St. Andrew and its annual Festival are mainstays of New Haven's Italian-American culture. The Ladies Society of St. Andrew, moreover, offers scholarships and makes donations to a food bank and a soup kitchen, among other worthy causes.[52]

Theresa Argento is an elder of New Haven's Italian community. A native of New Haven's Wooster Square neighborhood, she is the daughter of immigrants from Amalfi. Argento's late husband, Pasquale Argento, traced his descent to Atrani, a Campanian town near his wife's ancestral Amalfi. Theresa Argento has participated in Italian-American activities since her mother invited her to do so at the age of thirteen. Argento's daughter and granddaughter now contribute to the ongoing efforts to preserve and celebrate Italian-American culture. Theresa Argento herself has conducted a walking tour of the Wooster Square neighborhood for many years. She is the chairperson of the Amalfi–New Haven Sister City Committee.[53] Argento also serves as a director of the Columbus Day Committee of Greater New Haven, a position that recognizes her lengthy track record of community involvement.[54]

Patti-Jo Esposito is Theresa Argento's protégé. Ms. Esposito, who was born in 1967, became involved in the St. Andrew's Society around 2000. Her ancestors came to the United States from Amalfi and Atrani, and her grandparents were neighbors of Theresa Argento's. Moreover, her uncle, Andrew Pettola, and Argento's brother are lifelong friends. Patti-Jo Esposito's late father, Pete "Doc" Esposito, served as chairperson of the Society of St. Andrew Italian Feast. He was devoted to the feast and worked hard to make the annual event a success. Theresa Argento was the feast's co-chairperson at the time, and she had many telephone conversations with Pete Esposito over the years. (Mrs. Argento presented the eulogy at his funeral several years ago.)[55]

Now Pete Esposito's daughter, Patti-Jo, follows in her father's footsteps. She participates in Italian-American activities and serves as the publicity coordinator for the Society of St. Andrew Italian Festival. Patti-Jo Esposito, who lives in heavily Italian East Haven, draws meaning from her ancestral customs and traditions. Esposito says that her Italian-American work "keeps me grounded, knowing who I am and where I come from."[56] As one who venerates the Italian/American heritage of New Haven County, she articulates the connection between past and present, Italy and the United States: "How can I know where I am going if I don't know and respect where I came from?"[57]

✳ IV. Monsignor James Lisante, the pastor of St. Thomas the Apostle Church on Westminster Road in West Hempstead, New York, is a charismatic communicator and multimedia figure. The Irish-Italian pastor authors books, writes a newspaper column, records radio commentaries, and hosts a television program.[58] Nicholas and Cecilia Lisante raised their son ("Monsignor Jim" to his parishioners) in West Hempstead. The Brooklyn-born priest remembers moving into St. Thomas Parish as a young child in the late 1950s. At the time, it was mainly Irish and German, with relatively few Italians. Over the years, the parish became increasingly Italian as a result of the migration of Italian Americans to Nassau County, New York. Today four thousand families, who come mainly from Nassau County, participate in the parish, which is 60-plus percent Italian American. There are nine Masses on Sunday, along with an average of five funerals, four weddings, and four baptisms each week.[59] St. Thomas dates back to 1931; the parish celebrated its seventy-fifth anniversary in 2006.

Italian Americans currently exert a significant cultural influence in St. Thomas Parish. The Pastoral Council at St. Thomas is comprised of a diverse group of Italian Americans, Irish Americans, and Latino Americans. St. Thomas has a Padre Pio Prayer Group, and one thousand people come to the Annual Celebration of Padre Pio on August 20. One finds a shrine to Padre Pio, which includes a statue of the Italian saint, outside St. Thomas the Apostle Church. Moreover, there is a shrine to Saint Patrick, complete with a statue of the Irish saint, inside the church. A number of years ago some Irish Americans had become discombobulated by the Italian-American influence in the parish. Soon the St. Thomas parishioners erected the statue of St. Patrick; it was a gesture of respect for the Irish Catholics of West Hempstead. Monsignor Lisante himself points out that his parish includes many Irish-Italian families.[60] In sum, St. Thomas Parish demonstrates how Long Islanders from different ethnic groups can create a viable and vibrant faith community.

Italian Americans make up 14.4 percent of New York State's population. Richmond County, New York, is the nation's most heavily Italian county. People of Italian descent account for 37.7 percent of the residents in Richmond County, which is coextensive with Staten Island.[61] In the New York City metropolitan area, some notable bastions of Italian Americans include: Westchester County, New York (20.8 percent Italian), Nassau County, New York (23.9 percent Italian), and Suffolk County, New York (28.6 percent Italian). In Upstate New York, five metropolitan areas rank among the top 50 in America for having the largest numbers of Italian Americans: Buffalo–Niagara Falls (16.2 percent Italian); Rochester (16.7 percent Italian); Albany–Schenectady–Troy (16.9 percent Italian); Syracuse (15.7 percent Italian); and Utica–Rome (19.7 percent Italian).[62]

The Buffalo metropolitan area is home to a substantial Italian community; retired New York State Court of Claims Judge Mario Rossetti personifies this group's successes. A native of Worcester, Massachusetts, Rossetti moved with his family to Buffalo at the age of five during the 1930s. His parents were immigrants from Apulia, and his older brother had been born in Italy. In those days, there was discrimination against Italians outside of their ethnic enclaves. Things began to change for Buffalo's Italians when young Italian Americans (Rossetti among them) became educated and entered the professions. Mario Rossetti graduated from law school in his twenties. By contrast, his hard-working father, Joe Rossetti, had come to the United States with a second-grade education.[63] The younger Rossetti worked hard, too, and earned the respect and esteem of his legal colleagues in New York State.

Judge Rossetti's late wife, Helen Rossetti, was a pillar of the community until her passing in 2005. As a youth, Mario Rossetti met his future bride when he delivered newspapers to her family. She moved away from the neighborhood, but they kept in touch and were married in the late 1950s. Helen Rossetti spent much of her time on voluntary activities, as she reached out to people from different ethnic backgrounds and all walks of life. The well-liked Buffaloan sent "cards and notes to sick people" and in those cases where there was a "death in the family." Mrs. Rossetti, moreover, delivered "talks on bereavement to various social groups." She was "active in church activities," including Nocturnal Adoration and the Confraternity of Christian Doctrine. Helen Rossetti would "go to the shut-ins and give them communion," remembers Justice Rossetti. "She loved everybody," says her proud husband of 47 years.[64] Upon her passing, Mrs. Rossetti was mourned by the thousands of people whose lives she had touched in Buffalo and beyond.

Monroe County, New York, is another place with a sizable and influential Italian-American population; the last census found that 18.5 percent of Monroe County's 735,343 residents have Italian ancestry. The Monroe County suburbs of Rochester include such heavily Italian communities as Greece, Fairport, Penfield, Irondequoit, and East Rochester. Joseph Capogreco, a longtime resident of the Rochester area, is a well-known Italian-American figure in Upstate New York. A native of Siderno in the Province of Reggio Calabria, Capogreco moved to Rochester in 1954. He went to Upstate New York because his wife's family lived there.[65] Over the last 50-plus years, he has seen the Italian Americans of Monroe County make great progress.

Capogreco has known his spouse, Yolanda, since childhood. In fact, they grew up on the same street in Siderno. Capogreco's father-in-law, Domenic Meleca, worked in Rochester and his family, including the future Mrs. Capogreco, joined him in the United States in the postwar years. During the early 1950s Yolanda Meleca returned to Siderno to marry Joseph Capogreco, who had been a law student at the University of Rome. Capogreco followed the love of his life back to America, where he initially worked in a tailor shop and at a dry cleaner while attending the University of Rochester at night.

After graduating from the University of Rochester in 1959, Capogreco was employed as an educator in Rochester for thirty-two years. The Penfield, New York, resident taught Italian, Spanish, French, and Latin in the

Rochester public schools. He retired in 1992. This veteran teacher remembers that 75 percent of the students in his Italian-language classes were Americans of Italian origin. They often knew dialectal Italian. A tough grader and stern disciplinarian, Capogreco says, "I loved what I did." Today his legacy as an educator endures. Capogreco's former students are dentists, attorneys, architects, and engineers, among many professions and occupations. Whenever he and Mrs. Capogreco attend a wedding or some other social occasion in Rochester, they usually encounter one or two of his former students.

This warm and inclusive man contributes to Monroe County's civic life in different ways. Capogreco is a board member of the Metro Carlson YMCA of Rochester, a member of the Executive Board of the Opera Theatre of Rochester, and a past president of the Kiwanis Club of Penfield-Perinton. He currently serves as president of Rochester's Circolo Italiano di Cultura. In addition, he served as vice president of the Sicilian Sport Club (he was once the Club's "Man of the Year") and Director of Publicity for the Italian Civic League of Rochester. For the last forty-five years Joseph Capogreco has been part of Rochester's annual Columbus Day Celebration. And he has promoted Casa Italiana on Nazareth College's campus in Rochester, along with being one of the one hundred founders of the Italian American Community Center in Rochester.

Capogreco is also a multimedia figure. Over the years, he has written for such publications as *Il Progresso* and *America Oggi*. In 1994 Capogreco began to edit the "Pagina Italiana" of the Italian American Community Center's monthly newspaper in Rochester. Most prominently, this Calabrian-born American is the host and director of "Carosello Italiano" (Italian Carousel), a bilingual radio program that airs on Sunday mornings for three hours on Rochester's WROC Newstalk 950. Capogreco began broadcasting this program in 1967: Its content includes Italian news, Italian music, and interviews with guests.[66] Indeed, "Carosello Italiano" is a community institution, one that enjoys an enthusiastic listenership among Greater Rochester's large Italian-American community and beyond.[67]

V. Two or three times each year Gennaro Manzo would tell his grandson, Jerry Somma, a particularly poignant story about his youth in Italy.[68] Manzo was born on October 28, 1905; he grew up on Ventotene, an island near Naples. During Manzo's youth, his father, a fisherman, had an accident. When one of his fishing colleagues threw out the anchor during the workday, the elder Manzo's foot became entangled in the anchor rope. A doctor had to amputate the bottom half of his leg, and he could not work from that point onward. Thereafter, Gennaro Manzo's childhood essentially came to an end, as he began to assume some of the family's breadwinning responsibilities.

During this period, Manzo left school (he was in the fourth grade) to pick the family's crops so they would have enough food to eat. He had only a very old pair of shoes to wear when he went to work in the field, and his feet froze because of the harsh weather (the frost had come). When Gennaro Manzo related this narrative to his grandson, he would open his fists as if he were reliving it. "This was the only story that would make him cry when he told it," remembers Jerry Somma. Manzo spoke about his childhood experiences in such a way that his grandson could feel the ache and the cold that he had experienced decades earlier.

Gennaro Manzo came to the United States when he was seventeen years of age. Indeed, Manzo and his brothers, Sal and Vincent, all immigrated to America during a one-year period. As adults, they lived within three miles of each other in Brooklyn. Gennaro Manzo had been a presser in the Garment District, and he always insisted on having neatly pressed clothing. A strong believer in family, he and his wife, Assunta Manzo, lived in Bensonhurst, New York, with their daughter, Rose Somma, and her husband, Carmine Somma, and their children: Carmine, Susan, and Jerry. Jerry Somma, who was named for his grandfather and whose patron saint is San Gennaro, draws upon Gennaro Manzo's lessons in his personal life and business dealings. The forty-year-old Floridian's parents and grandparents strongly influenced his philosophy of life and appreciation of Italian customs and traditions. The Somma family's nightly dinners and Sunday meals were quite important to him. Their dining room was the place where he started to develop his world view and learned to express his opinions.

Jerry Somma's maternal grandparents, Assunta and Gennaro Manzo, played a central role in his childhood and young adult years. Their room was next to his bedroom in the Sommas' Bensonhurst residence. Assunta Manzo was ill during Jerry Somma's youth. Her two daughters cared for their ailing mother, as did her husband, Gennaro Manzo. Jerry Somma himself learned how to give diabetes injections to his grandmother at the age of nine or ten. Every day the young Brooklynite would go into his grandparents' room and sit on Gennaro Manzo's ottoman. The older man

and his grandson would talk for hours and hours. There were family celebrations as well as innumerable conversations and "life lessons" in Assunta
and Gennaro Manzo's room. After his wife's passing in 1981, Gennaro
Manzo wore a black tie every day of his life until he became sick. He came
down with Parkinson's disease in 1990, and he passed away in 1997 at the
age of ninety-two. Jerry Somma remembers his grandfather as a man of
dignity, a strong work ethic, and great love for his wife and family. He
describes the love in his family as "priceless."

Somma comes from a household in which the following advice was
paramount: "Whatever you do, take pride in what you do." "We are passionate people," observes Somma. This passion for food, family, and
music (particularly opera) undergirds what the former football player
describes as a "beautiful culture." Indeed, Manzo did much to shape his
grandson's personality and outlook on life. Jerry Somma remembers the
lessons in life that his grandfather shared with him. "He taught me about
character," says Somma, who admires how Manzo and his other Italian
relatives went through difficult times with integrity. "Today we should
never have to compromise our character," notes Somma, "if they did not
compromise it under those conditions." As a youngster, beginning when
he was eight or nine years of age, Jerry Somma shined his grandfather's
shoes every Friday night. Gennaro Manzo was a stickler for detail; he paid
his grandson fifty cents per shoe. In doing so, the older man underscored
the message of taking pride in your work.

The bond between Jerry Somma and his grandfather is something that
could not be verbalized. "We could communicate without talking," recalls
Somma. He used to speak Italian with his grandfather, but to no one else.
To be sure, Gennaro Manzo encouraged the use of English. Manzo, who
respected this country and the English language, had taught himself how to
speak and write English. He would tell his stories mainly in English, but
some of the content would be in Italian, too. Gennaro Manzo celebrated
each year the day (June 27) that he became a U.S. citizen. "This was a country that afforded him great opportunity," notes his grandson. Manzo, of
course, never forgot Italy. He corresponded with people on Ventotene each
week, and he sent packages containing jeans and chocolates to them. When
Rose and Carmine Somma visited Ventotene, the islanders knew Manzo's
grandchildren and great-grandchildren through his letters to them. Today
Jerry Somma wears a pendant that includes a photograph of his grandfather.
He remembers Gennaro Manzo as "a proud man and a strong man."

Jerry Somma moved from New York to Florida during the 1990s, yet the Jupiter, Florida, resident returns to Brooklyn regularly to see his parents and relatives. After he went to college in Nassau County, New York, Somma started his own business in 1996. For a time, he had three tobacco shops, including one in Tequesta, Florida. He sold these businesses around 2001. That year he and a friend, Bill Fagnano, "talked about how much we loved it down here" and "what we missed" in the Northeast. They missed the "authentic street festivals" that one finds in New York and other northeastern states.

Therefore, Bill Fagnano and Jerry Somma formulated the idea for an ethnic celebration: the Feast of Little Italy Italian Festival. Fagnano is the Chairman of the Board of the Feast of Little Italy Italian Festival. Jerry Somma, moreover, serves as the organization's President. Their work on the festival is "a labor of love." The Feast of Little Italy was held for the first time in 2003 over Memorial Day Weekend in West Palm Beach, Florida. The event was a success, despite some rain, "tremendous heat," and a competitive weekend. Fagnano and Somma both live in Jupiter. So they decided to hold the Feast of Little Italy at Jupiter's Abacoa Town Center, a venue that is ideal for family events, during the fall.

The Feast of Little Italy has elicited an excellent reaction from the local media, the community, and its business sponsors. These sponsors—Sorrento Cheese among them—play an important role in keeping the annual event free of charge (there is no admission fee). Somma underscores the teamwork among the 100-plus vendors and other festival participants. The Feast of Little Italy is an "authentic street festival," an affordable and enjoyable event with a "tremendous children's area." It includes wine seminars, cooking demonstrations, much popular entertainment, a wide array of options for food and drink, and numerous other ways in which to enjoy Italian-American culture. Each year the Feast of Little Italy draws an average of 60,000 people, including many families, over a three-day period. Somma estimates that 50 percent of the festival attendees are Italian Americans. "Everybody gets to be Italian for the weekend," says this inclusive and outgoing entrepreneur. The most recent Feast of Little Italy Italian Festival was held in Abacoa Town Center in Jupiter, Florida, on November 7, 8, and 9, 2008.[69]

Due to the Feast of Little Italy's success, the Festival organizers recently created another three-day event, the Taste of Little Italy, in Port St. Lucie, Florida. It took place for the first time on February 8, 9, and 10,

2008, and drew forty thousand attendees. The Taste of Little Italy is now an annual event in Port St. Lucie.[70] Both Jupiter and Port St. Lucie have sizable Italian-American communities. Many residents of these areas originally came to Florida from the Northeast during the 1970s, 1980s, and 1990s. For these Floridians, the Feast of Little Italy and Taste of Little Italy help to recreate the Italian ambience that exists in so many towns and cities in New York, New Jersey, Connecticut, and elsewhere.

❀   ❀   ❀

With the passage of time, many Italian Americans who were shaped by their lives in predominantly Italian neighborhoods have gone on to live in other communities. John Scara and his Italian-American friends from Staten Island have a remarkable story of brotherhood that dates back more than seven decades.[71] Scara, who was born on April 16, 1932, grew up in the Rosebank section of Staten Island, a heavily Italian area during his childhood and young adult years. This close-knit community in the east-central part of New York City's smallest borough nurtured Scara and his peers. Even though most of them have not lived on Staten Island for years, they remember Rosebank, their hometown, with great fondness today.

Scara describes the Rosebank of his youth:

> We all lived on the same street only doors away from each other. Nearby on the street was an Italian market, also a baker, a fruit and vegetable store, a butcher, and a candy store. A few houses down the street was the shoe repair shop. On many summer evenings, all our mothers would be seated outside on the front stoop. The bakery would start up and we could smell the bread. We would get ten cents and run into the bakery oven area and purchase a loaf right out of the oven. We would run back to our mothers, who had plenty of butter or olive oil to smother on the bread. I can still smell the bread. Life was simple then, but things like this bonded us forever.

Fast-forward many years—and these Rosebank natives share a nostalgia for yesteryear as well as the cultural similarities and generational ties common to men from their generation. "We lived through World War II," notes John Scara, a resident of Deerfield Beach, Florida. These men all remember the rationing and blackouts during World War II. Moreover, Scara and his compatriots all fought in Korea, worked hard in their careers, married and raised their families, and now enjoy comfortable and well-deserved retirement lifestyles. Their successes parallel the broad gains made by people of Italian origin throughout our nation. Today these seven-tysomething Staten Island natives call themselves "the Rosebank Boys."

All of the Rosebank Boys are Italian, and everyone is from Rosebank. They strongly believe in the importance of family, friendship, and community. Accordingly, these lifelong friends refer to each other by their boyhood names. There are six living members of this venerable fraternity: Joe Capobianco (Joe Jills), Michael DeMonte (Micky Dee), Bob Litrell (Tonto), Pat Pepe (Patsy Be Beep), John Scara (Scara), and Al Somma (Albie). In 2006 two gentlemen—Andy Nuzzi (Andy Gump) and Joe Guzzi (Joe Goon)—passed away. With one exception, the Rosebank Boys have moved away from the old neighborhood, but they have kept in touch with each other over the years.

John Scara and the five living Rosebank Boys maintain close ties, some six and seven decades after they grew up together. The Rosebank Boys now live in different parts of the country, as in South Florida and Toms River, New Jersey. Bob Litrell, to be sure, still lives in Rosebank in the house where he spent his childhood. While there are hundreds of miles separating these longtime friends, they remain in close contact through their frequent telephone conversations. "There is a real bond there," according to John Scara. As importantly, the Rosebank Boys have regular reunions—sometimes in South Florida, other times on the Jersey Shore. The same men who played together at the ages of three, four, and five, and who walked to school together as boys, now see each other at weddings, funerals, and reunions. During their reunions in New Jersey, they smoke cigars, catch crabs, enjoy Italian meals, use childhood names, and banter with each other.

When they get together, the Rosebank Boys share their memories of growing up on Staten Island. "We relive" things, says Scara. When he sees his friends, their mothers and fathers come to mind for him. "The conversations," Scara notes, "are always about our youth and the sad part is how we keep losing dear friends. But we are happy and content with our lives and our love for one another. It is a great time for us and the excitement of our reunions never diminishes." These gatherings take on a special poignancy now that two of the Rosebank Boys have passed away. As Scara writes, "The Rosebank Boys are a very good example of the Italian Americans who were raised in tradition and loyalty." "We are very proud of our town and heritage," continues Scara. "We fought in wars and came back to raise children who are now becoming leaders in their communities and churches. It was a poor neighborhood but rich with love for one another."

Chapter 11

GOVERNING AMERICA

S everal years ago, then-Arizona Governor Janet Napolitano created an initiative to provide every one of Arizona's first-grade students with a children's book. Private donors endorsed the governor's creative idea and funded the initiative with $445,000 in contributions.[1] This program resonates with immigrant parents, who want to see their children learn English. However, they often do not have the resources to purchase books for their youngsters. Now elementary school students regularly approach the governor in supermarkets and thank her for the children's books that they have received due to her initiative. In fact, they often inform their governor that this volume is the only book they have at home. Napolitano herself draws a parallel between the experiences of today's immigrant children and those of her Italian-immigrant ancestors a century ago.[2]

Napolitano's Italian relatives "came from near Naples" to the United States during the "first part of the 1900s."[3] The future governor herself was born in New York City on November 29, 1957. She grew up in a household where her family observed Italian customs and followed Italian traditions. Janet Napolitano credits her parents, Jane Napolitano and Dr. Leonard Napolitano, for giving her the values and encouragement that led her to commit her life to public service. Dr. Leonard Napolitano has spent much of his professional career promoting access to health care in New Mexico, where he cofounded and served as Dean of the University of New Mexico School of Medicine.[4] Janet Napolitano lived in Pittsburgh and Albuquerque during her youth.[5]

A top graduate of Santa Clara University and the University of Virginia

Law School, Janet Napolitano relocated to Phoenix, Arizona, in 1983. After serving as a law clerk to a federal judge, she practiced law for a decade there. Then Napolitano served as U.S. Attorney for the District of Arizona (1994 to 1998) and Arizona Attorney General (1999 to 2003). This avid sports fan, who particularly enjoys the Arizona Diamondbacks, became governor of Arizona in 2003, a position that she held until 2009 (when she took office as U.S. Secretary of Homeland Security).[6] Napolitano governed a fast-growing state, one with much ethnic, racial, and cultural diversity.[7] The Arizona governor highlights the importance of role models for different ethnic groups, including Italian Americans. She attends Italian-American events, has been to Italy on numerous occasions, and expresses pride in her Italian heritage.[8] Secretary Napolitano, to be sure, articulates an inclusive perspective that affirms and highlights the value of diversity. Overall, Janet Napolitano's compassion, competence, and visionary leadership made her one of the most popular and successful chief executives in Arizona history.[9]

The Democratic governor won plaudits from Arizonans for her focus on such matters as economic growth, public education, health care, disaster preparedness, and border security. She sought to provide opportunities for Arizonans of all ages, through her efforts to attract investment to Arizona, promote international trade, and enhance the Grand Canyon State's system of public education to prepare students for success in the global economy. Napolitano supported and promoted funding for full-day kindergarten in Arizona's public schools. Her accomplishments in the health-care field include the CoppeRx Card (a prescription discount plan for seniors) and expanded health insurance coverage for small businesses and individual Arizonans. She also has focused on preparing for and dealing with Arizona's droughts and fire seasons. Napolitano champions border security and law enforcement, too; she spearheaded the drive to form the Arizona Counter-Terrorism Information Center.[10]

The Napolitano administration's emphasis on fiscal responsibility appealed to Arizonans across the political spectrum. "When Governor Napolitano took office in January 2003, the state faced a billion dollar deficit," notes the governor's official biography.[11] "In that first year in office, she erased that deficit without raising taxes or cutting funding for public schools or other vital services."[12] Napolitano's fiscal approach won the approval of many Republican-leaning independents and even some Republicans in Arizona, two demographic groups whose members are typically skeptical of the Democrats' economic policies.

Public service matters to Secretary Napolitano in part because it gives her "the ability to touch a lot of lives" and the opportunity to affect many subject areas over the long term.[13] Napolitano's popularity in Arizona stems, in part, from her hard work, informality, emphasis on results, and commonsense manner. She has sound political instincts, as evidenced by her refusal to accept a $65,000 pay increase in the past.[14] Throughout 2005 and 2006 her approval ratings were so high that no big-name GOP figures wanted to challenge her. Then, in November 2006, Janet Napolitano won reelection to the Arizona governorship by the impressive margin of 63 percent to 35 percent. This moderate Democrat's popularity in a Republican-leaning state reflects a significant consensus in Arizona that Napolitano's policies work well. Her leadership abilities led *Time* magazine in November 2005 to name her one of "America's Five Best Governors."[15] Napolitano, moreover, was the 2006–2007 Chair of the National Governors' Association (NGA); she previously served as the NGA's vice chair.[16]

Arizona's chief executive from 2003 to 2009 is a savvy politico as well as a top-flight leader. Indeed, she contends that the national Democratic Party "has to broaden its base geographically and in terms of issues."[17] Secretary Napolitano increasingly receives national attention, a testament to her executive abilities and willingness to transcend partisan and ideological differences in pursuit of pragmatic solutions to policy issues. For years now the national media have mentioned her as a prospective presidential contender. And Napolitano received attention in the media as a potential running mate for Democratic presidential nominees John Kerry (2004) and Barack Obama (2008), respectively. Her bright political future is enhanced by her extensive travels around America.[18] Most recently, Janet Napolitano's experience in governance led President Barack Obama to choose her to be part of his Cabinet as the Homeland Security secretary.

I. Anna C. Verna became president of the Philadelphia City Council in 1999, the first woman ever to hold this powerful position. Verna has been a member of the Philadelphia City Council since 1975, when she won the election that year to succeed her father, William A. Cibotti, who died in office as the Second District's councilmember. Verna, a South Philadelphia native and current resident, represents Center City, South Philadelphia, and Southwest Philadelphia in the Second Council District. She is socially moderate and fiscally conservative. An advocate of tax reform and affordable housing, this Democrat of Italian origin enjoys a good reputation for dedicated leadership and constituent service. In addition, Verna is a respected figure in Philadelphia's Italian-American world, where she serves as the Columbus Civic Association's Vice President and the yearly Columbus Day Parade's Chairwoman, among other positions.[19] It is altogether unsurprising that an Italian American would play such an important role in Philadelphia's politics, considering that the Philadelphia metropolitan area is home to the nation's second-largest concentration of Italians.

People of Italian descent have participated in American politics and government since the beginning of U.S. history. While their numbers led politicians to take note of them in the Northeast, urban Midwest, and other parts of the country during the first decades of the twentieth century, the Italian immigrants and their descendants were not especially mobilized or prominent in the political arena at this time. By the 1960s, however, they had become an important voting bloc, one whose complex views on cultural and economic issues made it difficult to classify them (as a group) in an ideological or partisan sense.[20] As recently as the 1970s, Italian Americans identified heavily with the Democratic Party, an outgrowth of that party's traditional concerns for ethnic constituencies and less-affluent workers. With increasing affluence and the integration of Italian Americans into mainstream America, though, they have shifted increasingly toward the Republican Party. "Today 35 percent of Italian Americans say they are Republicans, 32 percent are Democrats, and the remaining 33 percent, Independent," notes one source.[21] Italian Americans currently participate in the electoral process in significant numbers: They make up a sizable percentage of the electorates of such states as New York, New Jersey, Connecticut, Massachusetts, Rhode Island, and Pennsylvania.[22]

Americans of Italian descent are now an essential part of our nation's politics and government. Going back as far as the 1770s, two Italian Americans signed the Declaration of Independence. In the post–World War II era, we began to see people of Italian origin become increasingly prominent in the political arena. Today Italian Americans regularly become governors of states, members of the president's cabinet, and members of the U.S. Congress.[23] Former Pennsylvania Senator Rick Santorum served as chairman of the Senate Republican Conference Committee in the 107th, 108th, and 109th Congresses, a position that made him the third highest-ranking member of the GOP Senate majority. The list of Italian Americans who currently wield power in national politics and government includes such figures as U.S. House Speaker Nancy Pelosi, the American Association of Retired Persons CEO William Novelli, and U.S. Supreme Court Justices Samuel Alito and Antonin Scalia.

Americans from Italian backgrounds, to be sure, regularly win elected positions in the United States. While there is pride in the Italian-American community when a person of Italian ancestry is elected to office, Italian Americans do not necessarily vote for candidates with Italian surnames.[24] These days most politicos from Italian backgrounds run for office as individuals *who happen to be Italian* rather than as *Italian-American candidates*. Boston in particular and Massachusetts in general are places where Italian Americans have won significant offices by forming multiethnic coalitions. Earlier this decade observers took note that Robert Travaglini became President of the Massachusetts Senate in 2003 and Salvatore DiMasi was elected Massachusetts House Speaker in 2004. Italian Americans had never held the top legislative positions in Massachusetts before. These milestones, along with the prominence of State Auditor Joseph DeNucci, Boston Mayor Thomas Menino, Boston City Clerk Rosaria Salerno, U.S. Representative Michael Capuano, and others, symbolized the advances of Italian-American politicians in the Bay State.[25]

Italian Americans have won statewide or significant offices—or run well for these elected positions—in many states with relatively few people of Italian origin. Such states include Hawaii, Idaho, Iowa, Kentucky, Minnesota, New Mexico, Washington, West Virginia, Wisconsin, and Wyoming.[26] Wyoming, meanwhile, is 3.1 percent Italian. The Equality State regularly elects Italian Americans to statewide office, as in Democrat Teno Roncalio, who once held Wyoming's at-large U.S. House seat, and Republican Michael Enzi, who handily won U.S. Senate races in 1996, 2002, and 2008. Wyoming made history in 2007, when Governor Dave Freudenthal chose John Barrasso, an Italian-American Republican, to replace the late Craig Thomas in the U.S. Senate.[27] "According to the National Italian American Foundation," notes *Congressional Quarterly*, "this will be the first time that both of a state's two senators have been of Italian stock."[28] Senator Barrasso easily defeated his Democratic challenger in the November 2008 election.

Earlier this decade, Joe Manchin III's overwhelming victory in the West Virginia gubernatorial race in 2004 merited attention for its milestones.[29] "An Italian-American, a Catholic and the grandson of immigrants, Joe Manchin's pedigree reads very differently than that of any previous governor," writes Chris Stirewalt.[30] Only 3.9 percent of West

Virginians have ancestral ties to Italy. Governor Manchin, to be sure, is attuned to public opinion in his state: *Rasmussen Reports* noted survey data with Manchin's 79 percent approval rating in 2006.[31] And he won reelection by an overwhelming margin last year.

Until the 2008 presidential election cycle, there had never been a serious, credible Italian-surnamed person who had declared and run for the White House in either political party. Al Smith, the four-term governor of New York and 1928 Democratic presidential candidate, was the son of a German-Italian father and an Irish-English mother. However, his surname gave no clue as to his Italian heritage and he himself did not seem to identify as Italian (or part Italian) publicly.[32] To be sure, the book, *Italians in America*, describes his accomplishments as follows: "Smith became the first Italian-American governor of New York in 1919. In 1928 he went down in history as the first U.S. presidential candidate of Italian descent, losing the race to Herbert Hoover."[33] Similarly, *The Italian American Experience* notes: "Alfred Emanuel Smith's multiethnic ancestry of Irish, English, German, and Italian qualifies him as an Italian American governor."[34]

Since the 1980s Italian Americans have surfaced periodically as prospective candidates for president or vice president. Geraldine Ferraro, of course, was Democratic presidential nominee Walter Mondale's running mate in 1984; the three-term Democratic congresswoman from Queens became the first Italian-surnamed member of a major party's national ticket. Analysts had thought that Lee Iacocca and Mario Cuomo would have been strong candidates for the White House, but neither man ultimately sought the position. Throughout much of 2007, Republican Rudolph Giuliani was the front-runner for the GOP presidential nomination in 2008. In addition, Colorado Congressman Tom Tancredo, the grandson of Italian immigrants, participated in the 2008 Republican presidential contest before he withdrew from the race in December 2007. He regularly received national attention for his hard-line positions on immigration policy and criticisms of multiculturalism.[35]

II. "As a kid in Brooklyn in the 1930s, all the Califanos in the phone book were relatives," remembers Joseph A. Califano Jr.[36] Califano was born on May 15, 1931, in Brooklyn to an Italian-American father, Joseph A. Califano Sr., and an English/Irish mother, Katherine Gill Califano. He grew up in a Catholic household, one in which Irish and Italian customs and traditions contributed to the rich, nurturing environment that his parents created for him, their only child. Califano recalls that there were a sizable number of Califano family functions with Italian themes— Christmas, New Year's, Easter, and Sunday night dinners (two to three times per month). At the same time, he remembers that there was an "enormous sense of being American" in his home. Joseph Califano Sr. abstained from speaking Italian around his son. The younger Califano, meanwhile, had "mainly Irish teachers," who reinforced his sense of being American, at the Catholic schools (St. Gregory's, Brooklyn Preparatory High School, and Holy Cross College) that he attended for sixteen years.[37]

Since the early 1960s Califano has enjoyed a remarkable career in American public life. A top graduate of Harvard Law School, the Brooklyn native served in the U.S. Navy and later worked as a Wall Street lawyer before entering governmental service in 1961. Between 1961 and 1965 he held a series of positions of ever-increasing importance and responsibility in the U.S. Defense Department. This work involved him in such issues as civil rights, Cuba policy, and tensions in the Panama Canal Zone.[38] Then, in 1965, Califano became President Lyndon Johnson's "chief domestic advisor." In this capacity, the precocious New Yorker worked for President Johnson from 1965 to 1969 to implement his expansive vision of the Great Society programs. To do so, he focused on a wide variety of pressing social issues, ranging from civil rights to economic matters.[39] According to the historian Robert Dallek, "Califano was such a quick study and so devoted to the Great Society programs that, within six months of coming to the White House, he sometimes became a surrogate President."[40]

Likewise, the historian Irving Bernstein describes Califano's tenure in the White House:

A young man who could win the high esteem of Cyrus Vance, Robert McNamara, and Lyndon Johnson was, obviously, special. Joe Califano had the essential qualities: high intelligence, loyalty, probity, command of language, an easy manner that made friends quickly, enormous energy and diligence, great curiosity, and management skills. Like the President, he believed that government could be used to broaden democracy in order to raise those at the bottom of the social order. At the same time, Califano was a political pragmatist. As with his boss and the best kids on the streets of Brooklyn, he held no prejudices based on ethnicity or religion. While it is difficult to imagine two people more different than Lyndon Johnson and Joe Califano, they meshed almost perfectly. The President came to rely on him heavily and put him in charge of major crises. Further, at moments when Johnson was under great strain he would turn to Califano for personal support.[41]

After Johnson retired from the Presidency in 1969, Califano has remained in the public eye through his high-profile lawyering, government service, and think-tank leadership. During his post–White House legal career, he found himself once again involved in some of the most compelling events of our time, particularly Watergate. In fact, he served as the *Washington Post*'s legal counsel during the Watergate years and sued the Committee to Re-elect the President in civil court on behalf of the Democratic National Committee. Califano reentered public life to serve as President Jimmy Carter's Secretary of Health, Education, and Welfare (HEW) from 1977 to 1979, a position that enabled him to affect social policy in a significant number of fields. After he left the Carter administration, Califano served on blue-chip corporate boards and enjoyed a reputation as a premier Washington attorney.[42] Then, in 1992, he retired from practicing law and founded the National Center on Addiction and Substance Abuse (CASA) at Columbia University. Califano currently serves as CASA's Chairman and President.[43]

When asked by an interviewer about the events and accomplishments that make him proudest, this father of three children cites the importance of his family, of course, as well as a number of policy achievements. When it comes to policy matters, Califano is proud of his work on spearheading the Great Society programs in the 1960s.[44] Moreover, he takes particular pride in "starting the anti-smoking campaign in 1978" during his tenure at HEW.[45] The legendary Washington figure also notes that, as HEW Secretary, he signed regulations related to section 504 of the Rehabilitation Act of 1973, in order to promote accessibility for persons with handicaps in public places.[46] And Califano cites the decision that he made as HEW Secretary to enforce the "Title IX regulations for women's athletics" to promote equal opportunities for women in intercollegiate sports.[47] Finally, Califano describes his work at CASA during the last 17 years as a very significant factor in his professional career.[48] He documented the first seven decades of his life in a readable and historically important memoir, *Inside: A Public and Private Life* (2004).[49]

Califano has been a significant Italian-American role model since the 1960s, one whose successes helped to herald the emergence of Americans of Italian origin in U.S. mainstream culture and institutions. President Johnson liked to showcase Califano and Jack Valenti for Italian-American audiences to signal to them that he felt favorably inclined toward Italian Americans and their interests. There were few prominent Americans of Italian descent at the highest levels of the U.S. government at that time. Thus, when Califano served in the White House, Italian-American groups regularly invited him to march in parades and go to dinners, among other activities. (Johnson deployed Califano on various occasions to curry favor with Catholic voters as well.)[50] Decades later, this former cabinet secretary continues to receive attention as a pioneering figure for Italian Americans.

Joseph Califano evinces a deep appreciation for what is possible in the United States. On the last page of text in his memoir, he writes: "I believe that the American dream is nourished by the openness of our society—the reality that anyone can do anything, anyone can grow up to be president. That dream has survived civil war, two world wars, a depression, racial strife, half a century of cold war with communist nations, and the terrorist attack of September 11, 2001."[51] Indeed, Califano's life and personal story highlight the possibilities that now exist for members of groups (the Catholics, the Irish, the Italians) that once experienced outsider status in America.

III. Frank Carlucci was understandably delighted when President George W. Bush named Colin Powell to be U.S. Secretary of State in December 2000. Powell, after all, had once worked for him on three separate occasions in government; Carlucci recognized and nurtured the future four-star general's exceptional potential.[52] To this end, Powell's autobiography, *My American Journey*, includes a number of positive passages about—and references to—Carlucci. One such sentence can be found on page 389 of *My American Journey*: "The man who had done so much to shape my life, Frank Carlucci, and so much to save the Reagan-Bush presidency by rehabilitating the NSC after Iran-contra, was leaving too."[53] In fact, Carlucci's public service during the Reagan administration capped a distinguished career in diplomacy and public service.

The Carlucci clan has been contributing to America ever since the former defense secretary's paternal grandfather, also named Frank Carlucci, came from Italy to the United States during the late 1800s. The Italian-born Frank Carlucci arrived in America as a stonecutter with little money, and he brought seven or eight of his siblings to the United States as well.

He set up a construction company, one that worked on part of Ellis Island, the steps at Arlington National Cemetery, the Hotel Casey in Scranton, Pennsylvania, and a church and the courthouse in Wilkes-Barre, Pennsylvania. His grandson and namesake, Frank C. Carlucci, was born in Scranton on October 18, 1930, and reared in Wilkes-Barre. The American-born Frank Carlucci is a native of the Wyoming Valley of Pennsylvania, one who has always had an awareness of his Italian heritage and background.[54]

"In my lifetime," observed Carlucci in a 2004 interview, "I have seen being an Italian go from being a stigma to an asset."[55] During his youth, he recalls "riding on a streetcar and being called 'a dirty wop.'"[56] There was "mild" discrimination in those days; it was "tolerable," remembers Frank Carlucci, "but it existed."[57] On a lighter note, the Ivy League alumnus describes how he speaks with his hands and gesticulates much during his speech, a hallmark of Italian and Italian-American culture. Carlucci's rise to power began early, when he enrolled at the age of twelve at Wyoming Seminary, a boarding school in Kingston, Pennsylvania.[58] Then he went to Princeton University, where he graduated with a bachelor's degree in 1952, and then went directly into the military during the Korean War.[59]

Between 1952 and 1986, Carlucci served his country with distinction on a number of fronts. He served in the U.S. Navy as a lieutenant (Junior Grade) from 1952 to 1954 and attended Harvard Business School during the mid-1950s. Thereafter, he was a Foreign Service Officer for twenty-six years. Carlucci also served as assistant director and, later, director of the Office of Economic Opportunity (1969 to 1971). Then he was the Office of Management and Budget's associate director and deputy director (1971 to 1972), Undersecretary of the U.S. Department of Health, Education, and Welfare (1972 to 1974), and U.S. Ambassador to Portugal (1975 to 1978). Later, Carlucci served as deputy director of Central Intelligence (1978 to 1981) and deputy secretary of Defense (1981 to 1983). From 1983 to 1986 he was Sears World Trade, Inc.'s president and then chairman and chief executive officer.[60] His record in these important positions made him a well-known and well-respected figure in Washington.

The need for seasoned leadership in the aftermath of the Iran-contra affair led Carlucci to reenter government in late 1986. Upon becoming President Ronald Reagan's National Security Adviser in 1986, he "restructured the National Security staff" and, by the end of his tenure in 1987, restored the credibility and trustworthiness of the National Security

Council.[61] When Caspar Weinberger retired as Secretary of Defense in 1987, Carlucci succeeded him and held this position until 1989. It was a critical time to be defense secretary because of the geopolitical considerations involving the Soviet Union in the waning days of the Cold War. According to Carlucci, the U.S. "intelligence reports accurately predicted the size of the Soviet military," but "not the Soviet economy."[62] Carlucci remembers how he "started parallel discussions with the Soviet military" and he went to the Soviet Union and met with his Soviet counterparts.[63] On the domestic front, Carlucci dealt with budgetary issues, congressional relations, base closings, and many other matters during his tenure as the sixteenth Secretary of Defense.[64]

Carlucci's wisdom derives from his decades at the pinnacles of American business, diplomacy, and government. The main lesson he offers is: "We are not an island."[65] "The world can change very fast," notes this veteran of Portugal's transition to democracy and the end of the Cold War.[66] He characterizes U.S. educational institutions as America's "greatest national-security asset."[67] When it comes to the Cold War, Carlucci writes: "History will judge Ronald Reagan for his vision and his strength of purpose in pursuing that vision. He knew that the way to peace was to negotiate, and that the only way to negotiate was through strength. Step one was to restore our strength and to label the U.S.S.R. for what it was. Step two was then to engage them in serious negotiations on a number of fronts. George Shultz provided superb advice and great negotiating skills, but it was Ronald Reagan who supplied the determination and the leadership."[68]

Today Carlucci can look back with pride on a career that combines an impressive record of government service with a significant history of leadership in the realm of global finance and commerce. Among his many professional activities, Carlucci served as chairman of the board of directors of Nortel Networks from 2000 to 2001.[69] Most prominently, he reentered the business world as vice chairman of the Carlyle Group, the respected private-equity firm, in 1989. Then, in 1993, the veteran diplomat and high-ranking government official became chairman of the Carlyle Group, a position that he held until 2002. From 2002 to 2005, Carlucci was chairman emeritus of the Carlyle Group.[70] These days he continues to offer—and be consulted for—his sage advice and expertise on numerous issues related to national security and international affairs.

IV. In July 1994 Leon Panetta, who was then the director of the Office of Management and Budget, made history when he became President Bill Clinton's second chief of staff. No American of Italian descent had ever held this powerful position before. By doing so, Panetta immediately became part of the pantheon of Italian-American trailblazers.[71] Clinton demonstrated significant confidence in Panetta's management abilities when he named him to be chief of staff. During his two and one-half years as White House chief of staff, this son of Italian immigrants won plaudits for the focus, efficiency, and discipline of the White House staff. At that time, relatively few Italian Americans had served at such high levels of American government: Panetta held two cabinet-level positions during the Clinton administration.

Leon Edward Panetta was born on June 28, 1938, in Monterey, California. His parents, Carmelo and Carmelina Panetta, were immigrants from the Province of Reggio Calabria. They arrived in the United States during the 1930s. The future Washington heavyweight grew up in a "home of immigrant Italians" with the "basic customs," as in "eating fish on Christmas Eve" and "Christmas dinner with family." The Panettas would "make gnocchi" and "prepare gnocchi for Christmas Day." During his childhood, Panetta spent much time with his grandfather (he knew him as his "Nonno"). The elderly gentleman taught his grandson to speak Italian. This linguistic skill came in handy when Leon Panetta himself went to Calabria in 1956 and he became acquainted with his Italian cousins. The contact between the American and Italian Panettas has "continued over the years." Leon Panetta and his wife, Sylvia Panetta, have three sons, all of whom have visited Italy and spent time with their Calabrian relatives.[72]

Leon Panetta's Italian heritage—from which he derives certain basic values ("love of family," the "importance of family," and "hard work")—is integral to his life and career. As a young man, he was an employee at his family's restaurant. Then, after Carmelo and Carmelina Panetta sold the restaurant, he worked on the Carmel Valley farm that they owned. During his youth, Panetta asked his parents as to why they left their native land for the United States. Carmelo and Carmelina Panetta replied that they did so because they could offer their children a "better life in this country." The Panettas found opportunities in Monterey, California, a town with a substantial Italian-American population.[73] Education was important in Leon Panetta's family; he graduated with a bachelor's degree (*magna cum laude*) from Santa Clara University in 1960. He received his J.D. from the Santa Clara University Law School three years later. And from 1964 to 1966, he served in the U.S. Army with distinction.[74]

During his twenties, Leon Panetta began his career in public service, one that would take him to the pinnacle of American government. He traces his interest in public service to three sources. Firstly, his parents encouraged him to "give back" to his country and community. Secondly, Panetta's two years in the U.S. Army cemented his sense of duty and "giving back" to one's country and community. Thirdly, President John F. Kennedy's visionary leadership inspired him to become involved in public service.[75] Beginning in the 1960s, Leon Panetta has enjoyed a record of continuous achievement in his professional life.

As a young man, Panetta worked in a variety of appointed positions in government. In 1966 he began his career in public service with a staff position working for Republican Senate minority whip Thomas Kuchel. Later, he took a position at the U.S. Department of Health, Education, and Welfare in 1969. After a short time, he was named HEW's director of the Office for Civil Rights. Panetta energetically enforced the laws pertaining to "civil rights and equal education" and resigned this position in 1970 rather than submit to political pressure to be less committed to racial equality. He then worked for New York City mayor John Lindsay as his executive assistant. Panetta, who changed his partisan affiliation from Republican to Democrat in 1971, returned to Monterey the same year.[76]

After he practiced law in Monterey for five years, Panetta won election to the U.S. House in 1976. From 1977 to 1997 Panetta worked, once again, in the federal government. He served in Congress from 1977 to 1993, where he represented the Central Coast of California. As a member of Congress, Panetta focused on health, budget, education, environmental, and civil rights issues. Between 1989 and 1993, the Californian chaired the U.S. House Budget Committee. During the Clinton Administration, he served as director of the U.S. Office of Management and Budget (1993 to 1994) and chief of staff to the President (1994 to 1997).[77]

In a 2004 interview, Panetta pointed to several highlights from his career in public life. For one, he cites his tenure as director of the Office for Civil Rights at HEW, where he steadfastly backed anti-discrimination initiatives. Panetta, moreover, is proud of his sixteen years in Congress.[78] His leadership on the House Budget Committee helped result in "the balanced budget that eliminated the deficit."[79] In addition, Panetta authored the legislation that created the Monterey Bay National Marine Sanctuary.[80] And he cites with pride his "legislation that established Medicare and Medicaid reimbursement for hospice care for the terminally ill."[81] As OMB director, too, he played a "large role in the [Clinton administration's] economic plan," particularly the resulting "fiscal discipline" that led to a "balanced budget" and a budget surplus.[82] Finally, as White House Chief of Staff, Panetta "was the principal negotiator of the successful 1996 budget compromise, and was widely praised for bringing order and focus to White House operations and policy making."[83]

Throughout his life, Leon Panetta has drawn strength from his Italian heritage and family background.[84] He writes:

> Italy has contributed more to the world than any nation in history. One way to understand the importance of these contributions would be to see what would be left if we took everything Italian from the world. What a loss for music, art, engineering, design, literature, and life's little luxuries—good food, fine wine, and high fashion. And what a loss for the United States, which would no longer have an estimated twenty million Americans of Italian descent, the children and grandchildren of the Italian immigrants who came to this country more than a century ago.[85]

Today Leon Panetta continues his remarkable record of leadership and public service. Currently, he spends much of his time at the Leon and Sylvia Panetta Institute for Public Policy at California State University, Monterey Bay. He and his wife, Sylvia (the granddaughter of northern Italian immigrants), are the founders and directors of the Institute, which dates back to December 1998.[86] Meanwhile, his name surfaced as that of a prospective California gubernatorial candidate in 1998, 2003, and 2006. Leon Panetta also teaches at California universities and serves on various task forces as well as corporate and nonprofit boards, among his many professional responsibilities. Recently, he was a member of the Iraq Study Group, a role that reflected his status as an elder statesman and exemplified his contributions to American democracy.[87] And in January 2009 President Barack Obama chose Panetta to be director of the Central Intelligence Agency.

V. Then-U.S. Secretary of Veterans Affairs Anthony J. Principi was the 2003 honoree of Il Circolo, The Italian Cultural Society of the Palm Beaches in Florida. Principi's aunt and uncle, Vera and Fred Princiotta, are members of Il Circolo. The Deerfield Beach, Florida, residents told their nephew about this important Italian cultural organization. Therefore, in 2002, Principi attended and spoke at Il Circolo's annual gala. Al Marzelli, Il Circolo's president at the time, asked him to be the honoree at the organization's 2003 gala, an honor that he accepted with dignity and graciousness.[88]

In 2003 Il Circolo recognized Anthony Principi at its yearly gala that took place at The Breakers. The Palm Beach event was attended by a number of his family members, including his wife, Elizabeth, his mother, sisters, aunt, and uncle.[89] "He projects sincere appreciation for what he was able to accomplish in this country," notes Il Circolo's Sally Valenti of Principi, "and gives thanks to his Italian upbringing for maintaining the dedication and hard work ethic it takes to achieve success."[90] Principi delivered a moving and powerful acceptance speech at the 2003 gala, one that celebrated the Italian culture and heritage and resonated with the Il Circolo members.[91] "I remember his speech as a great reflection on our heritage, with a truly inspirational message," recalls Dr. James Guttuso, who was then the president of Il Circolo.[92]

Anthony Principi is the son of an immigrant of Italian origin. His father, Antonio Principi, arrived in the United States from the Mendoza region of Argentina during the early 1920s; he was descended from Piedmontese immigrants who had gone to South America. Principi's mother was born in New York City. Her parents came from San Fratello, Sicily.[93] Antonio Principi served in the U.S. military during the Second World War. After the war, he operated a New York City business that sold electrical supplies. Anthony Principi was born on April 16, 1944. During his childhood, Principi lived in "heavily Italian" East Harlem, a solidly Italian Bronx neighborhood, and, finally, a New Jersey community that had a smaller percentage of Italian Americans than in East Harlem and the Bronx.[94]

This second-generation American himself has strong ties to Italian-American culture. "I am Italian American through and through," says Principi.[95] He looks at the indicators of one's Italian ancestry (e.g., food, culture, and family values) as a "very important part of life." His Italian heritage affects his outlook in terms of such matters as values, family, tradition, and the Catholic Church. Principi, who spent much of his time as a child with his Nonna, speaks with pride of his Italian heritage. He is a devoted family man: Anthony Principi and his wife, Elizabeth Principi, are the parents of three sons.[96] In addition, he maintains ties to Italy and once served as "a foreign exchange officer with the Italian Navy."[97] Today he is an important role model for Italian Americans, having served as a member of President George W. Bush's Cabinet from 2001 to 2005.

Principi graduated from the U.S. Naval Academy in 1967, and he began a professional career that led him to spend many years in Washington. A veteran of the Vietnam War, Principi was decorated for his heroism in combat. After graduating from Seton Hall University Law School in 1975, Principi was part of the Judge Advocate General's Corps in the U.S. Navy. He went to Washington in 1980, where he worked in government over the next 15 years. His curriculum vitae for the 1980s includes top positions with the U.S. Senate Armed Services Committee and the U.S. Senate Committee on Veterans' Affairs. Then he served as deputy secretary of Veterans Affairs (1989 to 1992) and acting secretary of Veterans Affairs (1992 to 1993). From 1993 to 1995 he was the U.S. Senate Committee on Armed Services' Republican staff director and chief counsel. Apart from his extensive experience in government, Principi also worked as a business executive and practiced law. While a private citizen during the Clinton administration, he chaired the Commission on Servicemembers and Veterans Transition Assistance.[98] The Navy veteran enjoys public service, in part because one has "the opportunity to make a difference in people's lives."[99]

Anthony Principi became U.S. Secretary of Veterans Affairs in 2001, at a time when the Department of Veterans Affairs (VA) faced significant challenges. The Californian entered the position as someone who was respected by members of both political parties as well as activists and observers of veterans' affairs. It was a difficult time to become the VA secretary because the number of veterans eligible to use the VA facilities was surging and straining the VA's capacity to take care of them. Principi is a proven administrator, one who ran the federal government's second-biggest bureaucracy for four years. This challenging job involved difficult but necessary decisions about who was eligible for care at VA facilities. Yet Principi generally received plaudits for his principled leadership, his accessibility to activists, veterans' groups, and members of Congress, and his frequent travels to various states to inspect VA facilities and listen to veterans' concerns.[100]

When Principi reviews his four years as VA secretary, he points to a number of improvements for veterans. Firstly, there was a significant increase in funding (from $48 billion to $71 billion) for the U.S. Department of Veterans Affairs between 2001 and 2005.[101] Secondly, Principi describes how an additional one million veterans received health care in the VA while he was Secretary. Thirdly, the Principi team focused on improving the VA's productivity, in terms of processing benefit claims and the "delivery of services in health care."[102] Indeed, these positive results during Principi's four-year tenure as Veterans Affairs Secretary led to widespread praise from veterans' groups and observers of veterans' issues.[103]

Now in his sixties, Principi continues to play an active role in governmental affairs. In 2005 President Bush named him to be the chairman of the Defense Base Closure and Realignment Commission (BRAC), a politically sensitive assignment that directly affected the lives of thousands of Americans and the economies of numerous American communities.[104] He remains focused on veterans' issues, including the efforts to give young veterans the assistance they need to reenter the civilian world after their military service.[105] Meanwhile, Americans of Italian origin regularly celebrate and recognize Principi because of his distinguished record of public service and profound gratitude for the opportunities that exist in America.

VI. When Pellegrino Rodino Sr. came to the United States as a teenager in 1898, he had no friends, relatives, or acquaintances in America. A member of a peasant family in Atripalda, a village in Italy's Province of Avellino, Pellegrino (or Peter) Rodino Sr. loved and honored the country that adopted him. He became a naturalized American citizen; his wife, Margaret Rodino, was an Italian American born in the United States. One of their children, Pellegrino (or Peter) Rodino Jr., was named for his father. The younger Rodino, who came into the world on June 7, 1909, in Newark, New Jersey, grew up in the First Ward of Newark, a close-knit, virtually all-Italian neighborhood. As a child, little Peter lost his mother to tuberculosis.[106] Peter Rodino Sr., therefore, became the substantial formative influence in his young son's life. Later, Peter Rodino Jr. recalled that his father, a toolmaker with little formal education, was a creative and inventive individual who loved opera and storytelling.[107]

Peter Rodino Jr. lived in accordance with his father's dictum: "Be decent, be just, and be honest."[108] He was a self-made man, one who graduated from the New Jersey Law School in 1937 and earned the Bronze Star as a result of his service in the U.S. Army from 1941 to 1946. This practicing attorney and member of the Democratic Party fell short in his first congressional bid in 1946, but he ran again in 1948 and won the first of twenty terms in the U.S. House. As a legislator, Rodino focused on constituency service and his legislative objectives. He revered the Constitution and spoke eloquently about the importance of good government. Rodino served in the U.S. House of Representatives from 1949 to 1989; for the last 16 years of his congressional career, he was chairman of the House Judiciary Committee.[109] In a 2004 interview, Peter Rodino Jr. remembered with particular pride how he had been a leader in three realms—the Nixon impeachment inquiry, civil rights, and immigration reform—as part of his lengthy career in public life.[110]

Rodino's nonpartisan and statesmanlike leadership of the House Judiciary Committee during the Watergate years culminated in the 1974 impeachment hearings that produced a bipartisan consensus in favor of President Richard Nixon's impeachment.[111] In 2005 one of his obituarists, Michael T. Kaufman, described him as someone "who impressed Americans with the dignity, fairness and firmness he showed as chairman of the impeachment hearings that induced Richard Nixon to resign as president."[112] Gerald M. Pomper analyzes Rodino's role in this complex constitutional drama and describes him as "A Hero of the House."[113] The Watergate crisis, to be sure, showcased the contributions of two Italian Americans—House Judiciary Committee Chairman Peter Rodino and Judge John J. Sirica—to American government.[114] "Rodino became a national figure after impeachment," notes Howard Fields.[115] In 1976 Democratic presidential candidate Jimmy Carter had Rodino on his list of prospective running mates, but the veteran politico took himself out of contention for this position.[116]

Besides Watergate, Peter Rodino won plaudits for, and took pride in, his stalwart support of civil rights during his decades in Congress. From 1949 to 1973, Rodino represented a majority-white constituency that was based in Newark; from 1973 to 1989 his congressional district in Newark and environs was majority-black. This liberal and inclusive lawmaker voted for civil rights and open housing when he had a mainly white constituency, positions that made him unpopular among some Italian Americans. He vigorously advocated on behalf of antidiscrimination initiatives and legislation, including civil rights, open housing, voting rights, affirmative action, and the Martin Luther King Jr. federal holiday, during the 1960s, 1970s, and 1980s.[117] "He [Rodino] played a decisive role in almost all civil rights legislation over three decades," notes Carol M. Swain.[118]

In her assessment of Peter Rodino and Lindy Boggs, two Caucasians who represented congressional districts with black majorities during the 1970s and 1980s, Carol M. Swain writes:

Peter Rodino and Lindy Boggs . . . used their seniority and committee positions to represent racial and political minorities. Their seniority allowed them to shape the national legislative agenda in ways that helped African Americans both in their districts and nationally. Both were considerably more liberal than the vocal white minorities in their districts, and both faced criticism for their active role on behalf of blacks. They persisted in their endeavors despite harassment of various kinds. After court decisions mandated majority-black districts, Rodino and Boggs held on to their seats because they had the trust of a majority of the district's voters. They maintained multiracial coalitions that withstood the assaults of black opponents who often sought to beat them using racially polarizing strategies.[119]

In addition to his leadership during Watergate and admirable record as a proponent of civil rights, Rodino was proudest of his legislation on immigration reform.[120] As Joel Millman writes: "Immigration was Rodino's bailiwick long before, and well after, Watergate."[121] He was a key proponent of the Hart-Celler Immigration Reform Act of 1965, which ended the discriminatory immigration regulations that favored Northern European immigrants over those from Southern Europe.[122] Rodino characterized the "national origins" legislation on immigration as being "undemocratic," and he worked very hard to repeal it.[123] More than two decades later, Rodino was again a leader in the efforts to reform America's immigration laws—this time with the Simpson-Rodino Immigration Reform and Control Act (IRCA) of 1986. Rodino supported amnesty for many undocumented immigrants, as he wished to minimize the worker exploitation and depressed wage scales that he believed resulted from a large number of low-wage, undocumented workers.[124]

Rodino was, of course, a patriotic American, one who evinced a deep respect for Italy and Italian-American culture. After he served in Italy during the 1940s as an officer in the U.S. Army, he visited the country of his ancestry on subsequent occasions. Back in the United States, Rodino represented a heavily Italian constituency for decades. The lifelong New Jerseyite sponsored the legislation to make Columbus Day a federal holiday. In addition, Peter Rodino met with many Italian premiers and foreign ministers over the years. He led numerous delegations to Italy as a Member of Congress, and he was involved in earthquake relief in Italy. This son of a poor Campanian immigrant also received the great honor of being named a Cavaliere di Gran Croce by the Italian government. Peter Rodino Jr. died on May 7, 2005, at his West Orange, New Jersey, residence; as an

American of Italian descent, he contributed significantly to our nation and its institutions.[125]

❋ ❋ ❋

The results of the November 2006 elections led to a significant milestone for Italian Americans: Nancy Pelosi, the House Democratic leader, became the Speaker of the U.S. House of Representatives after the Democrats retook control of Congress.[126] Pelosi, who was born in 1940, grew up in Baltimore. Her father, Thomas D'Alesandro Jr., was once the Mayor of Baltimore as well as a five-term congressman. Likewise, her brother, Thomas D'Alesandro III, served as Baltimore's chief executive. Pelosi herself moved to San Francisco during the 1960s, where she and her husband, Paul Pelosi, raised their five children. Nancy Pelosi served in several posts—she was California Democratic Party chairman from 1981 to 1983 and the Democratic Senatorial Campaign Committee (DSCC) finance chairman from 1985 to 1987—before entering electoral politics in San Francisco in 1987. That year she won a special election to serve in the U.S. House.[127]

Pelosi's principled liberalism, tireless fundraising, considerable political abilities, and focus on Democratic Party unity enabled her to win the respect and confidence of her congressional colleagues. As a member of Congress, Pelosi's committee assignments have included the House Appropriations Committee, the House Banking and Financial Services Committee, and the House Permanent Select Committee on Intelligence. The liberal lawmaker was elected House minority whip in 2001.[128] "Overwhelmingly elected by her colleagues in the fall of 2002 as Democratic Leader of the House of Representatives," reads Pelosi's congressional biography, "Nancy Pelosi is the first woman in American history to lead a major party in the U.S. Congress."[129] Then, in January 2007, she won election as U.S. House Speaker.

Nancy Pelosi is the highest-ranking woman and Italian American in the history of the U.S. Congress. "Pelosi is an edgy partisan whose cockiness inspires friends and rankles foes," according to *Congressional Quarterly*.[130] During the 110th Congress, the San Francisco Democrat moved vigorously to be a counterweight to the Republican administration. Like many national political leaders, Pelosi is a polarizing figure. In February 2007 *Rasmussen Reports* noted that "House Speaker Nancy Pelosi (D) is viewed favorably by 49 percent of American voters and unfavorably by 40 percent."[131] The survey also found that she had "the highest name recognition of anybody in the Congressional Leadership ranks" and was "the only Congressional Leader with a higher favorable total than unfavorable."[132] Pelosi, of course, is the third highest-ranking figure in American government. After Vice President Joe Biden she is second in line of succession to the presidency.

Of course, Pelosi appreciates her Italian heritage and she notes her historic role as the first woman and Italian American to become House Speaker.[133] In a recent speech, she said, "To this great nation, our families brought the hallmarks of Italian life: a deep faith, an abiding love of family, and a strong work ethic. No ethnic group has done more to reinforce American family values than Italian Americans. These values have allowed us to make extraordinary contributions in academics, the arts, business, science, and government."[134] Italian Americans often highlight Nancy Pelosi's achievements and significant power in U.S. government; however, her ideological positions and partisan affiliation do not resonate with all of her coethnics, many of whom are more conservative than she. At the same time she is one of our nation's most prominent Italian-American role models, a fact that transcends ideology and partisanship for some individuals, at least.[135]

While Nancy Pelosi made history on Capitol Hill, former New York City Mayor Rudolph Giuliani emerged in late 2006 and early 2007 as the top candidate for the 2008 Republican presidential nomination.[136] Giuliani, to be sure, invokes his Italian heritage and celebrates America for the opportunities that his Italian ancestors found here. He also emphasizes the contributions that they (and, indeed, all immigrants) have made to America.[137] In his best-selling book, *Leadership*, Giuliani writes: "When my grandfather Rodolfo Giuliani, for whom I am named, left Italy, over a hundred years ago, he set sail for America with only $20 in his pocket. He left his family, his home, everything that was familiar and safe. He saw the obstacles that faced him: treacherous journey across a dangerous ocean, coming to a place whose language he didn't understand. And yet Rodolfo and his wife and my other grandfather and grandmother all made the same choice to come here."[138]

A legendary former prosecutor, Giuliani is a native New Yorker who has had a distinguished career of public service. During the 1980s the New York University School of Law graduate served as associate attorney general (the number three position in the U.S. Justice Department) and then U.S. Attorney for the Southern District of New York before narrowly losing a race for mayor of New York City in 1989. Giuliani won the mayoralty of New York City four years later. During his time in office (1994 to 2002), Giuliani drew attention for his determined leadership and forceful management style. Until 9/11, the mayor's tenure was marked by a focus on quality-of-life issues and a significant decrease in the city's once-high crime rates.[139]

Giuliani's leadership in the aftermath of 9/11 significantly enhanced his stature and reputation.[140] "Giuliani is the closest thing in America to a mythic hero," wrote Nathan Vardi in 2006. "His reputation was forged in the refiner's fire of Sept. 11, which burned away the dross of what had been a successful but contentious two terms as New York City's mayor, a guy who reduced crime, yet picked fights with squeegee men and jaywalkers."[141] Vardi notes that Giuliani drew much praise for his courage, strength, and compassion after 9/11. Consequently, he became a formidable presidential candidate, one who led many Republican polls during 2007.[142] Giuliani's 2008 presidential bid was a significant milestone for Italian Americans: Zev Chafets described Rudy Giuliani as "the first serious presidential candidate in history with a vowel at the end of his name."[143] Yet this ethnic milestone received relatively little attention in the mainstream press. Giuliani's Italian heritage did not appear to have affected his campaign at all.[144]

Regardless, Giuliani faced a complicated path to the GOP presidential nomination in 2008. Some observers, after all, raised questions about the sixtysomething politico's temperament, personal life, business dealings, and his liberal leanings on certain social issues (particularly gun control, abortion rights, and gay rights). In his unsuccessful campaign to win the GOP primaries, Giuliani focused on his electability, stressed the closely related issues of terrorism and national security, promised to make right-of-center judicial appointments, and highlighted his conservative mayoral record on fighting crime, cutting taxes, and reforming welfare.[145] Nevertheless, Giuliani's campaign made strategic errors and he proved unable to connect with voters in the early Republican contests. After a distant third-place showing in the Florida presidential primary in late January 2008, Giuliani withdrew from the GOP presidential contest and endorsed Senator John McCain. He remains active in public life, although with a somewhat lower profile than before.[146]

Part IV

CONTEMPORARY ITALIAN-AMERICAN CULTURE

Chapter 12

CUSTOMS, TRADITIONS, AND HISTORY

Pearl Oliva remains true to the customs and traditions that her Italian-born parents brought with them from the Marches and Apulia to the United States.[1] Her father, Guido Oliva, and his parents, Teresa Seri and Giuseppe Oliva, left their home in Fano, a town in the Province of Pesaro in the Marches, and came to America in 1903. They settled in the Boston area. Guido Oliva was only six at the time; he had been born in 1897. The same year that the Olivas came to the United States, Guido Oliva's future wife, Michelina Luisi, was born in Lucera, a community in the Province of Foggia, in Apulia. At the age of seventeen, she departed from Italy for the United States (specifically, Massachusetts) in early spring. When she left Apulia, the flowers were in bloom there. She came to suburban Boston on April 19, 1921, to find "waist-high snow." Michelina Luisi resided with Jenny Schiavone, her first cousin, in Framingham, Massachusetts. She had planned to remain in America for only two years.

Soon after her arrival in the United States, the young Italian immigrant met her husband-to-be, Guido Oliva. One day she went for a Sunday afternoon stroll with Jenny Schiavone. During their walk, they encountered Mary Oliva Omiccioli. Mary Omiccioli, in turn, invited Michelina Luisi to come to the Oliva home for coffee to meet her mother, who took an interest in new arrivals from Italy. When Michelina Luisi went to the Oliva household on that Sunday afternoon, that is where she became acquainted with her future husband, Guido Oliva. Soon thereafter, Oliva asked his mother an important question: "How do you court a girl from

Italy?" His mother told him that "you write a note" to her. So Mrs. Oliva was pressed into service and wrote a letter to Michelina Luisi on behalf of her son. When Guido Oliva and his mother showed up at her residence, Luisi knew then that her suitor was "serious" and "respectable."

After a period of courtship, Michelina Luisi and Guido Oliva were married on October 8, 1922, at St. Tarcisius Catholic Church in Framingham. Pearl Oliva, one of their daughters, was born in Framingham on June 26, 1928. She and her older sister, Lillian, were immersed in Italian and Italian-American culture as children. In fact, they "learned Italian from the crib," as Michelina Luisi spoke Italian to her daughters. Seventeen months after her birth, Pearl Oliva's maternal grandmother (Maria Ianiro Luisi) came to the United States. Nonna Luisi communicated with her granddaughter, Pearl, only in Italian and took her to the ballet and to art museums. Guido Oliva, to be sure, "was a great dancer," one who "read poetry," appeared in plays, "trained boxers," and was himself a referee. He and his wife regularly attended the opera, too. During the 1920s, Guido (also known as Jack) founded the Citizens Club where he prepared Italian immigrants to become citizens.

In 1950 Guido Oliva started an Italian-language radio program that has been on the air more or less continuously since its creation. This program was known for many years as the "The Italian-American Hour." Pearl Oliva began helping her father with the show; ultimately, she produced the "Guido Oliva Italian-American Hour." Guido Oliva broadcast only in Italian during the 1950s, 1960s, and early 1970s. After her father's passing in 1972, Pearl Oliva succeeded him as the host of one of the longest-running radio programs in Italian-American history. Today she broadcasts the "Guido Oliva Italian Hour" on WSRO 650 AM in Framingham, Massachusetts, on Sunday mornings from 8:00 A.M. to 9:00 A.M. She plays Italian operas and oldies (Perry Como, Jerry Vale) and stays current with selections from the latest Italian hits; she also makes dedications ("Happy Birthday," "Happy Anniversary," "In Memoriam," etc.). In addition, there are Public Service Announcements and interviews on the "Guido Oliva Italian Hour." And Oliva's program includes the Entertainment Report with information about plays, films, ballet, and other cultural events. She toggles between Italian and English on her show.

Pearl Oliva has maintained her connections to Italy as an educator and in other realms. A longtime teacher, Oliva received her bachelor's degree from Framingham State College and a master's degree from Boston College. After teaching high school English for seven years, Oliva started teaching Italian at Framingham North High School in 1974. This Fulbright Scholar developed Framingham North High School's thriving Italian program until her retirement in 1994. (Oliva has made at least 80 visits to Italy.) Now the Massachusetts radio broadcaster and lifelong Framingham resident teaches Italian for adults on Monday and Thursday evenings through the Lincoln-Sudbury Adult Evening program. Her husband, too, is a native Italian: Pearl Oliva and Francis J. Cristofori were married on July 6, 2002, in Framingham's St. Tarcisius Church.

Francis Cristofori (people call him "Fran") was born in 1921 near Cento, a town between Bologna and Ferrara in the Po Valley. Cristofori came to Wellesley, Massachusetts, with his mother at the age of four months. His father, Oreste Cristofori, already back in Wellesley, had served in the U.S. Army during World War I and become an American citizen as a result. After the war, he went back to Italy and married Venusta Corticelli Cristofori. When Oreste Cristofori died in 1935, Venusta Cristofori took her three children (fifteen-year-old Fran Cristofori and his two younger siblings, Claire and Ron) back to Italy. The Cristoforis remained in Italy for one year and three months before they returned to the United States. Seven decades later, Fran Cristofori participates in numerous activities in Natick, Massachusetts. This World War II veteran is a member of the Sons of Italy and the Rotary Club of Natick and the head usher at his church, St. Patrick Catholic Church in Natick. Cristofori, who is known as "Friendly Fran the Pasta Man," manages the OSIA Francesco De Sanctis Lodge's Wednesday night pasta dinners in Natick.[2]

Pearl Oliva, meanwhile, describes her work to promote Italian-American culture as a "mission of zeal to keep the language going." Her mother, Michelina, passed away in 2000. Today Oliva is a "lector, commentator, and Eucharistic minister" at St. Tarcisius Catholic Church. She remains active in Italian-American cultural activities. For instance, Oliva "contributed stories and artifacts" to the Framingham Historical Society and Museum's exhibit ("Abbondanza: The Richness of Italian-American Life in Framingham"). She also received an award, "I Migliori in Mens et Gesta," in 2005 from the Pirandello Lyceum in Massachusetts. Her hometown of Framingham continues to have a sizable Italian presence: Thirteen and one-half percent of this suburban Boston community's 66,910 residents trace their roots to Italy. Every day Pearl Oliva works to preserve the Italian customs, traditions, and history in Massachusetts, as she draws upon her family's cultural heritage, here and in Italy.

❋I.	Susan Rienzi Paolercio grew up at the intersection of 116th Street and 1st Avenue, in the center of East Harlem in New York City. This granddaughter of Italian immigrants was born in 1951. "It was almost as if your entire family was the neighborhood," remembers Paolercio of her childhood. In East Harlem, she learned about Italian foods, Italian holidays, and the "respect for family" that typifies the Italian-American community. She could go to all kinds of Italian stores within easy walking distance of her East Harlem home—the bread shop, the fish market, the pork store, and the pasta place. For her K–8 education, she went to Our Lady of Mount Carmel Grammar School in East Harlem. Paolercio recalls a real sense of family and community. Her parents' close relatives all lived nearby, and she saw her aunts and cousins regularly. "Everyone's apartment was an extension of your own," remembers the New Yorker.[3]

Dinner time was an essential part of each day during her youth. Susan Rienzi Paolercio poignantly describes her family's kitchen table in the 1950s and 1960s:

> It was what you saw first upon entering our apartment. A simple Formica-and-steel table, with four chairs completing the set. We ate dinner at that table every night at 5:30 P.M., a place and time that was the core of my childhood. We ate, we talked, and we were a family. Our parents listened to my brother and me as we spoke about our day, and Mom filled us in on the neighborhood happenings: who was getting married, who was sick, who was moving, and whose daughter was having a baby. Dad talked about his job, and we knew the names of all his friends and coworkers; just the simple art of communicating. But it was so much more; looking back, it was a time of love and acceptance and safety. That plain kitchen table represented a shared, warm time, when we were fed food and love at every meal; to me they are inseparable.[4]

After she moved out of East Harlem in 1975, Paolercio has lived in Queens (Elmhurst and Bayside) and Westchester County, New York. She currently resides in Mount Vernon, New York, and operates her business in nearby Bronxville. For years Paolercio has participated in Italian-American activities. She is a NIAF Area Coordinator and involved with the Columbus Citizens Foundation in New York City and the Westchester Italian Cultural Center in Tuckahoe, New York. Paolercio has two sons, Michael and Joseph, in their twenties. They are 100 percent Italian. Each year she enjoys the Feast of Our Lady of Mount Carmel that takes place in East Harlem in July. It is a reminder of her "wonderful" childhood. Paolercio herself returns to East Harlem regularly to work at Rao's, the exclusive restaurant that is co-owned by her cousin, the actor and restaurateur Frank Pellegrino.[5]

Susan Rienzi Paolercio aptly notes that there are generational differences with regard to the Italian-American experience. She discusses, for instance, the changes in the lives of Italian-American women. This engaging entrepreneur and ethnic advocate reflects on her way of life vis-à-vis that of her mother, Elsie Rienzi, a homemaker and full-time parent. "Our lives are tremendously different," notes Paolercio. Her father, Ben Rienzi, passed away in 2004. He was "the keeper of the flame." Now she is losing her aunts and uncles, an unfortunate development that underscores the changes in Italian-American life and culture.[6]

The fiftysomething cultural preservationist describes how ethnic lifestyles and neighborhoods change. This evolutionary process is a natural part of life and stems, to some extent, from the prevalence of two-income families in contemporary Italian America. Yet Paolercio strives to keep the Italian-American culture and traditions alive, through her preparation of Italian foods, celebration of Italian holidays, promotion of the Italian language, trips to Italy, support for Italian-American organizations, and heartfelt belief in the sanctity of family time (she nurtures her sons and maintains close ties to her cousins).[7] At the same time, she marvels at the increasing popularity of Italian-American culture: "Everything Italian is new again."

Most younger Italian Americans were born, reared, and socialized in largely or wholly American cultural environments. Not surprisingly, then, the distinctive Italian customs and traditions are not as salient among Italian Americans as they once were among the Italian immigrants.[8] Yet people of Italian origin continue to preserve different aspects of their heritage in the United States, through their culinary traditions; wine production; support of opera; regular family gatherings on Christmas, Easter, and other special occasions; and much more.[9] Italian-American history, meanwhile, is now becoming part of the multicultural narrative that defines our nation's past, present, and future. But many Americans of Italian extraction, particularly in the younger generations, are completely American in their outlook and lifestyles. Older Italian Americans regularly lament that a large number of their coethnics have little connection to—or interest in—Italian and Italian-American customs and traditions.[10]

At the same time, we are seeing some resurgence of interest (what amounts to a modest ethnic renaissance) in Italian customs and traditions for Italians across America. Younger people and older folks alike are redis-covering, reinventing, and reconfiguring what it means to be Italian in America through their participation in festivals, organizations, cultural centers, Internet activities, and Catholic parishes with strong Italian influ-ences. Saint Leo Catholic Church, for instance, is an important cultural and spiritual landmark in Baltimore's Little Italy.[11] The Rev. Oreste Pan-dola Adult Learning Center at St. Leo's School helps to sustain the ethnic heritage of this neighborhood through its offerings: photography, bocce ball, oil painting, Italian pastries, Italian cooking, Italian card games, and Italian-language classes.[12]

Overall, our nation's Italian heritage continues to influence millions of Americans and their way of life. Salvatore DePiano, a native of Bridgeport, Connecticut, remembers that he learned about "integrity, honesty, dili-gence, loyalty, and respect for family and authority" at home from his Ital-ian parents.[13] In addition, Italian Americans may manifest their Italian heritage through their elaborate hospitality, ample gesticulating, demon-strative attitudes toward others, and in many other ways. Certain Italian-American traditions, including folk medicine and a belief in the *mal'occhio* or "evil eye," have largely disappeared here in the United States.[14] Bocce, though, remains a hallmark of the Italian-American experience and a com-mon activity at Italian-American clubs and festivals. One finds bocce courts in certain public parks and at some Italian-American clubs, among other locations.[15] In sum, there are plenty of middle-aged and elderly tra-ditionalists who still preserve the venerable Italian-American customs.

The diversity of Italian-American culture means that preserving the Italian heritage of our nation may mean different things to different peo-ple. While there are many pan-Italian celebrations of this ethnic heritage, the foods, customs, dialects, patron saints, and other cultural aspects for Italian Americans differ by their Italian regional backgrounds and even ancestral hometowns. For example, some Americans of southern Italian origin continue to discuss their Albanian roots and participate in organiza-tions to preserve the Italian Albanian heritage that one finds in parts of Sicily, Calabria, and Basilicata.[16] Sometimes the Italian traditions followed by Italian Americans are antiquated by the standards of contemporary Italy. "Owing to the lack of regular communication with the homeland that is a typical outcome of the immigrant experience, especially in the past, there are many instances of immigrant communities preserving customs that are no longer common in the old country," notes Philip F. Notarianni.[17]

To be sure, people from Italian family backgrounds are now completely American in most cases; central Nevada is one place where this integration has developed to the point that there is nothing overtly "Italian" about the Italian Americans there.[18] "Central Nevada's Italians are characterized more by their adaptability than by their retention of Italian cultural traditions," wrote Blanton Owen in 1992.[19] "There are no Italian social clubs, no bocce ball tournaments, no ethnic or religious celebrations and processions, no Italian restaurants and no Italian music or dance in Eureka or any other place in central Nevada today."[20] Indeed, the Italian Americans of Eureka, Nevada, exemplify this melting-pot approach.[21] "None of Eureka's Italian families have denied or forgotten their Italian ancestry," observes Blanton Owen, "but none consistently practice old-world cultural customs either; they exist in memory only, to be revived within each family according to each family's collective memory when desired."[22]

In different parts of the United States, there are Italian Americans who seek to preserve their ancestral heritage. Darryl and Amorette Capparelli, for instance, are "trying to bring back the customs." Darryl Capparelli "searches the Internet for Calabrian recipes," just like those his "grandmother might have used." Recently, his family started having Sunday spaghetti dinners. Amorette Capparelli, a native southerner and an "Italian by Marriage," supports and encourages her husband as he seeks to perpetuate Italian-American customs and traditions.[23] The Capparellis market Italian items, which include mugs, T-shirts, magnets, posters, and buttons, on the Web.[24] A native of the West Side of Chicago, Darryl Capparelli currently serves as Vice President of the Italian Cultural Association of Greater Austin.[25]

Cultural preservationists share stories and anecdotes about the inherent difficulties of preserving the traditional aspects of Italian-American culture. A priest in a western city told me how the parishioners at his Catholic church wanted an Italian Mass. When the priest celebrated Mass in Italian, he found that their knowledge of the language was so limited that they could not comprehend the service. Likewise, an Illinoisan related to me how younger Italian Americans tell her that they want to learn how to cook Italian foods. Then she holds a cooking exhibition to teach these skills—and no one comes to it. It can be very difficult, if not almost impossible, to preserve these ancestral customs and traditions among Americans who are three, four, and five generations removed from the Italian immigration experience. Still, there are plenty of cultural advocates who try to keep the Italian-American heritage alive.

Vivian Sagona, for one, believes strongly in the importance of promoting, preserving, and perpetuating Italian-American culture, traditions, and history. The lifelong Pueblo, Coloradan and her husband, Frank Sagona, undertake efforts to celebrate all things Italian-American in their own family.[26] Sagona explains her rationale for doing so: "I love being an Italian American, and I love the Italian traditions, the Italian language, and visiting Italy. I was blessed by having the most wonderful parents and grandparents as mentors. The greatest legacy I can leave to my children and grandchildren is to pass on my passion and love for the Italian heritage and language and to instill in them the importance of keeping it alive. If I, as a full-blooded Italian American, fail to do that, then I have disappointed my parents and grandparents and I just can't let that happen."[27]

Mrs. Sagona, who was born during the 1940s, describes her cohort's responsibility to make sure that the Italian-American culture remains vibrant here. "It is my generation that must keep our Italian heritage and language alive," says Vivian Sagona.[28] The challenge of doing so is accentuated by the fact that many Italian Americans of her generation have children and grandchildren who live miles away in different cities and states. To this end, she outlines the ways in which she celebrates her family's ancestral heritage:

- I encourage my children and grandchildren to join—and to be active members of—Italian-American organizations.
- I encourage my children and grandchildren to celebrate the Italian religious holidays with recipes used by my mother and grandmother.
- I share stories with my children and grandchildren about their grandparents and great-grandparents.
- I introduce them to Italians from Italy and encourage them to correspond with them. My husband and I have taken trips to Italy and have taken our granddaughter there.[29]

II. Michael Pastore relates a story about wine and coffee from dinner time during his childhood in 1934. Pastore, who was about six years old then, sat between his parents, who propped him up with cushions. His mother sat on his left, and his father was on his right. "My mother got up and walked around the table to the stove," remembers Pastore. "She picked up the coffee pot and brought it back to the table and then she began pouring coffee for my father." Pastore wanted some *caffè* too. "Ma, can I have some coffee?" he asked her. His father responded by wagging his finger about two inches from young Michael's face: "You're too young for coffee. Drink your wine." The Pastore family usually had homemade red wine with dinner—Pastore's grandfather made it for them.[30]

A resident of Portland, Maine, Michael Pastore began drinking wine each dinner "at a young age." By the age of six, he was a regular wine drinker. The Pastores drank alcohol in moderation, as they had been socialized by their Italian cultural heritage to do so. Later, in basic training during his military service, Michael Pastore met three Italian-American fellows from Brooklyn who shared his philosophy regarding alcohol consumption.[31] Many Italian Americans, after all, would relate to Pastore's anecdote about wine and coffee. Time and time again, older Americans of Italian descent have told me about how their cultural affinity with wine led them to have a responsible attitude toward drinking as teenagers (compared to some of their non-Italian classmates). After all, as Edward Albert Maruggi writes: "Wine is central to life in the Italian family as well as in the Italian community at large, and is considered a staple as a food and a beverage."[32]

Wine was part of the culinary legacy that the Italian immigrants brought with them from Italy to the United States. Most Italian immigrants during the period of mass immigration came from the rural, less-affluent regions of Italy. Consequently, they arrived in America with their rural foodways and, as importantly, a desire to enjoy an adequate and varied supply of food (which had not been available to them in their homeland).[33] These immigrants valued the culinary choices possible in America. Meat consumption had been rare among the less-affluent groups of Italians, while these same individuals ate meat regularly here in the United States. In fact, meat consumption increased proportionately as they rose up the socioeconomic ladder. Certain traditions related to food continue for Italian Americans (expansive gardens, large and sumptuous meals) that reflect and stem from the opportunities the Italian immigrants found here.[34]

The Italian immigrants to the United States encountered food choices and more abundance than had been the case for them in Italy. Among the Italian newcomers, there was an emphasis on food, particularly macaroni or pasta, in their homes. Recurring concerns for them in Italy—namely, the issues of food scarcity and the all-too-real possibility of hunger—were largely nonissues for them in the United States. The Italian/Americans soon created cuisines that fused certain staples from southern Italy with the dishes and foodstuffs of central and northern Italy and took into account American ingredients and "styles of consumption." Ethnic cuisines, of course, functioned as an important element in Italian/American community building and identity development.[35]

Their culinary options in the United States, quite simply, signaled progress for the Italian immigrants. Hasia R. Diner writes:

> Food, and the ever present danger of hunger, drove the exodus of men and women from Italy who wanted to eat better and who resented their dependence upon others to feed them. In America *they* ate what *they* wanted. They took foods once denied to them, and reveled in consumption. They ate better, not just than they had, but than their social superiors had. By feasting every day in America upon Italy's holiday foods they made those foods more than just good. They made them sacred, symbolic of their communities and of American abundance. They measured the changes they had experienced in status and well-being by inventing new foods and calling them Italian. Food embodied where they had come from and what they had achieved.[36]

Decades later, the immense popularity of Italian cuisine in the United States provides tangible evidence as to how the Italian immigrants and their descendants have gradually become an indispensable part of the mainstream American culture. This was not always the case, of course, although spaghetti and tomato sauce has been a mainstream dish since the 1920s.[37] Italian Americans in their sixties and beyond will sometimes relate stories about how they had Italian food items in their lunches that made them stand out from their American classmates. More than a few Italian-American youths once carried their "ethnic" lunches to school in brown lunch bags that were stained with grease on the bottom, due to the rich, fatty, and delicious Italian foods inside those bags. Their lunches were lovingly prepared by Italian mothers who made meals for their children in accordance with decades and even centuries of Italian traditions.

These mothers were often unaware of the social stigma that might attach to their children's "ethnic" lunches. Indeed, the smell, taste, texture, and appearance of the Italian foods often marked Italian-American students as odd, alien, strange, and different in various contexts during the 1930s, 1940s, and 1950s. Some Italian-American youths were embarrassed by and even ashamed of their Italian lunches. The egg-and-pepper sandwich that one enjoyed in an Italian home did not always play as well in the lunchroom of an American school. One sixtysomething Italian-American woman told me that she would dump her lunch in a vacant lot on her way to school in the Bronx. By doing so, she wanted to minimize any sense of difference from her non-Italian classmates. Likewise, Italian Americans relate stories of having traded Italian foods (say, frittata or prosciutto sandwiches) for American fare at school decades ago.

At the same time, there were instances where non-Italian youths were curious about the Italian foods and sometimes found them appealing. By the 1970s these foods had become popular with Americans from all ethnic backgrounds. During the early 1970s, Paul Andriulli's high school classmates in Paterson, New Jersey, sometimes purchased his delectable Italian lunches from him. He used the proceeds to eat foods, as in chicken pot pies, that he would not have sampled otherwise.[38] Now, of course, students may eat Italian-American cuisine unblinkingly because it is generally seen as *American* food, almost as "all American" as hot dogs and apple pie.

In the 1970s, 1980s, and 1990s Italian cuisine surged in popularity, both at the elite and mass-market levels, in the United States. Italian foods are currently enjoyed by Americans from all ethnic groups, sold in supermarkets across our nation, and served at elite and mass-market restaurants alike. It is a never-ending source of irony to middle-aged and elderly Italian Americans that these once-inexpensive foods, which include polenta and pasta with garlic and olive oil, can be pricey today. Now there are mass-market offerings—the Italian Chicken sandwich at Burger King and the Frescata Italiana deli sandwich at Wendy's, for example—that draw upon the Italian connection to appeal to consumers.

Of course, one now regularly hears about the salutary aspects of the "Mediterranean diet." Health-conscious chefs and consumers have popularized the "Mediterranean diet" in the United States and beyond. It draws heavily upon traditional Italian cuisine, particularly from rural southern Italy, and such essentials as bread, herbs, cheese, pasta, tomatoes, and olive oil. The foods eaten by poor Italians a century ago now receive the approval of dietitians and physicians. Indeed, Italian regional cuisine has achieved significant popularity among American gourmets in recent years. These regional cuisines typically feature items that once were consumed by Italian peasants (*contadini*), including polenta, bruschetta, and focaccia.[39] As Luisa Del Giudice notes, "traditional Italian foodways are gaining gourmet status, just as Italian Americans were largely forgetting their own 'country' cooking."[40]

Food is an excellent example of how Italian and American-influenced Italian items have become quintessentially American. Pizza, a popular American food, symbolizes how Italian-American cuisine has become an integral, even indispensable, part of American culture since the 1950s.[41] Pizzerias (Dominos and Pizza Hut, among them) dot the land, pizzas fill the frozen-foods aisle in supermarkets, and slices of pizza compete with hamburgers and hot dogs for our attention at convenience stores. Americans also consume tiramisù, provolone, martinis, Caesar salads, mozzarella cheese, and Ghirardelli chocolates, along with such packaged foods as Michelina's dinners and Chef Boyardee products. Moreover, we eat commodified forms of Italian-American food at Sbarro, Fazoli's, Quiznos, the Olive Garden, Carrabba's Italian Grill, Romano's Macaroni Grill, and Maggiano's Little Italy, along with thousands of trattorias, mom-and-pop pizzerias, and high-end restaurants.

Italian food and cooking are quite popular among Americans as a group. The Italian-American celebrity chefs—e.g., Mario Batali, Lidia Matticchio Bastianich, Giada De Laurentiis, Rocco DiSpirito, Mary Ann Esposito—simultaneously reflect and contribute to this trend. There are such publications as *Italian Cooking & Living* and numerous Italian cookbooks (some of which focus on pan-Italian cuisine, others on Italian regional specialties). Much of the food that we commonly identify as "Italian" in the United States, particularly in terms of fast food, is actually Italian American. Of course, there are Italian-American businesses and companies that satisfy the need for Italian foodstuffs in the United States. Brioschi, Medaglio d'Oro, and Sorrento Cheese, to name three brands, have high name recognition among Italian Americans.

There continue to be thriving Italian bakeries, delis, and other businesses that cater to both "Italian" and "American" clienteles. Today you have to be in a heavily Italian area (the Italian Market in South Philadelphia, 18th Avenue in Brooklyn, or Harlem Avenue in Chicagoland) to see Italian bakeries, butcher shops, and the like, rather than all-purpose Italian markets. There are even some chain Italian stores, which include Claro's Italian Market (six outlets in southern California); Rubino's Italian Foods (ten markets in and around Rochester, New York); and Doris Italian Market & Bakery (a chain of six such establishments in South Florida). A number of Italian-American entrepreneurs market their wares on the Internet in what my father describes as "virtual delis."

Some of the Italian businesses are owned and operated by recent Italian immigrants, who add their contemporary Italian sensibilities to Italian/American culture. Emilio and Marina Milani, immigrants from Moricone, a town in Lazio, are the proprietors of Milani Italian Pastry and Bakery in Northford, Connecticut. Marina Milani's brother, Francesco Antonelli, works with her and her husband, Emilio Milani, a veteran pastry maker, in this well-regarded bakery. The Milanis moved to the United States in 1993. Initially, they owned a cafe in Fairfield, Connecticut. After selling this establishment, the Milanis started their current business. Milani Italian Pastry and Bakery serves a marketplace that values the Italian taste and style of its products and the proprietors' emphasis on using natural ingredients.[42]

III. Dr. Gloria Ricci Lothrop remembers how FBI agents visited her mother, Maria Angeli Ricci, regularly during World War II, and that they complimented her meticulously tended garden.[43] Maria Angeli Ricci merited this attention and these visits because she was on the government's "B list" of people to watch. A poet and newspaper columnist, Ricci had been the assistant director of the Italian Language Schools for young people in southern California in the prewar years. Therefore, the FBI reviewed and translated all of her poetry and newspaper columns. Maria Angeli Ricci, in fact, was an "enemy alien" for a time during World War II, one who carried an identification booklet. She was subject to a restrictive series of rules and regulations, which banned her from having flashlights, shortwave-radio capacity, photographs of military installations, and pages with writing in invisible ink. In addition, she faced a prohibition on travel outside her home for more than five miles in any one direction.

A lifelong resident of southern California, Dr. Gloria Ricci Lothrop was born in Los Angeles County in 1934. Her parents were immigrants from Lucca, and she learned to speak Italian from them. Lothrop herself has used her Italian linguistic skills to translate various articles and documents over the years. After receiving her undergraduate degree, she taught at Sacred Heart High School in Los Angeles (1956 to 1960) and Beverly Hills High School (1960 to 1964). Lothrop went to India on a Fulbright Scholarship in 1963. The poverty of South Asia affected her in such a way that she decided to change her career path after returning to the United States. She chose to pursue graduate studies. After earning her doctorate in history from the University of Southern California in 1970, Lothrop embarked on a distinguished academic career that culminated in her holding the W. P. Whitsett Chair in History at California State University–Northridge in Northridge, California.

Over the last four decades, Lothrop has compiled an enviable record of academic scholarship and community leadership that focuses frequently (but not exclusively) on Italian American–related subjects. The Pasadena, California, resident regularly participates in southern California's Italian-American activities, addresses various civic and professional organizations about Italian-American topics, and is cited and quoted by scholars and journalists alike. Her lengthy list of publications includes such works as *Fulfilling the Promise of California: An Anthology of Essays on the Italian American Experience in California* (2000) and *The Land Beyond: Italian Migrants in the Westward Movement: An Anthology of Essays on the Italian Settlers' Experience in the American West* (2007).[44] Through all of her professional activities, this top-notch social historian continues to broaden our understanding of the Italian-American contributions to this nation's culture and history.

These contributions receive increasing recognition in American academic research. Much valuable scholarship on the Italians of the United States has been published by the American Italian Historical Association, "an interdisciplinary association for the study of the Italian American experiences."[45] Italian-American history is one of the disciplines that informs our nation's Italian-American Studies programs. These programs, many of which exist at academic institutions in the Northeast, typically take an interdisciplinary approach to the study of Italian Americans. Students enroll in courses as part of the Italian American Studies Program at SUNY–Stony Brook, the John D. Calandra Italian American Institute at Queens College, CUNY, and similar programs at other academic institutions.

When it comes to the history of Italian Americans and other ethnic groups, the historical narratives are constantly evolving and developing—a reflection of the times in which we live and changing societal attitudes. In recent years, the Italian-American experience during World War II has resulted in a flurry of scholarship, including the book, *Una Storia Segreta: The Secret History of Italian American Evacuation and Internment during World War II*.[46] Similarly, the story of Sacco and Vanzetti continues to receive significant attention from historians.[47] "Precisely 80 years on," wrote William Grimes in 2007, "the Sacco-Vanzetti case still resonates like a mournful chord. Almost instantly elevated to the status of myth, the trial and execution of the anarchists Nicola Sacco and Bartolomeo Vanzetti remains one of the blackest pages in the American national story, a cautionary tale of lethal passions fueled by political fear and ethnic prejudice."[48]

Books are one way that we learn more about the history of Italian Americans. These works range from scholarly monographs to self-published autobiographies. In particular, Arcadia Publishing's *Images of America* series provides accessible and well-written photographic books, some of which highlight specific Italian-American communities. A number of such places have been featured as part of this ever-expanding series, including Albuquerque; Chicago; Detroit; Greater Cincinnati; Indianapolis; Milwaukee; Newark, Belleville, and Nutley; New Orleans; Newport and Northern Kentucky; Pittsburgh and Western Pennsylvania; and the Santa Clara Valley. These works of popular history trace the Italian-American story from the era of mass immigration to the present.

In addition, information is disseminated about Italian Americans through exhibitions and documentaries. Exhibitions are a popular and accessible means of exposing the public to facets of Italian-American history. "Not many people know about the Italians of the East Bay," contends Kathleen Maggiora Rogers, as she reflects on the San Francisco Bay Area. Therefore, Rogers helped to put together a traveling photo exhibit (*Con Le Nostre Mani: Italian Americans at Work in the East Bay*) earlier this decade.[49] Meanwhile, we are seeing documentaries that highlight the history of Italians in America. Some of these recent contributions to Italian Americana include *Our Italian Story*; *Italians in America—Our Contribution*; *Linciati: Lynchings of Italians in America*; *And They Came to Chicago: The Italian American Legacy*; and *Beyond Wiseguys: Italian Americans and the Movies.*

The Italian-American dimension of U.S. history is also recognized at a number of research centers and cultural heritage sites. The Immigration History Research Center at the University of Minnesota is America's preeminent repository of material concerning Italian-American ethnicity and the Italian immigration experience.[50] Researchers can also practice their craft using such resources as the Italian American Collection at the Senator John Heinz History Center in Pittsburgh, Pennsylvania, and the Italian American Collection in the San Francisco History Center at the San Francisco Public Library. Similarly, one can learn about Italian-American history at a variety of cultural heritage sites. These locations include the

Italian American Museum (Manhattan), the Italian Cemetery (Colma, California), the Museo ItaloAmericano (San Francisco), the Historic Italian Hall and Museum (Los Angeles); the Garibaldi-Meucci Museum (Staten Island, New York), the National Italian American Sports Hall of Fame (Chicago), the American Italian Heritage Museum and Cultural Center (Albany, New York), and the American Italian Renaissance Foundation Museum and Library (New Orleans).

Of course, there are varying and different perspectives on Italian-American history; many observers, particularly those outside the academy, enthusiastically celebrate their heritage largely uncritically. As part of her reflections in *Were You Always an Italian?*, the author Maria Laurino describes how she strongly dislikes books and documentary films that, in her opinion, are overly positive, celebratory, and sentimental about Italian-American history and family life.[51] Laurino writes: "These pasta/pizza/*paesano* tales embroider the myth of the '*italiano*,' reshaping disparate character traits into a singular folkloric image, rendering us indistinguishable from each other, playing the Muzak of ethnicity."[52]

Much of Italian-American family history is passed down from generation to generation at home. Older folks may tell their descendants about the family's culinary heritage, describe the immigration narrative of their relatives, discuss instances of anti-Italian prejudice and discrimination that occurred decades ago, and take pride in the role that they and their ancestors have played in building communities over the years. People, too, may share treasured family photos and recipes with their descendants. Mary Jane Naro Lankford's grandchildren, for instance, wanted a cookbook with her Italian recipes. Lankford, a Sicilian-American native of Lorain, Ohio, compiled this cookbook and gave it to them as a gift for Christmas.[53] Such examples demonstrate that interest in Italian-American customs exists even among some fourth-, fifth-, and sixth-generation Americans of Italian extraction.

There are numerous written accounts of Italian-American history that come from members of the community itself. Americans of Italian origin write autobiographies, family histories, the stories of Catholic parishes and ethnic enclaves and neighborhoods, and treatments of specific Italian and Italian-American subjects. Take Russell Bonasso of Fairmont, West Virginia. A charismatic man with a passion for social justice, Bonasso is an author, entrepreneur, and newspaper columnist, one who stresses the importance of family, hard work, and education. Over the years, the members of his large family have earned an impressive number of under-graduate and graduate degrees. The 87-year-old's books and oral recollec-tions describe the tough working and living conditions that the Italian immigrants and their children experienced in the West Virginia coal mines and coal camps decades ago.[54]

Carolyn Kantor, a resident of Carbon County, Utah, comes from a family with a heritage of coal mining, too.[55] In an unpublished manu-script, this granddaughter of Italian immigrants reflects on her family's experiences in Utah. She writes:

> We came to Utah looking for a better life. We didn't always find it. Instead of a Promised Land, we often found prejudice, low pay, and intolerance. But we were too stubborn to leave just because things were tough. We stayed and wove our blood and sweat into the fabric of Utah. Anyway we had been tested in the cauldron of time and knew that what we had found here was as good as it gets. When we were faced with a situation that led us to the end of our rope, we just tied a knot and hung on. We could always make a pot of spaghetti, get out the harmonica and play a few tunes, sing some songs, and do a few rounds of the polka.[56]

Carbon County, Utah, is a rich source of Italian-American history in the Mountain West.[57] People from Italian family backgrounds accounted for 9.2 percent of Carbon County's 20,422 residents in the 2000 census. The Italian-American population there includes a significant percentage of northern Italians as well as southern Italians.[58] Today one finds Italian-sur-named individuals in leadership positions throughout Carbon County. For example, Norma Procarione, whose ancestors come from northern Italy, serves as the Librarian at Price City Library in Price, Utah.[59] Overall, there is a great deal of ethnic diversity among the European Americans in this sparsely populated county in east-central Utah, due to the mines that brought many immigrants to the region during the Industrial Era.

Larry Hyatt shares an anecdote that demonstrates how, after decades of integration and the accompanying adjustment issues, Carbon Countians from many different European backgrounds now have a singular American identity. Hyatt is a resident of Helper, Utah, who volunteers in the small town's Western Mining and Railroad Museum. He chats with everyone who visits the museum. A tourist from California came in one day, where-upon Hyatt told her: "We had approximately thirty-five nationalities in the area." She looked at him strangely. "How many nationalities are there now?" the Californian asked this amiable promoter of local history. Hyatt responded, "Just one." She looked at him strangely again. "We're all Americans," he told her.[60] The descendants of Helper's immigrants from long ago are now Utahans and Americans, in yet another example of how a common American identity erases ethnic and cultural differences over time.

茶　茶　茶

The Italian Cultural Society in Sacramento, California, is on the forefront of the efforts to preserve the Italian cultural and linguistic heritage in the Golden State.[61] William Cerruti, a Sacramento attorney, founded the Italian Cultural Society in 1981. This grandson of Genoan immigrants is a native of an Italian neighborhood in East Sacramento. Today William Cerruti and his wife, Patrizia Cinquini Cerruti, are leaders of Sacramento's Italian-American community. Mr. Cerruti serves as executive director of the Italian Cultural Society and chair of the California Italian-American Task Force. Among its many objectives, the Task Force is focused on requiring that Italian-American history be included in the curriculum for California's public school students. Patrizia Cinquini Cerruti, meanwhile, is director of the Italian Cultural Society's Italian Language School. Mrs. Cerruti immigrated to the United States from Tuscany at the age of ten in 1970; now she takes tours of Californians to Italy.

Since 1981 the Italian Cultural Society has developed into a thriving community institution, one that sponsors a wide range of activities. The Society offers travel tours to Italy; cultural programs (films, lectures, performances, the annual Festa Italiana, and more); a language school with four hundred students each quarter; cultural and language programming for youths; and its bimonthly newsletter, *Altre Voci*, with a circulation of ten thousand households. The Italian Cultural Society's $300,000-plus annual revenues allow it to be self-sustaining. Its leaders are consciously inclusive: They create no barriers related to gender or ethnicity for membership or, for that matter, even emphasize membership. Consequently, the Society's activities draw in people from other ethnic groups as well as Italian Americans who do not participate in membership organizations. Most recently, the Italian Cultural Society spearheaded a successful campaign to raise funds to build the Italian Cultural Center in Sacramento. This facility opened in 2007.

Writing in 2006, William Cerruti described the Italian Cultural Center's purpose:

The new Center is our endgame. We have been successful in creating or recreating the sense of community and the social-cultural programming that represented the life of our Italian community in the past. The social and cultural connections that existed among us in the past have faltered. The Italian neighborhoods and all that went with them have waned and pretty much disappeared here and elsewhere. But there is a revitalization effort apparent across the US and I receive reports of Italian community after Italian community rebuilding their physical presence and neighborhoods.

Our new center is located in a suburban area where we have determined there are concentrations of Italian Americans. Our goal is to build the Center where this middle-class concentration exists, according to our mailing lists and the zip codes on our newsletter distribution. We hope, since the Center is being built in such a desirable and affordable area, that the Italian Americans will move into the district and establish businesses, as well as a new social and cultural life for our people.

That is our future and we hope that it will be the future of other Italian American communities. To rebuild their center and all that goes with it. Some may say it's late and it is, but it is happening across the nation and it is the only place we have left to go. If we are to have a future, this is it.[62]

In Albany, New York, meanwhile, Philip J. DiNovo is one of our nation's foremost Italian-American cultural preservationists. Over the last thirty years, he estimates that he has spent more than twelve thousand hours working on Italian-American activities.[63] The Albany native is 100 percent Sicilian. His wife, Mary, is of Roman origin, and she hails from Schenectady, New York. DiNovo, a retired professor, read Richard Gambino's *Blood of My Blood* during the 1970s.[64] This book, coupled with the memory of his Italian-immigrant grandparents, inspired him to become involved in efforts to promote the Italian-American culture. To this end, DiNovo founded the American Italian Heritage Association (AIHA) in 1979.[65] "Our goals are to record and preserve our Italian heritage and culture," according to the AIHA's mission statement.[66] Its members come from four nations and thirty-eight states of the United States.

DiNovo is the AIHA president and editor of the American Italian Heritage Association *Digest*. He is also a member of the National Board of the Italian Folk Art Federation of America. The Sicilian American has written about Italian-American culture and history for various publications around the nation. In retirement he works full-time on Italian-American activities. This community elder is passionate about his heritage and he inspires many people with his dedicated leadership. At times, DiNovo becomes understandably frustrated by the indifference that some members of the Italian-American community show toward the AIHA's work to preserve the history of their ethnic group.

Due to the efforts of DiNovo, the AIHA members, and others, the American Italian Heritage Museum and Cultural Center will open soon in Albany.[67] This institution succeeds the Italian Cultural Center and Museum in Utica, New York, that existed from 1985 to 1998. The first floor of the American Italian Heritage Museum and Cultural Center is a museum with "seven rooms that tell the Italian immigrant experience and highlight the contributions of Italian Americans." The second floor of this building, moreover, houses the Italian Cultural Center (where there will be a hall, a library, an art gallery, and a classroom where Italian language, genealogy, cultural, and cooking classes, among others, will be held). Looking toward the future, Philip J. DiNovo sees this institution as a means of keeping the Italian-American culture alive. "It may be our last opportunity because we won't have this chance again," observes DiNovo.

Chapter 13

PEOPLE OF FAITH

The birth of the Italian Republic on June 2, 1946, is a date that members of the Abruzzo and Molise Heritage Society of the Washington, D.C., Area commemorated with a dinner dance in 2004. One hundred sixteen of the Society's members, friends, and guests turned out for its Festa della Repubblica Dinner Dance on the evening of Saturday, June 26, 2004. The dinner dance was held at Holy Rosary Catholic Church's Casa Italiana on Third Street in Washington. General Pasquale Preziosa, the Italian Embassy's Defense and Air Force Military Attaché, delivered the dinner's keynote address. After dinner, the guests danced and listened to music throughout the evening.[1] In addition to this event, the Society holds a Ferragosto picnic each August, as it commemorates another important Italian holiday (Assumption/Ferragosto).[2] The Society itself is one of Holy Rosary Church's social groups.[3]

Holy Rosary Church draws Italian and Italian-American parishioners from throughout the Washington, D.C., metropolitan region. The church dates back to 1913; originally, it was a territorial parish for Italian immigrants in Washington's Little Italy. The Scalabrini Missionaries assumed responsibility for the parish in 1960, and Holy Rosary continues to be very Italian and Italian American. There is a weekday Mass in English, along with three Sunday Masses: two English Masses (9:00 A.M. and 12 noon) and one Italian Mass (10:30 A.M.). The church cosponsors Washington's Festa Italiana in July—and it publishes *Voce Italiana* (Italian Echo), a twelve-page newspaper. Indeed, Holy Rosary Church is a cultural landmark for Italians and Italian Americans in northern Virginia, southern Maryland, and Washington, D.C.[4]

Holy Rosary has numerous parish associations, prayer groups, and social groups for Italian Americans. Members of the parish associations and the Padre Pio Prayer Group come from a variety of Italian regional backgrounds. Certain prayer groups remain dominated by people from specific places in Italy, as in the St. Gabriel Society (Abruzzesi Americans), the St. Anthony Society (the Pugliese town of Roseto Valfortore), and the St. John the Baptist Society (Castelluccio Valmaggiore, a town in Puglia). Holy Rosary hosts numerous Italian-American social groups, including the Catholic War Veterans, Circolo della Briscola, the Abruzzo and Molise Heritage Society, the Roseto Valfortore Social Club, the Associazione Lucchesi Nel Mondo (Tuscany Club) of Washington, D.C., the Lido Civic Club, and FIERI DC.[5] These societies and prayer groups perpetuate, to some extent, the customs and traditions of the parishioners' forebears.

Casa Italiana (Italian House) is adjacent to—and part of—Holy Rosary Church. This social and cultural center is a gathering place for Italians, Italian Americans, and Italophiles in Washington, D.C., and environs. Casa Italiana opened in 1981. It regularly hosts Italian and Italian-American cultural activities and special events, including dances and dinners. In addition, social, cultural, and religious groups rent Casa Italiana for their Italian-related affairs.[6] The Casa Italiana Cultural Center is home to the Casa Italiana Language School, which offers "a full range of courses in Italian grammar and conversation, arts, and culture taught by native Italian speakers."[7] In sum, Casa Italiana reflects and enhances the ties that Holy Rosary's parishioners have to Italian and Italian-American culture.

The pastor of Holy Rosary Church balances the pastoral needs of his Italian and Italian-American parishioners. Father Lydio F. Tomasi is the current pastor of Holy Rosary Church. This native of Vincenza, Italy, holds a doctorate in sociology from New York University. Moreover, he served as director of the Center for Migration Studies in Staten Island, New York, for thirty-three years. Upon becoming the pastor of Holy Rosary Church in 2006, his biography noted that "Father Tomasi will also address changes and intergenerational transformations in the religious, ethical and cultural values of Italian Americans and all Americans."[8] A Scalabrini Father, Tomasi personifies the international orientation of his religious order. He continues the tradition of having Italian-born priests minister to Holy Rosary's parishioners.[9]

Despite some cultural differences, there is interaction between the Italian Americans and the Italians from Italy who worship at Holy Rosary

Church. In addition to the Italian Americans, there is a sizable population of Italian parishioners at Holy Rosary. (Both demographic groups are represented on the Parish Council.) The Italian nationals of Holy Rosary include people from the Italian Embassy, the World Bank, and the International Monetary Fund, in addition to Italian scholars who conduct research at the National Institutes of Health. Vatican Embassy personnel celebrate Holy Rosary's weekly Italian Mass on Sunday mornings. Second- and third-generation Italian Americans predominate at the English Masses on Sundays.[10] All three Masses draw large crowds. Holy Rosary is an unusual Italian-American church, in that its membership includes large numbers of Italian nationals as well as Americans of Italian descent. These dynamics result in a vibrant parish community.

I. The Feast of St. Gerard occurs every October at St. Lucy's Catholic Church in Newark, New Jersey, "the National Shrine of St. Gerard."[11] This annual cultural and religious event began at St. Lucy in 1899, five years before Gerard Maiella was canonized in 1904. During St. Gerard's Feast, there is a novena. The Italian Mass on the Sunday morning of the Feast, moreover, draws overflow crowds. The "church seats 732, but there are 1,200 people at the Mass," reports Monsignor Joseph Granato, the longtime pastor of St. Lucy's Church. The Feast takes place in St. Gerard Plaza in front of St. Lucy's (which includes a chapel for St. Gerard). In a venerable Italian-American Catholic tradition, the Feast still includes a procession through the neighborhood around St. Lucy's Church, whereby "people pin money on the statue" of St. Gerard as part of their "Prayer for a Favor" or "Thanksgiving for a Favor."[12]

Monsignor Granato describes St. Gerard as a "very powerful intercessor for this area." His parish includes many men named Gerard and many women named Geraldine. "Young women who are having trouble conceiving pray to St. Gerard for help conceiving," says Granato. "And they do conceive." "Each year there are more than one hundred newborn babies and more than one hundred expectant mothers," continues Monsignor Granato. Another reason that women pray to St. Gerard is "for healthy babies." Granato notes that "we give away sixty thousand medals of St. Gerard" annually; there is a new design on the medal each year. Also, he and his colleagues bless handkerchiefs with St. Gerard relics and distribute these items to people who request them. In fact, there is an easel at St.

Lucy's Church with letters from happy mothers and the photographs of their babies who were born after they prayed to St. Gerard.[13]

The Feast of St. Gerard has helped St. Lucy's Church, socially and financially. "This church would not have survived without the Feast of St. Gerard," notes Monsignor Joseph Granato. The 1950s and 1960s were difficult years for his parish, when many parishioners left Newark for the suburbs.[14] Now St. Lucy Parish is mainly Italian American and Hispanic. Italian Americans account for more than 50 percent of the parishioners, a large number of whom live in the suburbs and still come back to the church.[15] There is an Italian Mass on Sunday mornings that draws fifty people, on average, while Spanish Masses are celebrated on Sundays and Tuesday nights. At St. Lucy's Church, there are various feasts, devotions, and statues. These feasts honor St. Anthony (June), Our Lady of Mount Carmel (July), St. Rocco (August), Our Lady of the Assumption (August), St. Michael (September), and St. Gerard (October).[16]

Monsignor Joseph Granato's grandparents were immigrants from Campania, and he grew up near St. Lucy's Church. His parents were married at St. Lucy's, a parish that dates back to 1891. Granato himself has served the parish community of this Newark institution since his ordination in June 1955. Of his parishioners, Monsignor Granato says, "They are fiercely loyal. They are supportive. They are devout." In 2003, there were 80 weddings, 150 funerals, and 415 baptisms at St. Lucy, which has a Chapel of Perpetual Eucharistic Adoration. The baptisms, a sign of the parish's future, were 50 percent Italian and 50 percent Hispanic that year. "This parish is still heavily Italian-American in character," concludes Monsignor Joseph Granato, who values his parishioners from all ethnic backgrounds.[17]

The Italian immigrants and their descendants in New Jersey and beyond were, of course, strongly influenced by their religious experiences in Italy.[18] Mary Elizabeth Brown writes, "Three demographic factors shaped religious experience in Italy and carried over into immigrant religious experience in the United States."[19] For starters, the Italian immigrants came from a predominantly Catholic nation, one "without much religious pluralism."[20] "Second," as Brown points out, "although Italy is largely Catholic, there are tremendous regional variations in its Catholicism."[21] The southern Italian immigrants in particular had religious cultures that differed from American Catholicism.[22] "Their religious culture was characterized by an emphasis on lay-led, communal rituals, the annual feast day celebrations of town patron saints, and a folk culture of anticlericalism," writes Mary Elizabeth Brown.[23]

Finally, gender affected how the Italians approached and observed Catholicism. Brown writes: "Women were the links between the family and official Catholicism, the ones who were more regular in attendance at Mass and at devotions such as the rosary."[24] Italian men, to be sure, participated in other Catholic activities. "Men were the leaders of the lay-based, communal religious practices, the ones who organized the annual celebration of the patron saints' feast days," observes Mary Elizabeth Brown.[25] The Italian-immigrant population in the United States was heavily male during the late 1800s and early 1900s; therefore, these individuals were often unaccustomed to attending Mass regularly and engaging in other expressions of official Catholicism.[26]

As numerous historians have documented over the years, the Italian immigrants' transition into American Catholicism was somewhat difficult. The historian Jay P. Dolan writes: "The Italians offered the classic example of one group's practice of religion being misunderstood and consequently labeled by others as pagan superstition. Italian Catholicism was rooted in the confraternity and festive celebrations in honor of popular saints, rather than regular attendance at Mass and frequent reception of the sacraments. This shocked many American clergy—the Irish especially—and led to a litany of complaints, criticisms, and even conflict."[27] Even today, some elderly and middle-aged Italian Americans still recount stories of being outsiders in their parishes and parochial schools.

Yet the Italian immigrants and their descendants transplanted their distinctive faith traditions onto American soil and laid the basis for a vibrant Italian-American Catholicism that persists to this day. "The migrants re-created the lay-led, communal religion they had known in Italy," writes Mary Elizabeth Brown.[28] The Italian immigrants created mutual-benefit societies, organized celebrations of feast days for their ancestral patron saints, and in other ways preserved and perpetuated their religious traditions.[29] "The American environment shaped the development of the Italians' religious practice," observes Brown.[30] Not surprisingly, contemporary Italian-American Catholics seem to be similar to other Catholics when it comes to Mass attendance and other observances of Catholicism.[31]

Decades after the mass immigration from Italy to the United States, Italian-American Catholics still observe some of the religious practices and traditions that they and their ancestors brought with them from the Old World. There are novenas, processions, devotions to specific patron saints and the Madonna, and other specific dimensions of Italian-American Catholicism. Older Italian Americans often celebrate the patron saints from their ancestral villages, towns, cities, and regions in Italy.[32] Many Catholic parishes have religious societies and church festivals that are Italian or Italian American in character—or at least influenced by Italian and Italian-American culture. The Italian national parishes that once existed in many parts of America are now often ethnically diverse in character. Some Americans see themselves as Italian Catholics or Italian-American Catholics, not just Italian/American or Catholic; their faith is part of how they self-identify in an ethnic sense.

Currently, many Italian-American Catholics, particularly the members of the younger generations, are very secular in their outlook and faith practices. There are fewer and fewer ways in which contemporary Italian Americans practice Catholicism that differentiate them from other Catholics.[33] It seems that the solid, if not vast, majority of Italian Americans continue to be at least nominally Roman Catholic. Many Italian Americans are ancestrally Catholic and may have been baptized in the Church, but they do not attend Mass regularly. To be sure, much of the intermarriage by Italian Americans across ethnic lines has occurred within the Catholic community.

II. Eugene (Gene) Fedeli and Shirley Martignoni Fedeli are devout Catholics, whose activities span two Catholic churches in their hometown of Rockford, Illinois.[34] They are officially members of the Cathedral of St. Peter in Rockford and, at the same time, they participate in the faith community at St. Anthony of Padua Church, Rockford's heavily Italian parish.[35] "Gene and I were baptized at St. Anthony," notes Shirley Fedeli. "But as the boundaries changed in our diocese, I became a member of the Cathedral of St. Peter and when I married Gene he joined that parish due to our boundaries." With the easing of such rules, the Fedelis began participating in activities (the Columbus Day Mass, celebrations of St. Lucy, and other events) at St. Anthony Church because they wanted to support Italian cultural-preservation efforts. They also remain active members of the St. Peter's parish community.

The Fedelis are linchpins of Rockford's Italian-American community.

Gene Fedeli's parents, Maria Piazzalunga and Alberto Fedeli, were immigrants from Lombardy who arrived in Rockford during the 1920s. Shirley Martignoni Fedeli's parents were Catherine Domino (an American of Sicilian descent) and Peter Martignoni (an American who traced his ancestry to Lombardy). Gene Fedeli, who was born in 1936, repeated the first grade because he did not speak English, only Lombardian dialect. Mr. Fedeli also speaks standard Italian. As a boy, Gene Fedeli would never collect money from the lady on his paper route who reportedly gave the *mal'occhio* to her enemies. He would take what she owed to him out of his earnings. As an adult, Gene Fedeli worked at Barnes International, Inc. Mrs. Fedeli, meanwhile, is a retired educator and 1957 graduate of Rockford College. She and her husband have one daughter, Lisa Fedeli Hughes, and one granddaughter, Alexandra Hughes.

Gene Fedeli and Shirley Martignoni Fedeli are deeply involved, as a team, in many of Rockford's Italian-American activities. These outgoing and friendly Illinoisans write grant proposals for various schools, programs, and museums in Rockford and environs. Gene Fedeli serves as co-chairman of the Greater Rockford Italian American Association (GRIAA) and he is part of several GRIAA committees. The Fedelis and a colleague coedit the *Pappagallo*, the publication of GRIAA. Shirley Martignoni Fedeli, meanwhile, chairs three GRIAA committees: Culture and Education, the Columbus Day Mass, and the *Pappagallo*. In addition, she is the founder of the Amici Italiani Dance Troupe and the president of the Board of Directors of the Ethnic Heritage Museum in Rockford. Shirley Martignoni Fedeli and her husband now spend much of their time working on Italian and Italian-American projects.

These lifelong Rockford residents are creative exponents of the Italian-American cultural heritage. Mrs. Fedeli has been known to bring Sicilian puppets, an old broom from northern Italy, and other Italian artifacts with her to teach schoolchildren about Italian history and culture. Gene Fedeli, an expert palm weaver, is devoted to preserving this venerable art; he gives workshops on palm weaving in various parts of the Midwest. Mr. Fedeli, moreover, plays bocce and he continues the Italian custom of greeting men by kissing them on both cheeks. The Fedelis also contribute to cultural exchanges with Italians from Italy. During one such exchange in 2007, the Fedelis took visiting youths from Ferentino (Rockford's sister city in Italy) on a tour around northern Illinois.

Now in their early seventies, the Fedelis remain faithful to many Italian and Italian-American customs and traditions. Gene Fedeli, for instance, tends a substantial flower garden in the backyard of his home. The Fedelis regularly visit Italy, too. Gene Fedeli traces his ancestry to the Lombardian town of Cairate. The 2006 calendar for the Comune di Cairate in Lombardy included entries of Cairatese families from Argentina, Belgium, Brazil, France, Paraguay, Switzerland, and the United States. The Fedelis were featured as the June 2006 calendar entry; they represented the Americans. Recently, Mrs. Fedeli prayed to God and St. Lucy so that her cataract surgery would go well. Her prayers were answered. She and her husband are currently working on "a DVD of photos of St. Joseph Altars," and they already have 300 such altar photos. As pious Catholics, Gene Fedeli and Shirley Martignoni Fedeli integrate their faith traditions and Italian ancestry together seamlessly.

Today the Italian-American Catholic heritage continues to enrich many American communities. In the future, fewer and fewer Catholic parishes will have a distinctly Italian-American character, even as more and more parishes will have an identifiable Italian-American presence. Due to the current demographic trends, there are relatively few parishes becoming more Italian in the Northeast and Midwest. However, in the South and West, it is not uncommon for a parish to increase its Italian-American population from a small, almost nonexistent, percentage to a larger one in response to migration patterns. Such states as Arizona, Florida, and Nevada are home to Catholic parishes with growing Italian-American populations. The heavily Italian parishes will continue, in all likelihood, to feature Italian cultural and religious traditions.

One such parish is St. Dominic Roman Catholic Church in Brooklyn, New York. Seventy percent of the parishioners at St. Dominic Parish are Italians and Italian Americans. Many of them are older Italian Americans whose children have left the area. The parish dates back to the 1970s, and it includes twenty-five hundred active parishioners. On Sundays, there are three English Masses, one Italian Mass, and one Spanish Mass. (Thirty Italians, on average, attend the daily Italian Mass at St. Dominic Parish and approximately four hundred folks come to the Sunday Italian Mass.) Father Gaetano Sbordone, the pastor of St. Dominic, is the Brooklyn-born grandson of Campanian immigrants. Deacon Carlo Mellace of St. Dominic Church is an immigrant from Calabria who came to the United States in 1979; he heads the Italian Apostolate of the Diocese of Brooklyn.[36]

At St. Dominic, there are many faith activities, including singing, prayers, devotions, processions, and pilgrimages to certain shrines in the Northeast. Three Italian regional groups (the Apulians, Sicilians, and Calabrians) account for many of St. Dominic Parish's Italians and Italian Americans. In this parish, for instance, St. Joseph is celebrated with three dishes (one from Apulia, one from Sicily, and one from Calabria) to take into account the traditions of each of the three major Italian regional groups. "We maintain traditions that are disappearing in Italy," say Father Gaetano Sbordone and Deacon Carlo Mellace. When Italians from Italy come to Brooklyn, they reportedly marvel at the deep expressions of faith that they see in New York.[37]

Saint Anthony of Padua Parish in Youngstown, Ohio, meanwhile, continues to be a heavily Italian-American faith community. "The parish was founded in 1898 and served the needs of a large Italian population who immigrated to Youngstown to work in the steel mills," according to one parish history. "It is the oldest Italian parish in the Mahoning [V]alley."[38] Monsignor John DeMarinis, the pastor of St. Anthony, is the son of Italian immigrants and a Youngstown native who holds a master's degree in modern Italian history. Five hundred families are part of St. Anthony of Padua Parish. Ninety-five percent of the parishioners at St. Anthony are Italian Americans, particularly those individuals whose ancestors come from the Basilicata region.[39]

According to DeMarinis, the pastor and his parish are "very much aligned with Italian customs and traditions." His parishioners continue to be devoted to Saint Anthony, with a Feast of Saint Anthony that includes a large Mass, a statue of the saint, and a procession. Indeed, the Italian heritage is an important part of parish life. This heritage includes such Italian-American culinary staples as sweet pizzas, Easter bread, calamari in a jar, and the annual spaghetti dinner. Monsignor DeMarinis includes Italian proverbs in the church bulletin, too. Even today, there are some ethnically endogamous marriages involving Italian Americans in Saint Anthony of Padua Parish.[40]

Similarly, Our Lady of the Rosary Catholic Church in San Diego's Little Italy continues to be a thriving faith community with deep roots in Italian-American culture.[41] An Italian National Parish, the church was consecrated in 1925 and built by fishermen who taxed themselves twenty-five cents per ton of fish. Now the parish is largely composed of second- and third-generation Italian Americans, many of whom have Sicilian ancestry. It is "open to everyone," emphasizes Father Steven Grancini, the pastor of Our Lady of the Rosary. The parish draws Italian Americans from different parts of San Diego, who go there for Masses, baptisms, weddings, ceremonies, funerals, festivals, and parish activities.[42]

The Italian Catholic traditions remain alive and well at Our Lady of the Rosary Church. In fact, young people are joining the parish societies and, by doing so, maintaining these traditions. The different feasts at this church take into account the origins of the parishioners, particularly their ancestral hometowns in Sicily. Every feast has its own procession. The marchers stop the procession at certain points, turn the statue of a saint toward various houses, and people pin money on it. There are songs and prayers in Sicilian and Italian for the Novena of St. Anthony and the Madonna del Lume. In addition, there is an Italian Mass on the first Sunday of each month and at the festivals, too. As Father Grancini describes how his parishioners strongly support their church in terms of renovations and other matters, he concludes: "There is a family spirit in the parish."[43]

III. The Most Reverend Nicholas DiMarzio, Bishop of Brooklyn, has long focused on issues involving migrants and immigration, from testifying before Congress to negotiating with Fidel Castro for the release of political prisoners. After earning a doctorate in Social Work Research and Policy from Rutgers University in 1985, he spent six years as the Executive Director for Migration and Refugee Services at the U.S. Conference of Catholic Bishops (USCCB) in Washington, D.C. From 1998 to 2001 the Newark, New Jersey, native served as Chairman of the Migration Committee for the USCCB. DiMarzio is currently a member of the Pontifical Council for the Pastoral Care of Migrants and Itinerant People and previously served as a member of the Global Commission on International Migration.[44] He frequently writes about immigrants and immigration issues and, on occasion, has received some negative feedback from native-born Americans for doing so.[45]

This grandson of Italian immigrants was born on June 16, 1944, in Newark. Bishop DiMarzio's Italian-born grandparents came as young people to New Jersey. In fact, his maternal grandparents lived with DiMarzio's family while he was growing up in Newark. They spoke dialectal Italian. According to Bishop DiMarzio, the Italian-American Catholics of his youth exhibited "a lot of devotion" and "a little bit of anti-clericalism." During the last twenty years, he has heard periodically that

Italian Americans are proud to see bishops of Italian descent.[46] His record of leadership includes such positions as Auxiliary Bishop of Newark (1996 to 1999), Bishop of Camden (1999 to 2003), and Bishop of Brooklyn (2003 to the present). Presently he is the spiritual leader of one of North America's most diverse groups of Catholics, many of whom are immigrants or the children of immigrants.[47]

As the Bishop of Brooklyn, Nicholas DiMarzio has myriad civic, pastoral, and administrative responsibilities. The Diocese of Brooklyn encompasses the boroughs of Brooklyn and Queens, an area with nearly five million residents. DiMarzio is a significant civic figure in Brooklyn and Queens, due to his important position and respected professional background. As a pastoral leader, he articulates the Church's teachings and reaches out to the area's Catholics. To this end, he regularly visits the parishes in his diocese. As an administrator, he oversees the Catholic parishes, hospitals, high schools, and grammar schools in Brooklyn and Queens.

Nicholas DiMarzio embraces his diocese's remarkable ethnic, racial, cultural, and religious diversity. As of 2004, the Diocese of Brooklyn had 20 Creole Masses, 30 Polish Masses, 45 Italian Masses, and 120 Spanish Masses. The Bishop's Pastoral Letters will appear in English, Spanish, and several other languages. DiMarzio takes note of the particular holidays and feast days that matter to Catholics in his diocese: Boxing Day (December 26), for example, is an important holiday for Guyanese Americans. When it comes to how the Bishop allocates his limited time, he notes that one needs to "balance the need for attention and love in the family." Some groups require more attention than others at a particular time.[48]

The Italian-American cultural heritage matters to Bishop DiMarzio, of course. The Diocese of Brooklyn includes a sizable and visible Italian-American Catholic community, and DiMarzio himself reports that he speaks Italian "fairly well." He is the American Liaison to the Italian Bishops Conference.[49] DiMarzio was also one of the honorees at the Italian American Museum Gala and Awards Ceremony 2006. And he participated in the efforts "to establish an Italian Chapel in honor of Our Lady of Pompei in the Basilica of the National Shrine of the Immaculate Conception in Washington, D.C."[50] The Diocese of Brooklyn has been a traditional bastion of Italian-American Catholics over the years. It is fitting, then, that Bishop Nicholas DiMarzio adds to the diocese's rich multicultural history through his inclusive and culturally sensitive style of leadership.

Immigration is a significant issue that affects virtually every American institution—and the Catholic Church is no exception. Indeed, the Church is often on the forefront of this issue, due to the demographics of its parishioners and the positions of certain Catholic leaders (Cardinal Roger Mahony of Los Angeles has been particularly visible in his advocacy of immigrants' rights). During the period of mass immigration from Italy, the Missionaries of Saint Charles–Scalabrinians came to the United States to serve the Italian immigrants and their descendants. Over the years the Scalabrinians specialized in helping the Italian immigrants; now they also work with Spanish-speaking immigrants and other non-Italian groups. The Scalabrini Fathers are not all Italians anymore, either.[51] Today there are numerous Catholic parishes that were once heavily Italian, but now they have sizable Latino populations.

There are complex ethnic dynamics at Our Lady of Mount Carmel Church in Melrose Park, Illinois, a heavily Italian-American suburb of Chicago. The novena, devotions, processions, and festivals at Mount Carmel were all Italian until the 1970s. During the 1970s and 1980s Spanish-speaking Catholics began coming to the parish; now they account for a solid majority of this particular faith community. Father Louis Gandolfi, a Scalabrinian and native Italian, recently served as pastor of Our Lady of Mount Carmel in Melrose Park. He speaks English, Spanish, and Italian. As pastor of Our Lady of Mount Carmel, Father Gandolfi recorded his voicemail message in three languages—and he referred to himself as Father Louis, Padre Luis, and Padre Luigi. In fact, one can attend the parish's Sunday Masses in three different languages: English, Italian, and Spanish.[52]

Mount Carmel in Melrose Park is currently a heavily Latino (60 to 65 percent Mexican) parish with a sizable Italian-American presence. The Italian-American parishioners are mostly elderly, while their children return to Melrose Park for special feasts. As one might expect from a well-established ethnic group, the Italians are disproportionately responsible for the financial support of the parish. Yet Hispanic Catholics account for the preponderance of weddings, baptisms, and quinceañera celebrations there. At the same time, there are many funerals for Italian-American parishioners. "Integration of the groups is very slow," notes Father Louis Gandolfi. He reports that there are "no fights" between the Latinos and the Italians, but "the underlying division is clear." Ministry to two different ethnic groups requires empathy, awareness, knowledge, and understanding, says Gandolfi.[53]

St. Peter's Italian Catholic Church in Los Angeles is another traditionally Italian parish in a multiethnic community.[54] Father Giovanni Bizzotto,
a Scalabrini Father, recently served as the pastor of St. Peter's. A native
Italian, Bizzotto has worked with Catholics in Canada, Mexico, and the
United States. The area around St. Peter's was once a heavily Italian neighborhood, and the Church dates back to 1904. Currently St. Peter is a trilin-
gual (English, Spanish, Italian) parish. When he served as the pastor there,
Father Giovanni Bizzotto's voicemail message was in three languages:
English, Spanish, and Italian. The parish's population of Italian Americans
is scattered throughout the Los Angeles metropolitan area.[55]

Many important events in Italian Los Angeles take place at St. Peter's
Italian Catholic Church, a significant community institution for Italian
Americans in southern California. "People come here for special occasions," reports Father Bizzotto. Parties and festivities bring the Italians
back to the Church. Fifty Italian organizations meet at the Casa Italiana
adjacent to St. Peter's. According to Father Bizzotto, the Casa Italiana is
the "crib" of Italian-American Los Angeles. The weekly 11:00 A.M. Italian
Mass at St. Peter's draws 80 to 100 people on a regular basis and 300 to
400 people on a feast day. There is "a good core of Italian people coming
here," said Bizzotto in a 2004 interview. The parish has a Hispanic mission and includes Latino, Filipino, Chinese, and Vietnamese parishioners.
"We are open to everybody," Bizzotto told the Italians during his pas-
torate. "We are all people of God."[56]

IV. "Justice" is the overarching theme of Sister Margaret
Galiardi's life and work. Indeed, the Long Island, New
York, resident reads and interprets the Gospel as offering a "radical egal-
itarian message."[57] In 1964 she joined the Dominican Sisters of Amityville
in New York. Since then Galiardi has spent more than four decades educating, serving, and advocating on behalf of others. Her curriculum vitae
includes nearly a decade of service at the Intercommunity Center for Justice and Peace in Manhattan. Galiardi currently works at Homecoming,
an organization located in Amityville, New York, where she focuses on
Earth-based spirituality. Sister Margaret, who has a master's degree in
theology, notes that such environmental issues as delicate ecosystems, the
loss of topsoil, and global warming matter much to her.[58] Galiardi's book,
Encountering Mystery in the Wilderness: One Woman's Vision Quest (2004),

details her perspective on how we human beings relate to and interact with the environment.[59]

Sister Margaret Galiardi is an Italian American who has held significant offices in the Dominican Order. A native of New York City, she was born in Brooklyn on December 14, 1946. Her mother and father were American-born Italians of Abruzzese and Barese descent, respectively. From 1995 to 2001 she served as Director of Ministry, an elected position, for her Congregation. During those years Sister Margaret Galiardi also became the Dominican Order's Co-Promoter of Justice for North America. In this capacity, she served as a member of the Dominican International Commission for Justice, Peace, and the Integrity of Creation. Galiardi's work took her to Belgium, Bolivia, Cuba, the Dominican Republic, El Salvador, France, Guatemala, Hong Kong, Iraq, Israel, Italy, Nicaragua, the Philippines, and Spain.[60]

In her leadership role with the Dominican Order, Galiardi developed an acute awareness of international perceptions of U.S. foreign policies. Globally, she felt hostility toward her and U.S. government policies when she attended regional meetings and international conferences. "The work on justice and peace in this country has changed some perceptions of Dominicans in the developing countries regarding their brothers and sisters here," says Sister Margaret Galiardi.[61] When she and some of her colleagues traveled to Iraq in February 2000, their trip showed that not every American supported U.S. policies toward this Middle Eastern nation.[62] Galiardi heard about the impact of years of sanctions from the Dominican Sisters in Iraq. The Iraqi nuns were quite surprised to learn about the number of Americans and different groups that opposed the sanctions.[63] Galiardi herself testified to Congress about her Iraqi experiences in 2002.[64]

This American with a global world view remembers a particularly moving anecdote from her 2000 trip to Iraq. It occurred while she prayed in the lobby of her hotel. Galiardi's copy of the New Testament was on the table in front of her. She was looking out at the water when an elderly Iraqi man, dressed in traditional attire, came toward her. He had the Arabic prayer beads that one carries with him when he recites the Ninety-Nine Names of God in the Qur'an (it is a devotion). The Iraqi man greeted Sister Margaret in Arabic. She greeted him in kind. Then he held up his prayer beads: The quizzical look on his face signified that he wanted to know if she knew what they were. Sister Margaret nodded her head. In response, the devout Muslim bowed and pointed his prayer beads to her Scriptures simultaneously. Then both he and she bowed to one another in recognition of their shared bond of faith and humanity. It was a human connection "across barriers of language, culture, gender, age, and political alignment," says Sister Margaret Galiardi.[65] She personifies the increasingly significant role that people from Italian family backgrounds play in representing American Catholics throughout the world.

In recent years, Italian Americans have become prominent figures in the U.S. Catholic Church's leadership. The American Church hierarchy was traditionally dominated by Irish Americans. Anecdotal evidence suggests that some Italian Americans felt their coethnics were excluded all too often from leadership positions in this significant American institution. Now the expanding ranks of Italian Americans in the Church leadership parallel their rise throughout American society.[66] At this time, Italian Americans occupy roles of considerable influence in the American Catholic Church as priests, bishops, archbishops, and cardinals. There are three Italian-American Cardinals: Cardinal Anthony Bevilacqua, the archbishop emeritus of Philadelphia, Cardinal Roger Mahony, the archbishop of Los Angeles, and Cardinal Justin Rigali, the archbishop of Philadelphia.

Cardinal Justin Rigali serves as the spiritual leader of the area that includes one of America's largest concentrations of Italian-American Catholics. His paternal grandfather, Luigi Rigali, was born in 1851 in the Province of Lucca. One of twelve children, Rigali came to the United States for the first time about 1869. Luigi Rigali resided in Holyoke, Massachusetts, where he married an Irish-American woman. The Cardinal's father, Henry Rigali, was born in Holyoke in 1887. He graduated from Holy Cross College in 1910.[67] Henry Rigali and his wife, Frances Rigali, had seven children. Their seventh child, Justin, was born in April 1935 in Los Angeles. The future cardinal grew up in the City of the Angels, and he attended seminaries in southern California. After his Los Angeles ordination in April 1961, Rigali went to study and work in Rome.[68]

A talented linguist who speaks impeccable Italian, Cardinal Rigali lived in Italy for thirty years. He began his graduate studies in Rome in October 1961. Except for a three-and-a-half-year period, Rigali made his home in Rome from late 1961 until early 1994. Consequently, this grandson of an Italian immigrant has a particularly compelling perspective on the connections between Italy and the United States, the Italians and the Italian Americans. During his time in Italy, Rigali gained insights into "what the Italians left" and "what they went through" over the years.[69] Further, he learned about "their outlook" and "their ways of doing things."[70] The distinguished American Catholic leader notes that he holds the Italian culture in "immense esteem."[71]

For three decades, Cardinal Rigali held influential Vatican positions of importance and authority. After earning a doctorate in canon law from Rome's Pontifical Gregorian University in 1964, he served in the Vatican Secretariat of State's English-language section. Rigali spent three and one-half years working at the Vatican Embassy in Madagascar. Then, from February 1970 to August 1978, he served as Pope Paul VI's English-language translator, as well as the director of the Vatican Secretariat of State's English-language section. A friend to Pope John Paul II, this well-traveled Vatican official held a number of prominent positions during the pontificate, e.g., President of the Pontifical Ecclesiastical Academy, Secretary of the Congregation for Bishops, and Secretary of the College of Cardinals. Moreover, in 1985, Rigali received the honor of being named Titular Archbishop of Bolsena.[72]

Cardinal Rigali returned to the United States in 1994, when Pope John Paul II appointed him the archbishop of St. Louis. Rigali served as the spiritual leader of Catholics in St. Louis for nine and one-half years.[73] "He worked long hours and earned a reputation as a micro-manager, an excellent fund-raiser and a serious canon lawyer," notes one observer of his years in St. Louis.[74] Rigali forcefully advocated on behalf of the poor and worked tirelessly to abolish Missouri's death penalty. In addition, he vigorously spoke out in favor of the pro-life position.[75] One highlight of Rigali's tenure in St. Louis was Pope John Paul II's Pastoral Visit in January 1999. Rigali personally invited the Pope to come to St. Louis. Then he coordinated the arrangements for John Paul II's immensely successful visit there.[76] Indeed, the Holy Father's trip to St. Louis was "the only such visit to a single diocese in the United States during the pontificate."[77]

In 2003 Rigali was named the archbishop of Philadelphia and, later in the year, he became the only American on the Pope's list of thirty-one new cardinals.[78] In his pastoral duties and management responsibilities as Archbishop of Philadelphia, the Cardinal strives to be "solicitous" and "attentive" to the spiritual needs of the 1.5 million Catholics who live in the five-county region of the Archdiocese of Philadelphia.[79] The region encompasses 270 parishes in southeastern Pennsylvania; it includes Bucks, Chester, Delaware, Montgomery, and Philadelphia counties. In the last federal census, Italian Americans accounted for 504,056, or 13.1 percent, of the 3,849,647 people in these five counties. Overall, Rigali emphatically articulates an inclusive message that resonates with southeastern Pennsylvania's Catholics in general and Italian-American Catholics in particular.

Italian Americans figure prominently among the ranks of Greater Philadelphia's Catholics. They identify with Rigali because of his Italian heritage. "Many Italian Americans in Philadelphia tell me they're happy I'm here," reports the Cardinal.[80] Indeed, he speaks of the importance of transmitting Italian-American culture from one generation to the next. There are fourteen Italian national parishes in the Archdiocese of Philadelphia, with 34,000 to 35,000 Catholics in those parishes today. The Archdiocese of Philadelphia also includes "eight or nine other parishes" with sizable percentages of parishioners from Italian family backgrounds.[81] "It is the Italian national parishes," notes Cardinal Rigali, "that actually preserve the Italian American usages in their parish life."[82]

The Cardinal is a hands-on leader of southeastern Pennsylvania's multitudinous Catholics. He visits every one of the Archdiocese's 270 parishes. Rigali, who spends each Sunday in a different parish, enjoys meeting and speaking with the parishioners. His Eminence thrives on the multicultural dimension of his pastoral outreach. He attends such events as a celebration to mark a Polish national parish's one-hundredth anniversary.[83] And in January 2005 he presided over and delivered the keynote address at the twenty-second Annual Interfaith Service in Remembrance of Rev. Dr. Martin Luther King Jr. in Philadelphia.[84] Furthermore, Rigali notes that the "Church collaborates with the community in many areas."[85] The Catholic schools, for instance, serve many non-Catholic students.[86] In sum, Cardinal Rigali's extraordinary record of leadership exemplifies the significant contributions that Italian Americans make to the U.S. Catholic Church as well as the global Church.

V. From 1995 to 1998, the president (Bishop Anthony M. Pilla) and the vice president (then-Bishop Joseph A. Fiorenza) of the U.S. Conference of Catholic Bishops were Italian Americans.[87] This was a significant milestone for Americans of Italian origin. Both of Bishop Pilla's parents, George Pilla and Libera Nista, came from Collesannita, a town in the Province of Benevento directly east of Naples. George Pilla and Libera Nista met in Cleveland, Ohio. Their son, Anthony Pilla, was born in November 1932, and he remembers a childhood that included family activities, Catholic feast days, and their membership in an Italian parish (Holy Rosary). He admires the older Italian priests who "did a great job of establishing credibility for the Italo-Americans." They helped the immigrants in many ways, by assisting them in finding jobs, obtaining a good education, and even getting them out of trouble.[88]

Anthony Pilla grew up in an Italian-American community, one in which the *paesani* referred to each other as "cousins." He and his family spoke Italian at home. His grandmother never even learned to speak English. Bishop Pilla describes the conscious dimensions of his Italian heritage in terms of "family values," Italian traditions, "respect for elders," "taking care of each other," and "weddings and funerals." The Cleveland native delineates such factors as a "certain compassion for people" and "hospitality and welcome" as being elements of his Italian heritage, too. Italian family traditions continue to be important for the Pillas, and they gather every Sunday at Anthony Pilla's brother's home for lunch. In addition, the Pillas use family recipes that are handed down through the generations; Anthony Pilla notes that his brother and his niece still can tomatoes in accordance with family traditions.[89]

"Certainly my heritage impacts everything I do," says Bishop Pilla, "including religious issues."[90] His perspective has been affected by the stories and experiences of intolerance involving the Italian immigrants. Bishop Pilla remembers his father telling him about "prejudice in the workplace" and, to some extent, in society. As a youth, he heard about what it was like to be "considered imported scab labor." The bishop himself heard the words *wop* and *dago* for the first time when he went to public school, and he remembers that some of his classmates exhibited anti-immigrant bias and anti-Catholic bias. He also takes note of the stereotyping of Italians, particularly with regard to the Mafia.[91] Today Pilla holds the important Italian title of Grand'Ufficiale and he has been honored by the Bishop Anthony M. Pilla Program in Italian American Studies at John Carroll University in Cleveland, Ohio.[92]

Pilla served as Bishop of Cleveland from 1981 to 2006. He was ordained in Cleveland in 1959. After working briefly as an associate pastor in Cleveland, he taught at St. Charles for fourteen years. Then he served as Secretary for Clergy and Religious under then-Bishop Hickey for six years before becoming Auxiliary Bishop (1979 to 1980) of the Diocese of Cleveland. Pilla became Bishop of Cleveland in January 1981. The Ohioan notes that he was a trailblazer for Italian Americans as the Bishop of Cleveland; in fact, he was the "first non-Irish or non-German bishop in the history of this diocese."[93] People of Italian descent make up a significant percentage of Greater Cleveland's Catholic population.

Indeed, Anthony Pilla has seen dramatic changes occur for Italian Americans over the years. In 1979, when he became an auxiliary bishop in the Diocese of Cleveland, it was very rare to find Italian Americans on Cleveland's civic and corporate boards. By 2004, it was very rare to find civic and corporate boards that did not have (or had not had) Italian-American members. Bishop Pilla reflects on the progress that he has observed over the years, as indicated by the Italian-American lawyers, doctors, and CEOs that one sees in Cleveland and environs today.[94] Italian Americans, to be sure, are proud of Bishop Pilla. They "relate to me," he said in a 2004 interview.[95]

As Bishop of Cleveland, Pilla had significant duties and responsibilities. In this capacity, he was responsible for the spiritual lives of 900,000 Catholics, particularly the "proper transmission of Church teachings in the schools and otherwise." The Diocese of Cleveland includes 234 parishes and a school system with 60,000 students. Moreover, it is a significant social-service provider, one that serves 3 million meals per year. Every day as bishop, Pilla was out in the community in his multiethnic, multiracial diocese. He notes that there are sixty-three ethnic groups, including sizable numbers of Eastern Europeans, represented in the Diocese of Cleveland. He always sought to be present for significant events for the different ethnic groups.[96] "Whenever necessary," says Bishop Pilla, "I try to bring people together." The Bishop, too, indicated that it was important to him to "try to get people to work collaboratively with each other."[97]

In keeping with the large Catholic presence in Cleveland and environs, Anthony Pilla was one of Cleveland's most important figures during his twenty-five years as Bishop of Cleveland. Bishop Pilla is deeply interested in the efforts to bridge the urban-suburban gaps that sometimes develop in Cleveland and the other traditionally industrial cities of the Midwest and Northeast. One component of his bridge-building efforts involves urban-suburban partnerships between parishes. In addition, Cleveland's Catholic leaders try to affect policy with regard to urban-planning issues for the entire metropolitan region. The Roman Catholic Church—and the parochial schools in particular—are very important to the health of Cleveland's neighborhoods.[98] Pilla's initiatives on these issues are a significant part of his legacy; the well-regarded prelate retired as Bishop of Cleveland in 2006.

Archbishop Joseph A. Fiorenza, who led what was then the Diocese of Galveston-Houston, succeeded Anthony Pilla as president of the U.S. Conference of Catholic Bishops in 1998. His father, Anthony Fiorenza, was born in Sicily in a town near Palermo, and he came to the United States when he was thirteen or fourteen. His mother, Grace Galiano, hailed from a Sicilian-immigrant family in Texas; she was a native of the Lone Star State. Archbishop Fiorenza himself was born in January 1931 in Beaumont, Texas.[99] Most of Beaumont's Italians were Sicilians who came through the Port of New Orleans or, in some cases, Galveston. Archbishop Fiorenza reports that his "parents and grandparents were all Sicilians."[100]

Joseph Fiorenza's Beaumont upbringing melded the Italian and Catholic aspects of his family background. He was taught by the Dominican sisters in a Catholic elementary school and a Catholic high school. Archbishop Fiorenza recalls that his family "followed the regular Italian customs and traditions that our people brought with them." They ate traditional Sicilian foods, including spaghetti on Sundays. On St. Lucy's Day, they followed the custom of "not eating any wheat bread of any type." The archbishop recalls eating Italian cookies and delicacies as a youth. He remembers how Beaumont's Italians enjoyed the Sicilian-style pizza (thick crust with anchovies) and different types of Italian doughnuts and Italian cream cakes. In those days, St. Joseph's Parish in Beaumont was an Italian national parish. Fiorenza himself has always connected his Italian heritage to the Catholic Church. "I have always perceived my faith and heritage together," says Joseph Fiorenza.[101]

The prominent prelate notes that his parents wanted their children to assimilate into American society. After his grandparents died, speaking Sicilian was less common in his family. Fiorenza recalls no "overt prejudice" against Italians in Beaumont. There was a little name calling now and then, to be sure, and people in the community looked at the Italians as being "not quite American" during the 1930s and 1940s. In any event, the Italians of Beaumont exhibited a reticence about displaying overt indications of their Italian ancestry (the Italian flag, for instance) in the years before World War II. Fiorenza, of course, is "very proud" of his Italian heritage. The archbishop states that Italians have done so much to make the "beauty of God's world more resplendent."[102]

Fiorenza's biography includes pastoral, academic, and administrative positions. He was ordained in 1954. His career encompassed pastoral service in four different parishes in Houston, a stint as a Professor of Medical Ethics at Dominican College, Houston, and eight years as Administrator, Sacred Heart Co-Cathedral, Houston. From 1972 to 1973, he served as Vice Chancellor of the Diocese of Galveston-Houston and then, from 1973 to 1979, as Chancellor of the Diocese of Galveston-Houston. In 1979 Fiorenza was named and installed as Bishop of San Angelo. In 1984 he was named—and in 1985 he was installed—as Bishop of Galveston-Houston. As the bishop, he also served as the USCCB vice president (1995 to 1998) and USCCB president (1998 to 2001).[103] In December 2004 Galveston-Houston went from being a diocese to an archdiocese, due to its rapidly growing population of 1.3 million Catholics. At this time Fiorenza became the Archbishop of Galveston-Houston. After retiring in February 2006, he is now the Archbishop Emeritus of Galveston-Houston.[104]

In a 2004 interview, Fiorenza stated, "The Church in this part of the United States has become well known and well respected."[105] People look to the Church "to give leadership" on such matters as justice, race relations, capital punishment, the "respect for life," and reforming the criminal justice system. He notes that the Church should serve "the marginalized, the poor, those who do not have the same kind of access to those things that most citizens take for granted."[106] Houston's Catholic community is racially and ethnically diverse, too. Fiorenza notes that the different communities worship together. Many parishes in the Archdiocese of Galveston-Houston have three predominant ethnic groups: Latinos/Vietnamese/Anglos or Latinos/African Americans/Anglos. Fiorenza says "the diversity is a blessing." Furthermore, he notes: "We must remain united in the same faith."[107]

Italian Americans continue to play an important role in leading the Archdiocese of Galveston-Houston.[108] When Fiorenza initially came to Houston, there were two or three Italian restaurants in the entire city. Since the 1960s the Houston area has received Italian-American migrants from throughout America. When Fiorenza first became a bishop in 1979, there were not many Italian-American bishops then. He describes how there have been many more Italian-American priests since the 1960s and, consequently, more bishops of Italian extraction.[109] In 2006 Daniel DiNardo succeeded Fiorenza as Archbishop of Galveston-Houston; another Italian American, Bishop Emeritus Vincent Rizzotto, is also part of the archdiocesan leadership.[110]

❀   ❀   ❀

One finds plenty of Italian Americans who belong to different faith traditions besides Catholicism. Some Italian immigrants, to be sure, arrived in the United States as Protestants and members of other faith communities. Others left the Catholic Church once they arrived here because of such factors as intermarriage with non-Catholic spouses, the anticlerical attitudes they brought with them from Italy, dissatisfaction with particular Catholic parishes and clergy, and proselytizing by Protestant missionaries in Italian neighborhoods. The Protestants' efforts to win converts among the Italian immigrants met with varying success in different parts of the United States.[111]

Italian Americans from non-Catholic faith traditions report that they have many interesting experiences. Since Catholics are the largest group within Italian America, some individuals automatically assume that virtually everyone from an Italian background is Catholic. One Italian-surnamed American (who "grew up a Methodist") told me that he is "automatically assumed to be Catholic." Similarly, an Italian-American Baptist of my acquaintance reports that she and her family members sometimes experience feelings of being outsiders among both Baptists and Italian Americans. To be sure, the number of Americans of Italian descent with non-Catholic religious beliefs seems to be increasing.

Italian Americans are found in the Church of Jesus Christ of Latter-day Saints, particularly in Utah. Dr. Ed Morrell, a member of the Utah Valley Sunrise Rotary Club in Provo, Utah, reports that his wife, Norma Toronto Morrell, is one-quarter Italian. Her grandfather was Giuseppe Efisio Taranto (Joseph Toronto).[112] Toronto, who lived from 1816 to 1883, played an important role in nineteenth-century Mormon history. The Bella Sion Web site describes him as follows: "The first native Italian (and Roman Catholic) to join the Church of Jesus Christ of Latter-day Saints in this dispensation. Toronto was a friend and employee of Brigham Young for many years and became one of the heroes of the Nauvoo Temple story."[113] Ed Morrell cites his wife's ancestral heritage in the context of a broader discussion of the Italian-American presence in Utah.

Terri Nicole Sawyer, a past president of the Utah Valley Sunrise Rotary Club, is herself married to someone of Italian descent. Her husband, Robert Sawyer, comes from Italian stock, as his mother, Joyce Mezzonatto Sawyer, is 100 percent Italian. Robert and Terri Nicole Sawyer are Latter-day Saints who named their son, Rocky, for Porter Rockwell.[114]

Young Rocky's namesake occupies a significant place in LDS history; he served as "the bodyguard to Joseph Smith and Brigham Young." Smith and Young were "the first two Mormon prophets of this time," notes Terri Nicole Sawyer.[115] In sum, people of Italian origin, while not a large percentage of the Church of Jesus Christ of Latter-day Saints, continue to be valued members of this particular American faith community.

People of the Jewish faith are represented in Italian America, too. For example, Rabbi Barbara Aiello is an American of Italian origin from South Florida. She now lives in Italy, where she seeks to spur a resurgence of Italian Jewish culture.[116] Due to Italy's venerable Jewish presence, some American Jews of Italian descent are themselves descended from Jews in Italy.[117] Jewish immigration from Italy is not the only source of Italian America's Jewish population, however. As Jack Nusan Porter writes: "There are no figures regarding the number of Italian American Jews because defining an Italian American Jew is complex. It can include Jews who came from Italy to America or Italians who converted to Judaism or those who married Jews."[118] In the northeastern states and in South Florida, one sees numerous communities with sizable Jewish and Italian-American populations. Overall, Italian-American Jews make significant contributions to our nation in such realms as the arts, sciences, academia, and business.[119]

Methodism is another faith tradition that has deep roots in the Italian-American community. The Reverend James Thomas Carrico was a Methodist minister for more than four decades.[120] His paternal grand-mother's devout Methodism led the Indianapolis native to become involved in the Methodist Church's youth league. That is where he met his spouse, Betty Jane Mock. The Carricos, both of whom came from Indianapolis, were married in 1941. Betty Jane Carrico is a Butler University graduate who once taught in a one-room schoolhouse. Reverend Carrico held a master's degree from Garrett Evangelical Theological Seminary in Evanston, Illinois. Mark Carrico remembers his father, whose surname means "carriage driver" in Sicilian, as a man who "was always proud of his heritage." James Thomas Carrico came from a family where the values of faith, hard work, and self-sufficiency were paramount.[121]

Reverend Carrico spent his career as an ordained minister in Illinois, Indiana, and Wisconsin. A devoted family man, he and his wife had six children. Reverend Carrico retired after forty-two years as a full pastor, whereupon he became a visitation pastor in Whitefish Bay, Wisconsin, and then a visitation pastor in Bradenton, Florida. (His sermons took real-life situations and related them to God.) Finally, the Carricos went to live at Evergreen Retirement Community Center in Oshkosh, Wisconsin, a facility that is associated with the Methodist Church. For nine years James Thomas Carrico took care of his wife, who has Alzheimer's, before his passing in 2006. His youngest son, Mark Carrico, recalls how his father touched the lives of many people. Consequently, the Oshkosh service for him was standing-room only.

Besides Methodism, the Baptists have a long and venerable tradition of drawing some Italian Americans, one that dates back more than one hundred years. Ralph and Helen Kern are devout Baptists who value Italian-American culture. Mr. Kern hails from Fort Wayne, Indiana, and he is of Northern European and American Indian extraction. His wife, Helen Kern, grew up in the Washington Heights section of Manhattan. Her mother was a Del Mese and her father traced his ancestry to England and Ireland. Mrs. Kern's family was one of the few Protestant families in her New York neighborhood. Since the late 1990s she and her husband have been members of the Italian American Cultural Society of El Paso. Helen Kern herself has served as secretary of the Italian American Cultural Society of El Paso since 2000. Ralph Kern himself takes Italian lessons each month before the organization's meeting.[122] Both of the Kerns enjoy their involvement in Italian-American activities.

Chapter 14

PRESERVING AND
CELEBRATING
AMERICA'S
ITALIAN HERITAGE

In April 2005 Jerry Colangelo was appointed to serve as managing director of the USA Basketball Men's Senior National Team for the 2008
Beijing Olympics. This role, in his mind, directly involved the legacy
of his Italian-immigrant grandparents and the opportunities that his family has had in the United States.[1] "It is a great opportunity for me to give
back," noted Colangelo in a September 2005 interview, as he reflected on
his appointment to this position. After all, his grandparents came to the
United States in 1910; nearly one hundred years later, he observed that he
would be helping the United States to triumph in the 2008 Olympics.[2] As
managing director of the USA Basketball Men's Senior National Team
from 2005 to 2008, Colangelo guided the selection of the team members
and coaching staff, along with the Olympians' preparatory activities (particularly exhibition games and an extensive training regimen).[3] He received
rave reviews for his hard work to improve the standing of Team USA, as
the American basketball stars earned a gold medal in Beijing.[4]

Jerry Colangelo's paternal grandparents, Rosina and Giovanni Colangelo, probably had never heard of basketball when they left Naples for the
United States in 1910. Rosina Colangelo (née Morella) came from Faeto, a

village east of Naples in Apulia. Giovanni Colangelo hailed from Monteleone, a nearby village. After their arrival in the United States, the Colangelos settled in Chicago Heights, a south suburb of the Windy City. Rosina
Colangelo was a midwife with Old World remedies, while Giovanni Colangelo worked hard at a variety of jobs. In fact, he built Jerry Colangelo's
childhood home in the "Hungry Hill" section of Chicago Heights out of the
wood from railroad boxcars. Rosina and Giovanni Colangelo's son, Levio
(Harry) Colangelo, lived upstairs with his wife, Sue, and their children in a
living space smaller than the size of Jerry Colangelo's current office in
Phoenix.[5] The future sports legend was born on November 20, 1939.

"Growing up in an Italian-American neighborhood," to be sure, gave
Colangelo his foundation.[6] "Mine was a typical Italian upbringing; we
shared everything with one another, knew everybody's business, our sense
of family extended far beyond our four walls, and we felt safe and secure
and loved," remembered Jerry Colangelo in his 1999 memoir.[7] Chicago
Heights was a working-class community with steel mills and a textile factory. Colangelo delivered newspapers to every home in the neighborhood.
A leader among the neighborhood youths, he always felt very connected
to his Italian roots and his ancestral heritage. "I've taken the *Roots* thing
very seriously my whole life," reflects Colangelo.[8] His Italian-American
upbringing—and its lessons of family, loyalty, and hard work—helped
him to achieve many accomplishments.[9]

"Sports were a vehicle" that gave Jerry Colangelo access to higher education and news exposure on a local basis. The University of Illinois graduate and former collegiate basketball star reports that he is the "first person in my family and my extended family to go on to school."[10] After he
spent two seasons working with the Chicago Bulls, Jerry Colangelo, his
wife, Joan Colangelo, and their children left Chicagoland for Phoenix,
Arizona, in 1968.[11] As his biography notes:

> Jerry Colangelo arrived in the Valley of the Sun in 1968 to take over the expan-
> sion Phoenix Suns NBA franchise as the youngest general manager in profes-
> sional sports and has since guided the Suns into one of the most successful
> organizations in the NBA. He brought Major League Baseball to the Valley in
> 1998 and was chairman of the 2001 World Champion Arizona Diamondbacks.
> Colangelo was the key element in facilitating the move of the NHL's Winnipeg
> Jets to the Valley of the Sun to become the Phoenix Coyotes. Colangelo was
> also on the founding committee for the WNBA, and the Phoenix Mercury were
> one of the league's inaugural teams in 1997.[12]

In 2004 Colangelo sold the Phoenix Suns franchise for $400 million.[13] Indeed, "I have been involved in a couple of billion dollars worth of deals," notes the Phoenix civic leader.[14]

During the past four decades, Jerry Colangelo has played a significant role in the NBA's growth. "With the Suns, his roles have included general manager, head coach, president, managing general partner, chief executive officer and now chairman," according to his biography.[15] Colangelo served as chairman of the NBA Board of Governors and, in 2004, he was inducted into the Naismith Memorial Basketball Hall of Fame.[16] He credits two factors, among others—his "foundation in the old neighborhood" and "God gave me some abilities"—for his significant successes over the years. Colangelo emphasizes that "I still see myself as a guy from Hungry Hill."[17] He maintains close ties to Chicago Heights, as indicated by the town's Jerry Colangelo Gymnasium and his role as grand marshal of the community's Independence Day parade in 1998.[18]

Not all that many years ago, Jerry Colangelo's grandparents came to the United States with "knapsacks on their backs." Their legacy hit home for him in particular when he was an Ellis Island Medal of Honor winner in 2000.[19] Today Colangelo is a leader of such institutions as the National Italian American Sports Hall of Fame and the National Italian American Foundation. He himself was inducted into the National Italian American Sports Hall of Fame in 1994. In 1996 the longtime Arizonan received the NIAF Special Achievement Award in Sports/Business; soon thereafter he became a member of the NIAF Board.[20] Then, in 2005, Colangelo was chosen to be a vice chair of NIAF, an appropriate position for someone who "takes pride in the Italian heritage."[21] In their personal life, he and Joan Colangelo seek to transmit an appreciation of the Colangelo family's Italian background to their four children and ten grandchildren, who come from multiethnic backgrounds.[22]

Jerry Colangelo himself goes to Italy every year, and he and Mrs. Colangelo visited his ancestral villages for the first time in 1979. That year the first person the Colangelos met in Monteleone, Italy, was a lady on a donkey; her surname was Colangelo. In Monteleone's parish rectory, Jerry Colangelo located the baptismal record of his great-grandfather, Rocco Colangelo. The same day he and Joan Colangelo went to Faeto, his grandmother's hometown. There the Americans met an elderly couple in their nineties. After they identified themselves, the village elders started screaming because they had known Rosina in her youth. That day Jerry

Colangelo discovered that his family's pasta sauce originates in Faeto. "It was one of the greatest days of my life," recalls Colangelo.[23] Indeed, this grandson of Italian immigrants has made his mark in the broader culture of the United States, but he has never forgotten his roots in Italy and the Italian-American community.

I. Every year there is an impressive series of social and cultural events at the Italian American Club of Livonia in Livonia, Michigan.[24] The Club's signature events include the St. Louis Annual Dinner Dance (January), Carnevale (February), Pasquetta (springtime), Ferragosto (August), Festa del Vino (September), Columbus Day (October), the Memorial Mass (November), and a host of holiday events (the Santa Brunch, Christmas Luncheon, and Christmas Sing-a-Long). These activities have enriched the culture of Livonia and environs since 1977, the year in which the Italian American Club of Livonia was founded by a group of Italian-American locals.

The Club has its headquarters and holds events at its 26,000-square-foot facility at 39200 Five Mile Road in Livonia. This venue houses the Italian American Club of Livonia, the Italian American Banquet and Conference Center of Livonia, and the Italian American Club of Livonia Charitable Foundation. Italian Americans represent a significant percentage of the population in Livonia, a pleasant community in west suburban Detroit. Many Club members have roots in Detroit—they moved outward as Italian Americans and other European Americans left the central city for the suburbs during the postwar years.

The Italian American Club of Livonia, as with so many large ethnic organizations across the country, is a repository of Italian-American culture. There are 895 family memberships in the Club, according to Mary Galasso, the current president of this important community institution. (Mrs. Galasso and her Italian-born husband, Mario Galasso, are deeply involved in Greater Detroit's Italian-American community.) Most members of the Italian American Club of Livonia are American-born Italians, but there is a critical mass of Italian immigrants among the membership, too. Nick Giammarco, who describes himself as a "humbly proud" member of the IACL, reflects on the club's meaning to him, his family, and his compatriots.[25] "Often the club is simply our piazza," says Giammarco.

"We are there due to the innate need for Italians to share their passion for life and their love for their family and friends."[26]

Throughout the Detroit metropolitan area and, indeed, throughout the United States, there continues to be a venerable tradition of Italian-American clubs, societies, and organizations.[27] The Web site "Italian Los Angeles" nicely describes the various types of these groups: Culture & Heritage Associations; Genealogy; National Organizations (Heritage, Service, Philanthropy); Pan-Italian Clubs; Patron Saint Societies; Professional Associations; Religious Associations; Town & Regional Clubs; Womens' Clubs; and Other.[28] These organizations have different memberships based on such factors as age, gender, education, social class, and Italian regional origins. In addition, many major American cities continue to have institutions that serve as gathering places for Italian Americans, e.g., Casa Italiana (Los Angeles) and Casa Italia (suburban Chicago).

There is a wide range of organizational activity among Italian Americans. At the national level, Americans of Italian origin receive representation from such entities as the National Italian American Foundation; the Order Sons of Italy in America; the Italic Institute of America; FIERI, an organization for young Italian-American professionals; and UNICO National, the premier Italian-American service organization. Two of the biggest annual events in Italian America are OSIA's National Education and Leadership Awards (NELA) Gala in May and the NIAF Gala in October. The leaders of Italian-American organizations often have been involved in Italian-American activities for decades.

As a rule, though, most Italian Americans do not belong to any ethnic organizations.[29] Many folks with Italian backgrounds celebrate their heritage with family and friends, not in the communal settings offered by clubs, societies, and organizations. At the same time, these institutions play a major role in promoting Italian cultural events and activities and a positive image of Italians in communities across America. The Internet, meanwhile, has created new forms of Italian-American organizational activity, whereby Americans of Italian descent participate in communities of interest that transcend geography.

While most Italian-American groups mainly recruit middle-aged and elderly members, some organizations focus on young people. Il Club Italiano at Westchester Community College in Valhalla, New York, is one such group. The student members of Il Club Italiano and their faculty

mentor, Professor Carlo Sclafani, offer events and activities that promote
and preserve the Italian language, culture, and heritage on campus and
beyond.[30] Some Italian-American organizations exist at the secondary
school level. For instance, there are several ethnic clubs at Calvert Hall
College High School in Towson, Maryland, including the Italian Club
and the Irish Culture Club. The students in the Italian Club and the Irish
Culture Club compete in a bocce tournament each year.[31] Such activities
and organizations highlight how young European Americans, many of
whom are three, four, and five generations removed from the immigrant
experience, are recognizing their ancestral heritage.

To be sure, Italian-American institutions and cultural activities exist in
places with relatively few Italian Americans, including Idaho, the Cincinnati metropolitan area, and Memphis, Tennessee. Idaho's Italian-American organizational activities include the Italian American Club of Boise;
the OSIA Bonaventura Lodge #2814—Post Falls, Idaho; and the Idaho Italian Festival. In the Cincinnati, Ohio, area, one finds such outlets as the
United Italian Society of Greater Cincinnati and the newspaper *La Voce
Italiana*, and Newport Italianfest in Newport, Kentucky. Farther south,
Memphis, Tennessee, has long had a vibrant and venerable Italian-Amer-
ican community, as indicated by the presence of the UNICO Memphis
Chapter, Holy Rosary Catholic Church, the Memphis Bocce Club, the
Memphis Italian-American Society, and the Memphis Italian Festival.

Wisconsin, too, has a respectable Italian-American organizational
presence, even though people from Italian backgrounds constitute only 3.2
percent of the state's population. While there are many Wisconsin communities with a negligible Italian-American presence, other places have
higher-than-average Italian percentages—Cumberland (14.1 percent Italian), Kenosha County (10.8 percent Italian), and Iron County (19.2 percent Italian), among them. Perhaps most prominently, Italian Americans
account for 4.5 percent of the nearly 1.7 million residents of the Milwau-
kee-Racine metropolitan area. The Italian Community Center in Milwaukee sponsors Festa Italiana, which enjoys a well-deserved reputation
for being one of North America's most vibrant and best-attended ethnic
festivals. Every July this popular event draws a large number of visitors to
Milwaukee's lakefront.[32]

There are numerous Italian-American organizations in Wisconsin.
WisItalia is a statewide group that promotes the teaching of the Italian
language and Italian culture throughout the Badger State.[33] Outside of

southern Wisconsin, one finds such organizations as the Italian Men's Club (Wausau), Club Italo/Americano (Greater Green Bay), and the Gogebic and Iron County Paisano Club (Gogebic County, Michigan, and Iron County, Wisconsin). In Madison, Wisconsin's state capital and second largest city, Italian Americans participate in the Italian Workmen's Club, the Italian-American Women's Club, and CIAO! (Cultural Italian American Organization). Greater Milwaukee, in particular, is a bastion of Italian-American activity, with the Giuseppe Garibaldi Society, the Italian Community Center of Milwaukee, the Marche Group of Milwaukee, the OSIA Filippo Mazzei Greater Milwaukee Lodge #2763, the Pompeii Men's Club, the Pompeii Women's Club, the Santa Rosalia Society, and the UNICO–Wisconsin Chapter. And in southeastern Wisconsin, one finds two venerable organizations: the Italian-American Society (Kenosha) and the Roma Lodge (Racine).[34]

Let us focus now on the Roma Lodge in Racine, Wisconsin. The Roma Lodge is an impressive facility that hosts regular community events and parties as well as many activities and functions for its members.[35] In addition, the Roma Lodge Italian Festival each July attracts people from a wide range of ages and ethnic backgrounds to a vibrant community celebration in downtown Racine. Virtually everything at the festival is made by lodge members. Don Cicero currently serves as president of the all-male Roma Lodge—and his spouse, Rosemary Cicero, is a past president of the Vittoria Colonna, the women's group there. The Roma Lodge's leadership, too, includes Jerry Perona, who serves as the organization's secretary and edits the Roma Lodge newsletter. He and his wife, Judy Perona, are active in the Italian-American community of southeastern Wisconsin.[36]

Jerry Perona offers the following reflections on the meaning of the Roma Lodge to him and his family and, more broadly, the members as a group. Perona writes:

> I joined Roma Lodge at age 43. Though many of my wife's relatives were members for many years, time and other commitments kept me from joining. Though I was well versed in the activities the Lodge sponsored, it was an invitation of a friend of mine that prompted me to become a member.
>
> It was then that I discovered the real importance of Roma Lodge to the Italian-American community in Racine and Kenosha. Its special events, festivals, social gatherings, and other programs serve as a bridge between the Italian customs with which we were familiar and the American style of life. It provides an

opportunity to preserve what is important to us of our Italian heritage and to express the importance of that Italian heritage to the community at large.

The Lodge has gained great visibility in the community which may be what contributes to its ability to continue to draw young men as members. Because of this I am confident those things that I appreciate most about the Lodge will continue in the future.[37]

As the older Italian-American organizations alternately thrive, survive, or fade into history, some communities have newer Italian-American institutions that reflect the resurgence of interest in America's Italian heritage. The remarkable Westchester Italian Cultural Center in Tuckahoe, New York, typifies this trend.[38] Likewise, as Italian Americans move to different parts of the country, there is ethnic activity in places where it has not existed before. In fact, retirement destinations often offer several options for those who wish to participate in ethnic clubs. Take the southern suburbs of Phoenix, where Italian Americans (many of them retirees) participate in such organizations as the Solera Columbus Club, the Sunbird Italian American Club, and the Sun Lakes Italian-American Club.

In 2007, a group of Italian Americans formed the Villaggio Italian Club in Villaggio, a retirement community in Lake Worth, Florida. Rosemarie Falcone serves as co-chair of the Villaggio Italian Club's Italian Heritage Committee. The New York native describes her motivations for becoming involved in the Villaggio Italian Club:

> I joined for the memories. Only fellow Italians know what it was once like to have EVERY Sunday dinner with all the "Italian" trimmings at 2 P.M. The entire family sat around the table enjoying Momma and Nonna's cooking, naturally giving them both well earned accolades. Afterward, we played our favorite card game SCOPA. I was thrilled to be playing with the adults!! Nonno Peppino would always win the pot of nickels.
>
> Now get togethers happen only on holidays, because we're all too busy to be a family. My sister lives in Rome, Italy, my brother in New York. I miss the simpler times.
>
> I also miss my grandparents terribly. I love talking about them and learning what their lives must have been like through the stories revealed by the other club members.[39]

Similarly, Frank Popolizio and his wife, Diane Popolizio, of North Branford, Connecticut, maintain a rock-solid connection to their ancestral heritage and continue to be strongly Italian in their orientation.[40]

They do so without regularly participating in Italian-American organizations, however. These fortysomething civic leaders (both of whom have served as president of the Rotary Club of North Branford) treasure the stories and anecdotes about their Italian forebears. As importantly, they keep a number of Italian customs and traditions alive at home. When their children were very young, they sang Italian lullabies to them that have been transmitted from generation to generation in their families. They taught Italian games to them, too. The Popolizios, not surprisingly, are a close-knit family. They cherish the memory of Diane Popolizio's late parents—Addison Beckwith and Eleanora Omicioli Beckwith, while Frank Popolizio's parents, Eugene Popolizio Sr. and MaryAnn Citerella Popolizio, live near their children and grandchildren.

Food is an important way for members of the Popolizio clan to maintain their Italian heritage. Frank Popolizio makes excellent stuffed artichokes based on a recipe that his grandmother taught to him. Moreover, Diane Popolizio bakes crescia, an Easter bread that comes from the Marches. And on Christmas Eve, they have the traditional seven-fish dinner for the seven Sacraments. When Frank and Diane Popolizio are not preparing delectable foods at home, they enjoy dining at Portofino's Restaurant and Bar ("our favorite Italian restaurant") in New Haven. Also, they regularly order pizzas from Pepe's, Modern Apizza, and Sally's Apizza, three well-known New Haven pizzerias. In sum, Frank and Diane Poplizio were both reared by parents who valued their Italian heritage—and this is something they have successfully passed on to their own children.

II. Amulio Masini has been a member of the OSIA Giuseppe Verdi Lodge in Mechanicsville, Virginia, since the 1950s. Masini himself is a native of Tuscany. In 1921 his father came to the United States. After working here for six years, the elder Masini returned to Italy and brought his wife and young son, Amulio, to America in 1927. At that time, the Richmond Italians were predominantly Tuscan in origin. During the postwar era, the Richmond area has seen the in-migration of people from southern Italian backgrounds. Now the Giuseppe Verdi Lodge encompasses northern and southern Italians alike; it dates back to 1944. As of 2005, the Lodge's one hundred members were mainly middle-aged and elderly with an average age of sixty.[41]

As the historian of the Giuseppe Verdi Lodge, Masini offered these reflections about its history in 2005:

> I am eighty-six years old and almost the last of the old members of the Club. When I was small and my family belonged to the Lodge, it was a congregation of Italian families. There was a lot of ethnic bias at the time and families were hesitant to socialize with the general public. Therefore, these families joined Italian societies for socializing, fraternizing, entertainment, and to discuss their everyday problems. Some Lodges even had medical and funeral provisions because families in those days either had no insurance or could not afford it. So actually, the Lodge provided security, socializing, and fraternizing.
>
> Things have changed considerably. We no longer have to worry about ethnic bias and discrimination and now, the second and third generations are spreading out more into society in general, and the clubs are evolving more into social clubs that are more generally charity oriented. We continuously work for Social Justice, and have drives for different charities. We try to keep the interest in our heritage alive, but I am afraid that, as generations pass, some of the ideals of long ago are beginning to fade. However, as a social club, we can continue to be a credit to society and continue our work as Americans with Italian roots.[42]

Today the Giuseppe Verdi Lodge's members are a mixture of native Virginians and transplants from the Northeast. These residents of the Richmond area come together for fellowship and also "to learn about their heritage." The Lodge participates in Greater Richmond's civic and community activities to promote positive images of Italian Americans. These activities include scholarships, charity drives, and involvement in various community events.[43] Indeed, the Giuseppe Verdi Lodge and the two other Italian groups in metro Richmond—the Italian-American Cultural Association and the Italian American Business and Professional Societa—organize the Richmond Italian Street Festival each year.[44] These activities highlight the continuing importance of the Italian heritage and culture in Virginia's capital city.

The future of Italian-American clubs, societies, and organizations varies dramatically, considering that their membership is often middle-aged and elderly. Many such groups face the issue of how to attract and retain younger members. Widespread intermarriage, decades of assimilation, the growing distance in time from the immigrant generation, and the lack of any tangible connections to the Old World culture simply diminish the relevance of these clubs, societies, and organizations for many younger Americans of Italian descent. Likewise, Italian Americans in their twenties, thirties, and forties often are focused on their family and professional responsibilities and do not have the time necessary to participate in such associations. Certain Italian-American groups are relaxing males-only and Italian-only membership rules, due to changing societal attitudes and the prospect of declining membership.

Some Italian-American organizations limit their membership to Italian Americans and "Italian-By-Marriage" spouses, whereas others welcome non-Italians as social, associate, or even full members. The Italian American Club of Maui has two categories of membership: "The Famiglia" (people with any amount of Italian ethnicity by blood or marriage) and "the Amici" ("anybody who embraces the Italian culture").[45] "The Famiglia have the right to vote and be elected to office," according to Dr. James Vitale, a club cofounder. He estimates that one-third of the Italian American Club of Maui's current members do not have any Italian ancestry.[46]

Throughout the nation, many Italian-American clubs, societies, and organizations have non-Italian members and sometimes leaders (who are often the spouses of Italian Americans). Take Bill Casey, for instance; the Irish-German native of Long Island served as the president of the Italian-American Club of Greater Greenville in South Carolina.[47] This organization has a particularly inclusive membership policy. According to its Web site, "The Italian-American Club of Greater Greenville is open to anyone who is Italian-American, or is married to an Italian-American, wants to be Italian-American, thinks like an Italian-American, or would just like to hang out with a bunch of Italian-Americans."[48]

In Nebraska, OSIA leader Charles Turco and his colleagues demonstrate how viable Italian-American organizations welcome members of different ethnic backgrounds. Turco himself is one-half Sicilian; his mother had no Italian heritage. Today he and his German/Czech-American wife, Ann Turco, live in Omaha's traditionally Italian neighborhood. The Turcos have a lengthy history of involvement in the Sons of Italy. They point out that the Associate Members of OSIA in Nebraska may be from non-Italian ethnic backgrounds. Their inclusive attitude helps to explain why the Sons of Italy continues to thrive after being in Nebraska since 1919. Charles Turco, the Nebraska State President of OSIA for more than two decades, grew up on 5th Street in what was Omaha's Little Italy during the 1940s and 1950s. His father, Joseph Turco, was a longtime OSIA member.[49]

Charles Turco himself has been involved in the Sons of Italy for many years. He notes that the lodge's Thursday lunches and Friday dinners draw many indiviuals to the Sons of Italy Hall in Omaha. The Lodge's annual events include a summer picnic and a golf tournament. Each year the Sons of Italy in Nebraska also offers scholarships to young people. Charles Turco himself helps with community benefits and other charitable events whenever he can do so. Younger people continue to become involved in the Sons of Italy in Omaha (many children participate in the organization's activities), and the annual summer picnic is a key recruitment event. All of Ann and Charles Turco's grandchildren hold memberships in the Sons of Italy.[50]

Indeed, there are Italian-American families with multiple generations who have been involved in the Order Sons of Italy in America. Therese Quattrocchi Simpson, who was born in 1929, grew up in a family with a strong tradition of participating in the Sons of Italy in her native Connecticut. She has been a driving force behind the OSIA Bradenton Lodge #2782 in Bradenton, Florida, a relatively new chapter. (Mrs. Simpson presently divides her time between Florida and Calabria.) Her children all participate in the lodge—and her son, John Martell, currently serves as its president. In addition, Simpson's good friend, Grace Toscano Stafford, who immigrated from Calabria to the United States during the 1950s, is a lodge member.[51]

Therese Quattrocchi Simpson describes her family's extensive history of involvement in the Sons of Italy:

> As for my experience with the SOI over the years, I don't ever remember NOT being involved. My father, Frank Quattrocchi, was Venerable for the Amerigo Vespucci lodge in Danbury, Connecticut, in the years 1936, 1938, 1946, and 1947. My mother was always a member of the Collona lodge because at that time the men's and women's lodges were separate. As children, my brother, Virgil, sister, Angie, and I attended many family-type functions—Christmas parties, New Year's events, and Columbus Day parades, etc. My parents were instrumental in bringing live entertainment to the lodge.
>
> When I moved to Florida, I felt a loss. About 2002, I read about a lodge forming in Bradenton and immediately joined. After a couple of years, most members decided it was not what they were looking for and voted to disband. My children, along with about three other members, decided we would keep

the charter and worked hard to recruit new members to satisfy the Grand Lodge rules. We made it and were meeting in various places, not knowing month to month where we would be holding our next meeting. This bothered me so much that I bought the building we now use and the lodge is only responsible for utilities. We now have about 35 members and are still growing.[52]

As with Mrs. Simpson, some of the most enthusiastic supporters of Italian-American organizations are individuals who want to preserve the heritage that they celebrated in their youth. By taking the initiative in this way, they help to preserve certain aspects of Italian-American culture that would otherwise be lost forever. Indeed, it is possible for these cultural preservationists to revitalize the Italian-American culture—at least in specific contexts—with a distinctly modern connection to contemporary Italy. Their emphasis on heritage and culture may surprise some observers because Italian Americans are so thoroughly integrated into mainstream American culture. Yet one can be proudly and emphatically Italian in America today without being seen as "un-American." Such dynamics stem from our multicultural sensitivities and the widespread acceptance and even celebration of so many aspects of Italian culture and Italian Americana.

III. Festa Italiana Seattle! is the "biggest, not the oldest" of the "sixteen ethnic and cultural festivals at Seattle Center." The multiday event dates back to 1988—it draws forty thousand people, on average, each year.[53] "Thirty percent of the attendees have some claim to Italian extraction," reports Dennis Caldirola, the longtime executive director of Festa Italiana. The Italian Americans from Seattle's different clubs and organizations work together on the festival, in part because they want to educate their progeny about their Italian heritage and culture. The ranks of these cultural preservationists include Italian software engineers, who have immigrated to the United States during the last twenty years.[54]

The Italian and Italian-American culture celebrated at Festa Italiana in Seattle is mostly that of Italy before the Second World War. Dennis Caldirola, who lived in Italy for three years and returns to his *paese* regularly, describes how the festival goers dance the tarantella, enjoy accordion music, and listen to songs that originate from the period between 1900 and 1940. "It is an era, a feeling," reports Caldirola. To be sure, Festa Italiana includes many modern aspects of Italian life, as in exhibitions on Italian photography, Italian sports cars, and Italian contemporary art. Italian foods—pizza chief among them—attract people to the festival. The attendees enjoy the numerous cooking demonstrations, along with the grape stomp, bocce tournaments for adults and children, and many other activities.[55]

Festa Italiana Seattle! counteracts any lingering stereotypes about Washington State's Italian Americans. Dennis Caldirola, who is the current secretary of the Italian Club of Seattle, points out that there are exhibitions at Macy's in conjunction with each of Seattle's sixteen ethnic festivals. The Italian exhibition—and the festival, of course—promote positive images of Italian Americans and their culture.[56] Indeed, someone who enjoys Festa Italiana's Italian puppet shows or sings along to "That's Amore" probably does not associate Italians with organized crime and other negative stereotypes. This popular ethnic festival, in sum, offers entertaining and educational diversions, whereby people from different ethnic backgrounds learn about Italy, Italian Americans, and Italian culture in an enriching and enjoyable environment.

Each year Festa Italiana Seattle! is one of the 400-plus festivals that celebrate the Italian-American heritage. Italian *feste* in the United States may be primarily secular or primarily religious in their sponsorship and orientation. To be sure, many of the largely secular festivals include a Catholic Mass on Sunday mornings. And the mainly religious festivals often have a secular component, too. Some patron saints continue to be widely celebrated through events and festivals in different parts of Italian America, including Saint Joseph (March 19), Santa Rosalia (July 15), Our Lady of Mount Carmel (July 16), San Gennaro (September 19), and Saint Lucy (December 13).[57] Some Americans of Italian origin, moreover, commemorate Italian events and holidays, including Carnevale, Italian Republic Day, and Ferragosto.

The Italian-American ethnic festivals incorporate the Italian, the American, and the distinctively Italian American. Festival organizers try to promote positive images of Italian Americans that offset stereotypes—and there is often lighthearted ethnic chauvinism at their events.[58] Italian-American festivals have flourished since the 1970s, as it has become more acceptable for Italians Americans to celebrate openly their ethnicity in public settings. Italian food, folk dancing, popular entertainment, and green-white-and-red imagery typify the standard Italian-American festival.[59] Furthermore, Italian-themed church festivals are often popular community events, as in the St. Coleman Italian Festival in Pompano Beach, Florida, each February and St. Anthony's Italian Festival in Wilmington,

Delaware, every June. Overall, many Italian-American festivals are enjoyed and frequented by people from a wide range of ethnic backgrounds. These festivals may be as American as they are Italian.

Two of the finest Italian festivals in North America take place in West Virginia: the West Virginia Italian Heritage Festival (Clarksburg) and the Upper Ohio Valley Italian Festival (Wheeling). There is no admission fee for either event, both of which rank among North America's best-attended and most exciting Italian-American festivals. The West Virginia Italian Heritage Festival and the Upper Ohio Valley Italian Festival showcase Italian and Italian-American culture, promote positive images of Italian Americans, and highlight how people from Italian family backgrounds are integrally American. These events are, in essence, a celebration of "being American," as my respondents noted during a roundtable discussion in Wheeling, West Virginia, in 2005.[60]

This is also the case for the Italian-American festivals in the Lake Superior Region, where many communities in northern Minnesota, northern Wisconsin, and Upper Michigan have a mining heritage.[61] In the Lake Superior Region, such festivals as Festa Italiana (Chisholm, Minnesota), Festival Italiano (Hurley, Wisconsin), and the Ishpeming Italian Fest (Ishpeming, Michigan) admirably preserve the Italian customs and traditions of this area. Today the Italian heritage of the Lake Superior Region continues to be relevant in former mining towns like Hurley, even as virtually everyone from Italian family backgrounds is now fully integrated into mainstream America. As Russell M. Magnaghi writes: "The legacy of the mining town experience remains with local Catholic churches, Italian restaurants and shops, clubs, summer family visits, and ethnic festivals."[62]

There are at least 448 Italian-American festivals in the United States each year. These popular celebrations of Italian heritage take place throughout the United States. According to the *Sons of Italy 2008 Italian Festival Directory*, such events are found in the following states: New York (91), New Jersey (70), Pennsylvania (66), Illinois (33), Massachusetts (32), California (30), Connecticut (22), Ohio (22), and Rhode Island (13). In addition, Italian-American festivals enrich the cultural scene in the District of Columbia and such states as Alabama, Colorado, Delaware, Florida, Hawaii, Idaho, Indiana, Iowa, Kentucky, Louisiana, Maine, Maryland, Michigan, Missouri, Nebraska, Nevada, Oklahoma, Oregon, South Carolina, Tennessee, Texas, Utah, Virginia, Washington State,

West Virginia, and Wisconsin.[63] "The biggest festival is the Feast of San Gennaro held every September in New York City, which attracts about one million people," according to the Sons of Italy.[64] In recent years, new festivals have developed (the Feast of San Gennaro in Los Angeles, among others) that highlight Italian and Italian-American culture.[65] These examples demonstrate how America's Italian heritage continues to be celebrated, albeit in ways that may sometimes surprise contemporary Italians in Italy.

For decades, Italian Americans have honored the Italian navigator Christopher Columbus as a means of emphasizing the contributions of Italians to the New World. Columbus, of course, is commonly regarded as the first European explorer to reach North America. Due to this milestone, Columbus enjoyed the status of an American icon—and Italian-American hero—in the years before the advent of Multicultural America.[66] "Italian Americans," writes Christopher J. Kauffman, "grounded legitimacy in a pluralistic society by focusing on the Genoese explorer as a central figure in the formation of their sense of peoplehood."[67] Since the 1960s, Columbus has been the subject of much controversy and many reevaluations of his role in exploring the Americas. With few exceptions, however, Italian-American organizations continue to honor Columbus for his role as a key historical figure in the history of the Western Hemisphere.

There are many organizations, place names, statues, monuments, and celebrations that recognize Columbus in the United States. Most prominently, the U.S. Columbus Day federal holiday is celebrated every October. Italian Americans often observe the Columbus Day holiday with parades, banquets, festivals, ceremonies, dinner-dances, and other commemorations. "Indeed," notes Luisa Del Giudice, "the contemporary celebration of Columbus Day (October 12)—the primary, institutionalized pan-Italian-American festival—has now become a self-celebration of this group's accomplishments and contributions to American society."[68] October, moreover, is a month to honor the Italian-American heritage (it is known, variously, as Italian Heritage Month, Italian American Heritage Month, Italian Heritage and Culture Month, and National Italian American Heritage Month) through a series of events, activities, and observances that highlight the Italian contributions to the United States and, more generally, the world.

IV. In Sarasota, Florida, and environs, the Gulf Coast Italian Culture Society promotes and celebrates all things Italian. During the high season in Florida each year, this organization holds a regular series of events that highlight Italian culture and preserve the Italian-American heritage. Its civic activities include scholarships for high-achieving college-bound high school students from Italian backgrounds and financial support for the youth groups associated with the Sarasota Ballet and the Sarasota Opera. As of November 2008, there were 256 GCICS members, most of whom traced their ancestry to Italy. Also, there is contact between the GCICS and two other Italian organizations in Sarasota: the Ausonian Society and Sarasota Italian Cultural Events. A number of Italophiles and Italian Americans in the Sarasota area belong to all three organizations.[69]

The GCICS as an organization—and many GCICS members—worked with the Sarasota Sister Cities Association in 2007 to make Treviso, Italy, a Sarasota Sister City. There were a series of events that welcomed a delegation of *trevisani* to Sarasota, including a dinner party that was co-chaired by Arthur Castraberti and Mary Amabile Palmer. The guest list for this well-attended event included Dr. Joseph Polizzi, the Ausonian Society's president, and Angel Algeri, the president of Sarasota Italian Cultural Events. And the multi-course dinner included Italian music that delighted the visitors. As a surprise, Beatrice Lugana Fumei, a native Italian and GCICS member, sang the Italian National Anthem for the guests. Later, as one of the Italian visitors reflected on the day (the dinner, the music, and other events), he said of the Gulf Coast Italian Culture Society members: "Have you noticed, they are more Italian than we are."

As the current president of the Gulf Coast Italian Culture Society, Mary Amabile Palmer works hard to keep *italianità* alive in the Sarasota area. Indeed, she has a lengthy record of service to this organization. Before she became the GCICS president, Palmer served in such capacities as GCICS secretary, vice president, newsletter editor, and chair of social and cultural events. A longtime resident of the Boston area who moved to Sarasota, Palmer is the author of *Cucina di Calabria: Treasured Recipes and Family Traditions from Southern Italy* (first published in hardcover by Faber & Faber in 1997).[70] This pioneering and delightful book about Calabrian cuisine remains in print today: The paperback edition was released by Hippocrene in 2004.[71] The essays and recipes in *Cucina di Calabria* led Palmer to receive the Pirandello Award in Boston.

Mary Amabile Palmer's capable leadership of the Gulf Coast Italian Culture Society draws upon her life experiences. A vivacious person who looks much younger than her eighty-three years, Palmer reminisces:

> I grew up not wanting to be Italian or even an Italian American. I wanted to be an American. While I had friends of every ethnic persuasion, any Italian friend had to NOT have an Italian accent, and had to use good grammar.
>
> It wasn't until I was nearly forty that I fell in love with my Italian heritage. It happened when I went to Italy for the first time. I was in love with everything about Italy: the people, the natural beauty of the country, the man-made beauty and the smarts that put it together way back to the Romans, the architecture, the arts, the music, and the food—glorious food. Whether you go to a three-star Michelin restaurant or a neighborhood trattoria, it doesn't matter; the food is always so good!
>
> When I came back I dreamed about Italy for a whole month, and occasionally thereafter. The second European country I visited was France (which I also loved, especially Paris), but I thought how glad I was that I had visited Italy first because my feeling for Italy was now a part of my being, forever. Over the next forty years, I visited almost every European country, parts of Asia, Australia, New Zealand, Israel, Egypt, and other nations. I loved them all, but my love for Italy was steadfast. Nine visits to Italy tops them all.
>
> I began to spread the word to my friends, but especially to my sons, now grown men, and my grandchildren. I found myself asking little Alex, for example, when he was eight, "Do you know who invented ice cream?" Because I was always pointing out something outstanding about Italian athletes, singers, actors, movie directors, the inventor of the Ferrari, Michelangelo, you name it. His response was "I suppose you're going to tell me it was an Italian."
>
> I realized I was doing what my father had done when I was growing up—pointing out to me an endless number of outstanding Italian people: Enrico Caruso, Marconi, Toscanini. Now I was doing it too, not only with my grandchildren, but I write essays for an Italian newspaper entitled "Italian Culture" and include people like Hadrian, Monteverdi, Maria Montessori, Bernini, Puccini, Palladio, etc. I also provide GCICS members with a compilation of the year's essays annually, and of course, to my family as well. I want to share with everyone the glorious culture and accomplishments of Italians and Italian Americans of which I am so proud!

Palmer keeps the Italian-American culture alive with her grandchildren through her Italian cooking and family storytelling. Each of her grandchildren has cooked Italian cuisine with her and been photographed doing so. Her granddaughters, Jennifer and Katherine, have written about the Italian dimension of their experiences with their grandmother, something that delights her. Mary Amabile Palmer, too, took pride in how her grandsons Spencer and Alex visited Italy with their family in 2007. Over the years, she has bequeathed a sense of family history to her grandchildren. She tells them all about her Calabrian-immigrant parents, Giovanina (Jennie) Marino Amabile and Francesco (Frank) Amabile. The Amabiles canned and froze vegetables—and they gave bags of fresh vegetables to their neighbors and friends. Frank Amabile, in the best Italian tradition, had a substantial garden. He also brewed homemade wine, liquors, and root beer. These customs helped to inspire his younger daughter's interest in documenting authentic, traditional Calabrian recipes while it was still possible to do so.

In time-honored fashion, Mary Amabile Palmer has related the Amabile family's immigration narrative to her sons and grandchildren. Francesco and Giovanina Amabile came to America, as did so many Italian immigrants, "with the dream of having a better life for themselves and their children." Their older daughter, Domenica (Margaret), was eighteen months old when the Amabiles arrived on these shores. Immediately after coming to America, Jennie and Frank Amabile enrolled in a night school where they studied English. They transitioned "fairly easily" from living in a small Calabrian village to their new home (the industrial city of Schenectady, New York), according to Mary, their second daughter. She herself was born in Schenectady on December 27, 1925. "They were great parents, made good, long-lasting friends, and were kind, giving neighbors," she recalls. Years after their passing, Mary Amabile Palmer honors her parents' memory in many ways, including her involvement in the Gulf Coast Italian Culture Society.

The GCICS continues to flourish because of its dedicated members and leaders. These individuals—Italians and non-Italians alike—serve on committees, co-chair events, and contribute in other ways to the Society's functions. In my communications with Mary Amabile Palmer, the Society's current president, she spoke highly of the dedicated board members, too numerous to mention. But among them is Arthur Castraberti, who was a board member since the Society's inception and also served as vice president and president, and Pat and Marie Corsentino, who worked tirelessly for the Society—and who both served as president.

In addition, Palmer referred to several other individuals who have held various important roles in the Gulf Coast Italian Culture Society. Bob Long served on the organization's Board of Directors and as vice president. He is responsible for the creation and updating of the GCICS Web site (www.gcics.com). His wife, Linda Long, was also a board member and served as chairlady of the Scholarship Fund. Furthermore, Mary Amabile Palmer noted that Edith and Tony Zara are founding members of the GCICS. Edith Zara, in fact, has served on the GCICS board during its entire history. She is also the organization's Sunshine Lady, whose responsibilities include mailing cards to the members on important occasions. "She and Tony co-chair an event every year and are solid, dedicated, highly respected members," notes Mary Amabile Palmer. In addition, Ruth Napoliello served as a longtime GCICS board member and Membership Chairlady until her passing in 2007 at the age of ninety-three. "Ruth was Irish," remembered her friend, Mary, "but she loved everything Italian."

Palmer said she speaks for many in the GCICS who think of the organization "as family. When the members meet each other, after a warm greeting, they hug and kiss on both cheeks, just as they do with their own families." "Our members," she said, "are dedicated to continuing the traditions that their parents, grandparents, and even great-grandparents engrained in them with so much feeling." "This," she continued, "is true even if the people in Italy have moved on, and in some ways with perhaps less concern for maintaining all their ancestral traditions. But it makes sense, in a way—they don't have to be so involved. They are surrounded by Italian culture every day. We, on the other hand, need reminders of where we came from and who we are."

✿ ✿ ✿

Italian-American businesspeople and entrepreneurs have left their mark on the United States through their brand names, entrepreneurial creativity and innovation, and leadership of major American corporations. Americans from all ethnic backgrounds drink Gallo wine, relax in Jacuzzis, enjoy Ghirardelli chocolates, and eat sandwiches at Subway restaurants (Fred Deluca, the co-founder of Subway, is Italian American). Similarly, such Italian-American businesses as supermarkets, travel agencies, and, of course, restaurants contribute to the Italian-American cultural heritage of our nation. Take The Palms Restaurant in Rutland, Vermont, for example; this popular establishment has been in the Sabataso family for generations. Indeed, in most cities and towns across America, there are well-respected businesspeople and entrepreneurs from Italian family backgrounds who have gained prominence locally.[72]

The entrepreneur Leonard Riggio epitomizes the integral role that Italian Americans play in American business and, more broadly, American society. Their contributions are so thoroughly part of our national culture that the typical American thinks little, if at all, about them. As the driving force behind Barnes & Noble and GameStop, two of America's leading retail chains, Riggio helps to define what we read, how we play, and how we live.[73] "In addition," his biography says, "he is the chairman and principal shareholder of several privately held companies, including Barnes & Noble College Booksellers, serving more than five hundred college[s] and universities across America."[74] Nearly one hundred thousand people are employed by Riggio's various enterprises.[75]

The sixtysomething New Yorker's prominence highlights the complete integration of Italian Americans into our nation's mainstream. Leonard Riggio takes pride in his Italian-American background, but his ethnic heritage does not define how his customers relate to him or the products at Barnes & Noble, GameStop, Barnes & Noble College Booksellers, and his other businesses. As a rule, Riggio enjoys an enviable reputation as a role model in American business, and he is a sought-after speaker at colleges and universities and other venues around the United States. At the same time, Italian Americans recognize him as someone who represents their entire ethnic group in a variety of civic, philanthropic, and business contexts. In a conversation with me several years ago, one Italian-born man referred to "those Italian bookstores" when he described Barnes & Noble during our discussion.

Leonard Riggio is a native Brooklynite from a thoroughly Italian-American background. He was born on February 28, 1941, in New York City. His mother and maternal grandparents were the U.S.-born descendants of Neapolitan immigrants who arrived in the United States during the nineteenth century. His paternal grandparents came to America from Sicily between 1905 and 1910. Riggio himself grew up in Bensonhurst, Brooklyn. His "grandparents hardly spoke Italian in the house" and they wanted to "have their children speak the English language." The Italian-American youngsters "were trying hard to Americanize," remembers Riggio. As a result, none of the young people in Riggio's Brooklyn neighborhood spoke Italian. Nor did they feel any "connection to Italy" (which they viewed as a poor country at that time). To be sure, he and his compatriots were "proud of being Italian." His alma mater, Brooklyn Technical High School, was 15 percent Italian and even more heavily Jewish and Irish—demographics that reflected the community's population.[76] After Riggio graduated from Brooklyn Technical High School in 1958, he attended New York University and began his retailing career during the 1960s.

The entrepreneurial legend's signature business is Barnes & Noble, "the world's largest bookseller."[77] This widely admired American firm is a member of the Fortune 500 (the 446th largest U.S. company in 2007), with more than $5.4 billion in revenue during 2007.[78] Barnes & Noble enjoys a stellar reputation among North American consumers for its wonderfully varied selection of multimedia products—and welcoming atmosphere in which to browse, shop, and relax. Leonard Riggio currently serves as the Chairman of Barnes & Noble, Inc. His brother, Stephen Riggio, is the company's chief executive officer and vice chairman.[79] "My dream," says Riggio, "was to create a bookstore for the aspirants of the world, not just the already-arrived."[80] Indeed, Barnes & Noble has played a very significant role in making books accessible to the masses.[81]

While Riggio is best known for Barnes & Noble, he is having an equally significant impact on American culture with GameStop (the videogame company that he founded in 1987).[82] This thriving Fortune 500 retailer—it was 348th on the storied list in 2007—had $7.1 billion in revenue during 2007.[83] *Fortune* magazine sees three main reasons for GameStop's remarkable success. For starters, the store's managers and staffers establish rapport with their customers because they, themselves, are gamers. Secondly, GameStop has a well-developed network of retail stores, particularly in the United States. Thirdly, GameStop allows gamers to trade in their old games for new games, a policy that contributes significantly to the retailer's popularity. For these reasons, GameStop enjoys much cachet in the hotly competitive gaming world.[84]

Along with his business ventures, Riggio demonstrates leadership in various philanthropic endeavors and community institutions. Throughout the years, his volunteerism has included service on more than twenty non-profit boards. This generous patron of the arts believes strongly in good racial and ethnic relations. To this end, he is active in such organizations as the Children's Defense Fund and the Black Children's Community Crusade. His list of awards includes the Frederick Douglass Medallion, the Ellis Island Medal of Honor, the Americanism Award (the Anti-Defamation League), and honorary doctorates from Bentley College,

Long Island University, and Baruch College of the City University of New York. In addition, Riggio's induction into the Texas A&M Retail Hall of Fame and the Academy of Distinguished Entrepreneurs at Babson College recognizes his entrepreneurial accomplishments.[85]

Leonard Riggio supports the Italian-American community—and he continues to be one of our nation's leading Italian-American icons and role models. The devoted family man once served as president of the Columbus Citizens Foundation in New York City and as a board member of the National Italian American Foundation. And he received the 1998 NIAF Special Achievement Award for the Promotion of Literacy. "Italians have helped build this great country," notes Riggio.[86] Italians, he continues, have "heart and soul" as well as "generosity of spirit and love of fellow man." Notwithstanding his extraordinary successes, Leonard Riggio reports that he has confronted prejudice on the basis of his ethnic origin throughout his "entire life."[87] During an interview in 2005, Riggio described how he once encountered rumors of Italian "connections" and prejudicial questions ("Where did he get his money from?"). Such ethnic bias, not surprisingly, has lessened in recent years.[88]

Chapter 15

THE TIES THAT BIND

Seventeen-year-old Pietro Secchia left his Piedmontese hometown of Masserano in 1907 to go to the United States. He had just thirty dollars in his pocket when he arrived in the New World. More than eight decades later, his grandson, Peter Secchia, returned to Masserano to retrace his grandfather's steps before he, too, left Italy. But the second Secchia to make this trek did so as an American diplomat and entrepreneur, one who had just completed a highly successful stint as the U.S. envoy to Italy. Secchia departed Italy from Masserano because he remembered how his "grandfather had told him about leaving Italy and how sad it was for him." So on January 19, 1993, the outgoing American Ambassador to Italy began his reenactment of Pietro Secchia's departure from Italy decades before. On the evening of January 19, 1993 (his last night as ambassador), Secchia himself slept in the same Rongio farmhouse where his grandfather spent *his* final evening in Italy before he left for America.[1]

The following morning, Peter Secchia walked to the train station in Masserano (seventeen kilometers), just as Pietro Secchia had done in 1907. Distant relatives accompanied him for different parts of his trek. He carried a small bag duplicating his grandfather's material possessions. Passersby honked their horns and greeted Secchia with shouts of "Buon Viaggio" (Safe Trip) and "Bravo Cugino Pietro" (Well Done, Cousin Peter). Before leaving Masserano, Secchia stopped at the elementary school that his grandfather had attended for six years. The school officials brought out Pietro Secchia's report card for his illustrious American descendant. (These reports said: "Because Pietro could not afford the books assigned, he sat outside and watched through the window until the fifth grade.") Then Secchia took the train from Masserano to Genoa, where he drank from "the Fountain of Immigrants."[2]

Secchia's tenure in Rome came to an end on January 20, 1993, at 6:00 P.M. Roman time/12:00 noon Washington time. After his service as ambassador to Italy, Peter Secchia returned home to Michigan, where he continued his leadership in business and civic affairs. The aforementioned events, which were covered extensively by the Italian media, exemplified Ambassador Secchia's deep admiration and reverence for his grandfather. Pietro Secchia played a significant role in shaping his grandson's outlook and world view, and he passed on his admirable work ethic to his namesake. The younger Secchia currently keeps a copy of Pietro Secchia's ship manifest on the wall of his spacious office in Grand Rapids, Michigan.[3]

Ambassador Peter F. Secchia was born on April 15, 1937. The firstborn child of Cesare (known as Charlie) Secchia and Valerie Margaret Smith, the future Italophile grew up in Demarest, a small town in Bergen County, New Jersey. There were few Italian Americans in Demarest during the 1940s and 1950s. Secchia, in fact, remembers that he was the sole Italian-surnamed child in his first-grade class at Demarest Elementary School. World War II was difficult for his Italian-born grandparents, who, when not working, remained homebound much of the time because of nasty comments from their non-Italian neighbors. Pietro Secchia advised young Peter to "get an education," and he emphasized the importance of "saving, protecting, and providing for one's family."[4] Peter Secchia took his grandfather's advice and graduated from Michigan State University in 1963 after a four-year stint in the U.S. Marine Corps. Today this proud MSU alumnus holds six honorary doctorates.

Peter Secchia is a very successful entrepreneur, one whose signature business is Universal Forest Products (UFPI/NASDAQ). He joined the company in 1962 when it was a $1 million firm. Secchia, who is currently UFPI's Chairman Emeritus, bought control of the company in 1971; it had $12 million in annual sales at the time. UFPI went public in 1993.[5] By 2007, the profitable business ranked 705th of all U.S. companies in terms of revenues, when UFPI's $2.665 billion in annual revenues made it the fifth-largest U.S. company in *Fortune*'s category for "forest and paper products."[6] Secchia rose from modest origins to become a wealthy man; he continues to be active in various business ventures and regularly receives professional honors. At the same time, he is a significant civic leader in

Grand Rapids and the state of Michigan, as well as a generous philanthro-pist (one who recently gave a multimillion-dollar gift to move the MSU College of Human Medicine to Grand Rapids).[7]

For many years, Secchia has been active in Italian-American affairs and Republican Party politics. A recipient of the Ellis Island Medal of Honor, Secchia is a founder and longtime member of the West Michigan Lodge of the Order Sons of Italy in America.[8] He played an integral role in cre-ating Festa Italiana in Grand Rapids, too; this vibrant ethnic festival pro-moted the Italian heritage and culture. OSIA later honored him with the National Education Leadership Award. He also received the organiza-tion's "Marconi Award" as the National Italian American of the Year. Moreover, his sizable contributions to the National Italian American Foundation led the advocacy organization to name its headquarters in Washington, D.C. "The Secchia Building." Secchia is a political heavy-weight, too. He advised and maintained a warm friendship with the late former President Gerald R. Ford.[9] Secchia's deep involvement in Repub-lican Party affairs included his leadership of the George H. W. Bush cam-paign in Michigan's 1988 GOP presidential primary.[10] The former Repub-lican National Committeeman also helped George W. Bush in this key contest.

President George H. W. Bush named Peter Secchia to be U.S. ambas-sador to Italy in 1989, a position where he served with distinction for three and one-half years. As ambassador, Secchia visited every Italian region, every Italian province, and approximately three hundred Italian cities, towns, and villages. An unassuming man with an energetic and youthful family, Secchia won plaudits from the Italian people during his tenure. The ambassador became deeply knowledgeable about Italian history, and he, his wife, Joan, and their four children learned to speak Italian. In reflecting on his tenure as ambassador, Secchia focuses on the warmth of the U.S.-Italian relationship at the governmental level and the personal level (his friends included former Italian Premier Giulio Andreotti and the late Sicil-ian prosecutor Giovanni Falcone).[11] In 1993 Secchia's remarkable record as Ambassador to Italy resulted in his receiving two important honors: the U.S. Department of State Distinguished Honor Award and the Cavaliere di Gran Croce (The Knight of the Great Cross) from the Republic of Italy.

Secchia continues to maintain close ties to Italy—and he remains very involved in Italian-American activities and organizations. The Michigan business titan regularly travels to Italy; he was a ten-year trustee and benefactor of John Cabot University in Rome, the alma mater of his son, Charles.[12] In 2005 he received the National Italian American Foundation (NIAF) Special Achievement Award for International Affairs.[13] And in 2005–2006, he served as the leader of the Italian-American efforts to rally support for Judge Samuel Alito's confirmation to the Supreme Court.[14] The Secchia family, meanwhile, continues to grow and thrive. Peter and Joan Secchia's four children live in Rome, Seattle, Shanghai, and New York City.[15] Now in his early seventies, Peter Secchia regularly receives the well-deserved accolades that accrue to someone who has built successful businesses, contributed significantly to his community, and bolstered trans-Atlantic ties between two longtime allies, Italy and the United States.

❋ I. Lido Cantarutti's parents came from Friuli.[16] His mother, Evelina Cantarutti, is an immigrant from Rodeano Basso (Comune Rive d'Arcano). His late father, Guido Cantarutti, was an immigrant from the neighboring village of Cisterna del Friuli (Comune Coseano). Guido Cantarutti "came here multiple times during the 1920s," and he worked in Pennsylvania and Ohio before heading to northern California. Evelina Cantarutti and her son, Carino (Reno), emigrated from Italy in 1935; they went directly to the West Coast, near Santa Cruz, California. Lido Cantarutti himself was born in Santa Cruz in 1939. The Cantaruttis soon moved from Santa Cruz to Richmond, California, in the East Bay. During World War II, the Cantarutti family was ordered out of the Bay Area because Guido and Evelina Cantarutti had not yet become naturalized Americans. They relocated to Asti, California, but Guido Cantarutti continued working in Richmond. During the postwar period, they mostly lived in the East Bay.

The Friuliani customs and traditions informed every aspect of life in the Cantarutti household. Lido Cantarutti remembers Friulian cuisine, Roman Catholicism, the Friulian dialect, and "so many nostalgic recollections" as vital parts of his childhood. His parents, after all, had "much affection for their relatives back home." They missed Friuli and Friulians. There were "certain religious holidays" (the Assumption in particular) that mattered significantly to the Cantaruttis. In addition, the Friulian cuisine was essential to their family life, with its cheese, polenta, sausage, radicchio, minestrone, prosciutto, red wine, beef and chicken stews, and occasional servings of pasta. Lido Cantarutti's Friulian-American upbringing influenced his outlook on the world in at least four ways: 1) family; 2) hard work; 3) values; and 4) humility.

Cantarutti maintains significant ties to Italy through his family, friends, and the cinema. The recipient of numerous honors in Italy and the United States, he enjoys a good relationship with the Italian Cultural Institute in San Francisco. A holder of bachelor's (Phi Beta Kappa) and master's degrees in Language and Literature from the University of California–Berkeley, Cantarutti has taught Italian at the College of Marin for more than two decades. The former U.S. Army officer and businessperson regularly visits Friuli and encourages young Italian relatives to come to California. Currently, Lido Cantarutti serves as the director of the Italian Film Festival, a yearly event in Marin County, California.[17]

In 1985 Cantarutti became the key person responsible for this celebration of Italian cinema. The Italian Film Festival has grown dramatically under his leadership. Initially, it focused on the classics and "went from there to more contemporary films." At first, Cantarutti "sourced the films here in the U.S.A." Then he "started getting films from Rome." Cantarutti reports that he has "an excellent relationship with film distributors in Rome." The Italian movies are shown mainly at the Marin Center in San Rafael, California. The mission of the Italian Film Festival is "to entertain, but also to promote Italian films and culture," in Cantarutti's words. He finds this work to be "hugely satisfying and enjoyable."

Lido Cantarutti works on the Italian Film Festival throughout the year. He previews prospective films, books the films and theater, and puts together a promotional campaign with flyers, mailers, and press materials. The Marin County, California, resident has the films shipped from Italy to San Francisco. Each September, Cantarutti drives to the San Francisco International Airport to "pick up the prints" that arrive from Italy. The Festival takes place in October and November, and there is a volunteer group that assists him. He personally introduces each film and welcomes the audience to the show. The Italian Film Festival has a devoted cadre of viewers each year; the attendees hail from such places as Oakland, Berkeley, San Francisco, Marin County, and Sonoma County. This vibrant festival is part of the ongoing efforts throughout America to promote the Italian culture and language. Indeed, it illustrates how an Italian American (Lido Cantarutti) contributes to positive images of both Italy and the diasporic Italians at the same time.

As a group, the Italian immigrants and their immediate descendants in the United States once maintained substantial connections to Italy. During the late 1800s and early 1900s some Italian immigrants divided their time between Italy and the United States. These "birds of passage" would work in the United States for much of the year and then return to Italy in the winter months. Moreover, there were the returnees—Italians who went to America and decided to go home again.[18] In the United States, the Italian immigrants and their children often maintained close family ties to the Old Country and sometimes followed Italian events with great interest, particularly during such periods as the 1930s (when Italy invaded Ethiopia) and the Cold War (as in the hotly contested Italian presidential election of 1948). As time passed, though, the newer generations of Italian Americans generally had fewer family ties to the Old Country and interest in events there.[19]

Since the end of the mass immigration from Italy to the United States during the 1920s, Italian Americans have become progressively more "American" as a group and, consequently, less focused on Italian affairs. Italian-American observers will often cite World War II as a critical turning point that hastened the assimilation of the Italian immigrants and their descendants into American culture, as they sought to be seen as completely American and leave behind any aspects of their culture that distinguished them from mainstream America. (Italy, after all, was part of the Axis and an enemy of the United States from 1941 to 1943.)[20] For more than six decades now, the United States and Italy have been and continue to be close allies, two nations with excellent cultural, economic, and diplomatic relations.

Italy and the United States are both important players in the global economy. In 2006 U.S.-Italian trade amounted to $45.2 billion, as our imports from Italy substantially exceeded our exports to Italy. The United States had a trade imbalance with Italy of slightly more than $20 billion in 2006.[21] Presently, the Italians have nearly $12 billion in direct investment in the United States. At the same time, there is approximately $29 billion in direct U.S. investment in Italy.[22] Each year Americans contribute billions of dollars to the Italian economy through their tourism in Italy and purchases of Italian products (and vice versa).

Throughout America one finds people of Italian origin—and indeed individuals from many ethnic backgrounds—who develop and maintain extensive connections to Italy.[23] These Italophiles enjoy Italian art, music, culture, cuisine, and the myriad other aspects of *italianità*. Italian Americans often bring Italian singers and folk dancers to the United States to perform at Italian-American festivals and cultural events. High-ranking Italian guests, meanwhile, are prized attendees at Italian-American events, such as the NIAF Gala in Washington and the Columbus Day Parade in New York City each year. Italian-American organizations may also celebrate secular and religious Italian events and holidays, as in Carnevale, Italian Republic Day, and Ferragosto. And some Americans of Italian descent cheered Italy's ultimately successful bid to win the World Cup in 2006.

Today there are Americans who have spent decades promoting the Italian-American heritage and contributing to cultural exchanges between Italy and the United States. New York Supreme Court Justice Dominic Massaro, for one, enjoys an exemplary reputation for his distinguished career and extraordinary commitment to Italian Americana: events, activities, institutions, and organizations. Justice Massaro currently serves as President of the American Society of the Italian Legions of Merit, the officially recognized organization of Americans who have been decorated by the Italian Government. These individuals (the majority of whom are of Italian origin) work in the chivalric, diplomatic, and cultural arenas to sustain and perpetuate the Italian image and presence in the United States.

Italian diplomats, Minister Antonio Bandini among them, encourage and strongly support these types of efforts. Minister Bandini offers a fascinating perspective on American perceptions of Italy and the relationship between Italians and Italian Americans. A native of Emilia-Romagna, Bandini knows the United States well. He was an exchange student through the American Field Service as a teenager in 1965, when he spent a year at a Pennsylvania high school. Later, Bandini studied at the Johns Hopkins University European Centre in Bologna. A diplomat since 1974, Bandini has worked in Italy, Libya, France, Eritrea, Lebanon, Switzerland, and the United States. His distinguished record of diplomatic leadership includes a three-year stint as Italian ambassador to Eritrea. Bandini served as Italian vice consul in Newark from 1977 to 1980, and he became Italian consul general in New York in July 2003. His four-year tenure in this position concluded in July 2007.[24]

Bandini's work required him to represent Italy in the States of New York, Connecticut, and New Jersey (eight counties fell under his jurisdiction) as well as in Bermuda.[25] One issue is perception. While the image of Italy is quite positive in the American mindset, Bandini points out that there is an "over-focus on some aspects." Industrial machinery is the top Italian export, by far, to the United States. But many Americans "do not know much about Italian industrial potential," says Bandini. Likewise, Italy's pharmaceutical researchers contribute to innovations in the American marketplace, a fact that does not always receive much attention here. Besides working on issues of perception, Bandini oversaw such institutions as the Italian Cultural Institute, the Italian Trade Commission, the Italian Government Tourist Board, and the Italy-America Chamber of Commerce. Bandini also focused on education. The Government of Italy co-finances Italian-language instruction for thirty thousand students in New York, New Jersey, and Connecticut.[26]

The consul general was deeply involved in the Italian-American communities of the Tri-State Area. He points out that there are many Italian-related activities in New York, with Casa Italiana at New York University and the Italian Academy at Columbia University along with Italian-American programs at such institutions as Queens College, Rutgers University, SUNY–Stony Brook, Seton Hall University, Montclair State University, and the City University of New York. As a rule, the consul general attended two to four events each weekday. One daily event, on average, involved the Italian-American community. (Other events usually focused on cultural and "trade-related" matters.)[27] Minister Bandini's presence was coveted at Italian-American events as a speaker and/or honored guest, and his photograph often appeared in *America Oggi* and the *Italian Tribune*.

Bandini regularly highlighted issues that matter to and interest Italians and Italian Americans alike. The "rediscovery" of the Italian language by Italian Americans is one such topic. Likewise, Italian issues (e.g., the drive to protect Italy's interest in the context of the reform of the United Nations Security Council) are important to the members and leaders of many Italian-American organizations. Still, Bandini notes that, for all their common roots, Italians and Italian Americans have developed "separate identities," a reality that governs their relationship. "It is important to know each other, but not to pretend we are the same," says Bandini. Over the years he has watched with interest as Americans of Italian origin have developed a sense of unity and a common identity.[28]

As the consul general, Bandini periodically found himself educating Italians about Italian-American culture. In some respects, Italians at times have a patronizing attitude toward their American brethren. They note that spaghetti with meatballs is a culinary dish with no ties to Italy, even though it is quintessentially Italian American. Bandini tells Italians that spaghetti with meatballs is not a "deterioration" in culture. Rather, the

Italians did not have ground meat at the time in Italy, while the Italian Americans encountered ground meat in America and created this new dish as a result. Of the Italian-American heritage, he correctly observes, "It is a different identity, a different culture."[29]

Bandini offers a positive and inclusive perspective on the Italian-American experience, one that values the diversity of the Italian diaspora. To this end, he emphasizes the quality of life and the well-kept neighborhoods that typify Italian-American communities. The former consul general also sees similarities between the Italian and Italian-American approaches to the world. Both groups are "living in a pleasant, beautiful environment." Italians and Italian Americans, too, have "a profound respect for manual skills," and they "take pride in doing something well." Finally, Bandini notes that heritage is important to Italians and Italian Americans.[30]

II. In 2004 Angela Bizzarro and her younger siblings, JoAnn Mikulec and John A. Graziano, decided to visit Italy. They did so after losing their parents, Lena Graziano and John B. Graziano Jr., the previous year. (Lena and John Graziano were married for sixty-seven years and they died only five months apart.) The members of this close-knit Italian family traveled to Italy with their spouses, Dominick Bizzarro, Robert Mikulec, and Aleda Graziano. Their itinerary included a visit to John B. Graziano Jr.'s ancestral hometown of Bellona in the Province of Caserta, near Naples. He had lived there until he was sixteen. While this Italian/American had deep roots in Italy, he always insisted that his children speak English, as he wanted them to be fully American. At the same time, these children of an Italian immigrant developed a profound appreciation for their Italian heritage.[31]

Going to Bellona had particular significance for Mrs. Bizzarro and her family members. They went to the town hall in Bellona, whereupon Angela Bizzarro produced her father's birth certificate in order to learn more about his background. Once they arrived at the town hall, the American visitors indicated their interest in seeing the books that registered the births of town residents. During their visit, they conversed with an older Italian, who in turn helped them find someone who spoke fluent English. This English-speaking guide took Mrs. Bizzarro and her siblings to the home where their father and grandfather had lived and the church where they had been baptized. Thereafter, the Americans went to a local, family-owned restaurant. After they finished their meal, the kind restaurateurs drove to the autostrada and directed these heritage tourists to their next destination.[32]

Bizzarro and her siblings gained greater knowledge of their family's heritage, culture, and folkways after visiting Italy in general and Bellona in particular. Her brother, John A. Graziano, was the youngest child in the family, and he could not always understand the things his father did. After going to Bellona and interacting with the locals, however, he thoroughly understood his father's outlook, approach, and perspective. Here in the United States, Angela Bizzarro and her husband, Dominick Bizzarro, have imparted a strong connection to Italian/American culture to their children (who are 100 percent Italian). For instance, Mr. and Mrs. Bizzarro still prepare the traditional seven-fish dinner for their family on Christmas Eve.[33] In sum, the experiences of Angela Bizzarro and her family members resemble those of other Italian Americans who have visited Italy to learn more about their family histories.

During recent decades, there has been much interest among Americans in learning more about their ancestral backgrounds, genealogical details, and Old World origins. Researching one's genealogy and family history requires patience, diligence, and perseverance. Family historians use documents and oral histories, among other source materials, to practice their craft.[34] Genealogical research can enhance the accuracy of one's family stories and legends. Until they began conducting such research, some Italian Americans in Louisiana said their ancestors came from Palermo because they boarded the ship for the New World there. In fact, they journeyed from their towns and villages to Palermo, but this distinction had been lost in time.[35]

There are many ways in which Italian Americans research their genealogies and family histories. The Internet has been an invaluable resource, one that allows researchers to network with each other and share information in ways that were not possible twenty years ago. The Web site offering access to Ellis Island/Port of New York Records enables people to view and print the ship manifests from the fabled port of entry.[36] Visiting Italy is a significant part of researching one's genealogy and family history in many cases.[37] Some Americans even research their family crests and coats of arms. Family historians may contact parish priests in Italy, go to their ancestral hometown(s), and check baptismal and municipal records there. For Italian Americans, going to the Old Country can be an emotional experience, one in which they learn helpful details that flesh out their family stories and sometimes gain greater insights into their own lives.

Susan DeFazio became deeply involved in genealogy and family history after her father's passing in 2001.[38] Thereafter, the Des Moines, Iowa, resident sent an Italian-language form letter about her genealogical research to one dozen DeFazios in Bianchi, the Calabrian village where the DeFazios have a presence. In 2003 she received a telephone call from a distant cousin in Bianchi, who invited her to visit Calabria. Susan DeFazio went to Bianchi later that year with her cousin, Barb (Angotti) Ferguson, from Cedar Rapids, Iowa, whom she met doing genealogy online. They stayed with their Italian relative for the duration of their visit to Bianchi. This trip to Italy enabled the two Iowans to enhance their knowledge of genealogy and family history.

Since 2001 Susan DeFazio has come into contact with her relatives via e-mail in such places as Paris, Geneva, Toronto, Alberta, and the Sydney area. "Recently I met my relatives from Australia in Italy and took them to Bianchi," says DeFazio. The Italian American's pronounced interest in her heritage even led her to undergo DNA testing—and for years she has been quite involved with several Italian genealogy Web sites. DeFazio, in fact, published her family tree on Ancestry.com. Therefore, her name comes up as a source when people type in a family name or a town name that relates to the DeFazio family history.

Consequently, she receives e-mails from people who are researching their genealogies and family histories. In one case, Susan DeFazio gave a family photo to one of her correspondents in Italy. This Italian and her Canadian brother had never seen a picture of their grandfather before. There were tears streaming down her face when she saw his photograph for the first time. Her brother in western Canada viewed this photograph, too, after Susan DeFazio sent it to him via e-mail. Such examples indicate how genealogical research can result in enriching and heartwarming experiences.

There are numerous stories about the enjoyment and emotional sustenance that Italian Americans derive from heritage tourism. Calabresi in America, an organization for people of Calabrian descent, sponsors trips to Italy each September. "Many people discover the hometowns where their parents come from," says Renato Turano.[39] Likewise, Doug Pozzo reports that he has visited his father's ancestral village in the Piedmont. He even saw the well that is the source of his surname.[40] Moreover, in 2005 Carlo Giraulo took photos of the apartment where his maternal grandfather was born in Bisceglie, Bari, Italy.[41] "I felt very emotional when I was there," recalls Giraulo. "The feeling of standing where my grandfather grew up and played as a child one hundred years before was almost overwhelming. It brought tears to my eyes and still does today when I think of it."[42] These examples illustrate the ways in which Americans of Italian origin value their genealogy and family histories.

Italians may be surprised to learn that Italian Americans know the layouts of their ancestral towns, villages, and communities without ever having visited them before. Take the case of Father John Richetta, who remembered in a 2004 interview how the people in Pavone, his mother's Piedmontese hometown, marveled at how well he was able to recount the exact layout of the city on his first visit there decades ago. He told them that his mother had spoken of Pavone so often during his childhood that it had left an indelible imprint on his mind.[43] Similarly, George Silvestri Jr. echoes these themes with regard to his first visit, in 1963, to Partigliano, his ancestral Tuscan village. "It was like I had been there," says Silvestri. He felt this way because he had heard "so many descriptions" of Partigliano during his youth.[44]

Americans from a wide variety of ethnic backgrounds enjoy visiting Italy, studying there, and even living there. In 2006, for instance, 2,201,000 Americans went to Italy; the same year, 533,000 Italians came to the United States.[45] Italian Americans usually feel very welcome in Italy and enjoy their Italian experiences tremendously. They delight in the realization that their customs, traditions, mannerisms, and linguistic expressions often owe something to Italy. Many Americans of Italian origin, to be sure, never visit Italy. Some have no desire to do so. Others do not wish to allocate their resources in this way. And some might like to do so, but they are not especially fond of international travel. While Italian Americans who visit Italy may come away feeling much more ethnic pride—and greater knowledge of their Italian roots and heritage—they usually realize how American they are once they go to the Old Country.[46]

In an article published in *Fra Noi*, Bob Masullo reflected on how Italians relate to Italian Americans. This Bronx native, longtime journalist, and grandson of Italian immigrants and his wife, Eileen, lived in Italy for one year in 2005–2006.[47] At the conclusion of their sojourn in Italy, Bob Masullo wrote:

> Despite their general friendliness and liking of generic Americans, Italians have next to no feeling of kinship for Italian Americans. They regard us (or our

ancestors) as people who left Italy and therefore severed all ties. This is not true of people to whom you are actually related, of course; Italians tend to treat blood relatives like royalty. But if you say to an Italian to whom you are not related, "I am Italian American," expect about as much of a reaction as if you told him or her, "You know, we have the same color eyes." They just don't care about us in this way.[48]

It sometimes puzzles Italian nationals when Americans of Italian extraction will often refer to themselves as "Italian," considering that most such individuals hold U.S. citizenship, speak English as their mother tongue, and rarely, if ever, visit Italy. The native Italians would view the individuals who describe themselves in this way as "Americans" or, perhaps, Americans with Italian ancestors. Similarly, Italian immigrants to the United States may describe themselves as "Italian Americans"; they will refer to the U.S.-born people of Italian extraction as the "American Italians." In any event, Italian immigrants to the United States often play an important role in mediating between the Italians in Italy and Italian Americans in ethnic newspapers, institutions, organizations, and other realms.

Italian Americans, meanwhile, sometimes identify with Italian cultural and linguistic traditions that date back to the Italy of yesteryear. Some "Italian" characteristics that Italian Americans may associate with contemporary Italy no longer exist there.[49] Indeed, certain aspects of early-twentieth-century Italy (e.g., dialectal Italian and particular cultural traditions) have been preserved in time here in the United States. Italian visitors to this country may be impressed by the Italian Americans' fidelity to the older Italian customs and traditions (the ones their ancestors brought with them to the New World). As one would expect, Italian culture has changed dramatically over the last century. "What we think of as Italian culture is constantly shifting, changing, and reinventing itself," notes Aldo Svaldi, the vice-president of the Tirolesi-Trentini del Colorado.[50]

III. David Gratta is a native-born American who has been an Italian citizen since his birth in 1954.[51] Gratta, however, was born in Mobile, Alabama, and grew up in southern Mississippi. His paternal grandparents, Antonio Gratta and Giuseppina Fulciniti Gratta, were natives of the Town of Palmeriti in the Province of Catanzaro, who arrived in the United States during the early 1900s. Antonio Gratta became a U.S. citizen in 1934, while Giuseppina Gratta "never became a U.S. citizen." Gratta's late father, James Vincent (Vincenzo) Gratta, was born in Massachusetts in 1913. He was an Italian citizen from birth because he had been "born to Italians residing abroad," according to Italian law. When he married Ada Belle Butler, a native of Wayne County, Mississippi, in 1944, she became an Italian citizen, too. Their son, David Middleton Gratta, was born ten years later; he received Italian citizenship as a birthright on the grounds that he was "born to two Italian citizens residing abroad."

Throughout David Gratta's youth, his father taught him about his Italian heritage. His son remembers these lessons well:

> My father always instilled an appreciation of Italian cooking in our household, and he told Italian childhood stories, including those about "The Evil Eye," when I was young. I was also aware of the Italian Christmas tradition of La Befana. Our household followed the traditional Italian form: that of the father being the head of the family, but my mother being the center of it. My father taught me some of the historical aspects of Italy, such as the historical significance of Rome, and its contributions to government and Western civilization. It was from him that I initially learned about how Rome established the first Republic, and had a true Senate. From my earliest youth I learned of the very special place Italy holds in the pages of history, by inspiring the establishment of free republics throughout the world.

In his life, David Gratta has lived mainly in communities in the Deep South where there are few people of Italian origin. This grandson of Calabrian immigrants is a longtime Mississippian. During the early 1960s he and his family moved to southern Mississippi. The Hattiesburg, Mississippi, resident earned his bachelor's degree from William Carey College and his master's degree from the University of Southern Mississippi. Today Gratta is a businessperson who works in the oil and gas industry. In addition, this recipient of an Italian knighthood (an honor conferred by Italian President Giorgio Napolitano) serves as a Consular Correspondent for the Consulate General of Italy, Miami, and the Italian Ministry of Foreign Affairs. After Hurricane Katrina in 2005, David Gratta helped to coordinate the delivery of relief supplies from Italy to Mississippi. He was also responsible for gathering important information about the status of Italian nationals who were on the Gulf Coast at the time of Hurricane Katrina.

As a Consular Correspondent of Italy, Gratta works tirelessly to see that Italian-language courses are offered in the Magnolia State's public schools, colleges, and universities. To this end, he founded the Italian

Language and Culture Foundation in 2004. "One of my missions is to raise awareness of the Italian language and culture to the state and one way to do that is to offer Italian in the schools," reports David Gratta.[52] Since 2002 the Italian cultural advocate has made what he describes as "tremendous progress" in facilitating the study of Italian in Mississippi's public schools.[53] Learning the Italian language has cultural—and economic—significance to Mississippians. Italy, after all, is an important market for Mississippi businesses: Gratta notes that "Italy is the largest European market for Mississippi wood products today." Looking toward the future, David Gratta and like-minded Mississippians hope to promote ever-greater trade and cultural exchanges between their state and Italy.

The Italian government itself has significant representation in the United States through its various offices in major American cities (the Italian Embassy in Washington, D.C., chief among them).[54] In this country, one finds such Italian institutions as the Italian Trade Commissions, Italian Cultural Institutes, Italian Government Tourist Boards, and Italy-America Chambers of Commerce. Moreover, the Italian Consulates in the United States provide significant services and play an essential role in promoting Italian culture, Italian business, and the Italian language here. There are Italian Consulates in Boston, Chicago, Detroit, Houston, Los Angeles, Miami, Newark, New York, Philadelphia, and San Francisco, while the Italian Embassy in Washington has a Consular Section.[55]

Dr. Gianfranco Colognato, who recently served as Consul General of Italy in Miami, had numerous duties and responsibilities in this position.[56] During his tenure as consul general, Dr. Colognato wrote:

> The first and most important duty of a Consul is to assist and protect the Italian citizens and their properties. In this frame, the Office acts as an Italian City Hall, where the Italians resident in the consular Jurisdiction (mine consists of the territories of Alabama, Mississippi, Georgia, South Carolina, Florida, Puerto Rico, The Bahamas, Cayman Islands, Turks and Caicos Islands, U.S. and British Virgin Islands, and other minor ones) may obtain their passports, certificates, registrations of births, marriages, deaths and other documents. We also issue visas to those who are required to obtain one to go to Italy, for tourism and other purposes. Besides these administrative activities we are also challenged with other not less important matters like, for example, the promotion of Italian products, the diffusion of the Italian language and culture, and the support of Italian companies that wish to enter the American market.[57]

Colognato brought a diverse background to his position in Miami. A native of Rome, he was born in 1942 and graduated from the University of Rome in 1968. From 1968 to 1975 Colognato worked in Asmara (in what is now Eritrea) as an Italian-language teacher and journalist and, later, as an Italian-language professor at Asmara University.[58] Colognato joined the Italian Ministry of Foreign Affairs in 1975. His diplomatic résumé includes positions in such nations as Libya, Sudan, Nigeria, Somalia, Germany, Switzerland, and the United States, along with several assignments in Rome. He has had an eventful career: In 1991, for instance, the veteran diplomat played an important role in mediating among the different factions in Somalia's civil war. Before coming to Miami in July 2003, Colognato had been the Italian Consul General in Cologne, Germany.[59]

As Italian Consul General in Miami from 2003 to 2007, Colognato was a leader of the efforts to support Italian culture and business throughout the southeastern United States. He attended many social, cultural, and business events in Florida, the most populous state in his consular jurisdiction. In recent years the consul general addressed audiences at such academic institutions as the University of Miami and Florida International University. Besides Florida, Colognato also traveled to the other parts of his consular jurisdiction, as in Mississippi and South Carolina.[60] In his diplomacy, he often met with businesspeople, cultural figures, and top political leaders. In doing so, Colognato promoted a positive image of Italy as an economic power, cultural beacon, and diplomatic force.

Italian-American leaders in the Southeast speak highly of Dr. Colognato's record as consul general in Miami. He has been accessible, receptive, and inclusive in his interactions with them. "I maintain very good relations with the Italian-American Associations and carefully monitor their activities," says Colognato.[61] "When a specific interest arises," continues the Consul General, "I am ready to work with them in the preparation and realization of their projects."[62] As his schedule permitted, Colognato regularly attended Italian-American events in Florida and beyond.[63] In 2007, moreover, Colognato was honored as "Man of the Year" by Il Circolo, The Italian Cultural Society of the Palm Beaches.

Floridians and other Americans regularly participate in cultural and political exchanges with Italians in Italy. In fact, Americans and Italians often try to build and develop relationships between specific American and Italian communities (often in the form of Sister City agreements).[64] The Italian Embassy and the Italian governmental institutions elsewhere in the United States allow Italy to foster closer ties to people of Italian ancestry throughout the world, including the United States. As Luisa Del Giudice notes: "Italy has, for a variety of political and economic reasons, become interested in its immigrants and in reestablishing active links with these communities."[65] "At the regional level as well," continues Del Giudice, "governments in Italy are becoming increasingly aggressive about forging direct links with their coregionalists abroad."[66]

The Italian government is making a concerted effort to harness the power of the Italian diaspora through its promotion of the Italian language and culture—and in other realms as well.[67] In 1992 Italy legalized dual citizenship for qualifying individuals. Then, in 2001, Italy introduced voting rights for the Italian citizens living abroad. And in 2006 and 2008 there were elections for the "overseas constituencies" in the Italian Parliament.[68] North America and Central America are currently represented by Basilio Giordano in the Italian Senate and Gino Bucchino and Amato Berardi in the Italian Chamber of Deputies. This development highlights the mutually beneficial relationship between the Italian government and the Italians living abroad.

In any event, it will be interesting to see how the two nations and peoples maintain their connections in the coming years. Observers of the Western European countries point to "Generation E," a group that includes young Italians.[69] "Compared with their parents and grandparents, their emotional and historical attachment to America is weakening," notes Howard LaFranchi.[70] This astute observer continues: "A similar estrangement is occurring in America, where links to Europe are loosening as family ties to the old Continent fall further back in time and new immigrant ties are more often to other continents. In the post-cold-war years and especially since 9/11, attention has increasingly turned from Europe to Asia and the Middle East."[71] Indeed, the distance between Italians and Italian Americans seems to be growing.

This challenge of maintaining and enhancing the ties between the United States and Italy is faced by Ronald Spogli, the current U.S. ambassador to Italy. In 2005, President Bush named the Los Angeles investment banker, whose Umbrian ancestors came to the United States in 1912, to be U.S. Ambassador to Italy. The Italian-speaking Spogli lived in Italy during his twenties and traveled extensively in the country before he became ambassador. He seeks to preserve the bond between his native land and his ancestral homeland.[72] "Older Italians have a debt of gratitude with the

United States because they remember what America did to liberate Italy from the Nazis and help rebuild it in the years following World War II," noted Spogli in 2005. "But younger Italians don't care about events so far in the past and have little direct experience with America, getting most of their information from the Internet and television. I don't want to see that good will towards America end," posited Spogli.[73]

❀ ❀ ❀

Turning now to a comparative perspective, Dr. Carmel Ruffolo offers a series of intriguing reflections on the contemporary Italo-Australian and Italian-American experiences. The thirtysomething microbiologist and native of Melbourne, Australia, is the daughter of Calabrian immigrants. Ruffolo's mother came to Australia as a young child, while her father was older when he arrived in Australia. Ruffolo's parents emphasized her Italian heritage at home. As a youth, she went to an Italian school on weekends in Melbourne. Carmel Ruffolo has always had "direct links to Italy" through her family and, now, her husband Jack Ruffolo's family (he is an American of Calabrian origin). In fact, she traveled to Italy during the 1970s and 1980s. Her family also has relatives in Chicago, whom they visit often. Ruffolo began coming to the United States at an early age, and so she was familiar with the nation that became her home in 1997.[74]

Ruffolo says that the Italians are more "mobilized in Australia" than in America. This engaging scientist describes the many Italian delis, numerous Italian clubs (one for each *paese*, it seems), and rich array of Italian activities that exist in Australia. Professor Ruffolo notes how Italians seem to retain their ancestral culture and heritage more so in Australia than in the United States. To this end, she recalls a vivid anecdote from when she was ten years old. The young Australian was playing with her Italian-American relatives in Chicago when she discovered (to her great surprise) that her playmates did not speak Italian. Another cultural difference involves visits to Italy. Many of the Italian Australians of Ruffolo's acquaintance have traveled to Italy, whereas Italian Americans often live their entire lives without ever going to Italy.[75]

Australians of Italian descent are now well integrated into Australian society, just as their Italian-American counterparts make up a vital part of U.S. mainstream culture. The scholar Loretta Baldassar notes how second-generation Italian Australians often enter the professions, a familiar trajectory of immigrant success that one finds throughout the Italian diaspora.

Italy, moreover, is glamorous in Australia now.[76] Baldassar writes: "The popularity of things Italian is connected to the relatively recent development of Italy's international reputation. No longer a country of mass emigration and poverty, Italy since the 1980s has been high on the list of affluent countries. In part due to Italy's affluence and in part due to Australia's policy of multiculturalism, many second generation Italians are quite comfortable expressing their *italianità* consciously and conscientiously."[77]

Carmel Ruffolo herself is a second-generation Italian Australian: This passionate proponent of preserving the Italian heritage draws upon her culturally rich background in Australia. As a youth, Italian television was always available to Ruffolo in her Melbourne home. Likewise, *The Age* and *Il Globo* received equal amounts of attention there. (Her wedding photo appeared in *Il Globo*.) Now Ruffolo, her husband, Jack, and their two children live in Kenosha, Wisconsin. A Ph.D. in medical microbiology, she teaches microbiology at the University of Wisconsin–Parkside. Today Ruffolo reflects on the prevalence of Italian culture in Australia and says, "You're over there and you take it for granted." This open-minded global citizen deeply appreciates her ethnic upbringing in Melbourne. Ruffolo characterizes America as "my second home" and maintains especially close ties to Chicago.[78]

Her cousin, Joseph Bruno, is a well-known and well-respected figure in Chicago's Italian-American community.[79] Bruno, a native of the Calabrian town of Marano Marchesato who was born in 1935, arrived in the United States in 1960. Since then he has built a significant reputation as a "master furniture artisan" and developed a roster of clients that includes several celebrities.[80] Sometimes Bruno reflects on the fixed nature of opportunities in the Calabria of his youth. In those years, one's station in life was usually defined by his family's socioeconomic status.[81] Bruno, himself, has always had a strongly held sense of community and a desire to create—and participate in—institutions that preserve Italian traditions and sustain Italian cultural events and activities.[82]

During recent decades, Bruno has emerged as a leader in Chicagoland's Italian-American affairs. His honors include the prestigious title of Cavaliere from the Italian government. He is a founding member of the Calabresi in America Organization and a longtime participant in the Casa Italia and Italian Cultural Center in Stone Park, Illinois. Furthermore, Bruno is president of the Società San Francesco di Paola and plays a significant role in the Festa Della Famiglia that honors San Francesco (Calabria's patron saint) every August in suburban Chicago.[83] "That is his way of bringing the Italian culture here—and honoring this venerable culture in the United States," observes Carmel Ruffolo.[84] She, her husband, Jack Ruffolo, and their family participate in the Feast each year, as do thousands of Americans from Calabrian backgrounds.

Carmel Ruffolo, too, emphasizes a global perspective in her day-to-day life. Ruffolo herself is multilingual: She speaks standard Italian and Calabrese in addition to English. During the summer of 2005, she returned to Calabria as part of a delegation from the University of Wisconsin–Parkside to the Università della Calabria. Her mother's hometown is Castrolibero and the town's mayor asked her to deliver a speech there. This address was a moving and emotional experience for Ruffolo. Castrolibero is "home" for her, a place where she has family ties and warm feelings for the community. At the same time, she came to Castrolibero as an Australian-born Italian who represented an American university. Ruffolo always wears her Calabrian pin, a gift from an Italian political figure, as an expression of her pride in being a Calabrian in the New World.[85]

Epilogue

THE FUTURE

E very December, Lucrezia Lindia gives the Rome, Milan, and Calabrian telephone directories to her Italian students at Eastchester
Middle/High School in Eastchester, New York.[1] Each student
picks someone from the directory and sends a letter (in Italian) to that
person asking her or him about how s/he celebrates the holidays. Then, in
late January, the letters from Italy start arriving for Lindia's students.
Many Italians respond to their American correspondents, and they
describe their holiday plans in Italian. Through the letter-writing exercise,
Lindia gives the young people an opportunity to practice their Italian and
learn about Italian culture. It is one of the inventive teaching techniques
that she uses to educate and motivate her students.

Lindia (née Gioia) was born in Calabria. She came to the United States
at age nineteen in 1970 with an elementary-school teaching diploma from
Italy. The chic, multilingual Italian entered the Lenox Hill School and
enrolled in a special adult program for people who wanted to learn English. She was the valedictorian of her class there. Lindia then attended
Lehman College in the Bronx for three years and received a B.A. (Phi
Beta Kappa). Later, she went to Fordham University to earn a Master's of
Science in Bilingual Education. In addition, Lindia has an administrative
degree and certification in Spanish. A former Montessori School teacher
and administrator, Lindia is a veteran K–12 educator who also teaches
courses at such institutions as Middlebury College, Westchester Community College, and SUNY–New Paltz.

Lucrezia Lindia is married to Francesco Lindia, a fellow Calabrian and
educator who came to the United States in the 1970s. A tall, muscular man

with blond hair and blue eyes, Mr. Lindia appears German to many Americans. In fact, he is often mistaken for German until people hear him speak, reports Francesco Lindia. He had a great-grandfather who was 6'6", a height that is very unusual in Calabria. Francesco Lindia initiated the Italian program at Eastchester Middle/High School in 1980. Today Francesco and Lucrezia Lindia are both members of Eastchester's faculty in this affluent community in Westchester County, New York. The Lindias reside nearby in Greenwich, Connecticut. Their two twentysomething children, Fabio Massimo and Melissa, live in Manhattan and work in the financial-services industry.

Italian is Eastchester Middle/High School's top world language. Hundreds of Eastchester students enroll in Italian courses during each school year, and there are five Italian teachers in Eastchester's thriving Italian program. Eastchester offers Italian as a language due to the community's Italian-American population, but also as a result of the educators' creative efforts to encourage students to enroll in the language program. The Italian-language classes in Eastchester undoubtedly reinforce the feelings of kinship between Italian Americans and their Italian cousins, due to the significant focus that the Lindias and their colleagues place on Italian culture and folkways. Indeed, two reasons that Eastchester students enroll in Italian courses relate to their cultural affinity with Italy and their desire to speak with Italian kinfolk.

Young scholars in Eastchester learn much about Italian and Italian-American culture in Lucrezia Lindia's Italian-language courses. She teaches her students about such varied topics as sports, Carnevale, and Columbus and "The Encounter." And she regularly involves her students in cultural activities. In October 2004, for instance, Lindia brought Italian folk singers/dancers to perform at her school. Each school year the proud Calabrian spends three weeks on the topic of immigration, specifically internal Italian migration, intra-European immigration by Italians, and Italian immigration to the United States. This topic resonates with Eastchester residents, as Italian Americans constitute far and away the largest ethnic group there. Americans of Italian descent account for 34.6 percent of the Town of Eastchester's 31,318 residents. Around 60 percent of Eastchester's Italian students are Italian Americans.

As one of the nation's most prominent Italian-language teachers, Lucrezia Lindia spends countless hours outside the classroom on curriculum development, professional activities, and academic research. She serves as president of the Italian Teachers' Association (it covers Westchester County and the five boroughs of New York City), a chapter of the American Association of Teachers of Italian. Furthermore, Mrs. Lindia is one of the AATI's two regional representatives for New York. She regularly presents and publishes papers on educational topics, too. This recipient of the Association of Italian American Educators' Outstanding Educator of the Year Award works constantly with her colleagues throughout the nation to develop new and more effective pedagogical techniques. She recently co-authored an Italian-language textbook for middle/high school students, for example.[2] A consultant to the New York State Education Department, Lucrezia Lindia actively participates in New York City's Columbus Day Parade every October. Indeed, this über-teacher is "charming, indefatigable and heroically energetic," as one journalist describes her.[3]

The Lindia family maintains close ties to Italy. Lucrezia Lindia has a home in Calabria, and she teaches a course in Italy every summer. In their lives, Lucrezia and Francesco Lindia focus on the Italian language and culture. Their American-born children speak fluent Italian. Many of the Lindias' students in Eastchester are native-born Italian Americans who seek to reconnect with their ancestral homeland by learning the Italian language—and celebrating Italy's customs and traditions. Through their work to promote the Italian language and culture, the Lindias allow Italian Americans to preserve and perpetuate the Italian part of their heritage. At the same time, they help Americans learn about Italy and Italian Americans. Francesco and Lucrezia Lindia are Italians and Americans: Consequently, they serve as bridge-builders between two nations, two peoples, and two cultures.

I. Students with Italian surnames often enroll in Professor Alan Balboni's classes at the Community College of Southern Nevada. Italian Americans, after all, constitute nearly seven percent of the population in Clark County, Nevada. When Balboni calls the roll of his students each semester, he pronounces the Italian surnames as they would be pronounced in Italy. Balboni says that some of his Italian-American students seem surprised when he does so, as if they had never heard their names pronounced this way before. He notes that such a reaction is to be expected, considering that these young adults may be only one-quarter Italian. The assimilation process, observes Balboni, has proceeded to the point that there is essentially nothing "Italian" about some of his Italian-American students except their surnames. They have grown up in households where their parents focus little, if any, attention on ethnic issues.[4]

Today most Italian Americans are now virtually indistinguishable from other Americans in so many respects. Some Italian Americans do not view this development as being unilaterally positive. One man, a resident of western New York, told me that he sees the widespread assimilation of Italian Americans as a double-edged sword. Italians now have excellent opportunities to succeed in different endeavors, to be sure. At the same time, however, the warm, close-knit ethnic culture of his youth no longer exists. Therefore, this particular individual laments that Italian Americans have "assimilated to the point that we have lost our Italian heritage." This is especially true as Italian Americans become ever more variegated in their ethnic identities and the distance from the Old Country grows ever greater. Meanwhile, the gap between what is "Italian" (from Italy) and "Italian American" (how we Americans interpret, recognize, and celebrate our Italian heritage) will certainly grow larger with the passage of time.

In the future, we are going to see more instances in which Italian Americans remember their heritage with pride, even as it does not define who they are in their day-to-day lives. A young person may say he is *lucchese*, but not even know where Lucca is on the map.[5] Someday his identification with Lucca may lead him to visit the Tuscan city with his wife (a non-Italian, in all likelihood) and their children. Still, contemporary Tuscan culture is never going to influence his life and outlook much, if at all. In the coming years, though, some younger Italian Americans might yearn for the "ethnic" nature of their forebears' lives. I heard about the story of an Italian-American woman whose ancestors had been here three or four generations. At a multicultural event in the late 1990s, she observed the various activities and remarked to her Italian-born friend, "I wish I were ethnic."[6]

Of course, a young person does not have to be completely Italian to identify with her or his Italian heritage or, for that matter, to act and feel "Italian." Thomas Ragona's granddaughter, Gianna Lisette, is one-quarter Italian, one-quarter Slovak, and one-half Mexican. When she comes to visit her grandparents, she says, "Grandma, I want some macaroni. I'm Italian." Gianna is named for an Italian model—and Ragona stresses her Italian heritage to her.[7] Similarly, Ann and Charles Turco proudly cite the Italian characteristics of their grandchildren. Joseph Anthony Turco is one-eighth Italian. Ann Turco reports that her little grandson speaks with his hands, just as his father does. Max, another of the Turcos' grandsons, is three-eighths Italian. Charles Turco recounts with pride that Max enjoys pasta very much; the teenager chose "Salvatore" as his confirmation name.[8] These types of reactions will become ever more significant in the coming years, as few young Italian Americans will be fully Italian.

It is common to hear about young Americans who emphasize their Italian ancestry. "My brother's kids say they're proudly Sicilian as strongly as their grandfather might have," notes Monsignor Dominic Bottino.[9] Similarly, Ronald DiVecchio relates how his Polish-surnamed grandson identifies with his Italian roots. The young man tells his grandfather that he may learn to speak Italian in the future.[10] Vince Pardo's young granddaughter is one-half Korean, one-quarter Sicilian, and one-quarter Anglo. She often describes herself as Italian, reports her grandfather.[11] Anecdotal evidence suggests that young adults from ethnically mixed backgrounds regularly identify with their Italian heritage. Each year thousands of young Italian Americans visit Italy, while others spend college semesters studying there. Some Americans of Italian origin even relocate to Italy to live and work.

Many Italian Americans seek to pass their ancestral customs and traditions on to their grandchildren. Linda and Gerry Sepe grew up in Italian Catholic neighborhoods, which were nurturing places steeped in ethnic culture and traditional values. The Sepes' children learned from their parents to respect and appreciate Italian-American culture and values. Now the transplanted Texans have grandchildren—and they feel especially strongly about the importance of sharing their customs and traditions with the next generation.[12] Anecdotal evidence suggests that numerous Italian Americans from their generation feel the same way.

To this end, Nicholas Maiolo wrote and directed a play (*Due Cuori—Two Hearts*) to commemorate the 100th anniversary of the Order Sons of Italy in America. He and his grandchildren acted in the production four years ago. In doing so, Maiolo imparted the Italian heritage and culture to the youths while upholding the central tenet of Italian-American life: the primacy of family.[13] Although many young Americans of Italian origin focus little attention on the traditions of the past, it is not uncommon to find youths (like Maiolo's grandchildren) who embrace their ethnic heritage with great passion and enthusiasm.

Grant "Micheli" Scalise is a young American of Sicilian descent who seeks to preserve his ancestral and linguistic heritage. Scalise learned to speak fluent Sicilian as a teenager. A native of Brush, Colorado, Scalise knew only a few words of Sicilian when he was age fifteen in 2000. He spent his summers as a youth with his Sicilian-American grandparents, Martha and Carl Scalise, in Rockford, Illinois. During the summer of 2000, Scalise found an Italian textbook at their home, and it sparked his interest in learning Italian and Sicilian. Soon he taught himself rudimentary Italian and Sicilian from books. On a frequent basis, Grant Scalise peruses Sicilian dictionaries to refine and enhance his linguistic abilities. Moreover, he reads novels and watches Jay Leno and tries to translate the dialogue into Sicilian.[14]

Scalise is a creative proponent of Sicilian culture. He prefers to be called "Micheli," the Sicilian form of "Michele." In addition, the young linguist notes that his surname is spelled "Scalisi" in Sicily and "Scalise" in the United States. From 1900 to 2004, there were no interactions between the American Scalises and their Sicilian relatives. Then, in 2004, Grant Scalise contacted his relatives in Sambuca and went to Sicily for two months. The following year, a number of family members (his twin aunts, his grandparents, his father, and his stepmother) accompanied him to Sicily. The Sicilians find Scalise's unusual cultural odyssey to be quite interesting: His Sicilian media coverage includes newspaper articles and segments on a television program. Currently, he seeks to chronicle the regional variations in the Sicilian dialects and compile a Sicilian dictionary à la *Webster's Dictionary*.[15]

Throughout our country, Italian Americans have progressed to the point that relatively few people in the United States would criticize them for openly celebrating their culture and heritage. Up until the 1970s, though, such a focus on Old World traditions did not meet with approval from many Americans. Then, as now, Italian Americans focused largely on achieving success in the mainstream. They did so with wonderful results. Now that Italian Americans are a vital part of the American mainstream, Americans from other ethnic backgrounds usually enjoy, support, or at least tolerate expressions of Italian ethnicity in many realms of U.S. society. Currently, thousands of Italian-American youngsters study the Italian language in America's public and private schools; their parents and grandparents are often monolingual English speakers.

❧II. In 2006, an elderly man from the Mountain West asked me if I had ever been called a *wop*. My answer was negative, of course. The question took me by surprise: For someone in his thirties, the term has, thankfully, disappeared from contemporary American English. It is a historical curiosity. Indeed, this gentleman's question indicates how far the Italians of America have come during the years. Apart from some Mafia innuendoes and implications that Italian Americans are not especially "successful" as a group, Italian Americans encounter few overt instances of verbal bias anymore. But this particular individual had endured overt bias and prejudice as a young man. By recollecting his experiences, he reminded me of the progress that people of Italian origin have made in America.

Despite the tremendous economic success of Italian Americans, they still experience some disparities in certain sectors of American society. In 2005 the Order Sons of Italy in America published a study that documented how Italian Americans are underrepresented in the ranks of federal judges.[16] Thus far there has never been a U.S. president of Italian descent either. But such disparities are usually overshadowed by the remarkable progress of Italian Americans in so many societal institutions. Take the U.S. Supreme Court, for instance. "I never thought I would see the day when there were two Italians on the Supreme Court," remarks Judge Mario Rossetti.[17] The New York jurist remembers that he was delighted when Antonin Scalia joined the nation's highest court in 1986.[18]

Turning now to history, Italian-American icons, events, and figures continue to be part of our national story. Columbus may not be as popular as he once was, but there are other, emerging Italian-American icons and narratives. The composer/conductor Henry Mancini was recently honored on a U.S. postage stamp, as was the World War II hero John Basilone. Even so, there are still Italian-American contributions to U.S. history that remain obscure. As the book *Italians in America* points out, "Very few people know that scores of Italian-American women lost their lives in the Triangle Shirtwaist Company fire of 1911 or that the inspiring World War II image of Rosie the Riveter was based on factory worker Rosie Bonavita."[19] Most recently, the topic of Italian-American internees during World War II has received increasing amounts of attention. Older Italian Americans often note that Italian Americans were a vital part of the Greatest Generation during World War II.

In the first decade of the twenty-first century, one finds Italian-American heroes receiving more recognition than ever before. Sergeant John Basilone is one of the Italian community's best-known icons. His name graces landmarks and Sons of Italy lodges in different parts of America, among other forms of recognition and veneration. At the same time, there is a growing movement within Italian America to honor the contributions of the nineteenth-century American artist Constantino Brumidi. Washington, D.C., civic activist Joseph N. Grano is Chair of the Constantino Brumidi Society; he plans, organizes, and advocates on behalf of efforts to recognize Brumidi's accomplishments and commemorate his role in American culture.[20] (In 2008 President George W. Bush signed the Constantino Brumidi Congressional Gold Medal Act.) As time goes by, scholars, community activists, and ethnic advocates continue to uncover new Italian-American icons and stories to honor, recognize, and celebrate. Today people of Italian origin regularly note Italian-American firsts, pioneers, trailblazers, and role models.

For a time in late 2005 and early 2006 Italian Americans held the three highest positions in the U.S. military. In 2004 Lieutenant General Raymond Odierno began serving as Assistant to the Joint Chiefs of Staff. (His tenure in this position ended in 2006.) Then, in 2005, General Peter Pace and Admiral Edmund P. Giambastiani Jr. became the chairman and vice chairman of the Joint Chiefs of Staff, respectively. It was symbolically fitting that this significant milestone for Italian Americans merited little attention (in an ethnic sense) in the mainstream media. The Italian-American press, of course, devoted coverage to it. But the ethnic nature of these appointments simply was not newsworthy outside of the Italian community.

By 2005, Italian Americans had reached a point where their ascension to the highest levels of one of America's preeminent institutions did not elicit surprise from anyone. In fact, many Americans would see Pace's name (which means "peace" in Italian) as a monosyllabic Anglo-Saxon word—they would not pronounce it in the Italian fashion (PAH-chay). Pace's official biography notes that he was the first Marine named chairman or vice chairman of the Joint Chiefs. But his biography does not mention his ethnicity.[21] Similarly, *Newsweek* pictured Lieutenant General Raymond Odierno and his son, Captain Anthony Odierno, on the cover of the magazine's June 20, 2005, issue and featured them in the issue's lead story about fathers and sons who serve in the military. The *Newsweek* cover piece on Lieutenant General Odierno, whose troops were responsible for the capture of Saddam Hussein, and Captain Odierno, who lost an arm in Iraq, nicely described the family's commitment to the military, but the article never discusses the Odiernos' Italian family background.[22] In the eyes of the journalists, they were simply Americans.

The tendency to "mainstream" Italian Americans dates back more than two decades. Numerous analysts comment on how the Italian-American prominence in sports, business, and other realms is simply unnoteworthy anymore. "By the 1980s, assimilation of Italian Americans into American life was so complete that little attention was paid to ethnic origin," noted Jerre Mangione and Ben Morreale in 1992, as they discussed Italian-American sports figures.[23] Similarly, few people outside the Italian-American community ever take note of a new Italian-American CEO. "But there were dozens of other CEOs of Italian ancestry in the 1980s and 1990s, so many that no one bothered to count," observed Michael Barone in 2001.[24] With few exceptions, Italian-American figures receive accolades and acceptance from the general population; their Italian background is incidental in the eyes of the American public. Italian Americans may take note of an ethnic icon, but the individual is not necessarily viewed as "ethnic" by the rest of the population.

The nomination of Judge Samuel Alito to the Supreme Court in 2005 brought such issues into play again. Some observers challenged the Alito nomination on the grounds that the Court lacked sufficient racial and gender diversity. During the confirmation process in late 2005 and early 2006, Alito's Italian ancestry was front and center, but it was not a defining issue or characteristic by any means. Newspaper articles regularly mentioned the fact that Judge Alito's father immigrated to the United States from Italy.[25] And there were Web sites, public events, organizations, newspaper advertisements, and other activities devoted to mobilizing Italian Americans for Judge Alito.[26] Nonetheless, senators in several heavily Italian states (e.g., New York, New Jersey, Rhode Island) opposed the Alito nomination when it came to a vote in January 2006. Apparently, they were not concerned that Italian-American voters might hold such a vote against them. When Alito took his seat on the Court in early 2006, the Italian-American press published celebratory articles and commentaries about his ascension to this prestigious position.

Yet Italian Americans are now so much part of the mainstream that some members of the community question whether there is even a need to emphasize identifiable role models. Such individuals are particularly important, goes this line of reasoning, when a group is emerging on the American scene and needs to be taken seriously. After decades of advances, however, Italian Americans do not always focus on each milestone that involves an individual of Italian descent. The historian Gloria Ricci Lothrop, for one, sees no need to count regularly the number of Italian Americans in particular leadership positions. Lothrop takes great pride in her Italian heritage, but she does not focus on measuring progress for people of Italian origin by citing prominent figures or tallying the Italian surnames in a given context.[27] This distinguished scholar's viewpoint indicates that role models and explicit recognition on an ethnic basis are not matters of paramount importance to all Italian Americans.

茶 茶 茶

In the coming years, the Italian-American influence will touch the lives of more Americans than ever before, even as that influence becomes increasingly American and less Italian in many respects. Through intermarriage, the diffusion of Italian Americans throughout our country, and the general dissemination of Italian-American culture in the media, a growing number of Americans will have some sort of familiarity with Italian Americans and Italian Americana. Every year, for instance, the number of Americans with Italian blood almost certainly grows larger. Fully Italian individuals, meanwhile, account for a smaller and smaller percentage of the Italian-American community. And people of Italian ancestry can be found in appreciable numbers in more towns, cities, places, and institutions than ever before.

As the years pass, the last Italian immigrants who came here during the period of mass immigration from 1890 to 1924 will no longer be with us. It is still possible to speak to some of these intrepid pioneers, and to hear the stories of Italy and their early years here in America that they share with others. Second-generation Italian Americans (those whose parents came here as immigrants during the 1890–1924 period) share equally engaging and poignant anecdotes and stories about the immigration and integration experiences. Those stories are often surprising for baby boomers and their descendants, who have grown up in an affluent society—one in which Italian Americans face virtually limitless opportunities. Such first-person narratives will only be available to us for a limited time.

Older Italian Americans sometimes cite a sound recording, "The Joy of Growing Up Italian," as an example of the days gone by and what they wish to remember and even recapture.[28] "The Joy of Growing Up Italian" is a reflective story told by an anonymous narrator, who is the grandson of an Italian immigrant. He describes the world of Italian Americans in transition, from the vantage point of a second-generation American who grew up in ethnic communities during the 1940s and 1950s and then went on to college and success in the professional world. The narrative serves as a simple but elegant paean to Italian food, family, and a way of life that no longer exists. It celebrates the richness of Italian-American culture and family life. Reading this narrative and listening to this sound recording can be an emotional experience for older Italian Americans, as they reflect on their childhood experiences and the interconnected families and neighborhoods of the past.

Throughout the United States, there are many activities and initiatives that seek to promote, preserve, and perpetuate the Italian-American heritage, culture, and traditions. Museums perform this role well. Similarly, scholars, archivists, community activists, and family members record and preserve oral histories. Tom Profenno of the Italian Heritage Center in Portland, Maine, frequently records the oral histories of elderly Italian Americans in the Pine Tree State.[29] Future generations of students, academics, genealogists, and others will benefit from such efforts to capture the priceless and poignant stories of Italian-American elders.

In an important essay, "Are Italian Americans Just White Folks?" Rudolph J. Vecoli reflects on the nature and meaning of Italian-American ethnicity.[30] Vecoli writes:

> Beyond the personal significance of the Italian American experience in which I am willy-nilly a participant, as a humanist I argue for the intrinsic significance of that experience. It is an epic story of a diaspora, the story of the tragedies and triumphs of millions, the story of generations struggling to reconcile the old and the new. It is neither grander nor meaner than the story of other migrant peoples, *but it is our story*. Knowledge of that story can enrich and inspire our lives; it can provide us with a center and a compass in these turbulent times.[31]

Already, the history of Italian Americans is being analyzed for insights into how contemporary immigrant groups will adjust to and integrate into American culture and society. Michael Barone, for example, draws comparisons between the Italian-immigrant experience and that of Latino immigrants today.[32] We can expect to see a greater number of such comparisons in the coming years. The Italian-American story, after all, is one with many positive, affirming, and heartwarming aspects. Indeed, Italian Americans contribute immeasurably to our society in virtually every institution at almost every level. At bottom, their story is a quintessentially American narrative of faith, family, and work.

It is a beautiful story.

It is an inspiring story.

It is an American story.

And fundamentally, it is a story that belongs to each and every one of us, regardless of our ethnic background.

Notes

Prologue: American and Italian

1. Gr. Uff. Frank D. Stella, interview by author, Detroit, Michigan, December 1, 2004.
2. "St. Ubaldo Day—La Festa dei Ceri: Jessup, PA." www.stubaldoday.com/history.html.
3. Stella, interview.
4. Ibid.
5. Ibid. Today this predominantly white community of 4,718 continues to be heavily Italian. The last census found that Jessup is 42.5 percent Italian, 20.2 percent Irish, and 18.5 percent Polish.
6. Stella, interview.
7. Ibid.
8. To learn more about The F. D. Stella Products Company, go to www.fdstella.com.
9. Stella, interview.
10. Robert Ankeny, "Stella: Detroit's main go-to guy; Entrepreneur wields huge influence," *Crain's Detroit Business*, November 1–7, 1999, 1, 56.
11. Stella, interview; "Ellis Island Medal of Honor: Frank D. Stella." www.neco.org/awards/recipients/frankstella.html.
12. Stella, interview; David Barkholz, "Pavarotti to the pope: Stella's connections strong in Italy," *Crain's Detroit Business*, November 1–7, 1999, 56.
13. Stella, interview.
14. Ibid.
15. For an excellent source of information about Italian America, see Salvatore J. LaGumina et al., eds., *The Italian American Experience: An Encyclopedia* (New York: Garland Publishing, 2000).
16. Cataldo Leone et al., *Italians in America: A Celebration* (Washington, D.C.: Mockingbird Press and Portfolio Press/National Italian American Foundation, 2001), 1–13; Jerre Mangione and Ben Morreale, *La Storia: Five Centuries of the Italian American Experience* (New York: HarperPerennial, 1993), 3–27; Phylis Cancilla Martinelli, "Population," in Salvatore J. LaGumina et al., eds., *The Italian American Experience: An Encyclopedia* (New York: Garland Publishing, 2000), 497–498.
17. Michael Barone, *The New Americans: How the Melting Pot Can Work Again* (Washington, D.C.: Regnery Publishing, 2001), 126.
18. Ibid., 144; George Pozzetta, "Italian Americans," in Judy Galens, Anna Sheets, and Robyn V. Young, eds., *Gale Encyclopedia of Multicultural America*, vol. 2 (New York: Gale Research, 1995), 770; Salvatore J. LaGumina, *The Humble and the Heroic: Wartime Italian Americans* (Youngstown, N.Y.: Cambria Press, 2006), 192–203.
19. Barone, *The New Americans*, 148.

20. Pozzetta, "Italian Americans," 771.

21. Richard D. Alba, "Identity and Ethnicity among Italians and Other Americans of European Ancestry," in Lydio F. Tomasi, Piero Gastaldo, and Thomas Row, eds., *The Columbus People: Perspectives in Italian Immigration to the Americas and Australia* (Staten Island, N.Y.: Center for Migration Studies and Fondazione Giovanni Agnelli, 1994), 28.

22. Ibid; The Order Sons of Italy in America, *A Profile of Today's Italian Americans: A Report Based on the Year 2000 Census Compiled by The Sons of Italy* (Washington, D.C.: Order Sons of Italy in America, Fall 2003), 4.

23. Zoë Kashner, ed., *The World Almanac and Book of Facts 2007* (New York: World Almanac Books, 2006), 600.

24. When it comes to the topic of assimilation, the issue of generations arises for Italian Americans. As Richard D. Alba writes: "*Generation*, of course, refers to distance in descent from the point of immigration into the United States. (By convention, generations are numbered starting with the immigrants as the 'first,' so that their children are the 'second,' their grandchildren are the 'third,' etc.)." Richard D. Alba, *Ethnic Identity: The Transformation of White America* (New Haven, Conn.: Yale University Press, 1990), 5.

    It is common for Americans of Italian origin, at least in the vernacular, to consider the children born in the United States of immigrant parents as first-generation, not second-generation, Americans. In this book, I follow the generational schema offered by Alba. At the same time, I respect the descriptive practices of those who see the American-born generation as starting the generational cycle here, e.g., the son of an Italian immigrant who characterizes himself as a first-generation American. Such references continue to be prevalent among Italian Americans, particularly with the individuals who want to emphasize their immigrant heritage.

25. Rudolph J. Vecoli, "Are Italian Americans Just White Folks?" in A. Kenneth Ciongoli and Jay Parini, eds., *Beyond* The Godfather: *Italian American Writers on the Real Italian American Experience* (Hanover, N.H.: University Press of New England, 1997), 312.

26. Paul Andriulli, interview by author, Portland, Maine, October 15, 2006.

27. Vecoli, "Are Italian Americans Just White Folks?" 317, 320.

28. Peter Balistreri, interview by author, Milwaukee, Wisconsin, March 7, 2006.

29. Father John J. Richetta, interview by author, Kenosha, Wisconsin, October 20, 2004.

30. Ibid.

31. To learn more about Kenosha, see "Kenosha, Wisconsin." *Wikipedia, the free encyclopedia.* http://en.wikipedia.org/wiki/Kenosha,_Wisconsin.

32. Kenosha's St. Joseph High School now offers Italian-language courses, too.

33. Lisa Guido, interview by author, Kenosha, Wisconsin, September 22, 2004.

34. Professor Carmel Ruffolo, interview by author, Kenosha, Wisconsin, May 22, 2006; "UW–Parkside signs exchange agreement with Italian university," *UW–Parkside Communique*: June 30, 2004; Carmel Ruffolo, "Celebrating our Italian heritage, Part 1," *UW–Parkside Communique*: November 1, 2005.

35. During my speaking tour on Italian-American progress, I engaged in dialogue with people in different parts of America and elsewhere in the world. I addressed audiences in the following states: Alabama, Arizona, Arkansas, California, Colorado, Connecticut, Delaware, Florida, Georgia, Illinois, Indiana, Iowa, Kansas, Kentucky, Louisiana, Maine, Maryland, Massachusetts, Michigan, Minnesota, Mississippi, Missouri, Montana, Nebraska, Nevada, New Hampshire, New Jersey, New Mexico, New York, North Carolina, North Dakota, Ohio, Oklahoma, Pennsylvania, Rhode Island, South Carolina, South Dakota, Tennessee, Texas, Utah, Vermont, Virginia, West Virginia, Wisconsin, and Wyoming. In addition, I spoke about the Italian-American story in Australia, Canada, Ireland, Lebanon, the United Arab Emirates, and the United Kingdom.

    This Italian-American speaking tour was self-funded. I always traveled to the venues at my own expense. Moreover, I never accepted any honoraria for these talks.

36. Susan Rienzi Paolercio, telephone interview by author, August 4, 2006.

CHAPTER 1: COMING TO AMERICA

1. Ron Kantowski writes: "Andretti is a bon vivant who transcends his sport to the degree that he has become part of pop culture." Ron Kantowski, "Even at 64, Andretti doesn't idle," *Las Vegas (Nev.) Sun*, April 15, 2004.
2. According to *Wikipedia*, "The name *Mario Andretti* has become synonymous with speed in the United States, similar to Barney Oldfield in the early twentieth century and Stirling Moss in the United Kingdom." "Mario Andretti," *Wikipedia*. http://en.wikipedia.org/wiki/Mario_Andretti.
3. For background on Mario Andretti and his family, go to www.andretti.com and www.marioandretti.com. See, too, Mario Andretti, *Andretti* (San Francisco: Collins Publishers San Francisco, 1994); Gordon Kirby, *Mario Andretti: A Driving Passion* (Phoenix: David Bull Publishing, 2001).
4. Comm. Mario Andretti, telephone interview by author, October 4, 2005.
5. Ibid.; "Mario Andretti," *Wikipedia*.
6. Andretti, telephone interview.
7. Ibid.
8. "Mario Andretti," *Wikipedia*.
9. Andretti, telephone interview.
10. Kirby, *Mario Andretti*, 247.
11. Ibid.
12. Andretti, telephone interview.
13. Kirby, *Mario Andretti*, 247.
14. Andretti, telephone interview.
15. "Mario Andretti—The Family Business." http://sports.jrank.org/pages/149/Andretti-Mario-Family-Business.html.
16. Kantowski, "Even at 64, Andretti doesn't idle."
17. "Mario Andretti—The Family Business"; "Marco Andretti," *Wikipedia, the free encyclopedia*. http://en.wikipedia.org/wiki/Marco_Andretti.
18. Mario Andretti, telephone interview.
19. Josephine Bardelli, interview by author, Rockford, Illinois, June 5, 2006; Abbie Reese, "A lifetime in Rockford of family, fond memories," *Rockford (Ill.) Register Star*, April 7, 2005.
20. Bardelli, interview.
21. Ibid.; Reese, "A lifetime in Rockford of family, fond memories."
22. Bardelli, interview.
23. Ibid.; Reese, "A lifetime in Rockford of family, fond memories."
24. Donna R. Gabaccia, *Italy's Many Diasporas* (Seattle: University of Washington Press, 2000). See, too, Lydio F. Tomasi, Piero Gastaldo, and Thomas Row, eds., *The Columbus People: Perspectives in Italian Immigration to the Americas and Australia* (Staten Island, N.Y.: Center for Migration Studies and Fondazione Giovanni Agnelli, 1994); Thomas Sowell, *Migrations and Cultures: A World View* (New York: Basic Books, 1996), 140–174.
25. Donna R. Gabaccia, "Race, Nation, Hyphen: Italian-Americans and American Multiculturalism in Comparative Perspective," in Jennifer Guglielmo and Salvatore Salerno, eds., *Are Italians White? How Race Is Made in America* (New York: Routledge, 2003), 45.
26. Joseph Lopreato, *Italian Americans* (New York: Random House, 1970), 33–35.
27. Ibid., 35.
28. Ibid.
29. Maldwyn Allen Jones, *American Immigration*, 2d ed. (New York: University of Chicago Press, 1992), 212–269.
30. Jones, *American Immigration*, 152–211; Jerre Mangione and Ben Morreale, *La Storia: Five Centuries of the Italian American Experience* (New York: HarperPerennial, 1993), 31–85.
31. Jones, *American Immigration*, 171.
32. Mangione and Morreale, *La Storia*, 86–164; Betty Boyd Caroli, "Return Migration," in Salvatore

J. LaGumina et al., eds., *The Italian American Experience: An Encyclopedia* (New York: Garland Publishing, 2000), 548–550.

33. Michael Petta, interview by author, Middleton, Wisconsin, April 25, 2007.

34. George Silvestri Jr., interview by author, Novato, California, August 26, 2005.

35. Ibid.

36. Jerre Mangione, *Mount Allegro: A Memoir of Italian American Life* (1942, reprint, New York: Perennial Library/Harper and Row, 1989), 50.

37. In Multicultural America, some Italian Americans describe whites with no discernible ethnic identity as "Anglos," a word that is more typically used in situations involving Latinos/Hispanics and non-Latino/Hispanic whites.

38. Matthew Frye Jacobson, *Whiteness of a Different Color: European Immigrants and the Alchemy of Race* (Cambridge, Mass.: Harvard University Press, 1998), 9.

39. See, e.g., Jacobson, *Whiteness of a Different Color*, passim; Rudolph J. Vecoli, "Are Italian Americans Just White Folks?" in A. Kenneth Ciongoli and Jay Parini, eds., *Beyond the Godfather: Italian American Writers on the Real Italian American Experience* (Hanover, N.H.: University Press of New England, 1997), 311–322; Jennifer Guglielmo and Salvatore Salerno, eds., *Are Italians White? How Race Is Made in America* (New York: Routledge, 2003); Thomas A. Guglielmo, *White on Arrival: Italians, Race, Color, and Power in Chicago, 1890–1945* (New York: Oxford University Press, 2004).

40. Jacobson, *Whiteness of a Different Color*, 57.

41. Ibid.

42. Ibid.

43. David Maraniss, *When Pride Still Mattered: A Life of Vince Lombardi* (New York: Simon and Schuster, 1999), 241–242.

44. One elderly Italian American, who looks as if she is of Northern European descent, reported to me that she has never experienced ethnic discrimination because she does not appear to be visibly "Italian."

45. John DeMary, interview by author, Rivesville, West Virginia, October 28, 2005.

46. Alfred Bossi, e-mail to author, May 25, 2007.

47. DeMary, interview.

48. Minnie Rote, interview by author, Rivesville, West Virginia, October 28, 2005.

49. Ibid.; DeMary, interview; Alfred Bossi, interview by author, Las Vegas, Nevada, June 14, 2005.

50. Bossi, interview; Bossi, e-mail.

51. DeMary, interview.

52. For some background on this topic, see William S. Egelman, "Education: Sociohistorical Background," in Salvatore J. LaGumina et al., eds., *The Italian American Experience: An Encyclopedia* (New York: Garland Publishing, 2000), 194–195.

53. Michael Barone, *The New Americans: How the Melting Pot Can Work Again* (Washington, D.C.: Regnery Publishing, 2001), 145; Salvatore J. LaGumina, "Politics," in Salvatore J. LaGumina et al., ed., *The Italian American Experience: An Encyclopedia* (New York: Garland Publishing, 2000), 483–484; Valentine Belfiglio and Salvatore J. LaGumina, "Wartime Military and Home Front Activities," in Salvatore J. LaGumina et al., ed., *The Italian American Experience: An Encyclopedia* (New York: Garland Publishing, 2000), 669–674; Janet E. Worrall and Rose D. Scherini, "World War II, Internment, and Prisoners of War," in Salvatore J. LaGumina et al., ed., *The Italian American Experience: An Encyclopedia* (New York: Garland Publishing, 2000), 702–705.

54. Cataldo Leone et al., *Italians in America: A Celebration* (Washington, D.C.: Mockingbird Press and Portfolio Press/National Italian American Foundation, 2001), 188.

55. Michele Tuberosa Misci, telephone interview by author, April 27, 2007; Michele Tuberosa Misci, e-mail to author, May 12, 2007.

56. Jerre Mangione and Ben Morreale, *La Storia: Five Centuries of the Italian American Experience* (New York: HarperPerennial, 1993), 373–394, 410–421; Richard Renoff, "Sports," in Salvatore J.

LaGumina et al., eds., *The Italian American Experience: An Encyclopedia* (New York: Garland Publishing, 2000), 608–615; Cataldo Leone et al., *Italians in America: A Celebration* (Washington, D.C.: Mockingbird Press and Portfolio Press/National Italian American Foundation, 2001), 99–163; Salvatore J. LaGumina, *The Humble and the Heroic: Wartime Italian Americans* (Youngstown, N.Y.: Cambria Press, 2006), 192–203.

57. Thomas J. Ferraro, *Feeling Italian: The Art of Ethnicity in America* (New York: New York University Press, 2005), 91.

58. See, e.g., Salvatore Primeggia, "Comedy," in Salvatore J. LaGumina et al., eds., *The Italian American Experience: An Encyclopedia* (New York: Garland Publishing, 2000), 130–137.

59. "Everybody Loves Raymond," *Wikipedia, the free encyclopedia.* http://en.wikipedia.org/wiki/Everybody_Loves_Raymond.

60. "Rocky," *Wikipedia, the free encyclopedia.* http://en.wikipedia.org/wiki/Rocky; "Sylvester Stallone," *Wikipedia, the free encyclopedia.* http://en.wikipedia.org/wiki/Sylvester_Stallone.

61. Sean Gregory, "Slam, Glam, Serena," *Time* 169 (May 28, 2007): 52; Beth Fouhy, "Clinton Likens Herself to 'Rocky,'" *Associated Press*, April 1, 2008.

62. This vignette draws upon the public record and my interviews with Mr. Pipitone: Gaspare Pipitone, interview by author, Queens, New York, December 9, 2004; Gaspare Pipitone, interview by author, Franklin Square, New York, June 22, 2006.

63. For the quotation and information about EPASA USA, go to www.epasausa.com.

64. See www.comitesnyct.com.

65. Loretta Baldassar, *Visits Home: Migration experiences between Italy and Australia* (Carlton South, Australia: Melbourne University Press, 2001), 32.

66. Borgna Brunner, ed., TIME *Almanac 2007 with Information Please* (Boston: Information Please/Pearson Education, 2006), 365.

67. U.S. Census Bureau, *Statistical Abstract of the United States: 2006* (125th ed.) (Washington, D.C.: U.S. Government Printing Office, 2005), Table 8.

68. Donato Federico, interview by author, Cape Coral, Florida, November 14, 2005.

69. The three paragraphs about the Guarnieri family draw upon my multiple e-mail communications with Rose Guarnieri and the following sources: Domenick and Rose Guarnieri, interviews by author, Santa Ana, California, June 12, 2005; Domenick and Rose Guarnieri, interviews by author, Fountain Valley, California, July 1, 2005.

70. Anthony Polsinelli, interview by author, Wheeling, West Virginia, October 29, 2005.

71. The Hon. Renato Turano, interview by author, Berwyn, Illinois, March 11, 2005; Paul Basile, "The right stuff," *Fra Noi* 46 (May 2006): 55.

72. Turano, interview.

73. Ibid.; Basile, "The right stuff."

74. Basile, "The right stuff."

75. Ibid.

76. Ibid.; Turano, interview; "From Our Family to Yours," www.turanobaking.com/turanofam.php.

77. To learn more about the American Bakers Association, go to www.americanbakers.org.

78. Turano, interview; Basile, "The right stuff"; Katherine Boyle, "Bakery magnate: New Italian Senator," *Medill News Service*, April 13, 2006.

79. Paul Basile, "Next stop, Rome!" *Fra Noi* 46 (May 2006): 121.

80. Turano, interview.

81. Basile, "The right stuff."

82. Turano, interview.

83. Basile, "Next stop, Rome!" 51, 120–121.

84. Ibid., 51, 121; "Vision for the Future," *Fra Noi* 46 (May 2006): 55. For more information about Senator Turano, go to www.renatoturano.com.

85. Basile, "Next stop, Rome!" 51.

86. Ibid., 121.
87. Ibid.
88. Pasquale Pesce, interview by author, Santa Ana, California, June 12, 2005.
89. Ramin Setoodeh, "The Island of Dreams," *Newsweek* 149 (May 21, 2007): 22.
90. John Scara, interview by author, Atlantis, Florida, November 18, 2006.
91. Mr. Marinelli discussed these experiences in his remarks at the Tirolesi-Trentini Del Colorado meeting in Westminster, Colorado, on July 12, 2006.
92. Ernest Marinelli, "Journey in Time," undated letter to author.
93. Ibid.
94. Ibid.
95. Ibid.
96. Ibid.
97. Barbara Tenaglia Abela, interview by author, Dunedin, Florida, February 20, 2007; Barbara Tenaglia Abela, e-mail to author, May 7, 2007.
98. For more information about LIADO, go to www.liado.net. My coverage of the San Gennaro Festa draws upon my interview with Julie Calabrese in Pinellas County, Florida, on November 15, 2005, and my interviews with Barbara Tenaglia Abela, Rosemary Blumberg, Julie Calabrese, Carole Cosenza, and Ann Pici in Dunedin, Florida, on February 20, 2007.

CHAPTER 2: STEREOTYPING, DISCRIMINATION, AND ACCEPTANCE

1. "The Order Sons of Italy in America (OSIA) provided the program's producers with statistics, reports and concrete examples of how the US entertainment industry stereotypes Italian Americans." "ABC's *20/20* Focuses on Hollywood Stereotyping of Italian Americans," Press Release, September 7, 2006. www.osia.org/public/newsroom/pr09_07_06.asp.
2. "Hollywood Stereotypes," Transcript of *20/20* Segment—September 8, 2006. www.osia.org/public/newsroom/pr09_07_06_transcript.asp.
3. Ibid.
4. Ibid.
5. Ibid.
6. Dr. Dona De Sanctis, interview by author, Washington, D.C., February 10, 2005.
7. Ibid.
8. Ibid.
9. "Dona De Sanctis Steps Down as OSIA Deputy Executive Director," *Italian America* 12 (Fall 2007): 27.
10. De Sanctis, interview.
11. Order Sons of Italy in America, *Italian American Crime Fighters: A Brief Survey* (Washington, D.C.: Order Sons of Italy in America, 2005).
12. Ibid., 4.
13. Ibid., passim.
14. De Sanctis, interview.
15. "Dona De Sanctis Steps Down as OSIA Deputy Executive Director."
16. Dona De Sanctis, "Time to Say 'Good Bye,'" *Sempre Avanti*, October 2007. This article was reprinted in *The Alfano Digest*, June 29, 2008.
17. Ibid.
18. Ibid.
19. David Maraniss, *When Pride Still Mattered: A Life of Vince Lombardi* (New York: Simon and Schuster, 1999), 242.
20. Ibid., passim.
21. Salvatore J. LaGumina, *Wop!: A Documentary History of Anti-Italian Discrimination in the United*

States (Toronto: Guernica, 1999); Salvatore J. LaGumina, "Anti-Italian Discrimination," in Salvatore J. LaGumina et al., eds., *The Italian American Experience: An Encyclopedia* (New York: Garland Publishing, 2000), 16–17; Paul Budline, dir., *Anti-Italianism: Discrimination and Defamation in the History of Italian Americans* (South Orange, N.J.: Alberto Italian Studies Institute, Seton Hall University, 2005).

22. LaGumina, "Anti-Italian Discrimination," 16.

23. Ibid., 17.

24. Ibid., 16–17.

25. Luciano J. Iorizzo and Salvatore Mondello, *The Italian Americans*, rev. ed. (Boston: Twayne Publishers, 1980), 290; Richard Gambino, *Vendetta: The True Story of the Largest Lynching in U.S. History* (Toronto: Guernica, 2000); Dominic J. Pulera, *Sharing the Dream: White Males in Multicultural America* (New York: Continuum, 2004), 21–23.

26. LaGumina, "Anti-Italian Discrimination," 19. George De Stefano discusses the stereotypes of Italian Americans in contemporary popular culture. In his 2006 book, *An Offer We Can't Refuse*, he writes: "Members of this large, apparently growing, and highly visible ethnic group have distinguished themselves in business, politics, medicine, sports, entertainment, and the arts. But in popular culture Italian Americans are depicted mainly via several related stereotypes: as vicious criminals (any mafia movie or TV show), boorish and bigoted lowlifes (see the films of Spike Lee), or lovable buffoons (studly and stupid Joey Tribianni on TV's *Friends* and its spin-off, *Joey*. These types are by no means mutually exclusive; Tony Soprano's character incorporates all three." For this quotation, see George De Stefano, *An Offer We Can't Refuse: The Mafia in the Mind of America* (New York: Faber and Faber, 2006), 12.

27. William B. Helmreich, *The things they say behind your back* (1982; reprint, New Brunswick, N.J.: Transaction Publishers, 1989), 38–58.

28. Donald Tricarico, "Labels and Stereotypes," in Salvatore J. LaGumina et al., eds., *The Italian American Experience: An Encyclopedia* (New York: Garland Publishing, 2000), 320.

29. Ibid., 319–321; LaGumina, "Anti-Italian Discrimination," 18–19.

30. De Stefano, *An Offer We Can't Refuse*; Peter Bondanella, *Hollywood Italians: Dagos, Palookas, Romeos, Wise Guys, and Sopranos* (New York: Continuum, 2004); Thomas J. Ferraro, *Feeling Italian: The Art of Ethnicity in America* (New York: New York University Press, 2005), 107–127; Fred Gardaphé, *From Wiseguys to Wise Men: The Gangster and Italian American Masculinities* (New York: Routledge, 2006).

31. Donald Tricarico, "Labels and Stereotypes," 320.

32. Thomas Reppetto, *American Mafia: A History of Its Rise to Power* (New York: John McCrae/Henry Holt and Company, 2004); Thomas Reppetto, *Bringing Down the Mob: The War Against the American Mafia* (New York: John McCrae/Henry Holt and Company, 2006).

33. Reppetto, *Bringing Down the Mob*, 3.

34. Ibid.

35. Reppetto, *American Mafia*; Reppetto, *Bringing Down the Mob*.

36. Reppetto, *Bringing Down the Mob*, 4.

37. For a comprehensive treatment of New York's Mafia families, see Selwyn Raab, *Five Families: The Rise, Decline, and Resurgence of America's Most Powerful Mafia Empires* (New York: Thomas Dunne Books/St. Martin's Press, 2005).

38. Tricarico, "Labels and Stereotypes," 319–321.

39. Ibid., 320.

40. Ibid., 320–321.

41. Emil Bagneschi, interview by author, San Mateo, California, August 26, 2005; Emil Bagneschi, e-mail to author, July 21, 2007.

42. Bagneschi, interview.

43. Jim Rahilly, interviews by author, Sun Lakes, Arizona, December 6, 2005 and December 5, 2006; Jim Rahilly, e-mail to author, July 20, 2007.

44. Jim Rahilly, e-mail to author, April 15, 2007.

45. Rahilly, e-mail, July 20, 2007.

46. Cristogianni Borsella, for one, cites current instances of anti-Italian prejudice in his recent book. See Cristogianni Borsella, *On Persecution, Identity, and Activism: Aspects of the Italian-American Experience from the Late 19th Century to Today* (Wellesley, Mass.: Dante University Press, 2005).

47. See, e.g., Zogby International, *Teen Survey: Testing the Influence of Media on Racial Stereotypes* (Utica, N.Y.: Zogby International for the National Italian American Foundation, 2000).

48. Rocco Caporale, "Social Class Characteristics," in Salvatore J. LaGumina et al., eds., *The Italian American Experience: An Encyclopedia* (New York: Garland Publishing, 2000), 600.

49. Maria Laurino, *Were You Always an Italian?: Ancestors and Other Icons of Italian America* (New York: W. W. Norton and Company, 2000), 42; Stefano Luconi, "Cuomo, Mario M. (b. 1932)," in Salvatore J. LaGumina et al., eds., *The Italian American Experience: An Encyclopedia* (New York: Garland Publishing, 2000), 161; Michael Barone, "Italian Americans and American Politics," in A. Kenneth Ciongoli and Jay Parini, eds., *Beyond* The Godfather: *Italian American Writers on the Real Italian American Experience* (Hanover, N.H.: University Press of New England, 1997), 248–249.

50. Stefano Luconi, "Giuliani, Rudolph W. (b. 1944)," in Salvatore J. LaGumina et al., eds., *The Italian American Experience: An Encyclopedia* (New York: Garland Publishing, 2000), 269.

51. Ibid.

52. See, e.g., Erica-Lynn Huberty, "What's in a Name: Confessions of a Mafia Princess," in Barbara A. Arrighi, ed., *Understanding Inequality: The Intersection of Race/Ethnicity, Class, and Gender* (Lanham, Md.: Rowman and Littlefield Publishers, 2001), 36–39.

53. George Silvestri Jr., interview by author, Novato, California, August 26, 2005; George Silvestri Jr., e-mail to author, July 23, 2007.

54. William Cerruti, interview by author, Sacramento, California, August 25, 2005.

55. Rudolph J. Vecoli, "Are Italian Americans Just White Folks?" in A. Kenneth Ciongoli and Jay Parini, eds., *Beyond* The Godfather: *Italian American Writers on the Real Italian American Experience* (Hanover, N.H.: University Press of New England, 1997), 320.

56. Matthew Frye Jacobson, *Roots Too: White Ethnic Revival in Post-Civil Rights America* (Cambridge, Mass.: Harvard University Press, 2006), 244–245.

57. "David Chase, Creator: The Sopranos," www.hbo.com/sopranos/cast/crew/david_chase.shtml; "David Chase," *Wikipedia, the free encyclopedia.* http://en.wikipedia.org/wiki/David_Chase. For general information about *The Sopranos,* go to www.hbo.com/sopranos/.

58. Alessandra Stanley, "One Last Family Gathering: You Eat, You Talk, It's Over," *New York Times,* June 11, 2007.

59. Ibid.

60. For a nuanced viewpoint on Chase and *The Sopranos,* see Gardaphé, *From Wiseguys to Wise Men,* 150–164.

61. Mark Di Ionno, "For some proud Italians, 'Sopranos' cuts to the core," (*Newark, N.J.*) *Star-Ledger,* March 27, 2007; David Porter, " 'Sopranos' Leaves Mark on New Jersey; Show Ends 8-Year Run Sunday," *Associated Press,* June 10, 2007.

62. Raab, *Five Families,* 689–708; Reppetto, *Bringing Down the Mob,* 281–303.

63. De Stefano, *An Offer We Can't Refuse,* 9.

64. Ibid., 291.

65. De Stefano, *An Offer We Can't Refuse.*

66. Ibid., 349–350; "Victoria Gotti," *Wikipedia, the free encyclopedia.* http://en.wikipedia.org/wiki/Victoria_Gotti.

67. See, for example, *Gang Land News* (www.ganglandnews.com) and *Rick Porrello's American Mafia.com* (www.americanmafia.com).

68. Frederick C. Mish, ed., *Merriam-Webster's Collegiate Dictionary,* 11th ed. (Springfield, Mass.: Merriam-Webster, 2003), 746.

69. "Now," writes George De Stefano, "other ethnic crime syndicates, whether Russian, South American, or Asian, are commonly referred to as mafias." De Stefano, *An Offer We Can't Refuse*, 9.

70. David Sterritt, "An offer Hollywood can't refuse," *Christian Science Monitor*, March 4, 2005, 11–12.

71. See, e.g., Christian K. Messenger, *The Godfather and American Culture: How the Corleones Became "Our Gang"* (Albany: State University of New York Press, 2002).

72. Federico and Stephen Moramarco cite "*The Godfather* Trilogy" as a reason for celebrating America's Italian heritage in their book, *Italian Pride*. Federico and Stephen Moramarco, *Italian Pride: 101 Reasons to Be Proud You're Italian* (New York: MJF Books, 2000), 18–20.

73. Helmreich, *The things they say behind your back*, 51–52.

74. James Tognoni, interview by author, Milwaukee, Wisconsin, October 17, 2005.

75. Dr. Emanuele Alfano, telephone interview by author, February 15, 2005.

76. The Italian-American One Voice Coalition regularly receives media coverage for its antidefamation activities.

77. Alfano, telephone interview.

78. This quotation comes from the Italian-American One Voice Coalition's Web site (www.iaonevoicecoalition.org).

79. www.iaonevoicecoalition.org.

80. Alfano, telephone interview.

81. See, e.g., Dr. Emanuele A. Alfano, "*The Sopranos* Is Not *Just* a Television Show," April 21, 2007. www.iaonevoicecoalition.org/notjust.html.

82. Alfano, telephone interview.

83. Ibid.

84. During the early 1970s, the Italian American Civil Rights League made headlines as an antidefamation organization, even though its effectiveness was compromised by the Mob ties of some of its leaders. See Raab, *Five Families*, 184–200; Reppetto, *Bringing Down the Mob*, 86–105; Perry L. Weed, *The White Ethnic Movement and Ethnic Politics* (New York: Praeger Publishers, 1973), 51–62; Frank A. Salamone, "Italian American Civil Rights League," in Salvatore J. LaGumina et al., eds., *The Italian American Experience: An Encyclopedia* (New York: Garland Publishing, 2000), 300–302.

85. To learn more about the Commission for Social Justice, go to www.osia.org/public/commission/commission.asp.

86. See "Stereotype This! Debunking Hollywood's Italian Stereotypes and Myths." www.stereotypethis.com.

87. David Howard and John Murray, "Old Country, New City," *Waterbury (Conn.) Observer*, May 22–June 4, 1997.

88. Comm. Paola Bagnatori, interview by author, San Francisco, California, August 24, 2005. For more information about the Museo ItaloAmericano, go to www.museoitaloamericano.org.

89. www.museoitaloamericano.org.

90. Order Sons of Italy in America, *Italian American Crime Fighters*.

91. Raab, *Five Families*, 160–161, 213, 232–233.

92. Rudolph W. Giuliani with Ken Kurson, *Leadership* (New York: Miramax Books/Hyperion, 2002), 122.

93. Ibid., 196–197.

94. Ibid.

95. Louis J. Freeh with Howard Means, *My FBI: Bringing Down the Mafia, Investigating Bill Clinton, and Fighting the War on Terror* (New York: St. Martin's Press, 2005), 63–83, 119–138.

96. Freeh with Means, *My FBI*, 168.

97. Ibid., passim.

98. Ibid., 138.

99. "Lawrence Auriana, President of Columbus Citizens Foundation, Assails Bias and Prejudice in Entertainment and Political Circles," *PRNewswire*, November 9, 2005.
100. Peter Balistreri, interview by author, Milwaukee, Wisconsin, March 7, 2006.
101. Ibid.
102. Ibid.
103. Ibid.

CHAPTER 3: SUCCEEDING IN AMERICA

1. General Anthony Zinni, interview by author, Arlington, Virginia, October 28, 2004.
2. Zinni, interview.
3. Ibid.
4. Ibid.
5. Ibid.; Tom Clancy with General Tony Zinni and Tony Koltz, *Battle Ready* (New York: G. P. Putnam's Sons, 2004), 417–419. In 2000 Conshohocken, Pennsylvania, was 30.4 percent Irish, 24.2 percent Italian, 15.8 percent Polish, and 15.5 percent German.
6. Clancy with Zinni and Koltz, *Battle Ready*, 418.
7. Zinni, interview.
8. Clancy with Zinni and Koltz, *Battle Ready*, passim; General Tony Zinni and Tony Koltz, *The Battle for Peace: A Frontline Vision of America's Power and Purpose* (New York: Palgrave Macmillan, 2006), passim.
9. Clancy with Zinni and Koltz, *Battle Ready*, 3–15, 303–353.
10. Ibid., 312.
11. For more information about General Zinni, go to his Web site (www.generalzinni.com).
12. Clancy with Zinni and Koltz, *Battle Ready*; Zinni and Koltz, *The Battle for Peace*.
13. Zinni, interview.
14. Ibid.
15. Unless otherwise noted, the material in this vignette about Arthur Castraberti and his family comes from the public record and the following sources: Cav. Arthur Castraberti, interview by author, Sarasota, Florida, November 16, 2005; Cav. Arthur Castraberti, telephone interviews by author, September 30, 2006 and December 8, 2006.
16. For more information about Prince Pizzeria & Bar, go to www.princerestaurant.com.
17. The quotation comes from the following article: Kathy McCabe, "Rescue boats take to streets of Saugus," *Boston Globe*, May 18, 2006.
18. Arthur Castraberti, e-mail to author, September 12, 2006; "Saugus Chamber of Commerce," *Wikipedia, the free Encyclopedia*. http://en.wikipedia.org/wiki/Saugus_Chamber_of_Commerce.
19. Steven Castraberti graduated from Williams College. Paul Castraberti, moreover, is an alumnus of Yale University. And Linda Castraberti earned her undergraduate degree from Boston College and a graduate degree from Babson College.
20. Rocco Caporale, "Social Class Characteristics," in Salvatore J. LaGumina et al., eds., *The Italian American Experience: An Encyclopedia* (New York: Garland Publishing, 2000), 598.
21. Ibid.
22. Ibid.
23. William S. Egelman, "Education: Sociohistorical Background," in Salvatore J. LaGumina et al., eds., *The Italian American Experience: An Encyclopedia* (New York: Garland Publishing, 2000), 193–194.
24. Ibid., 193, 194, 196, 197; Caporale, "Social Class Characteristics," 599.
25. The material in this chapter's coverage of the DiNovo family draws upon the following sources: Professor/Cavaliere Philip J. DiNovo, interviews by author, Albany, New York, June 23, 2006 and October 3, 2006; Professor/Cavaliere Philip J. DiNovo, telephone interview by author, October 5, 2006; Professor/Cavaliere Philip J. DiNovo, e-mail to author, November 4, 2006.

26. Michael Barone, *The New Americans: How the Melting Pot Can Work Again* (Washington, D.C.: Regnery Publishing, 2001), 146.

27. Ibid.

28. Barone, *The New Americans*, 146.

29. The Order Sons of Italy in America, *A Profile of Today's Italian Americans: A Report Based on the Year 2000 Census Compiled by The Sons of Italy* (Washington, D.C.: Order Sons of Italy in America, Fall 2003).

30. Caporale, "Social Class Characteristics," 596.

31. To be sure, the Italian immigrants and their descendants had opportunities that did not exist for people of color in the years preceding Multicultural America.

32. Mary Joe Kaumo, interview by author, Rock Springs, Wyoming, July 11, 2006; Flora Bertagnolli, interview by author, Rock Springs, Wyoming, July 11, 2006.

33. Kaumo, interview.

34. I addressed the Rotary Club of Rock Springs and the Tyrolean Trentini of Wyoming in Rock Springs, Wyoming, on July 11, 2006.

35. Mary Joe Kaumo, interview.

36. Shirley Albertini, interview by author, Rock Springs, Wyoming, July 11, 2006; Professor Diane Albertini, interview by author, Rock Springs, Wyoming, July 11, 2006; Professor Diane Albertini, e-mails to author, September 25, 2006 and December 29, 2006.

37. "Teno Roncalio." *Wikipedia, the free encyclopedia.* http://en.wikipedia.org/wiki/Teno_Roncalio.

38. Caporale, "Social Class Characteristics," 596, 597.

39. Ibid., 595–601.

40. Ibid., 597.

41. Father Vincent Bommarito, interview by author, Saint Louis, Missouri, January 14, 2006.

42. Ibid.

43. The three paragraphs about Mr. Schiro draw upon the public record, my telephone conversations with him, and the following source: Frank Joseph Schiro, interview by author, Milwaukee, Wisconsin, August 9, 2006.

44. Schiro's great uncle, the boxer Sammy Mandell, was Lightweight Champion of the World from 1926 to 1930. Frank Joseph Schiro, e-mail to author, June 5, 2007.

45. Patty Koch, interview by author, Jacksonville, Florida, November 18, 2005.

46. Mary McGarry, telephone interview by author, December 17, 2006; Mary McGarry, interview by author, Mentor, Ohio, September 11, 2007.

47. McGarry, telephone interview.

48. Ibid.; Lisa Dimberio Nelson, interview by author, Mentor, Ohio, October 19, 2006.

49. McGarry, telephone interview.

50. Nelson, interview.

51. Lisa Dimberio Nelson, e-mail to author, December 19, 2006.

52. On Italian Americans and the G.I. Bill of Rights, see Barone, *The New Americans*, 146.

53. The material in the paragraphs about Alessandra DiCicco Higgs draws upon my observations, telephone interviews with Ms. Higgs, and interviews with Ms. Higgs in Naples, Florida, on May 2, 2005, November 14, 2005, and February 19, 2007.

54. For more information about Valleluce, Italy, go to www.valleluce.com.

55. See "Alessandra Higgs: The Heart of Compassion," *Focus* 21 (2000): 25, 52.

56. Comm. Robert Barbera, interview by author, Los Angeles County, California, June 16, 2005. See, too, "Robert J. Barbera: Curriculum Vitae."

57. Robert Barbera, interview, June 16, 2005.

58. Ibid. To learn more about Barbera Properties, go to www.barberaproperties.com.

59. Robert Barbera, interview, June 16, 2005; Comm. Robert Barbera, interview by author, Monrovia, California, August 9, 2005.

60. Robert Barbera, interview, June 16, 2005.

61. Ibid.
62. Ibid.
63. Ibid.
64. Ibid.; "Robert J. Barbera: Curriculum Vitae." See, too, the Web site for the Americanism Educational League (www.americanism.org).
65. Robert Barbera, interview, June 16, 2005.
66. Ibid.
67. Ibid.
68. Robert Barbera, interview, June 16, 2005; Josephine Volpe Barbera, interview by author, Los Angeles County, California, June 16, 2005.
69. Josephine Barbera is a retired educator whose forebears come from Sicily and Apulia. Josephine Volpe Barbera, interview.
70. Josephine Volpe Barbera, interview; Robert Barbera, interview, June 16, 2005.
71. Robert Barbera, interviews; *Lingua Viva*, September–December 2005 (Los Angeles: Istituto Italiano di Cultura, 2005); Comm. Robert J. Barbera, telephone interview by author, November 21, 2005.
72. Anthony Noto, interview by author, Easton, Pennsylvania, June 20, 2006; Janet Noto, interview by author, Easton, Pennsylvania, June 20, 2006.
73. Ibid.
74. Anthony Noto, letter to author, December 6, 2006.
75. This material about the Mamana family draws upon my interviews with Julia Cericola Mamana and Dr. June Mamana in Easton, Pennsylvania, on June 20, 2006.
76. Dr. Julianne Mamana Boyd describes some of her father's professional honors: "During his thirty-nine years of service in the Easton schools, he was named the National Principal of the Year in 1961 and received the Educator's Medal of Honor from the Freedoms Foundation at Valley Forge in 1965." Dr. Julianne Mamana Boyd, e-mail to author, June 25, 2007.
77. Ibid.; Julia Cericola Mamana, interview; Dr. June Mamana, interview.
78. The Hon. Carole Heffley, interview by author, Easton, Pennsylvania, June 20, 2006; The Hon. Carole Heffley, letter to author, December 2006.
79. Pam and John Richetta, "Sette Luna Proves That the Moon's the Limit in the Small City," *Italian Tribune*, March 30, 2006, 4; "Richetta Elected President of Historic Pomfret Club," *Italian Tribune*, April 27, 2006, 4.
80. To learn more about "Tempo Italiano," go to www.tempoitaliano.net.
81. "The Tempo Italiano Story," www.tempoitaliano.net; John D. Richetta, telephone interview by author, October 14, 2004; John D. Richetta, interview by author, Easton, Pennsylvania, June 20, 2006; Pamela Richetta, interview by author, Easton, Pennsylvania, June 20, 2006.
82. "The Tempo Italiano Story."
83. Ibid.
84. John D. Richetta, interview; Pamela Richetta, interview.
85. Pam and John Richetta, "A Chapter Closes," *Italian Tribune*, June 28, 2007, 16.
86. Pamela and John Richetta, *Tempo Italiano Memories Cookbook* (Easton, Pa.: Richetta Promotions, 2005). See, too, Pam and John Richetta, "Recipes and Memories in Tempo Italiano Cookbook," *Italian Tribune*, July 21, 2005, 18.
87. Pam and John Richetta, "The Importance of Remembering Our Italian Roots," *Italian Tribune*, January 5, 2006, 4.

CHAPTER 4: THE ETHNICS

1. Gr. Uff. Joseph Maselli, interview by author, New Orleans, Louisiana, April 25, 2005.
2. Maselli, interview.

3. Ibid.; Evans J. Casso, *Staying in Step: A Continuing Italian Renaissance* (New Orleans: Quadriga Press, 1984), 84–85.

4. Maselli, interview.

5. Ibid.

6. Ibid.

7. Ibid.

8. Ibid. See, too, "Italian-American Digest." www.airf.org/pages/digest.html.

9. Maselli, interview. For more information about the American Italian Renaissance Foundation, go to www.airf.org.

10. Maselli, interview.

11. Joseph Maselli and Dominic Candeloro, *Images of America: Italians in New Orleans* (Charleston, S.C.: Arcadia, 2004).

12. Maselli, interview.

13. Casso, *Staying in Step*, 86.

14. Maselli, interview.

15. Ibid.

16. Ibid.

17. Ibid.

18. Ibid.

19. Ibid.

20. All the material in this vignette about Mr. Ragona comes from the following source: Thomas Ragona, interview by author, El Paso, Texas, January 10, 2005.

21. John D. Skrentny, *The Minority Rights Revolution* (Cambridge, Mass.: Belknap Press of Harvard University Press, 2002), 275.

22. Ibid., 275–314.

23. Ibid., 277.

24. To cast light on these issues, see, e.g., Jerre Mangione, *Mount Allegro: A Memoir of Italian American Life* (1942, reprint, New York: Perennial Library/Harper and Row, 1989); Maria Laurino, *Were You Always an Italian?: Ancestors and Other Icons of Italian America* (New York: W. W. Norton and Company, 2000); Gina Cascone, *Life al Dente: Laughter and Love in an Italian-American Family* (New York: Atria Books, 2003).

25. Richard D. Alba, *Ethnic Identity: The Transformation of White America* (New Haven, Conn.: Yale University Press, 1990), 1–30, 290–319; Mary C. Waters, *Ethnic Options: Choosing Identities in America* (Berkeley: University of California Press, 1990), 16–89.

26. Alba, *Ethnic Identity*, 306.

27. Waters, *Ethnic Options*, passim.

28. Richard D. Alba, "Identity and Ethnicity among Italians and Other Americans of European Ancestry," in Lydio F. Tomasi, Piero Gastaldo, and Thomas Row, eds., *The Columbus People: Perspectives in Italian Immigration to the Americas and Australia* (Staten Island, N.Y.: Center for Migration Studies and Fondazione Giovanni Agnelli, 1994), 21–44.

29. Remo Minato, telephone interview by author, July 27, 2005.

30. Jessica Lyons, "It's a Family Thing; A New Generation of Monterey Italians Is Keeping the Tradition Alive," *Monterey County Weekly* (November 21, 2002).

31. Ibid.

32. Ibid.

33. Ibid.

34. Their Italian regional origins continue to take precedence over the panethnic Italian/American identity for many older people in Portland, Maine. Tom Profenno, interview by author, Portland, Maine, September 16, 2005.

35. See, e.g., "Polentone," *Wikipedia, l'enciclopedia libera*. http://it.wikipedia.org/wiki/Polentone; "Terrone," *Wikipedia, l'enciclopedia libera*. http://it.wikipedia.org/wiki/Terrone.

36. The Hon. Frank Guarini Jr., interview by author, Jersey City, New Jersey, October 5, 2004.

37. Ibid.; The Hon. Frank Guarini Jr., e-mail to author, July 8, 2008.

38. Guarini, interview; The Hon. Frank Guarini Jr., telephone interview by author, February 13, 2007.

39. Guarini, interview.

40. Ibid.; "Guarini, Frank Joseph, Jr., (1924–)," *Biographical Directory of the United States Congress, 1774–Present*. http://bioguide.congress.gov/scripts/biodisplay.pl?index=G000511; Michael Barone and Grant Ujifusa, *The Almanac of American Politics 1992* (Washington, D.C.: National Journal, 1991), 805–807; Phil Duncan, ed., *Congressional Quarterly's Politics in America 1992, The 102nd Congress* (Washington, D.C.: CQ Press, 1991), 963–965.

41. Guarini, interview.

42. Ibid.

43. Guarini is presently "one of the principals" in the ongoing efforts that focus on "the reconstruction and redevelopment of the Jersey City waterfront." Furthermore, he notes: "I stayed in my hometown to help bring a renaissance to Jersey City, which had seen hard times." Guarini, telephone interview.

44. The Hon. Marge Roukema, interview by author, Bergen County, New Jersey, June 23, 2005.

45. Ibid.

46. Ibid.

47. Ibid. For Dr. Roukema's perspective, see Richard Roukema, *Spouse of the House* (Ridgewood, N.J.: BooksByBookends, 2000).

48. Ibid.; Michael Barone and Richard E. Cohen with Charles E. Cook Jr., *The Almanac of American Politics 2002* (Washington, D.C.: National Journal, 2001), 991–993; Brian Nutting and H. Amy Stern, eds., *CQ's Politics in America 2002: The 107th Congress* (Washington, D.C.: CQ Press, 2001), 637–638.

49. Roukema, interview; Barone and Cohen, *The Almanac of American Politics 2002*, 991; Nutting and Stern, eds., *CQ's Politics in America 2002: The 107th Congress*, 637.

    Congresswoman Roukema also sponsored the Child Support Act, a pro-family initiative that "required divorced spouses (usually fathers) to financially support their children, even when they move to another state." The Hon. Marge Roukema, telephone interview by author, November 28, 2005.

50. Roukema, interview.

51. See the "Roukema Center for International Education" Web site at www.ramapo.edu/international.

52. Unless otherwise noted, all the information in this vignette about the TanCreti family comes from the following source: Dave TanCreti, interview by author, Des Moines, Iowa, February 20, 2005.

53. In the 2000 census, Rock Valley, Iowa, had 13 Italian-American residents, who constituted 0.5 percent of the 2,686 residents of this predominantly Dutch town.

54. Professor Alan Balboni, interview by author, Las Vegas, Nevada, June 14, 2005.

55. Joseph Ordornez, interview by author, Pinellas County, Florida, November 17, 2005.

56. Al Noto, interview by author, Tampa, Florida, November 19, 2005; Josie Noto, interview by author, Tampa, Florida, November 19, 2005; Pete Noto, interview by author, Tampa, Florida, November 19, 2005.

57. Nicholas P. Ciotola, *Images of America: Italians in Albuquerque* (Chicago: Arcadia Publishing, 2002), 8.

58. Ibid., 45, 66.

59. For more information about the Isleños, go to the Los Isleños Heritage and Cultural Society's Web site (www.losislenos.org).

60. W. Phil Hewitt, *The Italian Texans* (1973; reprint, San Antonio: University of Texas Institute of Texan Cultures at San Antonio, 1980), 5–6.

61. For background on Lama, see "A true American success story." www.tonylama.com/craftsman ship/history.asp.

62. Richard Apodaca, telephone interview by author, November 13, 2004.

63. Sister M. Lilliana Owens, *Reverend Carlos M. Pinto, S. J., Apostle of El Paso, 1892–1919* (El Paso, Texas: Revista Catolica Press, 1951), 35–58.

64. Enrique Medrano, interview by author, El Paso, Texas, January 8, 2005. For a biography of Father Pinto, see Owens, *Reverend Carlos M. Pinto.*

65. Medrano, interview.

66. Enrique N. Medrano, "Some of Father Carlos M. Pinto's Noteworthy Accomplishments," Unpublished paper, May 22, 2002, 5–7.

67. Father Rafael Garcia, telephone interview by author, January 31, 2005.

68. See, e.g., Federico and Stephen Moramarco, *Italian Pride: 101 Reasons to Be Proud You're Italian* (New York: MJF Books, 2000); Peter D'Epiro and Mary Desmond Pinkowish, *Sprezzatura: 50 Ways Italian Genius Shaped the World* (New York: Anchor/Rand, 2001).

69. Toni Andriulli, interview by author, Portland, Maine, September 16, 2005.

70. Some people also ascribe the phenomenon of "wannabes" to the gangster image on television and do not necessarily view it as a positive development.

71. Frank Ferraro, interview by author, Raleigh, North Carolina, January 18, 2006.

72. Lorraine Ali, "Laughter's New Profile," *Newsweek* 139 (April 22, 2002): 61.

73. Wayne Parry, "Some Arabs to change names," *Baltimore Sun,* March 24, 2002.

74. Daniel Cotroneo, interview by author, Saint Paul, Minnesota, August 8, 2006.

CHAPTER 5: MARRIAGE AND FAMILY LIFE

1. The seven paragraphs about the DeRenzo family and the Noll family draw upon my communications with Mrs. Terry Noll: Terry Noll, interview by author, Easton, Pennsylvania, June 20, 2006; Terry Noll, telephone interview by author, August 3, 2006; Terry Noll, e-mails to author, December 16, 2006, January 10, 2007, and February 5, 2007.

2. In 2000 Italian Americans accounted for 11.3 percent of Birdsboro, Pennsylvania's population of 5,064 residents.

3. Marlene Noll married a man, Rolando "Ron" DelVillano, from Sterling Heights, Michigan. DelVillano traces his ancestry to the same part of Italy as his wife's maternal grandparents. They met each other through her Uncle Tony, who also lives in Sterling Heights. Today Marlene and Ron DelVillano have three children: Vincenzo, Lucia, and Marco. They reside in the Detroit metropolitan area.

4. The Hon. Rosaria Salerno, interview by author, Boston, Massachusetts, April 5, 2005. In addition, I learned much about the Salerno family from my interview with JoAnn Serpico in Berwyn, Illinois, on March 11, 2005.

5. Brenda Warner Rotzoll, "Frank J. Salerno, co-owned funeral homes," *Chicago Sun-Times,* August 11, 2000.

6. Ibid.

7. The Hon. Rosaria Salerno, e-mail to author, June 19, 2007.

8. Salerno, interview.

9. Richard N. Juliani, "Family Life," in Salvatore J. LaGumina et al., eds., *The Italian American Experience: An Encyclopedia* (New York: Garland Publishing, 2000), 209–210.

10. Elizabeth G. Messina, "Women in Transition," in Salvatore J. LaGumina et al., eds., *The Italian American Experience: An Encyclopedia* (New York: Garland Publishing, 2000), 688.

11. Juliani, "Family Life," 209–211.

12. Rosalie Galasso Caputo, telephone interview by author, May 2, 2006.

13. Carlo Giraulo, interview by author, Portland, Maine, September 16, 2005; Carlo Giraulo, e-mails to author, April 2, 2007 and April 12, 2007.

14. Shirley Sinclaire, interview by author, Saint Paul, Minnesota, August 8, 2006.

15. Lisa Del Torto, interview by author, Oldcastle, Ontario, Canada, November 8, 2006; Lisa Del Torto, e-mail to author, April 16, 2007.

16. Frank Agostini, interview by author, Sand Springs, Oklahoma, May 21, 2006.

17. Juliani, "Family Life," 211.

18. Messina, "Women in Transition," 687–694; Bridget Oteri Robinson, "Women in the Workforce," in Salvatore J. LaGumina et al., eds., *The Italian American Experience: An Encyclopedia* (New York: Garland Publishing, 2000), 685–687.

19. Juliani, "Family Life," 211–212.

20. The paragraphs about the extended Basalone family draw upon the following sources: Dan Basalone, interview by author, Los Angeles, California, January 14, 2005; Carmen Basalone, interview by author, Los Angeles, California, April 16, 2005.

21. Michael Barone, *The New Americans: How the Melting Pot Can Work Again* (Washington, D.C.: Regnery Publishing, 2001), 146–147.

22. See, e.g., Nick J. Mileti, *Closet Italians: A Dazzling Collection of Illustrious Italians with Non-Italian Names* (No city: Xlibris, 2004), 282–283, 292–293, 296–297, 302–303, and 332–333.

23. Richard D. Alba, "Assimilation," in Salvatore J. LaGumina et al., eds., *The Italian American Experience: An Encyclopedia* (New York: Garland Publishing, 2000), 43.

24. Richard D. Alba, *Ethnic Identity: The Transformation of White America* (New Haven, Conn.: Yale University Press, 1990), passim; Mary C. Waters, *Ethnic Options: Choosing Identities in America* (Berkeley: University of California Press, 1990), passim.

25. I learned about this story during my visit to Erie, Pennsylvania, on June 12, 2006.

26. Thomas Ragona, interview by author, El Paso, Texas, January 10, 2005; Thomas Ragona, e-mail to author, February 9, 2007; Thomas Ragona, telephone interview by author, April 19, 2007.

27. Ragona, interview.

28. The paragraphs about the Battista family draw upon my interviews with Alice Battista, Bill Battista, and Bob Battista in Madison, Wisconsin, on December 21, 2006, as well as my telephone conversation with Alice and Bill Battista on February 15, 2007, and an e-mail from them on March 31, 2007.

29. In the early 1980s, Joe and Anita Battista moved from King of Prussia to Bridgeport, Pennsylvania (they spent their winters in Florida), and attended Our Mother of Sorrows Church with the Nasielski family. During the late 1990s and until his passing in 2002, Joe Battista volunteered to help make the stuffed cabbage rolls at the Our Mother of Sorrows Festival every summer. He even devised a cabbage-coring machine to make the process more efficient.

30. All the material in the paragraphs about Jill Rose and her family comes from the following sources: Jill Rose, interview by author, Taylors, South Carolina, November 19, 2006; Jill Rose, telephone interview by author, December 20, 2006; Jill Rose, e-mails to author, December 21, 2006 and January 16, 2007.

31. During a vacation earlier this decade, Jill Rose and one of her sons videotaped Frank Conti speaking about his life story. Rose interviewed her father, while her son videotaped the event for posterity.

32. Juliani, "Family Life," passim.

33. Ibid., 212.

34. Michael Pastore, telephone interview by author, February 21, 2006.

35. Marianne Dalfonso Reali, e-mail to author, August 14, 2006.

36. Flora Bertagnolli, interview by author, Rock Springs, Wyoming, July 11, 2006; Mary Joe Kaumo, interview by author, Rock Springs, Wyoming, July 11, 2006; Flora Bertagnolli, telephone interview by author, December 14, 2006.

37. George Silvestri Jr., interview by author, Novato, California, August 26, 2005.

38. Ibid.

39. The quotations and information in the three paragraphs about the Maggiora family come from the following sources: Kathleen Maggiora Rogers, interview by author, San Francisco, California, August 24, 2005; Kathleen Maggiora Rogers, e-mails to author, December 11, 2006, January 21, 2007, and August 16, 2007.

40. Stephanie Angle Lanzolla, interview by author, Raleigh, North Carolina, January 18, 2006; Vincent Lanzolla, interview by author, Raleigh, North Carolina, January 18, 2006.

41. Ibid.

42. Stephanie Angle Lanzolla and Vincent Lanzolla, e-mail to author, May 4, 2007.

43. Ibid.

44. Unless otherwise noted, all the material in this vignette comes from the public record and the following source: Andrew A. Lioi, *Rosaria's Family: The Family of Bruno and Rosaria Lioi, An Italian Immigrant Family* (Baltimore: Gateway Press, 1997). My account also draws upon the following sources: Andrew Lioi, interview by author, Baltimore, Maryland, September 12, 2006; Gerry Lioi, interview by author, Baltimore, Maryland, September 12, 2006.

45. Lioi, *Rosaria's Family*, 350.

46. Carl Carani, interview by author, Highwood, Illinois, September 21, 2006; Nancy Carani, interview by author, Highwood, Illinois, September 21, 2006.

47. Leon E. Wynter, *American Skin: Pop Culture, Big Business, and the End of White America* (New York: Crown Publishers, 2002), 279.

48. Angelina Renzi, telephone interview by author, August 3, 2006; Hank Marcello, interview by author, Providence, Rhode Island, October 16, 2006; Angelina Renzi, interview by author, Atlantis, Florida, November 18, 2006.

49. Dominick Filipponi, interview by author, New Port Richey, Florida, February 20, 2007; Joan Filipponi, interview by author, New Port Richey, Florida, February 20, 2007; Dominick Filipponi, e-mail to author, April 1, 2007.

CHAPTER 6: NAMING PRACTICES

1. Maria Antonia Peri Sack, "The Americanizing of Italian Names," *Il Pensiero*, 2004.

2. Ibid.

3. Ibid.

4. Ibid.

5. Marianne Peri Sack, interview by author, Saint Louis, Missouri, January 14, 2006; Marianne Peri Sack, questionnaire to author, January 14, 2006.

6. Peri Sack, "The Americanizing of Italian Names."

7. Ibid.

8. Eleanore Berra Marfisi, *Soprannomi: Nicknames of "The Hill"* (St. Charles, Mo.: RC Printing Services, 2005).

9. Ibid.

10. The quotations about Italian-American naming practices come from the second page in the section entitled "History" at the beginning of Marfisi, *Soprannomi*. There are no numbers on these pages.

11. Marfisi, *Soprannomi*, passim.

12. James Tognoni, interview by author, Milwaukee, Wisconsin, October 17, 2005.

13. John Marino, e-mail to author, July 18, 2006.

14. John Marino, interview by author, Washington, D.C., February 10, 2005.

15. Ibid.

16. Ibid.

17. Ibid.

18. Marino, e-mail.

19. Marino, interview.
20. For information about Italian surnames, see J. N. Hook, *Family Names: How Our Surnames Came to America* (New York: Macmillan Publishing Company, 1982), 191–201.
21. John Philip Colletta, *Finding Italian Roots: The Complete Guide for Americans*, 2d ed. (Baltimore: Genealogical Publishing, 2003), 20.
22. Ibid., 21.
23. Ibid., 20.
24. For a brief overview of Italian-American naming practices, see Colletta, *Finding Italian Roots*, 20–22.
25. Jessie Piscitello, interview by author, Easton, Pennsylvania, June 20, 2006; Jessie Piscitello, letter to author, August 2, 2006.
26. Carlo Giraulo, interview by author, Portland, Maine, September 16, 2005; Carlo Giraulo, e-mail to author, July 25, 2006.
27. Romana Antonelli, interview by author, Westminster, Colorado, July 12, 2006.
28. John Terravecchia, interview by author, Bedford, New Hampshire, September 15, 2005; Tina Terravecchia, interview by author, Bedford, New Hampshire, September 15, 2005.
29. John Terravecchia, e-mail to author, June 3, 2007. To learn more about Hampshire First Bank, go to www.hampshirefirst.com.
30. Dr. James Guttuso, interviews by author, Boca Raton, Florida, May 2, 2005 and November 13, 2005.
31. Dr. James Guttuso, e-mail to author, July 17, 2006.
32. Guttuso, interviews.
33. Ernest Manzo, interview by author, Clearwater, Florida, November 15, 2005.
34. Emil Bagneschi, interview by author, San Mateo, California, August 26, 2005; Emil Bagneschi, questionnaire to author, August 26, 2005.
35. Hugo Tagli, telephone interview by author, June 16, 2005.
36. Ronald Little, interview by author, Raleigh, North Carolina, January 18, 2006; Ronald Little, e-mail to author, August 9, 2006; Ronald Little, letter to author, September 28, 2006.
37. Calogero Cascio, interview by author, Franklin Square, New York, June 22, 2006.
38. Carlo Dalla, interview by author, Westminster, Colorado, July 12, 2006.
39. Carmine Russo, interview by author, Winchester, Virginia, June 21, 2006.
40. Nick J. Mileti, *Closet Italians: A Dazzling Collection of Illustrious Italians with Non-Italian Names* (No city: Xlibris, 2004), 352–353.
41. Ibid.; "Alicia Keys," *Wikipedia, the free encyclopedia.* http://en.wikipedia.org/wiki/Alicia_Keys.
42. Mileti, *Closet Italians*, 32–33.
43. Ibid., 214.
44. Ibid.
45. For the profile of Hulk Hogan, see Mileti, *Closet Italians*, 320–321.
46. To learn more about Livermore, see Peter Burrows, "HP's Ultimate Team Player," *BusinessWeek* (January 30, 2006): 76–78.
47. Remo Minato, telephone interview by author, July 27, 2005.
48. John Buffa Koch, interview by author, Jacksonville, Florida, November 18, 2005; Patty Koch, interview by author, Jacksonville, November 18, 2005.
49. Lucy Basso Smith, interview by author, Dunedin, Florida, November 15, 2005; Lucy Basso Smith, e-mails to author, March 15, 2007, March 25, 2007, and June 13, 2007.
50. Basso Smith, e-mail to author, March 15, 2007.
51. Adam Lashinsky, "Is This the Right Man for Intel?" *Fortune*, April 18, 2005.
52. Frank Sagona, interviews by author, Pueblo, Colorado, December 2, 2005 and July 13, 2006.
53. Michael Illia, interview by author, Pismo Beach, California, August 23, 2005.
54. Gr. Uff. Joseph Maselli, interview by author, New Orleans, Louisiana, April 25, 2005.

55. Truby Chiaviello, "Don't Let the Last Name Fool You," *F&L Primo* 6 (June/July 2005): 5–6.
56. Ibid., 5.
57. Ibid.
58. Ibid.
59. Ibid., 5–6.
60. Ibid., 5.
61. Jennie Michelon, interview by author, Rockford, Illinois, November 1, 2006.
62. Giovanna Michelon became Jennie Michelon when she entered elementary school. Her teachers gave the name "Jennie" to her. Jennie Michelon, interview by author, Rockford, Illinois, September 5, 2007.
63. Michelon, interviews.
64. Vincent Damian Jr., interview by author, Coral Gables, Florida, January 28, 2005.
65. Ibid.
66. Ibid.
67. Ibid. See Pietro di Donato, *Christ in Concrete* (1939; reprint, New York: New American Library, 2004).
68. Damian, interview.
69. Ibid.
70. Vincent Sposato III, interview by author, Sand Springs, Oklahoma, May 21, 2006.
71. Richard Floreani, interview by author, Bedford, New Hampshire, September 15, 2005.
72. John Illia Jr., interview by author, Las Vegas, Nevada, June 14, 2005.
73. George Silvestri Jr., interview by author, Novato, California, August 26, 2005.
74. Frank Sagona, interview by author, Pueblo, Colorado, July 13, 2006.
75. Dalla, interview.
76. Dr. James J. Divita, e-mail to author, November 28, 2005.
77. Ibid.
78. Ibid.
79. Armando De Marino Jr., interview by author, Franklin Square, New York, June 22, 2006.
80. Pasquale Pesce, interview by author, Santa Ana, California, June 12, 2005.
81. Comm. Joseph R. Cerrell, interview by author, Los Angeles, California, April 15, 2005.
82. Ibid.
83. Comm. Joseph R. Cerrell, e-mail to author, June 19, 2006.
84. Colletta, *Finding Italian Roots*, passim.
85. Monsignor Dominic Bottino, interview by author, Hammonton, New Jersey, October 12, 2005.
86. Peter Balistreri, interview by author, Milwaukee, Wisconsin, March 7, 2006.
87. Dr. Pete DePond, interview by author, Vienna, West Virginia, October 29, 2005; Dr. Pete DePond, telephone interview by author, November 22, 2005.
88. Ibid.; Dr. Pete DePond, e-mail to author, November 22, 2005.
89. Judge Richard Marano, interview by author, Bridgeport, Connecticut, June 24, 2005; Judge Richard Marano, telephone interview by author, July 11, 2005.
90. Ralph Tambasco, interview by author, Indianapolis, Indiana, March 13, 2006.
91. Michael Tambasco, interview by author, Indianapolis, Indiana, March 13, 2006.
92. Marianne Reali, interview by author, Portland, Maine, September 16, 2005.
93. Maria Baroco, telephone interview by author, December 13, 2006.
94. Ferraro is not the respondent's real name. I use a pseudonym to protect his privacy.
95. Mario Bertagna, e-mail to author, July 28, 2005.
96. Marano, interview.
97. Frank Sagona, interview, December 2, 2005; Frank Sagona, interview, July 13, 2006.
98. Michael Salardino, telephone interview by author, August 11, 2005; Michael Salardino, interview by author, Pueblo, Colorado, December 2, 2005.

99. Richard Apodaca, telephone interview by author, November 13, 2004; Richard Apodaca, interview by author, El Paso, Texas, January 7, 2005.

CHAPTER 7: LANGUAGE AND CULTURE

1. Translated into English, the chant has the following meaning: "The Befana comes at night/with her shoes all torn/dressed Roman style/long live the Befana!" Josephine Maietta provided me with this translation.
2. The information in the paragraphs about Cav. Josephine Maietta draws upon my interviews with Ms. Maietta in New York in 2004 and 2006, as well as our periodic telephone conversations and e-mail communications—and some biographical materials that Ms. Maietta kindly shared with me.
3. To learn about "Souvenir d'Italia," go to www.wrhu.org.
4. Josephine Maietta, personal communication.
5. The Web site of AATI LI (www.aatili.org) is a good source of information about this organization.
6. Ray Boggio, interview by author, Glendale, California, December 15, 2004. See, too, the Piemontesi nel Mondo Southern California Web site (www.pnmsocal.org).
7. Boggio, interview.
8. Ibid.
9. Ibid.
10. Kathleen Maggiora Rogers, interview by author, San Francisco, California, August 24, 2005.
11. For information regarding the Piedmontese classes, see www.piemontesinoca.com/study.php.
12. Kathleen Maggiora Rogers, e-mail to author, August 8, 2007. See Bobby Tanzilo with Gian Piero Morano and Vincenzo Marchelli, comp., *Rèis Monfrin-e: Poesie e canson an Piemontèis* (Milwaukee: Monferrini in America and San Francisco: Associazione Piemontesi nel Mondo of Northern California, 2007).
13. Joseph A. Tursi, "Italian Language in America," in Salvatore J. LaGumina et al., eds., *The Italian American Experience: An Encyclopedia* (New York: Garland Publishing, 2000), 307.
14. Ibid.
15. Ibid., 307–308; Frances M. Malpezzi and William M. Clements, *Italian-American Folklore* (Little Rock, Ark.: August House Publishers, 1992), 44.
16. Malpezzi and Clements, *Italian-American Folklore*, 44.
17. Michael La Sorte, *La Merica: Images of Italian Greenhorn Experience* (Philadelphia: Temple University Press, 1985), 159–188.
18. Malpezzi and Clements, *Italian-American Folklore*, 49–50; Michael Barone, *The New Americans: How the Melting Pot Can Work Again* (Washington, D.C.: Regnery Publishing, 2001), 144–145.
19. Tursi, "Italian Language in America," 308; Linda Santarelli Susman, "Linguistic History of Italian Dialects in the United States," in Salvatore J. LaGumina et al., eds., *The Italian American Experience: An Encyclopedia* (New York: Garland Publishing, 2000), 340–341.
20. Susman, "Linguistic History of Italian Dialects in the United States," 341.
21. U.S. Census Bureau, *Statistical Abstract of the United States: 2006* (125th ed.) (Washington, D.C.: U.S. Government Printing Office, 2005), Table 47.
22. For a list of the Italian-language Masses in the United States, go to www.masstimes.org.
23. Andrea Mantineo, interview by author, Westwood, New Jersey, December 7, 2004. See, too, www.americaoggi.info.
24. Ibid.
25. Tursi, "Italian Language in America," 308; Vincent A. Lapomarda, "Italian American Press," in Salvatore J. LaGumina et al., eds., *The Italian American Experience: An Encyclopedia* (New York: Garland Publishing, 2000), 509–518; Christopher Newton, "Radio," in Salvatore J. LaGumina et al., eds., *The Italian American Experience: An Encyclopedia* (New York: Garland Publishing, 2000),

532–533; Angela D. Danzi, "Station WHOM in New York," in Salvatore J. LaGumina et al., eds., *The Italian American Experience: An Encyclopedia* (New York: Garland Publishing, 2000), 533–535.

26. Nicholas Joseph Falco, "Successors to the Italian Newspaper," in Salvatore J. LaGumina et al., eds., *The Italian American Experience: An Encyclopedia* (New York: Garland Publishing, 2000), 619–621.

27. Newton, "Radio," 532–533.

28. See the Web site for ICN Radio (www.icnradio.com) to learn more about this network.

29. Newton, "Radio," 533.

30. For more information about Luigi Aiello and his radio programming, go to www.laiello.com.

31. Bill Guida, " 'La Voce D'Italia'; Italy native celebrates more than a quarter century on American airwaves," *Kenosha (Wis.) News*, March 25, 2008.

32. Ibid.

33. Ibid.

34. "Italics TV Magazine." http://qcpages.qc.edu/calandra/italics/index.html.

35. "About Italian American Network." www.italianamericannetwork.com/ianet/index.php?page=company.

36. Ibid.

37. Richard Floreani, interview by author, Bedford, New Hampshire, September 15, 2005; Richard Floreani, e-mail to author, August 24, 2006.

38. Richard Floreani, e-mail to author, March 5, 2008.

39. Professor Christopher Kleinhenz, interview by author, Madison, Wisconsin, October 21, 2004; Professor Christopher Kleinhenz, e-mail to author, May 31, 2008.

40. U.S. Census Bureau, *Statistical Abstract of the United States: 2006*, Table 256.

41. Kleinhenz, interview.

42. Ibid; Kleinhenz, e-mail.

43. Maria Grante Roos, interview by author, South Miami, Florida, January 27, 2005.

44. Ibid.; Lucrezia Lindia, e-mail to author, July 13, 2006.

45. Kleinhenz, e-mail; Kleinhenz, interview.

46. Kleinhenz, e-mail.

47. Lisa Guido, interview by author, Kenosha, Wisconsin, September 22, 2004.

48. Rosalie Galasso Caputo, telephone interview by author, May 2, 2006.

49. Roos, interview.

50. Ibid.; Maria Grante Roos, e-mail to author, May 22, 2008.

51. Roos, interview.

52. Antonella Albano, interview by author, Naples, Florida, January 26, 2005.

53. Kleinhenz, e-mail; Kleinhenz, interview.

54. Kleinhenz, e-mail.

55. This paragraph draws upon my interviews and e-mail communications with Bruna Petrarca Boyle in 2004, 2005, 2007, and 2008.

56. Kleinhenz, e-mail; Kleinhenz, interview.

57. Nelly Furman, David Goldberg, and Natalia Lusin, *Enrollments in Languages Other Than English in United States Institutions of Higher Education, Fall 2006* (Modern Language Association—Web publication, November 13, 2007), 13, 14. www.mla.org/pdf/06enrollmentsurvey_final.pdf.

58. To learn more about the American Association of Teachers of Italian, go to www.aati-online.org.

59. Kleinhenz, e-mail.

60. Tursi, "Italian Language in America," 308. The Arba Sicula Web site (www.arbasicula.org) is a useful source of information about this organization.

61. "Gaetano Cipolla," St. John's University. www.stjohns.edu/academics/undergraduate/liberal arts/departments/languages/faculty/bi_lang_cipollag.stj.

62. "Uncle Floyd Vivino's Italian American Serenade," *Italian Tribune*, February 15, 2007, 18.

63. Floyd Vivino, telephone interview by author, January 5, 2005.

64. Ibid.

65. Ibid.; Jim Beckerman, "Veni, vidi Vivino; Uncle Floyd, still wacky at 50, has become more of a tradition than a quirk," (*Bergen County, N.J.*) *Record*, August 20, 2002, at F1.

66. Vivino, telephone interview.

67. Salvatore Primeggia, "Comedy," in Salvatore J. LaGumina et al., eds., *The Italian American Experience: An Encyclopedia* (New York: Garland Publishing, 2000), 136.

68. Primeggia, "Comedy," 130–132.

69. Ibid.

70. Floyd Vivino, letter to author, July 8, 2008.

71. Primeggia, "Comedy," 130–133.

72. Ibid., 133–134.

73. Ibid., 134–136.

74. See, e.g., Joseph Fioravanti, "Pop Singers," in Salvatore J. LaGumina et al., eds., *The Italian American Experience: An Encyclopedia* (New York: Garland Publishing, 2000), 489–496.

75. "Eh, Cumpari!" *Wikipedia, the free encyclopedia*. http://en.wikipedia.org/wiki/Eh,_Cumpari!

76. Ibid.

77. Dean Martin, *All-Time Greatest Hits* (Los Angeles: Curb Records, 1990).

78. "That's Amore (song)," *Wikipedia, the free encyclopedia*. http://en.wikipedia.org/wiki/That's_Amore.

79. Ibid.

80. Unless otherwise noted, all the information in this vignette about Luisa Potenza comes from the public record and my interview with Ms. Potenza: Luisa Potenza, interview by author, Huntington, New York, December 9, 2004.

81. Luisa Potenza, e-mail to author, January 5, 2007.

82. For more information about "Italia Mia" and 1370 WALK–AM, go to www.1370walk.com.

83. Whenever Potenza goes to Italy, she purchases one dozen contemporary Italian compact discs that she later plays on her radio program.

CHAPTER 8: ITALIANS IN AMERICA

1. Gerald Browder Jr., e-mail to author, June 13, 2006.

2. See "Arturo Umberto Illia." *Wikipedia, the free encyclopedia*. http://en.wikipedia.org/wiki/Arturo_Umberto_Illia.

3. Gerald Browder Jr., e-mail; John Illia Jr., interview by author, Las Vegas, Nevada, June 14, 2005; Susan G. Browder, interview by author, Occidental, California, August 25, 2005.

4. Susan G. Browder, interview; Greg Browder, e-mail to author, June 17, 2006.

5. Greg Browder, interview by author, Occidental, California, August 25, 2005.

6. Gerald Browder Jr., e-mail.

7. Susan G. Browder, interview; John Illia Jr., interview.

8. Greg Browder, interview.

9. Gerald Browder Jr., e-mail.

10. Ibid.

11. Michael Illia, interview by author, Pismo Beach, California, August 23, 2005.

12. Ibid.

13. The material in the paragraphs about the Bussone family draws upon the public record and my interviews with Joseph and Evelyn Bussone in Sycamore, Illinois, on May 1, 2007, and my telephone conversations with Mr. Bussone.

14. Bussone has been recognized on various occasions for his civic leadership and fundraising activities. In 2000, for instance, he was honored by the Rockford Area Chapter of the National Society of Fund Raising Executives.

15. Phylis Cancilla Martinelli, "Scottsdale, Arizona," in Salvatore J. LaGumina et al., eds., *The Italian American Experience: An Encyclopedia* (New York: Garland Publishing, 2000), 585.

16. U.S. Census Bureau, *Statistical Abstract of the United States: 2006* (125th ed.) (Washington, D.C.: U.S. Government Printing Office, 2005), Table 46.

17. The Order Sons of Italy in America, *A Profile of Today's Italian Americans: A Report Based on the Year 2000 Census Compiled by The Sons of Italy* (Washington, D.C.: Order Sons of Italy in America, Fall 2003), 14–15.

18. Michael LaSorte, "Colonies in Small Towns," in Salvatore J. LaGumina et al., eds., *The Italian American Experience: An Encyclopedia* (New York: Garland Publishing, 2000), 126.

19. Jerome Krase, "Ethnic Neighborhoods," in Salvatore J. LaGumina et al., eds., *The Italian American Experience: An Encyclopedia* (New York: Garland Publishing, 2000), 199.

20. Salvatore J. LaGumina, "Regional Migration and Transplantation," in Salvatore J. LaGumina et al., eds., *The Italian American Experience: An Encyclopedia* (New York: Garland Publishing, 2000), 536–538.

21. Toni Andriulli, interview by author, Portland, Maine, September 15, 2005.

22. Rose Ann Rabiola Miele, interview by author, Boulder City, Nevada, December 5, 2006.

23. These insights draw upon my telephone interviews with Joseph Lo Casto in 2005 and 2006.

24. Andrew F. Rolle, *The Immigrant Upraised: Italian Adventurers and Colonists in an Expanding America* (Norman: University of Oklahoma Press, 1968). See, too, Andrew Rolle, "Introduction," in Gloria Ricci Lothrop, ed., *Fulfilling the Promise of California: An Anthology of Essays on the Italian American Experience in California* (Spokane, Wash.: California Italian American Task Force and the Arthur H. Clark Company, 2000), 15–20; Andrew Rolle, "The Immigrant Experience: Reflections of a Lifetime," in Gloria Ricci Lothrop, ed., *The Land Beyond: Italian Migrants in the Westward Movement: An Anthology of Essays on the Italian Settlers' Experience in the American West* (San Marino, Calif.: Patrons of Italian Culture, 2007), 13–19.

25. Rolle, *The Immigrant Upraised*, 6.

26. The Order Sons of Italy in America, *A Profile of Today's Italian Americans*, 14.

27. Ibid.

28. Armando Delicato, *Images of America: Italians in Detroit* (Charleston, S.C.: Arcadia, 2005), 117, 127.

29. Ibid., 127.

30. Ibid.

31. The Order Sons of Italy in America, *A Profile of Today's Italian Americans*, 14.

32. Ibid.

33. Patricia Anderson, interview by author, Baldwin County, Alabama, November 15, 2006.

34. Maria Baroco, telephone interview by author, December 13, 2006.

35. Anderson, interview.

36. Baroco, telephone interview.

37. For an overview of Italian-American history in the American South, see Gary R. Mormino, "The South," in Salvatore J. LaGumina et al., eds., *The Italian American Experience: An Encyclopedia* (New York: Garland Publishing, 2000), 604–606.

38. Mormino, "The South," 604–605.

39. Ibid., 605.

40. The Order Sons of Italy in America, *A Profile of Today's Italian Americans*, 10–11.

41. Joseph Maselli and Dominic Candeloro, *Images of America: Italians in New Orleans* (Charleston, S.C.: Arcadia, 2004).

42. Ibid., 7.

43. Ibid.

44. Ibid.

45. Ibid., 83–92, 120.

46. The Order Sons of Italy in America, *A Profile of Today's Italian Americans*, 14.

47. Maselli and Candeloro, *Images of America: Italians in New Orleans*, 58.

48. See Kenny L. Brown, *The Italians in Oklahoma* (Norman: University of Oklahoma Press, 1980).

49. On Pete's Place, see Brown, *The Italians in Oklahoma*, 38–39.

50. "Italian Festival of McAlester, Oklahoma." www.italianfestival.org.

51. See www.italianamericansocietyoftulsa.com.

52. Salvatore Gargiulo, telephone interview by author, April 10, 2006; Salvatore Gargiulo, interview by author, Tulsa County, Oklahoma, May 21, 2006.

53. Scott Brogna, interview by author, Sand Springs, Oklahoma, May 21, 2006.

54. Mary Jo Tannehill, interview by author, Sand Springs, Oklahoma, May 21, 2006.

55. Frank Agostini, interview by author, Sand Springs, Oklahoma, May 21, 2006.

56. Tony Bacino, interview by author, Pueblo, Colorado, December 2, 2005; Kathy Bacino, interview by author, Pueblo, Colorado, December 2, 2005.

57. Ibid.

58. Russell Frank, " 'Get on One End of the Rope and Pull Together': Italian-American Life and Work in Pueblo, Colorado," in David A. Taylor and John Alexander Williams, eds., *Old Ties, New Attachments: Italian-American Folklife in the West* (Washington, D.C.: Library of Congress, 1992), 144–159; Paula M. Manini, "Shaping Tradition: The Saint Joseph's Day Table Ritual," in David A. Taylor and John Alexander Williams, eds., *Old Ties, New Attachments: Italian-American Folklife in the West* (Washington, D.C.: Library of Congress, 1992), 160–173.

59. Tony Bacino, interview. See, too, "Tony Bacino," *Pueblo Chieftain*, February 2, 2008.

60. See, e.g., Ed Quillen, "Welcome to Kolorado, Klan Kountry," *Colorado Springs Independent* (May 22, 2003); Frank, " 'Get on One End of the Rope and Pull Together': Italian-American Life and Work in Pueblo, Colorado," 146, 147.

61. Kathy Bacino, interview.

62. Tony Bacino, interview.

63. Ralph Montera, interviews by author, Pueblo, Colorado, December 3, 2005 and February 9, 2006.

64. Ibid.

65. Kathy Bacino, interview.

66. This material draws upon my e-mails, interviews, and telephonic communications with Michael Salardino in 2005, 2006, 2007, and 2008.

67. Father Ben Bacino, interview by author, Pueblo, Colorado, July 13, 2006. See, too, Manini, "Shaping Tradition: The Saint Joseph's Day Table Ritual," 160–173.

68. Salardino, interviews.

69. Michael Salardino, e-mail to author, November 11, 2007.

70. Ibid.; Michael Salardino, interview by author, Pueblo, Colorado, September 26, 2007.

71. Dr. James Vitale, telephone interview by author, July 16, 2005.

72. Ibid.

73. Phylis Cancilla Martinelli, "Population," in Salvatore J. LaGumina et al., eds., *The Italian American Experience: An Encyclopedia* (New York: Garland Publishing, 2000), 497.

74. Martinelli, "Scottsdale, Arizona," 585–586.

75. Blanton Owen, "The Melting Pot Works: Italians in Central Nevada," in David A. Taylor and John Alexander Williams, eds., *Old Ties, New Attachments: Italian-American Folklife in the West* (Washington, D.C.: Library of Congress, 1992), 48–67; Alan Balboni, "The Italians," in Jerry L. Simich and Thomas C. Wright, eds., *The Peoples of Las Vegas: One City, Many Faces* (Reno: University of Nevada Press, 2005), 147; Albin J. Cofone, "Reno's Little Italy: Italian Entrepreneurship and Culture in Northern Nevada," in Gloria Ricci Lothrop, ed., *The Land Beyond: Italian Migrants in the Westward Movement: An Anthology of Essays on the Italian Settlers' Experience in the American West* (San Marino, Calif.: Patrons of Italian Culture, 2007), 187–201.

76. Owen, "The Melting Pot Works," 49.

77. Balboni, "The Italians," 145–163; Alan Balboni, *Beyond the Mafia: Italian Americans and the Development of Las Vegas* (Reno: University of Nevada Press, 1996).

78. Balboni, *Beyond the Mafia*, xix.

79. See Gloria Ricci Lothrop, "California's Italians: A Promise Fulfilled," in Gloria Ricci Lothrop, ed., *Fulfilling the Promise of California: An Anthology of Essays on the Italian American Experience in California* (Spokane, Wash.: California Italian American Task Force and the Arthur H. Clark Company, 2000), 233–273.

80. Dr. Gloria Ricci Lothrop, interview by author, Pasadena, California, April 17, 2005; Dr. Gloria Ricci Lothrop, telephone interview by author, April 24, 2008.

81. Donald Donato, telephone interview by author, November 3, 2005.

82. Lothrop, "California's Italians: A Promise Fulfilled," 261–262.

83. Gary Mormino and Ilaria Serra, *Italian Americans and Florida* (Boca Raton, Fla: Center for Interdisciplinary Studies, Florida Atlantic University, 2003); Gary R. Mormino, *Land of Sunshine, State of Dreams: A Social History of Modern Florida* (Gainesville: University Press of Florida, 2005), passim.

84. Mormino, "The South," 605.

85. The Order Sons of Italy in America, *A Profile of Today's Italian Americans*, 14–15.

86. Michael Barone and Richard E. Cohen, *The Almanac of American Politics 2006* (Washington, D.C.: National Journal Group, 2005), 392.

87. Julia Lawlor, "Snowbirds Flock Together for Winter," *New York Times*, February 2, 2007.

88. The information in this paragraph comes from a roundtable discussion at the Italian American Club of Greater Clearwater in Clearwater, Florida, on November 17, 2005.

89. John Buffa Koch, interview by author, Jacksonville, Florida, November 18, 2005; Patty Koch, interview by author, Jacksonville, Florida, November 18, 2005.

90. Julie Calabrese, interview by author, St. Petersburg, Florida, November 15, 2005.

91. Dominick Filipponi, interview by author, New Port Richey, Florida, February 20, 2007; Joan Filipponi, interview by author, New Port Richey, Florida, February 20, 2007.

92. http://cabriniosia.com. I accessed and viewed this Web content in 2007.

93. Members of the OSIA Frances Cabrini Lodge #2723 shared these anecdotes with me in Winchester, Virginia, on June 22, 2006.

94. John Buffa Koch, interview; Patty Koch, interview.

95. Robert Calvisi, telephone interview by author, December 8, 2005.

96. Marge DeBenedetto, telephone interview by author, July 7, 2006; Marge DeBenedetto, e-mail to author, March 27, 2008.

CHAPTER 9: ETHNIC NEIGHBORHOODS

1. For a history of Ybor City, see Gary R. Mormino and George E. Pozzetta, *The Immigrant World of Ybor City: Italians and Their Latin Neighbors in Tampa, 1885–1985* (Gainesville: University Press of Florida, 1998).

2. Vince Pardo, interview by author, Tampa, Florida, November 16, 2005; John Spoto, interview by author, Tampa, Florida, November 16, 2005.

3. Josie Noto, interview by author, Tampa, Florida, November 19, 2005; Pete Noto, interview by author, Tampa, Florida, November 19, 2005.

4. Mormino and Pozzetta, *The Immigrant World of Ybor City*, 132–134.

5. Ibid., passim.

6. Pardo, interview; Mormino and Pozzetta, *The Immigrant World of Ybor City*, 16–42.

7. Mormino and Pozzetta, *The Immigrant World of Ybor City*, 120.

8. Ibid., passim.

9. Ibid., 188–197.

10. For background on Vince Pardo's family history, go to http://vincepardo.net.

11. Pardo, interview.

12. Ibid. The L'Unione Italiana Web site (www.italian-club.org) offers information about the Italian Club of Tampa.

13. Pardo, interview.

14. Ibid.

15. Ibid.

16. Ibid.; Vince Pardo, e-mail to author, February 14, 2008.

17. Pardo, interview.

18. Ibid.; Vince J. Pardo, "The Winemaking Tradition," *Cigar City Magazine* (November/December 2005): 44–45.

19. Mormino and Pozzetta, *The Immigrant World of Ybor City*, 297–316. See, too, "Ybor City Development Corporation." www.tampagov.net/dept_ybor_city_development_corporation/index.asp.

20. The title of this chapter replicates that of the following source: Jerome Krase, "Ethnic Neighborhoods," in Salvatore J. LaGumina et al., eds., *The Italian American Experience: An Encyclopedia* (New York: Garland Publishing, 2000), 198–204.

21. Janet Cercone Scullion, interview by author, Pittsburgh, Pennsylvania, October 26, 2005.

22. Ibid.

23. Ibid.; Dennis Scullion, interview by author, Pittsburgh, Pennsylvania, October 27, 2005.

24. Visit www.bloomfieldlive.com to learn more about the Bloomfield Preservation and Heritage Society.

25. Cercone Scullion, interview; Janet Cercone Scullion, e-mail to author, February 15, 2008.

26. "Little Italy Days," www.shoppingbloomfield.com/little-italy-days/.

27. Ibid.

28. Krase, "Ethnic Neighborhoods," 198–204; Judith N. DeSena, "Community Issues," in Salvatore J. LaGumina et al., eds., *The Italian American Experience: An Encyclopedia* (New York: Garland Publishing, 2000), 137–138; Albin J. Cofone, "Reno's Little Italy: Italian Entrepreneurship and Culture in Northern Nevada," in Gloria Ricci Lothrop, ed., *The Land Beyond: Italian Migrants in the Westward Movement: An Anthology of Essays on the Italian Settlers' Experience in the American West* (San Marino, Calif.: Patrons of Italian Culture, 2007), 192–193.

29. Krase, "Ethnic Neighborhoods," 199.

30. See www.newcityamerica.com.

31. Marco Li Mandri, e-mail to author, December 11, 2007.

32. Marco Li Mandri, interview by author, San Diego, California, December 16, 2004.

33. For more information about San Diego's Little Italy, go to the Web site of the Little Italy Association (www.littleitalysd.com).

34. Li Mandri, interview.

35. See www.littleitalysd.com.

36. Li Mandri, interview.

37. See www.littleitalyredevelopment.org.

38. Laurie Penca, interview by author, Cleveland, Ohio, October 26, 2005.

39. Ibid.

40. For more information about San Francisco's North Beach neighborhood, go to www.sfnorthbeach.org.

41. Marsha Garland, interview by author, San Francisco, California, August 24, 2005; Marsha Garland, e-mail to author, December 13, 2007.

42. Ibid.

43. Garland, interview.

44. Ibid.

45. Ibid.

46. Ibid.; Marsha Garland, e-mail to author, December 17, 2007.
47. Garland, interview; Garland, e-mail to author, December 13, 2007.
48. Erla Zwingle, "Boston's North Enders," *National Geographic* 198 (October 2000): 50–67.
49. Ibid., 66.
50. Matthew A. Paolelli and Craig Tiede, "Economic upswing in Little Italy comes with a price," *Medill News Service*, December 1, 2005.
51. Ibid.
52. Ibid.
53. Ibid.
54. Ibid.
55. Ibid.
56. Ibid.
57. Jeanine Botta, "The Italian Experience in Howard Beach," *Italian Tribune*, September 29, 2005, 11.
58. Michael Powell, "Rethinking Who They Are; Census Shows People Are Declining to Report Their Heritage," *Washington Post*, May 25, 2002, A10.
59. Reverend Canon Matthew Mauriello, telephone interview by author, July 28, 2005; Reverend Canon Matthew Mauriello, interviews by author, Bridgeport, Connecticut, September 13, 2005 and August 10, 2007.
60. Ibid.
61. Ibid.
62. This material comes from the roundtable discussion that the Reverend Canon Matthew Mauriello graciously convened at Holy Rosary Catholic Church in Bridgeport, Connecticut, on August 10, 2007.
63. Ibid.
64. Mauriello, telephone interview; Mauriello, interviews.
65. Roundtable discussion, Holy Rosary Catholic Church.
66. Angie Staltaro, "Growing Up Italian on Bridgeport's East Side," Unpublished essay, August 10, 2007.
67. Mauriello, telephone interview; Mauriello, interviews.
68. Gina Carbone, " 'Sopranos' a mob hit to many," *Portsmouth (N.H.) Herald*, September 14, 2002.
69. "Akron neighborhoods," *Wikipedia, the free encyclopedia.* http://en.wikipedia.org/wiki/Akron_Neighborhoods.
70. DeSena, "Community Issues," 137.
71. Judith N. DeSena, "Intergroup Relations: Italian Americans and African Americans," in Salvatore J. LaGumina et al., eds., *The Italian American Experience: An Encyclopedia* (New York: Garland Publishing, 2000), 297–299.
72. Dennis J. Starr, "Trenton's Chambersburg," in Salvatore J. LaGumina et al., eds., *The Italian American Experience: An Encyclopedia* (New York: Garland Publishing, 2000), 639–640.
73. Ronald DiVecchio, interviews by author, Erie, Pennsylvania, October 27, 2005 and June 12, 2006.
74. Ibid. For more information about St. Paul Roman Catholic Church, go to www.stpaulrc-erie.com.
75. DiVecchio, interviews.
76. Vincent A. Lapomarda, "Maine's Little Italys," in Salvatore J. LaGumina et al., eds., *The Italian American Experience: An Encyclopedia* (New York: Garland Publishing, 2000), 354–355.
77. Ibid. For more information about St. Peter's Roman Catholic Church in Portland, Maine, go to www.stpeterschurchportland.org.
78. Lapomarda, "Maine's Little Italys."
79. Ibid.
80. Marianne Dalfonso Reali, interview by author, Portland, Maine, September 16, 2005.
81. Marianne Dalfonso Reali, e-mail to author, February 7, 2008.

82. Cofone, "Reno's Little Italy: Italian Entrepreneurship and Culture in Northern Nevada," 187–201.

83. Ibid., 201.

84. Dennis Caldirola, telephone interview by author, July 28, 2005.

85. Kathleen Fantazzi, interview by author, Wheeling, West Virginia, October 29, 2005.

86. "Kathleen J. Fantazzi." www.gkt.com/attorneys/kfantazzi.htm.

87. Fantazzi, interview.

88. "My cousin," notes Kathleen Fantazzi, "had a mural put on the wall of her house in South Philadelphia, which depicts the parish church, May procession, etc. It includes a rendering of my youngest daughter, Lori, in her communion dress at age 6." Kathleen Fantazzi, e-mail to author, February 28, 2007.

89. "South Philadelphia," *Wikipedia, the free encyclopedia.* http://en.wikipedia.org/wiki/South_Philadelphia.

90. Dominic Pulera, *Visible Differences: Why Race Will Matter to Americans in the Twenty-First Century* (New York: Continuum, 2002), 133–135.

91. "South Philadelphia," *Wikipedia, the free encyclopedia.*

92. Ibid.

93. Angelo Dundee, interview by author, Pembroke Pines, Florida, May 6, 2005.

94. Angelo Dundee with Bert Randolph Sugar, *My View from the Corner: A Life in Boxing* (New York: McGraw-Hill, 2008), 17.

95. Ibid.

96. Ibid., 17–19; Dundee, interview.

97. Dundee, interview; Dundee with Sugar, *My View from the Corner*, 20–42.

98. Dundee with Sugar, *My View from the Corner*, 21.

99. For the quotation, see Dundee with Sugar, *My View from the Corner*, 22.

100. Dundee with Sugar, *My View from the Corner*, 39–42.

101. Dundee, interview; Angelo Dundee, telephone interview by author, July 5, 2008.

102. Ibid.; Dundee with Sugar, *My View from the Corner*, 18, 50.

103. Dundee, interview.

104. Dundee with Sugar, *My View from the Corner*, passim.

105. Thomas Hauser, *Muhammad Ali: His Life and Times* (New York: Simon and Schuster, 1991), 36.

106. Dundee, interview; Dundee with Sugar, *My View from the Corner*, passim.

107. Dundee, interview.

108. Ibid.; Dundee with Sugar, *My View from the Corner*, 308.

109. Dundee with Sugar, *My View from the Corner*, 308.

110. Edward LaGuardia, telephone interviews by author, January 31, 2005 and February 7, 2005; Dr. Adriano Comollo, telephone interview by author, February 13, 2005. See, too, Tony Caputo's Market & Deli (www.caputosdeli.com) and the Italian Center of the West (www.italiancenterofthe west.com).

111. LaGuardia, telephone interviews.

112. Scott Helman, "The soul of a South Side machine; Group may give Clinton a boost," *Boston Globe*, January 3, 2008.

113. Ibid.

114. Patricia Civitate, correspondence with author, February 14, 2005.

115. I learned much about the Italian-American heritage of Des Moines from the participants in a roundtable discussion at the Italian-American Cultural Center in Des Moines, Iowa, on February 20, 2005.

116. Civitate, correspondence. See, too, www.IACCofIA.org.

117. Supervisor John Mauro, interview by author, Des Moines, Iowa, February 21, 2005.

118. Ibid.

CHAPTER 10: THE ITALIAN BASTIONS

1. The quotation can be found at www.njitalia.nj.gov.

2. Michael Barone and Richard E. Cohen, *The Almanac of American Politics 2006* (Washington, D.C.: National Journal Group, 2005), 1094.

3. Monsignor Dominic Bottino, interview by author, Hammonton, New Jersey, October 12, 2005.

4. Ibid. For more information about the Diocese of Camden, go to www.camdendiocese.org.

5. Bottino, interview.

6. Thomas, "Census: Americans moving away from ancestry."

7. "Freeholder Joseph H. Vicari." www.ocean.nj.us/PersonDetailPage.aspx?Name=JosephVicari.xml.

8. Mario Delano Jr., interview by author, Asbury Park, New Jersey, October 12, 2005.

9. Ibid. For more information about the Italian American Association of the Township of Ocean, go to www.iaato.com.

10. Unless otherwise noted, the material in this vignette draws upon my telephone interviews with Joseph Lo Casto in 2005, 2006, and 2007.

11. "Our Mission Statement," OSIA Giuseppe Verdi Lodge #2818. www.giuseppeverdilodge.com.

12. Ibid.

13. Tim Chavez, "Italian wants to bring a little bit of mother country to 'Mayberry,'" (*Nashville, Tenn.*) *Tennessean*, February 23, 2005; Bonnie Burch, "Sons of Italy is yet another reflection of growing diversity," (*Nashville, Tenn.*) *Tennessean*, January 4, 2006.

14. "U.S. Counties with High Percentage of Italian Americans." www.niaf.org/research/2000_census_2.asp.

15. "Italian ancestry by city—ePodunk." www.epodunk.com/ancestry/italian.html.

16. Vincent Lanzolla, interview by author, Raleigh, North Carolina, January 18, 2006.

17. Marie Spinner, interview by author, Raleigh, North Carolina, January 18, 2006.

18. I visited a wide variety of American communities with small Italian populations.

19. Laura Frappollo, interview by author, Winchester, Virginia, June 22, 2006.

20. These observations come from my conversations with Italian Americans who are members of the OSIA Frances Cabrini Lodge #2723 in Winchester, Virginia, on June 22, 2006.

21. For more information about the DaVinci Center for Community Progress, go to www.davincicenter.org.

22. "Welcome to The DaVinci Center!" www.davincicenter.org.

23. "About The DaVinci Center." www.davincicenter.org.

24. Ibid.; John Deluca, interview by author, Providence, Rhode Island, October 16, 2006.

25. "About The DaVinci Center."

26. Ibid.

27. Ibid.

28. Barone and Cohen, *The Almanac of American Politics 2006*, 1472–1475; Carmela E. Santoro, "Rhode Island," in Salvatore J. LaGumina et al., eds., *The Italian American Experience: An Encyclopedia* (New York: Garland Publishing, 2000), 550–552.

29. All the material in my paragraphs about the Manni family comes from my multiple e-mail communications with Angelina Renzi and the following sources: Angelina Renzi, telephone interview by author, August 3, 2006; Angelina Renzi, interviews by author, Atlantis, Florida, November 18, 2006 and February 20, 2007.

30. Renzi's oldest son, Paul, "was in a horrible accident and died at the age of 44." "He was a great family man and was a talented intellectual in engineering and business," remembers his mother. "I mourn this loss, not only to me, but to society." Angelina Renzi, e-mail to author, January 3, 2007.

31. Mary Marcello's husband, retired Colonel Angelo Marcello, served as the Director of Public Works under Rhode Island Governors Christopher Del Sesto and John Chafee. Their son, retired Major General John J. Marcello, spent 32 years in the military. The Army veteran and West Point graduate is now the President and CEO of the Allied Defense Group.

32. Bruna Petrarca Boyle, interview by author, Chicago, Illinois, November 19, 2004; Bruna Petrarca Boyle, interview by author, Kent County, Rhode Island, April 4, 2005; Bruna Petrarca Boyle, interview by author, Narragansett, Rhode Island, April 5, 2005.

33. Ibid.; Bruna Petrarca Boyle, telephone interview by author, March 11, 2007.

34. "Hartford's Neighborhoods: South End." http://hartford.omaxfield.com/soend.html.

35. Ibid.

36. The Order Sons of Italy in America, *A Profile of Today's Italian Americans: A Report Based on the Year 2000 Census Compiled by The Sons of Italy* (Washington, D.C.: Order Sons of Italy in America, Fall 2003), 14.

37. William Cockerham, "The Most Italian State in the Nation? Guess," *New York Times*, December 30, 2001, Sect. 14CN, p. 6.

38. G. Scott Thomas, "Census: Americans moving away from ancestry," *Tampa Bay Business Journal*, October 4, 2002; David Howard and John Murray, "Old Country, New City," *Waterbury (Conn.) Observer*, May 22–June 4, 1997.

39. "U.S. Counties with High Percentage of Italian Americans."

40. Catherine Killoran, telephone interview by author, July 5, 2006. I spoke at the New Milford Senior Center in New Milford, Connecticut, on October 18, 2006.

41. Sando Bologna, *The Italians of Waterbury: Experiences of Immigrants and Their Families* (Waterbury, Conn.: Sando Bologna, 1993); Sando Bologna and Richard M. Marano, eds., *Growing Up Italian and American in Waterbury: An Oral History* (Waterbury, Conn.: Sando Bologna and Richard M. Marano, 1997).

42. Anita Bologna, interview by author, New Haven County, Connecticut, June 24, 2005; Sando Bologna, interview by author, Waterbury, Connecticut, June 24, 2005; "Sando Bologna," www.bronsonlibrary.org/filestorage/33/SandoBologna.gif; "Learning How to Learn," in Sando Bologna and Richard M. Marano, eds., *Growing Up Italian and American in Waterbury: An Oral History* (Waterbury, Conn.: Sando Bologna and Richard M. Marano, 1997), 69–76.

43. This paragraph draws upon my interview and e-mail communications with Anita Bologna.

44. Judge Richard Marano, interview by author, Bridgeport, Connecticut, June 24, 2005; "Waterbury Offered Opportunity," in Sando Bologna and Richard M. Marano, eds., *Growing Up Italian and American in Waterbury: An Oral History* (Waterbury, Conn.: Sando Bologna and Richard M. Marano, 1997), 57–58.

45. For more information about the Pontelandolfo Community Club, go to www.ponteclub.com. See, too, Bologna, *The Italians of Waterbury*, 91–93; Howard and Murray, "Old Country, New City."
    I visited the Pontelandolfo Community Club in Waterbury, Connecticut, on June 25, 2005, and interviewed Antonio Rubbo Sr., the Club President, as well as Mario D'Occhio and Giuseppe Geloso. In addition, this paragraph draws upon the insights of Nicholas Rinaldi, a Club officer (Nicholas Rinaldi, interview by author, Shelton, Connecticut, September 13, 2005).

46. For more information about New Haven's Italian-American population, see Nancy N. Cassella and William V. D'Antonio, "New Haven," in Salvatore J. LaGumina et al., eds., *The Italian American Experience: An Encyclopedia* (New York: Garland Publishing, 2000), 403–405.

47. Barone and Cohen, *The Almanac of American Politics 2006*, 362–364; Jackie Koszczuk and H. Amy Stern, eds., *CQ's Politics in America 2006: The 109th Congress* (Washington, D.C.: CQ Press, 2005), 206–207.

48. Theresa Argento, interview by author, New Haven, Connecticut, September 13, 2005; Patti-Jo Esposito, interview by author, New Haven, Connecticut, September 13, 2005.

49. Cassella and D'Antonio, "New Haven," 403.

50. Argento, interview.

51. Cassella and D'Antonio, "New Haven," 403.

52. Argento, interview; Esposito, interview.

53. Argento, interview.

54. Ibid. To learn more about the Columbus Day Committee of Greater New Haven, go to www.columbusdaynewhaven.org.
55. Esposito, interview.
56. Ibid.
57. Patti-Jo Esposito, letter to author, April 18, 2007.
58. For more information about Monsignor Lisante and St. Thomas the Apostle Catholic Church, go to www.msgrlisante.org and www.stthomasapostle.org.
59. Monsignor James Lisante, telephone interview by author, March 2, 2005.
60. Ibid.
61. "U.S. Counties with High Percentage of Italian Americans."
62. The Order Sons of Italy in America, *A Profile of Today's Italian Americans*, 14, 15.
63. Judge Mario Rossetti, telephone interview by author, May 1, 2006.
64. Ibid.
65. All of the information in the paragraphs about Joseph Capogreco comes from the public record and my multiple interviews (in person and by telephone) with Mr. Capogreco in 2005, 2006, and 2007.
66. "Carosello Italiano with Joseph Capogreco." http://italiancarousel.net.
67. Capogreco receives e-mails from listeners throughout the United States as well as from such nations as Australia, Belgium, Canada, Colombia, Italy, Kuwait, Malta, Mexico, Russia, and Spain.
68. The material in the paragraphs about Jerry Somma, the Manzo and Somma families, and the Feast of Little Italy draws mainly upon the following source: Jerry Somma, interview by author, Jupiter, Florida, February 18, 2007.
69. To learn more about the Feast of Little Italy Italian Festival, go to www.feastoflittleitaly.com.
70. The Taste of Little Italy Web site (www.tasteoflittleitaly.net) offers information about this event.
71. All the information in the paragraphs about John Scara and the Rosebank Boys draws upon my meetings and e-mail communications with Mr. Scara in 2006, 2007, and 2008.

CHAPTER 11: GOVERNING AMERICA

1. The Hon. Janet Napolitano, interview by author, Phoenix, Arizona, January 13, 2005; Terry McCarthy, "A Mountaineer on the Political Rise," *Time* 166 (November 21, 2005): 32.
2. Napolitano, interview.
3. Ibid.
4. Ibid.; "Janet Napolitano—Governor of Arizona." www.governor.state.az.us/BioJN.asp.
5. "Janet Napolitano—Governor of Arizona"; Michael Barone and Richard E. Cohen, *The Almanac of American Politics 2006* (Washington, D.C.: National Journal Group, 2005), 91.
6. Ibid.
7. Stephen Ohlemacher, "Arizona Tops Nevada as Fastest Growing State," *Associated Press*, December 22, 2006.
8. Napolitano, interview.
9. For more information about Governor Napolitano's administration, go to www.azgovernor.gov.
10. "Janet Napolitano—Governor of Arizona."
11. Ibid.
12. Ibid.
13. Napolitano, interview.
14. Chip Scutari, "Napolitano nixing raise could pay dividends; Low salary may scare off '06 GOP hopefuls," *Arizona Republic*, July 25, 2005.
15. McCarthy, "A Mountaineer on the Political Rise," 30, 32–34.

16. For more information about the National Governors' Association, go to www.nga.org.

17. Sasha Abramsky, "Blue-ing the West," *Nation* 284 (January 22, 2007): 28.

18. McCarthy, "A Mountaineer on the Political Rise," 32, 34.

19. "Anna C. Verna," *Wikipedia, the free encyclopedia.* http://en.wikipedia.org/wiki/Anna_C._Verna; "Biography of Councilwoman Verna." www.phila.gov/citycouncil/verna/biography.html.

20. Leone et al., *Italians in America*, 79–97; Michael Barone, "Italian Americans and American Politics," in A. Kenneth Ciongoli and Jay Parini, eds., *Beyond* The Godfather: *Italian American Writers on the Real Italian American Experience* (Hanover, N.H.: University Press of New England, 1997), 245–250.

21. Leone et al., *Italians in America*, 200.

22. There are relatively few districts and jurisdictions where Italian Americans account for a majority of the electorate.

23. Frank J. Cavaioli, "Governors," in Salvatore J. LaGumina et al., eds., *The Italian American Experience: An Encyclopedia* (New York: Garland Publishing, 2000), 270–275; Salvatore J. LaGumina, "Politics," in Salvatore J. LaGumina et al., eds., *The Italian American Experience: An Encyclopedia* (New York: Garland Publishing, 2000), 480–486.

24. Barone, "Italian Americans and American Politics," 250.

25. Frank Phillips and Jenna Russell, "DiMasi said to secure speakership; Reaches deal with rival on tenure length," *Boston Globe*, September 26, 2004; Jennifer Peter, "Italians take over in Boston," *Washington Times*, October 8, 2004.

26. For a brief description of this phenomenon, see Barone, "Italian Americans and American Politics," 245.

27. CQ Staff, "Barrasso a Conservative Republican, Much in the Mold of Predecessor Thomas," *CQ Politics.com*, June 22, 2007.

28. Ibid.

29. Chris Stirewalt, "Quietly breaking old barriers; Manchin's strength shows a change in West Virginia," *Charleston (W.Va.) Daily Mail*, May 11, 2004, 4A. See, too, Barone and Cohen, *The Almanac of American Politics 2006*, 1785–1786.

30. Stirewalt, "Quietly breaking old barriers."

31. "West Virginia Senate: Byrd Flying to Reelection with 33 Point Lead," *Rasmussen Reports*, September 11, 2006.

32. According to Robert A. Slayton, "He [Al Smith] considered himself to be Irish, but technically speaking, on his father's side, the grandparents were German and Italian. He was considered, prior to John Kennedy, the best-known and most important Irish politician in the US on a national level." "Booknotes: *Empire Statesman: The Rise & Redemption of Al Smith* by Robert Slayton," Booknotes.org, May 13, 2001. www.booknotes.org/Transcript/?ProgramID=1613.

33. Leone et al., *Italians in America*, 82.

34. Cavaioli, "Governors," 270.

35. On Tancredo's views and political career, see Barone and Cohen, *The Almanac of American Politics 2006*, 337–339; Koszczuk and Stern, eds., *CQ's Politics in America 2006*, 192–193; Tom Tancredo, *In Mortal Danger: The Battle for America's Border and Security* (Nashville: WND Books, 2006); Holly Bailey, "A Border War," *Newsweek* 147 (April 3, 2006): 22–25; Sridhar Pappu, "Walking A Hard Line On Campaign Trail in Iowa; Can Anti-Immigration Fervor Keep Tancredo in the Race?" *Washington Post*, August 11, 2007, at C1.

36. The Hon. Joseph Califano, interview by author, New York, New York, December 6, 2004.

37. Ibid.; Joseph A. Califano Jr., *Inside: A Public and Private Life* (New York: Public Affairs, 2004), ix–x, 3–44.

38. Califano, *Inside*, 45–150.

39. Ibid., 151–187; Joseph A. Califano Jr., *The Triumph and Tragedy of Lyndon Johnson: The White House Years* (New York: Simon and Schuster, 1991).

40. Robert Dallek, *Flawed Giant: Lyndon Johnson and His Times, 1961–1973* (New York: Oxford University Press, 1998), 295.
41. Irving Bernstein, *Guns or Butter: The Presidency of Lyndon Johnson* (New York: Oxford University Press, 1996), 319.
42. Califano, *Inside*, 188–455.
43. Ibid., 455–463, 479–481, 485–486, 493. For more information about CASA, go to www.casacolumbia.org.
44. Califano, interview.
45. Ibid. On the anti-smoking initiative, see Califano, *Inside*, 354–358, 368, 493.
46. Califano, interview. For information about this topic, see Califano, *Inside*, 338–341.
47. Califano, interview; Califano, *Inside*, 341–342.
48. Califano, interview.
49. Califano, *Inside*.
50. Califano, interview; Califano, *Inside*, 170, 386.
51. Califano, *Inside*, 494.
52. The Hon. Frank Carlucci, interview by author, McLean, Virginia, October 6, 2004.
53. For Powell's perspective on Carlucci, see Colin L. Powell with Joseph E. Persico, *My American Journey* (New York: Random House, 1995).
54. Carlucci, interview.
55. Ibid.
56. Ibid.
57. Ibid.
58. Ibid.
59. "SecDef Histories—Frank Carlucci." www.defenselink.mil/specials/secdef_histories/bios/carlucci.htm.
60. Ibid.
61. Carlucci, interview.
62. Ibid.
63. Ibid.
64. "SecDef Histories—Frank Carlucci."
65. Carlucci, interview.
66. Ibid.
67. Ibid.
68. Frank C. Carlucci, "Tribute from Frank C. Carlucci," in Ronald Reagan, *A Shining City: The Legacy of Ronald Reagan* (New York: Simon and Schuster, 1998), 124.
69. "Lynton R. Wilson Becomes Nortel Networks Chairman of the Board; Frank C. Carlucci Retires as Chairman," News Release, April 26, 2001.
70. To learn more about The Carlyle Group, go to www.thecarlylegroup.com. See, too, "The Carlyle Group Names Louis V. Gerstner Jr. Chairman; Frank Carlucci to Become Chairman Emeritus After Nine-Year Tenure as Chairman," Press Release, November 21, 2002; Emily Thornton, "Carlyle Changes Its Stripes," *BusinessWeek* (February 12, 2007): 46–50, 57–59.
71. LaGumina, "Politics," 484; Cataldo Leone et al., *Italians in America: A Celebration* (No city: Mockingbird Press and Portfolio Press, 2001), xii, 88, 93.
72. The Hon. Leon Panetta, telephone interview by author, October 13, 2004.
73. Panetta, telephone interview.
74. "Leon Panetta," *Wikipedia, the free encyclopedia.* http://en.wikipedia.org/wiki/Leon_Panetta.
75. Panetta, telephone interview.
76. "Leon Panetta," *Wikipedia, the free encyclopedia.*
77. Ibid.
78. Ibid.; Panetta, telephone interview.

79. Panetta, telephone interview.

80. Ibid., "Leon E. Panetta: Institute Director." www.panettainstitute.org/people.html. I accessed and viewed this page in 2007.

81. Ibid. The quotation comes from the following source: "Leon E. Panetta: Institute Director."

82. Panetta, telephone interview.

83. "Leon E. Panetta: Institute Director."

84. Panetta, telephone interview.

85. Leon Panetta, "Foreword," in Cataldo Leone et al., *Italians in America: A Celebration* (No city: Mockingbird Press and Portfolio Press, 2001), xii.

86. Panetta, telephone interview. For more information about the Panetta Institute, go to www.panettainstitute.org.

87. "Leon Panetta," *Wikipedia, the free encyclopedia*; "Leon E. Panetta: Institute Director."

88. Sally Valenti, e-mails to author, February 4, 2006 and March 11, 2007.

89. Ibid.

90. Valenti, e-mail to author, February 4, 2006.

91. Ibid.; Dr. James Guttuso, e-mails to author, February 2, 2006 and March 11, 2007. My impressions of Il Circolo's 2003 gala also draw upon the following sources: Dr. James Guttuso, interviews by author, Boca Raton, Florida, May 2, 2005 and November 13, 2005. I also thank Dr. Guttuso for sharing the text of the Hon. Anthony Principi's February 2003 speech to Il Circolo with me.

92. Guttuso, e-mail to author, March 11, 2007.

93. The Hon. Anthony Principi, interview by author, Washington, D.C., November 10, 2004.

94. Ibid.; Suzanne Gamboa, "VA secretary thinks of his sons when he visits war wounded," *Army Times*, January 6, 2004.

95. Principi, interview.

96. Ibid

97. Ibid

98. "Secretary of Veterans Affairs Anthony Principi." www.whitehouse.gov/government/principi-bio .html.

99. Principi, interview.

100. Gamboa, "VA secretary thinks of his sons when he visits war wounded"; Sydney J. Freedberg Jr., "Can You Fix It, Tony?" *National Journal* 33 (January 27, 2001): 273; "A Standout at a Back-Burner Department," *National Journal* 35 (January 25, 2003): at p. 291; "'Bureaucracy Can Indeed Work,'" *National Journal* 35 (January 25, 2003): 293.

101. Principi, interview; Finlay Lewis and Otto Kreisher, "Principi touts record funding for veterans," *San Diego Union-Tribune*, December 10, 2004, A27.

102. Principi, interview.

103. See, e.g., Lewis and Kreisher, "Principi touts record funding for veterans"; Rick Maze, "Nicholson to succeed Principi as VA secretary," *Army Times*, December 9, 2004; "Vietnam Veterans of America Thanks Secretary Principi for Four Years of Exemplary Service," *U.S. Newswire*, December 9, 2004, at p. 1.

104. Anthony Principi, "Commission weighed defense and economic values in our decisions," *USA Today*, September 14, 2005, 10A; Gordon Lubold, "Walter Reed woes spur new scrutiny for base-closing plan," *Christian Science Monitor*, March 21, 2007. For more information about the 2005 Defense Base Closure and Realignment Commission, go to www.brac.gov.

105. Rick Maze, "Young vets? high jobless rate shows aid needed, panel told," *Army Times*, December 18, 2006.

106. The Hon. Peter Rodino Jr., interview by author, West Orange, New Jersey, October 7, 2004. See, too, Howard Fields, *High Crimes and Misdemeanors: The Dramatic Story of the Rodino Committee* (New York: Norton, 1978), 9-10; Joel Millman, *The Other Americans: How Immigrants Renew Our Country, Our Economy, and Our* Values (New York: Viking, 1997), 62-63.

107. Rodino, interview.

108. Ibid.

109. Ibid; "Rodino, Peter Wallace, Jr., (1909–2005)," *Biographical Directory of the United States Congress: 1774–Present.* http://bioguide.congress.gov; Michael Barone and Grant Ujifusa, *The Almanac of American Politics 1988* (Washington, D.C.: National Journal, 1987), 756–759; Alan Ehrenhalt, ed., *Politics in America, The 100th Congress* (Washington, D.C.: CQ Press, 1987), 965–968.

110. Rodino, interview.

111. Ibid.; Fields, *High Crimes and Misdemeanors*; Gerald M. Pomper, *Ordinary Heroes and American Democracy* (New Haven, Conn.: Yale University Press, 2004), 31–57.

112. Michael T. Kaufman, "Obituary: Peter Rodino, 95, chairman in Nixon hearings," *International Herald Tribune*, May 9, 2005.

113. Pomper, *Ordinary Heroes and American Democracy*, 31–57.

114. Michael Barone, "Italian Americans and American Politics," in A. Kenneth Ciongoli and Jay Parini, eds., *Beyond* The Godfather: *Italian American Writers on the Real Italian American Experience* (Hanover, N.H.: University Press of New England, 1997), 249; Michael Barone, *The New Americans: How the Melting Pot Can Work Again* (Washington, D.C.: Regnery Publishing, 2001), 120, 147–148, 192; Joseph A. Califano Jr., *Inside: A Public and Private Life* (New York: PublicAffairs, 2004), 297–298.

115. Fields, *High Crimes and Misdemeanors*, 300.

116. Ibid.; Rodino, interview; Pomper, *Ordinary Heroes and American Democracy*, 49.

117. Rodino, interview. See, too, Carol M. Swain, *Black Faces, Black Interests: The Representation of African Americans in Congress*, 2d ed. (Cambridge, Mass.: Harvard University Press, 1995), 170–171, 179–189.

118. Swain, *Black Faces, Black Interests*, 187.

119. Ibid., 188–189.

120. Rodino, interview.

121. Millman, *The Other Americans*, 62.

122. Ibid., 60–69; Rodino, interview.

123. Rodino, interview.

124. Millman, *The Other Americans*, 106–107, 130.

125. Rodino, interview; Kaufman, "Obituary: Peter Rodino, 95, chairman in Nixon hearings"; Adam Bernstein, "Rep. Peter Rodino, 95; Presided Over Nixon Impeachment Hearing," *Washington Post*, May 8, 2005, C11; Bruce Shipkowski, "Peter Rodino Jr., 96; led hearing on Nixon impeachment," *Boston Globe*, May 8, 2005.

126. "First Italian American Speaker of the House," *Italian Tribune*, November 16, 2006, 1.

127. Ibid.; Barone and Cohen, *The Almanac of American Politics 2006*, 185–189; Koszczuk and Stern, eds., *CQ's Politics in America 2006*, 86–87; "Biography: Congresswoman Nancy Pelosi, California, 8th District." www.house.gov/pelosi/biography/bio.html.

128. Ibid.

129. "Biography: Congresswoman Nancy Pelosi, California, 8th District."

130. Koszczuk and Stern, eds., *CQ's Politics in America 2006: The 109th Congress*, 86.

131. "Pelosi 49% Favorable, Other Congressional Leaders Panned by Voters," *Rasmussen Reports*, February 5, 2007.

132. Ibid.

133. "First Italian American Speaker of the House," 6.

134. Ibid., 1.

135. Russell Contreras, "Elevation of House speaker speaks to pride; Pelosi's rise cheers area's Italian-Americans," *Boston Globe*, November 30, 2006.

136. To learn more about Giuliani's life, career, and perspective, see Rudolph W. Giuliani with Ken Kurson, *Leadership* (New York: Miramax Books/Hyperion, 2002).

137. Giuliani with Kurson, *Leadership*, xvii.
138. Ibid.
139. For a recent overview of Giuliani's life and career, see Jonathan Darman, "Master of Disaster," *Newsweek* 149 (March 12, 2007): 24–33.
140. Darman, "Master of Disaster," 31; Nathan Vardi, "The Company He Keeps," *Forbes* 178 (November 13, 2006): 140.
141. Vardi, "The Company He Keeps," 140.
142. Ibid.
143. Zev Chafets, " 'Stallion' Rudy," *New York Post*, March 21, 2007.
144. Ibid.; Seth Gitell, "Benvenuto, Giuliani," *New York Sun*, June 5, 2007. To be sure, in a story about the diversity of the 2008 presidential candidates, *USA Today* noted the historic nature of Giuliani's candidacy for Italian Americans. See Susan Page, "2008 race has the face of a changing America," *USA Today*, March 12, 2007, at 1A.
145. Darman, "Master of Disaster"; Eric Pooley, "A Rudy Awakening," *Time* 169 (February 19, 2007): 42–43; Ryan Sager, "Giuliani Will Meet the Right," *New York Sun*, March 1, 2007; Dan Balz, "Giuliani Has No Real Chance with GOP Voters . . . or Does He?" *Washington Post*, March 4, 2007, at A1; Salena Zito, "Why Rudy?" (Pittsburgh, Pa.) *Tribune-Review*, March 10, 2007; David Von Drehle, "Why Is Rudy Smiling?" *Time* 169 (April 2, 2007): 34–38; June Kronholz, "Giuliani Support Hints at Shift; Emphasis on Defense, Not Social Issues, Attracts Some Republicans," *Washington Post*, July 5, 2007, A4.
146. Michael Powell and Michael Cooper, "For Giuliani, a Dizzying Free-Fall," *New York Times*, January 30, 2008; Michael Leahy and Michael D. Shear, "For Giuliani, the Trip South Started Early," *Washington Post*, January 30, 2008, at A1; Eric Lipton, "Giuliani Will Return Diminished, but Not Finished, Associates Say," *New York Times*, February 1, 2008.

CHAPTER 12: CUSTOMS, TRADITIONS, AND HISTORY

1. The paragraphs about Pearl Oliva and her family draw upon the following sources: Pearl Oliva, interview by author, Framingham, Massachusetts, April 5, 2005; Pearl Oliva, telephone interviews by author, December 13, 2004 and August 17, 2005.
2. Francis J. Cristofori, interview by author, Framingham, Massachusetts, April 5, 2005.
3. Susan Rienzi Paolercio, interview by author, New York, New York, October 20, 2005; Susan Rienzi Paolercio, telephone interview by author, August 4, 2006.
4. Susan Rienzi Paolercio, "Our Kitchen Table," in Frank Pellegrino, *Rao's Recipes from the Neighborhood* (New York: St. Martin's Press, 2004), 130. See pages 130 and 131 of this book for the full text of Paolercio's evocative essay.
5. Paolercio, telephone interview.
6. Ibid.
7. Ibid.
8. For an overview of these issues, see Richard D. Alba, "Assimilation," in Salvatore J. LaGumina et al., eds., *The Italian American Experience: An Encyclopedia* (New York: Garland Publishing, 2000), 41–44.
9. See, e.g., Joy Davia, "Ways of old enliven rich Italian heritage; Pride runs deep among the generations here," *Rochester (N.Y.) Democrat and Chronicle*, October 28, 2006.
10. "We had nothing, but we had everything": This is how one older gentleman from Boston's North End put it as he reflected on the bygone days. Erla Zwingle, "Boston's North Enders," *National Geographic* 198 (October 2000): 60.
11. Dianne Francesconi Lyon, "Baltimore's Little Italy," in Salvatore J. LaGumina et al., eds., *The Italian American Experience: An Encyclopedia* (New York: Garland Publishing, 2000), 51.
12. For more information about this community institution, go to www.pandola.baltimore.md.us.

13. The Hon. Salvatore DePiano, interview by author, Bridgeport, Connecticut, August 10, 2007.

14. Frances M. Malpezzi and William M. Clements, *Italian-American Folklore* (Little Rock, Ark.: August House Publishers, 1992); Luisa Del Giudice, "Folklore, Folklife," in Salvatore J. LaGumina et al., eds., *The Italian American Experience: An Encyclopedia* (New York: Garland Publishing, 2000), 237–245.

15. For a list of bocce courts in the United States, go to www.ibocce.com/locations.html.

16. Maureen M. Daddona and Richard Renoff, "Italian American Albanians," in Salvatore J. LaGumina et al., eds., *The Italian American Experience: An Encyclopedia* (New York: Garland Publishing, 2000), 299–300.

17. Philip F. Notarianni, "Places of Origin: Calabresi in Carbon County, Utah," in David A. Taylor and John Alexander Williams, eds., *Old Ties, New Attachments: Italian-American Folklife in the West* (Washington: Library of Congress, 1992), 78–79.

18. Blanton Owen, "The Melting Pot Works: Italians in Central Nevada," in David A. Taylor and John Alexander Williams, eds., *Old Ties, New Attachments: Italian-American Folklife in the West* (Washington: Library of Congress, 1992), 48–67.

19. Ibid., 52.

20. Ibid.

21. Ibid., 54.

22. Ibid.

23. Darryl Capparelli, interview by author, Round Rock, Texas, February 12, 2006; Amorette Capparelli, interview by author, Round Rock, Texas, February 12, 2006.

24. For more information about the Capparellis' Italian items, go to www.cafepress.com/italian things.

25. Darryl Capparelli, interview.

26. Vivian Sagona, interview by author, Pueblo, Colorado, July 13, 2006.

27. Vivian Sagona, e-mail to author, October 1, 2006.

28. Ibid.

29. Ibid.

30. Michael Pastore, interview by author, Portland, Maine, September 16, 2005; Michael Pastore, telephone interview by author, February 21, 2006.

31. Ibid.

32. Edward Albert Maruggi, "Wine Making Tradition," in Salvatore J. LaGumina et al., eds., *The Italian American Experience: An Encyclopedia* (New York: Garland Publishing, 2000), 678.

33. Luisa Del Giudice, "Foodways and Food," in Salvatore J. LaGumina et al., *The Italian American Experience: An Encyclopedia* (New York: Garland Publishing, 2000), 246; Hasia R. Diner, *Hungering for America: Italian, Irish, and Jewish Foodways in the Age of Migration* (Cambridge, Mass.: Harvard University Press, 2002), 21–47.

34. Diner, *Hungering for America*, 48–83.

35. Ibid.

36. Ibid., 83.

37. Harvey Levenstein, "The American Response to Italian Food, 1880–1930," in Carole M. Counihan, ed., *Food in the USA: A Reader* (New York: Routledge, 2002), 75–90; Harvey Levenstein, *Paradox of Plenty: A Social History of Eating in Modern America*, rev. ed. (Berkeley: University of California Press, 2003), 29–30, 51–52, 122, 223, 229–230.

38. Paul Andriulli, interview by author, Portland, Maine, October 15, 2006.

39. Del Giudice, "Foodways and Food," 247, 248.

40. Ibid., 248.

41. Levenstein, *Paradox of Plenty*, 122, 229–231, 232, 233–234, 249.

42. Elisabeth Strillacci, "A taste of Italy just next door," *North Haven (Conn.) Citizen*, April 8, 2008.

43. This vignette about Dr. Gloria Ricci Lothrop draws upon the public record and my four inter-

views with her in Los Angeles County, California, in 2005, our telephone conversations over the years, and the biographical information that she provided to me.

44. Gloria Ricci Lothrop, ed., *Fulfilling the Promise of California: An Anthology of Essays on the Italian American Experience in California* (Spokane, Wash.: California Italian American Task Force and the Arthur H. Clark Company, 2000); Gloria Ricci Lothrop, ed., *The Land Beyond: Italian Migrants in the Westward Movement: An Anthology of Essays on the Italian Settlers' Experience in the American West* (San Marino, Calif.: Patrons of Italian Culture, 2007).

45. For more information about the American Italian Historical Association, go to www.aihaweb.org.

46. Lawrence DiStasi, ed., *Una Storia Segreta: The Secret History of Italian American Evacuation and Internment during World War II* (Berkeley, Calif.: Heyday Books, 2001). See, too, Ronald Takaki, *Double Victory: A Multicultural History of America in World War II* (Boston: Little, Brown and Company, 2000), 132–136; U.S. Department of Justice, *Report to the Congress of the United States: A Review of the Restrictions on Persons of Italian Ancestry During World War II* (Washington, D.C.: U.S. Department of Justice, 2001). www.usdoj.gov/crt/Italian_Report.pdf.

47. William Grimes, "Prejudice and Politics: Sacco, Vanzetti and Fear," *New York Times*, August 15, 2007.

48. Ibid.

49. Kathleen Maggiora Rogers, interview by author, San Francisco, California, August 24, 2005.

50. Rudolph J. Vecoli, "Immigration History Research Center," in Salvatore J. LaGumina et al., eds., *The Italian American Experience: An Encyclopedia* (New York: Garland Publishing, 2000), 294–295.

51. Maria Laurino, *Were You Always an Italian?: Ancestors and Other Icons of Italian America* (New York: W. W. Norton and Company, 2000), 30–31, 52–53.

52. Ibid., 31.

53. Mary Jane Naro Lankford, interview by author, Dunedin, Florida, February 20, 2007.

54. This material draws upon my interview with Russell Bonasso in Marion County, West Virginia, on October 29, 2005, as well as our correspondence and periodic telephone conversations.

55. Carolyn Kantor, interview by author, Price, Utah, September 25, 2007.

56. Carolyn Kantor, unpublished manuscript, 2007.

57. On Carbon County's Italians, see Notarianni, "Places of Origin: Calabresi in Carbon County, Utah," 68–79; Steve Siporin, "Folklife and Survival: The Italian-Americans of Carbon County, Utah," in David A. Taylor and John Alexander Williams, eds., *Old Ties, New Attachments: Italian-American Folklife in the West* (Washington: Library of Congress, 1992), 80–93.

58. Notarianni, "Places of Origin: Calabresi in Carbon County, Utah," 70.

59. Norma Procarione, interview by author, Carbon County, Utah, September 25, 2007.

60. Larry Hyatt, interview by author, Price, Utah, September 25, 2007.

61. The paragraphs about the Italian Cultural Society draw upon the public record, materials from William Cerruti, and the following source: William Cerruti, interview by author, Sacramento, California, August 25, 2005.

62. William Cerruti, e-mail to author, June 11, 2006.

63. Unless otherwise noted, the material in the last three paragraphs of this chapter comes from the public record and my interviews with Professor/Cavaliere Philip J. DiNovo, both in Albany, New York, and by telephone, and our e-mail communications in 2006, 2007, and 2008.

64. Richard Gambino, *Blood of My Blood: The Dilemma of the Italian-Americans* (Garden City, N.Y.: Doubleday, 1974).

65. To learn more about the American Italian Heritage Association, go to www.aiha-albany.org.

66. "American Italian Museum and Cultural Center, Albany NY." www.americanitalianmuseum .org/History_AIHA.htm.

67. See the American Italian Museum and Cultural Center Web site (www.americanitalian museum.org).

CHAPTER 13: PEOPLE OF FAITH

1. Tony D'Onofrio, "Festa della Repubblica Dinner/Dance," AMHS Notiziario, July 2004. www .abruzzomoliseheritagesociety.org/July04AMSNotiziario.htm. I accessed and viewed this page in 2005.

2. For more information about the Abruzzo and Molise Heritage Society, go to www.abruzzomolise heritagesociety.org.

3. To learn more about Holy Rosary Church in Washington, see www.holyrosarychurchdc.org.

4. The material in this paragraph draws upon the information on the Holy Rosary Web site, as well as my observations when I visited the church on November 10, 2004.

5. www.holyrosarychurchdc.org/associations.htm.

6. "Casa Italiana Cultural Center." www.holyrosarychurchdc.org/casa.htm.

7. For the quotation, see the Casa Italiana Language School Web site (www.casaitaliana school.org).

8. "Meet Our Pastor: Reverend Lydio F. Tomasi, C.S., Ph. D.," www.holyrosarychurchdc.org/ pastor.html.

9. Father Tomasi's predecessor, Father Charles Zanoni, was born in the United States. He is an Italian American.

10. Father Charles Zanoni, interview by author, Washington, D.C., November 10, 2004. See, too, www.holyrosarychurchdc.org/history.html.

11. Monsignor Joseph Granato, interview by author, Newark, New Jersey, December 7, 2004. To learn more about Saint Lucy's Church, go to www.saintlucy.net.

12. Granato, interview.

13. Ibid.

14. Ibid.

15. Seventy to 75 percent of the students in the parish school are Latino. Granato, interview.

16. Granato, interview.

17. Ibid.

18. Mary Elizabeth Brown, "Religion," in Salvatore J. LaGumina et al., eds., *The Italian American Experience: An Encyclopedia* (New York: Garland Publishing, 2000), 538–542.

19. Ibid., 538.

20. Ibid.

21. Ibid.

22. Ibid.

23. Ibid.

24. Ibid.

25. Ibid.

26. Ibid.

27. Jay P. Dolan, *The American Catholic Experience: A History from Colonial Times to the Present* (Garden City, N.Y.: Doubleday and Company, 1985), 237.

28. Brown, "Religion," 539.

29. Ibid.

30. Ibid., 542.

31. Ibid.

32. Joseph A. Varacalli, "Saints," in Salvatore J. LaGumina et al., eds., *The Italian American Experience: An Encyclopedia* (New York: Garland Publishing, 2000), 563–568.

33. Brown, "Religion," 542.

34. Unless otherwise noted, the material in the paragraphs about the Fedelis comes from the public record and my interviews, telephone conversations, and e-mail communications with them in 2005, 2006, 2007, and 2008.

35. There is information on the Web about the Cathedral of St. Peter (www.stpeter-rockford.com) and St. Anthony of Padua Church (www.stanthonyrockford.com).

36. Father Gaetano Sbordone, interview by author, Brooklyn, New York, October 25, 2004; Deacon Carlo Mellace, interview by author, Brooklyn, New York, October 25, 2004.
37. Ibid.
38. "A History of St. Anthony Parish," www.girard.lib.oh.us/Community/anthist.htm.
39. Monsignor John DeMarinis, interview by author, Youngstown, Ohio, October 29, 2004.
40. Ibid.
41. For more information about Our Lady of the Rosary Roman Catholic Church, go to www.olrsd.org.
42. Father Steven Grancini, interview by author, San Diego, California, December 16, 2004.
43. Ibid.
44. "CURRICULUM VITAE: Most Reverend Nicholas DiMarzio, Ph.D., D.D."
45. Bishop Nicholas DiMarzio, interview by author, Brooklyn, New York, December 6, 2004.
46. Ibid.
47. For more information about the Diocese of Brooklyn, go to www.dioceseofbrooklyn.org.
48. DiMarzio, interview.
49. Ibid.
50. "Italian American Bishops Lead $2 Million Fundraising Effort to Construct New Italian Chapel At the Basilica of the National Shrine," www.nationalshrine.com. See, too, "Shrine to Honor Lady of Pompei," *Italian Tribune*, April 5, 2007, 1, 4.
51. Lydio F. Tomasi, "Missionaries of St. Charles—Scalabrinians," in Salvatore J. LaGumina et al., eds., *The Italian American Experience: An Encyclopedia* (New York: Garland Publishing, 2000), 384–385; Father Joseph Fugolo, interviews by author, Staten Island, New York, December 8, 2004 and May 18, 2005.
52. Father Louis Gandolfi, interview by author, Melrose Park, Illinois, January 18, 2005.
53. Ibid.
54. To learn more about St. Peter's Italian Catholic Church, go to www.stpeterschurchla.org.
55. Father Giovanni Bizzotto, interview by author, Los Angeles, California, December 17, 2004.
56. Bizzotto, interview.
57. Sister Margaret Galiardi, interview by author, Rockville Centre, New York, October 26, 2004.
58. Ibid.; Margaret Galiardi, O.P., *Encountering Mystery in the Wilderness: One Woman's Vision Quest* (San Antonio: Sor Juana Press, 2004), viii.
59. Galiardi, *Encountering Mystery in the Wilderness*.
60. Ibid., viii; Galiardi, interview.
61. Galiardi, interview.
62. Ibid.; Bart Jones, "Iraqis Focus Of Nuns' Fears; War Worries Inspire Campaign," *Newsday*, December 31, 2002.
63. Galiardi, interview.
64. Margaret Galiardi, O.P., "Dominicans Intervene at United States Congressional Hearing Regarding War with Iraq," October 11, 2002. www.franciscansinternational.org/news/article .php?id=67.
65. Galiardi, interview.
66. Mary Elizabeth Brown, "Church Leaders," in Salvatore J. LaGumina et al., eds., *The Italian American Experience: An Encyclopedia* (New York: Garland Publishing, 2000), 111–116; Rocco Caporale, "Social Class Characteristics," in Salvatore J. LaGumina et al., eds., *The Italian American Experience: An Encyclopedia* (New York: Garland Publishing, 2000), 597, 600; Gaetano L. Vincitorio, "Bernardin, Joseph Cardinal (1928–1996)," in Salvatore J. LaGumina et al., eds., *The Italian American Experience: An Encyclopedia* (New York: Garland Publishing, 2000), 60–61.
67. Cardinal Justin Rigali, interview by author, Philadelphia, Pennsylvania, January 21, 2005.
68. "Cardinal Justin Francis Rigali: Biography," www.archdiocese-phl.org/rigali/biorigali.htm; Patricia Rice, "Rigali Made Mark as Fund-Raiser," *St. Louis Post-Dispatch*, July 16, 2003, A9.

69. Rigali, interview.

70. Ibid.

71. Ibid.

72. "Cardinal Justin Francis Rigali: Biography."

73. Rice, "Rigali Made Mark as Fund-Raiser."

74. Ibid.

75. Ibid.

76. Barbara Watkins, "Pope's St. Louis visit offers lasting memories," *St. Louis Review*, October 10, 2003.

77. "Cardinal Justin Francis Rigali: Biography."

78. Bill Bergstrom, "Rigali known for quiet leadership, experience," *Houston Chronicle*, September 29, 2003, 12; David O'Reilly, "Rigali only American to be named cardinal," *Knight Ridder Tribune News Service*, October 22, 2003, at p. 1.

79. The quotations come from my interview with Cardinal Rigali. For more information about the Archdiocese of Philadelphia, go to www.archdiocese-phl.org.

80. Rigali, interview.

81. Ibid.; Cardinal Justin Rigali, letter to author, May 16, 2005.

82. Rigali, letter.

83. Rigali, interview.

84. Janae Hoffler, "In King's name, many faiths gather," *Philadelphia Tribune*, January 21, 2005, 1B.

85. Rigali, interview.

86. Ibid.

87. For information about the United States Conference of Catholic Bishops, go to www.nccbuscc.org.

88. Bishop Anthony M. Pilla, interview by author, Cleveland, Ohio, October 4, 2004.

89. Ibid.

90. Ibid.

91. Ibid.

92. See the Web page for the Bishop Anthony M. Pilla Program in Italian American Studies at www.jcu.edu/pilla/.

93. Pilla, interview. To learn about the Diocese of Cleveland, go to www.dioceseofcleveland.org.

94. Pilla, interview.

95. Ibid.

96. Ibid.

97. Ibid.

98. Ibid.

99. Archbishop Joseph A. Fiorenza, interview by author, Houston, Texas, October 12, 2004; "Archdiocese of Galveston-Houston/Most Reverend Joseph A. Fiorenza/Biography," www.diogh.org/bishops_fiorenza_bio.htm.

100. Fiorenza, interview.

101. Ibid.

102. Ibid.

103. "Archdiocese of Galveston-Houston/Most Reverend Joseph A. Fiorenza/Biography."

104. Ibid.; Tara Dooley, "New Archbishop, New Era; Mass marks major changes," *Houston Chronicle*, February 17, 2005, at p. 1.

105. Fiorenza, interview.

106. Ibid.

107. Ibid.

108. To learn more about the Archdiocese of Galveston-Houston, go to www.diogh.org.

109. Fiorenza, interview.

110. "Archdiocese of Galveston-Houston/Most Reverend Daniel N. DiNardo/Biography," www.diogh.org/bishops_dinardo_bio.htm; "Archdiocese of Galveston-Houston/Most Reverend Vincent M. Rizzotto," www.diogh.org/bishops_rizzotto_bio.htm.

111. Frank A. Salamone, "Protestantism," in Salvatore J. LaGumina et al., eds., *The Italian American Experience: An Encyclopedia* (New York: Garland Publishing, 2000), 519–520; Carmela E. Santoro, "Rhode Island," in Salvatore J. LaGumina et al., eds., *The Italian American Experience: An Encyclopedia* (New York: Garland Publishing, 2000), 551.

112. Dr. Ed Morrell, interview by author, Provo, Utah, September 25, 2007.

113. "BELLA SION—Biographies," www.bellasion.org/biogrf.html.

114. Terri Nicole Sawyer, interview by author, Provo, Utah, September 25, 2007.

115. Terri Nicole Sawyer, e-mail to author, October 20, 2007.

116. To learn more about Rabbi Barbara Aiello, go to http://rabbibarbara.com.

117. Federico and Stephen Moramarco, *Italian Pride: 101 Reasons to Be Proud You're Italian* (New York: MJF Books, 2000), 32–33; Jack Nusan Porter, "Italian American Jews," in Salvatore J. LaGumina et al., eds., *The Italian American Experience: An Encyclopedia* (New York: Garland Publishing, 2000), 302–303.

118. Porter, "Italian American Jews," 303.

119. Ibid., 302.

120. The paragraphs about the Carrico family draw upon the following sources: Mark Carrico, interview by author, Wausau, Wisconsin, March 12, 2007; Mark Carrico, telephone interview by author, July 24, 2007; Mark Carrico, e-mail to author, October 16, 2007.

121. "My father worked many jobs," remembers Mark Carrico. "One that always sticks in my mind was when he was a short order cook at the Snowball Diner in Indianapolis making nine cents an hour to pay for college." Carrico, e-mail.

122. Helen Kern, interview by author, El Paso County, Texas, January 9, 2005; Ralph Kern, interview by author, El Paso County, Texas, January 9, 2005.

CHAPTER 14: PRESERVING AND CELEBRATING AMERICA'S ITALIAN HERITAGE

1. Jerry Colangelo, interview by author, Phoenix, Arizona, September 28, 2005.

2. Ibid.

3. "Phoenix Suns CEO Jerry Colangelo to Head U.S. Basketball Team," *Italian Tribune*, July 21, 2005, 8.

4. Jerry Colangelo, "Olympics: Putting Together the U.S. Men's Basketball Team," *Washington-Post.com*, August 21, 2008; Nick Friedell, "Jerry Colangelo deserves credit for U.S.A. Basketball rebirth," *Yahoo! Sports*, August 23, 2008; Sean Deveney, "Colangelo deserves credit in Team USA's unselfish approach," *SportingNews.com*, August 24, 2008; Pete Thamel, "A Question in the Afterglow: What's Next for U.S. Men's Basketball?" *Rings Blog—NYTimes.com*, August 24, 2008.

5. Colangelo, interview.

6. Ibid.

7. Jerry Colangelo with Len Sherman, *How You Play the Game: Lessons for Life from the Billion-Dollar Business of Sports* (New York: Amacom, 1999), 12.

8. Colangelo, interview.

9. Ibid.

10. Ibid.

11. "SUNS: Jerry Colangelo Bio," www.nba.com/suns/news/jerry_colangelo_bio.html.

12. Ibid.

13. Colangelo, interview.

14. Ibid.

15. "SUNS: Jerry Colangelo Bio."

16. Ibid.; "Phoenix Suns CEO Jerry Colangelo to Head U.S. Basketball Team."

17. Colangelo, interview.

18. For an overview of Colangelo's life and perspective, see Colangelo with Sherman, *How You Play the Game.*

19. Colangelo, interview.

20. Ibid.; "Phoenix Suns CEO Jerry Colangelo to Head U.S. Basketball Team."

21. Colangelo, interview.

22. Ibid.

23. Ibid.

24. Unless otherwise noted, the material in the paragraphs about the Italian-American Club of Livonia draws upon the public record, my telephonic and e-mail communications with Mary Galasso in 2007 and 2008, the Web sites for the Italian American Club of Livonia (www.iacl.us) and the Italian American Banquet and Conference Center of Livonia (www.iabc-livonia.com), and my interviews with Mrs. Galasso and numerous Club members in Livonia, Michigan, on September 13, 2007. I visited and addressed the Italian American Club of Livonia in Livonia, Michigan, on that day.

25. Nick Giammarco, e-mail to author, September 18, 2007.

26. Ibid.

27. Luisa Del Giudice, "Folklore, Folklife," in Salvatore J. LaGumina et al., eds., *The Italian American Experience: An Encyclopedia* (New York: Garland Publishing, 2000), 245; John Andreozzi, "Organizations," in Salvatore J. LaGumina et al., eds., *The Italian American Experience: An Encyclopedia* (New York: Garland Publishing, 2000), 434–438.

28. "Clubs, Associations & Societies." www.italianlosangeles.org.

29. See, e.g., Richard D. Alba, "Identity and Ethnicity among Italians and Other Americans of European Ancestry," in Lydio F. Tomasi, Piero Gastaldo, and Thomas Row, eds., *The Columbus People: Perspectives in Italian Immigration to the Americas and Australia* (Staten Island, N.Y.: Center for Migration Studies and Fondazione Giovanni Agnelli, 1994), 32, 33.

30. Professor Carlo Sclafani, interview by author, Valhalla, New York, September 11, 2006.

31. Frank Passaro Jr., interview by author, Towson, Maryland, September 12, 2006.

32. See www.festaitaliana.com.

33. For information about WisItalia, go to www.wisitalia.org.

34. "Wisconsin Italian-American Organizations." www.wisitalia.org/pages/links/clubs.html.

35. To learn more about the Roma Lodge, go to www.romalodge.org.

36. This material draws upon my visits to the Roma Lodge, my attendance at the Roma Lodge Italian Festival, and my interviews and e-mail communications with Don and Rosemary Cicero and Judy and Jerry Perona in 2006, 2007, and 2008.

37. Jerry Perona, e-mail to author, October 1, 2008.

38. To learn about the Westchester Italian Cultural Center, go to www.wiccny.org.

39. Rosemarie Falcone, e-mail to author, September 20, 2008.

40. The paragraphs about the Popolizio family draw upon my interviews with Frank Popolizio and Diane Popolizio in North Branford, Connecticut, on March 14, 2007, and my e-mail correspondence with Frank Popolizio in 2007 and 2008.

41. Amulio Masini, questionnaire to author, August 9, 2005; Amulio Masini, interview by author, Mechanicsville, Virginia, September 10, 2006.

42. Masini, questionnaire.

43. Ibid. I visited and addressed the OSIA Giuseppe Verdi Lodge #315 in Mechanicsville, Virginia, on September 10, 2006.

44. See www.richmonditalianfestival.com.

45. Dr. James Vitale, telephone interview by author, July 16, 2005. For more information about the Italian American Club of Maui, go to www.italianamericanclubofmaui.com.

46. Vitale, telephone interview.

47. Bill Casey, interview by author, Taylors, South Carolina, November 19, 2006.

48. "Welcome to the Italian-American Club." www.iacgg.org.

49. Ann Turco, interview by author, Omaha, Nebraska, February 21, 2005; Charles Turco, interview by author, Omaha, Nebraska, February 21, 2005.

50. Ibid.

51. Therese Quattrocchi Simpson, interviews by author, Bradenton, Florida, February 17, 2007 and October 21, 2007. I presented programs about Italian-American topics at the OSIA Bradenton Lodge #2782 on February 17, 2007, and October 21, 2007.

52. Therese Quattrocchi Simpson, e-mail to author, June 10, 2008.

53. Dennis Caldirola, telephone interview by author, July 28, 2005. To learn more about Festa Italiana Seattle!, go to www.festaseattle.com.

54. Caldirola, telephone interview.

55. Ibid.

56. Ibid.

57. Mary Elizabeth Brown, "Religion," in Salvatore J. LaGumina et al., eds., *The Italian American Experience: An Encyclopedia* (New York: Garland Publishing, 2000), 538–542; Joseph A. Varacalli, "Saints," in Salvatore J. LaGumina et al., eds., *The Italian American Experience: An Encyclopedia* (New York: Garland Publishing, 2000), 563–567.

58. Denise Mangieri DiCarlo, "The Italian Festa in the United States as an Expression of Ethnic Pride," in Lydio F. Tomasi, Piero Gastaldo, and Thomas Row, eds., *The Columbus People: Perspectives in Italian Immigration to the Americas and Australia* (Staten Island, N.Y.: Center for Migration Studies and Fondazione Giovanni Agnelli, 1994), 79–88; Denise Mangieri DiCarlo, "Festa," in Salvatore J. LaGumina et al., *The Italian American Experience: An Encyclopedia* (New York: Garland Publishing, 2000), 222–225.

59. Del Giudice, "Folklore, Folklife," 239.

60. For information about these festivals, go to www.wvihf.com (the West Virginia Italian Heritage Festival) and www.italyfest.com (the Upper Ohio Valley Italian Festival).

I interviewed Stephen Pishner and Rachel Torchia of the West Virginia Italian Heritage Festival in Clarksburg, West Virginia, on October 28, 2005. The same day, I spoke about the themes of Italian-American progress at an event sponsored by the West Virginia Italian Heritage Festival in Clarksburg.

In addition, I participated in a roundtable discussion with leaders of the Upper Ohio Valley Italian Festival in Wheeling, West Virginia, on October 29, 2005.

61. Hurley, Wisconsin, resident Paul Sturgul, an elder law attorney and historian, researches the Italian-American presence in the Lake Superior Region and other historical topics. Mr. Sturgul is of Italian and Polish descent.

62. Russell M. Magnaghi, "Occupations of Italian Immigrants in Turn-of-the-Century America: Mining," in Salvatore J. LaGumina et al., eds., *The Italian American Experience: An Encyclopedia* (New York: Garland Publishing, 2000), 423.

63. "Sons of Italy Releases 2008 Festival Directory," Press Release, February 26, 2008. www.osia.org/public/newsroom/pro2_26_08.asp.

See, too, "The Sons of Italy 2008 Italian Festival Directory." www.osia.org/public/pdf/2008_festival_directory.pdf.

64. "Sons of Italy Releases 2008 Festival Directory."

65. See www.feastofla.org.

66. John Alexander Williams, "The Columbus Complex," in David A. Taylor and John Alexander Williams, eds., *Old Ties, New Attachments: Italian-American Folklife in the West* (Washington: Library of Congress, 1992), 196–209; Frank J. Cavaioli, "Christopher Columbus (1451–1506)," in Salvatore J. LaGumina et al., eds., *The Italian American Experience: An Encyclopedia* (New York: Garland Publishing, 2000), 129–130; Matthew Frye Jacobson, *Roots Too: White Ethnic Revival in*

Post–Civil Rights America (Cambridge, Mass.: Harvard University Press, 2006), 336–346; Dr. Joseph V. Scelsa, "Why We Honor Columbus," *Queens (N.Y.) Gazette*, October 11, 2006.

67. Cavaioli, "Christopher Columbus (1451–1506)," 130.

68. Del Giudice, "Folklore, Folklife," 238.

69. This account about the Gulf Coast Italian Culture Society draws upon multiple sources, particularly my e-mail communications and telephone conversations with Mary Amabile Palmer, the Society's current president.

I have visited Sarasota, Florida, on two occasions to learn about the Gulf Coast Italian Culture Society. On November 16, 2005, I interviewed a group of GCICS leaders in Sarasota at the home of Arthur Castraberti. And on October 21, 2007, I had numerous conversations with many GCICS members and officers at the Society's Welcome Back Brunch in Sarasota. I addressed the Society during the latter event.

70. Mary Amabile Palmer, *Cucina di Calabria: Treasured Recipes and Family Traditions from Southern Italy* (Boston: Faber and Faber, 1997).

71. Mary Amabile Palmer, *Cucina di Calabria: Treasured Recipes and Family Traditions from Southern Italy* (New York: Hippocrene Books, 2004).

72. See Jerre Mangione and Ben Morreale, *La Storia: Five Centuries of the Italian American Experience* (New York: HarperPerennial, 1993), 405–409; Luciano J. Iorizzo, "Business and Entrepreneurship," in Salvatore J. LaGumina et al., eds., *The Italian American Experience: An Encyclopedia* (New York: Garland Publishing, 2000), 73–83; Cataldo Leone et al., *Italians in America: A Celebration* (Washington, D.C.: Mockingbird Press and Portfolio Press/National Italian American Foundation, 2001), 47–77.

73. See the Web sites for Barnes & Noble (www.barnesandnoble.com and www.barnesandnoble inc.com) and GameStop (www.gamestop.com).

74. "Leonard Riggio," Barnes & Noble Booksellers. www.barnesandnobleinc.com/our_company/ management_team/leonard_riggio/leonard_riggio.html.

75. Ibid.

76. Leonard Riggio, telephone interview by author, April 20, 2005.

77. "Leonard Riggio," Barnes & Noble Booksellers.

78. "500 Largest U.S. Corporations," *Fortune* 157 (May 5, 2008): F-23, F-24.

79. See "Stephen Riggio," Barnes & Noble Booksellers. www.barnesandnobleinc.com/our_company/ management_team/steve_riggio/steve_riggio.html.

80. Riggio, telephone interview.

81. Ibid.

82. Devin Leonard, "GameStop Racks Up the Points," *Fortune* 157 (June 9, 2008): 108–110, 112.

83. "500 Largest U.S. Corporations," *Fortune* 157 (May 5, 2008): F-17, F-18.

84. Leonard, "GameStop Racks Up the Points," 108–110, 112.

85. "Leonard Riggio," Barnes & Noble Booksellers.

86. Riggio, telephone interview.

87. Ibid.

88. Ibid.

CHAPTER 15: THE TIES THAT BIND

1. Ambassador Peter Secchia, interview by author, Grand Rapids, Michigan, February 17, 2005. For additional biographical information about Amb. Secchia, go to www.secchia.com.

2. Secchia, interview.

3. Ibid.

4. Ibid.

5. "About UFP: Historical Timeline." www.ufpi.com/about/time2.htm. The Universal Forest Products Web site (www.ufpi.com) provides much useful information about this company.

6. "The *Fortune 1000* Ranked Within Industries," *Fortune* 155 (April 30, 2007): F-57.

7. "Secchia provides lead gift, Grand Action to help campaign as msu board launches plan to change the way medicine is taught, delivered," News Release, January 18, 2007.

8. Pietro Secchia was a longtime member of the Order Sons of Italy in America.

9. "Peter F. Secchia—Biographical Notes." www.wmwta.org/html/events.html. I accessed and viewed this page in 2006. "Ellis Island Medal of Honor: Peter F. Secchia." www.neco.org/awards/recipients/petersecchia.html.

10. Robert A. Rosenblatt, "2 Close Bush Allies in Line for Commerce Post," *Los Angeles Times*, December 6, 1991, D2.

11. Secchia, interview.

12. Ibid. For more information about John Cabot University, go to www.johncabot.edu.

13. "U.S. Ambassador & Business Executive Peter Secchia to be Honored at Italian American Gala in Washington, D.C.," *Italian Voice*, October 13, 2005.

14. David D. Kirkpatrick, "Advocacy Groups Prepare New Ad Campaigns on Alito," *New York Times*, January 3, 2006, A14.

15. Secchia, interview.

16. The material in this vignette about Lido Cantarutti and the Italian Film Festival draws upon the public record and the following source: Cav. Uff. Lido Cantarutti, interview by author, San Rafael, California, August 26, 2005.

17. For more information concerning the Italian Film Festival, go to www.italianfilm.com. In addition, this Web site contains biographical material about Mr. Cantarutti.

18. Betty Boyd Caroli, "Return Migration," in Salvatore J. LaGumina et al., eds., *The Italian American Experience: An Encyclopedia* (New York: Garland Publishing, 2000), 548–550; Jerre Mangione and Ben Morreale, *La Storia: Five Centuries of the Italian American Experience* (New York: HarperPerennial, 1993), 89.

19. Ernest E. Rossi, "Cold War: Italian Americans and Italy," in Salvatore J. LaGumina et al., eds., *The Italian American Experience: An Encyclopedia* (New York: Garland Publishing, 2000), 120–123; Ernest E. Rossi, "Cold War: U.S. Foreign Policy toward Italy," in Salvatore J. LaGumina et al., eds., *The Italian American Experience: An Encyclopedia* (New York: Garland Publishing, 2000), 123–125; Marco Rimanelli, "United States–Italian Diplomatic Relations, 1776–1945," in Salvatore J. LaGumina et al., eds., *The Italian American Experience: An Encyclopedia* (New York: Garland Publishing, 2000), 646–655.

20. See, e.g., Lawrence Di Stasi, "How World War II Iced Italian American Culture," in Ishmael Reed, ed., *Multi-America: Essays on Cultural Wars and Cultural Peace* (New York: Viking, 1997), 169–178; Salvatore J. LaGumina, *The Humble and the Heroic: Wartime Italian Americans* (Youngstown, N.Y.: Cambria Press, 2006).

21. C. Alan Joyce, ed., *The World Almanac and Book of Facts 2008* (New York: World Almanac Books, 2008), 67.

22. Ibid., 72.

23. Italian Americans have raised funds for Italy's periodic earthquake-relief efforts over the years.

24. Minister Antonio Bandini, interview by author, New York, New York, October 20, 2005; "Speaker of the Week: 11/29/05; Hon. Antonio Bandini—Consul General of Italy in New York." www.nyrotary.org/oospeakers/112905.asp. I accessed and viewed this page in 2006.

25. To learn more about the Consulate General of Italy—New York, go to www.italconsulnyc.org.

26. Bandini, interview.

27. Ibid.

28. Ibid.

29. Ibid.

30. Ibid.

31. Angela Bizzarro, interview by author, Pompano Beach, Florida, January 28, 2005.

32. Ibid.

33. Ibid.

34. Sharon DeBartolo Carmack, "Genealogy and Family History," in Salvatore J. LaGumina et al., eds., *The Italian American Experience: An Encyclopedia* (New York: Garland Publishing, 2000), 259–260. See, too, Sharon DeBartolo Carmack, *Italian-American Family History: A Guide to Researching and Writing About Your Heritage* (Baltimore: Genealogical Publishing Company, 1997; John Philip Colletta, *Finding Italian Roots: The Complete Guide for Americans*, 2d ed. (Baltimore: Genealogical Publishing Company, 2003).

35. Gr. Uff. Joseph Maselli, interview by author, New Orleans, Louisiana, April 25, 2005.

36. www.ellisislandrecords.org.

37. See, e.g., Frank Passaro, "Finding Nonno," *Glimpse* (Fall 2006): 34–39.

38. The sources for the paragraphs about Susan DeFazio and her family are: Susan DeFazio, interview by author, Des Moines, Iowa, February 20, 2005; Susan DeFazio, letter to author, May 16, 2005; Susan DeFazio, e-mail to author, January 21, 2008.

39. The Hon. Renato Turano, interview by author, Berwyn, Illinois, March 11, 2005.

40. Doug Pozzo, interview by author, Culver City, California, December 18, 2004.

41. Carlo Giraulo, telephone interview by author, August 25, 2005.

42. Carlo Giraulo, e-mail to author, January 23, 2008.

43. Father John J. Richetta, interview by author, Kenosha, Wisconsin, October 20, 2004.

44. George Silvestri Jr., interview by author, Novato, California, August 26, 2005.

45. Joyce, ed., *The World Almanac and Book of Facts 2008*, 79, 80.

46. Michael Pastore, for one, remembered in a 2005 interview that his father kissed the ground at Logan International Airport after he returned to the United States from a trip to Italy. Michael Pastore, interview by author, Portland, Maine, September 16, 2005.

47. Bob Masullo, "It was a very good year," *Fra Noi* 46 (June 2006): 19, 112.

48. Ibid., 112.

49. Masullo, "It was a very good year," 19.

50. Aldo Svaldi, interview by author, Westminster, Colorado, July 12, 2006.

51. Unless otherwise noted, the material in the paragraphs about Cav. David Gratta and his family comes from my telephone conversations and e-mail communications with Mr. Gratta in 2005, 2006, 2007, and 2008, as well as a questionnaire that he filled out for me in 2005.

52. Nikki Davis Maute, "Man's mission: Italian in schools," *Hattiesburg (Miss.) American*, January 2, 2005.

53. The quotation is from a personal communication with Mr. Gratta. See, too, "Officials Look to Expand Italian Language Program To Other Schools," News Release, August 22, 2008.

54. For a useful overview of the Italian diplomatic presence in the United States, go to www.ambwashingtondc.esteri.it.

55. There are Honorary Consuls, Honorary Vice Consuls, and Corresponding Consuls of Italy in different parts of the United States. The ranks of such individuals include Maria Scordo Allen, the Honorary Vice Consul of Italy in Denver, Colorado; Mario Daniele, the Honorary Vice Consul of Italy in Rochester, New York; and Cav. Joseph Delfino, the Corresponding Consul of Italy in Naples, Florida.

56. For information about the Consulate General of Italy–Miami, go to www.italconsmiami.com.

57. The Hon. Gianfranco Colognato, questionnaire to author, July 20, 2005.

58. "InGentibus—Dr. Gianfranco Colognato." www.ingentibus.org/en/about/Organization/cvs/Gianfranco_Colognato.htm.

59. Ibid.; Colognato, questionnaire.

60. Andy Kanengiser, "Italian pushed for Miss. classrooms; Leaders from Italy pledge financial support for pilot program," *(Jackson, Miss.)* Clarion-Ledger, August 21, 2004; Josh Gelinas, "Aiken leaders show Italian official what state has to offer," *Augusta (Ga.) Chronicle*, March 27, 2005.

61. Colognato, questionnaire.

62. Ibid.

63. Ibid.

64. For information about Sister Cities, go to www.sister-cities.org.

65. Luisa Del Giudice, "Folklore, Folklife," in Salvatore J. LaGumina et al., eds., *The Italian American Experience: An Encyclopedia* (New York: Garland Publishing, 2000), 241.

66. Ibid.

67. See "Italiani nel Mondo" at the Ministero degli Affari Esteri. www.esteri.it/MAE/IT/Italiani _nel_Mondo/.

68. See, e.g., Laura Smith-Spark, "Expat politicians find their feet in Rome," *BBC News*, May 12, 2006.

69. Howard LaFranchi, "Bush visits a Europe ever further away," *Christian Science Monitor*, February 18, 2005.

70. Ibid.

71. Ibid.

72. "New U.S. Ambassador to Italy Meets with Sons of Italy; Collaboration to promote stronger U.S.-Italy exchange in business and education discussed," OSIA Press Release, July 15, 2005. www.osia.org/public/newsroom/pr7_15_05.asp.

73. Ibid.

74. Professor Carmel Ruffolo, interview by author, Kenosha, Wisconsin, May 22, 2006.

75. Ibid.

76. Loretta Baldassar, *Visits Home: Migration Experiences between Italy and Australia* (Carlton South, Australia: Melbourne University Press, 2001), 27.

77. Ibid.

78. Ruffolo, interview, May 22, 2006.

79. For material about Bruno, see Dominic Candeloro, comp., *Voices of America: Italians in Chicago* (Charleston, S.C.: Arcadia, 2001), 73–80.

80. Patricia Gerlach, "The Fine Art of Furniture Finishing," *from house to HOME* 3 (Fall 2006): 22–23.

81. Cav. Joseph Bruno, interview by author, Stone Park, Illinois, October 23, 2006.

82. Professor Carmel Ruffolo, interview by author, Kenosha, Wisconsin, June 17, 2008.

83. Gerlach, "The Fine Art of Furniture Finishing"; Jim Distasio, "Crowning achievement," *Fra Noi*, n.d.; Jim Distasio, "Festa della Famiglia," *Fra Noi*, n.d.

84. Ruffolo, interview, June 17, 2008.

85. Ruffolo, interview, May 22, 2006.

Epilogue: The Future

1. All the material in this vignette comes from the public record and my interviews with Francesco and Lucrezia Lindia in Greenwich, Connecticut, and Westchester County, New York, in December 2004, September 2006, and March 2007. Ms. Lindia also answered a questionnaire for me; her answers inform the material that I write about her and Mr. Lindia.

2. Lucrezia G. Lindia and Gary A. Milgrom, *Italian for Communication Level II*, 2d ed. (Lancaster, Va.: Curriculum Press, 2005).

3. Francine Prose, "Immersed in Italian," *More* (March 2004): 72.

4. Professor Alan Balboni, interview by author, Las Vegas, Nevada, June 14, 2005.

5. Lisa Guido, interview by author, Kenosha, Wisconsin, September 22, 2004.

6. Daniela Johnson, interview by author, Narragansett, Rhode Island, April 5, 2005.

7. Thomas Ragona, interview by author, El Paso, Texas, January 10, 2005.

8. Ann Turco, interview by author, Omaha, Nebraska, February 21, 2005; Charles Turco, interview by author, Omaha, Nebraska, February 21, 2005.

9. Monsignor Dominic Bottino, interview by author, Hammonton, New Jersey, October 12, 2005.

10. Ronald DiVecchio, interviews by author, Erie, Pennsylvania, October 27, 2005 and June 12, 2006.

11. Vince Pardo, interview by author, Tampa, Florida, November 16, 2005.

12. Linda Sepe, interview by author, Round Rock, Texas, February 12, 2006.

13. Nicholas Maiolo, letter to author, May 12, 2006; Nicholas Maiolo, interview by author, Mechanicsville, Virginia, September 10, 2006. I thank Mr. Maiolo for answering my questions and sending the DVDs of his productions to me.

14. Grant "Micheli" Scalise, interviews by author, Rockford, Illinois, November 1, 2005 and May 3, 2006.

15. Ibid.

16. *Report on Italian American Federal Judges* (Washington, D.C.: Sons of Italy Commission for Social Justice, 2005).

17. Judge Mario Rossetti, telephone interview by author, May 1, 2006.

18. Ibid.

19. Cataldo Leone et al., *Italians in America: A Celebration* (Washington, D.C.: Mockingbird Press and Portfolio Press/National Italian American Foundation, 2001), dust jacket.

20. I thank Joseph N. Grano for sending useful materials to me about the efforts to honor Constantino Brumidi over the years.

21. "Chairman Joint Chiefs of Staff: General Peter Pace." www.jcs.mil/bios/bio_pace.html. I accessed and viewed this page in 2006. To be sure, General Pace celebrates his father's Italian-immigrant heritage. See Glenn Frankel and Daniela Deane, "General Speaks of Immigrant Father; Congressional Hearing Turns Personal," *Washington Post*, July 11, 2006, A3.

22. T. Trent Gegax and Evan Thomas, "The Family Business," *Newsweek* 145 (June 20, 2005): 24–31.

23. Jerre Mangione and Ben Morreale, *La Storia: Five Centuries of the Italian American Experience* (New York: HarperPerennial, 1993), 384.

24. Michael Barone, *The New Americans: How the Melting Pot Can Work Again* (Washington, D.C.: Regnery Publishing, 2001), 148.

25. See, e.g., David D. Kirkpatrick, "Court Nominee Presents Father as Role Model," *New York Times*, December 5, 2005.

26. David D. Kirkpatrick, "Advocacy Groups Prepare New Ad Campaigns on Alito," *New York Times*, January 3, 2006, A14.

27. Dr. Gloria Ricci Lothrop, interview by author, Pasadena, California, December 9, 2005.

28. The story is known as "The Joy of Growing Up Italian" or, less commonly, "The Joy of Growing Up Italian American." See "The Joy of Growing Up Italian American." www.italiamerica.org/id38.htm.

29. Tom Profenno, interview by author, Portland, Maine, September 16, 2005.

30. Rudolph J. Vecoli, "Are Italian Americans Just White Folks?" in A. Kenneth Ciongoli and Jay Parini, eds., *Beyond The Godfather: Italian American Writers on the Real Italian American Experience* (Hanover, N.H.: University Press of New England, 1997), 311–322.

31. Ibid., 319–320.

32. Barone, *The New Americans*, 117–192.

ACKNOWLEDGMENTS

G*reen, White, and Red* is the story of the seventeen million–plus Italian Americans and, more generally, a narrative that involves all of us as Americans in some way or another. As such, this book draws upon the stories of hundreds of people throughout the United States. Numerous individuals shared their insights with me, facilitated my contact with interviewees, invited me to speak in specific venues, and helped me to learn more about specific aspects of Italian-American culture and history.

It is, of course, impossible to cite everyone's story in the book or to mention all the individuals who coordinated my speaking appearances and shared their views, thoughts, experiences, and perspectives with me before, during, and after my presentations and in other contexts. Please note that I appreciate everyone's input very much.

In particular, I wish to thank the following:

Barbara Tenaglia Abela; Father Gianni Agostinelli; Frank and Sheri Agostini; Anthony Aiello; Luigi Aiello; Ricardo Alas; Antonella Albano; Professor Diane Albertini; Lilia Albertini; Shirley Albertini; Dr. Emanuele Alfano; Ida and John Alia; Maria Scordo Allen; Carlo Amodio; Patricia Anderson; Comm. Mario Andretti; Paul and Toni Andriulli; John Anello Jr.; Philip and Romana Antonelli; Richard Apodaca; Theresa Argento; Professor Carmen Argondizzo; Comm. Lawrence Auriana; Martha Bache-Wiig; Anthony and Kathy Bacino; Father Ben Bacino; Comm. Paola Bagnatori; Emil and Iris Bagneschi; Professor Alan Balboni; Peter Balistreri; Minister Antonio Bandini; The Hon. Peter Barca; Josephine Bardelli; Helen and Joseph Baroco; Maria Baroco; Judy

Cotone Barrows; Carmen and Dan Basalone; Paul Basile, Sister Ruth Battaglia; Alice and Bill Battista; Bob Battista; David Beccue and Valeri DeCastris; Kathy Becker; Bertha Belmontes; Mario Bertagna; Charlotte Wright Bertagnolli and Donald Bertagnolli; Flora Bertagnolli; Gerald Bertagnolli; Virgil Bertani; Joe Betzala; Alan Biondi; Joe Bisciglia; Graziella Bivona; Angela Bizzarro; Father Giovanni Bizzotto; Professor Benita Blessing; Rosemary Blumberg; Ray Boggio; Anita Bologna; Claire and Sando Bologna; Father Vincent Bommarito; Russell Bonasso; Karen Bonomo; Walter Borla; Alfred Bossi; Monsignor Dominic Bottino; Dr. Julianne Mamana Boyd; Bruna Petrarca Boyle and Vin Dudzik; Camillo Breggia; Nancy Brennan; Scott Brogna; Gerald Browder Jr.; Greg Browder; Susan G. Browder; Aimee Brown; Cav. Joseph Bruno; Tony Bruno; Vincent Bueti; Jerry and Rosemary Bullock; S. H. Bill Burgin; Debbie Buscaglia; and Evelyn and Joseph Bussone.

Barbara and Frank Caesar; Julie Calabrese; Patrizia Calce; Dennis Caldirola; Carmela Calia; The Hon. Joseph Califano; Linda and Robert Calvisi; Dr. Giuseppina Candia; Cav. Uff. Lido Cantarutti; Carol and Joseph Capano; Joseph and Yolanda Capogreco; Lisa Capogreco; Pasquale Capogreco; Richard Capozza; Amorette and Darryl Capparelli; Rosalie Galasso Caputo and Silvio J. Caputo Jr.; Carl and Nancy Carani; Josephine Carbone; Louis Carleo; The Hon. Frank Carlucci; Mark Carrico; Calogero Cascio; Bill Casey; Cav. Arthur Castraberti; Steven Castraberti; Mary Ann and Pete Cerminara; Comm. Joseph R. Cerrell; William Cerruti; Frank Cerullo; Truby Chiaviello; Madeline and Nick Ciani; Antonino Ciccotelli; Don and Rosemary Cicero; Grace Ciolino; Dr. A. Kenneth Ciongoli; Professor Gaetano Cipolla; Patricia Civitate; Geoffrey Claroni; Jerry Colangelo; Edith Cardiello Coleman; The Hon. Gianfranco Colognato; Dr. Adriano Comollo; Frank Cona; Leo Conoscente; Joyce Coopersmith; Alessio and Josephine Coppola; Marie and Pat Corsentino; Dr. Thomas Cortese Jr.; Carole Cosenza; James Costanzo; Daniel Cotroneo; Ray Crenna; Adam Crescenzi; Josephine and Nicholas Cristy; Michael Critelli; David Cuicchi; Dr. Frank D'Alessandro; Carlo Dalla; Professor Carol Damian and Vincent Damian Jr.; Mario Daniele; Joseph Dardis; Patricia D'Ascoli; Michael Davanzo; Marge DeBenedetto; Tom DeCarlo; Andrew Decker; Joseph DeFazio Sr. and Mary DeFazio; Susan DeFazio; Mary and Neil DeGoey; Mario Delano Jr.; Estelle Delfino and Cav. Joseph Delfino; Armando Delicato; Lisa Del Torto; John Deluca; Monsignor John DeMarinis; Armand De

Marino Jr.; John DeMary; Mary Ann De Meo; The Hon. Salvatore DePiano; Flora DePond and Dr. Pete J. DePond; Dr. Dona De Sanctis; Comm. Frank J. De Santis; Kathy De Santis; Alfred and Bernice De Simone; Dott. Guerino D'Ignazio; Dott. Gaetano Dileo; Bishop Nicholas DiMarzio; Mary DiNovo and Professor/Cavaliere Philip J. DiNovo; Alda Di Tomassi; Ronald DiVecchio; Dr. James Divita; Mario D'Occhio; Donald Donato; Frances and Jasper Drago; Ron Dudas; and Angelo Dundee.

Robin Easter; Patti-Jo Esposito; Giancarlo Fadin and Christine Zgradic; Antonio Faiolo; Rosemarie Falcone; Kathleen Fantazzi; Eugene Fedeli and Shirley Martignoni Fedeli; Donato Federico; Charles Ferraro; Frank Ferraro; Dominick and Joan Filipponi; Patrick Fiore; Frank Fiorentino; Archbishop Joseph A. Fiorenza; Richard Floreani; Michele Foffi; Father Thomas Foudy; Albert and Laura Frappollo; Sister Marianna Frigo; Cav. Dominic Frinzi; Marion Todd Frizzell; Father Joseph Fugolo; Emilio and Josephine Galassini; Mario and Mary Galasso; Sister Margaret Galiardi; Anthony Gallina; Marie and Salvatore Gambino; Father Louis Gandolfi; Jill Gant; Oscar and Santina Garcia; Father Rafael Garcia; Professor Fred Gardaphé; Phyllis and Salvatore Gargiulo; Marsha Garland; Gino Gaudio; Robert Gaudio; Giuseppe Geloso; Pat Gentile; Bob Giacoletti; Frank Giacoletti; Joe Giacoletti; Nick Giammarco; Don Giovanni; Carlo Giraulo; Nancy Gough; Father Gerald Grace; Monsignor Joseph Granato; Father Steven Grancini; Vincent Granito; Joseph N. Grano; Cav. David Gratta; Bob and Marie Graziano; Charles Greco; Chester Grossi; The Hon. Frank Guarini Jr.; Domenick and Rose Guarnieri; Vittorio Guerrera; Lisa Guido; Joseph Guido Sr.; Dr. James Guttuso and Lucy Guttuso; Dr. Henry Guzzo; Jane and Sheldon Hall; Asma Hasan; Seeme Hasan; Tommy Haws; The Hon. Carole Heffley; Thomas Hemman; Alessandra DiCicco Higgs; and Larry Hyatt.

Len Iaquinta; John Illia Jr.; Michael Illia; Gloria Ingleman; Phyllis Milozzo Jensen; Jean Jimenez; Daniela Johnson; Carolyn Kantor; Buddy and Mary Joe Kaumo; Helen and Ralph Kern; Paul Kienitz; Catherine Killoran; Dr. Lenny Klaver; Professor Christopher Kleinhenz; John Buffa Koch and Patty Koch; Edward LaGuardia; Judy and Sal LaLoggia; Mary Jane Naro Lankford; Stephanie Angle Lanzolla and Vincent Lanzolla; Cav. Wilma Laryn; Dr. Joseph Latona; Guido Leo; Viola Leone; Cav. Rosemary Licata; Franco Ligorio; Marco Li Mandri; Francesco and Lucrezia Lindia; Andrew and Gerry Lioi; Robert and Rosemarie Lippman; Monsignor James Lisante; Joseph Lo Casto; Diego Lodico; Vincent Lodico; Cav. Antonino and Lina Lombardo; Kathy Lombardo; Michelle Love; Gianna Lupo; Stewart Magnuson; Robert Maida; Cav. Josephine A. Maietta and Mauro A. Maietta; Nicholas Maiolo; Julia Cericola Mamana; Dr. June Mamana; Fred Manni; Andrea Mantineo; Ernest and Jeannette Manzo; Judge Richard Marano; Hank Marcello; Mary Marcello; Ernest and Pat Marinelli; John Marino; John Martell; Gr. Uff. Joseph Maselli; Amulio Masini; Justice Dominic Massaro; Bob Masullo; Reverend Canon Matthew Mauriello; Supervisor John Mauro; Mary McGarry; Monsignor John J. McInytre; Gabriela McNamara; Enrique Medrano; Peter and Virginia Megani; Claude and Delores Melito; Deacon Carlo Mellace; Ben Mercadante; Susan Mesko; Leon Metz; Mary Michele; Jennie Michelon; Rose Ann Rabiola Miele; Remo Minato; Michele Tuberosa Misci; Ralph Montera; Dr. Paul Montrone; Michael Moran; and Dr. Ed Morrell.

Anita and Pete Nanni; The Hon. Janet Napolitano; Lisa Dimberio Nelson; Arlene and John Newhouse; Terry Noll; Al Noto; Anthony and Janet Noto; Josie Noto; Pete Noto; Amelia (Amy) and Tony Odorisio; Pearl Oliva and Francis J. Cristofori; Joseph Ordornez; Anessa Otten; Mary Amabile Palmer; Sal Palmeri; Anthony Palmisano; Michael Palmisano; The Hon. Leon Panetta; Susan Rienzi Paolercio; The Hon. Leonard Paoletta; Dr. Carmine Paolino; Vince Pardo; Madison Parker II; Frank Passaro Jr.; Michael Pastore; Laurie Penca; Gayle Perez; Jerry and Judy Perona; Pasquale Pesce; Robert Petrolino Sr.; Michael Petta; Dennis and Tina Piasio; Ann Pici; Patricia Pickett; Bishop Anthony M. Pilla; Gaspare Pipitone; Marcella Pirlot; Jessie Piscitello; Stephen Pishner; Prof. Vincenzo Poerio and family; Anthony Polsinelli; Diane and Frank Popolizio; Eugene Popolizio Sr. and MaryAnn Citerella Popolizio; Luisa Potenza; Carmela Powers; Doug Pozzo; Fred and Vera Princiotta; The Hon. Anthony Principi; Norma Procarione; Josephine Profaizer; Tom Profenno; Thomas Ragona; Lawrence A. Ragone; Jim and Lucille Rahilly; Frank J. Rane; Maria Ranieri; Rosalie and Sal Ranieri; Grace Raso; Marianne Dalfonso Reali; Helen Redmount; Angelina Renzi; Mayor Joe Reorda; John D. Richetta and Pamela Richetta; Father John J. Richetta; Ray Ricossa; Cardinal Justin Rigali; Leonard Riggio; Anita Lombardi Riley; Nicholas Rinaldi; Therese Riordan, Dominic Rizzuti; Jean and Ranieri Rocchi; Joy Rodino and the Hon. Peter Rodino Jr.; Kathleen Maggiora Rogers; Alan Rolandi; Maria Grante Roos; Jill Rose;

Pat Rossacci; Judge Mario Rossetti; Judge I. John Rossi; Minnie Rote; Dr. Alfred Rotondaro; The Hon. Marge Roukema and Dr. Richard Roukema; Antonio Rubbo Sr.; Professor Carmel Ruffolo; Mario Ruffolo; Gene and Loretta Ruggeri; Angelo Rulli; Judy Rulli-Socha; and Vincent Russo.

James Sabatoso; Joan and Lou Sacchetti; Marianne Peri Sack; Frank and Vivian Sagona; Michael Salardino; The Hon. Rosaria Salerno; Ben Sanchez; Father Frank Sanfelippo; Ralph Sangiovanni; The Hon. Rick Santorum; Steve Sasso; Terri Nicole Sawyer; Father Gaetano Sbordone; Mayor Anthony Scaffidi and Millie Scaffidi; Grant "Micheli" Scalise; Helen and John Scara; Dan Scardino; Frank Joseph Schiro; Robert Scipione; Professor Carlo Sclafani; Dennis Scullion; Jack Scullion; Janet Cercone Scullion; John Sebaste; Ambassador Peter Secchia; Gerry and Linda Sepe; Jerome Sergi; JoAnn Serpico; Roseann Scalise Sheridan; George Silvestri Jr.; Therese Quattrocchi Simpson; Shirley Sinclaire; Lucy Basso Smith; Jerry Somma; Bernice and Floyd Sperino; Adriana and Carmelo Spinella; Marie Spinner; Betty Sposato; Vincent Sposato III; John Spoto; Grace Toscano Stafford; Angie Staltaro; Gregory St. Angelo; Gr. Uff. Frank D. Stella; Jennifer Stocker; Jim and Maria Stoddard; Paul Sturgul; Aldo Svaldi; Hugo Tagli; Michael Tambasco; Ralph Tambasco; Vito Tamboli, Dave TanCreti, Dr. Orazio Tanelli; Mary Jo Tannehill; Gloria Raso Tate; Ralph Tenuta; John and Tina Terravecchia; Dr. Giuseppe Tiradritti, James Tognoni, Rachel Torchia, Paolo Toschi, Luigi Tosti; The Hon. Renato Turano; Ann and Charles Turco, Joseph Tursi, Golby Uhlir; Dr. Francesca Valente; Sally Valenti; Jo Mera Varisco; Joseph and Marilyn Vecchio; Virginia Vencuss; Dr. James Vitale; Floyd Vivino; Dorothy and Joe Walesewicz; Dave Warren; Kent White; Tamara Sislak Williams; Father Charles Zanoni; Carol Zen; and General Anthony Zinni.

My travels and conversations with folks around the world brought me into contact with many wonderful and welcoming people. For example, Thelma Macaluso and her daughters, Susan Rubino and Christine Wenz, created a nice quilt for me titled, "Italian Roots to American Growth." This quilt is a touching reminder of our Italian heritage and the fellowship that one finds in the Italian Cultural Association of Greater Austin.

On a special note, I want to thank my teachers in Wisconsin's public schools for giving me the tools to read and write. In particular, I wish to express my appreciation to Ruth Kahl and Mary Sterken, whose guidance and mentoring were especially critical to my development as an elementary school student.

Ronald and Mary Lee Laitsch deserve credit, too, for successfully agenting my first two books, *Visible Differences* and *Sharing the Dream*. They played an important role in launching my literary career—and I will always be grateful to them. As importantly, I salute Frank Oveis, the editor of *Visible Differences* and *Sharing the Dream*, for his wisdom, foresight, and graciousness.

Since 2005 I have had the privilege of knowing Dr. Gloria Ricci Lothrop. Dr. Lothrop's deep knowledge of U.S. history, her insightful perspective on Italian Americana, and her commitment to inclusion for all ethnic and racial groups inspire me in my work and life.

On this project, I worked with Ariane C. Smith of Capital A Publications, LLC, who produced Dr. Lothrop's most recent book, *The Land Beyond*. Capital A Publications enjoys a well-deserved reputation for excellence, due to Ariane's creativity, exacting standards, and emphasis on producing high-quality books.

I am delighted that *L'Italo-Americano* is the publishing imprint for *Green, White, and Red*. *L'Italo-Americano*'s publisher, Comm. Robert J. Barbera, is a remarkable American success story, someone who salutes America for its great opportunities and, at the same time, celebrates his Italian heritage. He and his lovely wife, Josephine Volpe Barbera, are wonderfully gracious and honorable. At *L'Italo-Americano*, I also thank Mario Trecco, the Editor, and Laura Mesrobian, the Office Manager.

Now I would like to salute those who are by my side, day after day, and have followed the research and writing of this book particularly closely.

Rima Abou Mrad deserves recognition for having enriched my life in so many ways; her love, support, and encouragement are precious and invaluable to me. In addition, I want to thank the Abou Mrad family—especially Général Bahige Abou Mrad and Madame Marcelle Kiwan Abou Mrad; Ghassan Abou Mrad and Christina Saikaly Abou Mrad; Hani Abou Mrad and Karen Rizkallah Abou Mrad; Dr. Ghada Abou Mrad; and Rania Abou Mrad Jawhar and Nibal Jawhar—for welcoming and embracing me. Similarly, I would like to recognize Colleen Dolan-Greene and Trey Greene as well as Cornelia Baker for their graciousness and hospitality during my frequent visits to Detroit in 2008.

My relatives in Wisconsin and beyond have been consistently supportive and encouraging on this project and my other endeavors. In particular,

I would like to thank Darwin and Martha Cone; Trudy Lalor and John McShane; Hildegarde and Joseph Schroeder; Anna Marie Lux and Randall Kohl; and Gerard Lalor.

My sister, Maria Pulera, and brother-in-law, Rishi (Rish) Chaudhry, are amazing: Their love, support, generosity, enthusiasm, and hospitality nurtured me at every stage of this book. The Pulera family is blessed to have formed a union with the Chaudhry family. Specifically, I want to thank Rish and his parents, Dr. R. C. Chaudhry and Mrs. Sudesh Chaudhry, and his sisters, Dr. Anushka Chaudhry and Dr. Urshla Chaudhry, and his brother-in-law, Manish Bhasin.

My parents, Mr. Eugene Pulera and Dr. Margaret Lux Pulera, deserve a particular debt of gratitude for making this book possible. Their unwavering support, consistent encouragement, and loving home environment enabled me to research and write *Green, White, and Red*. Throughout my life, they have shaped my world view through their example—especially their compassion, their positive outlook, and their emphasis on inclusion and creating opportunities for all.

As an Italian American, my father takes great interest in his heritage. We spent countless hours discussing the topics in this book and traveled together many times to visit Italian-American delis, tour communities, interview respondents, and so much more.

I dedicate this book to my grandparents: Edward Laurence Lux and Elisabeth Weiter Lux; and Frank Joseph Pulera and Mary Puntillo Pulera. In everything that I do, I stand on their shoulders.

INDEX

 *Green, White, and Red: The Italian-American Success Story* by Dominic J. Pulera is set in Caslon Old Style type with Dalliance Flourish Ornaments. Design by Ariane C. Smith, Capital A Publications, LLC, Spokane, Washington. Printing by Sheridan Books, Inc., Chelsea, Michigan.